6 00

B&N

listed

A History of England in Eight Volumes

Founder Editor, Sir Charles Oman

Volume VII

ENGLAND SINCE WATERLOO

A History of England in Eight Volumes

I

ENGLAND BEFORE THE NORMAN CONQUEST
by Sir Charles Oman

II

ENGLAND UNDER THE NORMANS AND ANGEVINS
by H. W. C. Davis

III

ENGLAND IN THE LATER MIDDLE AGES
by Kenneth H. Vickers

IV

ENGLAND UNDER THE TUDORS
by G. R. Elton

V

ENGLAND UNDER THE STUARTS
by G. M. Trevelyan

VI

ENGLAND UNDER THE HANOVERIANS
by Sir Charles Grant Robertson

VII

ENGLAND SINCE WATERLOO
by Sir J. A. R. Marriott

VIII

MODERN ENGLAND, 1885-1945
by Sir J. A. R. Marriott

ENGLAND
SINCE WATERLOO

Sir J. A. R. Marriott

LONDON: METHUEN & CO LTD
NEW YORK: BARNES & NOBLE INC

First published October 2nd 1913
Reprinted fourteen times
Fifteenth Edition 1954
(with a new select bibliography
by M. R. D. Foot)
Reprinted 1957

15·3
CATALOGUE NO. (METHUEN) 3377/ʊ

PRINTED IN GREAT BRITAIN

INTRODUCTORY NOTE

BY THE GENERAL EDITOR

IN England, as in France and Germany, the main characteristic of the last twenty years, from the point of view of the
student of history, has been that new material has been accumulating much faster than it can be assimilated or absorbed. The
standard histories of the last generation need to be revised, or
even to be put aside as obsolete, in the light of the new information that is coming in so rapidly and in such vast bulk. But
the students and researchers of to-day have shown little enthusiasm as yet for the task of re-writing history on a large
scale. We see issuing from the press hundreds of monographs,
biographies, editions of old texts, selections from correspondence,
or collections of statistics, mediaeval and modern. But the
writers who (like the late Bishop Stubbs or Professor Samuel
Gardiner) undertake to tell over again the history of a long
period, with the aid of all the newly discovered material, are
few indeed. It is comparatively easy to write a monograph on
the life of an individual or a short episode of history. But the
modern student, knowing well the mass of material that he has
to collate, and dreading lest he may make a slip through overlooking some obscure or newly discovered source, dislikes to stir
beyond the boundary of the subject, or the short period, on
which he has made himself a specialist.

Meanwhile the general reading public continues to ask for
standard histories, and discovers, only too often, that it can
find nothing between school manuals at one end of the scale
and minute monographs at the other. The series of which this
volume forms a part is intended to do something towards meeting
this demand. Historians will not sit down, as once they were
wont, to write twenty-volume works in the style of Hume or
Lingard, embracing a dozen centuries of annals. It is not to
be desired that they should—the writer who is most satisfactory

in dealing with Anglo-Saxon antiquities is not likely to be the one who will best discuss the antecedents of the Reformation, or the constitutional history of the Stuart period.   But something can be done by judicious co-operation : it is not necessary that a genuine student should refuse to touch any subject that embraces an epoch longer than a score of years, nor need history be written as if it were an encyclopædia, and cut up into small fragments dealt with by different hands.

It is hoped that the present series may strike the happy mean, by dividing up English History into periods that are neither too long to be dealt with by a single competent specialist, nor so short as to tempt the writer to indulge in that over-abundance of unimportant detail which repels the general reader. They are intended to give something more than a mere outline of our national annals, but they have little space for controversy or the discussion of sources, save in periods such as the dark age of the 5th and 6th centuries after Christ, where the criticism of authorities is absolutely necessary if we are to arrive at any sound conclusions as to the course of history.   A number of maps are to be found at the end of each volume which, as it is hoped, will make it unnecessary for the reader to be continually referring to large historical atlases—tomes which (as we must confess with regret) are not to be discovered in every private library. Genealogies and chronological tables of kings are added where necessary.

C. OMAN

PREFACE

ANYONE who has attempted the task of writing the history of a crowded period in a given number of pages will judge leniently some at least of the many defects of this book. Of its defects—more particularly its sins of omission—no one can be so conscious as the author. Many paragraphs have had to be excised and some chapters to be omitted. But one thing I would crave permission to say. This is not a long book, still less can it pretend to be a great book, but it is at least the fruit of prolonged study and reflection. I began the accumulation of materials more than twenty years ago; some few sections of the book were actually written fifteen years ago, and during the intervening period the subject—in one or other of its varied aspects—has been rarely absent from my mind. The delay in the execution of my task has not only given me the opportunity for reconsideration and reflection, but has enabled me to utilize many authorities of first-rate importance only recently made available. Among these I regard the *Letters of Queen Victoria* as of primary significance for the period 1837-1861. Invaluable also (though utilized by previous writers) are Greville's *Journals*, the Creevey and Croker Papers, the Melbourne Papers, and above all the Peel Papers. The Canning Letters (ed. Bagot) have thrown considerable light upon an earlier period (1800-1827), while for the latest period (1860-1901) the historian is confronted with an ever-accumulating mass of materials in the shape of Biographies, Memoirs, Diaries, Letters, and Papers.

Among a large number of such publications I would particularly mention the *Life of Lord Palmerston*, begun by Lord Dalling and completed by Mr. Evelyn Ashley; Lord Morley's *Life of Gladstone*, Lord Fitzmaurice's *Life of Lord Granville*, Mr. Holland's *Life of the Duke of Devonshire*, Mr. O'Brien's *Life of C. S. Parnell*, and the *Memorials of Roundell Palmer, Earl of Selborne*. The Novels of Disraeli seem to me hardly less worthy of study than his Speeches, and his brilliant *Life of Lord George Bentinck ;* but Mr. Monypenny's volumes appeared too late for me to use.

The plan of this work does not permit the parade of the apparatus of " original research," and I have had to keep " references " within narrow limits, but for years I have been a student of the original materials for the history of the nineteenth century, and if the results of this saturation are not apparent in the text, my critics must hold responsible either my lack of literary skill or the concentrated form of the narrative. Of secondary authorities also I have made full use, and I wish to acknowledge a special debt to the laborious work of Sir Spencer Walpole and the brilliant volumes of Mr. Herbert Paul. With the conclusions of both writers I have found myself frequently at variance, but no historian of this period can afford to neglect their works. I should like to add, as an act of piety, that it was the attractive pen of Mr. Justin McCarthy which first aroused my boyish interest in this period. I hope that I have not failed to acknowledge any specific debts, but in a work which has extended over a long period of time, especially if it has formed the basis of teaching, one can never be sure. For any un-acknowledged borrowings, either of thought or expression, I ask pardon.

The reader will perceive that I have frequently abandoned strict chronology. All that I have to say of India, for example, will be found in Chapters XIV., XV., and XXIV., and, as far as possible, I have treated Foreign affairs apart from the details of domestic politics. I am aware of the objections to this method, but the advantages seem to me to outweigh the disadvantages.

The book has been read in type-script by Professor Oman, the General Editor, and by the Rev. Alfred B. Beaven, late Head Master of Preston Grammar School. Both these scholars have made valuable suggestions, and to both my grateful thanks are due. I have also to acknowledge the courtesy of the pro-prietors and editors of the *Quarterly Review* and the *Fortnightly*

Review in permitting me to utilize articles which I have contributed to these *Reviews*. In the compilation of the Index I have been assisted by my wife.

J. A. R. MARRIOTT

April 7th, **1913**

NOTE TO SECOND EDITION

A FEW misprints and errors have been corrected, and a few recently published works have been added to the bibliography. Among these the most important are the biographies of Lord Clarendon and Lord Lyons by Sir Herbert Maxwell and Lord Newton respectively, and to them I have given some references mainly in Chapters XII., XIII., and XXII. Judgments to which exception was taken by obviously competent reviewers have been carefully reconsidered, and in one or two cases have been modified ; but to one category of complaints I am compelled to present an adamantine front. Reviewers who complain that this or that movement has been scantily treated, or this or that man insufficiently noticed, ought in fairness to bear in mind limitations of space, and address themselves to my publisher. It would have been far easier for me to have disposed my matter in three volumes rather than in one.

It is, however, eminently satisfactory to observe that most of such criticisms cancel out, proving that, in a period so recent, relative values have still to be adjusted. Similarly in regard to another category of criticisms. One important journal heads its review " A Tory on England " ; another, of opposite complexion, declares that the author " appears himself to be a democrat " ; a third affirms that the " book is a substantial effort to write impartial history," and adds that " it fails because Mr. Marriott is a historian and therefore cannot be impartial ".

b

Such conflict of criticism may well leave an author contented. To one accusation only, if it were just, should I be sensitive : that the book gives "nothing about the Imperial sentiment ". Of its justice I am more than willing that readers of the book should judge. For the rest, an historian of the nineteenth century must needs offend some susceptibilities which he would fain respect ; he is compelled to excise much that is of interest to himself, and to disappoint almost every reader who has special hobbies or pet heroes. He may deem himself fortunate if the offence proves to have been distributed impartially, and if he is convicted only of such omissions as would, if remedied, have involved the transgression of inevitable limitations, or—still worse—a sacrifice of perspective and proportion. One sentence I am constrained to add. I should be grossly insensible to generosity if I failed to acknowledge, with sincere gratitude, the cordial reception generally accorded to this work by my confrères and critics, not least by those who are and know themselves to be politically opposed to the author.

J. A. R. MARRIOTT

WORCESTER COLLEGE,
22nd June 1914

NOTE TO THIRTEENTH EDITION

FOR this edition the book has been subjected to a thorough revision, but mainly in respect of small points of style. In substance the book remains in its original form. I am conscious that its " angle " may be derided as hopelessly " Victorian ". Such criticism would not perturb me : it is evidently proper that the tone should accord with that of the period under review ; nor is it certain that the social, economic, and political presuppositions of the " Victorian era " will not in the long run prove less unsound than it is to-day fashionable to assume.

J. A. R. MARRIOTT

December 1944

TABLE OF CONTENTS

BOOK I

THE AFTERMATH OF WAR, 1815-1832

CHAPTER I

CHAPTER II

CHAPTER III

xi

CHAPTER XIV

CHAPTER XV

CHAPTER XVI

CHAPTER XVII

BOOK III

DEMOCRACY AND EMPIRE

CHAPTER XVIII

CHAPTER XIX

CHAPTER XX

CHAPTER XXI

CHAPTER XXII

CHAPTER XXIII

CHAPTER XXIV

AFGHANISTAN, SOUTH AFRICA AND IRELAND (1878-1880)

CHAPTER XXV

THE GLADSTONE ADMINISTRATION—IRELAND AND EGYPT— (1880-1885)

CHAPTER XXVI

GENEALOGICAL TABLE

LIST OF MAPS

BOOK I

THE AFTERMATH OF WAR, 1815-1832

CHAPTER I

INTRODUCTORY

ENGLAND emerged from the great war the most powerful nation in the world. Compelled by the action of the French Republic to take up arms in 1793, she had sustained the struggle, almost without pause, for a quarter of a century—not seldom single-handed. Again and again she had been deserted by her allies. Again and again they had been encouraged, partly by her liberal subsidies, partly by her dogged resolution, partly by her unbroken supremacy at sea, to recombine to resist the domination of the new Charlemagne. Her steadfastness, courage, and endurance at last reaped the appropriate reward. Impotent to assail English power at sea, foiled in his attempt to ruin her commerce, baffled by the national spirit which he had himself aroused in Germany and Spain, overwhelmed under Russian snows, and finally conquered by the genius of Wellington, Napoleon was at last driven into exile, and Europe was at peace.

The task of the soldiers ended, that of the diplomatists began. Over the settlement which they effected at Paris and Vienna, England naturally exercised a powerful influence. Her own material acquisitions seem, however, at first sight to be incommensurate with the sacrifices she had made in the common cause. Russia reaped a rich harvest in Poland and on the Baltic littoral; Austria exchanged her embarrassing heritage in the Netherlands for much-coveted provinces in Northern Italy; Prussia underwent a territorial readjustment which definitely determined her political destiny; Sweden was partially consoled for her losses on the Baltic by the acquisition of Norway; the Dutch Stadtholder absorbed Belgium, and the King of Sardinia annexed Genoa. Compared with the substantial gains of her principal allies the compensations obtained by Great Britain might appear inadequate; in reality, as will presently appear, they were scarcely less pregnant with future possibilities than those of Russia, Prussia, or Austria. Her attitude in the negotiations which preceded the peace was consistent with her unselfish activities throughout the war. Her first anxiety was to secure a settlement which should be at once equitable and permanent. Captious critics are apt to assume that neither result was actually attained. It is

1

commonly asserted that the diplomatists were inspired solely by the spirit of reaction ; that they ignored the new and vital forces generated during the last twenty years ; that they paid excessive deference to the convenience of rulers and too little to the rights of subjects ; that they were solicitous for the principle of equilibrium but careless as to that of nationality ; in fine, that they erected a flimsy structure upon unstable foundations. Criticism in the light of after events is easy. The task of the diplomatists was exceptionally difficult. Their first and most obvious duty was to erect the strongest possible barrier against a recurrence of the devastating flood from which Europe had so lately emerged. It is not pretended that they were entirely successful ; the ill-assorted union of Belgium and Holland lasted only fifteen years ; the territorial partition of Italy, and the constitutional settlement of Germany were not destined to much greater permanence ; but at least it may be claimed that the peace of Europe was not again seriously disturbed for more than a generation.

English gains   Great Britain had not much personal interest in the territorial reconstruction in Europe. She retained the island of Malta as an additional guarantee for her naval supremacy in the Mediterranean ; she accepted the protectorate of the Ionian Isles, which Bonaparte had intended to use as stepping-stones to the East ; in the Northern Seas she acquired Heligoland, and she employed her dominant influence to induce France to bind herself, without loss of time, to concert with the British Government " the most effectual measures for the entire and definitive abolition of a commerce so odious and so strongly condemned by the laws of religion and nature " as the slave trade. For the rest England sought her compensations further afield.

British India, doubled in extent under the rule of Lord Wellesley (1798-1805), was beginning to exert a powerful influence upon the policy of the homeland. The retention in 1815 of the Mauritius, of Ceylon, and above all, of Cape Colony, was significant of this new influence. These acquisitions, although valuable in themselves, were primarily important as stages on the highway to India.

The West Indies were, in 1815, regarded as hardly less important than the East. And not without reason. Out of the total exports of £58,624,550 [1] no less than £7,218,057, or little less than one-eighth, went to the West Indies. The retention, therefore, of Trinidad, St. Lucia, Demerara, and Essequibo meant more than the present generation is wont to realize.

Substantial in amount and significant in direction as these acquisitions undoubtedly were, no one can pretend that they afforded excessive compensation for the sacrifices which Great Britain had made during the prolonged contest with France. To many they seemed ridiculously inadequate. But be this as it may, it is at least incon-

---

[1] Porter, *Progress of the Nation*, p. 477 (ed. 1912).

testable that the war left England with prestige enormously enhanced, with power unbroken, and Empire extended.

These things were not bought without price. If England reached in 1815 the zenith of political and military prestige, she touched the nadir of industrial dislocation and social discontent. That a great war is invariably followed by a period of economic recoil has become a commonplace of historical generalization. But the recoil of 1815 was unprecedently severe and unusually prolonged. For this there were many reasons, which will demand detailed investigation later on. For the moment it must suffice summarily to point out that the period of the great war was coincident with that of the Industrial Revolution. Thanks to a series of remarkable mechanical inventions, England, which had for centuries been a granary and a sheepfold, was suddenly transformed into the workshop of the world. Parallel to the manufacturing revolution, and practically coincident with it, there had taken place in agricultural methods changes which revolutionized the rural economy of England. Down to the outbreak of the war more than half the parishes in the country were cultivated on the " open field " system ; and the results as regards aggregate yield, were, by general consent, disastrous. During the reign of George III. no less than 3,200 Enclosure Acts were passed, and more than six million acres were enclosed. Improved methods of cultivation and of stock breeding were introduced ; farms were consolidated ; capital was embarked in agriculture, and science was called in to reinforce the old rule of thumb. Thanks to this agricultural revolution, England was able not merely to feed a rapidly increasing population at home, but to export her produce to the continental countries rendered sterile and desolate by the ravages of war. Hardly less important than the revolution in manufacturing and agricultural methods was the immense development during the same period in means of communication. While " Turnip " Townshend and Coke of Holkham, Ellmann of Glynde, Bakewell and Arthur Young multiplied a hundred-fold the productiveness of the soil ; while Kay and Hargreaves, Arkwright and Crompton, Cartwright and Watt, revolutionized the textile industry ; Brindley and the Duke of Bridgewater, Telford and Macadam, gave to labour a new mobility and facilitated enormously the exchange of commodities. Down to the accession of George III. England, in regard to means of transport, was the most backward country in Western Europe. The first Canal Act was not passed until 1755 and the roads were scandalously bad.[1] At the date of the accession of Queen Victoria England possessed 4,000 miles of navigable waterway ; the trunk roads were improved out of recognition ; steam navigation had begun, and two lines of rail had been laid down.

With the economic, social, and political results of these changes

Economic distress and social unrest

The Industrial and Agrarian Revolutions

---

[1] *Cf.* Arthur Young, *Tours in Great Britain, passim.*

this volume must be largely concerned : the stupendous increase of aggregate wealth ; the rapid growth of population and the significant changes in its distribution ; the rise of new industries and the growth of cities ; the development of means of communication ; the expansion of over-sea trade—these things suggest some at least of the clues which may enable the student to track the maze presented by the history of the nineteenth century. For the historian of this period is confronted by a task different in kind from that which impedes the student of the Middle Ages. He is baffled not by paucity, but by redundance of material. His function, consequently, is selective rather than accumulative.

Main lines of development in nineteenth century

It may be well, therefore, to indicate at the outset the more important lines of development upon which in this complicated period attention should be concentrated.

The nineteenth century may be summarily described as the period of Democracy and Empire, Science and Industry. It witnessed a fourfold revolution : Political, Social, Economic, and Intellectual. From the political standpoint the period falls naturally into three great divisions, corresponding to three striking changes in the centre

Growth of Democracy

of political gravity. The years between 1815 and 1832 witnessed the close of the rule of the aristocratic oligarchy which had governed England, and in the main with conspicuous success, for a century and a half. The Reform Act of 1832 dethroned the landed aristocracy and committed supreme power to the commercial classes. The full effect of the change was not, however, discernible for a generation. Until the death of Lord Palmerston (1865) England continued to be governed, despite an extended franchise and a radical redistribution of constituencies, by a knot of great families who had ruled it since 1688. But by 1865 the era of middle class rule was itself drawing to an end. In 1867 a second shifting of the centre of political gravity occurs. By Disraeli's famous " leap in the dark " (1867) the mass of the town artisans were admitted to the parliamentary franchise. By Gladstone's Act of 1884 the same privilege was conferred upon the rural labourers. Again, however, it will be seen that a generation had to elapse before the newly enfranchised classes found their political feet and inaugurated the era of " Democracy ". Not until the beginning of a new reign and a new century did political supremacy effectively pass from the bourgeoisie to the manual worker. Nor must the importance of the Press and the Platform in this connection be ignored.

Local government

The growth of the democratic principle was not, however, confined to the Imperial Government of Great Britain. A similar development is observable in the local government of the Motherland and in that of the more important Colonies. The reform of Municipal Corporations in 1835 ; the re-introduction of the elective principle into County government in 1888 and into District and Parish govern-

ment in 1894, mark the main stages in the first case ; the attainment Colonial
of " responsible " government by Canada (1840), by the several self-government
Australasian Colonies (1850-1890), by the Cape Colony (1872), and by
Natal (1893) are the most important examples of the latter. The
advent of Democracy must, therefore, be regarded as one of the
primary interests of the period under review.

Hardly less significant is the shifting of the centre of social and
economic gravity. The Act of 1832 administered the *coup de grâce*
to the political ascendancy of the landed gentry. The legislation of
Sir Robert Peel (1841-1846) combined with the immense development
of facilities for transport, similarly put an end to their economic Social
changes
supremacy. Ascendancy passed from the owners of land to the
owners of capital, as it is now, in turn, passing from the owners of
capital to the possessors of business brains and skilled hands. Both
changes are accurately reflected in the history of legislation. The
owners of capital asked nothing of the State but abstention from
interference—a fair field and freedom from restraint. But the
philosophical ascendancy of Bentham, and the political supremacy
of the " Manchester School " were of comparatively short duration.
The introduction of machinery ; the supersession of the hand-worker ;
the development of the factory system ; the concentration of population in unregulated towns ; in a word—the Industrial Revolution
raised problems that were both new and puzzling. To solve them State interference
the interference of the State was invoked, and the result is seen in a
long series of parliamentary statutes. Acts for the restraint and
supervision of child labour and female labour in factories and workshops ; for the improvement of the sanitary conditions under which
the poor live ; for the education of their children and for their own
protection from accidents, may be cited as characteristic illustrations
of this tendency.

To the same industrial revolution we must look also for the The
genesis of new economic problems. If, as is claimed, the Revolution economic
problem
solved the problem of " production," it must be admitted that it of "distribution ".
accentuated, if it did not create, the problem of " distribution ". So
long as the household was largely self-sufficing ; so long as industry
was organized on the " domestic " system ; so long as there was little
differentiation of economic functions and the machinery of exchange
was crude, the problem of distribution was held in abeyance. But
when the landowner was parted from the capitalist, the manufacturer
from the farmer, and both from the hand-worker, disputes naturally
arose as to the share of the total product which each could equitably
claim. In such a contest the individual workman had little chance
against the capitalist-employer. Hence the necessity for the organ- Trade
ization of labour and the initiation of collective bargaining. Until Unions
1824, and in a modified degree until 1871, the law was steadily
opposed to " combination," but economic pressure gradually wore

down the resistance of legislative restraint, and the legalization of trade unions forms one of the most significant chapters in the economic history of the nineteenth century.

Co-operation   Trade Unions, however, though effective as a palliative, offer no permanent solution of the problem of distribution and no sound basis for industrial peace. The Co-operative movement has a wider scope. The idea of " Co-operation " was born in the fertile brain of Robert Owen, but it was first embodied in successful experiment by a working class Society at Rochdale in 1844. As a distributive agency, the Co-operative movement has attained gigantic proportions and has proved an unqualified success. But it has done more than provide the working classes with sound commodities at reasonable prices. By its democratic system of control it has initiated thousands of working men into the mysteries of business management and has taught them the importance of the functions of capital ; by its automatic machinery for saving it has inculcated not merely the virtues but the possibilities of thrift ; but it has not solved, and it cannot solve, the problem of wealth-distribution.

The same principle applied, in a variety of forms, to the difficult art of production has made a gallant effort in this direction. It were idle to pretend that it has attained, in this sphere, a complete, or even a very large measure of success. There have been many experiments, watched with sympathy by all who realize the gravity of the problem, and many failures. In the simpler form of " profit sharing " some success has indeed been achieved, and even in the more complex and elaborate form of " labour co-partnership " there has been more success than is commonly supposed. But progress has unfortunately been retarded by the singular reluctance of Co-operators to recognize the market value of business brains. Signs are not wanting that lessons learnt in the hard school of experience are being taken to heart ; that Co-operators are beginning to appreciate the increasingly important part which direction plays in modern industry, and to face the fact that efficient direction cannot be obtained unless the market price is paid. As soon as this truth permeates the Co-operative body we may look for rapid progress in the domain of production.

Socialism   Thus far the recognition of the economic importance of the *entrepreneur* has been tardy, and, meanwhile, a third solution of the problem has obtained increased support among the working classes of this, as of other countries. Robert Owen was the father not only of Co-operation, but of English socialism. The modern socialist, however, impatiently brushes aside both Co-operation and Trade Unionism as mere palliatives. In his view the panacea for all social and economic ills is to be found in the nationalization of all the instruments of production, transport, distribution, and exchange. Private ownership of land, of capital, of warehouses, of machinery of railways, steamships, canals, tramways, etc., is to cease, and industry is to be organized exclusively by the State. It would be out of place to attempt here a critical examination of this or any other proposed solution of the economic problem of the nineteenth century, but no history of the period can ignore either the insistent nature of the problem itself or the marked effect upon legislation and administration of the persistent effort to discover a solution. The abandonment of the dogmas of the Benthamite School ; the breakdown of the principle of *laisser faire ;* the multiplication of governmental functions, and the intrusion of the State into domains hitherto deemed sacred to the individual—this has been for good or evil a marked feature of the latter portion of the period under review.

The nineteenth century will, however, stand out not merely as the age of Industry but as the age of Science. With the purely intellectual achievements of Science this work cannot concern itself ; but no attempt, however summary, to estimate the forces which have gone to mould the destinies of modern England can fail to take account of the growth of the scientific spirit and the application of the scientific method. Science has not only permeated thought ; it has influenced legislation and has revolutionized the arts of production. The whole mental outlook of the world has been profoundly modified by scientific generalizations. The results of laboratory research are applied in the workshop, and the steed of Science is harnessed to the car of Industry.[1] *Science and industry*

From Science it is, happily, an easy transition to Religion. The ecclesiastical movement of the century seems to have followed three distinct but ultimately convergent directions. It is expressed, first, in the successful agitation for the abolition of religious " tests ". These tests were mainly the work of Elizabethan and Caroline statesmen, and their object was to associate the State with the Anglican Establishment, and to identify active citizenship with adherence to the Church of England. One of the most characteristic features of the legislation of the century has been the removal of the limitations thus imposed. In illustration of this tendency it is sufficient to cite the repeal of the Test and Corporation Acts (1828) ; the Catholic Relief Act (1829) ; the admission of Jews to Parliament (1858) ; the Education Act of 1870 with its conscience clause, and the Act for the abolition of University Tests (1871). *The ecclesiastical movement. Abolition of tests*

It is not without significance that the surrender of a privileged political position by the Church of England has been coincident with a period of remarkable activity within the borders of the Church itself. The earliest years of the century witnessed a great Evangelical revival which derived its chief inspiration from Cambridge ; the middle period was remarkable for the Neo-Catholic or Tractarian *Religion and Theology*

---

[1] *Cf.* on this point the suggestive remarks of Mr. A. J. Balfour, *The Nineteenth Century* (Cambridge Press, 1900).

movement which is particularly associated with Oxford, and, later still, the liberal or latitudinarian view found distinguished exponents in such men as F. D. Maurice, Arnold of Rugby, Dean Stanley, and Jowett. Closely connected with the last movement is the attempt, now common to all schools of Theology, to apply the scientific and historical method to Biblical interpretation and exegesis.

Educa-
tion
Not less noteworthy is the fact that the age which witnessed the abolition of Ecclesiastical tests witnessed also a complete change in the attitude of the State towards the education of the poor. Down to 1833 this was regarded as the exclusive concern of the Churches. Not until that year did the State vouchsafe any assistance to the two great voluntary societies which were attempting to cope with this increasingly difficult problem. In 1839 a Committee of the Privy Council was appointed to supervise the work of these societies.[1]

Not, however, for another generation did the State itself seriously undertake the function of educating the children of the poor. And by that time its educational conscience had been aroused in other directions. The appointment in 1850 of two Royal Commissions to inquire into the state, discipline, studies, and revenues of the Universities of Oxford and Cambridge marks the real beginning of State interference with Higher Education ; the appointment of the Public Schools Commission in 1861, and of Lord Taunton's Commission in 1864 indicated similar concern as to Secondary Education.

Foreign
and Co-
lonial
policy
These topics by no means exhaust the interest and significance of the Victorian era. Constitutional, economic, social, educational and ecclesiastical reforms must necessarily fill a large space in any volume devoted to the history of the nineteenth century. But they must not be permitted to engage exclusive attention nor to obscure the importance of the part played by Great Britain upon the stage of European and world politics.

The Revolution of 1688 marked an important crisis in the relations of England and the continent, and during the whole of the succeeding century (1688-1815) this country played a conspicuous if not a dominating part. The accession of the Dutch Stadtholder to the English throne ; the resounding victories of Marlborough and Rooke ; the command of the Mediterranean first asserted after the capture of Gibraltar and Minorca ; active participation in the so-called wars of succession, Spanish and Austrian ; a long series of defeats inflicted upon France in three several continents ; above all, the leadership of many coalitions in the Revolutionary and Napoleonic wars, contributed to give this country a pre-eminent position among the Powers of Europe.

But the essential significance of English activity during this period was missed by contemporary observers and, for many genera-

---

[1] *The British and Foreign School Society* and *The National Society* which had been established respectively in 1807 and 1809.

tions, by historical critics. It may be an hyperbole to declare, with Sir John Seeley, that we conquered half the world in a fit of absence of mind. Nevertheless Seeley performed a real historical service in teaching us to scrutinize motives and estimate broad results : he reduced to order the chaos of the eighteenth century ; he showed that in the apparently disconnected and meaningless contests of that period there was a profound and consistent tendency, and that events seemingly miscellaneous and unrelated were in reality making towards a definite and important goal. That goal was Colonial Empire : supremacy in India and the New World.

After 1815 the political focus was consciously adjusted. Great Britain had tended to withdraw from interference in matters which concern Europe only, and concentrated her attention upon questions of world politics. She exchanged, in short, a foreign for a colonial policy. Not one of the innumerable wars in which, since 1815, she engaged was really European in significance and scope. The one apparent exception—the Crimean war—was an exception which strictly proves the rule. She fought in India, in Afghanistan, in China, in South Africa, in Egypt, in New Zealand, in Canada—in every quarter of the globe except in Europe. If the actual fighting in the Crimean war took place on European soil, it was the Asiatic, not the European, interests of Great Britain which were immediately involved. *World politics*

The moral of a bare recital such as this is unmistakable. The centre of political gravity for the British Empire during the nineteenth century unquestionably shifted. Great Britain could no longer be regarded primarily as a European power but as the Mother of a bevy of daughter lands—the President of an informal federation of free nations scattered throughout the world.

The pages that follow will disclose the growth of that Empire. Its history falls, to an extent not generally realized, within the period allotted to this volume.

The great disruption of 1783 left us without any English Colonies save Newfoundland and some of the West Indian islands. The history of British Canada dates from the immigration of loyalists from the United States in 1783, but for many years the progress of the new Colony was slow, and in 1815 Englishmen and Frenchmen together numbered less than 350,000 souls. Cape Colony had become by 1815 a British possession, but not until 1820 did it begin to be a British Colony. Australia, rediscovered by Captain Cook in 1768, was utilized, after the loss of the thirteen Colonies, as a penal settlement, but not until 1821 was any part of it opened to free immigration. In India the foundation of a British Empire had been laid broad and deep by Clive and Warren Hastings in the eighteenth century, and by 1815 much of the superstructure had been raised by Cornwallis and Wellesley. But India, though an imperial asset of *Colonial expansion* supreme value, never has been and never can be a British Colony—a field for the expansion and multiplication of the British race.

Egypt   Intimately connected with British Dominion in India is the position which this country has been compelled to assume in Egypt. British statesmen were, however, characteristically slow to realize the connection. France perceived it long ago. So far back as 1738 a brilliant French diplomatist—D'Argenson—published a project for the reorganization of the Ottoman Empire, which included, *inter alia*, the acquisition of Egypt by France, and the cutting of a canal from the Levant to the Red Sea which should belong in common to the whole world. More than a century was to elapse before the idea of D'Argenson was embodied in the great enterprise of Lesseps. It is, however, worthy of note that when in 1788 the Emperor Joseph II. and the Czarina Catherine II. were meditating a partition of Eastern Europe, they suggested that Egypt should be thrown as a sop to France. At the close of the century Napoleon determined that the acquisition of the sop should no longer be delayed. In his campaign against Great Britain he realized from the outset that Egypt was a vital point. " Really to destroy England we must make ourselves master of Egypt." [1]   But England was curiously lethargic in awakening to the fact which loomed so large before the eyes of Frenchmen. In 1840 and again in 1853 Nicholas I. of Russia pressed the question upon the attention of the English Court and the English Cabinet. In his statesmanlike diagnosis of the Eastern problem he invariably insisted that England's interests must be safeguarded by the acquisition of Egypt. But neither in 1840 nor in 1853 would England listen to the Russian proposals based upon the recognition of this fact.

The Suez Canal   The opening of the Suez Canal in 1869 revolutionized the situation. The Mediterranean, which for four hundred years had been a mere backwater of commerce, rapidly regained the position it had lost. But the canal was the work not of England, but of France. In 1875 Disraeli secured for England a controlling influence in the canal by the purchase of the Khedive's shares. It was a masterstroke of policy, imperfectly appreciated at the moment, and was followed up in 1878 by the acquisition of Cyprus. At last England was awakening from her lethargy in regard to Egypt. The critical moment arrived in 1882. France declined to share in the task of the restoration of order, the dual control was virtually abolished ; and the suppression of Arabi's rebellion was followed by the establishment of a thinly veiled British Protectorate in 1883. In the same year troubles broke out in the Soudan which, after many vicissitudes and more than one tragedy, was finally conquered in 1898, apparently against the will, and palpably against the initial inclination of the conqueror. Great Britain has thus been compelled, greatly to her

[1] Bonaparte to the Directory, August 16th, 1797.

own advantage and not less to the advantage of the people whom she rules, to assume a dominant position in Egypt and the Soudan.

There remains one other topic which will demand detailed treat- Ireland ment in this volume. The Irish question is never very far from the surface of English politics. Ministries come and ministries go, but the Irish problem confronts them impartially. When Wellington won his victory at Waterloo, Ireland was just midway between the Union and Catholic Emancipation. The Catholic agitation was crowned with success in 1829, and for ten years O'Connell gave his Whig allies their chance. They failed to take it, and in 1841 the Repeal agitation was inaugurated. This culminated in the " Young Ireland " rebellion of 1848. But the central fact of Irish history in the nineteenth century is the great famine of 1845-1846. It changed the face of the country and accentuated many problems which are still in process of solution. Among these the most insistent is the agrarian problem which, with rare and short intervals, occupied the attention of the Imperial Legislature from 1850 until the close of the century. During the 'sixties the agrarian movement was compli- cated by the Fenian outbreak, and by the successful agitation for the disestablishment and disendowment of the Anglican Church in Ireland. During the late 'seventies, and throughout the 'eighties, it was closely intertwined with the Parnellite movement and the demand for legislative independence.

It is not pretended that the preceding analysis is in any sense exhaustive. But in a period so crowded with detail it may, perhaps, conduce to lucidity if some emphasis is laid at the outset upon the main points to which, in the pages that follow, the reader's attention must be primarily directed. Perhaps we are as yet too near the events of the nineteenth century to see them in their true perspective, or to assign to them the precise significance which, in the eyes of posterity, they will ultimately assume. Provisionally, however, we may hazard the conjecture that the characteristic differentia of English history since Waterloo will be found in the conjoined ascen- dancy of Science and Industry, in the advent of Democracy, and in the extension of Empire.

CHAPTER II

PEACE WITHOUT PLENTY. POLITICAL, ECONOMIC, AND SOCIAL DISLOCATION

(1815-1822)

The
Prince
Regent

WHEN Wellington won his victory at Waterloo, the Prince of Wales had been for nearly five years Regent of Great Britain and Ireland. After more than one temporary lapse into insanity, George III. had been finally bereft of reason in 1810, and since then had lived in complete retirement at Windsor, under the guardianship of his devoted wife. His eldest son, now Prince Regent, was perhaps the least reputable member of a family whose common stock of virtue was not superabundant. By no means devoid of ability, not lacking in dignity, and possessed of considerable personal charm,[1] he had nevertheless deservedly forfeited the affection and even the respect of his people. For the vindictiveness with which he pursued his wife there may have been reason, but nothing can excuse his undutiful behaviour to his father or his harshness towards his only legitimate child.

A shameless voluptuary, a reckless spendthrift, a hard drinker, and a confirmed gambler, his conduct was a constant embarrassment to his ministers and a terrible example to his subjects; but his correspondence with the leading statesmen[2] of the time proves that he had an ample measure of political sagacity and no little shrewdness in his judgment of men. He had received the allied Sovereigns in 1814 with a dignity and hospitality worthy of a unique occasion, and his visits to Ireland (1821) and Scotland (1822) afforded evidence of his power to conciliate goodwill when he chose to exert himself to that end. But it cannot be denied that the Crown lost both political power and social prestige during his reign as Regent and King.

The
Liverpool
Ministry

The Prince's early attachment to the Whigs had sensibly cooled since his accession to a position of greater responsibility, and although he had opened negotiations with their aristocratic leaders in 1812, he was probably relieved when the overtures proved sterile.

Lord
Liverpool

On Spencer Perceval's death in 1812 the Premiership, together with the leadership of the Tory party, had passed to Lord Liverpool. Robert Banks Jenkinson, second Earl of Liverpool, belongs to a class of statesmen whom we are pleased to regard as typically English. Born in 1770, and educated at the Charterhouse and Christ Church, he entered Parliament as member for Rye in 1790. He served his official apprenticeship under Pitt, and his administrative experience

---

[1] Queen Victoria's recollection of him was " large and gouty, but with a wonderful dignity and charm of manner ".—*Letters*, i. 16.

[2] *Cf. e.g.* Yonge, *Life of Lord Liverpool, passim.*

was exceptionally large and various. Before his accession to the Premiership he had filled all three Secretaryships of State : at the Foreign Office under Addington he was responsible for the Treaty of Amiens ; he was at the Home Office under Pitt from 1804-1806, and again under the Duke of Portland from 1807-1809 ; and as Secretary for the Colonies and War (1809-1812) he was immediately responsible for the conduct of the war in the Peninsula. He was not included in the ministry of " All the Talents," but he was regarded —particularly by the King—as more than a possible candidate for the Premiership in 1807, and again, when Perceval was preferred to him, in 1809.

After Perceval's assassination there were prolonged negotiations with Wellesley and Canning on the one side, and with the Whig leaders, Grenville, Grey, and Moira, on the other. Ultimately, however, Lord Liverpool formed a Government which differed little in personnel from that of his predecessor. Selected as a safe compromise in 1812, Lord Liverpool succeeded in retaining office with satisfaction to his friends and the goodwill of his opponents for nearly fifteen years. That he was ever in the front rank of English statesmen no one will affirm ; but he was an admirable administrator ; he filled the highest offices in the State with dignity and efficiency ; he spoke with lucidity and good sense ; he was conciliatory to his opponents, and he held together his own party as no one else at that time would have done.

Of Lord Liverpool's colleagues the most prominent were the Lord Chancellor and the Secretaries of State for Foreign and Home affairs. John Scott, first Earl of Eldon, was throughout his political life a consistent and unbending Tory of the deepest hue. The younger of two remarkable brothers [1] he entered the House of Commons through the good offices of Lord Thurlow, in 1782. He became Solicitor-General in Pitt's administration in 1788, Attorney in 1793, Chief Justice of the Common Pleas in 1799, and Lord Chancellor, under Addington, in 1801. He held that office until after Pitt's death in 1806. To the grief of the King he refused to be associated with " All the Talents," but he returned to the Woolsack under Portland in 1807 and for twenty years never quitted it. Despite former differences he enjoyed the confidence of the Regent not less completely than that of George III., and to the end of his life was the typical representative of that school of Toryism which detested the idea of change or reform. *Lord Eldon*

Far inferior to the Chancellor in ability but belonging to the same school of Toryism was the Home Secretary, Lord Sidmouth. Canning's merciless lampoons have tended to obscure the substantial merits of " Dr." Addington. An admirable Speaker of the House of *Lord Sidmouth*

---

[1] The elder, William Scott, Lord Stowell, was one of the most eminent lawyers who ever sat as Judge in the Admiralty Court.

Commons Addington was dragged in 1801 from a position he adorned to occupy one to which he was manifestly unequal. But though he could not fill Pitt's shoes as Premier, Addington was by no means the fool that contemporary satire would suggest.

As Home Secretary during the critical years 1812-1821 he must at least have the credit of having performed an exceedingly unpopular duty with unflinching courage and exemplary firmness. Whether he was statesman enough to comprehend causes as well as to deal vigorously with effects is a matter of dispute on which something must presently be said.

Lord Castlereagh Incomparably more interesting as a personality than either Sidmouth or Eldon was the Secretary of State for Foreign affairs— Robert Stewart, Viscount Castlereagh. That contemporaries should have undervalued his merits and achievements is not perhaps remarkable ; for Castlereagh with all his splendid endowments of character and intellect was entirely lacking in personal magnetism.

> Stately in quiet high-bred self-esteem,
> Fair as the Lovelace of a lady's dream.

Lord Lytton's lines do no more than justice to his remarkable dignity, but he had none of the arts which make for general popularity. Himself devoid of enthusiasm, and too honest to affect a quality he did not possess, he naturally failed to evoke it among his followers. " He is," said Cornwallis, " so cold that nothing can warm him." The very qualities which gave him his ascendancy in the councils of Europe militated against his success in the British Senate. His calm, unruffled, and passionless judgment commanded the respect of continental diplomatists ; his curious lack of oratorical skill invited the sarcasm of his parliamentary opponents. But his special misfortune was that throughout his career he should have been overshadowed in popular estimation by the brilliant gifts of his great rival Canning, and posterity has been slow to correct the misapprehension of contemporaries.

For a quarter of a century Castlereagh played an important part in English politics ; for ten years he was the real ruler of England and one of the arbiters of Europe. As Chief Secretary for Ireland he was largely responsible for the suppression of the rebellion and mainly instrumental in carrying the Act of Union. He was Secretary of State for the Colonies and War under Pitt in 1805, and again under Portland (1807-1809). But his real work was done at the Foreign Office, and it is by his ten years' administration of that great department that his reputation must stand or fall. Coming into office at a moment (1812) when Napoleon's power though threatened was still unbroken, it was his task to maintain the European coalition during the most critical years of the whole war, and to represent Great Britain in the negotiations for peace. He reached the zenith of his fame as a statesman in the year of Waterloo. The last seven years of his life, with which alone we are concerned in this volume, were not only an anti-climax in his career ; they added much to his contemporary unpopularity, and they detracted seriously though unjustly from his posthumous fame.

Such were the men to whom at a critical time the destinies of the country were confided. The task before them was one of appalling complexity. They were called upon immediately and simultaneously to restore equilibrium to the national finances ; to relieve the pressure of taxation ; to enter upon the gigantic task of liquidating the national debt ; to alleviate distress and to maintain social order— and all this at a moment of slackening trade and of diminishing revenue. Rarely indeed, if ever, in our history has social discontent been more pronounced or economic distress more general than in the years immediately following upon the Peace of 1815. *The task of the Ministry*

For this there were many reasons. A proverbial aphorism associates " Peace " with " Plenty " ; experience teaches, on the contrary, that the conclusion of a great war is invariably followed by a period of suffering and want. But never has the economic recoil of Peace been so marked as in the years between 1815 and 1822. For this fact the duration and severity of the struggle which ended at Waterloo would alone be sufficient to account. But all the effects of protracted war were, in this case, accentuated by the coincidence of an economic revolution without parallel or precedent in magnitude and scope. *Reasons for general distress*

During the long war a new England had come into being, and it is hardly matter for surprise that rulers and ruled were alike distracted by the phenomenon ; that they were slow to diagnose the unfamiliar diseases of the body politic and slower still to devise appropriate remedies. *The new England*

When the French Republic declared war upon Great Britain in 1793 it had at its back a population of over 26,000,000 souls. To oppose to this the United Kingdom could command perhaps 14,000,000 people, of whom a discontented Ireland claimed between 3,000,000 and 4,000,000.[1] By 1815 the population of the United Kingdom despite the drain of the war had leapt up to 19,000,000— an increase of 35 per cent. in twenty-two years. Such an increase was without precedent in this country. Before 1751 it is believed *Population*

---

[1] Statistics of population in Great Britain are only approximate previous to 1801 when the first official census was taken. No precise estimate can be formed of Irish population till 1821. The population of the chief towns of the United Kingdom at the end of the war in 1816 : London, 1,100,000 ; Dublin, 180,000 ; Manchester and Salford, 140,000 ; Glasgow, 125,000-130,000 ; Liverpool, 120,000 ; Birmingham under 100,000 ; Bristol, 80,000 (once the second city in England) ; Leeds, 70,000-80,000 ; Sheffield, 60,000-70,000 ; Plymouth, 50,000-60,000 ; Portsmouth, 50,000-60,000 ; Norwich, 40,000 (once the third city).—*Report of Poor Law Commission* (1909), p. 304. For a discussion of population statistics *cf.* an interesting paper by E. C. K. Gonner (*Statistical Journal*, 1913).

that the largest decennial increase of population was about 3 per cent. Between 1791 and 1801 it was 11 per cent., between 1801 and 1811 14 per cent., and between 1811 and 1821 no less than 18 per cent. Well might the benevolent Malthus be alarmed. This phenomenal increase in population was due to the coincidence of prolonged war and economic revolution. There was a simultaneous demand for men for the arts of war and the arts of commerce. Artificial stimulus was followed by corresponding depression. With the Peace came a cessation of demand both for men and for commodities, and the market was suddenly glutted. This phenomenon was neither unnatural nor unprecedented, but in this case industrial dislocation was intensified by the peculiar conditions of the recent war.

Foreign trade   For the last twenty years England had been the only country in Western Europe free from the devastating effects of military operations. She had consequently been called upon to supply the commercial needs of the whole world, and, thanks to the recent improvements in agriculture and in manufacturing industry, she was in a position to do so. The result was seen in a totally unprecedented expansion of foreign trade. In 1792 the total imports amounted to £19,659,358 and the exports to £18,336,851. In the last year of war imports rose to £32,987,396, while the exports reached the amazing total of £58,624,550. But England had not merely secured a virtual monopoly of manufactures ; she had also become the carrier of the world. Since Napoleon's famous Berlin Decree and the British retort embodied in the Orders in Council no ship could sail the seas except under the British Flag. The extent to which England had become the entrepôt of international trade may be gauged by the statistics of foreign and colonial produce re-exported from this country. Re-exports, which in the last year of peace (1792) amounted to £6,568,349, rose in the last year of war to £19,157,818.

Revenue   The national resources kept pace with the expansion of trade and the growth of population. The revenue collected by Pitt in 1792 amounted to no more than £19,859,123. The same taxes produced in the last year of war no less than £45,000,000. But those taxes were, of course, wholly inadequate to the service of the State. During the twenty-three years between 1793 and 1815 over £65,000,000 a year was on the average raised for public purposes, and during the last two years the expenditure reached the appalling total of £105,943,727 (for 1813) and £106,832,260 (for 1814).

Growth of debt   An heroic effort was made to meet expenses as far as possible out of revenue. Thus, while in 1793 the tax revenue was, as we have seen, under £20,000,000, by 1815 it had risen to £72,210,512—the largest sum ever raised by taxation in Great Britain until the Crimean war. But no modern State could have carried on the Napoleonic war, still less have sustained by lavish subsidies an European coalition, without recourse to loans. Hence the charge for debt (interest and management) which in 1793 amounted to less than £9,500,000 had swollen by 1815 to over £31,000,000. The capital sum of the debt had increased in an even more appalling degree : from £239,663,421 in the former year to £831,171,132 in the latter.[1] Opinions differ as to the policy of Pitt and his successors at the Treasury in raising the loans required in stock of a low denomination, but on the whole the system is generally condemned. Between 1793 and 1801 the average rate at which 3 per cent. stock was issued was £57 7s. 6d. per £100 stock. Between 1803 and 1815 the average price obtained was £60 7s. 6d. Had the financiers of that day had the courage to raise money at something more nearly approaching the market price—say 5 per cent.—the burden upon the shoulders of posterity would have been sensibly lightened and the sacrifices demanded of contemporaries not appreciably increased.

Those sacrifices could not under any circumstances have been otherwise than heavy. Nevertheless, during the greater part of the war they were sustained with remarkable cheerfulness. Employment was abundant ; trade was advancing by leaps and bounds ; high prices diffused an air of general if delusive prosperity. But during the last five years of the struggle the economic outlook darkened ominously. The rigours of the Continental System and the British retaliations began to tell ; war with the United States (1812-1814) still further dislocated trade ; while in Great Britain itself several bad harvests caused the price of wheat to fluctuate violently. Between 1808 and 1813 the average price of wheat was over £5 a quarter, and in the summer of 1813 it touched 171s. Before Christmas of the same year it had dropped to 75s. *Variations in prices*

Among many causes which contributed to high prices and still more to violent fluctuations one deserves special mention. Since the crisis of 1797 cash payments had been suspended at the Bank of England and an enforced paper currency had been in circulation. As a consequence innumerable country Banks had sprung up—some of them reared upon very unstable foundations. Between 1797 and 1814 more than 700 such Banks came into existence, but more than a third of them stopped payment in the critical years 1814 and 1815. Inflation of the paper currency naturally followed upon the suspension of cash payments and the multiplication of Banks ; but until the closing years of the war the effects were less marked than might have been anticipated. In 1810 there were £25,000,000 of notes in circulation and the premium on gold rose to £8 7s. 8d. per cent. In 1813 it rose to £29 4s. 1d. and the gold value of a £5 note fell to £3 10s. In 1815 the premium fell to £13 9s. 6d. and the gold value of a £5 note rose consequently to £4 6s. In the face of such violent *Currency disturbances*

---

[1] These are MacCulloch's figures ; Porter's vary but immaterially.

2

fluctuations no prudence could avert commercial ruin ; trade was reduced to a mere gamble, and violent oscillations in prices inflicted dire hardship alike upon producer, retailer, and consumer.

Administration of the Poor Law

It may be doubted, however, whether amongst all the factors which contributed to the prevailing misery there was any single one so potent as the mistaken kindness which inspired the administrators of the Poor Law. The first half of the eighteenth century is one of the bright periods in the history of English pauperism. When George III. came to the throne the total sum expended on the relief of the poor amounted to no more than £1,250,000, or 3s. 7d. per head of the population. The last twenty years of the century witnessed the legislative abolition of the " Workhouse test " and a sensible slackening in the strictness of administration. The example of the Berkshire magistrates who, in 1795, decided to supplement wages out of the rates was so generally followed throughout the South of England as to elevate the resolution of a local bench to the dignity of an " Act of Parliament ". The notorious " Speenhamland Act " contained an elaborate schedule, by which income was to be apportioned to family. The policy embodied in this " Act " has been vigorously assailed and cannot on economic grounds be defended. It stimulated population ; it encouraged idleness ; it depressed wages, and it rendered still harder the hard lot of the thrifty and independent labourer. The seed flung carelessly broadcast at the close of the eighteenth century produced an abundant harvest of demoralization and misery in the second and third decades of the nineteenth. The cost of poor relief had risen to 8s. 11d. per head in 1803 and to 13s. 1d. in 1811. The annual expenditure on poor relief which in the first year of George III.'s reign was £1,250,000, averaged during the last five years of the reign over £7,000,000, and the economic burden was, perhaps, the least of the evils this expenditure entailed.

The situation in 1815

Such were the outstanding features of the situation by which the rulers of England were confronted after the conclusion of the great war : a labour market congested and dislocated ; trade suddenly arrested after a period of abnormal inflation ; a gigantic debt ; a falling revenue ; a disordered currency ; a peasantry demoralized by reckless administration of relief ; a populace discontented and ripe for disturbance ; all classes involved in a common ruin : landlord and tenant-farmer, capitalist and manufacturer, banker and merchant, skilled artisan and agricultural labourer.

To those who can attribute all the prevailing misery to the fatuous policy of a selfish oligarchy the above analysis will seem superfluously elaborate.[1] To those who refuse to accept this facile

---

[1] Cf. e.g. Dr. J. F. Bright (English History, iii. 1330), who writes of the Tory Government : " It cannot be said that they were urged by patriotic motives. Throughout their conduct had been dictated by the interests of their class. . . . The same motive of class aggrandizement which detracts from the virtue of the foreign policy of this Ministry underlay the whole administration of home affairs.

explanation and desire to trace surface effects to underlying causes it may be helpful. Certain it is that without a clear apprehension of the social and economic situation in 1815 there can be no fair criticism of the policy pursued by the Government of the day, and no real clue to the complex problems by which they were confronted.

Under these circumstances it was singularly unfortunate that Lord Liverpool should have committed the Exchequer to Vansittart. Despite some financial experience and much personal amiability he was obviously unequal to the office at a time of almost unparalleled responsibility. He had neither a strong grip on economic principles nor sufficient business ability to atone for the lack of it. Muddle-headed as a thinker he was blundering as an administrator. The leading dogma of his economic creed was a blind belief in the virtues of irredeemable paper money ; the chief plank in his financial pro-gramme was the maintenance of the Sinking-fund even at the cost of fresh loans. *Van-sittart*

In the Budget of 1816 Vansittart had to provide for an expendi-ture of over £66,000,000. Apart from the Property tax, which then stood at 2s. in the £ and yielded about £15,000,000 a year, he could reckon on receipts of over £58,000,000. He proposed, therefore, to reduce the Property tax to 1s. But the Opposition regarded this as a very imperfect fulfilment of repeated pledges, and raised a strong protest. Brougham,[1] whose brilliant parliamentary career dates from this time, led the attack upon Vansittart with extraordinary persistency and skill. Like his nominal leaders Ponsonby and Tierney, Brougham refused the proffered remission of 1s., and de-manded that as the war was over the war tax should be altogether abandoned. The Government was beaten by a majority of 37, and Vansittart, deprived of his expected £7,500,000 was faced with a large deficit. Defeated on the Property tax, he decided to surrender as well the " war malt tax "—an additional 2s. per bushel on malt imposed in 1804. This concession cost him an additional £2,700,000. Even under these circumstances the Sinking-fund was sacrosanct, and Vansittart solved his difficulties by borrowing £11,500,000 with one hand, while he paid £15,000,000 into the Sinking-fund with the other. Such scrupulosity might be magnificent, but it was not sound finance. *Budget of 1816*

The year 1816 is, nevertheless, memorable for a financial trans-action of permanent significance. Ireland had become to all intents and purposes insolvent, and it was decided that the only permanent solution of her difficulties was to be found in the consolidation of the *Consoli-dation of British and Irish Exche-quers*

There was an incapacity to look at public affairs from any but a class or aristo-cratic point of view." Even Sir Spencer Walpole, to whose *History of England from 1815* I wish to acknowledge my obligation, is not free from this prejudice. *Cf. e.g.* vol. i. p. v, Preface.

[1] Henry Brougham entered the House oi Commons as member for Camelford, 1810 ; out of Parliament, 1812-1815 ; brought in for Winchelsea, 1815.

British and Irish Exchequers. This natural sequel to Pitt's political
Union was actually consummated in January, 1817, and conferred an
immense though unappreciated boon upon the poorer country.

For Great Britain, as a whole, the outlook was exceedingly gloomy.
But the clouds were momentarily dispelled by the auspicious marriage
of the Princess Charlotte and the success which attended the naval
expedition to Algiers.

Marriage of the Princess Charlotte   On May 2nd, 1816, the Princess Charlotte Augusta, heiress to the
throne and the only legitimate grandchild of George III., was married
to Prince Leopold George Frederick, younger brother of the reigning
Duke of Saxe-Coburg. Her refusal to marry William, Prince of
Orange, foiled Castlereagh's favourite project ; but it did not
diminish her general popularity, and her marriage to Prince Leopold
was heartily acclaimed by those who hoped at no distant date to be
her subjects. The House of Commons voted £60,000 for the
Princess's trousseau and settled £60,000 a year upon her.

Expedition to Algiers   In August, Lord Exmouth was despatched in command of a large
naval force to chastise the Dey of Algiers for a recent outrage upon
the British flag and to compel him to abandon the practice of
Christian slavery. The naval operations were conducted with
brilliant success ; the objects of the expedition were completely
attained, and a death-blow was given to the barbarous and piratical
custom of reducing captives to slavery.

Marriage bells and brilliant feats of arms might temporarily relieve,
but they could not permanently dissipate the prevailing gloom.

Agricultural distress   Bad harvests and violent fluctuations of prices were bringing
widespread ruin upon agriculturists. In the hope of assisting them
the Legislature in 1815 prohibited the importation of wheat until
the price reached 80s. a quarter. But this afforded no relief when,
as in 1816, the price fell to 52s. 6d. It is easy to blame farmers for
their folly in taking leases at rents calculated upon war prices, and
to condemn landlords for extortion. But, meanwhile, the greatest of
English industries appeared to be threatened with imminent ruin.
Reports received by the Board of Agriculture in response to a circular
letter issued in 1816 attest the severity of the crisis.[1] Farmers, who
a few years ago were competing eagerly for farms, were sending in
notices to quit, and many farms were unlet ; mortgagees found it
difficult to realize ; credit was collapsing ; Banks were failing in all
directions ; substantial farmers were becoming parish paupers. And
while the producer was ruined the consumer derived no benefit. In
December, 1816, wheat which in the spring had fallen to 52s. 6d.
rose to 103s. Agriculture had become a mere gamble.[2]

[1] The questions and answers will be found in a State Paper of singular interest
reprinted in *Annual Register*, Chronicle, pp. 459-469. *Cf.* also Prothero, *Pioneers
and Progress of English Farming*, pp. 89 *seq.*
[2] " I assure you the landed people are getting *desperate* : the universality of
ruin among them or distress bordering on it is *absolutely* unparalleled." C. C.
Western, M.P., to Creevey (Feb. 17th, 1816).—*Creevey Papers*, i. 252.

If landlords and farmers were ruined, merchants and manufac- Depres-
turers were in no better plight. "The Citizens," wrote the Master sion of
of the Mint, "have lost all their feelings of pride and richness and trade
flourishing fatness, trade is gone, contracts are gone, paper credit is
gone, and there is nothing but stoppage, retrenchments and bankruptcy." [1] Wellesley-Pole did not exaggerate the gravity of the
situation, nor are the causes of it obscure. The war, as we have seen,
had encouraged reckless capital expenditure. Traders, as is their
wont, looked no further than their noses. The inevitable happened.
With the restoration of normal conditions the continental demand for
English goods rapidly slackened ; prices came down with a run ;
production was paralysed, and thousands of hands were turned adrift
to swell the army of the unemployed.

The crisis was particularly severe in the industries which had been
stimulated by the demand for war stores. The iron and coal trades
were especially depressed. Out of thirty-four furnaces in South
Staffordshire twenty-four were out of blast, and whole villages were
reduced to starvation. Similar stories came from Newport, Tredegar,
Merthyr Tydvil, and other growing towns of Monmouthshire and
South Wales, whilst thousands of iron workers and colliers were
suddenly thrown out of work.[2]

The natural consequences ensued. As William Cobbett himself Epidemic
observed : "When men are in distress they are out of humour : they of dis-
have not time and are not in a disposition to listen to reason ".[3] order
Because bread was at famine prices the existing supplies of corn were
diminished by incendiaries. Because work was scarce, machinery
was smashed and factories were destroyed. From all parts of the
country came reports of violence and crime. In the Eastern counties
there was an alarming amount of unrest and disorder. Barns and
ricks were burnt to the ground ; thrashing machines and other
agricultural implements were publicly burned ; bakers' and butchers'
shops were attacked, and angry mobs demanded " bread or blood " ;
cargoes of wheat and potatoes intended for export were seized ;
immense damage was inflicted upon property, and Littleport, in the
Isle of Ely, presented the appearance of a town " sacked by a be-
sieging army ". Nor was the unrest confined to the agricultural
counties. The Tyneside colliers, the Preston cotton-weavers, the
Wiltshire cloth-workers, the Monmouthshire and Staffordshire iron-
workers, the jute-workers of Dundee,—all alike were in ferment,
demanding more employment, higher wages, and cheaper food.

The agitation was not exclusively economic. It began to assume Political
agitation

[1] Wellesley-Pole to Bagot, July 30th, 1816.—Bagot, *Canning and his Friends*,
ii. 33.
[2] *Annual Register* (1816), *passim.* In illustration of the general scarcity of
money it is stated (*A.R.*, Chronicle, p. 54) that two Claudes for which 1,000 guineas
each had been paid in 1813 were sold for 80 and 70 guineas respectively.
[3] *Political Register*, December, 1815.

a political complexion. With the cries for more work and cheaper
food, there began to mingle demands for universal suffrage and
annual Parliaments. Demagogues like "Orator" Hunt, brilliant
pamphleteers like William Cobbett added fuel to the flames, and
Byron exhausted his powers of mordant sarcasm in pouring contempt
upon the Government. Cobbett's *Political Register* was at the end
of 1816 reduced from 1s. to 2d. and began to exercise an unbounded
political influence. Political clubs sprang up like mushrooms. The
"Hampden" clubs, founded by Major Cartwright in 1815, began
to formulate many of the demands afterwards embodied in the
"Charter". The "Spencean Philanthropists" preached communistic
doctrines to hungry mobs. In the background we can discern the
more sinister figures of political conspirators and even assassins,—
men of the type of the Watsons and Thistlewood.

Meeting in Spa Fields In the winter of 1816 London itself was alarmed by an outbreak
of disorder. On November 15th a meeting was organized in Spa
Fields, Bermondsey, to call attention to the sufferings of the "distressed manufacturers, artisans, and others of the Cities of London
and Westminster, the Borough of Southwark, and parts adjacent,"
and after much wild talk was adjourned to December 2nd. Rumours
gained ground of an organized attack upon the Government; of
plots to seize the Tower and the Bank, and to seduce the Army.
Undoubtedly there was much inflammatory language: mobs assembled
bearing tricolour badges, and men talked of a Committee of Public
Safety. On December 2nd the adjourned meeting was held in Spa
Fields; the mob, inflamed by speeches from the Watsons, made off
to Clerkenwell and Smithfield, sacked a gunsmith's shop at Snow
Hill, and armed with their booty marched through Cheapside and
invaded the Royal Exchange. Courageously confronted by Matthew
Wood, the Lord Mayor, their further progress was arrested and after
some time order was restored.

Reform petition from the City Corporation But behind the mob serious political forces were in operation.
Precisely a week after the Spa Fields meeting, the Corporation of
London formally addressed the Prince Regent. They declared that
"the distress and misery which for so many years has been progress-
ively accumulating, has at length become insupportable," and that
"the commercial, the manufacturing, and the agricultural interests
are equally sinking under its irresistible pressure, and it has become
impossible to find employment for a large mass of the population".
They ascribed the distress and discontent to "rash and ruinous wars,
unjustly commenced and pertinaciously persisted in," to gross
extravagance in war and peace, and above all to "the corrupt and
inadequate state of the representation of the people in Parliament".
They begged the Regent to urge upon Parliament measures "for
making every practicable reduction in the public expenditure and
restoring to the people their just share and weight in the Legislature ".

The Prince Regent did not add to his popularity by the severe snub which he inflicted upon the petitioners, and as he returned from the opening of Parliament (Jan. 28th, 1817) the windows of his coach were smashed.

On the reassembling of Parliament, Ministers were confronted by a menacing situation. Political agitation was clearly supervening upon the social disorder arising from economic distress. Would it under these circumstances be wise, or even possible, to embark upon the path of reform? Might not concessions be interpreted as weakness?[1] Was it not imperative to begin with the restoration of social order? But would not repression drive the moderates into the arms of the extremists? The secure wisdom of posterity may suggest that the way of safety lay in a judicious combination of strong administration and timely reform. But such a policy would have demanded a precise diagnosis of the situation. No Ministry could safely plunge into the sea of reform without previously ascertaining the strength and direction of the currents and cross-currents they would have to encounter. Was the country ripening for revolution? Would reform arrest or precipitate it? Were the sporadic outbreaks of disorder due to the intolerable pressure of economic distress, or evidences of a settled design to overturn the existing order? Such were the questions confronting the Executive, and no fair-minded critic will be quick to blame Lord Liverpool and his colleagues if they were not answered with the assurance and wisdom which come only from a knowledge of the event.

The policy of the Government, 1817

The Prince Regent's speech at the opening of Parliament (Jan. 28th) referred to " the attempts which have been made to take advantage of the distresses of the country for the purpose of exciting a spirit of sedition and violence ". Secret Committees were immediately appointed in both Houses, and on February 18th and 19th their *Reports* were laid before Parliament. The Committees, after an investigation of the information at the disposal of the Executive, were clearly impressed with the gravity of the situation. They held that both in London and in the provinces—notably in the manufacturing districts of Lancashire, Leicestershire, Derby, Nottingham, and Glasgow—there was clear evidence of a deliberately planned revolutionary movement. They deplored the multiplication of political clubs and societies and the dissemination of inflammatory publications which not only demanded advanced political reforms, such as universal suffrage and annual elections, but aimed at " the plunder and division of all property "; which taught that " the landowner was a monster to be hunted down," and that worse than the landowners were the fund-holders, " rapacious creatures who take from the people 15d. out of every quartern loaf." [2]

[1] *Cf. e.g.* Walter Scott to J. W. Croker (March ,1817). " We are all shocked at your giving your mob so much head."—Croker, i. 99.

[2] *Lords Journals,* ii. p. 41.

Repres-
sive
measures
In view of these *Reports* Sidmouth and Castlereagh had little difficulty in persuading Parliament to suspend the Habeas Corpus Act for four months (Mar. 3rd-July 1st), and to pass further Acts to prohibit the holding of seditious meetings, to prevent the seduction of the Army and Navy from their allegiance, and to provide for the security of the Regent's person. More keenly criticized was a letter issued by Lord Sidmouth to the Lord Lieutenants (Mar. 27th) urging the Magistrates to issue warrants for the apprehension of persons charged before them upon oath with the publication of " blasphemous and seditious pamphlets and writings," and to compel them to give bail to answer the charge. The circular was regarded as an insidious attack upon the liberty of the Press, and though prosecutions were numerous, convictions were few. The most notorious and most damaging fiasco was the prosecution (Dec. 18th) of an antiquarian bookseller named Hone, who had published certain profane parodies, such as *The Sinecurist's Creed*. Despite the efforts of the Attorney-General and Chief Justice Ellenborough to secure a conviction, Hone induced the jury to acquit him, and the popularity of the verdict was unmistakable.

Insurrec-
tionary
move-
ments
Meanwhile, agitation was renewed in the North and Midlands. Early in March large meetings of working men organized in Manchester were dispersed by the authorities, and on March 29th some thousands of the agitators set out upon a journey to London which, from the fact that the men carried blankets, is known as the " March of the blanketeers ". The march was arrested and the men dispersed before they had got many miles out of Manchester.

More serious but still abortive was an " insurrection " planned by a man named Brandreth in the Midlands on June 10th. Some alarm was created by the march of armed rioters in Derbyshire and Nottingham, but the rioters were easily dispersed by the yeomanry, the ringleaders were arrested and paid for their criminal folly with their lives.

In consequence of these renewed disturbances Secret Committees were again appointed (June 3rd) in both Houses, and the Committees found " but too many proofs of the continued existence of a traitorous conspiracy for the overthrow of our established government and constitution and for the subversion of the existing order of society ". Before the prorogation Parliament renewed until March 1st, 1818, the suspension of the Habeas Corpus Act.

Death of
Princess
Charlotte
The harvest of 1817 was an exceptionally good one, and in the autumn things quieted down. But before the year ended the whole nation was plunged into mourning by the death in childbirth of the Princess Charlotte (Nov. 6th). Her death not only removed a popular Princess but rendered the succession to the Crown in the direct line exceedingly precarious. Of George the Third's thirteen sons and daughters not one had a legitimate child. The eldest collateral

descendant, William, Duke of Gloucester, was also childless. Under these circumstances the duty of the Royal Dukes was obvious, and in the following year (1818) four Royal marriages were solemnized. The Duke of Clarence married the Princess Adelaide of Saxe-Meiningen ; the Duke of Cambridge the Princess Augusta of Hesse-Cassel ; the Duke of Kent the Princess Victoria of Saxe-Coburg, widow of Charles Prince of Leiningen, while the Princess Elizabeth married Frederick Landgrave of Hesse-Homburg. It is significant that despite the great anxiety as to the succession the House of Commons should have shown itself exceptionally parsimonious in making provision for the Royal bridegrooms. A modest grant of £10,000 a year proposed for the Duke of Clarence was reduced to £6,000, and in high dudgeon refused by him as totally inadequate ; [1] grants of a similar amount were made to the Dukes of Cambridge and Kent in the teeth of strong opposition, while a proposal for an addition of £6,000 to the Duke of Cumberland, who had lately married, was actually rejected. So low had the prestige and popularity of the Crown been brought by the Prince Regent and his brothers.[2]

When Parliament reassembled on January 27th, 1818, the Regent was able to congratulate the country upon a marked improvement in the financial situation. A good harvest was followed by a distinct revival in trade and that again by a subsidence of disorder. The Government was able therefore to dispense with the exceptional powers bestowed upon the Executive by the suspension of the Habeas Corpus Act. The Act of the previous session lapsed on March 1st, and has never since that day been re-enacted in England. It was deemed necessary, however, to obtain an Act of Indemnity for all those who had, in virtue of the powers conferred upon them by the suspensory Act, detained suspects in custody or had suppressed " tumultuous and unlawful assemblies ". The Indemnity Act, though a natural sequel of the suspension Act, and in accordance with precedent, was not passed without fierce debate in both Houses. The necessity for such an Act is a striking testimony to the way in which the principle of Habeas Corpus has intertwined itself with the fibres of the English constitution.

It was at this time that Parliament showed its concern for the impaired morals of the people by voting the sum of £1,000,000 towards the erection of new churches. At the same time it demonstrated its steadfast adherence to the principles of Wilberforce by

Session of 1818

Grants for religious and phil- anthropic objects

---

[1] " Besides a Settlement such as is proper for a Prince who marries expressly for a succession to the throne, the Duke of Clarence demands the payment of all his debts which are very great and a handsome provision for each of his natural children."—Creevey, i. 268. Reported conversation with Duke of Kent.

[2] " They (the Princes) are the damnedest millstone about the necks of any Government that can be imagined. They have insulted, *personally* insulted, two-thirds of the gentlemen of England, and how can it be wondered at that they take their revenge upon them in the House of Commons."—Wellington ap. Creevey, i. 277.

granting £400,000 to the Spanish Government to compensate the Spaniards for their abolition of the slave trade. Having done so much for religion and humanity Parliament could await its dissolution with serenity. Sir Francis Burdett sought to disturb its closing days by a motion in favour of universal suffrage, annual Parliaments, electoral districts, and vote by ballot, but he failed to secure a single vote in its favour. Parliament was dissolved on June 10th.

General Election of 1818

The General Election was attended with unusual excitement, over one hundred constituencies being contested. The Opposition could make but little impression upon the compact Tory majority, but several notable fights ended in their favour. Romilly and Burdett were returned after a violent contest for Westminster ; in the City Sir William Curtis, a Tory member, who had sat for twenty-eight years, lost his seat, and three Whigs with one Tory were returned ; Brougham vainly attempted to win Westmoreland from the Lowthers ; and there were stiff fights in Wilts, Herefordshire, Devonshire, Kent, and Lincolnshire. In all, the Whigs gained about thirty votes. " The recent Elections plainly show that the people are no longer under the guidance of shallow pretenders to constitutional learning, or base dealers in vulgar sedition : and that even the most respectable zealots of reform have failed to estrange them from their natural leaders." [1] Such was the complacent comment of a great Whig organ on the results of the General Election of 1818.

The Opposition in Parliament

Notwithstanding these victories in the country the Opposition was very far from being an effective Parliamentary force. The Whig party was indeed hopelessly disorganized and divided. In the House of Lords Lord Grenville held aloof in haughty isolation ; in the House of Commons the front rank had of late been terribly thinned by the hand of death. Whitbread, to the deep regret of all good men, died by his own hand in 1815 ; George Ponsonby, the titular leader of the Whig party, and Horner in 1817 ; Sir Samuel Romilly, like Whitbread by suicide, in 1818. Tierney succeeded Ponsonby in the leadership, but Burdett and the small group of Radicals owed him no allegiance, and even his nominal lieutenants were frequently in revolt. By far the ablest man in the party was Henry Brougham, but his restlessness, egotism, tactlessness, and vanity, to say nothing of his unpopularity, rendered him impossible as leader.[2] Tierney, though held up to ridicule by Creevey, was conciliatory and popular, and divided the party less than any other leader who could, at the moment, have been selected.[3]

Meeting of new Parliament, 1819

When the new Parliament met on January 14th, 1819, the speech

---

[1] *Edinburgh Review*, June, 1818 (xxx. 204), where the Whig gains are put at " nearly 30 ".

[2] *Cf. e.g.* Bagot, June, 1816, to Canning : " What a Gin-drinking, straggling, corderoy scoundrel he seems to be ".

[3] *Cf.* Creevey, *passim*. Creevey nicknamed him " Mother Cole," a character in one of Foote's farces. For explanation *cf.* Creevey, i. 327.

from the Throne reported with satisfaction " a considerable and progressive improvement of the revenue ". The Master of the Mint (Wellesley-Pole) wrote in similar strain to his friend Charles Bagot : " the revenue flourishes, the reductions are great, the country is quiet, and all the world is at peace ".[1]

The complacency of the Government was short-lived : for the year 1819 was destined to see the Peterloo Massacre, and the passing of the *Six Acts*. But for the moment the talk was all of the currency. Sydney Smith wittily complained that " he got nothing now in Town but soup and bullion ". On February 2nd Tierney moved for the appointment of a Committee on the state of the circulating medium and on the continuance of the *Bank Restriction Act*. But on the motion of the Chancellor of the Exchequer a Secret Committee was preferred. Presided over by Robert Peel, and including such men as Vansittart, Castlereagh, Canning, Tierney, Wellesley-Pole, Huskisson, and Sir James Mackintosh, the Committee presented its report to the House on April 5th and May 6th.

Peel's reputation as a financier dates from his appointment as Peel chairman of this remarkable Committee. Born in Lancashire on February 5th, 1788, he was little more than thirty at this time. The eldest son of a man who made an enormous fortune in the Lancashire cotton trade,[2] he belonged by birth to the new aristocracy of commerce. His father, the first Sir Robert, was a first-rate business man, a stout Tory, an enthusiastic supporter of Pitt and his policy, a subscriber of £10,000 to the French War Fund, and the author of the first of a long series of Factory Acts. The elder Peel was convinced that the prosperity of England rested upon three main foundations : the Corn Laws, the Protestant Establishment, and inconvertible paper. In this creed the younger Robert Peel was reared. Educated at Harrow and Christ Church he was brought into the House of Commons in 1809 as member for Cashel, an Irish Borough picked up for him by his father, and burdened with only twelve constituents. Attached to the Tory party he served his official apprenticeship as Under-Secretary for War and the Colonies under Spencer Perceval, and for six years (1812-1818) was Chief Secretary for Ireland in the Liverpool Ministry. To Canning's chagrin he was elected as the representative of the University of Oxford[3] in 1817, and in the following year he resigned the Chief Secretaryship. His appointment as chairman of the Bullion Committee in 1819 was

---

[1] January 12th, 1819. *Cf. Canning and his Friends*, ii. 87.

[2] According to Greville (ii. 128) the elder Peel started in business without a shilling, and left to his eldest son £22,000 a year in land and £450,000 in the funds ; £250,000 a-piece to five younger sons ; and £60,000 a-piece to three daughters. In his lifetime he allowed his eldest son £12,000 a year and spent £3,000 a year himself.

[3] Peel owed his selection to the fact that he opposed while Canning favoured Catholic emancipation.

rightly regarded as an immense compliment to so young a man, and marked his admission to the front rank in his Party and in the House of Commons.

Resumption of cash payments

Peel entered upon his task with an open mind. In 1810 he had voted against the proposal for the resumption of cash payments, as recommended by Horner's Committee ; but circumstances had changed. Reference has already been made to the grave inconvenience resulting from the violent fluctuations in prices. The Bank Restriction Act was unquestionably one of the contributory causes of these fluctuations, and Peel's Committee reported strongly in favour of the gradual resumption of cash payments. A masterly speech from Peel persuaded the House to a unanimous acceptance of the Report ; it was resolved that cash payments should be gradually resumed, and that from May 1st, 1823, the Bank should pay its notes in gold. So strong was the position of the Bank that cash payments were in fact resumed two years before the stipulated date—on May 1st, 1821. That the resumption inflicted some temporary hardship on individuals is not to be denied, but it is none the less true that few Acts, if any, have contributed more powerfully to the stability of English commerce and the maintenance of English credit than the Bullion Act of 1819.

Reform proposals in the House of Commons

This Act was the only important legislative achievement of the first session of the new Parliament. But resistance to reform was clearly weakening in the House of Commons. Grattan's motion in favour of Catholic emancipation was rejected in a full House only by a majority of two, while that of Lord Archibald Hamilton demanding a Select Committee to investigate the state of Scottish representation was actually carried. On the other hand, Burdett's attempt to pledge the House to consider the question of parliamentary reform in the ensuing session was heavily defeated.

Agitation in the country

Although the House of Commons declined to take the Reform question seriously, the temper of the country was rapidly rising. Political agitation was, as usual, powerfully stimulated by economic distress. The improvement in trade manifested in 1818 was not maintained. Clouds again gathered on the commercial horizon. The number of bankruptcies increased ominously ; wages fell ;

1819

complaints of unemployment grew louder, and in the early summer great meetings were held at Glasgow, Ashton-under-Lyne, Leeds, Stockport, and elsewhere. A meeting at Birmingham held on July 12th and attended by more than 15,000 persons adopted the novel expedient of electing Sir Charles Wolseley, a Staffordshire Baronet, as " legislatorial attorney and representative of Birmingham ". But while the proceedings at Birmingham were tinged with farce those at Manchester resulted in grim tragedy.

Peterloo

On August 16th a vast meeting took place in St. Peter's Fields, now in the very heart of the great city of Manchester. From all the

neighbouring districts of Lancashire and Cheshire the men came in
their thousands; "many of them in regular marching order five
deep"; all preceded by flags surmounted with caps of liberty and
bearing various mottoes such as "No Corn Laws," "Annual Parliaments," "Universal Suffrage," "Vote by Ballot". The number
present was roughly computed at 80,000. Hardly had the chairman,
"Orator" Hunt, mounted the hustings when the Yeomanry with
drawn sabres charged into the dense throng to effect his arrest. In
an instant all was confusion. Crowds of people were trampled under
foot; eleven were killed; a few were sabred to death; three or
four hundred were more or less severely injured. Hunt and various
associates were arrested and committed for trial by the Lancashire
magistrates, and after various postponements were convicted at
York, not of high treason, as was originally intended, but on a charge
of "conspiracy to alter the legal frame of the Government and constitution of these realms, by force and threats, and with meeting
tumultuously at Manchester, with 60,000 persons, armed with sticks".
Hunt was sentenced to two years and six months' imprisonment,
Samuel Bamford and two other defendants to a year's imprisonment.
In each case they were required to find sureties to be of good behaviour during a further term of five years.

Meanwhile, congratulations poured in upon the victors of
Peterloo. The local magistrates returned thanks "to the Commanders, Officers and men of all the Corps who had taken part in
the actions of the day," particularly expressing their gratification
"at the extreme forbearance exercised by the Yeomanry when
insulted and defied by the rioters". The Regent expressed his "high
approbation" of the "exemplary manner" in which the Yeomanry
"assisted and supported the civil power," and Lord Sidmouth
conveyed the message "with great satisfaction".

In other quarters other views prevailed. Subscription lists were
opened in London and Liverpool for the victims of the "Manchester
massacre"; meetings were held at Norwich, Westminster, Bristol,
Liverpool, Nottingham, and York; some simply asked for inquiry,
others strongly censured the conduct of the Manchester authorities
and the Ministry. The great meeting at York was attended by
Lord FitzWilliam who was in consequence dismissed from the Lord
Lieutenancy of the West Riding. Still more significant was the
action of the Common Council of London who, on September 9th,
asserted "the undoubted right of Englishmen to assemble together
for the purpose of deliberating upon public grievances"; insisted
that the Manchester meeting was "legally assembled" and that its
proceedings were "orderly and peaceable," and finally expressed
their "strongest indignation" at the "unprovoked and intemperate"
conduct of the authorities.

In view of the rising excitement of the nation the Ministry took The Six
Acts

the wise step of summoning Parliament in the autumn. It met on
November 23rd, and a week later Lord Sidmouth outlined the proposals of the Government. After much debate and formal protests
from Lord Grey and other Whig Peers, but with the entire concurrence of Lord Grenville and his friends, the " Six Acts " became law.
The titles of these Acts sufficiently indicate their import. They were
designed (1) to prevent delay " in the administration of justice in
cases of misdemeanour " ; (2) " to prevent the training of persons in
the use of arms and the practice of military evolutions " ; (3) " for
the prevention and punishment of blasphemous and seditious libels " ;
(4) " to authorise Justices of the Peace in certain disturbed counties
to seize and detain arms " ; (5) " to subject certain publications to
the duties of stamps upon newspapers, and to make other regulations
for restraining the abuses arising from the publication of blasphemous
and seditious libels ; and (6) " for more effectually preventing seditious
meetings and assemblies ". Much violent criticism has been expended upon these Acts, and Castlereagh in particular has been held
up to the execration of posterity for the part which he took in passing
them through the House of Commons. But to three out of the six,
the first, second, and fourth, no serious objection can be taken. The
third, after remaining for some years a dead letter, was repealed in
1830. The duration of the Act for the prevention of seditious
meetings was expressly limited to five years, and that for the seizure
and detention of arms to a little more than two. Tierney found in the
proposals of the Executive " an evident determination to resort to
nothing but force ". That " force is no remedy " is a favourite
aphorism with orators in opposition. That it is no permanent
remedy is true ; but it is equally true that occasions arise when its
application is essential to the existence of civilized society. Whether
such an occasion had arisen in 1819 is a question which the historian
of to-day should be slow dogmatically to decide—at any rate against
the prevailing opinion of contemporaries.[1]

Death of
the King
and
Queen

Before Parliament reassembled in 1820 the longest reign hitherto
recorded in English history had come to an end. Death had been
busy of late in the ranks of the Royal family. The Princess Charlotte
died in 1817, the Queen in 1818, the Duke of Kent on January 23rd,
1820, and a week later (Jan. 29th) the poor old King himself was
released from his living tomb. His death evoked an outburst of
affectionate loyalty from all classes of his subjects. For the last ten
years, indeed, George III. had been nothing more than a shade
dragging out a melancholy existence at Windsor, bereft of reason,
sight, and hearing. But it was not forgotten that for fifty years he
had played a large if not a brilliant part upon the political stage, and
had represented with remarkable fidelity the views—not to say the

[1] " The Legislative enactments of 1819 ; to them we must, in no small degree,
ascribe the quiet state of the country in 1820."—*Annual Register*, 1820, p. 3.

prejudices—of the great majority of his subjects. No one can pretend that he was a great ruler ; but he was eminently a good man, and his homely virtues and his simple life, his dauntless courage and shrewd wit, his untiring industry, his generosity and kindliness won him general affection and respect.

Little respect or affection was entertained for his successor ; and whatever remnant of either sentiment survived was dissipated in the first months of the new reign. For more than a year after George the Fourth's accession the public mind was almost exclusively occupied with the scandalous relations of the King and Queen. " The discussion of the Queen's business," wrote Greville, " is now become an intolerable nuisance in society ; no other subject is ever talked of. It is an incessant matter of argument or dispute what will be done and what ought to be done. All people express themselves tired of the subject, yet none talk or think of any other." [1]   *George IV. (1820-1830)*

For the moment, however, attention was diverted from the King to his Ministers. On February 23rd the country was startled by the news of the conspiracy to which for bloodthirsty folly there had been no parallel since the days of Guy Fawkes. Arthur Thistlewood and a band of fanatical associates had planned to get rid of the whole of the detested Tory Cabinet at one murderous stroke. A Cabinet dinner to be held at Lord Harrowby's house in Grosvenor Square on February 23rd was the occasion selected for the execution of a plot which had been long maturing. The Government were in possession of complete information through one of their spies named Edwards. The Ministers instead of dining with Lord Harrowby remained at Fife House, while the conspirators, twenty or thirty in number, were surprised in the midst of their preparations at Cato Street, Edgware Road. They offered armed resistance, and slew the first constable who entered the stable where they were assembled. The police arrangements had been bungled and only nine arrests were made ; the leader and fourteen associates escaped ; but Thistlewood and several others were captured next morning. Brought to trial in April on a charge of high treason all the prisoners were convicted and sentenced to death. Thistlewood and four of his accomplices were executed on May 1st ; the other six were respited and transported for life. As to the guilt of the prisoners there was and is no question ; the extent of the conspiracy is more difficult to determine. Greville declares that the plan was to fire a rocket from Lord Harrowby's house after the destruction of the Cabinet, as a signal for a general rising ; that the Bank was to be attacked, and the gaols thrown open Whether any such signal would have been obeyed is doubtful.   *Cato Street Conspiracy, Feb. 23rd, 1820*   *The police*

The natural alarm excited by the Cato Street Conspiracy was intensified in April by an insurrectionary movement in Glasgow and the neighbouring districts. The organizers called upon " the people

[1] June 25th, 1820 (i. 32).

of England, Scotland, and Ireland to come forward and effect a revolution by force ". The force, however, was lacking, and the " insurrections " which took place at Bonnymuir and elsewhere were suppressed without difficulty.

The period of lawlessness and disorder ushered in by the peace of 1815 culminated in the Cato Street Conspiracy. The few remaining years of that Tory ascendancy, which had now lasted for more than half a century, were comparatively tranquil. For this there were several reasons. The worst of the economic crisis was over, and trade, abnormally stimulated by the war, was gradually restored to a more healthy condition. The reconstruction of the Liverpool Ministry in 1822 and the infusion of a more liberal element into the Cabinet gave hope of reasonable and moderate reform. Some credit also must be given—though it is unfashionable to do so—to the firmness with which the principles of law and order had been vindicated by Sidmouth and Castlereagh. It was of course the business of the Opposition to oppose—in public, but in private even opponents admitted the success of their policy. " Everybody agrees," wrote a strong Whig, " that the Doctor has done his part well." [1] Nor must it be forgotten that in the early years of the new reign the public mind was diverted, first, by a Court scandal of exceptional magnitude, and later by absorbing questions of foreign policy. Before we can discuss the latter a word must be said of the former.

Queen
Caroline

If the perspective of History were determined by contemporaries it would be necessary to devote a whole chapter to the " Queen's business ". But large as this business looms in the memoirs and diaries of the day, the modern Historian may compress the sordid and unsavoury details into a paragraph. When the Prince of Wales, in 1795, married the Princess Caroline of Brunswick, a bad man was mated to a frivolous, foolish, and unattractive woman. The marital connection hardly survived the formal marriage, and even before the birth of the Princess Charlotte husband and wife had ceased to live together. In 1806 the Whig Ministry humoured their patron by appointing a Secret Committee to conduct a " delicate investigation " as to the behaviour of the Princess, but nothing worse than levity was proved against her, and in 1814 she withdrew to Italy. Exasperated by her exclusion from Foreign Courts, and by the omission of her name from the English Liturgy, she returned to England in June, 1820, to claim her rights as Queen, to annoy the King, and to embarrass the Ministry. Ever since the death of Princess Charlotte her father had been increasingly anxious for a divorce, and spies had been employed to obtain the necessary evidence. On his accession to the throne the King pressed the Ministers to institute proceedings, but, anxious to avoid the inevitable scandal, Lord Liverpool resisted

[1] Lyttelton to Bagot, ap. Bagot, *Canning and his Friends*, ii. 37 (Dec. 30th 1816).

the King's wishes, though he promised to meet them should the Queen return to England. The time for the fulfilment of his promise had now come.

Received by the populace with indiscriminate enthusiasm, the Queen posed as a distressed and persecuted woman. Her most valuable asset was in reality the shameless life and political unpopularity of her husband. The Whigs also were quick to perceive the opportunity of snatching a party advantage from the embarrassments of the Government. "Some of the Opposition," wrote a Tory lady, "are behaving shamefully." "Not only the mob," wrote the Whig Lyttelton, ("don't be deceived by what your Tory friends tell you to the contrary), but people of all ranks, and the middle classes almost to a man, and I believe the troops too, side with the Queen."[1] It was true. On June 6th the King insisted that the House of Lords should institute an inquiry into his wife's conduct. Efforts at compromise conducted, on the King's part by Wellington and Castlereagh, on the Queen's by Brougham, her Attorney, and Denman her Solicitor-General, broke down on two points—the question of reception at Foreign Courts and on that of inclusion in the Liturgy. The Lords' Committee reported that the evidence demanded a solemn inquiry, and on July 8th Lord Liverpool introduced a Bill of Pains and Penalties to deprive the Queen of her title and dissolve her marriage. The Bill came on for second Reading on August 17th, and the Queen's trial (for such in effect it was) was protracted through the autumn. An immense volume of conflicting evidence was taken; Brougham conducted the defence with consummate skill; the second Reading was carried by a majority of 28 (Nov. 6th), the third Reading only by 9. Liverpool accepted the division as a sign of defeat, and amid delirous manifestations of popular enthusiasm the Bill was dropped. "I have never met anyone of any kind who believes her to be innocent," wrote Croker to Peel.[2] Croker moved in Tory circles, but he probably reflected the privately expressed opinions of those best qualified to judge. Even the Queen's friends were by this time disposed to recite the prayer of the famous epigram :—

> Gracious Queen, we thee implore
> Go away, and sin no more.
> Should that effort be too great,
> Go away—at any rate.

In the following session (1821) the House of Commons voted her an annuity of £50,000, but she did not live to enjoy it. On the refusal of the Privy Council to allow her to be crowned with the King, she foolishly attempted to force her way into the Abbey (July 19th, 1821). A few weeks later her unhappy life came to an end (Aug. 7th). She had already outlived her transient popularity, and the tide was

[1] *Canning and his Friends*, ii. 98.   [2] *Correspondence*, i. 177.

3

turning in the King's favour. His Coronation in July was not only celebrated with extravagant magnificence,[1] but appeared to evoke some popular enthusiasm. In August he paid a visit to Ireland, where he exerted to such good effect his undoubted powers of fascination that Lord Dudley declared that " if he had stood for Dublin he might have turned out Shaw or Grattan ".[2] Scarcely less enthusiastic, though less tumultuous, was his reception in Scotland a year later. In London he was never seen in public during the last seven years of his life. He feared the ridicule which might be excited by his dropsical bulk, and spent most of his time with Lady Conyngham at Brighton—a shameless voluptuary to the end.

Reconstruction of the Government

Lord Liverpool's Ministry was severely though, perhaps, undeservedly shaken by the " Queen's business ". There were, moreover, indications that the period of repression was passing away, and that Parliament was prepared to resume the work of constructive legislation interrupted by the outbreak of the French Revolution. Canning left the Cabinet in January, 1821, in consequence of his inability to concur in the policy of the Government towards the Queen. He was thus free to give his powerful support to Plunket's Catholic Emancipation Bill, which was carried through the Commons in 1821, only to suffer extinction in the House of Lords. A similar fate befell Canning's own Bill in 1822, designed to permit Roman Catholic Peers to sit and vote in the House of Lords. While Canning and Plunket were thus active on behalf of the Roman Catholics, Lord John Russell was pressing forward the cause of Parliamentary Reform. In 1820 his Bill for withholding Writs from Grampound, Penryn, Camelford, and Barnstaple, passed the Commons ; his resolution in favour of reform was supported by a large minority in 1821, and in the same session his Bill for the Disfranchisement of Grampound was actually carried, though the Peers insisted on giving the seats to the County of York instead of the Borough of Leeds. In 1822 Sir James Mackintosh succeeded in pledging the House of Commons to a reform of the Criminal Law. These things were indicative of the rising tide of opinion both at Westminster and in the country at large.

Not less suggestive were the changes in the Ministry itself. In 1822 Lord Sidmouth, who had stolidly and courageously borne the brunt of his colleagues' unpopularity, was succeeded at the Home Office by Peel ; Lord Wellesley accepted the Lord Lieutenancy of Ireland ; Plunket, the strenuous advocate of Catholic claims, became Attorney-General,[3] and C. W. Wynn succeeded Bragge Bathurst at the Board of Control. In 1823 the Ministry was further strengthened. especially on the financial side. by the substitution of F. J. Robinson

---

[1] The King's Crown cost £54,000 and his robes £24,000.
[2] Quoted by Brodrick, *Political History of England*, vol. xi. p. 197.
[3] For Ireland.

for Vansittart at the Exchequer, and by Huskisson's appointment to the Board of Trade. But most important and most significant of all was the change at the Foreign Office and in the Leadership of the House of Commons. In 1822 Castlereagh, who in 1821 had by his father's death become Marquis of Londonderry, died by his own hand. Lord Liverpool promptly offered both the vacant offices to Canning. The latter had recently been persuaded to accept the Governor-Generalship of India, and was just on the point of leaving England to assume his new duties. He decided, however, to accept Lord Liverpool's offer, and for the next five years Canning was the real ruler of England and a great power in affairs of Europe.[1]

[1] Brougham's comment on the event is curiously at variance with received opinion : " Canning succeeds to Foreign Office, Lead of the House, etc.—in short, all of Castlereagh except his good judgment, good manners, and bad English ". —Creevey, ii. 249.

CHAPTER III

ENGLAND AND EUROPE. THE HOLY ALLIANCE. CASTLEREAGH AND CANNING
(1815-1830)

Castle-
reagh and
Canning

THE persistent legend that English foreign policy underwent a violent deviation in 1822 is no longer accepted by competent historians. But it is none the less true that the accession of Canning to the Foreign Office was an event of real significance alike for England and for Europe. In order to gauge adequately its importance, it will be necessary to survey the course of English foreign policy since the conclusion of the war.

Relations
with the
Great
Powers,
1815-1822

At no period in her history have the relations of Great Britain with the Continental Powers been so intimate as during the decade which followed Waterloo. Such intimacy was not merely natural but inevitable. England it was who had formed and financed successive coalitions against Napoleon Bonaparte ; who, thanks to Castlereagh, had prevented at Chatillon the disruption of the last coalition on the eve of final victory ; who, thanks to Wellington, had secured at Waterloo the ultimate overthrow of the common enemy. Her Minister was largely responsible for the terms of the settlement of 1815, and her General commanded the joint army of occupation which guaranteed their execution. That England should intervene more closely and more continuously than usual in the concerns of continental Europe is, therefore, a matter neither for surprise nor reproach.

The Holy
Alliance

Nor is it wonderful that the allied Sovereigns and their Ministers should have welcomed this opportunity to put international relations on a more satisfactory basis. In this laudable ambition the *Holy Alliance* had its genesis. Few diplomatic efforts have incurred more odium or more ridicule. And neither is wholly deserved. Its author, the Czar Alexander of Russia, was a curious mixture of shrewdness and mysticism, of lofty ideals and calculating ambition. In its origin the Holy Alliance was a genuine attempt to apply the principles of Christian ethics to international politics ; to revive the idea of a confederacy of nations and to rebuild the European polity upon a religious basis. According to the terms of the original scheme announced by the Czar in September, 1815, the Sovereigns of Russia, Austria, and Prussia bound themselves " agreeably to the words of Holy Scripture which commands all men to live as brothers, to remain united in the bonds of true and indissoluble brotherly love ; always to assist one another ; to govern their subjects as parents ; to maintain religion, peace, and justice. They consider themselves

but as members of one and the same Christian family commissioned
by Providence to govern the branches of one family. They call on
all powers who acknowledge similar principles to join this Holy
Alliance." The Regent of England, not being a Sovereign, was
technically ineligible for membership in the alliance, but he wrote to
his " brothers " to express his cordial assent to the " sublime principles " enunciated by the Czar. The Sovereigns of France, Spain,
and the two Sicilies subsequently gave it their adherence. Metternich
regarded the whole transaction with cynical contempt ; Castlereagh,
to whom enthusiasm of any kind was unintelligible, described it as a
" piece of mysticism and nonsense," and was led to doubt the sanity
of the Czar ; Canning was more suspicious as to his sincerity. _Cor-
ruptio optimi pessima._ Representing, in its original conception, a
noble if impracticable ideal, the Holy Alliance so rapidly degenerated
as to justify the worst suspicions of Canning. In its practical
working, after 1818, it came to mean an attempt to direct the internal affairs of the several States, by means of periodical conferences,
in the interests of autocracy and reaction.

In the Holy Alliance itself England, as we have seen, had no formal part. But closely connected, though not to be confounded with
it, was the Quadruple Treaty concluded on November 20th, 1815,
between Great Britain, Austria, Prussia, and Russia. Specifically
based upon the Treaties of Chaumont (March 1st, 1814) and Vienna
(March 25th, 1815), this Quadruple Alliance was primarily the work
of Castlereagh. The High Contracting Parties, " wishing to employ
all their means to prevent the general tranquillity (the object of the
wishes of mankind and the constant end of their efforts) from being
again disturbed ; desirous, moreover, to draw closer the ties which
unite them for the common interests of their people " solemnly
renewed their adherence to the Treaties of Chaumont and Vienna,
mutually guaranteed the second Treaty of Paris, and finally, in order
to " facilitate and to secure the execution of the present Treaty and
to consolidate the connections which at the present moment so closely
unite the four Sovereigns for the happiness of the world," agreed to
" renew their meetings at fixed periods . . . for the purpose of consulting upon their common interests and for the consideration of the
measures which at each of these periods shall be considered the most
salutary for the repose and prosperity of nations and for the maintenance of the Peace of Europe ". [1] Such were the principal stipulations of the famous document which laid the foundation of the
Concert of Europe, and continued to exercise a great though diminishing influence upon international relations for the next thirty years.

With the principle of Concert it is difficult to quarrel, yet unless
it were carefully worked and vigilantly watched, danger lurked in
the scheme. That Castlereagh was not blind to the danger is clear

The Quadruple Alliance, Nov. 20, 1815

[1] Hertslet, _Map of Europe by Treaty_, i. 372-375.

from the warning which he addressed to the foreign missions before the close of the year : " In the present state of Europe it is the province of Great Britain *to turn the confidence she has inspired to the account of peace* by exercising a conciliatory influence between the Powers rather than put herself at the head of any combinations of Courts to keep others in check ".[1]   These words suffice not merely to define the policy of Great Britain, but also to acquit Castlereagh of the charge—uncritically reiterated—of having " tied England to the tail of the Holy Alliance ".   Canning's appreciation of the danger lurking in " Government by congresses " may have been more acute than Castlereagh's, and his language was certainly more emphatic, but Canning was not Foreign Secretary and Castlereagh was.   To have broken up the European Concert attained by infinite pains and not yet convicted of reactionary tendencies, would have been, on the part of the responsible Minister, an act of unpardonable levity. Castlereagh's policy was a combination of co-operation and vigilance, and few can now doubt that it was statesmanlike and sound.

The Congress of Aix-la-Chapelle, 1818   Three years passed and the Quadruple allies found themselves in conference at Aix-la-Chapelle (Sept.-Nov. 1818).   The Sovereigns of Russia, Austria, and Prussia were present in person.   Among the accredited diplomatists were Castlereagh and Wellington, Metternich from Austria, Hardenberg and Bernstorff from Prussia, Nesselrode and Capo D'Istria from Russia.   The Duke of Richelieu, Prime Minister of France, was also admitted to plead for the evacuation of France by the allied troops.   The consideration of this question was indeed the primary purpose of the Congress.   The Treaty of Paris had provided that " the military occupation of France might cease at the end of three years " if the allies approved.   The decision really rested with the Duke of Wellington, and the Duke advised that the " army of occupation might, without danger to France herself and to the peace of Europe, be withdrawn ".   The Congress accepted his advice ; France, backed by the great financial houses of Baring and Hope, entered into renewed engagements for the payment of the unliquidated claims of the allies, and by the end of the year not a single foreign soldier was encamped upon the soil of France. At the same time France was formally readmitted to the polite society of Europe, and thus the Quadruple Alliance of 1815 was converted into the " Moral Pentarchy " of 1818.

Not, however, in its original form.   Three years had sufficed to confirm the suspicions of the English Cabinet.   The spirit of reaction had already manifested itself, not obscurely, in France and Germany, still more violently to the south of the Alps and the Pyrenees.   The greatest circumspection was, therefore, displayed by the English representative at Aix-la-Chapelle lest the Alliance of 1815 should be utilized in the interests of repression.   By a Secret Protocol dated

[1] December 28th, 1815.—*Castlereagh Correspondence,* xi. 105.

November 15th, 1818, the Quadruple allies agreed to renew their engagements of 1815 as regards France, and to confer " on the most effectual means of arresting the fatal effects of a new revolutionary convulsion with which France may be threatened ".[1] They even provided for the disposition of the allied forces in such an event.[2] But there was to be no general European league which could justify regular interference in the internal concerns of independent States. On this point the English Cabinet was emphatic. Lord Liverpool had a wholesome fear of Parliament before his eyes. " We must recollect," as he wrote to Castlereagh, " in the whole of this business, and ought to make our allies feel that the general and European discussion of these questions will be in the British Parliament." Castlereagh on his side pathetically complained that the Czar Alexander " having only passed *one day* in a Polish Parliament has no very clear notions of what can be hazarded in a British House of Commons ".[3] In the result, however, the Alliance of 1815 was renewed in much more general terms. The allied Sovereigns expressed " their invariable resolution never to depart either among themselves or in their relations with other States from the strictest observation of the principles of the right of nations ".[4] In a Protocol of the same date (Nov. 15th, 1818) it was specifically laid down that there should be no stated or periodical meetings, but that if necessary a meeting should be arranged *ad hoc*—with the further important proviso that, in the case of meetings called to consider the affairs of any of the minor States, " they shall only take place in pursuance of a formal invitation on the part of such of those States as the said affairs may concern, and under the express reservation of their right of direct participation therein ". " The weight of England," wrote Lord Stewart to Lord Liverpool, " has been prodigious at this meeting." [5] In this attempt to safeguard the smaller States from the officious benevolence of the Holy Alliance, it is not difficult to trace the hand of the British representative. Indeed, to Castlereagh and to Castlereagh alone Europe owed the manifest failure of the Congress of Aix " to provide the transparent soul of the Holy Alliance with a body ".[6]

[1] Wellington, *Supplementary Despatches*, xii. 835-837.
[2] *Ibid.*   [3] Castlereagh to Bathurst, October 4th.
[4] Declaration of the five Cabinets, November 15th, 1818.—*Annual Register*, 1819, p. 135.
[5] Stewart to Liverpool, October 20th, 1818. Stewart adds an interesting sentence : " The dislike between the Emperor of Russia and Metternich renders the latter inefficient to transact delicate points with him ; Hardenberg, from his infirmities and declining weakness, is incapable of taking a prominent line ; Bernstorff is kept in the background by Hardenberg, and the Minister of the Emperor pretends to see the delicate points in a different light from his master : hence, had it not been for the unwearied labour of my brother and the Duke of Wellington, their repeated conferences with the Emperor personally, it is evident that no progress would have been made ".
[6] I deliberately repeat here a statement made in a former work, *George Canning and his Times* (p. 85), despite the strictures it has incurred from a very competent critic (Temperley's *Canning*, p. 142). I used and use " Castlereagh " in this connection, not as Mr. Temperley appears to suppose in contradistinction to Canning, but as synonymous with Great Britain whose chief representative he was.

Castlereagh's Foreign Policy, 1818-1822   The attitude maintained by Castlereagh during the remainder of his life was entirely consistent with that which he assumed during the momentous negotiations at Aix-la-Chapelle. When, for example, in 1819 Metternich showed his intention to employ the machinery of the German Bund for the purpose of suppressing liberty of thought and speech in the several States of the German Confederation, Castlereagh entered an emphatic protest. The Carlsbad Decrees issued by the Germanic Diet at the bidding of Metternich in 1819 appeared to him to be a distinct infringement of the rights of Sovereign States, and as such to be repudiated by the allied Powers.

Precisely the same principles inspired his policy in regard to the insurrectionary movement which in 1820-1821 broke out in Spain, Portugal, and Naples, and which, but for his firmness, would probably have involved a general European conflict.

Revolutions in Southern Europe   In no country in Europe had the shock of reaction after 1815 been felt so violently as in Spain. Ferdinand VII., of all the Spanish Bourbons the most contemptible, had been welcomed back to the throne with limitless enthusiasm. But not even Spanish loyalty was proof against the combination of weakness and cruelty which he displayed. By 1820 his popularity was exhausted ; the flag of insurrection was unfurled at Cadiz, and from an orgy of reaction the Spaniards characteristically plunged into an orgy of revolution. From Spain the revolutionary infection spread to Portugal and Naples. Alexander of Russia was burning to throw a Russian army into the Peninsula ; Metternich was determined to restore order in Southern Italy. Both hoped to obtain for their several enterprises the sanction of the allied Powers. In regard to Naples, Austria had by treaty a certain right of interference ; in regard to Spain, Alexander had no rights save such as could be deduced from the principles accepted at Aix-la-Chapelle. Castlereagh was determined that the latter should not be perverted to that end. As regards Russian intervention in Spain he was successful, but against his wishes a Conference to consider the whole situation met at Troppau (Oct. 20th, 1820).

Congress of Troppau   At Troppau Lord Stewart held a watching brief for Great Britain, but in the deliberations of the Congress the latter took no formal part. The policy of Great Britain as defined by Lord Castlereagh was from first to last unequivocal and consistent. If Austrian interests were threatened by events in Italy, Austria might intervene to protect them, provided that " she engages in this undertaking with no views of aggrandisement " and that " her plans are limited to objects of self-defence ".[1] But to anything in the nature of concerted action on the part of the Pentarchy Castlereagh was unalterably opposed. Not that he was in any sense a friend to revolu-

[1] Castlereagh to Stewart, September 16th, 1820.—*Castlereagh Correspondence*, xii. 311.

tion. His primary, if not his sole, consideration was the maintenance
of the peace of Europe, and that peace was, in his judgment, less
likely to be jeopardized by domestic revolution than by the armed
intervention of the Great Powers. The Czar, however, was falling
more and more completely under the influence of Metternich, and on
November 19th, 1820, the three Eastern Powers promulgated the
Protocol of Troppau. This famous document set forth with startling
explicitness the doctrines of the Holy Alliance. " States," it declared, " which have undergone a change of Government due to
revolution, the result of which threatens other States, *ipso facto*
cease to be members of the European Alliance, and remain excluded
from it until their situation gives guarantees for legal order and
stability. . . . If, owing to such alterations, immediate danger
threatens other States, the Powers bind themselves, by peaceful
means, or if need be by arms, to bring back the guilty State into the
bosom of the Great Alliance."

Conscious, perhaps, of the alarm the declaration would be likely
to excite, and certainly aware of Castlereagh's suspicious attitude,
the Eastern Sovereigns issued an explanatory circular (Dec. 8th,
1820). They asserted that " the Powers have exercised an undeniable right in concerting together upon means of safety against
those States in which the overthrow of a Government caused by
revolution could only be considered as a dangerous example, which
could only result in a hostile attitude against constitutional and
legitimate Governments," and expressed a confident hope that " the
goodwill of all right-minded men will no doubt follow the allied
Courts in the noble Arena in which they are about to enter ".[1]
France expressed a general assent, but Castlereagh, on behalf of
Great Britain, declined to become a party to the measures which
would be " in direct repugnance to the fundamental laws of this
country ". Further, in a circular despatch of great vigour (Jan. 19th,
1821), while admitting the individual right of Austria to interfere in
Naples he denounced the principles enunciated at Troppau on the
ground that they " would inevitably sanction . . . a much more
extensive interference in the internal transactions of States than
. . . can be reconcilable either with the general interest or with the
efficient authority and dignity of independent Sovereigns ".[2]

Castlereagh's despatch created a profound sensation in the
continental Chancelleries ; but despite his protest a mandate was
given to Austria to crush the Neapolitan revolt. An army of 80,000
marched, practically without resistance, upon Naples ; the wretched
King Ferdinand was restored, vengeance was exacted from all who
had taken part in the recent disturbances, and the principles of
legitimacy were triumphantly vindicated.

While Austria found congenial occupation in Italy, France was

[1]Hertslet, i. 659.   [2] *Ibid.*, 664.

itching to go to the assistance of Bourbon absolutism in Spain. On the pretext of establishing a *cordon sanitaire* against an epidemic of yellow fever (Aug. 1821), France gradually massed 100,000 men on the Pyrenean frontier. The Eastern Courts were by no means opposed to French intervention, but before it could be formally sanctioned an even more threatening cloud had appeared on the diplomatic horizon.

The East-ern ques-tion In March, 1821, Europe was startled by the news that the Greeks under Prince Alexander Hypsilanti had raised the standard of revolt in Moldavia. Owing to the discouraging attitude of the Czar, the Moldavian rising proved to be a mere flash in the pan. But in the Morea and the Ægean Islands the Greek revolt quickly attained the dimensions of a national insurrection. The Greeks made no secret of their ambition : the Ottoman Turk was to be driven out of Europe, and the Byzantine Empire to be restored at Constantinople. On both sides the struggle was conducted with the utmost ferocity : outrages on the one side called forth cruel reprisals on the other, and it became increasingly difficult for the Powers in general and for Russia in particular to stand oloof.

The Czar's position was one of peculiar embarrassment. As founder of the Holy Alliance, as partner of Prince Metternich in the Troppau Protocol, he was the sworn foe of revolution ; as the Pro-tector of the Greek Church and the traditional friend of Turkey's enemies, he was impelled to interference on behalf of the Greeks. Moreover, Russia had at the moment her own quarrel with the Turk. There was the utmost danger that the two quarrels, in their origin distinct, would merge into one, and that Russia would use the Greek insurrection to further her own traditional ambitions.

Castle-reagh's policy Such an issue would have been in Castlereagh's judgment en-tirely repugnant to British interests, and on July 16th, 1821, Castle-reagh (now Lord Londonderry), availing himself for the first time of a unique privilege, addressed directly to the Czar a letter which adroitly turned against the Czar his own principles, and laid down with admirable explicitness the line which British policy was thence-forth to follow. His supreme object was to stop the isolated inter-vention of the Czar. In this he was entirely successful.[1] But the atmosphere continued to be explosive ; the peace of Europe hung by a very slender thread. How long could Russia be restrained from crossing the Pruth, and France from crossing the Pyrenees ? How long could England refrain from recognizing the belligerent rights, if not the independence, of the Spanish Colonies in South America ? These were the questions which once more brought the Powers into conference at Vienna and Verona in the autumn of 1822. At that conference England was to be represented by the Foreign Minister

---

[1] The letter, which is an admirable example of Castlereagh's adroitness as a diplomatist, may be read in full in his *Correspondence*, xii. 403-408.

himself, but until he could arrive her interests were to be confided to the Duke of Wellington. Castlereagh, therefore, fortunately for his own reputation, drafted an elaborate memorandum, which conclusively attests his own sagacity and foreshadows the policy adopted in its entirety by Canning.

In the discussion on the Italian question England was to take no part, " lest by doing so she should appear to admit the justice of a proceeding against which from the outset she had protested ". In regard to the Eastern question, every effort was to be made to reconcile the differences between Russia and Turkey, and " then, and not till then," the condition of Greece might be considered. The recognition of the Greeks as a *de facto* Government had become almost inevitable, but the British plenipotentiary was to " stand aloof " from any engagement with the allies either to accept the Greek Government as that of an independent State, or to compel the submission of Greece herself to the Porte by force of arms. As regards the domestic revolution in Spain, " that is a matter with which, in the opinion of the English Cabinet, no foreign power has the smallest right to interfere ". *(margin: Castlereagh's memorandum)*

The case of the revolted Spanish Colonies was different : " Over by far the greater part of them Spain has lost all hold," and it is clear that " their recognition as independent States has become merely a question of time ". England, therefore, was to advocate the principle that, while no help should be given to revolting Colonies, every province which had actually established its independence should be recognized. But this must be a matter between Spain and England exclusively. " There is to be no concert with France or Russia or any other extraneous Power to effect it. Other nations may or may not come into the views which England entertains : but upon their approval or disapproval of her views, England is not in any way to shape her conduct." Finally, England is to urge the final suppression of the slave trade. The memorandum is a masterly exposition of the principles which from first to last inspired Castlereagh's policy : a strenuous insistence upon national independence ; abstention from interference in the domestic concerns of independent States ; and a frank recognition of the claims of new nationalities which had *de facto* established their independence.[1] Adopted by Canning, these principles were asserted by him with a vigour in action to which his predecessor could not pretend. *(margin: Old and New Spain)*

Castlereagh's course was run. Worn out by the twofold strain of Parliamentary leadership and diplomatic responsibility, his mind gave way, and on August 12th, 1822, he died by his own hand. *(margin: Death of Castlereagh)*

He had reached the climax of his career in 1815. Always devoid of personal magnetism, the last seven years of his life had filled to the brim the cup of his unpopularity. The brutal shouts of his

[1] Alison, *Castlereagh*, iii. 172.

enemies even desecrated the closing scene in Westminster Abbey. Brougham, indeed, was big enough to appreciate a fallen foe. " Put all their men together in one scale and poor Castlereagh in the other —single he plainly weighed them down." Creevey expressed, though with characteristic malevolence, the prevailing view among his opponents : " a worse, or if he had had talent and ambition for it, a more dangerous public man never existed ".[1] No English statesman ever incurred greater, or more undeserved unpopularity. His diplomacy was misunderstood, and it was his misfortune to be compelled, in addition, to bear the odium of the domestic policy of the Government. The financial blunders of Vansittart ; the repressive legislation of Sidmouth and Eldon ; the unsavoury business of Queen Caroline—for all these things Castlereagh was of course in part responsible, and in exceptional degree was made to suffer. And impartial history has only begun to do tardy justice to his qualities. Apart from the official biography of Alison, the memory of Castlereagh was left, for half a century, to the mercy of his opponents. But a reaction is clearly discernible.[2] One of the greatest of our Foreign Ministers," warmly testifying to his " courage, patience, and faultless sagacity," has declared him to be " that rare phenomenon—a practical man of the highest order who yet did not by that fact forfeit his title to be considered a man of genius ".[3]

Canning   The dual position which Castlereagh had held was pressed by Lord Liverpool upon the acceptance of Canning, and thus, at the age of fifty-two, Canning became, for the second time, Foreign Secretary, and, for the first time, Leader of the House of Commons. Born in 1770 and educated at Eton and Christ Church, Canning had hitherto had a singularly chequered political career. Entering the House of Commons as a disciple of Pitt in 1793, he was appointed in 1796 to serve his official apprenticeship under Grenville as Under-Secretary for Foreign Affairs. He became an Indian Commissioner in 1799, Joint Paymaster of the Forces in 1800, and in 1801 resigned office with Pitt. For the next three years he found the serious business of life in incessant intrigue against Pitt's successor, and his recreation in the manufacture of squibs to be fired off against the " Doctor ". The squibs did Addington little harm and Canning no good. On Pitt's return to power (1804) Canning became Treasurer of the Navy, and was thus fortunate enough to be connected with the Admiralty

[1] Creevey, ii. 44, 43.
[2] Cf. e.g. a typical Whig, Mr. George Brodrick : " He was a Tory in days when most patriots were Tories, and he was a Tory of the best type ".—Political History of England, xi. 200.
[3] Lord Salisbury, Biographical Essays, i. 49. The writer adds shrewdly and characteristically : " He might have maintained his policy with impunity if he would have done readier homage to the Liberal catch-words of the day. If he had only constructed a few brilliant periods about nationality or freedom, or given a little wordy sympathy to Greece or Naples or Spain or the South American republics, the world would have heard much less of the horrors of his policy."

during the critical year of the naval campaign against Napoleon. He resigned on Pitt's death (1806), and was not included in Grenville's Ministry, though its popular appellation, " All the Talents," could not, as Fox handsomely observed, be strictly applied to any Government from which Canning was excluded. In the following year Canning joined the Portland Ministry as Secretary of State for Foreign Affairs. Castlereagh became at the same time Secretary for the Colonies and War—an office which afforded ample opportunities for friction with the Foreign Minister. On neither side were they neglected.

Canning's first tenure of the Foreign Office (1807-1809) was memorable for the success with which he foiled the conspiracy of Tilsit ; for the unfortunate but unavoidable bombardment of Copenhagen ; and for the opening scenes of the Peninsula campaign. Into the causes which led to the unfortunate duel between Canning and Castlereagh, and to the break-up of the Ministry of which they were the main supports, it is unnecessary to enter.[1] It is sufficient to recall the fact that while Castlereagh returned to office as Foreign Secretary in 1812, and retained that office continuously for ten years, Canning never regained a foremost place in English politics during his great rival's life. Castlereagh, indeed, with great magnanimity offered to resign the Foreign Office in his favour on the formation of the Liverpool administration in 1812. Canning described the offer, without hyperbole, as " the handsomest ever made to an individual," but he declined to accept it without the leadership in the Commons, and for four years he was out of office. In 1816 he re-entered the Cabinet as President of the Board of Control, but his friendship with Queen Caroline rendered it difficult for him to remain a member of the Cabinet while her " business " was under discussion, and accordingly, in 1820, he resigned. All his colleagues and even the King parted with him, it would seem, with genuine regret, and the cordial letter addressed to him by Castlereagh proves that the old bitterness between these great men was largely assuaged.[2] Liverpool repeatedly pressed Canning's claims to re-admission upon the King,[3] but the latter was obdurate ; and Canning's career in English politics seemed to be definitely closed before it was well begun. It was under these circumstances that, in the summer of 1822, he accepted the Governor-Generalship of India, and was in the midst of preparations for departure when the death of Lord Londonderry opened once more the prospect of high office at home. The idea of India had, however, by this time laid its spell upon Canning, and it was, apparently, with real regret that he received the offer of the " whole inheritance ".

[1] Cf. vol. vi. of this work, p. 441. See also an interesting suggestion in Sir W. Napier's Life of Sir C. Napier, i. 40, and cf. Marriott, Castlereagh, c. xi.

[2] Stapleton, Canning and his Times, p. 319.

[3] Cf. Lord Liverpool's strong letter to the King, June 10th, 1821, and a still stronger one, June 29th.—Yonge, Liverpool, iii. 142, 148.

Anything less he had resolved to refuse.[1] " To the last day I hoped," he wrote to Charles Bagot, " that the proposal made to me might be one which I could refuse." It was not, and in 1822 Canning obtained his life-long ambition.

Canning's foreign policy   On his return to the Foreign Office Canning was confronted by three questions of immense difficulty—the Greek insurrection and the quarrel between Russia and Turkey ; the internal affairs of old Spain ; and the relations between Spain and her revolted Colonies in South America. To these was subsequently added a fourth : the position of the House of Braganza in Portugal and Brazil.

In regard to the first three he adopted without modification the instructions drawn up by Castlereagh. Wellington, who represented Great Britain at the Congress of Verona, told the Powers that while " there was no sympathy and would be none between England and revolutionists and Jacobins," England must insist on " the right of nations to set up over themselves whatever form of Government they thought best ". Above all, there must be no concerted intervention on behalf of absolutism in Spain. The protest of Wellington averted joint action ; it could not stop the intervention of France, and, despite all the efforts of Canning, the Duc d'Angoulême crossed the Bidassoa at the head of 100,000 men (April 6th, 1823).

Within a few months Ferdinand VII. of Spain was restored to his throne and his authority, and, under the protection of French troops, who remained encamped in Spain until 1827 he was able to wreak a terrible vengeance upon his enemies.

Foiled in Old Spain, Canning turned to the New, and " sought materials of compensation in another hemisphere ". He was resolved that if France had Spain, it should not be Spain with the Indies, and he " called the New World into existence to redress the balance of the Old ".[2] The situation in South America had indeed become intolerable. For outrages unnumbered upon British ships and traders no redress could be obtained from the Spanish Government. Spain, indeed, was impotent to control the action of her Colonies. With these Colonies, therefore, Canning determined to deal directly : to punish the privateers, and to recognize the independence of " those countries which appear to have established their separation from Spain ". Before the end of 1823 consuls were appointed to protect British interests in most of the principal towns ; in 1824 Great Britain recognized the independence of Buenos Ayres, Colombia, and Mexico, and in 1825 of Bolivia, Chili, and Peru.

Spain was powerless to resist Canning's will, but France was not. In 1823 it was rumoured that France meant to extend her intervention from the Old Spain to the New. France was bluntly informed that no such intervention would be permitted by Great Britain

---

[1] Letter to Lord Morley, August 26th. *Cf. Canning and his Times,* i. 31.
[2] Speech in House of Commons, December 12th, 1826.

(Oct. 1823), and the latter's attitude was supported by the United States. On December 2nd, 1823, President Munroe sent to Congress the famous message in which he declared " that any interference on the part of the great Powers of Europe for the purpose of oppressing or controlling the destiny of the Spanish American States, which had declared their independence, would be dangerous to the peace and safety of the United States, and would be considered as the manifestation of an unfriendly disposition towards them ".

In 1825 the Spanish Empire in South America was all but wiped out. The language and still more the action of Canning sealed the doom of the Holy Alliance, and ended the attempt to govern Europe by congresses. England had got little satisfaction from congresses : " We protested at Laybach ; we remonstrated at Verona. Our protest was treated as waste paper ; our remonstrances mingled with the air ; our influence, if it is to be maintained abroad, must be secure in the sources of strength at home ; and the sources of that strength are in the sympathy between the people and the Government." Canning's language was apt to be a trifle magniloquent ; but magniloquence was not with him a substitute for action.

This was proved conclusively in his dealings with Portugal. In all the complicated web of modern European history there is no more tangled skein than that provided by Portugal and Brazil.[1] The line taken by Canning is, however, tolerably clear, and with that alone, fortunately, we are concerned. In 1807, just after Canning had foiled the Tilsit conspiracy, Napoleon had issued an edict that the " House of Braganza had ceased to reign ". The Royal Family and Court made their escape in time, and transferred the seat of Government to Brazil. At the restoration of 1815 it was naturally expected that John VI. would return to Lisbon ; but he preferred Rio Janeiro, and Portugal was in effect reduced to the position of a dependency of its own colony. In 1820, the revolutionary contagion spread from Spain to Portugal, and John, in 1821 was reluctantly compelled to return to Europe to reassert his authority. In the following year (1822) the Brazilians threw off the yoke of the mother country, and proclaimed Dom Pedro, eldest son of John VI., as Constitutional Emperor of Brazil. Meanwhile, the successful intervention of France in the absolutist interest in Spain excited the hopes of the Portuguese reactionaries, who were led by the King's second son and heir, Dom Miguel. France was only too eager to extend her intervention from Spain to Portugal, and was restrained solely by the firm attitude of Canning. The Constitutionalists in Portugal applied for the assistance of English troops. This request Canning was compelled, conformably with his principles of non-intervention, to refuse. But he sent a British squadron to the Tagus, and made it

Canning and Portugal

---

[1] It is unravelled, as far as may be, by Mr. Edmondson ap. *Cambridge Modern History*, vol. x., c. x.

otherwise clear to France and to Europe that if England refrained from interference on behalf of the one party, France must refrain on behalf of the other. The ships, moreover, were found useful when, in April, 1824, Dom Miguel effected a *coup d'état* and virtually superseded his father. John VI. went on board the *Windsor Castle*, and from that vantage-ground effectually re-asserted his authority. Dom Miguel was exiled, order was restored, the Gallophils were deposed, and Canning triumphed. In 1825 Canning had the further satisfaction of bringing about a settlement of the long-standing difficulties between Portugal and Brazil. As a result of a conference in London a Treaty was signed (Aug. 29th, 1825), by which John VI. recognized the independence of Brazil, and " his best-beloved son Dom Pedro as Emperor ".

Six months later John VI. died (March 10th, 1826). The Emperor Pedro thereupon promulgated a constitutional charter for Portugal, but renounced his rights on the Throne in favour of his daughter, the Infanta Maria—a child of seven, who was to marry her uncle Miguel. But the Miguelists refused the compromise and appealed for help to Spain ; the party of the Regency appealed to England. To Canning intervention was one thing ; intervention to repel intervention was another. He waited only for the assurance that Spain meant to support the Miguelists by arms. This reached him on December 8th, and four days later he announced to Parliament that an English force was on its way to Portugal. Not an hour had been lost. " The precise information on which alone we could act arrived only on Friday last. On Saturday the decision of the Government was taken, on Sunday we obtained the sanction of His Majesty, on Monday we came down to Parliament, and at this very hour, while I have the honour of addressing this House, British troops are on their way to Portugal." In one of his most effective speeches Canning announced to Parliament and to Europe the principle on which the Government had acted. England had no wish to interfere on either side in Portugal, but neither would she permit anyone else to do so. The Holy Allies were scandalized, but Spain desisted from any further efforts to assist the Portuguese reactionaries. Canning's prompt and decisive action not only saved the liberal constitution in Portugal, but probably averted a European war. The English force remained in Portugal until April, 1828. Canning was now dead ; Dom Miguel had been appointed by his brother to the Regency in February, 1828, and, despite his oath of fealty to the Constitution, made no secret of his intention to exchange the Regency for the Crown. Wellington, who became Prime Minister in January, 1828, had always disliked Canning's foreign policy, refused to let English troops take side in domestic broils in Portugal, and insisted on their withdrawal. No longer restrained by their presence, Miguel flung aside all dissimulation ; all the Ministers at

Lisbon, except those of Rome and Spain, withdrew, and Portugal plunged into an orgy of reaction. Meanwhile, the Infanta Maria, dispatched from Brazil by her father in ignorance of the doings of Dom Miguel, was brought to England, where she was received as Queen of Portugal (Sept. 1828). In England she was joined by the leading Portuguese constitutionalists, and by some 3,000 to 4,000 military refugees. Wellington, anxious to maintain the strictest neutrality, was now in a position of great embarrassment. He had only too good reason to fear that England would be used as the base of the operations against the *de facto* Government of Portugal. Despite all his vigilance, an expedition did sail from England in January, 1829, for the Azores, but it was intercepted by an English squadron and effected nothing. Not until 1834 was the matter finally settled, when Miguel was compelled, by the joint action of the Western Powers, to sign the Convention of Evora, by which he renounced his rights to the Throne of Portugal, and left the way clear for his niece Donna Maria.

Of much greater importance than the affairs of Spain or Portugal, though of less immediate interest to the diplomatists at Verona, was the development of events in Eastern Europe. Here also Canning adopted and maintained the policy defined by Castlereagh. Both statesmen were friendly to the Greek cause, but both regarded the question primarily and properly from the point of view of British interests, and both used every endeavour to induce Turkey to agree with her Greek adversary quickly, lest Russia should get the opportunity of fishing in troubled waters. *Canning and the Eastern question*

For three years (1821-1824) the Greeks, despite fierce internal feuds, more than held their own against the Turks, but in 1824 the Sultan summoned to his aid Ibrahim Pasha, the son of his vassal, Mehemet Ali of Egypt. Ibrahim occupied Crete in 1824, and in the following year crossed to the Morea, where he " harried, slaughtered, and devastated in all directions ". The rumour ran that he meant to carry off all the Greeks who were spared by his ferocious troops into bondage in Egypt. From the first the Greek cause had been warmly espoused by the English people, partly from classical sentiment and partly from religious, partly from detestation of the Turk and not least in response to the eloquence of Byron. Volunteers had gone in their thousands not from England only, but from other Western nations and from the United States. Tidings of Ibrahim's deeds and intentions roused the Phil-Hellenist sentiment to the highest pitch. Meanwhile, in Greece itself the cause of the insurgents seemed desperate. Missolonghi [1] fell in 1826, after a year's heroic defence, to which English volunteers materially contributed, and in the following year, despite the efforts of Lord Cochrane, General Church, and others, Athens itself was compelled to surrender.

---

[1] Where Byron had died, April 19th, 1824.

4

How was the progress of events in South-Eastern Europe regarded by the Powers and the peoples of the West ? Metternich
never diverged for an instant from the line he had from the first
taken up ; the Greeks were lawless rebels and must be left to their
fate. Prussia, as usual, followed humbly in the wake of Austria. In
France, however, the Phil-Hellenist sentiment was not powerless,
and in England and Russia it might at any moment get beyond the
control of the respective Governments. In March, 1823, Canning
had been obliged, by the same logic of events as necessitated the
recognition of the South American Republics, to recognize the
Greeks as belligerents. As in the West, so in the East, the insurgents
took to piracy. British trade was suffering severely ; no redress
could be obtained from the nominal Sovereign, and none could be
asked at the hands of a non-recognized belligerent. " The recognition of the belligerent character of the Greeks," as Canning explained,
" was necessitated by the impossibility of treating as pirates a
population of a million souls, and of bringing within the bounds of
civilized war a contest which had been marked at the outset on both
sides by disgusting barbarity." [1]

Russia resented Canning's isolated action, and in January, 1824,
proposed " collective intervention ". Anxious to avoid encouragement to Greek " nationality," she suggested that Greece, including
the Archipelago, should be divided into three autonomous provinces,
on the model of Moldavia and Wallachia, nominally subject to
Turkish suzerainty but practically under Russian protection.[2] To
settle the details a conference was invited to meet at St. Petersburg.
The Porte was furious when it learnt the proposal, and in August,
1825, the Greeks themselves addressed Canning in an equally angry
protest. The plan, they complained, was one " for giving them over
bound hand and foot to the Turks," and they declared " that they
would perish to the last man rather than submit to be negotiated
about on such principles ". " Hereupon," wrote Canning,[3] " we say
halt." Sir Charles Bagot was accordingly withdrawn from the
conference at St. Petersburg, but nevertheless Canning assented to
a mildly worded offer of mediation, which was presented in a joint
note to the combatants in March, 1825. The Porte, flushed with
Ibrahim's victories, contemptuously refused the offer. The Greeks
in desperation turned once more to Canning, placed themselves
formally under British protection, and begged that Great Britain
would send them a King. The suggestion was, of course, inadmissible, and Canning made it clear to the Greeks that he could not
depart from his policy of strict, though benevolent, neutrality.

At this juncture the situation was profoundly affected by the

[1] Quoted by Alison Phillips ap. *C.M.C.* x. 186.
[2] *Cf.* Lane-Poole, *Stratford Canning*, i. p. 341.
[3] To Granville, November 15th, 1824.

sudden death (Dec. 1st, 1825) of the Czar Alexander. His successor
Nicholas was a man of different mould and temper. He had none
of Alexander's Western veneer, nor of his mysticism and sentiment ;
he was a Russian to the core. Alexander had clearly " discerned
the revolutionary march in the troubles of the Peloponese ". Nicholas
cared even less for the Greeks than his predecessor ; but he was even
more indisposed to allow the Porte to play fast and loose with Russia.
Canning was becoming convinced as to the necessity of a frank
understanding with that Court, the more so since Prince Lieven, the
Russian ambassador in London, had expressed the wish that Canning
" would take the question into his own hands, since Great Britain
was the only Power which could bring the state of affairs in Greece
to a satisfactory settlement ".[1]

To this end Canning induced the Duke of Wellington to undertake Protocol
a special mission to St. Petersburg to congratulate the new Czar on of St.
accession (Jan. 1826). The Duke was further charged to adjust, if Peters-
possible, the outstanding difficulties between Russia and Turkey, and April 4,
to arrive at an understanding with Russia on the Greek question. 1826
The result of the mission was seen in the signature (April 4th, 1826)
of the Protocol of St. Petersburg. By this Treaty the two Powers
renouncing any " augmentation of territory, any exclusive influence,"
or any preferential commercial advantages for themselves, agreed to
offer their mediation to the Porte. Greece, though continuing to
pay tribute to the Porte, was to become a virtually independent
State, to be governed by authorities chosen by itself, and to enjoy
" entire liberty of conscience and commerce ". To prevent collisions
in the future the Turks were to evacuate Greece, and the Greeks were
to " purchase the property of the Turks . . . on the Grecian continent
or islands ".

This Protocol must be regarded as a political triumph for Canning
and a personal triumph for Wellington, but it did nothing to adjust
the outstanding differences between Russia and Turkey. In regard
to these, the new Czar was determined to brook neither dallying on
the part of the Porte nor intervention on the part of the Powers.
He had already embodied his terms in an ultimatum despatched to
Constantinople (March 17th, 1826), and the Porte, temporarily embarrassed by the mutiny of the Janissaries, was compelled to accept
the Czar's terms in the Convention of Ackermann (Oct. 7th, 1826).

As regards Greece, on the other hand, the Porte, in the full tide
of triumphant barbarity, showed no signs of accepting any mediation
unless backed by force. Greece had already formally applied for it.
Accordingly in September, 1826, Canning proposed to the Czar
common action to enforce mediation upon the Sultan. If the Sultan
remained obdurate, the two Powers agreed to intimate to him that
" they would look to Greece with an eye of favour, and with a

[1] Stapleton : *Times*, p. 465, and Canning to Granville, November 8th, 1825.

disposition to seize the first occasion of recognizing as an independent State such portion of her territory as should have freed itself from Turkish dominion ".

Every effort was made to bring the other Powers into line; Metternich, however, left no stone unturned to frustrate Canning's policy, even to the extent of using backstairs influence to create mistrust between the Court and the Cabinet. Prussia followed Metternich's lead, but France concluded with Russia and Great Britain the Treaty of London (July, 1827). The public articles of the Treaty were substantially identical with the terms of the Protocol, in accordance with which an " immediate armistice " was to be offered to the belligerents. A secret article provided that the Porte should be plainly informed that the Powers intend to take " immediate measures for an approximation with the Greeks "; and that if within one month " the Porte do not accept the armistice . . . or the Greeks refuse to execute it " the High Contracting Powers should intimate to one or both parties that " they intend to exert all the means which circumstances may suggest to their prudence to obtain the immediate effect of the armistice . . . by preventing all collision between the contending parties . . . without, however, taking any part in the hostilities between them ".

Battle of Navarino   A joint note was presented to the Turk (Aug. 16th) who indignantly declined mediation. But by this time the control of events was passing from the hands of dallying diplomatists into those of plain sailors. The Admirals in command of the British and French fleets in the Levant were informed of the terms of the Treaty on August 7th. Sir Edward Codrington found them difficult of interpretation. Was he to use force or not ? He appealed to the British ambassador at Constantinople and, satisfied with Stratford Canning's answer, he sailed for the Morea. A large Egyptian fleet had meanwhile sailed with reinforcements for the Morea, and on September 7th joined the Turkish ships in Navarino Bay. The allied fleets of England, France, and Russia followed. Ibrahim was informed that none of his ships would be allowed to leave the harbour, and quickly discovered that the allied Admirals meant to enforce their orders. Foiled at sea he renewed his attack on land with increased ferocity. Of the atrocities he committed the sailors were all but eye-witnesses.[1] To remain passive was impossible, but agreeably to instructions there were to be " no hostilities ". The Turks, however, opened fire ; the battle became general, and before sundown on October 20th the Turko-Egyptian fleet " had disappeared, the Bay of Navarino was covered with their wrecks ".

Welling-ton's policy   The news of the battle of Navarino was received with amazement throughout Europe, and by the English Government with something like consternation. The sailors had indeed cut the Gordian knot

---

[1] *Cf. Narrative of Captain Hamilton* ap. Marriott, *Canning*, p. 131.

tied by the diplomatists, but they got no thanks in England for doing it. Canning was dead (Aug. 8th), and Wellington, who after five months' interval succeeded to his place, made no secret of his dislike of Canning's policy. The Turk with consumate impudence described Navarino as a " revolting outrage," and demanded compensation and apologies. Even Wellington was not prepared to go this length, but the King was made (Jan. 29th, 1828) to " lament deeply " that " this conflict should have occurred with the naval forces of an ancient ally," and to express " a confident hope that this untoward event will not be followed by further hostilities ".

The one anxiety of the new Government was to preserve the independence and integrity of the Ottoman Empire. No language could have been more nicely calculated to defeat this object. Turkey was, of course, encouraged to persist in her attitude towards Greece, and to renew her quarrel with Russia. Russia was permitted, and even compelled, to engage single-handed in war with the Turks. Thus all the fruits of years of diplomacy on Canning's part were carelessly dissipated in a few months by his successors.

The Porte, meanwhile, denounced the Convention of Ackermann, and declared a Holy War against the infidel (Dec. 20th, 1827). Russia, though with ample professions to the Powers of complete disinterestedness, accepted the challenge, and in May, 1828, 150,000 Russian troops under Wittgenstein crossed the Pruth. The Turks, to the amazement of Europe, made not only a stubborn but an effective resistance, but in July, 1829, Diebitsch, by a masterly march, crossed the Balkans and appeared before Adrianople (Aug. 19th). Constantinople was at his mercy. Kars and Erzeroum had already fallen, and the Sultan had no alternative but to accept the terms embodied in the Treaty of Adrianople.

In the long history of the Eastern question, the Treaty of Adrianople is inferior only in importance to those of Kainardji and Berlin. Russia restored her conquests, except the " Great Islands " of the Danube ; but her title to Georgia and the other provinces of the Caucasus was acknowledged ; all neutral vessels were to have free navigation in the Black Sea and on the Danube ; practical autonomy was granted to the principalities of Moldavia and Wallachia under Russian protection ; Russian traders in Turkey were to be under the exclusive jurisdiction of their own consuls, while, in regard to Greece, the Porte accepted the Treaty of London—thus virtually acknowledging its independence.

Treaty of Adrianople, Sept. 14th, 1829

The final settlement of the Greek question was referred to a conference which was to meet in London. It provided plenty of occupation to the diplomatists for some time to come, and not until 1831 was Lord Palmerston at last able to bring matters to a tolerably satisfactory issue. Greece was to be independent under the guarantee of Great Britain, France, and Russia. The frontier was, after much wrangling, fixed with some niggardliness at a line extending from the Gulf of Volo on the east, to Arta on the west. The form of Government was to be a constitutional monarchy, and the Crown having been declined, first by Prince John of Saxony, and then, after a momentary acceptance, by Prince Leopold of Saxe-Coburg, was ultimately accepted by Otto, second son of King Louis of Bavaria. Count Capodistrias, who had been virtually ruler of Greece, was assassinated in 1831, and the way was clear, therefore, for the new King who began his ill-starred reign in 1833.

The Treaties of Adrianople and London close a chapter in the history of English foreign policy, and more particularly in that section of it which is concerned with the unravelling of " that shifting, intractable, and interwoven tangle of conflicting interests, rival peoples, and antagonistic faiths that is veiled under the easy name of the Eastern question ".[1] The Duke of Wellington supposed that he had seen the beginning of the end of it. The Treaty of Adrainople he declared to be " the death-blow to the independence of the Ottoman Porte, and the forerunner of the dissolution and extinction of its power ". After the lapse of eighty years, few would be found to re-echo his confident prediction. The Duke, like the Czar Nicholas, unquestionably underrated the marvellous recuperative power of the sick man, and the adroitness with which he learnt to turn to account the jealousies of the Powers. Those jealousies still retard the solution of a problem to which the Hellenic rising added one more factor, and still mock the efforts of those who would fain give substance to the dreams, though they repudiate the methods of the Holy Alliance.[2]

[1] The phrase is Lord Morley's.
[2] These words were, of course, written before the events of 1912-13.

CHAPTER IV

THE LAST YEARS OF TORY RULE. SOCIAL AND FISCAL REFORMS.
CATHOLIC EMANCIPATION
(1822-1830)

AN attempt was made in the last chapter to explain the part
played by England in European politics during the years
which followed the Napoleonic wars. A secondary purpose was to
expose the fallacy which associates the substitution of Canning for
Castlereagh with a new era in English foreign policy. Despite their
contrasted temperaments, the two statesmen pursued a common end.
But if Canning did not introduce a new system into diplomacy, he
did enforce, together with colleagues Peel, Huskisson, and Robinson,
a new spirit in domestic legislation. The various manifestations of
that new spirit it is the purpose of the following pages to disclose.

It is usual to date the era of reform from the accession of the Recon-
Whig party to power in 1830. Then, as often, it happened that a struction of the
powerful stimulus was given to legislation by the electoral success of Liverpool
a party long excluded from office. But the causes of reform and Cabinet,
reaction go far deeper than mere party oscillations, and cannot be 1822-1823
satisfactorily explained by party triumphs. In this case the period
of stagnation closed not in 1830, but in 1822 ; the era of reform was
coincident not with the formation of Lord Grey's administration, but
with the reconstruction of that of Lord Liverpool.

The change of ministerial personnel in 1822-1823 was, as we have
seen, comprehensive and significant. Canning, it will be remembered,
succeeded Londonderry not only at the Foreign Office, but in the
leadership of the House of Commons ; Peel, with a reputation immensely enhanced by his skilful conduct of currency reforms, replaced
Lord Sidmouth (Addington) at the Home Office ; the support of
the Grenville Whigs was conciliated by the appointment of C. W.
Wynn as President of the Board of Control, and the hopes of the
Catholics were naturally raised by Lord Wellesley's acceptance of the
Lord Lieutenancy of Ireland, and still more by Plunket's appointment as his Attorney-General. Even more clearly indicative of
impending change of policy were the appointments to the Exchequer
and the Board of Trade. Vansittart, most incompetent of financiers,
was raised to the peerage as Lord Bexley, and receded into the
Chancellorship of the Duchy of Lancaster ; F. J. Robinson replaced
him at the Exchequer and was in turn succeeded at the Board of
Trade by William Huskisson.

Exceptionally strong in general administrative ability few
Cabinets, since the inception of parliamentary government, have

contained three more eminent financiers than Peel, Huskisson, and Robinson, while Canning himself, as his speeches and essays abundantly prove, had a firm grip upon economic principles.[1] The influence of these men is clearly discernible in the legislation promoted by the reconstructed Ministry.

Reasons for reforming activity

Quite apart, however, from changes in ministerial personnel, reforms of a drastic nature could not have been much longer delayed. During the last thirty years scarcely a single remedial measure had been placed upon the Statute-book. For this legislative stagnation no one in England was to blame. Twenty-five years had been more than fully occupied by the struggle against revolutionary and Napoleonic France. Pitt, an ardent administrative reformer, had wisely, though reluctantly, put aside a congenial task for something even more immediately important. It is unwise, as Windham said, to repair one's house in the hurricane season. So Pitt felt, and his reforming work, upon which he had made an excellent beginning during his first nine years of office, was postponed to a more convenient season. Upon twenty-five years of war there had supervened five years of economic distress and social agitation. The hurricane was still blowing, though from a different quarter. Once more reform was postponed. But since 1820 there had been a marked improvement in the situation. The worst of the commercial and financial crisis was obviously over ; trade revived ; social order was restored, and men's minds turned hopefully towards the prospect of legislative amelioration.

Questions to the fore

Several questions of first-rate importance insistently demanded a solution. The parliamentary success of Lord John Russell (1820-1821),[2] reinforced by the Yorkshire petition of 1823, proved that the question of electoral reform could not be much longer postponed. The inclusion of Canning and Plunket in the Ministry compelled Lord Liverpool to continue to treat Catholic emancipation as an " open question ". The inclusion of Huskisson was a pledge of fiscal reform. Mackintosh was exposing the ghastly barbarities of the criminal code ; Wilberforce and Fowell Buxton those of slavery. In the world of industry the Combination Laws pressed with peculiar severity upon the wage-earners, and some readjustment of the relations between Capital and Labour was imperatively required.

Reform of Criminal Code. Justice and police

The first question with which the new Ministers elected to deal was the scandalous condition of the criminal law. Peel's tenure of the Home Office was memorable for its amendment. Derided by Disraeli as a " burglar of other men's ideas," Peel certainly possessed in exceptional measure, the faculty of bringing to legislative fruition

---

[1] *Cf. e.g. Quarterly Review*, Nos. 8 and 9, containing reviews of pamphlets by Sir John Sinclair on the Currency question, now identified as the work of G. Ellis and Canning.—Marriott, *Canning*, p. 146.

[2] *Cf. supra*, p. 41.

the seeds sown by others.   In the reform of the criminal law, Romilly
planted, Mackintosh watered, Peel reaped the legislative harvest.
The condition of things before these men began their crusade was
nothing short of appalling.   For no fewer than 200 offences the death
penalty could still be legally inflicted ;   procedure was antiquated
and defective ;   the innocent were sometimes convicted ;   the guilty
constantly escaped.   The severity of the law of course defeated its
own object.   It blunted the moral conscience of the nation ;   it
obliterated the distinction between offences trivial and grave ;   it
encouraged serious and persistent crime ;   it failed to deter the casual
offender.   Criminal procedure was reduced to a farce.   Juries naturally refused to convict for petty offences, when conviction might cost
the offender his life.   Poachers and shoplifters were sentenced to
death by the score, but rarely suffered the death penalty.   Of 655
persons indicted for shoplifting between 1805 and 1807, 113 were
sentenced to death, but not in one case was the penalty enforced.
On the other hand, between 1811 and 1818 over 100 persons went to
the gallows for the crime of forgery.   But even before the efforts of
legislative reformers, humane practice had outrun barbarous precept.
During the last three-quarters of a century only 25 crimes out of a
possible 200 had actually evoked the extreme penalty.   But it was
high time that the law should be brought into accord with practice.
As a result of many years' labour Romilly carried two trifling amendments, and on his death (1818) Sir James Mackintosh kept the question
well to the fore.   In 1822 the House of Commons pledged itself, " at
an early period of the next session to take into its serious consideration the means of increasing the efficiency of the criminal code by
abating its rigour ".
      This pledge was handsomely redeemed by Peel.   During his first
tenure of the Home Office (1822-1827) no fewer than 278 Acts were
repealed, and such of their provisions as were still valuable were re-
enacted in eight new statutes.   One hundred felonies were by a
stroke of the pen removed from the category of capital offences, and
before he finally left the Home Office in 1830 he had the satisfaction
of knowing that the death penalty could no longer be pronounced,
much less enforced, except upon offenders convicted of serious crime.
This was Peel's most substantial achievement as Home Secretary,
but it was not the only one.   He abolished Benefit of Clergy in
criminal offences ;   he removed various scandals and anomalies in the
Marriage Laws ;   he improved the condition of the gaols ;   he reformed criminal procedure ;   he consolidated and amended no less
than 66 Acts relating to the constitution and functions of juries,
and, finally, he associated both his names imperishably with the
establishment of a new police force in the metropolis (1829).   It will
not be forgotten that during his second tenure of the Home Office
(1828-1830) Peel was also Leader of the House of Commons, and in

that capacity was responsible for the Catholic Emancipation Act. But apart from that his legislative record is sufficiently remarkable.

Peel's industry and enthusiasm were contagious. While he was busy at the Home Office, Robinson and Huskisson, steadily backed in the House by Canning, were effecting changes of the first magnitude in the commercial system of the country. Robinson, best known by the sobriquet of " Prosperity," was a sound economist and a capable administrator. His colleague deserves to rank among the greatest financiers this country has produced.

Born in 1770 William Huskisson was returned to the House of Commons in 1796, and served his apprenticeship at the Treasury under Pitt. On the latter's death he attached himself to Canning, with whom he resigned in 1809. Restored to office as Minister of Woods and Forests in 1814, he quickly established his reputation as one of the first financial authorities in the House. His pamphlets and speeches gave him an incontestable claim to a place on the Bullion Committee of 1819, and also upon the Committee which was appointed in 1821 to consider the question of agricultural distress. On the reconstruction of the Ministry he might naturally have aspired, as Liverpool frankly explained to the King, to the highest financial post.[1] But Canning induced him to accept the combined offices of Treasurer of the Navy and President of the Board of Trade, with the promise, speedily fulfilled, of admission to the Cabinet.

His influence upon his colleagues, and particularly upon Robinson, was soon apparent. Order and simplicity were introduced into the national accounts ; the Sinking Fund, dear to the heart of Vansittart, was shorn of its objectionable features, and only the realized surplus was applied to it. A large amount of taxation was remitted ;[2] the expenses of revenue collection were sensibly reduced ; the national debt was diminished at the rate of some six millions a year, and finally, advantage was taken of the improved credit of the country to effect a conversion of the 4 per cent. annuities.[3]

For these excellent results the credit belongs primarily to Robinson. But even more important were the commercial and fiscal reforms initiated by Huskisson himself. For the most adroit financier can effect little when the creation of national wealth is retarded by a vicious commercial system. To remove burdensome restrictions upon trade ; to stimulate production ; to encourage exchange ; to develop by every means in his power the economic resources of the country—these were the objects which Huskisson set himself to achieve.

---

[1] Yonge, iii. 212.

[2] *Cf.* Speech of the Chancellor of the Exchequer, March 13th, 1826.—Hansard, xiv. 130. Robinson showed that between 1815 and 1825 nett remissions of taxation amounted to £27,522,000. Between 1823 and 1825 the funded debt was reduced from £796,530,000 to £778,128,000 ; the unfunded from £36,281,000 to £31,703,000.

[3] Consols stood at about 90 ; and the 4 per cents., redeemable at par, at 102.

The Navigation or Trade Laws still lay at the roots of the old commercial system, though large inroads had already been made upon their integrity. Passed in 1651, 1660, and 1672 they continued for nearly 200 years to form the foundation of British Commercial Policy. Stripped of technical details, these Acts provided that no merchandise should be imported into England, Ireland, or any British plantation, from Asia, Africa, or America, in any but English-built and English-owned ships, navigated by an English commander and manned by a crew of which at least three-fourths were Englishmen. From European countries goods might be imported in English ships, thus defined, or, under discriminating duties, in ships belonging to the country in which the goods were produced. Aimed primarily at the mercantile supremacy of the Dutch, it cannot be denied that these Acts attained their object, and contributed largely to the commercial and naval ascendancy of Great Britain. They won, moreover, unstinted praise from Adam Smith,[1] who was magnanimous enough to prefer political to commercial considerations. On Ireland, no doubt, the Trade Laws pressed hardly until the Union ; but to the " plantations " they were not, in earlier years at least, a disadvantage. Every effort it is true was made to secure for the mother country the primary advantages of colonial trade. But it is not clear that the Colonies suffered by the process.[2] This much at any rate may be said in defence of the system assailed by Huskisson : it was avowedly inspired by " consideration of power," not by " consideration of plenty " ; it regarded security rather than wealth ; it preferred " defence to opulence " ; it was in harmony with the prevailing ideas economic and political, and it secured its end. Under it, England and her dependencies increased mightily in power and did not apparently lack " plenty ". Moreover, as time went on and occasion demanded, much of its apparent harshness towards the Colonists was mitigated in practice by a prudent carelessness on the part of authority. To this slackness George Grenville was the disastrous exception. His conscientious discharge of duty lost us our first colonial empire.

The successful revolt of the thirteen colonies dealt a mortal blow at the old system. Excluded from its benefits and exposed to its disadvantages, the Americans retaliated in kind. Retaliation led to negotiation, and by the Treaty of 1814 [3] " the ships of the two countries were placed reciprocally upon the same footing in the ports of England and the United States, and all discriminating duties

---

[1] " Some of the provisions of this famous Act may have proceeded from national animosity. They are as wise, however, as if they had been dictated by the most deliberate wisdom."—*Wealth of Nations*, bk. iv. c. ii.

[2] To this conclusion the best American opinion is steadily tending : see *e.g.* A. B. Hart and Prof. Channing, both quoted by Prof. Ashley (*Surveys Historic and Economic*), who shares the opinion. See also on this subject Hertz, *Old Colonial System*. [3] Treaty of Ghent.

chargeable upon the goods which they conveyed were mutually repealed ".[1] But apart from our own Colonies the face of America was changing rapidly. Brazil became independent of Portugal, and the Spanish Colonies were throwing off the feeble but galling yoke of the mother country. In a great speech delivered on March 31st, 1825, Huskisson agreed that these changes placed our own Colonies at a relative commercial disadvantage, and that the old commercial system must be abandoned if the political connection was to be maintained.[2] By legislation passed in 1822 a large, but in their view insufficient, measure of freedom had been granted to the Colonies.[3] The Reciprocity Act of 1825 extended the same principle to foreign countries. Power was given to the King in Council to conclude reciprocity treaties and to discriminate still further against countries which declined them. Under this Act treaties were concluded with all the important countries of the world, including our old rival the Netherlands. But though largely deprived of their sting, the Navigation Laws still remained upon the Statute-book, and by an Act of 1845 were actually consolidated and re-enacted. But it was an expiring policy. Against the prevailing spirit of *laisser faire* such restrictions could not, even theoretically, stand, and in 1849 they were entirely swept away. Thus was the policy of Huskisson carried to its logical conclusion. That an immense impulse was thereby given to the oversea trade of Great Britain is undeniable ; but it remains an open question whether in the process provisions still of some value to national security were not unnecessarily sacrificed.

Tariff Reform

But the relaxation of the Navigation Laws was only a part of the general commercial policy of Huskisson. A wholehearted theoretical free trader, he was convinced that " national prosperity would be most effectively promoted y an unrestrained competition not only between the capital and the industry of different lasses in the same country, but also by extending that competition as much as possible to all other countries ".[4] But he proceeded cautiously. Duties not exceeding £30 per cent. were substituted in some cases for absolute prohibition, in others for exorbitant but ineffective duties. Thus foreign manufactured silk and foreign gloves, articles hitherto prohibited but " to be bought in every shop," were admitted at a duty of 30 per cent. ; on cotton goods a uniform duty of 10 per cent. was substituted for duties varying from 50 per cent. to 75 per cent. ; on linens a fixed duty of 25 per cent. for duties varying from 40 per cent. to 180 per cent. ; on woollens 15 per cent. for 50 per cent. to 67½ per cent. ; and so on. Iron, copper, zinc, tin, lead, earthenware, glass, paper, bottles, printed books, and many other articles were

[1] Porter, *Progress of the Nation*, p. 395.   [2] Hansard, c. xii. 1098-1115.
[3] 3 George IV. c. 41, 42, 43, 44.
[4] *Cf.* Huskisson's great speech, March 25th, 1825.—Hansard, x. 1210 *seq.*

brought into Huskisson's comprehensive schedule. But imports were by no means to be free. Huskisson was a tariff reformer, not a tariff abolitionist. A tariff was devised primarily with a view to revenue ; incidentally to afford some measure of protection to the home producer, and some preference to the Colonies, and, not least, to kill the smuggling trade. " Let the State," said Huskisson, " have the tax which is now the reward of the smuggler, and let the consumer have the better and cheaper article without the painful consciousness that he is consulting his own convenience at the expense of daily violating the laws of his country." But while the State and the consumer were his first consideration, the interests of the manufacturer were not forgotten. If under the new tariff he had to face foreign competition, the simultaneous reduction of duties on raw material gave him a better chance of facing it successfully. Other changes were, about the same time, effected. Bounties on exports were gradually abolished ; laws forbidding the emigration of artisans and providing for the regulation of wages in the Spitalfields silk industry were repealed, and, most important of all, a serious effort was made to relieve the increasing tension between Labour and Capital by the repeal of the Combination Laws.

The English law had always regarded trade combinations of all kinds with extreme disfavour as " conspiracies in restraint of trade ". From the time of Edward I. to that of George IV. legislation directed against such associations had been practically continuous and conspicuously inoperative. In 1823 the Statute-book contained from thirty to forty enactments designed to prevent associations either of employers or employed. It was not, however, until the last years of the eighteenth century, when the economic results of the industrial revolution began to be felt, that Trade Unions, as now understood, became obtrusive. In 1800 a strenuous attempt was made by the legislature to crush them once for all. Under the Act of that year any artisan who combined with others to advance his wages, to decrease the quantity of his output, or to interfere with the management of the business, rendered himself liable to imprisonment. In a word, "the strike was a crime, the trade union was an unlawful association ".[1]

During the next twenty years, more particularly during the period of trade depression after 1815, the relations of Labour and Capital became steadily worse : the repeal of the " Spitalfields Act " and of the Act prohibiting emigration brought the whole question to the notice of Parliament, and a Select Committee, appointed in 1824, reported that the Combination Laws had not only " not been efficient to prevent combinations either of masters or workmen, but, on the contrary, had had a tendency to produce mutual irritation and distrust, to give a violent character to the combinations, and to render them highly dangerous to the peace of the community ".

[1] Dicey, *Law and Public Opinion*, p. 98.

Combina-
tion Acts
of 1824
and 1825
In accordance with the recommendation of the Committee a law [1] was passed repealing all the existing Acts against trade combination, and leaving masters and workmen alike absolutely free to combine. Hume and Francis Place [2]—a radical tailor—were responsible for this measure ; Huskisson regarded it as too sweeping. His fears were speedily realized ; the immediate results were disastrous. Several strikes occurred, accompanied by considerable violence and disorder, and in 1825 it was found necessary to pass a further Act which declared that combinations had been found " injurious to trade and commerce, dangerous to the tranquility of the country, and especially prejudicial to the interests of all who were concerned in them ". The common law of conspiracy was, consequently, reaffirmed ; a very limited right of combination was conceded ; but penalties were prescribed for violence, threats, intimidation, molestation, or obstruction by any person for the purpose of forcing a master to alter his mode of business, or a workman to refuse or leave work, or of forcing any person to belong to or conform to the rules of any club or association. [3] The general effect of this Act was to render Trade Unions non-legal but not necessarily criminal associations. As such they were excluded from the benefits of the Friendly Societies Act, and their funds were left at the mercy of dishonest officials. In this unsatisfactory position they remained for more than forty years.

General
prosperity
of the
country
Labour troubles though serious in themselves did not seriously retard the general economic recovery.

The wisdom of the measures promoted by Robinson and Huskisson was speedily vindicated by results. Gloomy prognostications were unfulfilled, and on the meeting of Parliament in 1825 Ministers were greeted with a chorus of congratulations. " Our present prosperity," said the mover of the Address in the House of Lords, " was a prosperity extending to all orders, all professions, and all districts." The debate in the Lower House was an echo of that in the Upper, and both were endorsed by the judgment of a highly competent contemporary observer. " Nearly all property had risen greatly in pecuniary value, and every branch of internal industry was thriving. Agricultural distress had disappeared ; the persons employed at the cotton and woollen manufactures were in full employment ; the various departments of the iron trade were flourishing ; on all sides new buildings were in progress of erection, and money was so abundant that men of enterprise, though without capital, found no difficulty in commanding funds for any plausible undertaking." A detailed statistical investigation substantiates these glowing generalizations, but only a few examples can here be quoted. The official value of the exports which in 1820 was £48,951,537 rose by 1830 to £69,691,303. Imports in the former year were £32,438,650, in the latter £46,245,241.

[1] 5 George IV. c. 95.   [2] *Cf.* Graham Wallas, *Life of Francis Place.*
[3] Wright ap. Dicey, p. 191.

The imports of foreign wool which amounted in 1820 to less than 10,000,000 lbs. in 1830 exceeded 32,000,000. The number of spinners employed in the manufacture of cotton rose in ten years from 68,257 (1821) to 135,742. Similar illustrations of expanding prosperity might be almost indefinitely multiplied.

The pace was at first too rapid. When trade is booming manu-facturers have no time to think; they act, and apparently to the end of time will act, as though the sun of prosperity would shine for ever, as though cyclical disturbances were unknown phenomena. Crisis of 1825-1826

To the improvidence of honest trade was added the folly and knavery of wild financial speculation. To the excitement thus en-gendered there had been no parallel since the bursting of the South Sea Bubble. No scheme was too fantastic to secure the support of the unwary. Over £174,000,000 of capital was subscribed for new companies during the year 1824 and the beginning of 1825; [1] 435 petitions for private bills were presented in the session of 1825, and no fewer than 286 became law; [2] money was exceptionally cheap, and banks and discounters were ridiculously complaisant. The in-evitable results ensued. As the year 1825 went on, the all too familiar symptoms of the coming storm began to manifest themselves. Demand slackened; stocks accumulated; prices came down with a run; banks took alarm; confidence was shaken; credit contracted, and by the end of the year England was in the throes of a terrible financial crisis.

On December 5th the great banking house of Sir Peter Pole & Co. suspended payment. As they kept the accounts of forty-four country banks the shock thus given to credit was tremendous. In the next few weeks seventy-eight banks, including five great London houses, closed their doors.

The Mint and the Bank of England did all they could to mitigate the severity of the crisis. Sovereigns were coined and issued at the rate of 150,000 a day, but the Bank itself was saved mainly by the accidental discovery of 700,000 £1 notes. After this the violence of the storm abated, but the Government felt compelled to propose legislation to prevent, if possible, its recurrence. The circulation of notes under £5 was prohibited—in England [3]—after February 5th, 1829, and an important measure was passed to give greater security to country Banks. Hitherto, under the charter of the Bank of England, no private bank might have more than six partners. All restrictions of this nature were now removed in the case of all banks, except those within sixty-five miles of London. Despite urgent pressure the Government refused, in the true spirit of Benthamite *laisser faire*, to issue Exchequer Bills, but they persuaded the Bank

[1] *Annual Register*, 1825, p. 2. [2] *Ibid.* p. 121.
[3] Scotland successfully resisted the prohibition of small notes : a result due largely to the *Letters of Malachi Malagrowther*, in which Sir Walter Scott showed himself no unworthy successor to Swift.

to advance £3,000,000 to merchants upon the security of their merchandise. These means did much to restore confidence to capitalists, but little to alleviate the sufferings of the wage-earners.

These sufferings during the winter 1825-1826 were acute. On the whole they were borne, on the testimony of the King's Speech, " with exemplary patience ". But, nevertheless, riots were reported from many manufacturing centres : from Norwich, Bradford, Trowbridge, Dudley, Carlisle, and all parts of Lancashire. In a single week over 1,000 power-looms were smashed in Blackburn and the neighbourhood, and throughout Lancashire the destruction of fixed capital was great.

Partial relaxation of Corn Laws.

Prolonged drought in the summer of 1826 added to the general discomfort, and in fear of deficient harvests, the Government hurriedly adopted two remedial measures. By the first, wheat stored in bonded warehouses was allowed to come into market on payment of a duty of 10s. per quarter. By the second, the Government was authorized temporarily to open the ports to a limited amount (500,000 quarters) of foreign oats and other grain.

Having passed these Bills Parliament was dissolved on June 2nd. The General Election created little excitement, but the two questions most in agitation were the Corn Laws and the Catholic claims. A brief autumn session was opened on November 14th in order to give Ministers an indemnity for further, though temporary, infringement of the Corn Laws.

Before Parliament reassembled the Duke of York, " most kind and best natured of Princes," [1] passed away (Jan. 5th, 1827). The King was anxious to succeed his brother as Commander-in-Chief, but Lord Liverpool insisted that the Duke of Wellington should have the post. It was his last exercise of authority as Prime Minister. Before the session was a week old he was struck down by apoplexy (Feb. 17th), and though death was not immediate he never recovered sufficiently to take any further part in politics.[2] It was said of him with truth by the American Minister that if he was not the ablest man in his Cabinet " he was essentially its head ". His mortal illness not only dissolved the Cabinet but broke up the party, which for years past had been kept together only by his authority and tact.

Canning's Ministry

Upon whom would his mantle fall ? " I think somehow," wrote Creevey,[3] " it must be Canning after all, and that then *he'll die of it.*" In both respects Creevey's forecast was accurate. But Canning's succession was by no means a foregone conclusion ; it was settled only after weeks of negotiation and intrigue, and it smashed into fragments the party to which he belonged. That Canning was incomparably the ablest man in the Cabinet and in the party goes without saying. But he had no strong political connection ; his

---

[1] Crocker, i. 360.

[2] Lord Liverpool died December 4th, 1828.   [3] ii. 106.

Catholic sympathies were not popular in the country; his liberal views were repugnant to the Upper House and his brilliant wit did not conciliate the Lower. " He rarely," it was said, " delivers an important speech without making an enemy for life." Because he talked so well men thought him a knave, as they thought Castlereagh a fool because he talked so badly. Eight Dukes signed a remonstrance to the King against his appointment as Prime Minister, and when it is remembered that Tory Peers returned over 100 members to the House of Commons,[1] the strength of the forces opposed to Canning will be appreciated. The day-to-day details of the struggle which ensued may be followed by the curious in the *Correspondence and Diaries* of J. W. Croker who was behind the scenes. They are more interesting than edifying.

Conscious of his own claims Canning informed the King " in plain terms that the substantive power of a Prime Minister he must have, and what's more, must be known to have ". But conscious also of his isolation in his own party, he advised the King to form an Anti-Catholic Ministry without him.[2] The King, with a just appreciation of Canning's value at the Foreign Office, suggested that Canning and Peel should serve under the Duke of Wellington. Canning declined, and on April 10th received His Majesty's commands to form a Government, and kissed hands as First Lord of the Treasury and Chancellor of the Exchequer. Of the members of the late Cabinet, Peel, Eldon, the Duke, Lord Bathurst, Lord Melville, and Lord Westmorland refused to serve in the new. Canning was consequently compelled to look to the Whigs for general support, though Lord Lansdowne and Tierney were the only prominent members of that party who entered the Cabinet.[3] Robinson, raised to the Peerage as Lord Goderich, became Colonial Secretary with the Leadership of the House of Lords; Lord Dudley went to the Foreign Office; Sturges Bourne kept the Home Office warm for Lord Lansdowne until July; Lord Harrowby retained the Presidency of the Council, and Huskisson that of the Board of Trade. Of the new appointments the most interesting were those of Copley, who as Lord Lyndhurst accomplished the amazing feat of ousting Lord Eldon from the Woolsack, and Palmerston who, retaining the Secretaryship-at-War,[4] for the first time entered the Cabinet. He seldom quitted it during the next thirty-five years.

Canning survived the attainment of his honourable ambition only long enough to taste the bitterness of power. A chill caught at the Duke of York's funeral fastened upon a constitution already undermined. His opponents gave him no peace. Peel stood aside in

Death of Canning, Aug. 8th, 1827

---

[1] For detailed list *cf.* Croker, i. 371.

[2] Greville, *Memoirs*, ii. 105.

[3] The Earl of Carlisle who joined the Ministry as Commissioner of Woods and Forests was admitted to the Cabinet as Privy Seal in July.

[4] Continuously held since 1809.

5

dignified aloofness, but the Tory underlings literally hunted him to death in the House of Commons, and in the Lords he was attacked with cruel acerbity by the leading Peers.[1] He managed with Huskisson's help to carry through the Commons an ingenious measure providing for a sliding scale on imported corn, but it was so emasculated by the Lords at the instance of Wellington that it was withdrawn. The broken session ended on July 2nd; on August 4th Canning was seized with mortal illness, and on the 8th he died at Chiswick.

Canning's reputation rests primarily upon his foreign policy. Proclaimed to the world in language not devoid of bombast, it was none the less conceived on sound lines and executed with unusual vigour. In a sense larger than he knew he " called a new world into existence to redress the balance of the old ". His contemporaries in Europe clung to the out-worn formulas and absolutist principles which had dominated diplomacy in the eighteenth century and had inspired the settlement of 1815. It is to the eternal credit of Canning to have perceived that the edifice built upon these foundations could not stand. More than this. He understood, as few did, that the ideas and forces which had emerged from the revolutionary chaos, ideas which continental statesmen were anxious only to repress, were fundamentally conservative in essence. Among these the most potent was that of nationality, and upon this Canning's policy was founded. Hence his memory as a diplomatist links itself with those of the great constructive statesmen, the Cavours and Bismarcks, whose work is characteristic of the nineteenth century. As a domestic reformer he must be classed with the enlightened statesmen of the pre-revolutionary epoch—the Pitts, D'Arandas, and Turgots. To reform in the narrower electoral sense he was opposed ; of administrative reform he was a keen advocate. The causes of religious equality, of slave emancipation, of free trade, of free labour lost in Canning one of their best and most effective friends.

Welling-   Goderich carried on Canning's administration during the recess.
ton's   There was some shuffling of places, and some new men were intro-
Ministry,
1829-1830 duced, but as the Ministry was practically still-born the details are unimportant. Goderich, after a fruitless effort to allay ministerial squabbles and jealousies, resigned on January 8th, 1828, never having met Parliament as Premier. The Duke of Wellington succeeded to the Premiership, and for a few months presided over a Cabinet which differed little in composition from that of his precedessors. The most important changes were the return of Peel to the Home Office with the lead of the Commons, and the appointment of Goulburn to the Exchequer. But the Canningites were not comfortable, and

---

[1] " Canning—the Tories—idiots that they were and never discovering that he was their best friend, hunted to death with their besotted and ignorant hostility." —Greville, ii. 185.

in the summer a considerable reconstruction was effected. To the undisguised relief of the Duke, Huskisson tendered his resignation as Colonial Secretary. Huskisson indeed was willing to be over-persuaded, but the Duke promptly closed negotiation. " It is no mistake ; it can be no mistake ; it shall be no mistake." Dudley, Palmerston, Grant, and Lamb followed Huskisson's example.

The weakness of the new Government in foreign policy has been already exposed.[1] Their domestic policy now claims consideration, but it cannot be understood without a clear appreciation of the position of their chief. The great Duke did not regard politics with the eye of the ordinary politician. Principles might be eternal, but positions were to be maintained only so long as they were tenable. Office meant to him not the achievement of ambition nor even a grasp upon opportunity, but the fulfilment of grim duty. Without this knowledge his conduct in high office might appear eccentric not to say unprincipled. In reality no politician was ever more simply and transparently conscientious. It was his duty to serve his King whether in the camp or in the senate, and no fear of criticism, no dread of inconsistency, could deter him from doing it.

The two years of Wellington's administration were memorable for three large measures of reform. The Test and Corporation Acts, enacted during the Anglican fervour of the Restoration, required every holder of office, civil or military, to receive the Sacrament according to the rites of the Established Church. Ever since 1727, following an example set by the sagacity of Walpole, an Indemnity Bill had been enacted annually [2] by Parliament, and thus Dissenters had been relieved of all penalties for violation of these laws. For a hundred years, therefore, the Acts had been inoperative, but they still galled the pride, though they did not hinder the ambition, of the Protestant Dissenters. In 1828 Lord John Russell carried against the Government a motion in favour of their repeal. Wellington and Peel bowed to the sense of the House, and despite bitter opposition from Sir Robert Inglis and Lord Eldon the Sacramental Test was abolished. There was, however, substituted a declaration, apparently void of offence, that office holders would do nothing " to injure or subvert the Protestant Established Church ". *(margin: Repeal of Test and Corporation Acts, 1828)*

The same session witnessed the enactment of a Corn Law, identical in principle with that which in the previous year Wellington's amendment had destroyed. A sliding scale was established under which a duty of 25s. 8d. was imposed when the price was at or below 64s., and the duty diminished to 1s. when the price rose to 73s. The sliding scale proved, however, only moderately successful ; it put too large a premium upon speculation. But the Government were now confronted by a problem even more difficult than that of the Corn Laws. *(margin: Corn Laws : a sliding scale)*

[1] *Cf.* pp. 52-54, *supra.*   [2] With four exceptions.

On the resignation of the Canningites, Mr. Vesey Fitzgerald was appointed to succeed Mr. Charles Grant at the Board of Trade. Fitzgerald was personally and politically one of the most popular men in Ireland, but he was, of course, a Protestant. Daniel O'Connell, though a Catholic, resolved to oppose his re-election for County Clare, and that resolution marked a turning point in the history of Ireland.[1]

But its significance must not be exaggerated. It is sometimes assumed, if not asserted, that now for the first time the assault was delivered against the virgin fortress of Protestant ascendancy. As a matter of fact, the outworks had been carried a generation ago; only the citadel remained untaken. By successive Acts of the Irish legislature,[2] passed between 1774 and 1792, most of the provisions of the " Penal Code " had been repealed, and most of the Catholic disabilities had been removed. By the Act of 1793 the Catholics were even admitted to the parliamentary franchise. Certain disqualifications remained : no Catholic could sit in Parliament, nor become a Sheriff, nor rise to the highest posts in the Army or at the Bar. But these pressed not so much upon the Catholic masses as upon the classes loyal for the most part to the English connection.

Pitt intended that a final and complete measure of emancipation should be a concomitant of the Act of Union. But for that avowed intention the opposition to the Union would have been less easily overcome. Pitt, however, counted without his Sovereign. The King refused all concessions to the Catholics ; Pitt resigned ; and the healing measure was deferred until it was too late to heal.

The Catholic question was not, however, permitted to slumber either in the Imperial Parliament or in Ireland. Motions were perpetually made in the House of Lords by Lord Grenville, Lord Donoughmore, and Lord Wellesley : in the Commons by Grattan, Plunkett, and Canning. Canning carried the House with him in 1812, and thenceforward, thanks mainly to the influence of Castlereagh, the question was officially regarded as an " open " one in the Liverpool Cabinet.

It was in Ireland, however, not at Westminster, that the decisive battle was fought and won, and the victory was due primarily to the genius of a single individual, Daniel O'Connell.

O'Connell was of all Irish leaders incomparably the greatest. He was magnificently endowed by nature for the part he had to play. A herculean frame, a keen intellect, a lambent humour, consummate eloquence, a voice at once sonorous and capable of the finest shades of expression, an enthusiastic temper, tenacity and adroitness combined : above all a perfect appreciation of Irish character. Born in

---

[1] The suggestion appears to have come from Sir David Roose, an Irish Tory. See *Correspondence of O'Connell*, ed. Fitzpatrick, i. 159.
[2] 1774, '78, '82, and '89.

1775, O'Connell became in 1810 Secretary to the Catholic Committee, and in 1823 founded and organized the Catholic Association. Suppressed by the Government in 1825 as " an unlawful combination and confederacy," the Association was ingeniously reconstituted by O'Connell and made its power felt in the Waterford election of 1826, when it broke down the political ascendancy of the Beresfords. Still more clearly was its power demonstrated in 1828.

O'Connell's triumphant return for County Clare created throughout Ireland intense excitement, and compelled the Wellington Government to face a situation which by general admission was fundamentally changed by that event. To refuse to Catholics the abstract rights of citizenship was one thing ; to decline to allow a duly elected Catholic to take his seat in the House of Commons was another.[1] Peel realized the dilemma in which the Government was placed. Lord Anglesey, their Lord Lieutenant, warned them that the hope of maintaining tranquillity in Ireland depended upon " the forbearance and the not very determined courage of O'Connell," and urged them, much as he abhorred the idea of " truckling to the overbearing Catholic Demagogues," to utilize the momentary calm to adjust the question.[2] By the end of the session of 1828 Peel had convinced himself that the Catholic question must be settled once for all, but he decided, and with obvious propriety, that for him to remain a member of the Government which must settle it was impossible. Moved, however, partly by his sense of the gravity of the crisis, partly by his loyalty to the Duke, above all by his conviction that he alone could carry an Emancipation Bill through Parliament he consented—perhaps to the detriment of his own reputation—to withdraw his resignation.

Parliament met on February 5th, 1829, and learnt to their amazement that the King recommended them not only to take " into deliberate consideration the whole condition of Ireland," but also " to review the laws which impose disabilities on His Majesty's Roman Catholic subjects ". To this speech the King had given " a reluctant assent," [3] and stipulated that the Relief Bill should not be introduced until the Catholic Association had been suppressed. A Bill to effect this object was passed rapidly through both Houses, but before the Royal assent was given the Association voluntarily dissolved itself.

Catholic Emancipation

The time had now come for the fulfilment of the pledge given in the speech from the Throne. On March 3rd the King made a final effort to avert surrender. The Ministers consequently resigned, and the King eventually and reluctantly gave way.

On March 5th Peel rose " as a Minister of the King and sustained

---

[1] *Cf.* the exceedingly acute remarks of John Keogh of Mount Jerome ap. *O'Connell Correspondence*, i. 160.
[2] Peel, *Memoirs*, i. 149.   [3] *Ibid.*, 310.

by the just authority which belongs to that character to vindicate
the advice given to his Majesty by a united Cabinet". The Bill
passed its second reading in the Commons by a majority of 180 and
in the Lords by 105. In the Lower House Peel made a gallant
attempt to defend the Bill upon its merits ; to the Peers Wellington
bluntly commended it as a preferable alternative to civil war. " I
am one of those," he said, " who have probably passed a longer period
of my life engaged in war than most men, and principally, I may say,
in civil war, and I must say this, that if I could avoid by any sacrifice
whatever even one month of civil war in the country to which I am
attached, I would sacrifice my life in order to do it." Such language
from the great soldier could not fail of its appeal : protests were
signed by the Duke of Cumberland, Sidmouth, Eldon, and thirty-six
other peers, but before the middle of April the Bill became law. It
contained various supposed securities against the spread of Roman
Catholicism, but as regards civil rights it was a large and generous
measure. Roman Catholics became eligible for almost all offices,
civil, military, parliamentary, and municipal, save those of Regent,
Lord Lieutenant, Lord Chancellor of England or Ireland, and one or
two others.

But this politic and generous concession was immediately followed
by a measure of wholesale, and, as it seemed, penal disfranchisement.
Emancipation had been won by the votes of the 40s. freeholders ;
their triumph was short-lived, for by a second Act of 1829 the qualification in Irish Counties was raised to £10, and the electorate was
thus reduced from 200,000 voters to 26,000.[1] It is true that for thirty
years the " forties " had been regarded as " practically nothing more
than a part of the live stock upon the estate of the landlord," who
created them for his own purposes. But in 1826, and until more
conspicuously in 1828, the cattle had strayed from the fold. The
" weapon," said Peel, " which the landlord has forged with so much
care and has heretofore wielded with so much success has broken
short in his hand ". The disfranchising Act was the result of this
miscarriage. Brougham regarded it " as the high price, the all but
extravagant price," of emancipation, but he was willing to pay it.
In Ireland it was regarded—and small wonder—as a surreptitious
attempt to cancel the effects of emancipation and to redress the
balance in the interests of the " Ascendancy " party.

Less intrinsically important, but not less irritating, were the
slights inflicted upon O'Connell himself. Despite his eminence at
the Irish Bar he was markedly passed over in the distribution of
" silk," and, even more unfortunately, he was compelled before
taking his seat to seek re-election for County Clare. He was not
opposed, and the re-election rendered necessary by technicalities was

[1] This is O'Connell's estimate, cited by O'Brien, *Fifty Years of Concessions*, i.
357. Lord Londonderry (*op. cit.* i. 353) put the number of freeholders at 191,000.

hardly more than formal, but it gave the agitator an opportunity which he did not neglect. " In my person," he declared, " the County of Clare has been insulted. To you is due the honour of having converted Peel and conquered Wellington." Such language may sound mere bombast to Englishmen : in Ireland it had its effect. Thanks in part to the adroitness of the agitator, in part to the tact-lessness of the English Ministries, emancipation did little to allay discontent in Ireland. Conceded in a reluctant spirit,[1] and carried with irritating concomitants, a healing measure may well fail to heal. Granted to Ireland in 1801 emancipation might have served to con-solidate the Union ; wrested from England in 1829, it was destined to inaugurate the agitation for repeal.[2]

Neither the King nor his Ministry long survived the Act of Catholic Emancipation. Apart from questions of foreign policy—already discussed—there was nothing in the remaining years of the King's reign to demand the attention of the historian. On June 26th, 1830, George IV. died after a prolonged illness, and his brother, the Duke of Clarence, succeeded to the throne as William IV. The change of Sovereigns was opportune. A bad man and a bad King, George IV. died unregarded and unrespected by his subjects. His successor, bluff, genial, and kind-heartedly eccentric, was commended to them alike by his profession and by his personality. And times were such that the cause of Monarchy needed all the adventitious aid it could command.[3]

Death of George IV., June 26th, 1830

Before the new reign was many weeks old the July Revolution had broken out in France ; the old Bourbon Monarchy had been finally overthrown ; a severe blow had been struck at the principle of legitimacy and therefore at the European settlement founded upon it ; Louis Philippe had been installed as a " Citizen King " ; Charles X. was in exile, and half Europe was in a state of turmoil and insurrection.

The July Revolution in France

[1] Peel's personal position is disclosed frankly and fully in his *Memoirs*, vol. i. Emancipation involved a painful sacrifice to him and some discredit to the University of Oxford. Peel felt bound to resign his seat and failed to secure re-election against Sir Robert Inglis. He immediately secured a seat at Westbury.

[2] In my account of Irish policy here and elsewhere throughout this work, I have occasionally borrowed from an article of my own in the *Fortnightly Review*, March, 1901.

[3] Greville, ii. 2, 4, and 65. " King George had not been dead three days before everybody discovered that he was no loss and King William a great gain." . . . " There never was anything like the enthusiasm with which he was greeted by all ranks ; though he has trotted about both town and country for sixty-four years, and nobody ever turned round to look at him, he cannot stir now without a mob, patrician as well as plebeian at his heels." . . . " The King seems to have be-haved perfectly throughout the whole business, no intriguing or underhand com-munication with anybody, with great kindness to his Ministers, anxious to support them while it was possible, and submitting at once to the necessity of parting with them. The fact is he turns out an incomparable King, and deserves all the encomiums that are lavished on him. All the mountebankery which signalized his conduct when he came to the throne has passed away with the excitement which caused it, and he is as dignified as the homeliness and simplicity of his character will allow him to be."

The events passing in France exercised an immense influence upon England and upon Europe; but the history of that reaction belongs to a new reign and a new Ministry. For the long spell of Tory administration was at an end, and Lord Palmerston, not Lord Aberdeen,[1] was responsible for the protection of British interests during the critical years which followed upon the revolution of 1830.

Close of the Tory Régime The Parliament elected in 1826 was dissolved, in consequence of the death of George IV., on July 24th, 1830. The General Election took place amid signs of unusual excitement; the Government lost fifty seats; Brougham was returned without trouble or expense to himself for Yorkshire, and two of Peel's brothers were defeated. On November 2nd the new Parliament was opened by the King in person, and Wellington at once made it clear that no measure of parliamentary reform could be expected from the existing administration. The attack was immediately opened in both Houses all along the line, and on November 16th the Ministry, having already suffered defeat on the question of the new Civil List, announced its resignation. The formation of the new Government was entrusted to Lord Grey.

The resignation of Wellington and Peel in 1830 closes a great epoch in English history. England had been ruled by a succession of Tory Ministries, virtually without break, for sixty years. Their rule was coincident with the most momentous period of modern history—a period which witnessed the loss of our first Colonial Empire, and the beginning of a second, the French Revolution and the Napoleonic wars, the Irish Union and Catholic Emancipation, the industrial revolution and the birth of a new England. The overthrow of the Wellington Admnistration was in the nature of things. The Tory party had ceased to stand for the old principles and was exhausted in personnel. In the pre-reform era the swing of the party pendulum was more deliberate than now, but it was nevertheless perceptible—at half-century intervals. Moreover, Peel and Wellington had made the fatal error of encouraging foes at the expense of friends. The old Tories were disgusted at the " Great Betrayal " of 1829 ; the new Whigs were stimulated to fresh hopes by the obvious weakening in the resistance to reform. The accession of a new Sovereign with Whig sympathies ; the overthrow of the legitimist régime in France ; the manifestations of liberal tendencies in Italy and Germany and Belgium—all these contributed to the overthrow of the old régime in England. But the vital issue which in 1830 divided parties was that of parliamentary reform. Wellington bluntly refused to touch the question. In his famous speech in the House of Lords he said emphatically that " he was not only not prepared to bring forward any measure of this nature ; but he would at once declare that, as far as he was concerned, as long as he held

---

[1] Aberdeen had succeeded Dudley at the Foreign Office, May, 1828.

any station in the Government of the country, he should always feel it his duty to resist such measures when proposed by others." [1]

That speech sealed the fate of the old Tory party and definitely closed the half-century of Tory rule.[2]

[1] For the whole speech *cf.* Hansard, 3rd ser., i. 52. The speech is almost an echo of Paley's words : " We have a House of Commons composed of 558 members, in which number are found the most considerable landowners and merchants of the Kingdom ; the heads of the army, the navy, and the law ; the occupiers of great offices in the State ; together with many private individuals eminent by their knowledge, eloquence, and activity. If the country be not safe in such hands, in whom may it confide its interests ? . . . Does any new scheme of re-presentation promise to collect together more wisdom or to produce firmer integrity ? "—*Moral Philosophy*, ii. 220 (quoted by Lecky, *Democracy and Liberty*, i. 7).

[2] 1770-1830, virtually unbroken save for Rockingham's three months' Ministry in 1782, the " coalition " of 1783, and the " Talents," 1806-1807.

BOOK II

THE REIGN OF THE MIDDLE CLASSES,
1832-1867

CHAPTER V

THE RULE OF THE WHIGS.   PARLIAMENTARY REFORM AND AFTER
(1830-1833)

**Lord
Grey's
Ministry**

THE supreme issue between parties at this moment was that of parliamentary reform. It was, therefore, appropriate that on the resignation of Wellington and Peel the formation of the new Ministry should be entrusted to Earl Grey. Born in 1764, the scion of an ancient Northumbrian house, and the eldest son of a distinguished soldier, he entered the House of Commons as Member for his native county in 1786. In 1792 he became the most influential spokesman of the *Society of Friends of the People*, and thence onwards for forty years was the foremost advocate of parliamentary reform. In 1792, 1793, and 1797 he had brought forward motions in the House of Commons, only to encounter a solid phalanx of opposition inspired to reaction by the dread example of France. But despite his long political career Lord Grey had little administrative experience. Less than two years at the Admiralty and the Foreign Office (1806-1807) represented the sum of his official life. Nevertheless, he was obviously marked out as the chief of a " Reform " Ministry, and the King's choice merely ratified general expectation. With four exceptions his colleagues in the Cabinet were all Peers, and the exceptions were not far removed from that order. Edward Geoffrey Stanley (eldest son of Lord Stanley, who was heir to the Earldom of Derby) became Chief Secretary for Ireland ; Lord Althorp was Chancellor of the Exchequer ; Mr. Charles Grant (afterwards Lord Glenelg) was President of the Board of Control, and Sir James Graham, a great territorial magnate, was First Lord of the Admiralty. The Secretaryships of State were all entrusted to Canningites : Lord Palmerston (Foreign), Lord Goderich (War and Colonies), and Lord Melbourne (Home). Huskisson also would doubtless have been included in the new Ministry but for his death by accident at the opening of the Manchester and Liverpool Railway (Sept. 15th. 1830). His absence seriously weakened Grey's Government in the department of Finance. With the possible exception of the Foreign Secretary, the most masterful personality in the Cabinet was Henry

Brougham, now elevated to the Peerage and the Woolsack.[1] Lord
Grey's own boast in regard to his Cabinet is said to have been that
in acreage it surpassed any previous record.[2] Whiggism was
certainly dying hard.

The situation which confronted Lord Grey's Ministry was not Social
devoid of difficulty. In Ireland O'Connell had already unfurled the Disorder
flag of " Repeal," and the troops had been called out (Oct. 1830) to
suppress the disturbances which marked the inauguration of the new
agitation. In England there were ominous signs of recrudescence of
the recent epidemic of social disorder. Luddites and rick-burners
were again to the fore. " Every post," writes Greville, " brings fresh
accounts of conflagrations, destruction of machinery, association of
labourers, and compulsory rise of wages. Cobbett and Carlile[3]
write and harangue to inflame the minds of the people, who are
already set in motion and excited by all the events which have
happened abroad." The new Ministry had not been in office two
days before they found it necessary to issue a proclamation offering
large rewards for the discovery of " offenders, rioters, or burners,"
and promising all the Lord Lieutenants assistance in the suppression
of disorder. Hampshire, Wilts, Berkshire, and Buckingham were
particularly conspicuous for crime and disturbance,[4] and in December
no less than 1,000 rioters, 700 of whom came from Hants and Wilts,
were brought to trial before a Special Commission at Winchester.
In January Carlile was convicted at the Old Bailey of " addressing
inflammatory language to the labouring classes," and was sentenced
to two years' imprisonment and a fine of £200. Cobbett, arraigned
on a similar charge, escaped punishment owing to the postponement
of his trial for six months. By that time the panic caused by
agrarian disorder had abated, and public interest was concentrated
upon the fate of the Reform Bill.

For some large measure of parliamentary reform the time was Parlia-
clearly ripe. It is true that there had been in recent years some mentary
slackening in the intensity of the demand. For whereas the year reform
1821 had produced a crop of nineteen petitions in favour of reform
and the year 1823 no less than twenty-nine, the years between 1824
and 1829 had produced none at all. Commercial prosperity is a
sure solvent of political agitation. But by 1830 prosperity was once
more waning, and interest in purely political questions was quickened
by the outbreak of revolution in France. In July the legitimist

---

[1] As Lord Brougham and Vaux. " Vaux et praeterea nihil," as the wits had
it. Greville's comment is characteristic : " The joy is great and universal ; all
men feel that he is emasculated, and drops on the woolsack as on his political
death-bed ; once in the House of Lords, there is an end of him, and he may rant,
storm, and thunder without hurting anybody."— i. 67.

[2] Parker's *Graham*, i. 90.

[3] Richard Carlile—a well-known Secularist .ecturer.

[4] *Cf.* for the " last labourers' insurrection " Mr. and Mrs. Hammond's *The
Village Labourer*, 1760-1832, a work which appeared too late for me to utilize.

Monarchy, which had been restored by the bayonets of the allies in 1815, finally tottered to its fall ; Charles X. was driven into exile, and Louis Philippe, Duke of Orleans, thanks mainly to the support of the Parisian bourgeoisie, was installed as " the Citizen King ". The shock thus given to the principle of legitimacy was felt in greater or less degree in most of the European States, in Poland, Italy, Germany, and most of all in Belgium.[1] Great Britain felt it least, but even here it gave renewed impulse to the cry for parliamentary reform.

Distribution of seats   That cry could no longer be stifled or ignored. Not since the middle of the fifteenth century had there been any general enactment in regard to the electoral franchise, and the Act of Henry VI., confining the county franchise to 40s. freeholders, had been reactionary and restrictive. The Tudors had greatly increased the numbers of the House of Commons by bestowing representation on Wales, and by the creation of numerous parliamentary boroughs, many of them towns of considerable importance. The Stuarts followed suit, but since the Revolution of 1688 there had been no alteration either in the franchise or in the distribution of seats in England and Wales.[2] But in the half-century before 1830 a new England had, as we have seen, come into being. Population which had been thin and scattered was not only increasing with great rapidity, but was also shifting in distribution. Towns which in Tudor and Stuart times had been important centres of trade were decaying into hamlets ; villages were growing into cities. The counties north of the Trent, which down to the eighteenth century were mostly poor and thinly populated, were becoming the centres of industrial activity. Bradford-on-Avon was yielding pride of place in the woollen trade to Bradford-on-Aire. Manchester and Liverpool, Leeds and Birmingham were quickly attaining to the pre-eminence which they have never since lost.

But electoral changes had not kept pace with economic development. Of the 203 parliamentary boroughs in 1831 no less than 115 were contained in the ten maritime counties between the Wash and the Severn and the County of Wilts, and of the 115 no less than 56 were on the tideway.[3] But this distribution, as Mr. Porritt points out, presents no paradox when the " social and industrial conditions of England up to the reign of Elizabeth are borne in mind ".[4] Any anomalies which had arisen were of comparatively " recent origin ". But they were sufficiently glaring. Such places as Old Sarum, Newtown (Isle of Wight), Gatton, Bramber, Bossiney, Beeralston, Hedon, Brackley, and Tregony, some of them hardly distinguishable

---

[1] The Belgian movement was, of course, " nationalist " rather than anti-monarchical, but the July Revolution in Paris, nevertheless, gave a powerful impulse to the Belgian movement.

[2] With a few unimportant exceptions The Scotch Union had brought 45, the Irish Union 100 additional members into the House of Commons.

[3] Porritt, *Unreformed House of Commons.*   [4] *Op. cit.* p. 85.

hamlets, returned two members apiece; Manchester, Birmingham, Leeds, Sheffield, Wolverhampton, Halifax, Bolton, and Bradford returned none.

The vagaries of the electoral franchise were not less bewildering The electoral franchise than those of the distribution of seats. The county members were elected on a uniform franchise by the 40s. freeholders; but in the boroughs the utmost variety prevailed. In some, known as "Scot and Lot Boroughs," all ratepayers were entitled to vote; in others only the hereditary "freemen"; in others only members of the municipal corporation; in others "potwallopers"; [1] while in others the franchise was attached to the ownership or occupation of particular houses known as "ancient tenements". But it is noticeable that even in boroughs where the franchise was theoretically wide, it was in practice narrow and confined. Thus in Gatton, where it was enjoyed by all freeholders and "Scot and Lot" inhabitants, there were only seven qualified to exercise it, and in Tavistock only ten. In the whole of England, Wales, Ireland, and Scotland, out of 16,000,000 people there were only 160,000 electors. It was alleged in 1793 by the *Society of the Friends of the People*, that out of 513 members for England and Wales 70 were returned by boroughs which had practically no electors at all, 90 by boroughs with less than 50, and a further 37 by towns with less than 100 voters apiece. According to another calculation 254 members were said to represent an aggregate constituency of less than 11,500. Bad in England, things were even worse in Ireland and Scotland. Out of the 300 members in the Irish House of Commons 216 represented boroughs or manors, and of these 200 were elected by 100 individuals and nearly 50 by 10. In Scotland sixty-six boroughs contained in the aggregate 1,450 electors; Edinburgh and Glasgow had 33 apiece; while the County of Bute out of a population of 14,000 possessed 21 electors, of whom only one was resident.

It was the restriction of the franchise which threw such enormous Influence and corruption power into the hands of the Government, of the great territorial magnates, and the Indian "Nabobs," and which contributed in large measure to the almost universal corruption prevailing in the borough constituencies. A vote was a possession far too valuable to be parted with except for a high consideration, and it has been estimated [2] that prior to 1832 not more than one-third of the members of the House of Commons represented "the free choice even of the limited bodies of electors then entrusted with the franchise". Sydney Smith, writing in 1821, declared that "the country belongs to the Duke of Rutland, Lord Lonsdale, the Duke of Newcastle, and about twenty other holders of boroughs. They are our masters." The statement was grossly exaggerated, but it had in it more than a

---

[1] All persons with a hearth of their own.
[2] By Erskine May, *Constitutional History*, i. 362.

semblance of truth. The Duke of Newcastle did in fact return eleven members, Lord Lonsdale nine, Lord Darlington seven, and the Duke of Rutland, the Marquis of Buckingham, and Lord Carrington six apiece. In 1780 the Duke of Richmond declared that not more than 6,000 men returned a clear majority of the House of Commons. A petition presented in 1793 on behalf of the *Friends of the People* by Grey declared that 357 members were returned by 154 patrons, of whom 40 were Peers. According to the detailed analysis of Oldfield, no less than 487 out of the 568 members of the House of Commons were, in 1816, nominees. Of the English members 218 were returned by the nomination or influence of 87 Peers ; 137 by 90 powerful commoners ; and 16 by the Government itself. Of the 45 Scotch members 31 were returned by 21 Peers, the remainder by 14 commoners. In Ireland 51 were returned by 36 Peers, and 20 by 19 commoners. Allowing a considerable margin for exaggeration in these various estimates, it is impossible in face of them to maintain that the pre-reform system was representative in anything but the crudest sense.

Gross corruption alike in the constituencies and among the elected or nominated representatives was the inevitable corollary of such a system. To the sale and purchase of seats the term cannot in fairness be applied. A seat was as much a marketable commodity in the eighteenth century as an advowson in the nineteenth, and the legitimacy of the transaction was recognized alike in Pitt's Reform Bill of 1785 and the Act of Union of 1800. In each case the value of a seat was estimated at over £7,000. Nor was this excessive, for sums far in excess of this amount were frequently spent on a parliamentary contest. Thus in 1768 the Bentincks and the Lowthers spent £40,000 apiece in contesting the counties of Cumberland and Westmoreland, while at York in 1807 the expenses of Lord Milton and of Mr. Lascelles are said to have amounted, in the aggregate, to the astounding sum of £200,000.

Repeated attempts were made to restrain these abuses, but with very imperfect success, and long before 1830 it had become obvious that nothing would really avail to cleanse the Augean stable short of a drastic redistribution of seats and a wide extension of the franchise.

In 1780 the *Society for Constitutional Information*, anticipating by sixty years the famous " points " of the Charter, demanded universal suffrage and equal electoral districts. Pitt in 1785 gave ministerial sanction to a scheme for extinguishing some of the "rottenest " of the boroughs, by compensating their owners and distributing their representatives among the counties and some of the largest towns. To admit the principle that a borough was property, saleable and purchaseable, was perhaps inexpedient, though it subsequently served to oil the wheels of the Irish Union, and the rejection of Pitt's Bill meant the postponement of reform for

nearly half a century. No one could think seriously of reform while
France was involved in Revolution, still less while the energies of the
nation were concentrated upon defeating Napoleon. But the flood
pent up for twenty-five years burst all barriers after 1815 with
results already described.

Throughout the autumn and winter of 1830-1831 there was a Reform
continuous agitation in favour of reform. The seed sown in many agitation
soils during the last half-century was rapidly ripening for harvest.
The philosophical radicalism of the Utilitarians ; the work of
Bentham, of James and John Stuart Mill, of Hume and others ; the
democratic liberalism of Francis Place ; the communism of Robert
Owen, all these were bearing fruit in the ferment of opinion and the
political organization which immediately preceded the Reform Bill
of 1831.

The first work of the Grey Ministry was to appoint a Committee Progress
to draft a Bill to " amend the representation of the people in England of the Re-
and Wales ". The Committee consisted of two members of the form Bill
Cabinet : Lord Durham and Sir James Graham ; Lord Duncannon,
the chief Government Whip, and Lord John Russell. To these, as
they were approaching the end of their labours, the Duke of Richmond
was added. Creevey declares that of the Bill, which is known to
history as his, Lord Grey " knew not one syllable till it was presented
to him all ready cut and dry ".[1] This myth has been finally exposed
by the publication of Graham's Memorandum on the proceedings in
the Committee of Four.[2] The original draft proposed by the Committee was substantially amended by the Cabinet who (1) struck out
the vote by ballot ; (2) retained septennial as against quinquennial
Parliaments ; and (3) substituted £10 for the proposed £20 rating
qualification in boroughs.

On March 1st Lord John Russell, though not yet a member of
the Cabinet, laid the ministerial proposals before the House of
Commons. They proved to be more drastic than even the most
sanguine Radicals had dared to hope. The first feature of the Bill
was a large measurement of disfranchisement. Sixty boroughs with
less than 2,000 inhabitants apiece, returning in the aggregate 119
members, were to be totally disfranchised ; the united boroughs of
Weymouth and Melcombe Regis were to lose two of their four
members ; 47 other boroughs, with more than 2,000 but less than
4,000 inhabitants, were to lose one member apiece. Thus 168 seats
were placed at the disposal of the Government. Enfranchisement
was on an adequate but less generous scale. Seven of the largest
represented towns like Manchester and Birmingham were to get 2
members apiece ; twenty more were to get 1 ; the London boroughs
to get 8 ; 57 were to go to the English counties ; 3 to Ireland, 5 to
Scotland, and 1 to Wales. The nett reduction in the numbers of

[1] ii. 264.   [2] Parker's *Graham*, i. 114 *seq.*

the House was to be 62. As to voting qualification there was an immense simplification. In the boroughs there was to be a £10 rating qualification, and freemen were to retain their votes. In the counties, copyholders and £50 tenants were added to the old 40s. freeholders. The Bill passed the second reading by a majority of only one. Before it was committed General Gascoyne carried, by a majority of eight, an instruction that there should be no diminution in the total number of representatives of England and Wales. On this rebuff the Ministry decided upon an immediate appeal to the country ; on April 22nd Parliament was dissolved in hot haste by the King, and amid the wildest excitement a General Election was held. The issue was as nearly isolated as it ever can be in English politics. " The Bill, the whole Bill, and nothing but the Bill," was the rallying cry of the Whigs. Their triumph was complete, and they came back with a majority of more than a hundred. The

The second Bill Reform Bill, with only a few minor changes, was reintroduced by Lord John Russell on June 24th, and on July 7th it was read a second time by a majority of 136 (367 to 231). The Tories fought it for two months in Committee, but before the end of September it was sent up to the Lords backed by a majority substantially undiminished. The Lords, after nearly a week's debate, threw it out (Oct. 8th) by a majority of 41 (199 to 158).

Reform riots The action of the Lords is said to have brought the country to the verge of revolution. There were serious riots in several of the large towns, notably in Derby, Nottingham, Worcester, Coventry, and—most serious of all—in Bristol. It is difficult to believe that these were the work of the classes about to be enfranchised. The Reform Bill, however, was looked upon only as an instalment. The political principle once admitted was to be the lever for far-reaching social and economic changes. Behind the Utilitarians were the Owenites. Social revolution was to come in the wake of political reform. The Whigs might persuade themselves that a measure so generous and comprehensive would be accepted by all parties as a final settlement. The Tories knew better ; so did the Radicals ; the Chartists best of all. Not otherwise can we explain the disturbances in the autumn of 1831. Commercial and agricultural distress and the dread of pestilence [1] doubtless added fuel to the flames, but the conflagration was due to a mass of economic and social discontent which had been accumulating during the last half-century. That discontent found, as we shall see, cold comfort in the clauses of the Act of 1832. But the immediate cry was for " the Bill ".

The third Bill Parliament was reopened on December 6th. A week later Lord John Russell introduced his third Reform Bill, this time in a shape considerably altered. The disfranchisement clauses were decidedly less rigorous, and were based not only on the principle of population,

[1] Cholera appeared in November.

but upon the number of inhabited houses, and the contribution of the town to the assessed taxes. More important still, the numbers of the House were to remain unchanged. The Bill passed rapidly through all its stages in the House of Commons, and before the end of March was launched upon its perilous voyage in the Lords.

Would the ship reach port safely ? In no responsible quarter was it believed that the Lords would yield without coercion, or the certain prospect of its application. If they gave the Bill a second reading it would only be with the intention of emasculating it in Committee. Under these circumstances some of the Cabinet were in favour of obtaining from the King an immediate guarantee that he would assent if necessary to the creation of a sufficient number of Peers to carry the Bill.[1] The King, however, demurred ; Lord Grey himself was reluctant, and the majority of the Cabinet decided to await events. In the Lords, thanks mainly to the attitude of the " waverers," the Bill was read a second time (April 14th) by a majority of nine (184 to 175). But on May 7th Lord Lyndhurst carried by a large majority (151 to 116) a motion in favour of postponing the clauses (with Schedule A) dealing with the disfranchisement of the smallest boroughs, until the rest of the Bill had been approved. The situation foreseen by Lord Durham, Sir James Graham, and other " stalwarts " in the Cabinet had actually arisen, and the Cabinet now advised the King to create as many Peers " as might ensure the success of the Bill in all its essential principles ". The King, though in favour of extensive reform, was strongly opposed on principle to the coercion of the Peers, and regretfully accepted the proffered resignation of the Ministry. The House of Commons expressed its confidence in the retiring Ministry by a large majority, and the country was profoundly agitated by the crisis. The King turned to Lord Lyndhurst, to Manners-Sutton (then Speaker of the House of Commons), and to the Duke of Wellington. Neither Lyndhurst nor Manners-Sutton could form a Ministry, but the Duke was willing to try in order " to save the Sovereign from the indignity of having so gross a violation of the Constitution imposed upon him ". But everything really depended upon Peel. No Ministry could now avoid a large measure of " Reform ". Not even to save the King and the Lords was Peel prepared to pledge himself to this. Negotiations broke down, and on May 14th the Duke advised the King to recall Lord Grey. For his own part the Duke promised that " in order to save His Majesty's personal honour as to the creation of Peers . . . he would . . . remove all pretence for such a creation by withdrawing his opposition ".[2] Greville's appreciation of the personal conduct of the two leading actors in this episode is not very wide of the mark. " Peel acted right from bad motives, the Duke

The House of Lords and the Crown

Resignation of Lord Grey's ministry

---

[1] *Cf.* Parker's *Graham*, i. 134 *seq.*
[2] For history of negotiations *cf.* Croker, ii. 153-169 ; Peel, i. 206 *seq.*

6

Its rein-   wrong from good ones." [1]   The Grey Ministry was reinstated, and
statement   the King in writing granted permission to Earl Grey " and to his
Chancellor Lord Brougham to create such a number of Peers as will
be sufficient to ensure the passing of the Reform Bill, first calling up
Peers' eldest sons ".   The battle was won.   The opponents of the
Bill in the House of Lords withdrew, and on June 7th the Bill received
the Royal assent.   The same session witnessed the passing of similar
Bills for the reform of the representation in Scotland and Ireland.

Summary   The changes effected by this legislation in its final shape may
of Reform   now be summarized.   First, as regards disfranchisement : 56
Act   boroughs with less than 2,000 inhabitants were totally disfranchised.
Of these 55 had two members each ; one, Higham Ferrers, had one ;
Weymouth and Melcombe Regis lost two of their four members ;
and 30 boroughs with less than 4,000 inhabitants lost one of their
two members.   Thus 143 seats were surrendered.   These were redistributed as follows : 65 to English and Welsh counties ; 44 to
twenty-two English boroughs (two each) ; 21 to single member
boroughs ; 8 to Scotland and 5 to Ireland.   The total numbers
therefore remained unchanged at 658.   In the boroughs a uniform
£10 household franchise was established, with the reservation of the
rights of resident freemen in corporate towns.[2]   In the counties the
old 40s. freeholders were reinforced by copyholders and long leaseholders, and by tenants-at-will paying a rent of £50 a year.   In
Scotland the county franchise was given to all owners of property of
£10 a year and to certain leaseholders ; in Ireland to owners as in
England and £20 occupiers.

The final and total result was the addition of some 455,000
electors to the roll—an addition which more than tripled the electorate.   In the towns political power was vested mainly in the
merchants, manufacturers, and shopkeepers ; in the counties in the
landowners and the farmers.   In addition to the clauses defining the
franchise and the distribution of seats, the Act of 1832 provided for
the formation of a register of voters, for the division of constituencies
into convenient polling districts, and for the restriction of the polling
to two successive days.

That the Reform Acts of 1832 constituted a great political and
parliamentary achievement will be denied by none.   Before, however, an attempt is made to estimate its real and permanent significance, a few words may be said as to the part played in the struggle
by individuals.

Conduct   Throughout the whole crisis the King's behaviour was, by general
of   consent, admirable.   Not only was his conduct entirely " correct "
William   in the constitutional sense, but " he bestowed much time and thought
IV.   in going over every part of the plan, examined its bearings, asked
most sensible questions ".[3]   Lord Grey himself bore similar testi-

---

[1] ii. 336.   [2] If existing prior to 1831.   [3] Creevey, ii. 216.

mony : " the King's noble conduct is indeed a just theme for praise, and entitles him to all our gratitude and all our zeal in his service ". To the general principles of the Bill he gave a cordial assent ; as to the means by which it was forced through one branch of the legislature he had grave misgivings.[1] How far they were justified is still a matter of controversy.[2] In the Commons the lion's share of the work fell to Lord John Russell, ably supported by Lord Althorp, but in the Cabinet they were strongly backed both by Graham and Lord Durham.

But neither the King's closet, nor the Cabinet, nor the Commons was the scene of the real conflict over reform. The key to the position was in the House of Lords. It was the Lords, not the Monarchy nor the Commons, who were fighting for their political lives. For a century and a half the Peers—partly in their own chamber, still more through their nominees in the Lower House—had been the real rulers of England. In 1832 they were called upon to surrender a trust which they had administered, on the whole, with conspicuous fidelity and success, albeit by methods which the public opinion of to-day regards as indefensible. That they were blind to the new forces —political, social, and economical—which the last half-century had generated may be imputed to them for stupidity, but not for unrighteousness. Nor can it be denied that their estimate of the results to be apprehended from reform was nearer the mark than that of their opponents. Lord Grey himself represented his proposals as " aristocratic " ; his colleagues hoped that an " effectual check would be opposed to the restless spirit of innovation " ;[3] the Whigs generally believed that the Bill was at once " conservative " and final in its terms. Nothing would have amazed them more than to learn that they were opening the flood-gates to the tide of democracy. " Neither the Whig aristocracy who introduced the first Reform Bill," says a philosophical writer, " nor the middle class whose agitation forced it through, conceived it to be even implicitly a revolutionary measure. The power of the Crown and of the House of Lords were to be maintained intact ; the House of Commons was to be more representative, but not more democratic than before. The change was regarded as one of detail, not of principle ; in no sense a subversion of the Constitution, but merely its adaptation to new conditions."[4] The Duke of Wellington judged it far more shrewdly : " there is no man who considers what the Government of

Conduct of the Lords

---

  [1] King Billy *hates* the Peer-making, but as a point of honour to his Ministers he gives them unlimited power."—Creevey, ii. 241.
  [2] Greville's opinion of William IV. had changed for the worse. Under date May 17th, 1832, he writes : " His ignorance, weakness, and levity, put him in a miserable light, and prove him to be one of the silliest old gentlemen in his dominions."—ii. 300.
  [3] Report of Cabinet Committee.
  [4] Dickinson, *The Development of Parliament*, p. 39—the whole essay is eminently worthy of attention.

King, Lords, and Commons is, and the details of the manner in which it is carried on, who must not see that Government will become impracticable when the three branches shall be separate, each independent of the other, and uncontrolled in its action by any of the existing influences ". It is true that the full force of the shock administered in 1832 was not felt for at least two generations. Despite organic change, the Government of England continued to be aristocratic in personnel at least until 1867. Nevertheless, it is a sound instinct which assigns to 1832 the real point of transition from Aristocracy to Democracy. The changes of 1867 and 1884 were implicit in the earlier revolution. That these changes were neither foreseen nor intended by Lord Grey and his colleagues is true, but it is nothing to the point. They opened the gates ; the capture of the citadel was merely a question of time.

The instinct, therefore, which led the Lords to resist to the last the proposals of reform was, from their own point of view, perfectly sound. With the passage of the Bill their political death-warrant was signed. That an " extensive measure " could have been much longer deferred few people on either side believed, and events have more than justified the general belief.

Though reform was inevitable, the Act by which it was accomplished was open to grave criticism. That it cruelly disappointed the hopes of the working classes was conclusively proved, firstly by the Chartist agitation, and secondly by their refusal to support Cobden and Bright in their crusade against the Corn Laws.[1] Neither then nor later had the Whigs any intention of satisfying democratic aspirations. Still less did their Bill satisfy the Philosophical Liberals. It was based not on principle but on expediency ; it darned and patched ; it abolished some of the more flagrant abuses, but it left innumerable anomalies ;[2] it broke the principle of aristocracy without admitting that of democracy ; representation was based neither on numbers, nor wealth, nor education ; worst of all, in view of the philosophers, no effort was made to secure representation for minorities.[3] None the less the Whigs had a great achievement to their credit, and if in 1848 the epidemic of Revolution left us scathless, we must thank the legislation of 1832 not less than that of 1846.

The General Election and the new Parliament

No time was lost in testing the temper of the new constituencies. After an interval no longer than was needed for the arduous work of registration, Parliament was dissolved on December 3rd, and the elections began forthwith. In some places rioting occurred, but on the whole the new machinery worked smoothly, and the elections were conducted without serious disturbance. The polls went, as

[1] See *infra*, pp. 112–3.
[2] According to Porritt (*op. cit.* i. 23) there still remained after 1832 " eighty-five avenues through which the parliamentary franchise could be reached " (some of these only respected the vested interests of the existing voters).
[3] *Cf.* Mill, *Representative Government*.

was to be anticipated, strongly in favour of the Ministerialists.
" Orator " Hunt was defeated at Preston, where, as in other ancient
boroughs, the effect of the Reform Act was to circumscribe the
constituency ; and Cobbett, though afterwards returned for Oldham,
failed to secure election at Manchester.

It is difficult to state with precision the disposition of parties in State of
the new Parliament. No two contemporary estimates agree. Nor parties
is this remarkable, for party lines were a good deal blurred. The
Conservatives (to adopt the name by which Croker had recently re-
christened the Tory party) numbered something between 143 and
167. The Ministerialists are variously estimated at anything
between 382 and 491, the latter figure including all who were not
Tories. But the Radicals numbered 71, and the Repealers 38, and
both were in opposition to Lord Grey's Government.[1] It was
deemed wise, in view of the crowd of inexperienced members, to have
an experienced Speaker in the chair. Manners-Sutton was, therefore, re-elected, though not without opposition from a handful of
Radicals and Repealers, led by Cobbett and O'Connell. Despite the
Speaker's authority there was, however, much confusion at the
beginning of the session. " For two nights and a half," says Croker,
" the vehemence and disorder was so great that people began to
think the National Convention was begun." [2] Things gradually
settled down, but the outer aspect of the House corresponded to a
real disintegration and confusion of parties. The most remarkable
feature of the new Parliament was the way in which Peel, with
amazing rapidity and dexterity, re-established his personal position.
" You will be placed in a new and, I fear, painful position in the
House of Commons." So Lord Aberdeen had written to him on the
eve of the session. The prediction was entirely falsified by the
event. Before the session was over Peel was the real master of the
House. " The fate of the Government was, and he knew it, in his
hands." Croker was right. Peel played his game with consummate adroitness.[3] Despite their great majority the Ministry was
from the outset weak, and rapidly grew weaker, but Peel kept them
in for two reasons : they were doing his work, and there was no
possible alternative. " What are we doing," he wrote to Croker

---

[1] The Rev. A. B. Beaven, whose authority on such points is unrivalled, has
closely scrutinized the votes of members returned to this Parliament, and he kindly
permits me to state that his final estimate of the strength of parties is as follows :—
Ministerialists (including 107 " Reformers " and 42 " Moderate Whigs ")   . 382
Radicals   71
Repealers   38
                                                                                          ———
                                                                                          491
Conservative   167
    This tallies closely with Mr. Gladstone's estimate of the strength of his own
party, as he puts the Conservatives at 160.
    [2] ii. 202.   [3] Cf. Greville, ii. 363, 377, 382 and passim.

(March 5th, 1833), " at this moment ?   We are making the Reform Bill work. . . . We are protecting the authors of the evil from the work of their own hands."   It was, as we shall see, no idle boast.

Work of the session   The King opened Parliament in person on February 5th, but his speech, despite the solemnity and significance of that occasion, was singularly colourless.   There was some reference to the affairs of Portugal, Holland, and Belgium ; the Parliament was reminded of its " anxious duty to promote by all practicable means habits of industry and good order among the labouring classes of the community ; and of the expiration of the Charters of the East India Company and of the Bank of England ".   But the bulk of the speech was devoted to Ireland.   Irish questions were, indeed, destined to dominate not only the speech but the session and the Parliament. Before proceeding to discuss them, it may be well to deal with other legislative achievements of the session.

New Charter for the East India Company   The East India Company had lost its commercial monopoly in India in 1813, and the opportunity was now taken for completing the work then begun.   The Charter was renewed for another twenty years, but only on condition that the Company confined itself to the task of political administration.   The monopoly of the China trade was to be abandoned ; trading operations in India were to cease ; Europeans were to be allowed to settle in India without hindrance, and natives were to be admitted to office.   To compensate for the loss of its commercial privilege the Company was to receive for forty years an annuity of £630,000, charged upon the revenues of India. A legal member was at the same time added by the appointment of Macaulay to the Governor-General's Council.

Bank Charter Act   The Charter of the Bank of England, last renewed in 1800, was to lapse in 1833.   It was now renewed for a further term of twenty-one years, but the conditions were considerably modified, and Parliament reserved to itself the right to revise them after eleven years. Despite strong opposition, the Bank of England was permitted to retain its most cherished privilege.   It remained the Banker of the Government ; it alone, among the London Joint Stock Banks, was allowed to issue notes, and those notes, except at the Bank of issue, were to be legal tender.   The last provision was erroneously interpreted as a partial return to inconvertibility.   As a fact, it represented a concession to the country banks and an attempt to avoid a recurrence of the dangers, more particularly the drain of gold, revealed in 1825-1826.   The convertibility of Bank of England notes remained, however, entirely unimpaired.

Legal reforms   Two useful legal reforms stand to the credit of the Lord Chancellor. One, for the abolition of fines and recoveries, greatly simplified the conveyance of land ; the second was an Act " for the better administration of justice in His Majesty's Privy Council ".   The Long Parliament, in its zeal against the " Star Chamber " and other prerogative courts, had swept away the greater part of the judicial business of the Council. But the latter still retained the supreme appellate jurisdiction for the over-sea dominions of the Crown. The multiplication of Colonies and Dependencies restored to the Council an importance of which the Long Parliament had never dreamt. Moreover, in 1832 the High Court of Delegates, established as the Supreme Court for ecclesiastical causes by Henry VIII., was abolished, and its jurisdiction was transferred to the Privy Council. But the procedure of the latter was haphazard. Accordingly in 1833 its judicial functions were transformed to a Committee consisting of the President of the Council, the Lord Chancellor, and such Privy Councillors as held or had held high judicial office, including, in ecclesiastical cases, such Archbishops and Bishops as were Privy Councillors. The constitution of the Court was further amended in 1871, and again in 1876. Since 1833 its business has rapidly increased with the development of the over-sea dominions, and it now occupies a position of immense importance in the machinery of Empire. In ecclesiastical affairs its jurisdiction has not been unchallenged.[1]

The first session of the first reformed Parliament is memorable in the history of elementary education. Down to 1833 the whole responsibility for the education of the children of the poor had been assumed by the Churches. The Church of England had done its work since 1811 through the National Society, founded by Andrew Bell; the British and Foreign School Society, founded by Joseph Lancaster and maintained for the most part by the liberality of Nonconformists, had been in operation three years longer. The Budget of 1833 provided for a Treasury grant of £20,000 a year in aid of elementary education. By a Treasury minute (August 30th, 1833) the administration of the money was entrusted to the two Societies already named; none of it was to be spent on the erection of schools, and no grants were to be made unless they were met by at least an equal amount of voluntary contributions. Though not in itself imposing, the grant laid the foundations of a gigantic edifice.[2] *The first education grant*

The Treasury grant for education was not the only evidence of concern for the welfare of the rising generation. Of even greater immediate significance was the acceptance of Lord Althorp's Factory Bill. During the last thirty years the conscience of the nation had become increasingly alive to the scandals connected with the employment of children in factories. Under the " apprentice system," parish apprentices were sent from the workhouses to the factories, there to be " used up " as the " cheapest raw material in the market ". The evils, moral and sanitary, connected with this " White Slavery," *The Factory Act*

---

[1] *Cf.* Halsbury (ed.), *Laws of England,* vol. ix.; Holdsworth, *History of English Law,* i. 292 *seq.*

[2] See *infra,* c. xxi. p. 328.

compelled the intervention of the State. Thanks mainly to the efforts of the first Sir Robert Peel, the " Health and Morals Act " was passed in 1802. The Act laid down certain sanitary regulations, and provided that the children should not be kept at work for more than twelve hours a day. But it applied only to legal apprentices. The result was to stimulate a traffic, in some senses still more hideous because more unnatural, between the mill owners and the parents. " Instead of parish apprentices," said Sir Robert Peel, " the children of the surrounding poor are preferred, whose masters, being free from the operation of the former Act of Parliament, are subjected to no limitation of time in the prosecution of their business, though children are frequently admitted there to work thirteen or fourteen hours a day at the tender age of seven years, and in some cases still younger ". Parliament could not resist this demand for investigation, especially when urged by such a representative cotton-spinner as the first Sir Robert. The Commons appointed a Committee in 1816, the Lords in 1819, and as a result the Second Factory Act (1819) was passed. No children under nine years of age were to go into a factory ; for children under sixteen the hours were limited to twelve, and night work was prohibited. But the Act referred only to cotton mills. Further restrictions were imposed by Sir John Hobhouse's Act of 1825, which provided for definite meal times and quarter holiday on Saturdays. The next stage was marked by the ten-hours agitation initiated by Richard Oastler and Michael Thomas Sadler. Sadler introduced, but failed to pass, a ten-hours Bill in 1831. At the General Election of 1832 this eminent Tory philanthropist was defeated at Leeds, and the parliamentary leadership of the movement was assumed by Lord Ashley, better known later as the Earl of Shaftesbury. Ashley reintroduced the ten-hours Bill early in the first session of 1833. The Government favoured counsels of delay, but, defeated in the House, adopted Ashley's Bill, and in a modified form passed it into law. Lord Althorp's Act, as it is generally designated, introduced several new principles into factory legislation. A distinction was drawn between " children " aged nine to twelve, and " young persons " (thirteen to eighteen). " Children " were not to work more than nine hours a day, or more than forty-eight a week, and were to spend two hours a day in school—the thin end of the " half-time " wedge ; " young persons " were limited to a sixty-nine hours' week, and neither for them nor for children was night work permitted. For the first time inspectors were appointed to see that the provisions of the Act were enforced. For a " middle-class " Parliament this was not a bad beginning. The cotton-spinners did not like it, but they were compelled to give way.

Slavery abolition   The benevolent interest of the new Parliament was not confined to the " White Slaves " at home. Of the rich legislative harvest gathered in this session the most remarkable crop was the Act for the

" abolition of slavery throughout the British Colonies ". The question had long been kept before the mind and conscience of the country by a band of single-minded philanthropists, such as Clarkson, William Wilberforce, Zachary Macaulay, and Fowell Buxton. Pitt and Fox lent their powerful support in the House of Commons, and in 1807 the traffic in slaves was legally prohibited. In 1823 Fowell Buxton introduced a motion in favour of the gradual abolition of slavery itself, and Canning, in the same year, issued a circular intended to secure the better treatment of slaves. The immediate result of this movement was not favourable to discipline in the West Indies. The planters were infuriated and talked of " independence " ; the slaves became restless and unruly. In 1833 the Government, grasping the nettle firmly, decided on total emancipation. All children under six years of age were to be freed immediately ; all who should hereafter be born were to be born into freedom ; slavery was to cease on August 1st, 1834, and the slave owners were to be compensated by a loan of £15,000,000. But between slavery and freedom there was to be an intermediate period of " legal apprenticeship " lasting for twelve years. During this period the freed slaves were to work for their former masters during three-fourths of their working week or day, in return for maintenance. During one-fourth of their time they were to be free to work for hire. This well-meant but complicated compromise did not stand. Before the Bill passed, the intermediate period was reduced from twelve years to seven, and ultimately it lasted only four. Instead of a loan of £15,000,000 the planters received an out-and-out compensation of £20,000,000. Of the ultimate economic effects of emancipation this is not the place to write, but it cannot be doubted that the free traders and abolitionists were over-sanguine. The Act of 1833 was based primarily not on economic, but on moral grounds. At the cost of real self-sacrifice the nation deliberately determined on an act of righteousness and benevolence. Nor was the appropriate reward withheld.

CHAPTER VI

IRISH AFFAIRS. O'CONNELL AND THE WHIGS
(1833-1837)

The Re-formed Parliament and Ireland FROM the foregoing record of fruitful legislative activity, it needs something of an effort to turn to the Irish policy of the Whig Government. But now and for many sessions to come Ireland filled the stage at Westminster, and determined the fate of more than one Ministry.

In 1832 the new electorate in Ireland returned 38 Repealers and 67 Unionists : but of the latter 37 favoured the extinction of tithes. Thus the country, as an Irish writer points out, had declared strongly against the tithes, and for the Union.[1] The Irish Executive was committed by Lord Grey to Lord Anglesey (as Lord Lieutenant) and **Stanley's Chief Secretaryship** Mr. Stanley as Chief Secretary. During the critical years 1830-1833 the latter was the virtual ruler of Ireland. Stanley was a man of brilliant parts : unsurpassed in debate, a vigorous administrator, clear-sighted within a limited range, and transparently honest. But he was absolutely devoid of that insight and imagination which are essential to a statesman who governs a dependency. Though thrice a Conservative Prime Minister, Stanley was a typical Whig. He was a devout and unquestioning believer in the English system of Government, and firmly convinced that its adoption was alone sufficient to secure to all the various races of mankind social happiness and political contentment. To Ireland he offered his blessing in the exact spirit of Cromwell's Proclamation (of 1649) : " We come by the assistance of God to hold forth and maintain the lustre of English liberty in a nation where we have undoubted right to do it ; wherein the people of Ireland (if they listen not to such seducers as you are) may equally participate in all benefits ; to use liberty and fortune equally with Englishmen, if they keep out of arms ". That any Irishman should be blind to the lustre of " English liberty," or slow to avail himself of " liberty and fortune " in an English sense is what no genuine Englishman has ever been able to understand. And such lack of understanding is probably an important part of the equipment of a governing race. Stanley was typically devoid of it. If the Irish would " keep out of arms," and refuse to listen to " seducers " like O'Connell all would be well. After thirty years of stagnation in domestic politics the Englishman was about to set his house in order. If Irishmen would behave nicely their house should be put in order too. They, too, should have an extended franchise and municipal self-government ; a reformed poor law, and a national

[1] O'Brien, *Fifty Years of Concession in Ireland*, i. 413.

system of education. But the irony of the situation was that for Whig reform of the English type—extended to Ireland with the best intentions—the average Irishman cared nothing.

During the decade that followed upon Catholic emancipation interest in Ireland was concentrated upon one question—presenting itself under various aspects. What was " emancipation " intended to mean ? Did it mean merely the admission of a few Catholic gentry to the Parliament at Westminster, or the inauguration of a Catholic administration in Ireland ? Would it secure the abolition of a system under which a literal tenth of the produce of all the poorest land in Ireland went to the support of a wealthy, heretical, and alien Church ? What is the " Irish question " ? asked Mr. Disraeli. " One said it was a physical question, another a spiritual ; now it was the absence of the aristocracy, then the absence of railways. It was the Pope one day, potatoes the next." During the early thirties the answer to this question was unequivocal. " The Irish question " was " Tithes ".

To the Irish peasant " Tithe " was hateful on many grounds. It **The Tithe** was an English institution, never having been known in Ireland until **question** the Synod of Cashel (1175) ; it was a badge of Protestant ascendancy, never having been exacted until the Reformation ; and it was a perpetually recurrent drain upon his scanty material resources. Thus the injury was partly material, and partly moral. " Tithe " was at once a drain upon his purse, a sear upon his conscience. No such argument availed for the Episcopalian farmer. But the Protestants, Episcopalian and Presbyterian alike, had managed in large measure to evade the impost.

" Tithe " was, of course, only part of a larger question. The **The Es-** position of the Established Church in Ireland was entirely anomalous. **tablished** It was magnificently endowed. To put its revenues at £800,000 a **Church in** year would probably be an under-statement. Yet despite its en- **Ireland** dowments, and despite the penal legislation of the eighteenth century, its adherents were proportionately fewer than they had been two centuries before. In 1834 the population of Ireland was close on 8,000,000. Of these 6,427,712 persons were Roman Catholics; 852,064 were Protestant Episcopalians ; 642,356 were Presbyterians, while 21,808 adhered to other forms of Protestant dissent.

" The Church of the 800,000 Protestant Episcopalians was established and endowed ; the Church of the 600,000 Presbyterians was endowed but not established ; the Church of the 6,000,000 Catholics was neither established nor endowed." [1]

" On an Irish Sabbath morning," says Sidney Smith,[2] " the bell

---

[1] O'Brien, *Fifty Years*, i. 372. To Mr. O'Brien's most valuable work I owe many of the statistics and quotations given above. For further information on this subject reference should be made to it.

[2] Quoted by O'Brien.

of a neat Parish Church often summons to worship only the parson and an occasionally conforming clerk, while 200 yards off, a thousand Catholics are huddled together in a miserable hovel, and pelted by all the storms of Heaven."

The immediate object of the Catholic peasant, however, was to get rid of the payment of " Tithe ".

In 1830 war was proclaimed. " Let your hatred of ' Tithe ' be as lasting as your love of justice." Such was the advice of the Catholic Bishop of Kildare, Dr. Doyle. Advice of this kind rarely falls upon deaf ears in Ireland. The fuel was already gathered ; it needed but a spark to ignite it. By 1831 all Ireland was ablaze. " Payment of tithes," says a contemporary account,[1] " was almost everywhere refused : the usual system of threats and murder was again set in motion ; the clergymen dared not ask, the willing occupier dared not pay." At the end of 1831 Committees were appointed in both Houses to investigate the question. The Committees recommended (1) an immediate grant by Government to the distressed clergy, and (2) a " scheme for the extinction of tithes and their commutation for a charge upon land ". On these lines Lord Grey's Government legislated in 1832. An Act was passed authorizing the Government to advance a sum not exceeding £60,000 to the Irish clergy, and to reimburse themselves by collecting the arrears from the tithe-payers. Later in the year Stanley obtained the sanction of Parliament to a second measure, making tithe-composition compulsory and permanent. Both measures were violently opposed by O'Connell. The first, he declared, would make the Lord Lieutenant " Tithe-Proctor-General for all Ireland " ; the second would only perpetuate abuses, while both would serve to buttress an institution which was hopelessly rotten and unsound.

Social order

Meanwhile the social condition of Ireland was going from bad to worse. The legislation of 1832 had served only to accentuate bad feeling ; no tithes could be collected ; a widespread system of " boycotting " was initiated ; the Executive was powerless, and by the end of the year anarchy was everywhere triumphant. Such were the circumstances under which the General Election of 1832 was held. O'Connell definitely unfurled the banner of Repeal, and Ireland returned forty-five members pledged to sustain him in his demands.

The King's Speech of 1833, after foreshadowing a tithe-commutation Bill and a Bill dealing with the Protestant Establishment, proceeded : " But it is my painful duty to observe that the disturbances in Ireland, to which I adverted at the close of the last session, have greatly increased. The spirit of insubordination and violence has risen to the most fearful height, rendering life and property

[1] *Annual Register*, 1831, p. 327.

insecure, defying the authority of the law, and threatening the most fatal consequences if not promptly and effectively repressed."

The debate on the Address was bitter and protracted. That crime was rife in Ireland O'Connell did not deny; but crime was due not to agitation but to misgovernment. O'Connell was answered by Stanley; and the answer of Stanley may be compressed into a sentence : " A Government, to be loved, must first be feared ". Reform-cum-coercion and undying resistance to Repeal—this was the programme of the Ministry.

On February 12th Lord Althorp introduced into the House of Commons a Bill dealing with the Temporalities of the Church in Ireland. It was a large measure involving, as originally drafted, a considerable dose of " disendownment ". Opinion, however, was not ripe for the acceptance of the principle of " appropriation," and this part of the Bill was subsequently dropped. The remainder of it after a stormy passage became law. Two Archbishoprics and eight Bishoprics were suppressed; first-fruits and Church cess were discontinued ; many sinecures were abolished ; some ecclesiastical incomes were reduced ; and a commission to deal with the surplus revenues of the Church was appointed. But on the main question victory rested with the Ascendancy party. Revenues were to be redistributed, but not alienated.

Church Temporalities Bill

On February 15th a Coercion Bill was introduced by Lord Grey into the House of Lords. It was admittedly of the severest character. Greville describes it as " a *consommé* of insurrection-gagging Acts, suspension of Habeas Corpus, martial law, and one or two other little hards and sharps ". Immense powers were committed to the Lord Lieutenant, and Ireland was to be temporarily governed by martial law. The debate in the Commons revealed the fact that the Ministry was divided as to the expediency of the measure. Althorp's speech in introducing it was singularly ineffective ; but Stanley in a great speech saved the Bill. Despite the opposition of Repealers and Radicals the Bill became law in April.

Coercion

The Session, however, sorely tried the cohesion of the Government, and before its close the Ministry was reconstructed. Lord Wellesley succeeded Lord Anglesey as Lord Lieutenant, while Stanley was replaced as Chief Secretary, first by Hobhouse and afterwards by Littleton.[1] But Stanley's promotion to the Colonial Office involved no change in the Irish policy of the administration. In opening the session of 1834, the King was able to congratulate Parliament upon a great improvement in the state of Ireland. That his words were not merely due to official optimism is proved alike by the private correspondence of the time, and by the public statistics of Ireland. Crime and outrage had undoubtedly diminished. The Castle had regained the upper hand ; but the causes of social disorder

[1] Lord Wellesley's son-in-law.

remained. Against the Union and against tithes the agitation was waged without remission. The King's Speech referred to both questions. It announced such a "final adjustment of the tithes . . . as may extinguish all just causes of complaint without injury . . . to any institution in Church or State". At the same time it declared His Majesty's "unalterable resolution . . . to maintain inviolate " by all the means in his power the legislative Union.

The action of the Ministry was unequal in resolution and consistency to the words of the King. There was indeed no faltering with the question of the Union. On April 22nd O'Connell moved for a Select Committee " to inquire and report on the means by which the dissolution of the Parliament of Ireland was effected ; on the effects of that measure upon Ireland ; and on the probable consequences of continuing the legislative Union between both countries ". The motion was defeated by a majority of 523 to 38.

The Church question

In regard to the Church problem the Ministry was less fortunate. The tithe question was still far from settlement ; and behind the tithe question loomed the whole question of the Irish Establishment. Late in 1833 Littleton had induced Parliament to vote £1,000,000 to the distressed tithe-owners, and to authorize the Government to collect the arrears. Early in 1834 a Bill was introduced for the commutation of tithes into a land tax payable to the State at the rate of 80 per cent. of their previous value. In the course of the debate Ministers were challenged on the larger question of appropriation. The challenge was variously answered by Stanley and Lord John Russell. The dissensions of the Cabinet stood revealed to the world. " Johnny," in more senses than one, had indeed " upset the coach." The Government agreed to the appointment of a Commission to inquire into the whole question of the position of the Irish Church. On this Stanley resigned. Sir James Graham, the Duke of Richmond, and the Earl of Ripon (formerly Lord Goderich) went with him. The Cabinet was temporarily patched up, but their troubles were by no means at an end. Hopelessly divided on the principle of " appropriation," they were still more divided on that of " coercion ". Stanley's Act of 1833 was to expire on August 1st. Some members of the Cabinet were opposed to its renewal at any rate in its entirety. Lord Wellesley was prepared to rule without it : Littleton undertook to " manage Dan ". His " management," however, was so clumsy as to bring the whole Government down like a pack of cards. The Cabinet insisted on the renewal of the Coercion Act ; O'Connell declared that he had been " tricked by Littleton " ; Littleton was obliged to resign ; Althorp followed ; Lord Grey refused to go on without Althorp ; and on July 9th his own resignation was announced. The Reform Ministry was at an end.

Fall of Lord Grey's Ministry

The great ship had gone to pieces on the Irish rocks. The immediate cause of the disaster was clearly the indiscretion of Littleton.

But the essential causes went much deeper. The Ministry as a whole had no clear mind on the Irish question, and in policy they were divided. For the actual course of administration Stanley, whether at the Castle or at the Colonial Office, was primarily responsible. With the best intentions in the world Stanley cannot be described as a "sympathetic" administrator, and he was cordially disliked by the Irish members. But whatever his shortcomings Stanley knew his own mind. He cannot be blamed for not knowing the minds of Littleton, Wellesley, Althorp, and Lord John. This double-mindedness was fatal to the Ministry of Lord Grey, and their failure in Ireland was neither unaccountable nor undeserved. To the general record of failure there was, however, one exception. Stanley must have full credit for having done more than any other individual to lay the foundations of a National System of education. His Bill was based upon the principle of " a combined literary and a separate religious education ". A Board was to be constituted by the Lord Lieutenant, composed partly of Protestants and partly of Catholics. The Board was to appoint teachers, authorize school-books, and to superintend the whole system of national elementary education. "Even the suspicion of proselytism" was to be " banished ". Four days a week were to be devoted to combined moral and literary, one or two to separate religious instruction. Finally, the parliamentary grant was to be withdrawn from the Kildare Street Society and bestowed upon the National Board. Stanley's Act has been the basis of elementary education in Ireland from that day to this, though the whole spirit of its administration has been altered. Stanley contemplated a " mixed " system. To this idea the whole genius of the Irish people, Roman Catholics and Protestants, is irresistibly opposed. And in this case the national genius has proved itself too strong for legislative intention and enactment. Throughout the length and breadth of Ireland, with very small exceptions, the school system is to-day not " mixed " but strictly denominational.

During the last months of Lord Grey's Ministry Ireland claimed a large but not an exclusive share of public attention. Apart from Ireland the session of 1834 was memorable : on the one hand, for a great legislative achievement, and on the other, for the evidence it afforded as to the existence of a new force in English politics. *Lord Melbourne's Ministry, July 17th-Nov. 15th 1834*

With the former we shall deal presently ; as to the latter a word may be said at once. The legislation of 1832, even more conspicuously than that of 1828,[1] made the Protestant Dissenter a really effective political force. It was clearly manifested in the new Parliament. Already in 1833 the House of Commons had permitted Mr. Pease—the first Quaker elected for 140 years [2]—to take his seat on making an affirmation. In the same session an Act was passed to

---

[1] Repeal of the Test and Corporation Acts.   [2] Erskine May, iii. 177.

enable Quakers, Moravians, and Separatists on all occasions to substitute an affirmation for an oath.   In 1834 the Dissenters petitioned for the exclusion of the Bishops from the House of Lords, and indeed for the complete separation of Church and State.   A Bill for the admission of Dissenters to University Degrees passed the Commons but was rejected in the Lords.   Other Bills for the relief of Dissenters from Church rates, for the removal of restrictions upon the celebration of marriages in Dissenting Chapels, and for the commutation of English tithes, did not get so far.

The new Poor Law   Few legislative achievements have had a more significant bearing upon the social and moral life of the people than the Poor Law Amendment Act of 1834.   For this legislation the Whig Ministers are entitled to unstinted credit.   No Government seeking only popularity would have touched the question ;   no Government genuinely concerned for the social and economic welfare of the people could have evaded it.

The great Poor Law of Elizabeth had conferred upon the indigent poor two rights :   upon the impotent the right to maintenance ; upon the lusty and able-bodied the right to be " set on work ". Appropriate to an era of paternal despotism and economic transition, the Act might have wrought much mischief but for the wisdom of administrators.   An amendment of 1722 [1] imposed a salutary restraint upon careless methods of relief, and virtually insisted upon the " Workhouse test ".   The last years of the eighteenth century witnessed a lamentable lapse from sound principles.   The administrators of that day were not, however, without excuse.   It was a time of economic transition, of high political excitement and of terrible suffering among the poorest class.   But the remedies applied proved even worse than the disease.   They led to the wholesale pauperization of the rural labourers.   Gilbert's Act of 1782 effected the first breach in good administration.   Though permissive in terms it was widely adopted, and its principles were still further enforced and rendered compulsory by the Act of 36 George III. (1796).   The " Workhouse test " was abolished, work was found for the workless, and allowances were made in aid of wages.   Lax administration was even more responsible than panic legislation for the wholesale demoralization which ensued.   " It guaranteed to every labourer not merely his life, but a living more plentiful than he could obtain in the open labour market.   It undertook that his means should increase with the increase of his family.   It acknowledged the duty of saving him from suffering irrespective of his own merits or demerits.   It gave practically to everybody who asked.   It charged not only the weak upon the strong, but the stupid on the skilful, the lazy upon the industrious, the drunken upon the sober, the dissolute upon the

[1] 9 George I. c. 7.

chaste, the honest upon the dishonest." [1]   This terrible impeachment
can be proved to the hilt from the Report of the Commission appointed
by Lord Grey's Government in 1832.[2]   The Commissioners, including
such men as Dr. Blomfield, Bishop of London, Dr. Sumner, Bishop
of Chester, Nassau Senior, Sturges Bourne, and Edwin Chadwick,
arrived at conclusions which can only be described as appalling.
Economic dislocation and social degradation went hand in hand.
Expenditure which in 1701 amounted to about £900,000 rose in 1802
to over £4,000,000, and ultimately, in 1818, reached the gigantic
total of £7,870,000, or 13s. 4d. per head of population.   Outdoor
relief was given in a bewildering variety of forms : by providing
gratuitous house room ; by money relief " in lieu of labour " ; by
" parish employment " ; by the " roundsman system " ; by the
" labour rates system " ; and most commonly of all by " make up "
or " bread money," by an allowance, that is, in aid of wages.   In
some parishes the poor rate exceeded 20s. in the £ ; [3] farms were
thrown up ; land went out of cultivation ; landlords, farmers, and
labourers were involved in a common ruin.   The wrong inflicted upon
the labourers who remained self-supporting and independent was
incalculable ; the debasement of the rest was matched only by their
discontent.

    Legislation followed immediately upon the Report of the Com-
missioners ; and neither came a moment too soon.   The assent given
to the Bill of 1834 was almost unanimous ; only 20 votes were
recorded against the second reading in the Commons, and 13 in the
Lords.   The general principle of the Act was that " the situation of
the person receiving relief should not on the whole be made really or
apparently so eligible as the situation of the independent labourer of
the lowest class ".   The control of poor relief was vested in a Board
of three Commissioners, upon whom immense discretionary powers
were conferred : they were to have power to order the erection of
workhouses ; the formation of unions of parishes, and the drafting
of regulations for outdoor relief.   In each Union the law was to be
administered by a Board of Guardians, consisting in part of members
elected by the ratepayers and in part by the Justices of the Peace.
The law of settlement was relaxed, and the bastardy law amended.
The core of the Act was the appointment of Poor Law Commissioners.
The first Commissioners were the Right Hon. Frankland Lewis, Mr.
Nicholls, and Mr. Shaw Lefevre, and it was these men who, together
with their Secretary, Mr. Edwin Chadwick, gave the colour to the
Act of 1834.   The Act itself was hardly more than a *cadre ;* every-
thing depended on the discretion of the Board.   For the success or
failure of the Act the Commissioners and their Secretary, not the

---

[1] Montague, *The Old Poor Law and the New Socialism*, p. 11.
[2] See Report of 1834, reprinted by order of the House of Commons in 1885.
[3] At Rye they were 21s. ; at Shipley (near Horsham), 27s. : at Cholesbury
Bucks, 32s.

legislature, were responsible. They saved England from the gravest
social and economic danger to which it had ever been exposed.
Their work—in particular the abolition of outdoor relief for the
able-bodied and the re-imposition of the " Workhouse test "—was
subjected to severe criticism. They themselves were denounced as
the " bashaws of Somerset House " ; as " concentrated icicles " ;
Tory Democrats like Disraeli combined with Radicals like Cobbett
and the all-powerful *Times* to assail the " Poor Law Bastilles " and
to abuse the " Poor Man's Robbery Bill ". The remedies applied
were indubitably caustic ; but not more caustic than the gravity and
prevalence of the disease demanded. No " rose-water surgery " (to
use Carlyle's phrase) could have sufficed. Financial ruin and moral
degradation had stared us in the face. To have saved rural
England from bankruptcy was much ; it was still more to have
restored to the English poor their moral dignity and economic independence.

Fall of the Whigs　　The Poor Law Amendment Bill was proposed by Lord Grey's
Ministry. Before it became law Lord Grey had resigned, and Lord
Melbourne had become Prime Minister. But the life of the new
Ministry was from the first precarious. Such strength as it possessed
was due mainly to Lord Althorp's personal hold upon the House of
Commons. By what was virtually a party plébiscite Lord Althorp
was induced to return to the Cabinet and the lead of the House ; the
" Derby Dilly " with its " three insides " remained in opposition ;
coalition with Peel and Wellington though suggested by the King
was wisely declined on both sides ; Lord Melbourne, therefore,
retained most of the colleagues of Lord Grey. Weak in Parliament
the new Ministry was not in favour at Court. The King never gave
it his confidence, and took the first opportunity of dispensing with its
services.

The opportunity came in November, 1834, with Lord Althorp's
succession to the Peerage. A new leader had to be found for the
Commons. Lord John Russell was proposed ; but the King told
Melbourne that Russell " would make a wretched figure " and that
" Abercromby and Rice were worse than Russell ". On November
15th " the town was electrified by the news that Melbourne's Government was at an end ". The mystery which for a long time enshrouded
the circumstances attending Lord Melbourne's dismissal has not even
now been entirely dissipated. " It is long since a Government has
been so summarily dismissed, regularly kicked out in the simplest
sense of that phrase." [1] Such was Greville's first impression, and it
has been very generally accepted. But it has now become clear that
Melbourne himself felt that the main prop of the Government was
removed by Althorp's accession to the Peerage, that he intimated to
the King the probability of a break-up of the Cabinet on the Irish

[1] Greville's *Journals*, iii. 147-8.

Church question, and that he was personally glad to be out of it.[1]
Palmerston's account of the matter is entirely corroborative : " We
are all out ; turned out neck and crop. . . . Melbourne wrote to the
King to say that as when he first took his present office he had
represented the influence of Althorp in the Commons as one great
foundation of the strength of the Government ; now that Althorp
was removed to the Lords by the death of his father, he deemed it
his duty towards the King to ask whether he wished him to propose
arrangements for supplying Althorp's place or whether he preferred
asking advice from other quarters." One of Lord Melbourne's
biographers goes so far as to say that " the King did what his Minister
invited him to do ".[2] Be this as it may, two things are certain :
that the King was anxious to be rid of his Ministers, chiefly from
apprehensions as to their Church policy ; and that the Prime Minister
was not sorry to be free of the troubles which he saw immediately
ahead of him.

Lord Melbourne himself bore the King's summons to the Duke of Sir
Wellington. The Duke advised His Majesty to entrust the formation Robert
of a Ministry to Peel, but Peel was at the moment in Rome, and in Ministry,
the meantime the Duke became Secretary of State for all departments. Novem-
The Great Seal was transferred to Lyndhurst, but for some weeks the ber, 1834-
Duke was literally sole Minister. On December 9th, Peel, having 18th,
travelled post-haste from Rome, kissed hands as First Lord of the 1835
Treasury. Negotiations were opened with Stanley, Graham, and
other seceders from the late Cabinet, but by preconcerted arrangement
the latter declined them. Peel, therefore, had to rely entirely upon
Conservatives. He himself took the Chancellorship of the Exchequer
the Duke took the Foreign Office, Goulburn the Home Office, and
Lord Aberdeen War and the Colonies. Lyndhurst again became
Lord Chancellor. Peel decided not to meet Parliament, but to appeal
to the electorate, and on December 30th Parliament was dissolved.

The election that ensued is remarkable chiefly for the address The Tam-
issued by the Prime Minister to the electors of Tamworth. That worth
manifesto marked an epoch in the history of English parties ; it laid manifesto
the foundations of the new Conservatism. In it Peel definitely
accepted the Reform Bill as " a final and irrevocable settlement of a
great constitutional question ". Nor was he opposed to the spirit of
the Act if properly understood and wisely interpreted. " If by
adopting the spirit of the Reform Bill it be meant that we are to live
in a perpetual vortex of agitation ; that public men can only support
themselves in public estimation by adopting every popular impression
of the day, by promising the instant redress of anything that anybody
may call an abuse . . . I will not undertake to adopt it. But if the
spirit of the Reform Bill implies merely a careful review of institutions,

---

[1] See Melbourne, *Papers*, 219-221, 225.
[2] H. Dunckley, *Melbourne*, p. 184.

civil and ecclesiastical, undertaken in a friendly temper, combining with the firm maintenance of established rights the correction of proved abuses and the redress of real grievances—in that case I can for myself and my colleagues undertake to act in such a spirit and with such intentions."

The education of the country to the new Conservatism was, however, a work of time. The General Election of 1835 raised the strength of the Conservatives from 150 to 270,[1] but not until 1841 did they find themselves in a clear majority.

The Irish question

The new Parliament met in temporary quarters at Westminster, both Houses having been destroyed by fire during the recess. The Opposition carried an amendment to the Address, but only by a majority of seven, and Peel decided that he would carry on the Government until Easter. But whatever Government was in office, Ireland, and particularly the Tithe question, demanded immediate attention. Sir Henry Hardinge, Peel's Chief Secretary, brought forward a measure which was a simplified edition of Littleton's Bill of 1834. "The urgency and magnitude of the evil render it," said the Chief Secretary, "absolutely necessary that Parliament should attempt to rescue society in Ireland from the disorganized state into which it has been thrown by the Tithe Question. Intimidation has been carried to such an extent as to render it utterly impossible to proceed with a collection of these dues." The Whigs, however, were determined not to allow the Tories to legislate on the tithe question without concurrently affirming the principle of appropriation. The whole question was formally raised by Russell. On the clear issue thus joined the Ministry was decisively defeated, and on April 8th Peel resigned. Melbourne came back to office, but for the next five years O'Connell was in power.

Melbourne's second Ministry

Melbourne's second Ministry did not differ widely in personnel from his first. Lord Palmerston returned to the Foreign Office, Charles Grant (afterwards Lord Glenelg) became Colonial Secretary, and Lord John Russell, with the lead of the Commons, went to the Home Office. Spring Rice became Chancellor of the Exchequer and Lord Lansdowne resumed the Presidency of the Council. One significant change was made. Brougham, whose restless vanity had contributed not a little to the fall of the Government in the previous autumn, was not invited to return to the Woolsack, and until January, 1836, the great Seal was in commission. Lord Cottenham (Pepys) was then appointed.

Municipal Corporation Act

The session of 1835 witnessed the enactment of one measure of first-rate importance. For the last three centuries the government of English towns had been growing more and more oligarchical, and more and more corrupt. Vested, from early times, in the general

---

[1] The Conservatives proper numbered only 232, but about 40 "moderate" Whigs steadily supported Peel.

body of rate-paying burgesses, town government gradually passed into the hands of a " Corporation " consisting generally of a Mayor, Aldermen, and Common Councillors. These governing bodies were as a rule self-elected, and their importance was enhanced by the fact that in them was vested, in many cases, the right of returning members to Parliament. The creation of new boroughs by the Tudors and Stuarts led to a great increase in the number of these close corporations. Charles II. and James II. made a determined effort to bring all the corporations under the direct influence of the Crown.[1] The effort was attended by very partial success, and was one of the contributory causes of the Revolution of 1688. But the abuses connected with municipal government were intensified rather than diminished during the eighteenth century. The rapid increase of many towns in wealth and population, the enhanced significance of parliamentary representation, gave to the oligarchical corporations an additional importance. A place on these exclusive bodies was eagerly sought for the pecuniary advantages it conferred. The Report of a Commission appointed in 1833 revealed a scandalous condition of affairs. Local administration, as now understood, was the last thing with which the governing bodies concerned themselves. Many of the corporations possessed considerable corporate property derived from land, leases of tithes, tolls of markets and fairs, octroi duties, and fees. In many they administered specific trust, in all they exercised valuable patronage. It is hardly too much to say that it was the prevailing rule that all property and most patronage was administered with a single eye to the advantage of the administrators. " The revenues of the Corporation are variously employed ; a great part is usually absorbed in the salaries of their officers and entertainments of the Common Council and their friends. . . . It is not often that much of the Corporate property is expended on police or public improvements. . . . In some towns large sums have been spent in bribery and other illegal practices of contested elections. During the election of 1826 the Corporation of Leicester expended £10,000 to secure the success of a political partisan and mortgaged some of their property to discharge the liability incurred. . . . Few Corporations admit any positive obligation to spend the surplus of their income for objects of public advantage. . . . At Cambridge the practice of turning the Corporation property to the profit of individuals was avowed and defended." [2] It is small wonder that the commissioners found it necessary to report that the existing municipalities " neither possess nor deserve the confidence or respect " of His Majesty's subjects, and that there prevailed " a distrust of the self-elected Municipal Councils whose powers are subject to no popular control " and a " discontent under the burthens of local

---

[1] *Quo Warranto.*
[2] *First Report on Municipal Corporation*, pp. 32, 45 *et seq.*

taxation, while revenues that ought to be applied for public advantage are diverted from their legitimate use, and are sometimes wastefully bestowed for the benefit of individuals, sometimes squandered for purposes injurious to the character and morals of the people ".[1]

The provisions of the Act of 1835 were of a drastic character. The constitutions of nearly all the old corporate boroughs (178 in number), except London, were remodelled on a uniform plan. The government was vested in a Mayor, Aldermen, and Councillors, the latter to be elected by all inhabitant householders who for the past three years had been rated to the relief of the poor. To the corporation was entrusted all the ordinary duties of local administration, and in particular the raising and expenditure of borough funds. These funds were to be subject to independent audit. The corporations had already lost (by the Act of 1832) their exclusive privilege in regard to parliamentary elections, and the Act of 1835 was a natural corollary of that great measure. Inspired by a similar spirit it achieved similar results. It registered the first and therefore the most important step in the democratization of local Government in England.

An Irish Municipal Bill was introduced in 1836 and again in 1837. On both occasions it passed through the House of Commons ; but was defeated in the Lords. Not until 1840 did it become law. Under its provisions fifty-eight corporations were abolished and ten were reconstituted on the basis of a ten-pound franchise. The same franchise had been adopted in the Scotch Act of 1833.

Apart from Municipal Reform the legislative energies of the second Melbourne Ministry were almost entirely concentrated upon Ireland.

Whig policy in Ireland Early in 1835 O'Connell defined the terms on which he was prepared to keep the Whigs in office. The question of repeal would be allowed to remain in abeyance, provided that the Whigs would press to a successful issue three measures : the appropriation of the surplus revenues of the Irish Church to national purposes ; an extension of the Irish suffrage ; and a sweeping reform of the Irish corporations. These terms formed the basis of the " Lichfield House Compact ". " Compact," says Russell,[2] " there was none, but an alliance on honourable terms of mutual co-operation undoubtedly existed. The Whigs remained as before the firm defenders of the Union ; O'Connell remained as before the ardent advocate of Repeal ; but upon intermediate measures on which the two parties could agree, consistently with their principles, there was no want of cordiality. Nor did I ever see cause to complain of O'Connell's conduct." The more straightforward course would have been to give O'Connell the office he undoubtedly desired. Brougham, it is certain, urged this course upon the Ministers. Equally certain is it, that whether Melbourne himself was prepared for it or not, the King's hostility to

[1] *Report*, p. 49.   [2] *Recollections and Suggestions*, p. 134.

his admission was immovable. Under a keen sense of disappointment O'Connell behaved, as Greville put it, " admirably well ". " It is intended," he writes, " to leave O'Connell out of the arrangement, and at the same time to conciliate him and preserve his support. In this they (the Ministers) have succeeded." O'Connell had his consolations. He missed, indeed, the opportunity for which he is said to have longed—the " opportunity of proving to the Protestants of Ireland that when in power he could and would do them justice " ; but at any rate he could secure his co-religionists from injustice. If he was not himself in office, he had approved those who were. Lord Mulgrave became Lord Lieutenant ; Lord Morpeth, Chief Secretary ; the law offices were placed in " sympathetic " hands, but the man who gave the " tone " to the Melbourne-O'Connell administration was the Under-Secretary, Thomas Drummond.

Whatever the verdict on his policy may ultimately be, Drummond himself was by general admission one of the most striking figures in the history of British rule in Ireland.

The difficulties confronting Drummond in Ireland were not slight. Thomas Throughout the country and among all classes the spirit of lawlessness Drummond was dominant ; the tithe war was being waged with undiminished bitterness ; faction fights were common ; disorder was rife ; justice was contemned, and the whole administrative system was utterly demoralized. Drum1ond's first work was to establish confidence n the administration of justice and inspire respect for law. " Extraordinary " powers he disliked and disclaimed. Coercion he believed to be demoralizing alike to subject and to ruler. But implicit obedience to the ordinary law he was determined, as far as in him lay, to exact—and from all parties.

That Drummond was entirely successful in the restoration of social order in Ireland cannot be asserted. He did all perhaps that even-handed administration could effect. But he was not master of the legislative machine at Westminster ; nor could he by a stroke of the pen work a revolution in the economic conditions of the people whom he ruled. All that man could do he did. He urged upon his superiors the pressing need of agrarian legislation, and he worked with superhuman energy to develop the industrial resources of the country. In popular imagination Drummond lives as the author of the famous aphorism, now happily a commonplace : " Property has its duties as well as its rights "—a reminder originally addressed to the magistrates of Tipperary. But his rule was brief. Worn out with labours, physical and mental, Thomas Drummond died in 1840. To say that he made mistakes is merely to affirm that he was human. Overhaste is the common fault of the idealist. Idealist and overhasty Drummond was. Nevertheless, his rule is a bright chapter in the sombre volume of Irish history.

While Drummond was toiling in Dublin, the Melbourne Government was industriously occupied in " ploughing the sands " at Westminster. The situation was no doubt difficult for the Ministers and especially for Lord John Russell. They had come into power on the principle of " appropriation," [1] O'Connell who kept them in power had declared that one word was worth the whole Bill. To drop " appropriation " would have been hardly decent ; to carry it through the House of Commons was difficult ; to carry it through the House of Lords was soon found to be impossible. Bill after Bill was rejected in the latter House. Ministers might storm ; the Peers smiled. They were in an impregnable position, for behind them was the solid body of English opinion. The Whigs depended upon O'Connell ; the Conservatives relied upon England. Under these circumstances " to fill up the cup " is only to drink to political disaster. Apart from " appropriation," Morpeth might have carried a satisfactory Tithe Bill in 1835. All parties had assented to the principles. The burden was to be transferred—in appearance at any rate—from occupier to owner ; the clergy were to lose some portion of their money, but to gain in security. Not, however, until 1838 were these principles actually embodied in legislation. In that year Ministers decided on a frank abandonment of appropriation, and the House of Lords, whose victory if temporary was complete, passed the Bill. Tithes were henceforth commuted into a permanent rent charge at the rate of 75 per cent. of their nominal value, and the large advances made to the clergy in lieu of arrears—amounting in all to a million of money—were wiped out. The Act was virtually identical with Hardinge's Bill of 1835 ; and its passing constituted a humiliating defeat for its authors, and a triumph for their opponents.

Irish Poor Law   The same session witnessed the passing of an Irish Poor Law. In Ireland, as in most Roman Catholic countries, there had been hitherto no legal provision for the relief of the poor. But about 1830 the terrible distress existing among the Irish peasantry attracted the attention of the Imperial Parliament ; various schemes for the amelioration of their lot were proposed, and in 1833 a commission was appointed to inquire into the whole subject. Language is too weak to describe the appalling state of things which their report revealed. The root of the difficulty was the same as that which confronts us in India to-day. Population had multiplied with astonishing rapidity. Comparatively good government had removed the natural check, while a stimulus had been supplied by priests and landlords. In three-quarters of a century the population of Ireland had nearly trebled. For six months out of the twelve one-third of this population, or 2,385,000 people, were on the verge of starvation. Something had to be done ; but what ?

---

[1] *I.e.* the appropriation of the " surplus revenue of the Irish Established Church in Ireland " to secular purposes.

The commissioners recommended a variety of palliatives : emigration, public works, model agricultural schools, reclamation of
waste-bogs, and the like. But they shrank (and herein they were
thoroughly representative of Irish opinion) from a poor law on the
English lines. The Government regarded the report as inconclusive,
and the recommendations as inadequate. They therefore sent over
to Ireland Mr. Nicholls—an English Poor Law Commissioner—to
make further inquiries. In six weeks he had presented his report,
and on that report the Government framed their Bill. The whole
country was to be divided into unions ; each union was to be administered by a Board of Guardians, consisting in part of *ex officio*,
in part of elected members ; for these boards no minister of religion
was to be eligible ; there was to be no law of settlement ; workhouses were to be erected ; the workhouse-test was to be absolute ;
there was to be no out-door relief ; indoor relief was to be given only
to the destitute. The Irish Act was the English Act of 1834, stripped
of the settlement principle and " out-door relief ". For four years it
was administered by English officials. The Act was amended in
1843, and again in 1847, mainly in an English direction. It has
never been popular in Ireland ; but on the whole it has achieved a
fair measure of success.

The contents of this chapter afford sufficient evidence that, Death of
during the first decade of Whig rule, Ireland was seldom far from the William
surface of English politics. But before the Irish Poor Law Bill and IV.
the Tithes Commutation Bill became law, an event of first-rate
importance occurred in England. On June 20th, 1837, William IV.
died ; the Crown of Hanover devolved upon his brother, the Duke
of Cumberland, and that of Great Britain and Ireland, upon his
young niece, Princess Victoria.

CHAPTER VII

THE FIRST YEARS OF THE NEW REIGN
(1837-1841)

Queen
Victoria

THE young Princess who was now called to ascend the throne was the only child of her parents. Her father was Edward Duke of Kent (1767-1820), the fourth son of George III. ; her mother was Victoria Mary Louisa (1786-1861), daughter of Francis Duke of Saxe-Coburg-Saalfeld and widow of the Prince of Leiningen, by whom she had a son and a daughter. The Duke of Kent was a man of considerable ability and high character ; a keen soldier and, unlike his father and brothers, a robust Liberal. He was genuinely interested in the movement for the abolition of slavery, was zealous for popular education and voted for Catholic emancipation. He died at a comparatively early age, just before his father, in 1820, leaving his widow and infant child [1] in circumstances which were almost straitened. The Duchess of Kent was a woman of strong not to say stern character and brought up her daughter both strictly and well. From her earliest years the young Princess was trained in habits of order, punctuality, obedience, and self-sacrifice. Her education was undertaken largely by the Duchess herself, assisted by Miss Lehzen, the Rev. George Davys,[2] and a large staff of masters for special subjects. Her political education, up to her accession to the throne, she owed mainly to her maternal uncle, Prince Leopold of Saxe-Coburg, who, but for the untimely and lamentable death of the Princess Charlotte, would himself have been Prince Consort of England.[3] But though docile and considerate the Princess from her early years " instinctively formed an independent judgment on any question that concerned her." [4] Prince Leopold she regarded as a second father, and the long series of letters which passed between them proves how well her confidence and affection were justified.[5] In 1827 the death of the Duke of York rendered the ultimate succession of the Princess almost certain. On the accession of the Duke of Clarence (1830) she became heir-presumptive, and in recognition of this fact Parliament voted to the Duchess of Kent an extra £10,000 a year. Seven years later the death of William IV. brought the Princess Victoria to the throne.

The situa-
tion

Just eighteen at the time of her accession, Queen Victoria was confronted with a difficult not to say a perilous situation. Canada

---

[1] Born May 24th, 1819.
[2] Afterwards Dean of Chester and Bishop of Peterborough (1839-1864).
[3] King of the Belgians, 1831.
[4] A. C. Benson, *Letters of Queen Victoria*, i. ; hereafter quoted as *Q.V.L.*
[5] *Q.V.L. passim.*

was in rebellion, and the language of contemporaries proves that they regarded its separation from Great Britain as a contingency by no means remote ; Ireland was not far removed from the state of Canada ; while in England the Chartist agitation was just coming to a head. Worst of all : the position of the monarchy was far from secure. Under George III. the throne was popular but not respected ; under George IV. it was neither ; William IV. " restored its popularity but not its dignity ". It was, therefore, the first task of Queen Victoria to re-establish the monarchy in the affections and respect of her people in general, and in particular to conciliate the support of the middle classes who, since 1832, had become the dominant power in the State. Consequently it was " supremely fortunate that the Queen by a providential gift of temperament thoroughly understood the middle-class point of view " [1]—a fact demonstrated in a thousand ways during the next half-century.

The young Queen was fortunate in the personality of her first Lord Mel- Minister. Lord Melbourne cannot be counted among the greatest of bourne English statesmen, but he has one supreme title to our gratitude : he guided Queen Victoria wisely, gently, and firmly in the paths of constitutional monarchy. The Queen was an apt pupil, but from the first hour of her reign the force of her own personality was apparent in all she did. Her Journal, June 20th, 1837, reads thus : " at nine came Lord Melbourne whom I saw in my room and *of course quite alone* as I shall *always* do all my Ministers. He kissed my hand and I then acquainted him that it had long been my intention to retain him and the rest of the present Ministry at the head of affairs and that it could not be in better hands than his. . . . I like him very much and feel confidence in him. He is a very straightforward, honest, clever, and good man." " How fortunate I am," she wrote to King Leopold, " to have at the head of my Government a man like Lord Melbourne. . . . He is of the greatest use to me politically and privately." The young Queen had need of all the help and encouragement which Melbourne could give her. His own position, was far from assured. In the General Election which ensued, the Conservatives still further improved their position, numbering 312 as against 273 in the previous Parliament. England and Wales gave them a clear majority of 20 against the Ministers, but Scotland and Ireland redressed the balance. Even with Radicals and O'Connellites, however, the Ministerialists could claim only a majority of 34.

A short autumn session was devoted to the settlement of the new The new Civil List. The result is of historic significance, as marking the Civil List climax of the gradual change which had been in progress since the Revolution. Down to that time there had been no discrimination between the revenue of the Crown and that of the nation. The institution of the Civil List under William III. was the first attempt

[1] *Q.V.L.* i.

to clear up the confusion. The process then begun was carried further under his successors. The total sum voted to the Crown was gradually diminished, but with each diminution the Crown was relieved of charges which belonged more properly to Parliament. George II. received the hereditary revenues with a parliamentary guarantee that if they fell short of £800,000 a year the deficiency would be made good by Parliament. George III. placed the hereditary revenues for the first time at the disposal of Parliament, and accepted in return the minimum Civil List of his predecessor of £800,000 a year. William IV., on his accession, surrendered to Parliament not only the " hereditary revenues," but also certain miscellaneous and casual sources of revenue. In return he received a Civil List of £510,000 a year, divided into five departments, to each of which a specific annual sum was assigned. At the same time the Civil List was further relieved of various extraneous charges. The process was completed on the accession of Queen Victoria. The Civil List was then fixed at £385,000 a year, distributed as follows : (1) Privy Purse, £60,000 ; (2) Household Salaries, etc., £131,260 ; (3) Royal journeys, etc., £172,500 ; (4) Royal Bounty, £13,200 ; (5) Unappropriated, £8,040. The Crown still continued to enjoy the revenues of the Duchies of Lancaster and Cornwall, the latter being part of the appanage of the Prince of Wales.[1] All other hereditary revenues were surrendered by the Queen to the nation, and the nation made an exceedingly good bargain. In 1837 the hereditary revenues amounted to less than £250,000 a year ; in 1900 they were worth £452,000 a year—more than sufficient to pay the whole Civil List. But the arrangement was in reality no less advantageous to the Crown than to the nation. The sum voted to the Queen proved indeed, in the later years of the reign, inadequate to the maintenance of the Royal state, but the Crown had its reward. Increase in national expenditure could no longer be ascribed either to the extravagance of the Court or to its desire to exercise illicit political influence.

The Canadian Rebellion   After the settlement of the Civil List Parliament was adjourned until February, but grave news from Canada led to its reassembling on January 16th. For some time past the condition of Canada had given rise to considerable anxiety. Many causes combined to excite discontent, more particularly in Lower or French Canada, but foremost among them was the constitutional difficulty. To understand this a brief retrospect is necessary. The Canada which passed under the dominion of Great Britain in 1763 was French. Twenty years later there was superadded a British Canada, due largely to the immigration of the " United Empire loyalists," the expelled " Tories " from the Colonies which had cast off the British connection and become the United States. Between French and English,

_____

[1] The former now (1911) produces about £60,000 a year ; the latter about £80,000.

Roman Catholics and Protestants, friction, before long, arose. This Pitt attempted to assuage in his *Canada Constitutional Act* of 1791, and, for the time being, with success. Under this Act Canada was divided into two Colonies : Upper and Lower, Ottawa and Quebec. In each there was to be a Governor, assisted by an Executive Council and a bi-cameral Legislature : a Council of nominees and an elected House of Representatives. In each land was set apart for the endowment of the dominant Church. For a time things went well, and in the war of 1812 the Canadians demonstrated their loyalty to Great Britain, as they had in the War of American Independence. But the Constitution of 1791 had one crucial defect : the Executive was in no way responsible to the Legislature. This defect, combined with fiscal and ecclesiastical difficulties, ultimately led to the breakdown of the Constitution. In Lower Canada, in particular, there was a prolonged conflict between the Assembly and the Executive. " Having no influence in the choice of any public functionary, no power to procure the removal of such as were obnoxious to it on merely political grounds, and seeing almost every office in the Colony filled by persons in whom it had no confidence, ' the Assembly ' had recourse to that *ultima ratio* of representative power, to which the more prudent forbearance of the Crown has never driven the House of Commons in England, and endeavoured to disable the whole machinery of Government by a general refusal of the supplies." [1] In Upper Canada the same root difficulty existed, but, not being complicated by racial differences, it presented itself in a less accentuated form. Led by a young Frenchman, Louis J. Papineau, a vain and self-seeking rhetorician, the French party in Lower Canada raised the standard of independence (1837). A party in Upper Canada, led by William Lyon Mackenzie, followed suit. In both Colonies the rebellion was ultimately suppressed without difficulty, but not before it had compelled the attention of the Home Government to the menacing condition of affairs in British North America. Hitherto the English Ministry had been disposed to minimize its significance. Early in 1838, however, they decided to suspend the Canadian Constitution and to send out Lord Durham as High Commissioner.

From a personal point of view, Durham's mission to Canada was a fiasco ; but the *Report* in which he embodied his views of the problem, and prescribed remedies for its solution, is the most valuable State paper ever penned in reference to the evolution of Colonial self-government. Lord Durham recommended the union of the two Provinces ; an increase in the numbers of the Legislative Council ; a Civil List for the support of the officials ; a reform of municipal government, and, above all, that the Colonial Executive should be made responsible to the Colonial Legislature. " We are not now to

Lord Durham's mission and Report

[1] Lord Durham, *Report on Canada*, p. 81 (ed. Lucas) ; *cf.* also pp. 73, 75, and 77.

consider the policy of establishing representative Government in the North American Colonies. That has been irrevocably done . . . the Crown must consent to carry on the Government by means of those in whom the representative body has confidence."[1] And again : " The responsibility to the United Legislature of all officers of the Government, except the Governor and his Secretary, should be secured by every means known to the British Constitution. The Governor . . . should be instructed that he must carry on his Government by heads of departments in whom the United Legislation shall repose confidence ; and that he must look for no support from home in any contest with the Legislature, except on points involving strictly Imperial interests."[2] Durham's *Report* is rightly regarded as the Magna Carta of Colonial self-government. The Home Government accepted, frankly and unreservedly, the principles it enunciated, and made it the basis of their policy. But unfortunately for himself, Durham was less circumspect in action than sagacious on paper. He had hardly set foot in Canada (May, 1838) before he outraged local feeling by the appointment of new and untried men to his Executive Council. That there was something to be said for a fresh start, for a council " free from the influence of all local cabals," is undeniable ; and Charles Buller has said it well.[3] The proceeding was not in excess of the dictatorial powers with which Lord Durham was endowed ; but that three out of four Councillors should be his own private Secretaries was regarded as a glaring abuse, and worse was to come. On June 28th the Dictator issued an Ordinance proclaiming an amnesty for all who had taken part in the late rebellion, with twenty-three exceptions. Of these, eight, who had pleaded guilty to high treason, were exiled to Bermuda, and fifteen others, including Papineau, who had fled from Canada, were forbidden to return to it on pain of death. A loud outcry against these high-handed proceedings arose both in the Colony and at home. The deportation of criminals to Bermuda was illegal, and the Imperial Government, therefore, decided to disallow the Ordinance, though they accepted a Bill to indemnify the author of it. Lord Melbourne was aghast at Lord Durham's indiscretion. His conduct, he wrote to the Queen, " has been most unaccountable. But to censure him now would either be to cause his resignation, which would produce great embarrassment, and might produce great evil, or to weaken his authority, which is evidently most undesirable."[4] Durham was deeply hurt at the disallowance of the Ordinance, and in the Proclamation announcing its disallowance he justified his own conduct and censured that of the Ministry at home. Having thus added to his original indiscretion he determined to resign. On November 1st, 1838, he left Canada, and on landing at Plymouth he boasted that he had " effaced

[1] P. 278.
[3] See Buller's *Sketch, op. cit.*, p. 343.
[2] P. 327.
[4] *Q.V.L.* i. 163.

the remains of a disastrous rebellion ". As a matter of fact, there was some recrudescence of insurrection in both Provinces immediately after his departure, but Sir John Colborne suppressed it with the loss of forty-five British soldiers, killed and wounded.

The Durham *Report* was published in 1839, and the Government, both in administration and legislation, acted forthwith upon its recommendation. To Poulett Thomson (Lord Sydenham), who succeeded Lord Durham as Governor-General, Lord John Russell wrote thus : " Your Excellency . . . must be aware that there is no surer way of earning the approbation of the Queen than by maintaining the harmony of the Executive with the legislative authorities ". In 1840 the Union Act was passed. It provided for the union of Ontario and Quebec ; for a Parliament of two chambers : a Legislative Council of not fewer than twenty persons nominated by the Crown for life, and an elected House of Representatives ; and for a Civil List. Of the responsibility of the Executive there was, curiously enough, no mention. The English practice was implicitly presupposed, but not until the Governorship of Lord Durham's son-in-law, Lord Elgin, was the principle explicitly affirmed. In 1847 formal instructions were sent to the Governor " to act generally on the advice of the Executive Council, and to receive as members of that body those persons who might be pointed out to him as entitled to be so by their possessing the confidence of the Assembly ". Thus was the central doctrine of Lord Durham's *Report* definitely and finally accepted as the ruling principle of Canadian Government. The same principle has since been extended to all the more important Colonies in the British Empire. Lord Durham's brilliant but erratic career was closed by death in 1840. Lord Melbourne declared that he " was raised, one hardly knows how, into something of a factitious importance by his own extreme opinions, by the panegyrics of those who thought he would serve them as an instrument, and by the management of the Press ". The principal author of the Reform Bill of 1832, and of the Canadian *Report*[1] of 1839, whatever his obvious failings, can hardly be so lightly dismissed.

The Government of Canada was not the only problem which Chartism troubled the first years of the Queen's reign. On May 8th, 1838, the London Working Men's Association published a summary of their demands in a document subsequently known as *The People's Charter*. The points on which they insisted were six : annual Parliaments ; manhood suffrage ; vote by ballot ; the abolition of the property qualification for members of Parliament ; payment of members according to " the wholesome practice of ancient times " ; and equal electoral districts. This programme was an exact reproduction of

[1] This is not the place for a discussion of the difficult question of the authorship of the Durham *Report*. " Wakefield thought, Buller wrote it, Durham signed it—" represents one estimate.

that which had been adopted in 1780 by the Society for Constitutional Information—a society founded by Major Cartwright and Horne Tooke, and patronized by Charles James Fox. Chartism, though newly baptised, was clearly, therefore, no new thing. "The matter of Chartism," said Carlyle, "is weighty, deep-rooted, far-extending; did not begin yesterday; will by no means end this day or to-morrow."

What then was the genesis and meaning of the movement which reached a climax in 1838-1839 ? "Chartism," said Carlyle again, "means the bitter discontent grown fierce and mad, the wrong condition, therefore, or the wrong disposition of the working classes of England. . . . Is the condition of the English working people wrong ? . . . Or is the discontent itself mad like the shape it took ? Not the *condition* of the working people that is wrong, but their disposition. . . ." Looking more closely we can discern that the Chartist movement represented a mass of accumulated discontent evoked by three causes : social, economic, and political. The most serious feature of that day was the entire dislocation of social life, due to the rapid increase in the wealth of the middle class and the consequently widening gulf between employers and employed. Down to the great industrial revolution England had been in a very real sense a *community*. The events of the previous half-century had, unhappily, dissolved that community, and had shattered the human ties which had bound man to man and class to class. As a result, England had become a mere aggregation of atoms, disorganized, discontented, and antagonistic. Thus, in 1845, Disraeli wrote of "two nations between whom there is no intercourse and no sympathy, who are as ignorant of each other's habits, thoughts, and feelings as if they were dwellers in different zones, or inhabitants of different planets ". In the picture which he drew in *Sybil* there may have been exaggeration, but it was the exaggeration of a truth, substantiated from such different quarters as *Mary Barton*, *Yeast*, and *Alton Locke*.[1] Not less serious than the social estrangement was the economic depression of the working classes, also due to the industrial changes of the last half-century. A series of mechanical inventions had given a marvellous impetus to production ; wealth was increasing with unprecedented rapidity ; foreign trade was advancing by leaps and bounds ; but the artisans and labourers complained that for them things were not better but worse ; that trade was more shifty ; employment less constant ; that wages were stationary or falling, and that food was getting dearer day by day. There was wealth in abundance, and created, as they thought, mainly by their labour, and yet many of them were starving. The problem seemed to them inscrutable. "In the midst of plethoric plenty, the people perish."

But this was not all. Chartism had yet another side. Primarily,

---

[1] *Sybil*, published 1845 ; *Mary Barton*, 1848 ; *Yeast*, 1848 ; *Alton Locke*, 1850.

indeed, it was a political movement, due to the disappointment of the
working classes at the limited scope of the Reform Bill of 1832.   For
the " Reform " agitation Chartists had, as we have seen, supplied
the driving power.   They looked, not unnaturally, for some share of
the political spoils.   They got nothing out of Reform except a lever
for future agitation.   Hence, when the Anti-Corn Law movement
was inaugurated by Villiers and Cobden and Bright, it was denounced
by the Chartist leaders as a middle-class manœuvre.   " If you give
up your agitation for the Charter to help the Free Traders," said
Thomas Cooper, " they will not help you to get the Charter.   Don't
be deceived by the middle classes again.   You helped them to get
their votes, but where are the fine promises they made to you ?
. . . And now they want to get the Corn Laws repealed not for your
benefit, but for their own."   We need not inquire as to the justice
of the indictment ; the words sufficiently indicate the temper of the
Chartists, and explain the nature of their demands.   Those demands,
as we have seen, were exclusively political.   That they were stimulated by Lord John Russell's declaration in 1837, that the Whigs
meant the Reform Bill to be a final settlement, is certain.   It was a
challenge to which the Chartists responded from a hundred platforms.
Great meetings were held at Birmingham, Manchester, and elsewhere, with the result, almost inevitable in such movements, that
the leadership fell into the hands of the more violent party.   Early
in 1839 a national convention met in London, and then the schism
between the " moral force " and the " physical force " Chartists
reached a climax.   Some of the " moderates " withdrew, and the
lead was definitely assumed by men like Stephens and Feargus
O'Connor, who were determined to attain their objects at the cost, if
need were, of armed insurrection.   Meanwhile, a monster petition,
embodying five out of the six points, was presented to the House of
Commons (June 14th, 1839) by Mr. Thomas Attwood, one of the
members for Birmingham.   A month later (July 12th) the House
refused even to consider it.   Once more Lord John expounded the
Whig view as to the " finality " of the Reform Bill, and taunted the
Chartists, not unjustifiably, with demanding constitutional revision
as a prelude to communism.

   There had already been serious rioting in Birmingham on July
4th, and three days after the refusal of the House to consider the
petition it was resumed on a more menacing scale (July 15th).   Still
more serious was the outbreak among the Monmouthshire miners in
the autumn.   Irritated by the arrest of Henry Vincent, " the
Chartist Demosthenes," and the harsh treatment meted out to him
in Monmouth gaol, the miners determined on his forcible release.
Led by John Frost, an ex-Mayor of Newport, who had been lately
dismissed from the magisterial bench for seditious speeches, the
miners planned an attack on the town and prison.   The attack

8

miscarried, the rioters were dispersed by a few dozen soldiers and special constables. Thirty Chartists were killed, many were wounded ; and their leader, Frost, and two companions were arraigned for high treason, were convicted, and sentenced to be drawn, hanged, and quartered. The sentence was commuted to one of transportation for life, and Frost was permitted in 1856 to return from Van Diemen's Land to England. By that time even the echoes of the Chartist riots had passed away. The disastrous fiasco of the " Battle of Newport " marked the collapse of " physical-force " Chartism. The petition was presented again to the House in 1842, and for a third time presented and rejected in 1848. In the latter year the " moral-force " party were the victims of a fiasco not less signal than that which eight years before had arrested the " physical-force " movement. Chartism was literally laughed out of court. Nevertheless, Carlyle was right : " The matter of Chartism will by no means end this day or to-morrow ". Of their political programme most of the " points " have been already attained, and already political power has been employed for the adjustment of those economic and social conditions in which, from the first, Chartism found its *nidus*.

The Jamaica Bill
The Chartist agitation was only one of the many embarrassments by which the Melbourne Ministry was beset. The Anti-Corn Law League came into being under the leadership of Villiers and Cobden in 1839 ; the Radicals and Tory Socialists spared no efforts to foment the agitation against the new Poor Law " Bastilles " ; the repeal movement was definitely inaugurated in Ireland in 1840. But it was a Colonial question which actually led to their resignation. The abolition of Colonial slavery naturally created friction between the West Indian planters and the Home Government. In April, 1839, the Government introduced the Bill to suspend the Constitution of Jamaica for five years, and to vest dictatorial powers in a Governor and two or three Commissioners. The Bill was carried only by a majority of five, and the Ministry, feeling it to be impossible to force it through Committee, announced their resignation.

The Bed-chamber question
To the girl-Queen the resignation of her first Prime Minister caused acute pain,—a truth which she had no mind to conceal either from the outgoing or the incoming Ministers.[1] But she steeled herself to send for the Duke, who persuaded her to confide the formation of a Ministry to Peel. Both to Wellington and Peel the Queen ingenuously confessed her confidence in Lord Melbourne, " who had been to her quite a parent ". The Duke was sympathetic ; Peel seemed to her " such a cold, odd man, she can't make out what he means ". " The Queen " (as she wrote to Melbourne) " don't like his manner after— Oh ! how different, how dreadfully different to that frank, open, natural, most kind, warm manner of Lord Melbourne." Peel's lack of sympathy and manners was largely

[1] *Cf. Q.V.L.* i. 194 *seq.*

responsible for the difficulty which ensued. Having succeeded in securing the assistance not only of Wellington but of Sir James Graham and Lord Stanley, he laid a list of his proposed Cabinet before the Queen, and at the same time intimated that it would be necessary to change the Household officers, including some of the Ladies. The Queen took alarm and flew to Melbourne for advice, and on it she acted. Peel insisted that it was essential that " he should have that public proof of your Majesty's entire support and confidence which would be afforded by the permission to make some changes in that part of your Majesty's Household which your Majesty resolved on maintaining entirely without change ". That the Household officers in Parliament should be changed was accepted as axiomatic. The Queen understood Peel to demand in addition that all her Ladies should be changed as well. This course she conceived to be as " contrary to usage," as it was certainly " repugnant to her feelings ". As a result, the Queen declined to give way, Peel resigned his commission, and to the great and undisguised joy of the Queen the Melbourne Ministry was reinstated. Lord Ashley's testimony to the entire good feeling of Peel is conclusive : " I am sure that no parent ever felt towards his own daughter a more deep sense of duty and affection than he did towards Queen Victoria," but that the Queen should be surrounded by Whig Ladies, relations and friends of the late Ministry seemed to him both unconstitutional and unreasonable. It is now clear that Peel would have been satisfied with *some* changes ; the Queen as regards the Ladies would have none.[1] On resuming office the Whig Cabinet took the unusual step of putting on record and communicating to the Queen the following minute : " That for the purpose of giving to an Administration that character of efficiency and stability and those marks of the constitutional support of the Crown which are required to enable it to act usefully for the public service, it is reasonable that the great offices of the Court and the situations in the Household held by members of either House of Parliament should be included in the political arrangements made on a change of Administration ; but they are not of opinion that a similar principle should be applied or extended to the offices held by Ladies in her Majesty's Household ".[2] It should be added that it was not long before the Queen learned to give her entire confidence to Peel, and that sixty years later she remarked to Sir Arthur Bigge (her Private Secretary), " I was very young then, and perhaps I should act differently if it was all to be done again ".[3]

It was no lust for office which brought Lord Melbourne back but a sheer sense of chivalry—an unwillingness " to abandon his Sovereign

Melbourne Ministry reconstructed

[1] See in particular, *Q.V.L.* i. 214, and Peel, *Papers*, i. 391-398.
[2] *Q.V.L.* i. 216. This paragraph was read by Lord John Russell in the House of Commons in the course of the ministerial explanation, May 13th.
[3] *Q.V.L.* i. 211.

in a situation of difficulty and distress ". It was not, as we have seen, a bed of roses to which he returned. In the House of Commons the Ministry was palpably weakening. They carried their new Speaker, Mr. Shaw Lefevre, against the Tory nominee, Mr. Goulburn, only by a majority of eighteen, and during the recess the Cabinet was reconstructed. Mr. Charles Grant, who had become Lord Glenelg in 1835, retired from the Colonial Office, Lord John Russell took his place, and was succeeded at the Home Office by Lord Normanby ; Lord Clarendon joined the Cabinet as Privy Seal, and Lord Morpeth as Chief Secretary for Ireland. Baring succeeded Spring Rice as Chancellor of Exchequer ; Macaulay, Lord Howick as Secretary-at-War, and Henry Labouchere, Poulett Thomson at the Board of Trade. But no reconstruction could permanently restore the waning popularity of the Ministry.

Penny Postage and other social reforms
The adoption of Penny Postage though provided for in the Budget of 1839 redounded not to the credit of Ministers but of Rowland Hill. The reduction of the stamp duty on newspapers to one penny (1836) ; the permission given to Dissenters to celebrate their marriages in their own Chapels (1836) ; the abolition of the use of the pillory, and the removal of a number of crimes from the category of capital offences—all these contributed sensibly to social well-being. Even more important was the creation (1839) of a new Committee of the Privy Council to supervise elementary education—a measure accompanied by an increase of the grant from £20,000 to £30,000 and by the appointment of inspectors. But the most pressing need, a supply of trained teachers, was not met. Russell did indeed propose the establishment of a Government normal school, but the opposition of the Church party was so fierce that the proposal was dropped. Even stripped of this clause the Bill was carried only by a majority of two.

Publicity of parliamentary proceedings
Less contentious, but not less significant were two changes calculated, if not designed, to bring members of Parliament more directly under the control of their constituents. In the old Houses of Parliament, destroyed by fire in 1834, there were no facilities for parliamentary reporters. To report speeches made in Parliament was then, as it always had been and still is, a breach of privilege ; but the practice had long been tacitly permitted. In the new parliamentary buildings special provision was made for reporters, and in 1840 legislative protection was accorded to their reports. In 1837 Messrs. Hansard, the printers to the House of Commons, were sued by J. J. Stockdale for a libel contained in a Parliamentary Paper.[1] The Courts decided in favour of Mr. Stockdale, and consequently in 1840 an Act was passed providing that on the production of a certificate from the Lord Chancellor or the Speaker certifying that the

---

[1] For details, which are of great importance, cf. Robertson, *Cases and Documents*, pp. 380 seq. ; Anson, *Law of Constitution*, i. 169-177.

publication **was** under the authority of either House, the Courts should stay proceedings. Thus the last barrier to the publication of debates was removed. One other step in the same direction was taken in 1836 when the House of Commons for the first time authorized the publication of Division Lists, an example followed by the Lords in 1857.

Not by such achievements, unobtrusive though solid, is the life The of a Ministry prolonged. In 1840 public interest was largely con- Queen's centrated on the marriage of the young Queen, and in connection marriage with this matter her Whig friends made more than one blunder. The Queen's choice of her cousin Prince Albert of Saxe-Coburg Gotha to be her Consort was largely due to the good offices of King Leopold, the uncle of both parties. Prince Albert and his elder brother were invited to visit England in 1836, and the Princess wrote ecstatically to King Leopold about the charms of the young Prince. On November 23rd, 1839, the Queen formally announced her engagement to the Privy Council, and on the opening of Parliament (Jan. 16th, 1840) repeated the announcement. It was received with mingled feelings by the nation. Every one sympathized with the Queen in the prospect of a marriage of affection, but there were in some quarters strange misgivings. " The ultra-Tories," wrote Stockmar, " are filled with prejudice against the Prince. . . . . They give out that he is a Radical and an Infidel." [1] The Whigs committed various inexcusable blunders. In announcing the marriage they omitted to state the fact that Prince Albert was a Protestant. A foolish turmoil arose in Parliament. Was the Prince a Roman Catholic or an Infidel ? It is difficult to understand Wellington's conduct in this matter, and still more difficult to defend it. But not less indefensible was the blundering of the Ministers. Stockmar had satisfied them as to the facts, and they had simply neglected to pass on the assurance to Parliament. With equal folly and carelessness, and in defiance of the express advice of Stockmar, they avoided an understanding with the Opposition leaders as to the amount of the Prince's annuity. The Ministers proposed £50,000, the sum enjoyed by the Queens Consort of George II., George III., and William IV. Colonel Sibthorp, an Ultra-Tory, moved to reduce it to £30,000 ; he was supported by the Radicals and by Peel, and carried his motion by a majority of 104. This was a serious rebuff to the Ministry and a source of profound and natural annoyance to the Queen. A third difficulty remained. The Queen wished her husband to have the style and precedence of King-Consort. The Ministers insisted, perhaps rightly, on following the precedent of Queen Anne's reign : but in the Bill for the naturalization of the Prince a clause was inserted giving him precedence on all occasions next after the Queen. Again the Whigs were likely to suffer defeat, and again for lack of

[1] *Memoirs*, ii. 22.

preliminary negotiations with their powerful opponents. Stockmar, acting as the Prince's representative, insisted that further rebuff must be avoided; the clause was withdrawn, and the Queen subsequently bestowed precedence on the Prince by an Order in Council. On February 10th, 1840, the marriage took place in St. James's Palace with great splendour and amid every sign of popular approbation. Later in the year an Act was passed, unopposed save by the Duke of Sussex, naming the Prince Regent, should the Queen die leaving issue.

Fall of the Melbourne Ministry, Sept. 1841   The life of the Whig Ministry was ebbing fast. But they suffered as much for their virtues as their sins. Nothing in their career did them more honour than the Poor Law and the Factory Act; but the former was denounced as inhuman alike by Radicals and Tories, while the latter alienated the Liberal manufacturers. Nor did they derive much credit from their Irish policy. From the Irish peasant it evoked little gratitude, and among the English middle classes it created mistrust. Moreover, the country now enjoyed the luxury of an alternative. The old Tory party had reeled for a time under the shock of 1832. Thanks, however, to the unfailing sagacity and patient skill of Peel, the phœnix of Conservatism arose before long from the ashes of Toryism. The " Tamworth Manifesto," conceived with admirable judgement, had reassured the country and reconstructed the party. Not since 1835 had the Whigs been really masters in their own house. Six weary and humiliating years of office they had endured, but without tasting the sweets of power. To what a position had they now come ? " The Right Honourable member for Tamworth," said Mr. Leader, the Liberal member for Westminster, " governs England ; the honourable and learned member for Dublin governs Ireland ; the Whigs govern nothing but Downing Street." Their Irish taskmaster had extorted a modicum of legislative work, and in return had been loyal to the " compact ". But his patience was exhausted and his own foothold insecure.

It was otherwise with Peel. His position was improving every day. For years past he had held the Whigs in the hollow of his hand. Except for the Queen's natural reluctance to part with her Ladies, the Whigs would have been ousted in 1839. Lord Melbourne's chivalry induced him to resume the irksome task. But the final release was now at hand. The Bill for the removal of the Jews' Civil Disabilities, though it passed the Commons, was rejected in the Lords ; the Government was defeated on the Budget in May, and, at the beginning of June, Peel carried by a majority of one a vote of no-confidence. The Government appealed to the country ; the elections went heavily against them, and on the assembling of the new Parliament amendments to the Address were carried against the Ministry in both Houses : in the Lords by seventy-two, in the Commons by ninety-one. In Ireland O'Connell's party was shattered.

Barely a dozen Repealers regained their seats, and not a single recruit was found. O'Connell himself lost his seat in Dublin ; his son was defeated in County Carlow.

On August 30th the Whig Ministers announced their resignation, and the Queen entrusted the formation of a new Government to Sir Robert Peel.

With characteristic chivalry and good sense Lord Melbourne strove to reconcile the Sovereign to her new Ministers. His success may be counted as his final act of service to his Queen and country, *Close of Melbourne's career*

He led the Opposition in the House of Lords until in October 1842, he was prostrated by a stroke of paralysis. By 1846 he was sufficiently recovered to attend a meeting of Peers at Lansdowne House, and, though personally opposed to the repeal of the Corn Laws, and moved to profound indignation by Peel's conversion,[1] he advised the Peers not to oppose repeal. He suffered a transient pang of disappointment at being left out of the Russell Ministry in 1846 ; but his health, as he himself acknowledged, was unequal to office, and in 1848 the end came.

His work was done. To him the Queen had served her political apprenticeship. Never forgetful of the lessons he taught, she had now found advisers who were worthy of the confidence she reposed in them. Among these the most constant was naturally Prince Albert. Of his " judgment, temper, and discretion " Melbourne formed " the highest opinion," and on relinquishing office he felt " a great consolation and security in the reflection that he left the Queen in a situation in which she had the inestimable advantage of such advice and assistance ".[2] He had the further satisfaction before his death of seeing the new reign fairly launched upon a voyage, if not of unruffled calm, at least of unprecedented prosperity.

---

[1] " Ma'am, it's a damned dishonest thing," was his comment to the Queen.— Greville.

[2] *Q.V.L.* i. 385.

CHAPTER VIII

THE FOREIGN POLICY OF LORD PALMERSTON
(1830-1841)

NO reference has been made in the last two chapters to the relations of Great Britain and her neighbours. For two reasons : on the one hand, because domestic politics during the period under review were sufficiently absorbing to entitle them to exclusive consideration ; on the other, because the foreign policy of the Whig Government can be rendered more intelligible by separate and continuous treatment.

Lord Palmerston

The responsibility for that policy attaches primarily to one of the most remarkable political personalities of the nineteenth century —Henry John Temple, third Viscount Palmerston in the peerage of Ireland. Born in 1784, Palmerston's life covers nearly two-thirds of the long reign of George III. ; the whole of that of George IV. ; the whole of that of William IV., and nearly half that of Queen Victoria. He sat in sixteen different Parliaments, under four different monarchs ; he was in the House of Commons for nearly sixty years ; in office for nearly fifty ; he was a member of every Ministry, except those of Peel and Lord Derby, between 1807 and 1865 ; he touches Pitt and Fox at one end of his life ; at the other he was the rival of Disraeli and the colleague of Gladstone. He started his political life as a Tory, and at the age of twenty-five was offered by Spencer Perceval his choice of the Exchequer or the Secretaryship at War.[1] He chose the War Office, and there he remained for nearly twenty years (1809-1828), serving under five Tory Prime Ministers. Of his successive Chiefs the one with whom he was in closest sympathy was Canning, and much of his own work at the Foreign Office represents an attempt to put into practice the principles he had imbibed from that statesman. In 1828 he seceded with other Canningites from Wellington's Administration, and in 1830 he joined that of Lord Grey as Foreign Secretary. Except for a few months (Dec. 1834 to April 1835) he remained at the Foreign Office without break for eleven years.

Palmerston's Foreign Policy

From Canning Palmerston inherited two problems of great intricacy : the one concerned Greece and the Balkan Peninsula, the other the Iberian. To the near Eastern question there was added during his own régime that of the Far East ; while much nearer home a delicate and difficult situation was created by the refusal of the Belgian Provinces to accept as permanent the settlement of 1814.

Of all the items in that Settlement there was none which gave

Autobiography ap. Lytton Bulwer, Appendix, p. 371.

greater satisfaction to its authors than the union of the whole of the Low Countries—the Austrian or Spanish Netherlands and the United Provinces—under the Sovereignty of the House of Orange. It had long been the dream of European diplomacy to erect a stout barrier between France and Germany. The project was particularly near the heart of Pitt, and it was actually accomplished by his disciple, Lord Castlereagh. The latter had intended, as a further guarantee for the security of British interests in the narrow seas, that the King of the Netherlands should marry the Princess Charlotte, the heiress to the British throne. That project was defeated by the firmness of the Princess, who preferred to wed the Coburg Prince who—by a curious turn in the wheel of fortune—subsequently became the first King of the Belgians. None the less, Castlereagh shared the satisfaction of the other Chancelleries at the consummation of their diplomatic handiwork in the new kingdom of the Netherlands.

One factor, unfortunately, was studiously ignored by the diplomatists of Vienna—the wishes of the peoples immediately concerned. The neglect of this elementary consideration proved fatal to the prolonged existence of the new barrier kingdom. Between the Dutch of the Northern Provinces and the Walloons and Flemings of the South there was little in common. Racially they were of course akin, but despite the large admixture of Flemish blood, the peoples of the Belgian Provinces were wholly French in sympathy, and for more than twenty years they had actually formed part of France. In creed and in historical tradition North and South were sharply divided, and this division was accentuated by commercial rivalry. Nevertheless, a wise and conciliatory policy on the part of the House of Orange, adopted in 1814 and steadily pursued, might have done much to obliterate differences, and to weld North and South into a united Power if not into a united People. Such policy was conspicuously lacking. King William was " one of those clever men who constantly do foolish things, and one of those obstinate men who support one bad measure by another worse ".[1] The Dutch, though numerically inferior,[2] treated Belgium almost as a conquered province. This absorption was strongly resisted by the Belgian patriots, and they found sturdy allies in the Clericals, who were specially incensed against the Calvinist authorities of Holland. Now, as in 1790, Clericals and Democrats combined against an alien ruler, and both found encouragement and opportunity in the general upheaval of 1830.

The French Revolution of July, though not intrinsically of first-rate importance, exercised a considerable influence on the neighbours of France, and particularly, as was natural, upon the Belgian Provinces. An insurrection broke out in Brussels on August 25th, and

[1] Dalling, *Palmerston*, ii. 2.   [2] Dutch, 2,281,789 ; Belgians, 3,777,735.

quickly spread to Liège, Louvain, Ghent, and other towns. The King offered a considerable measure of devolution, the Belgians demanded independence. The Holy Allies were strongly opposed to the destruction of a corner-stone of the edifice of 1814, but the Belgians found a warm friend in Palmerston who in November, 1830, succeeded to the English Foreign Office. Palmerston was convinced that a recognition of Belgian independence was the only alternative to its absorption by France. Of the two alternatives the latter appeared the more imminent. In 1829 Prince Polignac had, with the sanction of his master Charles X., drafted a plan for the reconstruction of the map of Europe as drawn in 1815. This included the acquisition by France of Belgium " as far as the Meuse, the mouth of the Scheldt, and the Sea," in particular the annexation of Antwerp.[1]

The change of Government in 1830 effected little modification in the essential ambitions of France, and they were thwarted only by the firmness and skill of Palmerston. On November 4th the Powers agreed, in conference in London, to impose upon Holland and Belgium an armistice. This was accepted, but the Belgian National Congress which met in the following week demanded Belgian independence, a monarchical form of Government, and the exclusion of the House of Orange-Nassau. Thereupon, Lord Palmerston induced the London Conference to accept in principle the independence of Belgium (Dec. 20th), and to lay down certain *bases de séparation*. Holland accepted the draft convention ; Belgium, on the contrary, incensed by the assignment of the whole of Luxemburg to Holland and also by the financial stipulations,[2] rejected it. In thus throwing down the glove to Europe the Belgians relied on the support of France, whose diplomacy at this juncture was far from straightforward.[3] On February 3rd, 1831, the Belgians took the bold step of electing as their King the Duc de Nemours, the second son of King Louis Philippe. Palmerston firmly refused to allow Belgium to become, with or without Luxemburg, a French province, and on February 17th Louis Philippe was induced to decline the Crown on his son's behalf. But it was not easy to find a suitable alternative. Prince Leopold of Saxe-Coburg, who had already refused the Crown of Greece, was suggested. The French Ministry was aghast. " Si Saxe-Coburg met un pied en Belgique, nous lui tirerons des coups de canon," was Marshal Sebastiani's first comment. But wiser counsels and the firmness of Palmerston prevailed. It was understood that Leopold would marry an Orleanist Princess, and on June 4th the Crown was offered to him. The London Conference agreed on certain modifications of the *bases de séparation*, and on June 26th Leopold accepted the Crown.

---

[1] Stockmar, *Memoirs*, i. 139.
[2] Belgium was to be responsible for $\frac{16}{31}$ of the public debt.
[3] See Dalling, *Palmerston*, ii. 22-139.

A wiser choice could not have been made ; but the difficulties which confronted the new monarch were appalling. Holland, hitherto acquiescent, refused the modifications in the *bases de séparations* upon which Leopold's acceptance of the Crown was conditional, and promptly declaring war marched 50,000 men into Belgium. Belgium, defenceless, appealed for succour to England and France. Louis Philippe immediately complied, and war between France and Holland—perhaps a European conflagration—was averted only by the good offices of Great Britain. Once more (Aug. 23rd) an armistice was accepted by the combatants, and once more diplomacy—particularly that of Palmerston—got its chance. But the situation was still full of peril for Belgium, for Europe, and for Great Britain. France was now in military occupation of Belgium, though Palmerston bluntly told her that she could remain there only on pain of war with England. Clearly, however, the French troops could not be withdrawn until the safety of Belgium, on the side of Holland, was secured. This was the crux of the situation. Only from France could Belgium obtain effective assistance ; yet France was only half-trusted by Belgium, while by England and the rest of Europe she was wholly mistrusted. How was France to be got out of Belgium without endangering the latter's new-won independence ? From this dilemma Palmerston extricated himself and Belgium with consummate adroitness. King Leopold undertook to raze the fortifications of Menin, Ath, Mons, Phillippeville and Marionburg ; the French thereupon withdrew, and the London Conference proposed a third scheme for the settlement of the outstanding difficulties between Holland and Belgium. The first (Jan. 1831) Holland had accepted and Belgium had refused ; the second (June 26th) Belgium accepted but Holland refused. The third (Nov. 15th) proposed that Luxemburg—the vital point in dispute—should be divided. To this Holland objected, and being still in possession of the cidadel of Antwerp refused to give way. France sent a force to besiege the citadel ; an English fleet blockaded the Scheldt. The citadel was heroically defended by General Chassé, and not until December 23rd, 1832, was he compelled to surrender. The Powers were now unanimous in their recognition of Belgian independence, and in May, 1833, Holland acquiesced. Not, however, until 1839 were the articles of November 15th embodied in a definite treaty between the two countries immediately concerned. Thus, thanks to the firmness of Palmeston, three definite results had been achieved : an essential part of the settlement of 1814 had been destroyed without a European war ; an independent Belgian Kingdom under a constitutional monarchy and a European guarantee, had been brought into being ; and France, though the most effusive and most effective friend of Belgium, had been compelled to forego any hope of territorial acquisition for herself.[1]

---

[1] The diplomatic correspondence will be found in Dalling's *Palmerston,* and much valuable comment in Stockmar's *Memoirs,* i. 8-11.

Affairs in Portugal and Spain From Belgium Palmerston's attention was next turned to the Iberian Peninsula. Nowhere did he show himself more indisputably the disciple of Canning than in regard to Portugal and Spain. It is difficult for us to appreciate, still less to share, the interest which the internal affairs of the Iberian Peninsula excited in the statesmen of that generation. Palmerston, like Canning, regarded it as the one available arena in which to countermine the absolutist tendencies of the Holy Alliance. It is true that, like his master, Palmerston paid lip-homage to the principle of non-intervention ; but in practice that principle wore very thin. It would indeed be difficult to prove that Palmerston was less zealous to intervene on behalf of Liberalism than were the Holy Allies on behalf of absolutism.

Between the situations then existing in the two countries of the Iberian Peninsula there was a curious parallel. In both, politics were in a very disturbed condition ; in both, the Liberals and Absolutists alike found champions in the Royal House ; in both, there was a young Queen under tutelage representing the cause of " constitutionalism " ; in both, there was an uncle claiming a throne in alliance with the forces of absolutism. In July, 1831, Dom Pedro, having abdicated the throne of Brazil in favour of his son, arrived in England, the real head-quarters of the Portuguese Constitutionalists. A year later he landed in Oporto to support his daughter Maria against the claims of his brother Dom Miguel. France and England had already been compelled to send fleets to the Tagus to afford protection to their respective subjects, and obtain satisfaction for outrages committed upon them. Under a thin veil of diplomatic decorum France and England were now united in an active alliance with the Constitutionalists against the Miguelists. Pedro's fleet was commanded by an Englishman, his army by a Frenchman ; and both in navy and army many Englishmen and Frenchmen served as " volunteers ". In the summer of 1833 Miguel's fleet was annihilated by Napier off Cape St. Vincent ; Petro entered Lisbon in July, and Donna Maria was crowned Queen.

Christinos and Carlists in Spain Events had been moving in a similar direction in Spain. On September 29th, 1833, Ferdinand VII. died, leaving a young widow and two young daughters. Until his marriage (*en quatrièmes noces*) with Maria Christina of Naples Ferdinand had been childless, and his brother Don Carlos had every prospect of succession to the throne. The latter's prospects were still further improved by the fact that since 1713 the Salic law had prevailed in Spain. But on Ferdinand's marriage with Christina he revoked this law by Pragmatic Sanction. Shortly afterwards a daughter, Isabella, was born, and on his death was declared Queen, with her mother Christina as Regent. Don Carlos—backed by all the forces of absolutism—protested against this feminine usurpation, and on October 4th, 1833, was proclaimed King. Christina was consequently compelled to fling herself into the arms of the Liberals, and granted a constitution known as the *Estatuto Real*. Palmerston's comment on these events is highly significant of the point of view from which he regarded all continental politics. " The triumph of Maria and the accession of Isabella will be important events in Europe, and will give great strength to the Liberal party." [1]

That party was still further strengthened by the conclusion (April 22nd, 1834) of a formal alliance between Great Britain, France, Spain, and Portugal. This treaty provided for joint action between the contracting parties for the expulsion of the Infants, Carlos and Miguel, from Spain and Portugal respectively. Palmerston was highly elated at the results of his diplomacy : " a capital hit and all my own doing ". His motives are clearly revealed in the following letter to his brother, William Temple : " I reckon this to be a great stroke. In the first place it will settle Portugal, and go some way to settle Spain also. . . . But, what is of more permanent and extensive importance, it establishes a Quadruple Alliance among the constitutional States of the West, which will serve as a powerful counterpoise to the Holy Alliance of the East. . . . I should like to see Metternich's face when he reads our treaty." The sting was in the tail. The Infants were to be expelled from Spain, less for the advantage of the Spaniards and the Portuguese than as a counterstroke to the Eastern Courts. In its immediate aim the alliance was undeniably effective. In May, 1834, Dom Miguel agreed, by the Treaty of Evora, to leave Portugal and renounce his claim to the throne, and in June Don Carlos retired to England. All this was the effect, in Palmerston's view, of his diplomacy. " Nothing ever did so well as the Quadruple Treaty ; it has ended a war which might otherwise have lasted months." The military situation was all in favour of the Infants. " but the moral effect of the treaty cowed them all ".[2]

It did not cow them for long. On the dismissal of the Melbourne Government in November, 1834, Palmerston congratulated himself on the results of his four years' work. " Portugal is settled ; Spain is safe ; Belgium cannot be ruined, though they may cripple it by putting high duties on the Scheldt." As regards Belgium and Portugal he had warrant for his satisfaction ; as regards Spain it was premature. With the details of the civil war in Spain, with the alternating successes of Carlists and Christinos, this work cannot concern itself. One point, however, demands notice. Between Palmerston and the Orleanist régime in France there had never been complete accord. As compared with the Courts of Berlin, Vienna, and St. Petersburg that of Louis Philippe was " Liberal," and, there- fore, worthy of encouragement from the Whig rulers of England.

---

[1] To W. Temple, October 8th, 1833. William Temple was British Envoy at Naples, 1832-1856.
[2] *Palmerston*, ii. 197.

But Palmerston was always suspicious of France in regard to Belgium, and the mistrust engendered there was intensified by French policy in the Peninsula. In Western Europe differences did not reach an acute stage until the Spanish marriage question emerged in 1846. But, long before that, the Anglo-French *entente* had been broken by the development of events in the East.

The Eastern question
When Canning died Great Britain held a commanding position in the affairs of Eastern Europe, but the fruits of his bold and sagacious diplomacy were to a large extent dissipated by the timorous policy of his successor. If, indeed, the Peace of Adrianople was, as Wellington averred, the death-blow to the independence of the Ottoman Empire in Europe, the blow was partly inflicted by the Duke himself. The abrupt reversal of the policy of Canning; the apology for Navarino and the withdrawal of England from joint action with Russia, gave to the latter a free hand to deal with the Ottoman Empire as she would. The natural result was seen in the Treaty of Adrianople.[1]

Mehemet Ali
During the next decade the danger to the integrity of the Ottoman Empire proceeded from another quarter. In order to suppress the Greek insurrection, the Sultan, as we have seen, had recourse to the dangerous expedient of calling to his aid a powerful and ambitious vassal. But for the intervention of the Powers, Mehemet Ali, the Albanian adventurer who ruled Egypt avowedly in the name of the Sultan, would have made short work of the Greeks. As it was he got his reward, ostensibly in the cession of Crete, much more in the improvement of his general position in the Ottoman Empire. Not content with this, Mehemet Ali in 1831 demanded for his son Ibrahim the Pashalik of Damascus. The Porte refused, and in 1832 Ibrahim attacked and conquered Syria, which, like Egypt itself, was under vassaldom to Turkey. The Sultan, in alarm, appealed to the Powers. England was pre-occupied. France adhered to the Napoleonic view in regard to Egypt. Russia alone was ready to go to the assistance of the Porte. But Russia's friendship was, not unnaturally, suspect at Constantinople. In December, 1832, Ibrahim inflicted a crushing defeat on the Turks at Konieh, and advancing through Asia Minor threatened Constantinople itself. The Sultan turned in terror to his only "friend," and Russian troops were landed on the Northern shore of the Bosphorus. Thereupon the Western Powers intervened, and compelled the Porte, in the Convention of Kiutayeh (May 5th, 1833) to buy off the hostility of Mehemet Ali by the cession of Syria and Adana.

Treaty of Unkiar Skelessi 1833
It was, however, the sequel which revealed the significance of the situation. On July 8th, 1833, Turkey concluded with Russia the Treaty of Unkiar Skelessi. This famous treaty virtually placed the Porte under the military protectorship of Russia, and converted the

[1] See c. iii. pp. 64 *seq.*

Black Sea into a Russian lake. Henceforward the Dardanelles were to be closed to all war vessels except those of Russia and Turkey. Palmerston was bitterly chagrined by the success of Russia, and firmly determined that it should not be repeated. Both at St. Petersburg and Constantinople he protested, though in vain, against the terms of the treaty. But the lesson was deeply impressed upon his mind, and the seeds of mistrust then sown were destined to yield a fateful harvest in Persia, Afghanistan, and the Crimea.

It was not long before the Eastern question was reopened. On the one hand, the restless ambition of Mehemet Ali had been scotched, not killed. On the other, the Sultan Mahmoud was bent upon recovering what he had lost both in prestige and territory. His army was reorganized under Moltke ; commercial treaties were concluded with Great Britain and other Powers, and an effort, apparently serious, was made to introduce Western civilization into the Turkish Empire. In 1838 Mehemet Ali refused the payment of tribute to the Porte, and proposed to make himself completely independent. The Sultan massed troops on the Euphrates : Ibrahim confronted him at Aleppo. On June 24th, 1839, the Turks were routed at Nissib, and shortly afterwards the Turkish fleet went over to the Egyptian Viceroy. At this supreme crisis in the fate of his Empire the old Sultan Mahmoud died and was succeeded by his son, Abdul Mejdid, a youth of sixteen. The whole Turkish Empire seemed to lie at the mercy of Mehemet. Not for the first time, however, the weakness of Turkey proved to be its strength. The Government of Louis Philippe was putting its money on Mehemet, and encouraging him in his most ambitious designs. But the rest of the Powers had no mind to permit the break-up of the Ottoman Empire, and the substitution of the powerful Mehemet for a feeble youth at Constantinople.

Palmerston, at once mistrustful and contemptuous of Louis Philippe, determined to take a strong line. He was not at all disposed to see Egypt under the protection of France, and Turkey under that of Russia. His colleagues in the Cabinet were strongly averse to a rupture with France. Palmerston did not desire it, but neither did he fear it. " It is evident," he writes to Bulwer,[1] " the French Government will not willingly take the slightest step of coercion against Mehemet Ali . . . anxious as we are to continue to go on with them, we are not at all prepared to stand still with them. They must therefore take their choice between three courses—either to go forward with us and honestly redeem the pledges they have given to us and to Europe ; or to stand aloof and shrink from a fulfilment of their own spontaneous declaration ; or lastly, to go right about and league themselves with Mehemet Ali, and employ force to prevent us and those other Powers who may join us from doing that which

[1] September 1st, 1839.

France herself is bound by every principle of honour and every enlightened consideration of her real interests to assist us in doing, instead of preventing from being done."

As to the future of Turkey, Palmerston was far from pessimistic. "All that we hear about the decay of the Turkish Empire and its being a dead body or a sapless trunk and so forth is pure and unadulterated nonsense." Given ten years of peace under European protection, coupled with internal reform, there seemed to him no reason why "it should not become again a respectable Power". For the moment two things were essential : Mehemet must be compelled "to withdraw into his original shell of Egypt," and the protection afforded to Turkey must be European, not exclusively Russian. These were the keynotes of Palmerston's policy in the near East. Several of his important colleagues, including Lord Melbourne and Lord John Russell, were against him ; they had more mistrust of Turkey and less of Mehemet ; but a threat of resignation from the Foreign Minister brought them into line with him, and on July 15th, 1840, he had the satisfaction of concluding the Treaty of London.

Treaty of London, July 15th 1840 Under this treaty the Sultan agreed to confer upon Mehemet the hereditary Pashalik of Egypt, and, for his life, the administration of Southern Syria, including the fortress of St. John of Acre, with the title of Pasha of Acre. Failing Mehemet's acceptance within ten days, the latter part of the offer was withdrawn ; failing acceptance within twenty days, the whole offer. The rest of the contracting Powers, Great Britain, Russia, Austria, and Prussia, agreed to force their terms upon Mehemet ; to prevent sea-communication between Egypt and Syria ; to defend Constantinople, and to guarantee the integrity of the Ottoman Empire.[1] Two questions remained : would Mehemet accept the terms ; if not, could he count upon the active assistance of France ?

England and France The Quadruple Treaty aroused the liveliest indignation in France. The Citizen King and his people had been bowed out of the European concert by Lord Palmerston. The will of Europe was to be imposed explicitly upon Mehemet ; implicitly upon Louis Philippe. Thiers, now at the head of the French Government, was all for defying the will of Europe. Warlike preparations were pushed on apace ; the army and fleet were strengthened, the fortification of Paris was begun, and for a moment it seemed probable that a great European conflagration would ensue. Palmerston was quite unmoved. He knew his man. He did not believe that Louis Philippe was "the man to run amuck, especially without any adequate motive ".[2] Bulwer, therefore, was instructed to tell Thiers, " in the most friendly

[1] For the important influence exercised upon Anglo-French relations by the mission of Baron Brunnow, cf. C.M.H. x. 564.
[2] To Bulwer, July 21st, 1840.

and inoffensive manner, that if France throws down the gauntlet we shall not refuse to pick it up ".[1] His confidence in his own judgment was not misplaced. His diagnosis of the situation was entirely accurate. Louis Philippe knew well enough that a European war would complicate the domestic situation in France, and might imperil his dynasty. The fiery Thiers was permitted to resign and was replaced by Guizot, the pacific Anglophil. Meanwhile, in Eastern Europe things were moving fast. Mehemet refused the terms embodied in the Quadruple Treaty, and the Powers, therefore, proceeded to impose their will upon him. An English fleet, supported by some Austrian frigates, bombarded Beyrout and Sidon, and compelled Ibrahim to retire from Syria. The capture by Sir Charles Napier of the great fortress of St. John of Acre, hitherto deemed impregnable, completed his discomfiture. Napier sailed on to Alexandria, and compelled Mehemet to restore the Turkish fleet, and to accept the terms of the Quadruple Treaty. France was invited to come into the general settlement, and on July 13th, 1841, a Second Treaty of London was concluded between England, Russia, Austria, Prussia, and France. Syria and Arabia were restored to the Porte ; Mehemet was confirmed in the hereditary Pashalik of Egypt under the suzerainty of the Sultan, and the Powers agreed that the Dardanelles and the Bosphorus should be closed to all foreign ships of war so long as the Turkish Empire was at peace. The Treaties of London must be regarded as a conspicuous triumph for Palmerston. The Treaty of Unkiar Skelessi was torn up ; Turkey was rescued from the hostility of Mehemet Ali and from the friendship of Russia ; France was compelled to acquiescence, and the will of Great Britain was imposed upon Europe.

It was not only in the near East that Palmerston was suspicious The far-of Russian ambition and alert in the protection of British interests. ther East The sequence of events which led up to the first of several tragedies in Afghanistan may be more appropriately described elsewhere.[2] It is well, however, to recall the fact that at the moment when Palmerston, in suspicion of Russian designs, was tearing up the Treaty of Unkiar Skelessi, Lord Auckland and the Indian Government were, in deference to the same sentiment, deposing Dost Muhammad in Afghanistan, and embarking upon the disastrous policy which, after the murder of Burnes and Macnaghten, culminated in the humiliating retreat from Kábul (1838-1843). The year which witnessed the tragedy of Kábul witnessed also the cession of Hong Kong to England (1841).

The Chinese War raises a very difficult and still unsolved problem The in political ethics. " A war more unjust in its origin, a war more China calculated in its progress to cover this country with disgrace, I do War, not know and I have not read of "—such was the uncompromising 1839-1842 opinion of Mr. Gladstone.[1] If we find its origin in an attempt on the part of greedy traders to force a noxious drug upon reluctant customers, few will disagree with Mr. Gladstone. There is, however, reason to believe that the opium traffic was an incident in, rather than the essential cause of, the quarrel. The Chinese were implacably hostile not merely to the importation of opium but to all foreign trade, and indeed to intercourse of any kind with foreigners. How far foreigners were bound to acquiesce in exclusion raised a nice question, and it was rendered nicer by the fact that the most valuable portion of the traffic which they desired to force upon the Chinese consisted of opium.

Be this as it may, the Chinese determined in 1837 to put a stop to the importation of opium, and despatched to Canton a special Commissioner—Lin—armed with plenary authority to use all necessary means to effect this purpose. Previous to 1833 the trade in opium had been regulated by the East India Company, in whom the monopoly was vested. The Company's Charter lapsed in 1833, and on its reissue the monopoly was abrogated. As a result the trade not only increased with great rapidity, but, being no longer regulated by a responsible corporation, involved many regrettable incidents. The anxiety of the Chinese to stop it was, therefore, perfectly intelligible, though the action of Commissioner Lin was in the highest degree arbitrary and high-handed. He demanded that all the opium in the possession of the English traders in Canton should be surrendered and destroyed, a demand to which Captain Elliott—the English Superintendent in Canton—ordered the merchants to accede. Consequently 20,283 chests of opium, worth between £2,000,000 and £5,000,000 sterling, were destroyed. In return, Elliot gave the merchants a bond on the English Government. Commissioner Lin next demanded that henceforward all vessels engaged in the trade should be confiscated, and all traders should suffer death. Elliot naturally refused these extravagant demands ; bade the merchants evacuate Canton ; himself withdrew to Macao, and called upon the Governor-General of India—Lord Auckland [2]—for armed assistance.

It would serve no useful purpose to recount in detail the ensuing acts of violence on both sides, the outrages, the reprisals, and recriminations which in 1840 eventuated in war. The whole business was, to say the least, unsavoury ; but, whatever the indiscretion of British agents and the lawlessness of British subjects on the spot, no blame attaches to the Home Government. Their views had been admirably expressed in a letter from Sir James Graham to Lord William Bentinck, the Governor-General of India :—[3]

" Trade with China is our only object ; conquest there would be as dangerous as defeat, and commerce never prospers when force is used to sustain it. No glory is to be gained in a victory over the Chinese. Our factory there can only thrive by a ready compliance

with the laws, the prejudices, and even the caprices of a nation
which we seek to propitiate, and the super-cargoes must not imagine
that great national interests are to be sacrificed to a spirit of haughty
defiance mixed with contempt for the laws and customs of an independent people.   Our grand object is to keep peace, and by the
mildest means, by a plastic adaptation of our manners to theirs, to
extend our influence in China with the view of extending our commercial relations.   It is not a demonstration of force that is required,
but proofs of the advantage which China reaps from her peaceful
intercourse with our nation.   We are therefore most unwilling to
send our ships of war to Canton. . . ." [1]

The sentiments are almost too obviously " correct ".   But it is Treaty of
easier to be " correct " at Whitehall than in the Far East, and the Nankin,
two nations drifted into a war, from which, as Graham truly said, no 1842
glory was to be reaped.   But though glory was absent from the war,
substantial advantages were embodied in the Treaty of Nankin by
which, in 1842, the war was brought to an end.   The Chinese agreed
to cede Hong Kong to England, to pay a sum of £6,000,000 sterling
as " ransom," compensation, and indemnity, and to open to the
trade of the world the five port towns (henceforward known as
Treaty Ports) of Canton, Amoy, Shanghai, Ningpo, and Foo-Chow-
Foo.   On the other hand, the Chinese, despite the plausible arguments of the English negotiators, refused to legalize the opium trade.
The result was that a huge smuggling trade in the drug sprang up ;
the profits derived from it were in proportion to the risks, and a
class of traders were attracted to it who gave much trouble in the
future alike to the Chinese and to the English Government.

At the time, however, the Treaty of Nankin was regarded with
not irrational satisfaction in England.   But before it was concluded
the Whig Ministry had fallen, and all the credit of the achievement
fell to their successors.   The same mail which brought the news of
the signature of the Treaty of Nankin brought the still more welcome
news of the recapture of Kábul.   The Conservative Ministry were in
luck.   Alike for the disasters in Afghanistan and the sordid mingling
of success and failure in China, the Whig Government was, in some
degree, responsible ;   whatever measure of party advantage accrued
from these events was credited to Sir Robert Peel.   Not inappro-
priately might Lord Melbourne have addressed to his successor the
words of Henry the Fourth as he bequeathed the Crown to Prince
Hal :—

> I myself know well
> How troublesome it sat upon my head :
> To thee it shall descend with better fruit,
> Better opinion, better confirmation ;
> For all the soil of the achievement goes
> With me into the earth.

How far the prediction was verified the next chapter will show.

[1] Parker, *Graham*, i. 150.

CHAPTER IX.

SIR ROBERT PEEL'S MINISTRY
(1841-1846)

The Premiership of Peel

ON the resignation of Lord Melbourne the Queen called upon Sir Robert Peel to form a Government, and the task was at once accepted. By general consent Peel had been, for some years past, the foremost figure in the House of Commons ; in debating power he was inferior only to Lord Stanley ; in administrative experience he was second to none ; his patience and sagacity had reconstructed his party, and in the esteem alike of his colleagues and of the constituencies no man stood higher. He was no courtier—an " odd shy man " was the Queen's first impression—but he gradually won the confidence of the Sovereign, while the Prince Consort became his firm disciple and sincere friend. In the Cabinet his supremacy was unquestioned, and over every department he exercised a personal supervision such as few Prime Ministers have attempted, and none perhaps has maintained. " We never," wrote his chief lieutenant, Graham, " had a Minister who was so truly a first Minister as he is. He makes himself felt in every department and is really cognizant of the affairs of each." " You have been Prime Minister," said Mr. Gladstone to Peel in 1846, " in a sense in which no other man has been it since Mr. Pitt's time."

The Cabinet

Nor was his pre-eminence due to the inferiority of his colleagues. On the contrary, the Conservative Cabinet of 1841 was exceptionally strong in administrative talent. The Duke of Wellington led the House of Lords without portfolio, though, in 1842, he became Commander-in-Chief ; Lord Lyndhurst became for the third time Chancellor ; Lord Aberdeen was Foreign, Lord Stanley Colonial, and Sir James Graham Home Secretary ; Mr. Henry Goulburn was at the Exchequer and Sir Henry Hardinge was Secretary at War. For obvious reasons there was more than the usual amount of reconstruction during Peel's term of office, and among the younger recruits thus introduced into the Cabinet in 1845 were Mr. Sidney Herbert and Mr. Gladstone. Though Peel was without a second, " his right-hand man " [1] was Sir James Graham. " Your cordial support and entire and unreserved confidence have been," wrote Peel to Graham in 1846. " my chief stay."

Condition of affairs

Capable as were the Cabinet and trusted as was their chief, the condition of affairs confronting them when they took office was exceedingly grave. Embarrassing wars in China and Afghanistán ; difficulties of various kinds in Canada, the West Indies, and South

[1] Rosebery, *Peel*, p. 52.

Africa; at home, terrible distress among the poor; acute commercial depression; much unemployment; a falling revenue and a rapidly mounting deficit. "Can there be," asked Peel in 1841, "a more lamentable picture than that of a Chancellor of the Exchequer seated on an empty chest, by the pool of bottomless deficiency, fishing for a Budget?"

Peel was determined not to wallow in the old economic ruts, but he wisely refused to make a premature disclosure of his policy, and after the re-election of Ministers Parliament sat only for a few weeks in the autumn of 1841. Goulburn borrowed a sum of £5,000,000, half of which was applied to meeting the deficit of the year, and half to the funding of Exchequer Bills. This necessary business done, Parliament was prorogued on October 7th.

The winter of 1841-1842 was one of the worst, in an industrial and economic sense, through which this country has ever passed. A series of bad harvests combined with the Corn Laws to raise the price of bread; and while prices were high wages were low. Bread was at 10d. to 1s. 2d. the quartern loaf; lump sugar cost 7d. to 8d.; tea 4s. to 8s. a pound, or more generally 6d. an ounce; currants 9d., and soap 6d.; butter and meat were relatively cheap, but neither of these articles formed an item in the diet of the labouring classes. Agricultural wages were 9s. to 10s. a week, without board, or 1s. to 1s. 6d. for unmarried labourers living in the house. Masons, bricklayers, painters, carpenters, and plumbers got about $3\frac{3}{4}$d. an hour or 18s. for a week of sixty-four hours. But, low as wages were, there were many who could not earn them. One person in every eleven was a pauper. In Manchester 8,666 persons had a weekly income of under $14\frac{1}{2}$d.; in Bolton there were 6,995 persons whose average earnings were 13d. a week; in Leeds there were 20,000 persons whose average earnings were under 1s., and in Stockport many people earned less than 10d. In Manchester 116 mills were stopped; in Bolton 30 out of 50, and in Stockport so few factories were at work and so many houses unoccupied that the town itself was described as being "to let". 1,500 houses were empty in Bolton, 2,000 in Preston; 12,000 families were supported by charity in Manchester, and in Birmingham one-fifth of the entire population were in receipt of poor-relief. From most of the manufacturing centres, from Paisley and Glasgow, Bury, Rochdale, Wigan, and Coventry came the same tale of unemployment, distress and starvation.[1] The condition of things was appalling, and many remedies were proposed. The Chartists prescribed electoral reform; Carlyle favoured a sort of industrial feudalism, combined with education and emigration; Peel believed that only by fiscal reform was it possible to stimulate industry, to mitigate distress, and to restore a balance between

The "Condition of England"

---

[1] Cf. Ashworth, Recollections of Cobden and the League; The Hungry Forties: Speeches of Sir James Graham in Parliament and much pamphlet literature.

revenue and expenditure. To fiscal reform, therefore, he devoted most of his thought and administrative energy during the next five years.

Tariff reform

The most urgent need of the moment was cheaper and more abundant food. " We must " (as Peel wrote to Croker) " make this country a *cheap* country for living." The session of 1842 opened on February 3rd, and the Queen's Speech recommended Parliament to consider " the state of the finances and the expenditure of the country " and more particularly " the laws which affect the imports of corn and other articles ". For some such announcement the country had been prepared by the resignation of the Duke of Buckingham, rightly regarded as the special representative of the agricultural interest in the Cabinet. The Duke of Buccleuch took his place as Lord Privy Seal. Lord Ellenborough had been appointed Governor-General of India in the previous October, and had been succeeded at the Board of Control by Lord Fitzgerald.[1] With a Cabinet thus partially reconstructed Peel addressed himself to the problem of tariff reform.

The Corn Laws

His first task was a revision of the Corn Laws. For a century and a half the conditions of wheat production had been an object of special concern to the Legislature. During the first half of the eighteenth century Parliament hoped to " prevent grain from being at any time either so dear that the poor cannot subsist, or so cheap that the farmer cannot live by growing it ".[2] The Act of 1689 provided for a bounty of 5s. when wheat fell below 48s. a quarter, and was successful both in stimulating tillage and maintaining a steady level of prices. The amending Act of 1773 was also intended to keep the price steady at about 48s., but proposed to do it by permitting free importation when the price rose above 48s. It was less successful than the Act of 1689, to the principle of which Parliament reverted at the end of the eighteenth century. The Act of 1791 aimed at keeping the price between 46s. and 54s. To this end a prohibitive duty was laid on imported corn when the price was under 50s. ; a bounty of 5s. was given when the price fell to 44s., and only a registration duty of 6d. was charged on importation when the price rose above 54s. This Act combined with the great war to give an unhealthy stimulus to wheat culture, but the Peace of 1815 threatened the whole agricultural interest with ruin. In the hope of averting it the Corn Law of 1815 was passed.

Up till this time the motive of the Legislature had been regulative rather than protective. The Act of 1815 introduced protection pure

---

[1] Better known as Mr. Vesey Fitzgerald—O'Connell's opponent in the Clare election of 1828.

[2] C. Smith, *Considerations on the Importation and Exportation of Corn* (1759), ap. Cunningham (*Growth of English Industry*, p. 723), to whose excellent account of the Corn Laws this chapter owes much.

and simple, the importation of foreign wheat being absolutely prohibited so long as the price was under 80s. The new Act did nothing
to steady prices ; it reduced agriculture to a gamble ; and it aroused
bitter and just resentment among the commercial and industrial
classes. To meet these difficulties Peel introduced his sliding scale
in 1828, based upon the principle that it was desirable to keep the
price at about 70s. When it rose above 73s. the import duty was
reduced to 1s. ; when the price was between 64s. and 69s. the duty
was 16s. 8d. ; under 64s. the duty was 25s. 8d. The plan was unsuccessful ; it encouraged speculative trade, demoralized the producer, and did not relieve the consumer. Profoundly impressed by
the social unrest and the economic distress Peel returned to the
subject in 1842. He had declared emphatically, in 1839 that " unless
the existence of the Corn Law can be shown to be consistent, not only
with the prosperity of agriculture and the maintenance of the landlord's interest, but also with the protection and the maintenance of
the general interests of the country and especially with the improvement of the condition of the labouring class, the Corn Law is practically at an end ". Nevertheless, he proceeded cautiously. He still
insisted on the maintenance of the sliding scale ; when the price was
at or over 73s., importation was to be subject only to the registration
duty of 1s. ; when it stood at 50s. to 51s. there was to be a maximum
duty of 20s. Between the two extremes there was to be a carefully
graduated scale of duties rising when the price fell, falling when it
rose. In proposing his scheme he disclaimed the intention of protecting class interests, but he insisted that it was " of the highest
importance to the welfare of all classes . . . that the main sources of
your supply of corn should be derived from domestic agriculture ".
He contended that we are " entitled to place such a price on foreign
corn as is equivalent to the special burdens borne by the agriculturists " and refused " to be a party to any measure the effect of
which would be to make this country permanently dependent upon
foreign countries for any very considerable portion of its supply of
corn ".[1] The scheme was ingenious but not popular. The agricultural interest was uneasy ; Lord John preferred and proposed a
fixed duty of 8s. ; Cobden and the League denounced the proposed
measure as a " bitter insult to a suffering nation ".[2] But Peel
carried his proposals by large majorities, and, taken in conjunction
with reduction of duties on imported cattle and meat, they must be
regarded as a substantial concession to the interests of the consumer.

Peel was not, however, unmindful of other interests. So sensible
indeed was he of the pressing and paramount importance of financial
reform that he himself as Prime Minister introduced the Budget on
March 11th, 1842. The statement had been awaited with exceptional

The Bud-
get of
1842

---

[1] For Peel's views in detail *cf. Memoirs*, ii. Appendix, pp. 327-357.
[2] Morley, *Cobden*, i. 221.

interest and curiosity. Nor was the House disappointed. The
Premier's speech marked an epoch in the fiscal policy of this country.
The situation was a difficult one. Mr. Baring, the out-going Finance
Minister, had tried to balance his accounts by a general increase of
duties in 1840, and by reducing them in 1841. Both expedients
appeared to be equally futile. The revenue showed itself hopelessly
inelastic ; trade was increasingly depressed ; the farmers, despite
protective duties, could not make agriculture pay ; the artisans
could not get work ; the mass of the people could not get sufficient
food. Peel had taken deeply to heart the example of his masters in
finance, Pitt and Huskisson ; he had weighed the argument of Sir
Henry Parnell and had mastered the evidence collected by the
import Duties Committee of 1840. Faced with a deficit of about
£2,350,000 on the accounts of the expiring year, he estimated that,
on the existing basis of taxation, he would have another deficit for
1842-1843 of £2,469,000. Thus the six years 1837-1843 would show
an aggregate deficiency of over £10,000,000. Expenditure, then as
always, showed a tendency to increase ; how was the balance to be
adjusted ?

The in-   Peel wisely refused to have recourse to any financial nostrums ;
come tax he was convinced that we had " arrived at the limits of taxation on
articles of consumption " ; he appealed, therefore, to the possessors
of property to allow him to impose—in the first instance for three
years—an income tax of 7d. in the £. This he anticipated would
yield £3,700,000. It would thus not only supply the deficiency in
the revenue, but would enable him " with confidence and satisfaction
to propose great commercial reforms which will afford a hope of
reviving commerce, and such an improvement in the manufacturing
interests as will react on every other interest in the country ; and by
diminishing the prices of the articles of consumption and the cost of
living " would compensate for the immediate sacrifice. Ireland was
to be exempted from the income tax but to pay an extra 1s. a gallon
on spirits and to pay something more for stamps. Finally, the export
duty of 4s. a ton paid by coal carried by foreign ships was to be
extended to coal carried in British ships. From these sources he
expected an additional income of £4,380,000, which would give him
a surplus of £1,800,000. On the other hand he proposed to sacrifice
£1,200,000 of indirect taxation by reducing the duties on 750 articles
in the tariff, and by repealing the export duties on British manufactures. The principles which underlay these changes in the tariff
were clearly stated by Peel himself. " With respect to raw materials,"
he said, " which constitute the elements of our manufacture, our
object, speaking generally, has been to reduce the duties on them to
almost a nominal amount. On half-manufactured articles, which
enter almost as much as the raw material into our domestic manufacture, we have reduced the duty to a moderate amount, and, with

regard to completely manufactured articles, our design has been to remove prohibition and to reduce prohibitory duties, so that the manufactures of foreign countries may enter into a fair competition with our own. The general result of this tariff will be materially to diminish the charge of living in this country."

No bolder proposals in finance have ever been laid before the House of Commons. They represented, as many more or less clearly perceived, the beginning of a revolution of which no man could see the end. The Whig opposition, led in the Commons by Lord John Russell, keenly contested the income tax proposals, but Peel, loyally supported by his party, carried them by a majority of 106.

The immediate results of Peel's reforms were at once more and less successful than he had anticipated. The yield of the income tax would have exceeded the estimate by about £1,200,000 had it been for a full year, but by a gross error of calculation the Exchequer only got six months revenue in the current financial year ; customs, excise, stamps, and taxes all fell short of the estimate, with the result that, in 1843, Mr. Goulburn had to confess to a deficit of over £2,200,000. But he and Peel stuck courageously to their guns, and, despite the deficit, proposed no alterations in taxation for 1843-1844. Their coolness and courage were amply vindicated. In 1844 the Chancellor of the Exchequer was able to announce a realized surplus of £2,095,428. The last two harvests had been good ; trade prospects were rapidly improving ; the prices of necessaries were falling. Consequently, after paying off the deficit of the previous year, Mr. Goulburn was able to remit taxation to the extent of £400,000 by abolishing or reducing the duties on glass, vinegar, currants, coffee, and wool, and reducing the stamp duty on marine insurances.[1] But the year 1844 was remarkable less for the remission of indirect taxation than for the enactment of two measures of immense importance to the financial stability and commercial credit of the nation.

Firstly, by a bold scheme of " conversion " the interest on no less than £250,000,000 of the consolidated debt of the country was reduced from 3½ per cent., immediately to 3¼, and, after ten years' interval, to 3 per cent., after which Consols were to be irredeemable for a further twenty years. By this means the country secured an immediate saving of £625,000 a year and an ultimate saving of £1,250,000 Thus the charge for debt which in 1842 was £29,434,891 was reduced in 1852 to £27,918,027. It again rose slightly in the years immediately succeeding the Crimean War, but by 1861 it was down to £26,142,606. That Goulburn was able to effect this successful conversion was due primarily to the fact that, since Peel came into power. the price of Consols had risen from 89 to 99, but also to the

Conversion of Consols

---

[1] The duty on raw materials was not henceforward to exceed 5 per cent. ; on articles partly manufactured not to exceed 12 per cent., and on wholly manufactured goods 20 per cent.

general sense of security and well-being diffused by the financial and commercial reforms of the Conservative Ministry.

Bank Charter Act of 1844

Not less important was the enactment, in the same year, of the Bank Charter Act. In 1819 Peel had himself passed a Bill establishing the principle that all Bank notes should on demand be payable in gold, but the Legislature had done nothing to secure that the practice should correspond with the precept. Country banks had frequently failed to meet their note obligations, and during two crises, those of 1825 and 1839, the Bank of England itself " had been exposed to great danger ".[1] Peel was anxious to complete the work he had begun in 1819 : to " put a check on improvident speculation and inspire just confidence in the medium of exchange ". To this end he adopted the view put forward by Mr. Jones Loyd, afterwards Lord Overstone, " a London banker of rare sagacity, who propounded the true principles of currency with a tenacity which confounded his adversaries and a lucidity which ought to have convinced them ".[2] The Act of 1844 contained three main provisions. By the first, the banking department of the Bank of England was absolutely separated from the issue department and the latter was placed under stringent regulations. By the second, the convertibility of all notes issued by the Bank was secured. The Bank was allowed to issue £14,000,000 of notes (the amount dictated by experience) against Government securities, but for every note issued beyond that amount it was to retain bullion, of which 75 per cent. was to be gold. By the third, the note issue of other banks was severely restricted. Private and Joint Stock banks established after the date of the Act were forbidden to issue notes at all ; old-established banks were limited to an aggregate issue of £8,500,000—the average amount in circulation during the years which immediately preceded the passing of the Act.

The principle of this famous Act has been fiercely assailed ; but, despite the fact that the Act had to be suspended in 1847, in 1857, and in 1866, experience has proved its soundness, and has vindicated the prescient wisdom of Lord Overstone and Sir Robert Peel. The English currency will " go anywhere " and, within the limits of its face value, will " do anything ". The principle of the Act was extended to Scotland and Ireland in 1845.

The Budget of 1845

In 1845 Peel again took personal charge of the financial proposals of the Government. The period of three years for which the income tax had been imposed had now expired ; the immediate purpose of its imposition had been attained ; the revenue—despite the large remissions of taxation—had practically righted itself. A weak Ministry and a short-sighted Minister would certainly have been content to let well alone. But Peel, emboldened by the success of his experiment, was determined to carry it further and to renew the income tax for a further period of three years—" not for the purpose

---

[1] Parker, *Peel*, iii. 134.   [2] Thursfield, *Peel*, p. 194.

of providing the supplies for the year, but distinctly for the purpose of enabling us to make this great experiment of reducing other taxes ". Given a 7d. income tax he estimated that he could count on a surplus of nearly three and a half millions. Almost the whole of this surplus he proposed to give away in remissions of indirect taxation. The details of his scheme were inspired by a fivefold object : to reduce the cost of living ; to cheapen the raw materials imported for the use of manufacturers ; to secure economy of collection ; to promote commercial enterprise, and to increase employment. Accordingly, sugar duties were reduced to the value of £1,300,000 ; 430 articles —among them silk, hemp, flax and furniture wood—were taken out of the tariff altogether, at a total cost of £320,000 ; all the remaining export duties, valued at £118,000 and the duty on cotton wool, £680,000, were abolished. Thus the customs revenue stood to lose £2,418,000. Excise was to lose £890,000 by the repeal of the auction duty and that on glass. The total amount of remission was thus nearly three times as great as that in 1842, while a new principle of great significance, that " of absolutely repealing instead of merely reducing duties was now introduced ".[1] Moreover, the income tax was imposed, no longer as a temporary expedient, to tide over a period of exceptional difficulty, but as a regular part of the fiscal system of the country, although Peel did express his belief that " at the end of three years we may be at liberty to discontinue it ". Population was increasing : capital rapidly accumulating, and Peel was convinced that if he could facilitate the application of that capital to new branches of industry and manufactures, the effect would be greatly to increase the demand for labour ; and with the demand for labour, to increase the consumption of articles subject to taxation. Consequently he predicted that there would be " a fair opportunity for the House to consider " at the end of the three years' period " whether this tax ought to cease ". The language was guarded. Lord John Russell might denounce the tax as one in which " inequality, vexation, and fraud were inherent," but Peel was clearly inclining to the view that though the country would " be at liberty," thanks to an expanding trade and an elastic revenue, to discontinue the impost, it would be doubtful wisdom to seize the opportunity.[2] Peel's prescience was not at fault. The revenue from customs and excise showed remarkable expansiveness, sufficient, had the free traders stayed their hands, to have enabled them to dispense with Peel's " temporary " expedient : but, despite hints and semi-promises, notably from Peel's greatest disciple in finance, the opportunity was never redeemed, and the income tax has become to an ever-increasing extent the sheet-anchor of our national finances.[3]

[1] Northcote, *Twenty Years of Financial Policy*, p. 67—a work of great value, to which this chapter owes much.   [2] Speech, February 17th, 1845.
[3] In 1841 direct taxes produced 27 per cent. of the national revenue : in 1861 83 per cent. : in 1901 50 per cent. ; in 1907 52 per cent.

The year 1846 was remarkable for other things than mere persistence in a policy already adopted, or even the extension of an accepted principle. But, leaving on one side for the moment the repeal of the Corn Laws and the consequent fall of the Ministry, it may be convenient to complete our review of the tariff reforms effected by Peel. The Budget of 1846, apart from the revision of the corn duties, was of unusual significance. Custom duties to the extent of over one million sterling were remitted. Towards this remission all classes were called upon to contribute. The manufacturers lost much of the protection which they had hitherto enjoyed. The duties on timber and tallow—important raw materials—were reduced ; but the protective duties on the coarser kinds of cotton, woollen, and linen manufactures were surrendered altogether, and those on the finer kinds were reduced ; on most other manufactured articles the duty was to be as near 10 per cent. as possible. The consumer further gained by a reduction of duties on soap, candles, boots, shoes, foreign spirits, cheese, butter, and hops. The farmer was to get his seeds cheaper, but had to face the free importation of live animals and all kinds of meat, to say nothing of corn.

That the tariff reforms of Peel were financially justified can be denied by no one cognizant of the facts. In the five years 1842-1846 taxes to the amount of £8,206,000, or nearly one-fourth of the whole Customs and Excise duties, were remitted, yet notwithstanding this gigantic remission Customs, Excise, Stamps, and Taxes yielded nearly £400,000 more in 1847 than they had in 1842 ; while on Customs and Excise alone the loss was under £50,000.[1] It was a remarkable achievement, bearing testimony alike to the astuteness of the Minister and to the expansive capacity of English trade.

For the moment, however, the financial achievement, memorable as it was, was overshadowed by the social and economic revolution, and the political disintegration involved in the repeal of the Corn Laws. The task of vindicating Peel's consistency on this matter must be left to the biographer. The amount of credit due to Cobden and others is also a theme for the monograph. We must confine ourselves to a brief and bare recital of the facts. The reputation of Peel and his colleagues never stood so high as in the summer of 1845 ; never did their hold upon office seem so secure. Peel was apparently in power for life, and nowhere were the prospects of the Government more hopeful than in Ireland, for whose social and economic amelioration Peel was busily devising a variety of schemes. Then, suddenly, the sky was overcast, men's hearts failed them for fear, and the spirits even of the careless were depressed by the sense of impending catastrophe.

---

[1] These figures are based on the *Analysis of Budgets*, ap. Northcote. Appendix A.

The causes of the great Irish famine are not obscure. The most obvious was the appalling rapidity with which during the last century and a half the people of Ireland had multiplied. Under Charles II. Petty estimated the population at little over a million—the census of 1841 gave the number at 8,175,124. But commercial and economic development had not kept pace with the growth of population. Every adventitious circumstance combined to encourage the latter. Early marriages were commended by the priests ; legislative encouragement to tillage led to the multiplication of small freeholds ; the enfranchisement of the 40s. freeholder had the same result. As a French writer puts it brilliantly and tersely : " Le proprietaire Irelandais vit ainsi pulluler sous sa main des fermiers, des electeurs, et des clients ; ce sol fut mutilé, bruyé, reduit en poudre ; chaque grain de sable representait une famille, une rente, un patronage ".[1] Were ever words more literally true ? Out of the 8,000,000 people in Ireland 4,000,000 depended for subsistence upon a single root. Well might economists curse Raleigh's "lazy root ". Its fecundity none could gainsay ; but its productiveness was only equalled by its precariousness. Rumours as to the presence of potato disease reached Peel early in August, 1845. During August and September he watched and inquired and always with deepening anxiety. " I never witnessed in any case," says the Duke of Wellington, " such agony." Not, however, until the middle of September was there apprehension as to the general failure of the crop in Ireland. Early in October the outlook became very serious. The Prime Minister clearly apprehended the situation. In 1846 at least half the Irish peasantry would have to be fed on corn. But the English corn crop, like the Irish potato crop, was a failure. On October 13th Peel wrote to Sir James Graham : " The accounts of the state of the potato crop in Ireland are becoming alarming. I have no confidence in such remedies as the prohibition of exports, or the stoppage of the distilleries. The removal of the impediments to import is the only effectual remedy." Two days later (Oct. 15th) even more emphatically to Lord Heytesbury : " We must consider whether it is possible by legislation or by the exercise of prerogative to apply a remedy to the great evil with which we are threatened. The application of such remedy involves considerations of the utmost magnitude. The remedy is the removal of all impediments to the import of all kinds of human food—that is the total and absolute repeal for ever of all duties on all articles of subsistence . . . you might remit nominally for one year ; but who will re-establish the Corn Laws once abrogated, though from a casual and temporary pressure ? " In Ireland itself the popular remedy was not to open the ports to imports, but to close them to exports. So reputable a writer as Sir G. Duffy does not hesitate to declare that the famine was " created not by the

[1] De Beaumont, *L'Irlande*, i. 5.

blight but by the landlords," who exported from Ireland the food of the people. Peel, however, held steadily on his course. Two distinguished experts—Professor Lindley and Dr. Lyon (afterwards Lord) Playfair—were sent over to Ireland to examine the facts on the spot. Their report confirmed the worst apprehensions. Peel felt that action could no longer be delayed. The Cabinet was summoned for October 31st. It sat for nearly a week continuously. " Four Cabinet Councils of unusual duration," says Disraeli, " were held in one week." On November 1st, Peel compelled his colleagues to face at once the question—

" Shall we maintain unaltered,

" Shall we modify,

" Shall we suspend—the operation of the Corn Law ? "

Before the end of the week the Prime Minister was compelled to warn the Queen as to " the probability of serious difference of opinion ". His own views were supported only by Sir James Graham, Mr. Sidney Herbert, and Lord Aberdeen, and already he began to consider the advisability of resignation.

The bare record of the *Memoirs* makes it clear that Peel felt his responsibility at this juncture almost too heavy for endurance. That responsibility was, however, somewhat lightened, and at the same time the hand of his colleagues was forced, by the publication (Nov. 22nd, 1845) of Lord John Russell's " Edinburgh Letter ". At last Lord John declared unequivocally for the policy of free imports.

By this time Peel himself was convinced that the Corn Laws must go. But his colleagues were not equally open to conviction, and it was at least doubtful how far " repeal " would be popular in Parliament and in the country at large. For years past Cobden and the League had been vigorously preaching their crusade. But the masses were not yet converted. Cobden himself frankly admitted that " so far as the fervour and efficiency of our agitation has gone, it has eminently been a middle-class agitation ".[1]

Cobden and Villiers were more successful with the Minister than with the masses.

The fissure in the Cabinet was, however, too deep for healing, and on December 5th, 1845, Peel wrote to the Queen " with a heart full of gratitude and devotion to your Majesty, but with a strong conviction . . . that in the present state of affairs he can render more service to your Majesty and to the country in a private than in a public station ".[2]

Ministeri-
al confu-
sion

The Queen, therefore, asked Lord John Russell to form a Ministry. Despite Peel's promise of support, however, Lord John, after nearly a fortnight of fruitless endeavour, was obliged to inform the Queen (Dec. 20th) of his inability to obey her commands, and (in Disraeli's phrase) " handed back with courtesy the poisoned chalice to Sir

[1] Morley, *Cobden*, i. 249.   [2] *Q.V.L.* ii. 56.

Robert ". Peel, deeply moved by the Queen's distressing dilemma, agreed at once to carry on the Government. " I will be your Minister, happen what may. I will do without a colleague rather than leave you in this extremity." Lord Stanley alone persisted in his resignation, and his place at the Colonial Office was taken by Mr. Gladstone. The Queen expressed to King Leopold her " extreme admiration of our worthy Peel, who shows himself a man of unbounded loyalty and courage and highmindedness, and his conduct towards me has been chivalrous almost, I might say." " We have indeed," she added, " had an escape, for though Lord John's own notions were very good and moderate, he let himself be entirely twisted and twirled about by his violent friends and all the moderate ones were crushed." [1] No words could more aptly summarize the events of the past fortnight : Peel's conduct was indeed entirely chivalrous and self-forgetful, and he had to pay the penalty. For the moment he was " in the highest spirits at having got Mr. Gladstone and kept the Duke of Buccleuch ".[2] Lord Ellenborough was also brought back into the Cabinet (Jan. 1846) as First Lord of the Admiralty.

The ministerial changes were few and simple, but Peel had now The Session of to face Parliament. On January 22nd the Queen opened Parliament in person. Her speech was strangely cautious and colourless. 1846 She referred to the prevalence of serious crime in Ireland ; lamented the imminence of famine ; expressed satisfaction at the enactment of measures " calculated to extend commerce, and to stimulate domestic skill and industry, by the repeal of prohibitory and the relaxation of protective duties," and recommended Parliament to consider whether the principles on which they had acted might not " with advantage be yet more extensively applied ".

After the moving and seconding of the Address Peel at once rose to make a statement as to his own position and that of his Government. He explained that their resignation in December was due immediately to the failure of the potato crop, in that it had forced an immediate decision upon the laws which governed the importation of grain. He confessed without shame his conversion to the principle of free trade ; a conversion strengthened by the experience of the last three years. During that period he had watched day by day the effect of the relaxation of duties, both on finance and on all the social interests of the country, and he felt justified in proceeding with the further removal of protecting duties. But he had not felt it proper that " the charge of altering the Corn Laws should devolve upon him as Minister of the Crown ". He then reviewed the events of the past autumn ; the increasing gravity of the news from Ireland ; the dissensions in the Cabinet; Lord John Russell's " Edinburgh Letter " ; the opposition of Lord Stanley ; the resignation of the Cabinet; Lord John's inability to form a Government; his own

---

Ibid. 75.   [2] Prince Albert's Memorandum, *Q.V.L.* p. 77.

retention of office, and determination to submit his proposals to Parliament. Finally, in a noble peroration, he dissipated the idea that he had any desire after serving four Sovereigns to cling to the imaginary " sweets " of office, protested his devotion to his Sovereign and his country, and vindicated his loyalty to the principles of true Conservatism. " To conduct the Government of this country is a most arduous duty. . . . It is no easy task to ensure the united action of an ancient monarchy, a proud aristocracy, and a reformed constituency. . . . I have thought it consistent with the Conservative policy to promote so much of happiness and contentment among the people, that the voice of disaffection should be no longer heard, and that thoughts of the dissolution of our institutions should be forgotten in the midst of physical enjoyment. . . . But . . . I will not stand at the helm during such tempestuous nights as I have seen, if the vessel be not allowed to pursue fairly the course which I think she ought to take. . . . I do not wish to be the Minister of England, but, while I have the high honour of holding that office, I am determined to hold it by no servile tenure. I will only hold that office upon the condition of being unshackled by any other obligations than those of consulting the public interests and of providing for the public safety."

Only one voice was raised in protest. It was that of Disraeli, whose hour for long-meditated revenge had come. In " an hour of gibes and bitterness " he denounced Peel's speech as " a glorious example of egotistical rhetoric," and his policy as a betrayal of the principles which had put him in power and the party which had kept him there. But the Address was carried without a dissentient voice.

The repeal of the Corn Laws

Five days later the Prime Minister unfolded his scheme in Committee. To its general principles reference has already been made : cheap raw materials for the manufacturer, but no protection against fair foreign competition ; cheaper seed for the farmer, but no protection against foreign meat or corn ; for all, cheaper living. The Corn Laws were not to be abrogated immediately in their entirety. The duty was to be reduced to 1s. after February 1st, 1849, but in the meantime it was to be 10s. when corn averaged less than 48s. a quarter, diminishing to 4s. when the price was 53s. or over.

The Protectionists, organized and led with consummate adroitness by Disraeli and Lord George Bentinck, made a brave fight, but they numbered less than 250, and on May 15th Peel carried the third reading of his Corn Bill by a majority of ninety-eight (327 to 229). Thanks to the great authority of the Duke of Wellington it was steered safely through stormy waters in the House of Lords, being read a third time on June 25th.

Defeat of Peel's Ministry

On the very same night the Ministry were defeated in the Commons on their *Life Preservation Bill* for Ireland by a majority of seventy-three. The Protectionists could not avert or even delay the repeal of the Corn Laws, but they could still take dramatic, not to say melodramatic, revenge upon the Minister. Not for the first time, as they believed, had Peel fouled his own nest, betrayed his principles, and befooled his followers. The majority against the Government was a motley one, made up of Tories and Whigs, Protectionists and Free Traders, Radicals and Repealers. The alliance was as infamous as it was short-lived, but to the author of it, the revenge was infinitely sweet. In the most vivid chapter of the most brilliant political biography in the language he has himself described the scene in the House. Peel sat grim on the Treasury bench " as the Protectionists passed in defile before the Minister to the hostile lobby. It was impossible that he could have marked them without emotion : the flower of that great party which had been so proud to follow one who had been so proud to lead them. . . . They had extended to him an unlimited confidence and an admiration without stint. . . . They had been not only his followers but his friends. . . . They trooped on ; all the men of metal and large-acred squires. . . . Sir Robert looked very grave. . . . He began to comprehend his position, and that the Emperor was without an army."[1]

Two days later Peel announced to the House the resignation of the Ministry in an elaborate, but not wholly felicitous speech.

Peel's ministerial career was at an end : but until his life was suddenly terminated by an accident in 1850 he remained, though not in office, undeniably in power. Without his steady support his successors could not have weathered the parliamentary storms. " I never knew a man in whose truth and justice I had a more lively confidence." Such a tribute from the Duke of Wellington, his sometime chief, his sometime follower, his life-long colleague, is conclusive. " The greatest member of Parliament that ever lived " was the verdict of his most virulent opponent. But opponent as he was, no one judged him with greater acumen or upon the whole more fairly than Disraeli. It is true that in debate he denounced him as " a burglar of other men's intellect ". " For between forty and fifty years, from the days of Mr. Horner to those of the honourable member for Stockport (Cobden), the right honourable gentleman has traded on the ideas and intelligence of others. His life has been one great appropriation clause . . . there has been no statesman who has committed petty larceny on such a scale." This is the exaggerated language of debate. But even in the calm of literary reflection [2] Disraeli denied to Peel gifts of prescience, imagination, or originality. He declared that " he had a dangerous sympathy with the creations of others," that he lacked the gift of true leadership ; that he was " really deficient in self-confidence ; that he was

Character of Peel

[1] Disraeli, *Life of Lord George Bentinck*, c. xvi. The second volume of Mr. Monypenny's *Life of Lord Beaconsfield* appeared only as these sheets were passing through the press, and I have therefore been unable to make use of it.

[2] *Cf. Life of Lord George Bentinck.*

10

a bad judge of character and had little knowledge of men ". But on the other hand he described him as " a transcendant administrator of public business, and a matchless master of debate in a popular assembly. . . . In the senate he was the readiest, easiest, most flexible and adroit of men. He played upon the House of Commons as upon an old fiddle." Where Disraeli blames he is apt to be captious, but his praise is both just and acute. We may allow that Peel was, in Bagehot's phrase, " prone to receive the daily deposits of insensibly changing opinion ". It constitutes one of his strongest titles to the name of a great parliamentary statesman. The complex parliamentary machine involves a division of labour. Cobden could never have carried the repeal of the Corn Laws, nor O'Connell Catholic Emancipation. They sowed the seed ; but it was Peel's strong brain and over-mastering will which enabled him to garner the parliamentary harvest.

Foreign policy and social reform
   In the foregoing pages attention has been concentrated upon the financial and fiscal reforms carried by Peel during his great Ministry. But the years between 1841 and 1846 were not devoid of other interests. Foreign affairs were, throughout the whole period, of secondary importance, thanks mainly to the personal friendship of Peel and Guizot, but it is important to note that the signature of the Treaty of Washington—better known as the Ashburton Treaty—effected, in August, 1842, a satisfactory settlement of a long outstanding dispute as to the boundary line between Canada and the United States ; and that, in 1846, the Oregon Treaty similarly settled the boundary on the Pacific Coast giving us undisputed possession of Vancouver Island. In India matters of great importance were in progress, but to these attention will be directed later.[1] At home, social questions were much to the front. The appalling facts revealed by a Commission of enquiry as to the employment of women and children in mines and collieries enabled Lord Ashley to carry, in 1842, a Bill which prohibited work underground for women, girls, and boys under ten years of age. The same Act laid down regulations for the prevention of accidents and limited the employment of apprentices. The sectarian bitterness of Roman Catholics and Nonconformists foiled the efforts of Sir James Graham to secure, in 1843, a modicum of education for pauper and factory children, but in 1844 he added one more to the lengthening series of Factory Acts. Under this Act the legal hours of labour in factories for children between the ages of eight and thirteen were further reduced to six and a half hours, children were obliged to attend school for three hours a day, and increased powers were conferred upon inspectors. In connection with this measure Graham incurred some ill-deserved unpopularity which was intensified in the following year by the disclosure of the fact that he had issued a warrant to the

[1]*Cf. infra,* c. xiv.

officials of the Post Office authorizing them to open the letters of the Italian patriot, Mazzini—then a political exile in England. Lord Aberdeen also shared the odium attaching to Graham's conduct in consequence of the fact that the brothers Bandiera—deserters from the Austrian navy, and martyrs in the cause of Italian independence were shot by the Neapolitan Government for participation in an insurrectionary movement. The Bandieras had been in correspondence with Mazzini, and when it was discovered that Mazzini's letters had been opened at the Post Office it was inferred—not unnaturally—that Lord Aberdeen had communicated information thus obtained to the Austrian or Neapolitan Governments. It has now been proved, but only within the last few years, that Aberdeen had no such information, and had therefore nothing whatever to do with the fate which overtook the brothers Bandiera. That Mazzini's letters were, for a few months, opened is true : but in permitting this to be done Graham merely exercised a discretion necessarily vested in the Secretary of State, though not, it is understood, frequently resorted to.[1] Graham was very fiercely assailed both in Parliament and in the Press, and felt deeply the imputations made upon his personal honour. To the particular incident an exaggerated importance was attached ; it was now agreed that however odious the duty thus imposed upon the Secretary of State, it is one with the occasional performance of which it is impossible, in the public interest, to dispense.

Of much greater permanent significance were the movements which at this time agitated both the Church of England and the Church of Scotland. The two movements, though widely divergent in their ultimate results, had, in a sense, a common origin. Both proceeded from parties in the Churches impatient of the somewhat conventional respectability which Ecclesiastical Establishments are apt to engender, and anxious to emphasize the spiritual character of the Christian society. The movement in the Scotch Church was eminently disruptive, and resulted in 1843 in the secession of nearly 400 ministers and the establishment of the " Free Church ". The immediate points in dispute were, on the one hand, the respective rights of lay patrons and parishioners in regard to presentation to benefices ; on the other the precise relation of the Civil and Ecclesiastical Courts. The secessionists, led by Dr. Thomas Chalmers and Dr. Welsh, insisted upon the rights of parishioners as against patrons, and upon the superior validity of the decrees of the Ecclesiastical Courts. According to Chalmers " the indispensable, the vital object at stake is the uncontrolled management of our own ecclesiastical affairs ". The disputes were of long standing ; but in 1842 an

Ecclesiastical movements

---

[1] On the whole matter *cf.* Parker, *Graham*, i. c. xix., and, in particular, some interesting correspondence published by Lord Stanmore (Lord Aberdeen's son), together with an article in the *Times*, August 24th, 1907.

appeal was made to the Government, and their decision in favour of lay patronage and the authority of the State unquestionably precipitated the secession described above.

The Oxford Movement.

The contemporaneous movement in the English Church was certainly not less important, so important indeed was it that the details must be sought in special monographs.[1] In this place a bare summary must suffice. In 1833 John Keble, at that time Professor of Poetry at Oxford, preached before the University a sermon on " National Apostasy ". In the same year John Henry Newman, like Keble a Fellow of Oriel College, published the first of a long series of *Tracts for the Times*. These were the men who, joined by Richard Hurrell Froude, Edward Bouverie Pusey, and others, lit a fire in Oxford which has since burnt brightly throughout the English-speaking world. Impatience of dogma ; mistrust of enthusiasm ; neglect of the pastoral office ; indifference to historical tradition ; exaltation of the virtues of sobriety of thought and respectability of demeanour ; these were the outstanding features of the Church of the eighteenth century, the Church whose apathy converted the Wesleyan revival into a schismatic secession ; these were the principles implicit in the " Erastianism " of the early Victorian Whigs. From these things the Tractarians were minded to deliver both the Church and the nation. Keble, Newman, and Pusey took up the task of educating their brethren of the Anglican Church at the point where it had dropped from the fingers of Archbishop Laud. Like the Arminians of the seventeenth century, they desired to vindicate the Catholic position of the Anglican Church ; to reassert its identity with the pre-Reformation Church in England ; to insist on the continuity of its Apostolical Succession ; to exalt the Episcopal Order ; to revive the ancient and stately ceremonial ; to emphasize the importance of the Sacraments ; to enhance the authority of a mediatorial priesthood.

It was almost inevitable that some men, having gone thus far in the direction of Catholicism, should be impelled to go further. *Tract XC*—on the Thirty-Nine Articles—was a notable advance on *Tract I*, and in 1845 the author of both joined the Church of Rome. But though Newman and W. G. Ward found the *Via Media* too slippery for them, Keble, Pusey, and thousands more, remained entirely loyal to the Church of England. For a time the secessions to Rome brought grave suspicion upon the Oxford Movement as a whole ; but the alarm gradually subsided, and the personal piety, the pastoral devotion, and the missionary zeal which were characteristic of the followers of Keble and Pusey, extorted the respect even of opponents and profoundly influenced both the life of the Church

[1] *Cf. e.g.* R. W. Church, *Oxford Movement ;* Mozley, *Reminiscences ;* Newman, *Tract XC* and *Apologia pro vita sua ;* Lives of Arnold (Stanley), Pusey (Liddon & Johnstone), Keble.

and the ideals of the nation during the latter half of the nineteenth century. The history of the Oxford Movement, is, however, too specialized for treatment here. It is time to get back to the main political stream. That stream carries us irresistibly to Ireland.

At no period during Peel's Ministry were Irish affairs very far in the background. The General Election of 1841 had, as we have seen, shattered O'Connell's party, and in the new House of Commons scarcely twenty Repealers found seats. Nevertheless O'Connell proclaimed early in 1842 that this was to be the " great repeal year ". O'Connell spared no pains to verify his prediction. Monster meetings were held in all parts of the country, and the repeal " rent "—a voluntary tax imposed for the purpose of sustaining the agitation— yielded no less than £48,000. A marked feature of the agitation, due partly to the influence of O'Connell himself and partly to the temperance crusade of Father Mathew, was the absence of crime and disorder. Nevertheless, the Government passed a Bill to regulate the use and sale of arms ; and prohibited the holding of a monster demonstration at Clontarf. The meeting was called for October 8th, 1843, the prohibition was issued only on the evening of the 7th. Thanks to O'Connell's immediate acquiescence in the order, and the perfect discipline of his followers, the meeting was abandoned, and much bloodshed was thereby avoided. The Government, however, showed a curious lack of appreciation of their debt to O'Connell. He and his son John and half a dozen associates were arrested, and after a trial which lasted for twenty-five days O'Connell was convicted, and ultimately sentenced to pay a fine of £2,000, to be imprisoned for twelve months, and to find sureties that he would keep the peace for some years. The imprisonment lasted only three months, as the House of Lords, on appeal, reversed the judgment. Their action completed the discomfiture of O'Connell; he came out of gaol a broken man ; his hold upon his compatriots was fatally loosened ; Peel's generous policy in 1845 had largely contributed to his collapse ; the visitation of 1846 confirmed it. On February 8th, 1847, O'Connell made his last speech in the House of Commons mainly in dumb show ; on May 15th he died at Genoa on his way to Rome. A great political organizer, a superb mob-orator, a devoted son of the Church, it was O'Connell's life-work to dethrone the territorial aristocracy and to crown in their place the Irish priesthood.[1]

Two years before O'Connell's death Peel had sent his " message of peace " to Ireland. Against repeal he was adamant ; but short of repeal there was no concession to Irish sentiment which he was not ready to consider sympathetically. In 1843 he appointed a strong Commission under the chairmanship of the Earl of Devon " to enquire into the state of the law and practice in respect to the

O'Connell and Repeal

Peel's Irish policy

---

[1] *Cf.* for a fine appreciation of O'Connell, Lecky, *Leaders of Public Opinion in Ireland.*

occupation of land in Ireland ". In 1845 the Devon Commission issued a report of first-rate importance, on the strength of which Stanley introduced a Bill recognizing the principle of compensation for unexhausted improvements. It was strenuously opposed and, after reference to a Select Committee, Stanley withdrew the Bill, to be amended and at a more convenient season reintroduced. The season did not recur for a generation.

Irish education   With his educational reforms Peel was more fortunate. He increased the grant for elementary education in 1844, and in the same year by the *Charitable Bequests Act* he made a wise concession to Roman Catholic sentiment. In 1845 he made further provision for Maynooth College—a seminary which had been established in 1795 for the education of Catholic priests. Aided from its inception by the State, the College had, since 1808, received £8,000 a year from the Government. Peel now proposed to make a donation of £30,000 for buildings, and to increase the annual grant to £26,000. To avoid the necessity for an annual discussion of the grant he further proposed to charge it upon the Consolidated Fund. This statesmanlike proposal was assailed with a hurricane of abuse. It blew simultaneously from several quarters : from parsimonious economists willing to vote money to Maynooth, provided the sum was meagre ; from logical secularists who disapproved of all ecclesiastical endowments, and from rigid Protestants who did not object to " endowments " but only to the " endowment of error ". Among the assailants of the Bill were Lord John Russell and Bright ; Macaulay, though supporting the Bill, assailed the minister. But Peel withstood the clamour and his " message of peace " was safely despatched. Unfortunately it failed of its purpose. The increased endowment of Maynooth produced a marked change—not wholly for the better—in the status of the Irish priesthood ; it did not diminish their hostility to England.

The " Godless Colleges "   The same year witnessed the passing of a Bill for the establishment of the Queen's Colleges at Belfast, Cork, and Galway. £100,000 was voted for their establishment and provision was made for an endowment of £21,000 a year. The root principle of the scheme as propounded by Sir James Graham was " the avoidance of all interference positive or negative in all matters affecting the freedom of conscience ". By Anglicans, like Inglis, the proposal was denounced " as a gigantic scheme of Godless education " ; by Roman Catholics as a measure " dangerous to the faith and morals of the people ". Nevertheless, Peel and Graham, cordially supported by the Queen, persisted in their scheme. The Colleges were set up and in 1850 were affiliated into the Queen's University of Ireland. But the scheme was only partially successful. With " undenominational " education the Irish Roman Catholics would have nothing to do ; the Belfast College prospered ; but the Roman Catholics in 1854 established in Dublin a University of their own which cut the ground from under the "Godless" Colleges of Galway and Cork, and, despite many well-meant but doctrinaire attempts, the question of University education in Ireland remained in an unsatisfactory and unsettled condition until 1908.

Before the close of the year 1845 every other question in Ireland The had, as we have seen, to be postponed to the immediate necessity of famine succouring the people from starvation. To this problem Peel and after addressed himself, if not with infallible wisdom, at least with unimpeachable energy. Early in December he purchased, through the Barings, £100,000 worth of maize from the United States and retailed it in Ireland at one penny a pound. He set up relief committees under a central organization in Dublin and devised a scheme for the employment of the people on public works. The usual results ensued. The pay was adequate and the "work" exceedingly attractive to the less strenuous characters. In December, 1846, 276,000 men were thus employed; by March, 1847, the number had risen to 734,000. Meanwhile the ordinary industries were starved of labour; "the fisheries," writes a contemporary, "were deserted and it was often difficult to get a coat patched or a pair of shoes mended". The experiment had palpably failed: other remedies had to be devised; but Peel's responsibility was by this time over; it was left to his successor to solve the problem. Of the many difficulties bequeathed to Lord John Russell none was more insistent.

CHAPTER X

LORD JOHN RUSSELL'S FIRST ADMINISTRATION. THE IRISH FAMINE AND ITS CONSEQUENCES
(1846-1852)

"THE nineteenth century," writes Mr. George Peel, " has witnessed the persistent vengeance of Ireland. We destroyed her manufactures in the eighteenth century ; in the nineteenth she has destroyed our Ministers." It is truly said, and of no Ministry is it more true than the great administration of Sir Robert Peel. His defeat in June, 1846, was due primarily, of course, to a desire for vengeance on the part of the Protectionists ; but it was the Irish Coercion Bill which gave them the chance of glutting it.

Lord John Russell's Ministry

Lord John Russell's Ministry did not differ widely in personnel from that of Lord Melbourne. He himself became First Lord of the Treasury ; Lord Lansdowne led the House of Lords as Lord President of the Council ; Lord Cottenham returned to the Woolsack, from which, in 1850, he retired in favour of Lord Truro ; Lord Palmerston resumed his place at the Foreign Office ; Lord Grey became Secretary for War and the Colonies, and Sir George Grey, Home Secretary ; Sir Charles Wood was Chancellor of the Exchequer, and Sir J. C. Hobhouse (afterwards Lord Broughton) was President of the Board of Control. Other Cabinet offices were filled by Lord Minto (Privy Seal), Lord Auckland (Admiralty), Lord Clarendon (Board of Trade), Lord Campbell (Duchy of Lancaster), Lord Morpeth (Woods and Forests), Lord Clanricarde (Postmaster-General), and Mr. T. B. Macaulay who for a few months was Paymaster of the Forces. The last named and the Lord Chancellor were the only members of the Cabinet who did not succeed to office by the Divine right of Whiggism. Eight of the fifteen were hereditary Peers, and the rest were, with two exceptions, closely connected with the Peerage. But the Ministry as a whole was undeniably rich, both in talent and experience.

The Irish famine and its consequences

Of the many difficulties by which Russell and his colleagues were confronted the most obtrusive was the condition of Ireland, and it may be well, therefore, to review the Irish policy of the new Government before proceeding to other topics. The executive in Ireland was confided to Mr. Labouchere, who had a seat in the Cabinet as Chief Secretary, and Lord Bessborough who succeeded Lord Heytesbury as Lord Lieutenant ; but much of the attention both of the Prime Minister and the Home Secretary was necessarily given to Irish business. The problem was sufficiently perplexing : the peasants had to be at once succoured and coerced : crime and famine were stalking hand in hand throughout the country. With neither peril did the new Ministry deal firmly. Though they had utilized " coercion " to turn out Peel they soon found that without it they dare not face the coming winter in Ireland. They introduced an Arms Bill, but taunted with inconsistency they dropped it, and Lord Bessborough was bidden to do his best with the ordinary law.

It was clear to demonstration that the remedies hitherto devised for a calamity unexampled in extent and severity had completely failed. Lord John therefore determined, in the first place, on a gradual discontinuance of the labour rate. It was costing the Government one million sterling a month, and to the Irish people was doing at least as much harm as good. On August 15th the Act expired, and this disastrous experiment was at an end.

But the Irish Executive were still responsible for feeding a nation. The Prime Minister believed that no permanent remedy could be devised which did not embrace an amendment of the poor law, a radical reform of the land sytem, and a large scheme of emigration. But such a legislative programme would occupy the Imperial Parliament for years, and meanwhile the Irish peasants had, day by day, to be saved, if possible, from death by actual starvation. Russell refused, and very properly, to relax any of the rules against the employment of " public " labour on the improvement of private estates ; but he agreed to advance money to improving landlords on easy terms ; he instructed the Lord Lieutenant to acquire for the Government waste lands, and to sell or let them when reclaimed in plots of moderate size ; he distributed a vast quantity of seed, and attempted to develop the fisheries in the West by the introduction of expert fishcurers from Scotland to give technical instruction to the natives, and by providing them with salt and tackle at cheap rates ; finally he determined to substitute relief by food for relief by labour. So severe and general was destitution that by June, 1847, no less than 3,020,712 persons were daily supported on Government rations. By the autumn of 1847, however, the worst was over ; after the winter of 1847-1848 the famine was at an end.

To succour a starving nation was no light task ; but the famine itself was the least complex of the problems which arose from the failure of the potato. To discuss exhaustively the results of the famine would be to compress into a chapter the history of Ireland during the last half century. But some of the immediate results may be summarized. The mere money cost of the calamity was appalling. In one year, 1846-1847, the loss on the oat crop and the potato crop was estimated at £16,000,000 ; the Irish Board of Works spent some £11,000,000 on relief ; there was a large augmentation of local rates, in addition (of course) to the vast sums lavishly poured out by the Imperial Government, by societies, and by individuals. To the landlords the famine was disastrous. One-third of them were totally ruined, with nothing before them but the cold comfort of the Encumbered Estates Court.

The Encumbered Estates Court

The establishment of this Court was another—almost inevitable—result of the famine. Erected by a statute passed in 1849 it commenced its sittings on October 25th of the same year. The Act gave to the vendor a " simple, short, inexpensive mode of selling and transferring land," and to the purchaser " the advantage of a parliamentary title, impeachable by no jurisdiction and valid in the face of the whole world ". Immediate advantage was taken of the new machinery afforded by the Act. Between October, 1849, and August, 1857, no less than 7,489 new proprietors (of whom 7,180 were Irishmen) obtained a " stake in the country " by this means while the total sum realized by these sales amounted to £20,475,956.[1] The Act was, therefore, far from inoperative, but its results greviously disappointed expectations. The old proprietors were swept away ; the new purchasers bought for profit ; no sentiment intervened to soften the relations between the new men and their tenants ; rents were raised ; defaulters were evicted, and the last state of the peasant was in many cases worse than the first. The final result of the measure was, therefore, to accentuate a difficulty it was intended to mitigate, and to render still more imperative a legalization of customary rights.

Poor Law Amendment Act (1847)

Closely connected with this land legislation was the amendment of the Irish Poor Law.[2] Under the pressure of the famine the administration of relief entirely broke down, and in 1847 the Law itself was amended. Outdoor relief was legalized ; the Boards of Guardians were required to appoint medical and relieving officers; owners were made liable to rates, and the Government took powers to dissolve Boards of Guardians for the non-performance or neglect of duties. On the other hand severe penalties were enacted against mendicants and vagrants, and it was provided—as a further test of destitution—that no occupier of more than a quarter of an acre of land should be entitled to relief.

The Poor Law Amendment Act had one curious result. It gave an additional stimulus to emigration. Between 1846 and 1851 over a million people left the shores of Ireland, and nearly a million died at home. In 1841 the population stood at 8,175,124 ; by 1851 it had fallen to 6,552,385. In the half century between 1831 and 1881 the Irish population decreased by 32 per cent., while that of England and Wales increased 87 per cent. So much for the economic results of the great visitation. It remains to examine its political and social consequences.

"Law and order"

The increase in the amount of serious crime was appalling ; the homicides increased from 170 in 1846 to 212 in 1847 ; firing at the

---

[1] See Sullivan, *New Ireland*, p. 142, quoted ap. O'Brien, *Fifty Years*.
[2] See *supra*, c. vi. p. 10 .

person from 159 in the former year to 264 in the latter, and—most significant of all as proving the political character of the agitation— thefts of arms increased from 611 in 1846 to 1053 in 1847. Murder followed murder with hideous regularity, and the assassins with equal regularity escaped detection. Lord Clarendon who had succeeded Lord Bessborough as Lord Lieutenant, asked the Cabinet in 1847 for further powers. Lord John held back, though his diagnosis of the situation was acute. " As to the source of all this crime," he writes to Clarendon on November 10th, " it is plain that the multitude consider the landlords as enemies to be shot ; the priests denounce them as heretics to be cursed ; and the assassin, having public opinion and what he considered as religion in his favour, has no remorse."

By this time the Parliament which was elected in 1841 had run its course, and in November, 1847, the new Parliament met. Lord John found himself at the head of 325 Liberals ; the Protectionists mustered 226, and the Conservative Free Traders 105. Peel steadily supported the Government who were thus emboldened to pass a stringent coercion Act. The Lord Lieutenant was authorized to proclaim " any disturbed districts, and in such districts to require licences for the carrying of arms, and to increase the police force at the cost of the locality ". Russell insisted, however, that coercion should not stand alone. Hence the Encumbered Estates Bill which, as we have seen, became law in 1849, and a second Bill to afford tenants compensation for improvements, which was thrown out. But, though the roots of disorder might not have been touched, the more distressing symptoms rapidly abated. The assassin began to be detected ; juries began to convict ; the law exacted a semblance of respect, and " the terror which reigned among the innocent was transferred (as a contemporary phrased it) to the guilty. But 1848 was at hand.

It would have been little short of miraculous if the " Year of Revolution " had passed without incident in Ireland. The trend of events had for some time been towards an armed insurrection. Ever since the fatal " Repeal Year " O'Connell had been losing ground ; " Young Ireland " had been coming to the front ; but so far the leader had been lacking. He was at last found in an Irish aristocrat of gentle birth and English breeding. Smith O'Brien was the son of an Irish baronet, a cadet of the Earldom of Thomond, a descendant of Brian Boru. Educated at Harrow and Cambridge he had entered the House of Commons in 1828 as Member for Ennis and, until 1832, gave a general support to the Tory Government. But in 1843 he joined the ranks of the Repealers, and in 1846 he headed a formidable secession and took with him a crowd of visionary enthusiasts, including such men as Thomas Francis Meagher. John Mitchel, and Gavan Duffy. Early in 1847 the Irish Confederation

" Young Ireland " and '48

was inaugurated. Its object was Repeal; its methods constitutional. But events were moving faster than Smith O'Brien. In
February, 1848, the Republic was again proclaimed in France and
the Tone-Fitzgerald farce was revived by Meagher and O'Brien.
Lamartine gave the Irish envoys a chilly welcome. Poet and
idealist though he was, he was also statesman enough to question
the wisdom of bartering the sympathy of England for an alliance
with "Young Ireland".

By this time, however, the movement in Ireland had become
sufficiently obtrusive to compel the English Government to take
action. To put the old treason law into operation against "Young
Irishmen" was to employ a sledgehammer to crush beetles. Early
in 1848, therefore, the Treason-Felony Act was passed and a large
number of offences were removed from the category of treason into
that of treason-felony. Smith O'Brien was arrested, but escaped
conviction through the disagreement of the jury; Mitchel—by far
the most daring and inventive of the confederate leaders—was on
May 27th sentenced to fourteen years' transportation, and deported
to Bermuda. His removal proved to be a fatal blow to the revolutionary party, though its immediate effect was to hurry his associates
into action. On July 21st a "War Directory" of five persons was
appointed in Dublin, and a few days later O'Brien formally raised the
standard of insurrection. The response was almost tragically disappointing. A few half-armed, half-starved peasants enrolled themselves under his banner, and on 29th July they attacked a small body
of police who took up a position in a house near Ballingarry. The
fight that ensued is known to history as the "Battle of Widow
McCormack's cabbage-garden". No great damage was done except
to the cabbages; the peasants dispersed; and within a week O'Brien
was arrested. The executive, meanwhile, had not been idle. Half a
dozen of the chief towns (including Dublin and Cork) with as many
counties had been proclaimed; the Habeas Corpus Act had been
suspended; a vast quantity of arms had been seized, and a proclamation had been issued offering £500 reward for the arrest of
O'Brien. Arrested on August 5th he was tried for high treason and
found guilty, and condemned to be "hanged, drawn, and quartered".
Despite his own protest the sentence was commuted, and he was
transported to Australia; Meagher shared his fate, and the Irish
"48" was at an end. Sonorously tragic in its opening, it had degenerated into farce, and was eventually killed almost as much by
ridicule as by "coercion".

The Queen's visit to Ireland   In August, 1849, Queen Victoria, accompanied by the Prince
Consort and their elder children, paid her first visit to Ireland.
Expensive ceremonial would, under the circumstances, have been an
outrage upon decency. The Queen with characteristic consideration
refused to allow it, and visited Cork, Dublin, and Belfast in her yacht.

The unaffected enthusiasm with which the Royal party was received more than atoned for the absence of ornate preparations and profoundly touched the Queen's heart.[1] The visit, unhappily not repeated for half a century, did something also to obliterate the painful and bitter memories of the last three years. A year later Russell proposed to abolish the Viceroyalty, but yielded somewhat weakly to the clamour which such a proposal inevitably creates. He succeeded, however, in carrying a Bill for a considerable extension of the Irish franchise.

In Ireland, therefore, the Ministry was at last sailing into smoother water. Apart from Ireland political interests centred in Lord Palmerston's conduct of foreign affairs. Before proceeding, however, to that topic it may be well to say something of the progress of affairs at home.

In their financial policy Russell and Sir Charles Wood adhered Finance steadfastly to the principles of Goulburn and Peel. In 1846 they abolished the preference hitherto given to the English Colonies and produced an extra £300,000 for the year's revenue ; but these results, in the view of Lord George Bentinck, were obtained " at a cost of ' imperial ' ruin so great as to be intolerable ".[2]

In producing their Budget for 1847, the Government was confronted by a strangely paradoxical situation. A year of exceptional distress and dislocation had yielded an overflowing revenue. The harvest had failed ; prices were high ; thousands of people had to be kept alive by public and private bounty, yet the Exchequer was full.[3] The cost of the famine for the current year was estimated at £8,000,000 which Wood justifiably raised by a loan obtained at £3 7s. 6d. per cent. The General Election which took place in the late summer of 1847 had little effect upon the balance of parties, but it had a significant bearing upon the fiscal question. The Liberals were in a majority of 99 over the Protectionists, but the balance was held by 105 Peelites. Macaulay lost his seat at Edinburgh owing to his vote on the Maynooth Bill ; but the Tariff Reformers were for the most part triumphantly returned : Villiers and Bright in Lancashire, Cobden for the West Riding.

The year 1847 was, however, less remarkable for a General Elec- The comtion, than for a commercial crisis of unusual severity. The cyclical mercial fluctuation of trade is now a phenomenon of common observation. panic of No one expects a " boom " to be prolonged indefinitely ; the lean 1847 years follow upon the fat with unfailing regularity. In 1847 the phenomenon was relatively unfamiliar and consequently more alarming. Apart from that, the crisis was exceptionally acute. A period of speculation and over-trading was, as usual, followed by stringency in the money market, and ultimately by collapse of credit. Prices

[1] Cf. Q.V.L. ii. 267.   [2] Disraeli, Bentinck, p. 339.
[3] For explanation of the paradox cf. an interesting passage in Northcote, op. cit., p. 83 seq.

fluctuated widely,[1] and the famine intensified the prevailing distress.
But the immediate cause of the crisis was the railway mania. In the
three years, 1844 to 1846, Parliament sanctioned a capital expenditure of £185,000,000, while the railway conpanies were, in November,
1845, anxious to raise no less than £700,000,000 of new capital.[2] No
country in the world could have stood the strain. The smash came
in the autumn of 1847. No fewer than 220 great houses failed, and
the total losses were estimated at £30,000,000. Consols (having
averaged 95¾ in 1846) fell to 78 ; the discount rate rose nominally to
8 per cent., [3] but even at that rate few could get accommodation.
On 25th October, however, the Government authorized the Bank of
England to infringe the terms of their Charter and to issue notes
without the legal reserve in specie. So successful was this action
that confidence was quickly restored, and no indemnity was actually
required.

The alarm of war   The panic of 1848 proceeded from another quarter. Our relations with France were uneasy ; the country believed itself to be
unprepared to resist invasion, and this, combined with the tiresome
war in South Africa, necessitated increased expenditure on armaments. On February 18th the Prime Minister himself introduced
the Budget and proposed to raise the income tax from 7d. to 1s.,
offering in return the abolition of the duty on copper ore. Within
a fortnight, however, the outbreak of the February Revolution in
Paris removed all cause for immediate alarm, and on February 28th
the Chancellor of the Exchequer proposed to drop the additional 5d.
A third edition of the Budget was produced at the end of June, and
a fourth on August 25th. These infirmities of purpose did not add
to the credit of the Government, but, thanks to improving trade,
they muddled through the year without embarrassment to the
Exchequer.

The Chartist Fiasco   Fortune favoured them in another direction. The year 1848 was
a period of anxiety not only in Ireland but in every quarter of continental Europe. The fire lighted in Paris spread with great rapidity.
Italy, Hungary, and Bohemia blazed simultaneously into revolution.
In Rome the Venice Republics were proclaimed ; and thrones tottered
in Vienna and many of the lesser German Courts. In England the
Chartists, quiescent since the collapse of the physical force movement
in 1839, were roused to renewed activity by Feargus O'Connor. They
prepared a gargantuan petition, embodying the " six points," and
organized a monster demonstration to be held in London on April
10th. On April 6th the Home Secretary prohibited the procession
to Palace Yard ; the Duke of Wellington was called in to advise the

[1] Within twelve months the price of wheat rose from 49s. to 102s. and again
fell to 49s. 6d.
[2] Walpole, *op. cit.* iv. 317.
[3] Within the twelve months it had been 3 per cent. and subsequently fell to
4 per cent.

Cabinet on April 8th ; 170,000 special constables were sworn in, and the Duke made adequate but unostentatious preparations to prevent the demonstrators from crossing Westminster Bridge. The wise and kindly precautions of the Government and the Duke saved the situation ; the Chartists drew back ; the monster petition was forwarded to the Palace of Westminster in a cab ; it was found on examination to contain less than half the estimated number of signatures, and many of these were palpably fictitious.[1] The tables were dissolved in laughter, and Chartism ceased to trouble the land. Though its immediate programme was exclusively political, the driving force behind it was economic. For the economic problem Peel had found a solvent, and the banner of Chartism was never again unfolded. Nevertheless, almost the whole of the political programme has now been carried out.

One valuable addition to the Statute-book may be conveniently mentioned here. In 1847 Lord Ashley[2] and Mr. Fielden, a Lancashire cotton-spinner and Member for Oldham, carried a Bill to limit the hours of labour for women and children in textile factories to ten hours. It was, according to one writer, " a victory of the people of England over official England " ;[3] according to another, it represented " the revenge of the landlords upon the manufacturers for reform and free trade ". There is an element of truth in both statements, though neither contains the whole truth. The apostles of *laisser faire* were naturally opposed to State interference with industry ; protectionists and philanthropists welcomed it. The main credit of the achievement was Lord Ashley's, though, in the House of Lords, the Bishops gave him loyal support.

The Manchester School, worsted in 1847, had their revenge in 1849 and 1850. The bottom had already been knocked out of the Navigation Laws by the legislation of the Tory Government of 1823 ;[4] they were finally repealed by the Whigs in 1849. Canada was complaining that the abolition of the Corn Laws rendered their wheat-growers powerless in face of American competition, and Graham roundly asserted that if the Bill were rejected Canada would secede. The Bill was carried without difficulty in the Commons, but in the Lords only by a majority of ten, of whom eight were Bishops. To insist that this measure confirmed the supremacy of Great Britain in the carrying trade is not to impugn the wisdom of those by whom the Navigation Laws were originally enacted ; the infant industry had long since outgrown the need of swaddling-clothes.

Ten Hours Act

Repeal of the Navigation Laws, 1849

---

[1] Among them were the names of the Queen, Prince Albert, Wellington, Russell, and Peel.

[2] Though temporarily without a seat in Parliament his support of the Bill was of incalculable value.

[3] The front Benches were on the whole against the Bill though the Prime Minister voted for it.

[4] See *supra*, pp.

The Australian Colonies Act

A further measure in harmony with the prevailing tenets of the Manchester School was enacted in 1850. New South Wales and other Australian Colonies aspired to the dignity of " responsible " Government attained ten years earlier by Canada. The Act of 1850 conferred upon them general powers enabling them virtually to settle their own form of Government. Acting on this permission New Zealand and New South Wales, together with the daughter Colonies of the latter—Victoria, Tasmania, South Australia, and Queensland —all framed " responsible " constitutions between 1854 and 1859. Western Australia followed suit in 1890.

The Great Exhibition of 1851

Less intrinsically important than these measures, but more immediately striking to the imagination, was the opening of the Great Exhibition of 1851. The initiation and successful completion of this enterprise was mainly due to the Prince Consort, who was a wholehearted disciple of the Manchester School. Of the principles of that school the Exhibition of 1851 was the apotheosis. It was intended not only to promote industry and commerce, but to inaugurate an era of international peace :—

> O ye the wise who think, the wise who reign,
> From growing commerce loose her latest chain,
> And let the fair white-wing'd peacemaker fly
> To happy havens under all the sky,
> And mix the seasons and the golden hours ;
> Till each man find his own in all men's good,
> And all men work in noble brotherhood,
> Breaking their mailed fleets, and armed towers,
> And ruling by obeying Nature's powers,
> And gathering all the fruits of earth and crowned with all her flowers.[1]

It is pathetic to think how soon the dream faded.

The Ministry loses strength

Gratifying as was the success of the Exhibition to the Queen and the Prince Consort ; hopeful, as it seemed, for the future of European peace, it did little to arrest the decay of the Russell Ministry. Conscious of increasing debility, Russell attempted in January, 1849, to induce Sir James Graham to fill the vacancy at the Admiralty caused by the sudden death of Lord Auckland. Graham had already (in 1847) declined the Governor-Generalship of India from Lord John, as he had previously declined it (in 1835) from Peel. He now declined a Peerage and the Admiralty. Chiefly on three grounds : he mistrusted Palmerston's foreign policy, he did not like " coercion " in Ireland, and he was dissatisfied with the progress of " retrenchment " under the Russell Ministry. Even more serious for the Government than the refusal of Graham was the death of Peel (July 2nd, 1850). To say that Peel was their strongest supporter in the House of Commons is to understate the case ; without Peel's favour they could not have survived for a week.

[1] Tennyson, *Ode Sung at the Opening of the International Exhibition.*

Apart from the embarrassment caused to the Ministry and its chief by the independence of Palmerston at the Foreign Office, there were not lacking other elements of weakness. They suffered defeat in the Lords on their Parliamentary Oaths Bill (1849); in finance they gave the impression of not knowing their own mind, an impression strengthened by their conduct of the Budget of 1850; on the subject of parliamentary reform the Prime Minister's own wishes were frustrated by the Cabinet; above all, there was unrest in the Churches.

In ecclesiastical administration Russell was a typical Whig of the eighteenth century. Himself a man of deep and unaffected piety, his ecclesiastical bias was towards Liberal Evangelicanism. But he was primarily an Erastian. Mr. Gorham's successful appeal to the Privy Council (1850) gave him, therefore, genuine pleasure on every ground. Dr. Phillpotts, Bishop of Exeter, had refused to institute Mr. Gorham to a benefice in that diocese on account of his erroneous views on baptismal regeneration. The Court of Arches supported the Bishop; the Privy Council, as ultimate Court of Appeal in ecclesiastical causes, declared in favour of Gorham. By the Tractarians the judgment was bitterly resented. And for two reasons. They questioned the right of a secular Court to pronounce judgment on a question of doctrine, and they disliked the particular doctrine held by Mr. Gorham. The heat engendered by this judgment has not yet entirely evaporated. But it would not be easy to set up a tribunal at once more efficient and more impartial. The Judicial Committee does not presume to decide whether a particular doctrine is false or true; it is merely invested with authority to declare whether such a doctrine is consistent with the formularies of the Established Church. *Ecclesiastical affairs*

The excitement aroused by the Gorham controversy was, however, partial and insignificant compared with the universal ferment into which England was thrown by an act of " Papal aggression ". On September 30th, 1850, Pope Pius IX., now restored to the Vatican by Republican France, issued a Bull dividing England into twelve territorial dioceses. Hitherto the Roman Bishops had been *in partibus*, but Father Wiseman was now created a Cardinal and Archbishop of Westminster, and the other Roman Bishops assumed territorial titles. " The thing itself, in truth, is little or nothing and does not justify the irritation. What has goaded the nation is the manner, insolent and ostentatious, in which it has been done." Thus Palmerston wrote to his brother, and his words described, with absolute precision, the situation. To Lord John the action of the Papacy seemed to be " insolent and insidious "; and the Prime Minister unquestionably represented in this matter the opinions of the great mass of his countrymen. But there was ambiguity in his assertion that the nation looked " with contempt on *The Roman Catholic hierarchy*

11

the mummeries of superstition," and to describe the Tractarians " as unworthy sons of the Church of England " was gratuitously offensive.

Ecclesiastical Titles Act

The alienation of the High Churchmen further weakened the Ministry, but they were strong enough in 1851 to pass the *Ecclesiastical Titles Bill*, which declared the Papal Bull null and void, and imposed heavy penalties on all who attempted to give effect to it. The tactlessness of Pius IX., Cardinal Antonelli, and Cardinal Wiseman was paralleled only by the exaggerated alarm it excited in England. Russell's Act, valuable as a vent to outraged feelings, remained a dead letter until it was quietly repealed in 1871.

The Ministry in dissolution

Meanwhile, the Prime Minister had attempted to escape from a situation of deepening embarrassment. In 1850 Disraeli, who on the death of Lord George Bentinck (1848) had become leader of the Conservative Party in the House of Commons, failed to carry a motion deploring the depression of agriculture only by twenty-one votes. In 1851 the majority against him fell to fourteen, and in the same session Mr. Locke-King carried against the Government, by 100 to 52, a motion for the extension of the county franchise. Thereupon Lord John tendered his resignation to the Queen (Feb. 21st). Lord Stanley refused to form a Cabinet until Russell had tried to effect a coalition with the Peelites. By the Queen's wish Lord John met Lord Aberdeen and Sir James Graham at Buckingham Palace, but the latter declined to make themselves responsible for the *Ecclesiastical Titles Bill*. The negotiations consequently broke down, and upon March 3rd the Russell Cabinet resumed office.

The end, however, was not long postponed. Another overture was made to Graham in September, equally without success ; Palmerston was dismissed from the Foreign Office in December, being succeeded by Lord Granville ; and in February, 1852, Palmerston turned out his late colleagues on a *Militia Bill*. Relations between Russell and Palmerston had become increasingly strained, but the latter administered his " tit for tat " with perfect good humour, and bore his late chief no malice. As Prime Minister Lord John was not a complete success. He was conscientious—almost to a fault—in the discharge of his duties, but keen as was his intellect his physical strength was unequal to the strain of coping with a colleague so masterful in temper, so ebullient in spirits, and so utterly regardless of official decorum as Lord Palmerston. In essential policy the two were not far apart ; in method and in manners they were poles asunder. From the first Russell had encountered many difficulties, and a greater and stronger man might well have failed to surmount them. Parties were in a state of solution ; discipline was relaxed in the House of Commons, and if Russell retained office for six years it was due less to the cohesion of his supporters than the the lack of it among his opponents. His most valuable asset was Peel's loyalty to

Free Trade, and the steady support which that statesman gave to the only Ministry which could maintain it.

Peel's death was a blow to the Government from which ultimate recovery was hopeless, and it was probably a relief to all concerned, not least to the Prime Minister. that its declining years were not unduly prolonged.

CHAPTER XI

GREAT BRITAIN AND CONTINENTAL POLITICS.
LORD PALMERSTON AND QUEEN VICTORIA
(1846-1852)

Foreign
policy,
1846-1852

DURING the administration of Sir Robert Peel foreign affairs were in the background. Lord Aberdeen and Guizot were on terms of exceptional cordiality, and their personal friendship did much to maintain a good understanding between Great Britain and France. So long as the two great Western Powers were friendly, international peace in Europe was not likely, in the middle years of the century, to be seriously endangered. With the return of Lord Palmerston to the Foreign Office all this was speedily changed. Foreign affairs immediately became of primary importance. It is true that the Minister himself repudiated bellicose intentions, and not less true that he was able, in 1851, to boast that " though events have happened in Europe of the most remarkable kind and attended with great commotions of public feeling, and great agitation in the social and political system of the Continent—although events have happened which have brought the interests of England . . . into opposition to the interests of other great and powerful nations, yet at least the fact is that . . . peace has been preserved ".[1] The claim was characteristic and not ill-founded. Nevertheless, the advent of Palmerston to power fluttered the dovecotes in more than one continental capital.

The
Spanish
marriages

Notably in Paris. For the tension which arose between the two countries the Government of King Louis Philippe was, however, almost equally responsible. The question of providing the little Queen Isabella of Spain with a husband had been for some time under discussion. Following the traditional policy of the Bourbons Louis Philippe was anxious to strengthen his dynastic connection with Spain. England objected to the idea of a French Prince becoming Prince Consort, but after an interchange of visits with the French Court in 1844 and 1845, Queen Victoria agreed to the engagement of the Duc de Montpensier, younger son of the French King, to Maria Louisa, younger sister of the Queen of Spain. It was, however, stipulated that the marriage should not take place until after the birth of an heir to the throne of Spain.[2] The young Queen was now (1845) in her sixteenth year ; her mother, the Regent, failing a French Prince, would have preferred a Coburg. Lord Aberdeen promised Guizot that such an alliance should receive no support from England, but in 1846 the Queen-Regent offered the Queen's

[1] Ashley. i. 272.   [2] *Cf.* Aberdeen to Peel ap. *Q.V.L.* ii. 52.

hand to Prince Leopold of Saxe-Coburg, a nephew of the King of the Belgians and a brother of the King of Portugal. Palmerston's mention of Prince Leopold's possible candidature in a Foreign Office despatch gave Louis Philippe a pretext for repudiating his promise, and on October 10th, 1846, the marriage of Queen Isabella to her cousin Don Franciso Duke of Cadiz and of her sister to Montpensier were simultaneously celebrated at Madrid. The Spanish Prince was a man notoriously unfit for marriage, and the news of the shameful proceeding caused the liveliest indignation in England. Not least at Court, for the Queen resented it as a personal breach of faith and deplored it as a wanton destruction of the *entente*. " Guizot's conduct," she wrote, " is beyond *all* belief shameful and so *shabbily* dishonest. . . . My feelings were and are deeply wounded." [1] The Spanish marriage question was, however, of transitory importance. Always unsavoury, and perhaps exaggerated at the moment, it lost whatever significance it ever possessed after the fall of the Orleanist dynasty in France.

The politics of the West quickly reacted on the East. The rupture of the Anglo-French *entente* gave Austria the opportunity, with the cordial assent of her Eastern neighbours, of extinguishing the independence of Cracow, the last remnant of free Poland. Against this annexation Lord Palmerston protested in vain. *(Austrian annexation of Cracow)*

In regard to Portugal, however, the Western Powers were still able to act in accord. Matters had not settled down in that unhappy country.[2] In May, 1846, the Miguelists again raised an insurrection, and only by the aid of an English fleet, acting in conjunction with the fleets of France and Spain, was the authority of Queen Maria and the ascendancy of the Constitutional party restored (1847). But for Palmerston's prompt intervention Queen Maria would have owed her restoration to Spain, and a severe check would have been concurrently administered to liberal principles and to English commerce. A project launched about this time for the eventual fusion of Portugal and Spain was sternly resisted by the English Minister.[3] *(Affairs in Portugal)*

Equally effective was his action in reference to the Swiss *Sonderbund*. Between 1830 and 1848 Switzerland was in a condition of perpetual unrest, and there seemed little probability that the Confederation would hold together. In 1832 the Union was threatened by the " progressive " cantons who formed the *Siebener Konkordat*, to secure the sanctity of their reformed constitution. In 1843 the seven Roman Catholic and more conservative cantons retaliated with the *Sonderbund*. The *Sonderbund* stood for religious education, the retention of the Jesuits, the maintenance of the monasteries, and the sanctity of the federal Pact of 1815. The conservative cantons could *(The Swiss Sonderbund, 1843-1847)*

---

[1] To King Leopold of Belgium, *Q.V.L.* ii. 128, 129, and *cf. passim*, vol. ii. chaps. xiii. xiv. xv

[2] See *supra*, p. 124.   [3] Ashley, i. 18-20.

count on the strong support of Metternich, with whose views Russia,
Prussia, and Sardinia were in full accord. Guizot and Louis Philippe
inclined in the same direction. English opinion, on the contrary,
was strongly influenced by Grote's letters to the *Spectator*, in favour
of the " progressive " cantons. Palmerston saw his opportunity of
paying off Louis Philippe for the Spanish trick, and Metternich for
the annexation of Cracow. His anxiety was twofold : to prevent
the intervention of the reactionary Courts in Switzerland, and to
secure the final expulsion of the Jesuits. He played his game with
consummate skill. He kept the ring for the Protestant cantons,
warded off the interference of the Powers, and he had the satisfaction
of seeing the forces of unionism and progress completely triumphant
(Nov. 1847). The *Sonderbund* was dissolved : the federal union was
consolidated, and Switzerland was finally delivered from the dangers
of foreign interference.

The year
of revolu-
tion

The *Sonderbund* episode served to intensify the mistrust felt by
Palmerston for the continental Courts—particularly that of Austria.
The moment was fast approaching when the Hapsburg dominions
were to pass through the revolutionary furnace. On every side they
were vulnerable : in Hungary, Bohemia, above all, perhaps in Italy.
Palmerston gauged to a nicety the situation in Italy, and in 1847
he despatched Lord Minto on a special mission to warn the Italian
Sovereigns of the coming cataclysm, and to advise them to avert

Italy in
1848

revolution by timely reforms. " You are instructed to say " (he
wrote to the English representatives at the Italian Courts) " that the
direction of the progress of reform and improvement is still in the
hands of the Sovereign, but that it is now too late for them to attempt
to obstruct reasonable progress " (Jan. 1848). " Yield to-day that
which is reasonably asked, and resist to-morrow that which you will
be borne out in resisting, but do not let us put ourselves in the wrong
to-day merely for fear that we may find ourselves in the right to-
morrow." [1] Nor must reform be obstructed, should the Sovereigns
decide to initiate it, by outside interference. In making this claim
on their behalf Palmerston showed himself the true disciple of
Castlereagh and Canning.

The Italian Sovereigns were not wholly inattentive to his advice.
In January King Ferdinand granted a constitution to the two
Sicilies ; the Grand Duke of Tuscany followed suit in February, and
early in March constitutions were established in Piedmont and in
Rome. But news had by this time reached Italy which caused all
thought of mere constitutional reform to be flung aside. The flood-
gates of revolution burst open in Paris. Louis Philippe pusillani-
mously abdicated on February 24th, and France proclaimed the
Second Republic. In March the waters reached Vienna ; revolutions
broke out in Austria. Hungary, Bohemia. and many parts of Germany;

---

[1] Palmerston to Minto ap. Ashley, i. 8.

Metternich himself was driven into exile. The news aroused the
greatest enthusiasm among Italian Liberals. Before the end of
March the Austrians were compelled to evacuate Milan ; Venice re-
established the republic under Daniel Manin ; Metternich's puppets
fled from their thrones in Modena and Parma ; Charles Albert,
King of Sardinia, placed himself at the head of the national movement ; the Grand Duke of Tuscany joined him ; even Ferdinand of
Naples was obliged to simulate adherence to the movement ; Lombard,
Venice, Parma, Piacenza, Modena declared by plebiscite for fusion
with Sardinia ; the union of North Italy, under the hegemony of
Sardinia, seemed in the twinkling of an eye to have been achieved.

The Italian *risorgimento* had no more cordial friend than England.[1] England
Palmerston favoured from the first the formation of an Italian federa- and the
tion, one unit of which should be a large North Italian Kingdom, move-
stretching from the Alps to the Adriatic, under the House of Savoy. ment
As for the Hapsburg Empire, he believed that it would be strengthened
rather than weakened by the surrender of the Italian provinces.
" I cannot regret," he wrote to the King of the Belgians, " the
expulsion of the Austrians from Italy. . . . Her rule was hateful to
the Italians and has long been maintained only by an expenditure of
money and an exertion of military effort which left Austria less able
to maintain her interests elsewhere. Italy was to her the heel of
Achilles, and not the shield of Ajax. The Alps are her natural
barrier and her best defence." [2] To Austrian rule elsewhere he was
no enemy : " North of the Alps we wish her all the prosperity and
success in the world ".[3] The Prime Minister shared the views of
the Foreign Secretary, though he expressed them with more reserve ;
to the Court, however, they were anathema. On July 1st, 1848, the
Queen wrote to Palmerston : " She cannot conceal from him that
she is ashamed of the policy which we are pursuing in this Italian
controversy ".[4] For one thing Queen and Ministers were alike
obviously unprepared—the remarkable recovery of the Hapsburg
power in Italy. On March 23rd, 1849, Charles Albert's last army
was crushed by Radetsky at Novara ; in August, Venice surrendered ;
the vassal Princes were once more restored in Central Italy ; the
Roman Republic had fallen before the assault of France in July ;
Pius IX. was restored to the Vatican ; King Ferdinand, or " Bomba "
as his subjects called him, was once more supreme in the two Sicilies.
On every side the revolutionary movement collapsed, and for another
decade the triumph of Austrian absolutism in Italy was assured.
Despite his strong sympathy for the Italian cause, and indeed for

[1] This fact has always been recognized in Italy itself, and the evidence has
lately been marshalled with great skill by Mr. W. R. Thayer, *Life and Times of
Cavour*, London, 1911.

[2] June 15th, 1848, Ashley, i. 98.

[3] To Ponsonby at Vienna, July 31st, 1848.

[4] *Q.V.L.* ii. 215, and *passim*, c. xvii.

that of " oppressed nationalities," wherever they were to be found, Palmerston preserved the formal neutrality of England with tolerable success. " Every post," he writes, " sends me a lamenting Minister throwing himself and his country upon England for help which I am obliged to tell him we cannot afford him." Nevertheless, the Woolwich Arsenal was permitted to supply the Sicilian insurgents indirectly with arms, and Palmerston allowed himself the luxury of pouring out his soul to a somewhat unsympathetic Ambassador at Vienna. " The Austrians," he wrote to Ponsonby (Sept. 9th, 1849), " are really the greatest brutes that ever called themselves by the undeserved name of civilized men. Their atrocities in Galicia, in Italy, in Hungary, in Transylvania are only to be equalled by the proceedings of the negro race in Africa and Haiti. . . . I do hope that you will maintain the honour and dignity of England by expressing *openly* and *decidedly* the disgust which such proceedings excite in the public mind in this country." [1] Small wonder that such vehemence excited the alarm of Palmerston's Royal mistress ; with the people, however, his popularity steadily increased.

The " judicious bottle-holder " The Minister was not content with words. He encouraged the Sultan to refuse to surrender Kossuth and other Hungarian refugees who had escaped into Turkey, and when the latter was threatened with war by Austria and Russia, he ordered the British fleet up to the Dardanelles. The French Republic acted in concert with Great Britain ; but, with or without allies, Palmerston was " resolved to support Turkey, let who will be against her in this matter ". He was prepared even for war, though he did not anticipate it. The despatch of the fleet " was, for the Sultan, like holding a bottle of salts to the nose of a lady who had been frightened ".[2] The bold policy was successful. But the pace set by Palmerston was becoming too hot for his colleagues. Neither to their qualms, however, nor to those of the Queen did he pay much heed. He regarded the Foreign Office as his *peculium*, and all intruders were politely warned off. The Prime Minister, though sympathetic in the main towards his colleague's policy, found it impossible to defend his methods. The Queen detested the end no less than the means. By Palmerston himself her remonstrances were ignored : Lord John, though no courtier, could not and did not treat them so lightly. He felt indeed, and told Palmerston, that the Queen's " uneasiness was not always groundless," and by the spring of 1850 he had made up his mind to remove his impetuous lieutenant from the Foreign Office.[3] His intention, however, was frustrated partly by the attack made upon the foreign policy of the Government by the Opposition leaders, and still more by Palmerston's superb vindication of it in the House of Commons, a vindication which put him on a pedestal of popularity.

[1] Ashley, i. 139. [2] To Lord Normanby, October 23rd, 1849.
[3] Walpole, *Russell*, ii. 43-48.

To that popularity nothing contributed more powerfully than *Civis Romanus Sum* Palmerston's enforcement of the claims of two British subjects against the corrupt and dilatory Government of Greece. At the hands of that Government, Mr. Finlay, the eminent historian, and Don Pacifico, a Portuguese Jew born in Gibraltar, had suffered unquestionable wrong. That Pacifico's own record was none of the best mattered nothing to the Foreign Secretary. Equally with Mr. Finlay he was a British subject ; his repeated and just demands for redress had been ignored at Athens. Lord Palmerston's own efforts were similarly vain, and he determined, therefore, to instruct the British Admiral " to take Athens on his way back from the Dardanelles ". Russia resented the pressure thus put upon King Otho, the *enfant gâté de l'absolutisme* ; the French President sulked, was offended by the refusal of his offer of mediation, and withdrew his Ambassador, Droun de Lhuys, from London. But Palmerston went on his way unheeding and quickly achieved the desired end. Not even in England were his methods universally approved. In the House of Lords Lord Stanley moved :—

" That while the House fully recognizes the right and duty of the Government to secure to her Majesty's subjects residing in foreign states the full protection of the laws of those states, it regrets to find . . . that various claims against the Greek Government, doubtful in point of justice or exaggerated in amount, have been enforced by coercive measures directed against the commerce and people of Greece and calculated to endanger the continuance of our friendly relations with other powers." Supported by Lord Aberdeen and Lord Brougham, the motion was carried by a majority of thirty-seven. In the Commons, on the contrary, a vote of confidence was carried, after four nights' debate, by a majority of forty-six. That result, was primarily due to Lord Palmerston's own speech. Holding the attention of the House for no less than four hours, the Minister offered an elaborate vindication of his whole work at the Foreign Office. In turn he passed in review his action in regard to Greece, Portugal, Spain, Switzerland, and Italy, defended the principles which could be traced throughout it, and challenged a verdict on the policy as a whole. One at least of his points was incontrovertible. " While we have seen thrones shaken, shattered, levelled, institutions overthrown and destroyed—while in almost every country of Europe the conflict of civil war has deluged the land with blood . . . this country has presented a spectacle honourable to the people of England and worthy of the admiration of mankind." Nor could his concluding question fail of its effect : " whether, as the Roman in the days of old held himself free from indignity when he could say ' *Civis Romanus sum*,' so also a British subject, in whatever land he may be, shall feel confident that the watchful eye and the strong arm of England will protect him against injustice and wrong ? " Peel, in the last speech he ever delivered, declared that Palmerston's speech " has made us all proud of him ". Lord John felicitously described him as " Minister of England ". He himself confessed to his brother that he had become " the most popular man that for a very long course of time " had held the Foreign Office.

The Queen's Memorandum

Lord Palmerston's triumph, though complete, was short-lived. Rhetoric might sway the House of Commons ; it had no effect whatever on the judgment of the Queen. She resented the Minister's treatment of the Crown ; she deplored his diplomatic methods ; and she profoundly mistrusted his aims. In particular she complained, and with reason, that the Minister gave her no time to master the contents of Despatches which she was called upon to approve. Palmerston, on his side, treated the Queen much as an old family solicitor is apt to treat a young lady client : her perusal and approval were to be taken for granted. The Queen's conception of her plain duty was diametrically opposed to this. She repeatedly complained not only to the Foreign Secretary, but to the Prime Minister. Neither to her remonstrances nor to his Chief's did Palmerston pay the least attention. The Queen urged his removal from the Foreign Office, and Russell acquiesced, but the issue of the Debate on June 29th warned him of the futility of attempting it at the moment. On July 28th the Queen again complained that " there is no question of delicacy and danger in which Lord Palmerston will not arbitrarily and without reference to his colleagues or Sovereign engage this country ". Ultimately, on August 12th, the Queen drafted a formal memorandum explaining " what it is she expects from her Foreign Secretary ". " She requires (1) That he will distinctly state what he proposes in a given case, in order that the Queen may know as distinctly to *what* she has given her Royal sanction ; (2) Having *once given* her sanction to a measure, that it be not arbitrarily altered or modified by the Minister ; such an act she must consider as failing in sincerity towards the Crown, and justly to be visited by the exercise of her constitutional right of dismissing that Minister. She expects to be kept informed of what passes between him and the Foreign Ministers before important decisions are taken, based upon that intercourse ; to receive the foreign despatches in good time, and to have the drafts for her approval sent to her in sufficient time to make herself acquainted with their contents before they must be sent off." [1]

Lord Palmerston professed penitence, promised amendment, and went on precisely as before. In the autumn General Haynau, an Austrian soldier who had earned a reputation for exceptional cruelty in Hungary, was mobbed and hooted in London by the draymen when he was visiting the brewery of Messrs. Barclay and Perkins. Palmerston had to apologize to the Austrian Ambassador, Baron Koller, but could not refrain from an expression of his opinion that

[1] *Q.V.L.* ii. 315.

Haynau's visit was " a wanton insult to the people of this country ". The Queen was seriously annoyed, and told the Minister that she could " as little approve of the introduction of lynch law in this country as of the violent vituperations with which Lord Palmerston accuses and condemns public men in other countries . . . without having the means of obtaining correct information or of sifting evidence ". The rebuke was a stinging one, but no candid person can affirm that it was unmerited. As spokesman of Great Britain among the nations Palmerston had great merits, and under a strong Prime Minister they might have been less obviously balanced by defects. As it was, the task of correction fell too often to the Crown, and the Crown cannot permit repeated warnings to be disregarded without loss of dignity. It was unfortunate that on the merits of the disputes between himself and the Court the Foreign Secretary was more often right than wrong. In regard to Italy, as in regard to Schleswig-Holstein and other questions, the Queen's views were indubitably biassed by personal and dynastic considerations. Of these Palmerston was not unnaturally intolerant, but no degree of certainty as to the unassailable correctness of his own attitude can justify Palmerston's disrespectful treatment of the Crown. Some part of his irritation was doubtless due to the fact that there was a Prince Consort behind the Throne, and behind the Prince a Baron Stockmar. It is true also that the Queen had not yet accumulated the experience which proved so valuable to her Ministers in the later years of her reign; but her grasp of European politics was already firm, and, apart from this, she had certain constitutional rights in regard to the conduct of foreign affairs which no Minister was at liberty to ignore.

Nor was Palmerston more complacent towards his colleagues and his Chief than towards the Sovereign. Throughout 1850 and 1851 there was increasing friction between the Prime Minister and the Foreign Secretary. It came to a head in October, 1851, when Kossuth, the leader of the Hungarian revolution, landed in England. It was announced that he was to be received by Lord Palmerston. Lord John insisted that the proposed interview would be " improper and unnecessary ", and in plain terms interdicted it. Palmerston hotly retorted : " I do not choose to be dictated to as to whom I may or may not receive in my own house ". The Cabinet supported the Premier, and Palmerston gave way ; but a few weeks later he received a Radical deputation which presented him with an address in which the Emperors of Austria and Russia were referred to as " odious and detestable assassins ". Not unnaturally, the Queen was intensely annoyed ; but the Premier, though he could not justify his colleague, still hesitated to dismiss him.

At last, however, even Lord John's forbearance was exhausted, or perhaps his timidity was overcome. News reached London on

The *Coup* December 3rd, 1851, of the military *coup d'état* by which Prince
d'état of Louis Napoleon virtually overthrew the Second Republic,[1] dissolving
Prince
Louis Na- the chambers by armed force and crushing their supporters at the
poleon barricades with ruthless severity. The Queen, learning of it on the
(Dec.
1851) 4th, enjoined the strictest neutrality ; the Prime Minister concurred,
and instructions in this sense were sent by the Foreign Office to
Lord Normanby.[2] The latter learned, however, from the French
Foreign Minister that Palmerston had already expressed approval of
the *coup d'état* to Count Walewski,[3] an approval which naturally
rendered his own position difficult. He embodied the facts in a
despatch which ultimately came before the Queen and the Prime
Minister. The latter entirely associated himself with the Queen's
displeasure, dismissed Palmerston from the Foreign Office, and, with
the Queen's cordial approval, appointed in his place Lord Granville.
A curiously incongruous offer of the Vice-royalty of Ireland was
caustically declined by Palmerston.

The matter has been endlessly discussed, but the facts are no
longer in dispute. It is clear that Palmerston cordially approved
the *coup d'état*—partly on the principle of self-defence, partly on the
ground that the existing constitution of France was unworkable ; it
is clear also that, while instructing Normanby to maintain a neutral
attitude in Paris, he allowed the French Government to know his
own opinion without reserve. That Normanby had grave cause for
complaint against the Foreign Secretary is certain. That Palmerston
had cause for complaint against Normanby is also probable. On
April 16th, 1850, Louis Napoleon said to Lord Malmesbury, a visitor
in Paris : " Your Ambassador, Lord Normanby, is intriguing against
me, although his Chief, Lord Palmerston, and some of your Cabinet
Ministry are in my favour. I believe Lord Normanby carries on a
private correspondence with Prince Albert to my detriment." [4] That
some of his colleagues, including the Prime Minister, shared his
opinions and were partners in his indiscretion was publicly affirmed
by Palmerston and not denied by them. But it is also true that in
such a matter a peculiar responsibility attaches to the Foreign
Secretary, and it can hardly be denied that the Queen had a fair
pretext for insisting on his dismissal.

Her own delight at the issue was unbounded. " I have the
greatest pleasure," she wrote to King Leopold, " in announcing to
you a piece of news which I know will give you as much satisfaction
and relief as it does to us and will do to the whole world. *Lord
Palmerston is no longer Foreign Secretary.*" [5] The Queen's pleasure

---

[1] The formal overthrow was a year later, December 1852.

[2] Our Ambassador in Paris.

[3] French Ambassador in London. He was an illegitimate son of Napoleon I.
and a great confidant of his nephew.   [4] See Malmesbury, *Memoirs*, p. 192,

[5] See on the whole matter Ashley, *Palmerston*, i. c. vii. ; *Q.V.L.* ii. c. xx. ;
Martin, *Life of Prince Consort*, ii. c. xliv. ; Walpole, *Russell*, ii. c. xxii. ; Argyll.
Autobiography, i. 348.

was shared at many Courts, particularly at Vienna. Schwarzenberg gave a ball, and an English attaché wrote : "these arrogant fools here actually think that *they* have overthrown Lord Palmerston ". German opinion was not unfairly reflected in the doggerel lines :—

> Hat der Teufel einen Sohn
> So ist er sicher Palmerston.

The whole matter gave rise to formal explanations in the House of Commons. The French *coup d'état* was not popular in England ; military plots are rightly disliked in a constitutional country ; the revelation of the Queen's Memorandum gave the Prime Minister a temporary—perhaps an unfair—advantage ; Palmerston, with some chivalry, declined a retort, and his reply was consequently ineffective and ill-received.[1] But, as already recorded, Russell's triumph was brief. For about two months he was master on his own quarter-deck, but in the first breeze the ship itself foundered.

The *coup d'état* induced a great deal of uneasiness in England ; a military monarchy led by unscrupulous men had replaced the weak republic ; the national defences were notoriously defective, and Russell, therefore, on February 16th, proposed a scheme for the reorganization of the militia. Palmerston carried an amendment to the Bill, the Ministry was left in a minority, and, treating the vote as one of no-confidence, resigned on February 20th.
Resignation of the Russell Ministry, Feb. 20th, 1852

The Queen called upon Lord Derby to form a Government. His party was in a clear minority in the House of Commons ; it had no assured majority in the Lords, and its leaders, after twenty years of Whig and Peelite administration, were entirely lacking in official experience. It was natural, therefore, that Lord Derby should look for help to the man who had turned out the late Government. Palmerston, however, would not join him " on account of Protection," [2] and Derby, therefore, had to rely exclusively upon inexperienced Conservatives. Lord Malmesbury succeeded Lord Granville at the Foreign Office, Sir John Pakington became Colonial Secretary, Mr. Walpole went to the Home Office. The Duke of Northumberland took the Admiralty and Lord St. Leonards the Woolsack. Lord Lonsdale who became Lord President of the Council and Mr. Herries who was President of the Board of Control were with their Chief the only Ministers who had ever held Cabinet office before. But of the new appointments incomparably the most interesting was that of Disraeli, who became Chancellor of the Exchequer and leader of the House of Commons. Well might Sir James Graham " give his grave head a portentous shake when he spoke of the novel precedent of a whole cargo of the rank and file
The first Derby Ministry, Feb. to Dec. 1852

His apologia is to be found in Ashley, i. c. vii. As usual it is strong on the merits of the case, but less conclusive as a reply to the criticism of the Queen and Russell.

[2] The phrase is Lord Malmesbury's. *Memoirs*, p. 229.

being carried down to Windsor to be made members of the Privy Council, before they could receive the seals of office ".[1] " All kinds of jokes," wrote Lord Malmesbury, " were made in respect of our being such novices in office." [2] Lord Derby himself referred to his team of young horses : " not one had ever been in harness before, and they went beautifully ; not one kicked among them ".[3]

Militia Bill
The new Government was clearly a makeshift ; an appeal to the country could not be long delayed ; and, until the constituencies had declared themselves, it was agreed that the policy of the Government, fiscal and otherwise, should be conceived, as far as possible, on non-controversial lines. Supported by Palmerston they passed with ease, to the chagrin of Russell, an Act for the reorganization of the militia. The scheme differed from the rejected scheme put forward by Russell in two respects : the new force was to be national instead of local, and it was to be recruited by voluntary enlistment, the compulsory ballot being reserved as a last resort.

Disraeli's first Budget
Disraeli's first essay as Chancellor of the Exechequer was eagerly awaited. His Budget, however, was framed necessarily on conventional lines : he renewed the income tax for twelve months, but for reasons stated above made no attempt to revive protectionist principles. Disraeli's own statement won the unstinted applause of the Free Traders who accepted it as a triumphant vindication of the policy pursued during the last ten years.

The General Election
The Parliament elected in 1847 was dissolved on July 2nd, 1852, but the General Election made little change in the balance of parties. In the new Parliament the Whigs and Radicals numbered 319, the Tories between 290 and 300, and the Peelites 40-50. Parliament met on November 4th, but the mind of the nation was set not on the vicissitudes of parties, nor on political conflicts, but on doing the last honours, with hearts unisoned by the sense of a national sorrow, to one who was always above the common party turmoil.

Death of the Duke of Wellington
On November 18th, the Iron Duke, who had died on September 14th, was laid to rest in St. Paul's Cathedral. The Sovereign and her people mourned in common for one who had served devotedly both Queen and country. Truly was the great Duke buried " with an Empire's lamentation " ; " to the noise of the mourning of a mighty nation ". " No man," wrote Lord Palmerston, " ever lived or died in the possession of a more unanimous love, respect, and esteem." Greville, who was no respecter of persons, noted the deference which all men paid to one who occupied a place unique among his countrymen. This tribute was due not only to the conqueror of Napoleon. but to one who in council was recognized,

---

[1] Argyll, *Memoirs*, i. 361
[2] Malmesbury, p. 234.
[3] " A very sorry Cabinet," was the Queen's description of it.—*Q.V.L.* ii. 450.

despite obvious limitations, as having a single eye to his Sovereign's and his country's interest :—

> Our greatest, yet with least pretence,
> Great in council and great in war,
> Foremost captain of his time,
> Rich in saving common-sense,
> And, as the greatest only are,
> In his simplicity sublime.

The elections had given no encouragement to Protection, and on November 11th, Disraeli announced that the principle was to be decently interred. For the militant Free Traders this was not enough. They demanded from the Derby Ministry not merely abandonment but recantation. On November 23rd Villiers proposed a motion to extort it, but Palmerston intervened, and the House contented itself with a pious affirmation of the principle. Protection, as Disraeli said, was not only dead but damned. But the respite secured to the Ministry by Lord Palmerston was of short duration. On December 3rd Disraeli submitted his Budget to the House of Commons. Protection was dead, but Peel's most bitter assailant felt it incumbent upon him to do something for the mourners. His scheme was highly ingenious and his exposition of it masterly. He proposed to conciliate the general consumer by gradual remission of half the tea duty ; to help farmer and consumer alike by remitting half the malt tax ; to assess income tax on one-third of the farmer's rental instead of one-half ; to distinguish between " earned " and " unearned income " by extending the downward limit to £100 of the former and £50 of the latter. He calculated that the readjustment of the income tax would make little difference in the yield, but the remissions of tea duty and malt tax were to be off-set by an extension of the house tax to houses assessed at £10 a year and the raising of the rate from 9d. to 1s. 6d. in the £. On this last proposal he was defeated, and Lord Derby's spirited but short-lived enterprise came to an end (Dec. 20th, 1852).

The end of Protection

CHAPTER XII

THE COALITION AND THE CRIMEAN WAR

(1852-1855)

The Coalition Ministry

IT was not difficult to get rid of Lord Derby and Disraeli ; it was less easy to replace them. The Whig party did not possess a majority ; still less did the Conservatives ; but the latter had buried Protection ; and there seemed, therefore, no adequate reason why the breach of 1846 should not be healed and why the Peelites should not join forces with Lord Derby. Had they done so, it is not impossible that the Crimean War might have been avoided. They preferred, however, coalition with the Whigs. But who was to form and lead their new Ministry ? Lord John was the acknowledged leader of the largest section of the House of Commons, but there can be no doubt that in rejecting his claim the Crown represented an all but universal sentiment. " Lord John will never again unite us, take my word for this." So Roebuck wrote to Graham.[1] Palmerston " could feel no confidence in his discretion or judgment as a political leader and could place no trust in his steady fidelity as a colleague ". The Queen, interpreting the situation with her unfailing discrimination, summoned two veteran Peers, Lord Lansdowne and Lord Aberdeen. The former was prevented by illness from obeying the summons, and Lord Aberdeen, yielding to the strong wishes of the Sovereign, of his friends, and of Lord Lansdowne himself, agreed to form a coalition Government. " The arrangement of offices under the Junction company has been very difficult." Thus wrote Lord John to Lord Panmure.[2] That it was so was due primarily to the indecision, the caprice, and vanity of Russell himself.[3] Had he declined to take any part in a Government of which he was not to be the head, his position would have been both honourable and intelligible. That it would have been highly embarrassing to the Sovereign, to his colleagues, and to the country must be admitted. Nor could he fail to perceive it. He had sufficient magnanimity to accept the sacrifice involved in the surrender of the Premiership, but not enough ever to forget that he had made it. His vacillation tried even the patience of Aberdeen. Now he would stand aside altogether ; now he would take the Foreign Office with the lead of the Commons ;[4] now he would lead without

Attitude of Lord John Russell

---

[1] Graham, ii. 161.

[2] *Panmure Papers*, i. 37.

[3] Gladstone speaks of his conduct in Cabinet as " most capricious and unhappy " (Morley, i. 450), and Morley also quotes a notable opinion by Sir F. Baring.

[4] Despite his assurance to Graham, August, 1852 : " I could not be leader in the House of Commons for a peer-premier ".

portfolio. Eventually he took the Foreign Office on the understanding that when Parliament met he would surrender it to Lord Clarendon. This arrangement was carried out, and Lord John retained his seat in the Cabinet and the leadership of the House, without portfolio. Such a solution of the difficulty was open to grave constitutional objection, and the Queen was not alone in resenting it. The Sovereign bluntly expressed to Lord John himself her displeasure that " so important an innovation in the construction of the Executive Government should have been practically decided upon by arrangement intended to meet personal wants under peculiar and accidental circumstances ".[1] Nor is it possible to assert that the rebuke, though severe, was undeserved. In striking contrast to the attitude of Russell was that of Palmerston who cheerfully accepted the Home Office and did admirable work there. The other Secretaryship of State—Colonies and War—went to a Peelite, the Duke of Newcastle, and the same group supplied a Secretary at War (Mr. Sidney Herbert), a Chancellor of the Exchequer (Gladstone), a First Lord of the Admiralty (Sir James Graham), and a Privy Seal, in the person of the young Duke of Argyll. In all, therefore, the Peelites secured six places in the Cabinet, including the Premiership. The Whigs got six—Lord Lansdowne, without portfolio, Lord Granville (President of the Council), Lord Cranworth (Chancellor), Sir Charles Wood (Board of Control), Lord John Russell and Sir William Molesworth (Commissioner of Works). The last named was regarded as the solitary representative of the Radical left wing ; while the thirteenth member—Palmerston—stood, in a party sense, alone.

The new Cabinet was exceptionally rich—perhaps over-rich—in administrative capacity, and several men of first-rate ability, notably Mr. Cardwell, had necessarily to be content with subordinate office, but it may be questioned whether their aggregate strength was at all equal to the sum of their individual capacities. " It is a powerful team," said Graham, " but it will require good driving. There are some odd tempers and queer ways among them, but on the whole they are gentlemen, and they have a perfect gentleman at their head, who is honest and direct and who will not brook insincerity in others." [2] The Duke of Argyll bears testimony to the fact that of all the Cabinets in which he sat none " worked more smoothly or with less individual friction ".[3] But England, as Disraeli shrewdly said, does not love coalitions, and the record of the Coalition of 1852 did not tend to enhance her affection.

A measure for the better Government of India (1853) brought Gladstone's first Budget a stage nearer the final substitution of the Crown for the Company, and threw open to public competition the Indian Civil Service. A get Bill for removing Jewish disabilities was carried through the

Commons, though it was rejected in the Lords, but the outstanding feature of the session of 1853 was Gladstone's first Budget.

This remarkable Budget was, in the first instance, unfolded to his Cabinet colleagues in " a conversational exposition which endured without a moment's interruption for more than three hours ". Well might the Duke of Argyll refer to this performance as " by far the most wonderful effort that I ever listened to from the lips of man ".[1] Gladstone's close and pellucid argument carried conviction to his colleagues just as a week later (April 18th) it compelled the admiring assent of the House of Commons. For nearly five hours the great orator held the rapt attention of the House while he expounded the boldest financial scheme submitted to Parliament since the days of Peel.

It was, primarily, an Income Tax Budget. The tax renewed for twelve months by Disraeli was about to expire. Ought it to be renewed at all, and if so, under what conditions ? There was a strong agitation in favour of a differentiation in the rate of the tax according to the source of the income. Gladstone had himself inclined originally to this view, and his first business in connection with the Budget was to convince himself that such differentiation would be destructive of the vital principle of the tax. His second business was to convince the Cabinet ; his third to convince the Commons. In all three tasks he was triumphantly successful. He admitted the grave defects of the income tax : its irregularity ; its unpopularity ; its inquisitorial character, and the temptations it offered to fraud. If the House bade him, he could and he would renounce it altogether, but he besought them " not to nibble at it " ; to retain it, if at all, " in a state in which it will be fit for service in an emergency ". For such emergencies it ought, in his view, to be reserved, and not to be regarded as a " permanent portion of our ordinary financial system ". He proposed, therefore, to renew it for seven years—for two years at 7d., for a further two at 6d., for three years at 5d.—and to look forward to its final extinction on April 5th, 1860. Meanwhile, he refused to differentiate between the sources of income ; he extended the tax to incomes between £150 and £100 a year (at the 5d. rate throughout), and he brought Ireland into the mesh. This was the first keynote of the Budget scheme. The second was the extension of the legacy duty to real property passing by Will, and to both personality and reality passing under Settlement. A third was an increase of the duty on Scotch and Irish spirits, and a revision of certain trade licenses. From all these sources Gladstone anticipated a surplus of some £2,000,000, and, counting on this, he proceeded to a bold application of the principles he had learnt from Peel. He took 123 articles out of the customs tariff altogether, and he reduced the duty on 133 more, notably that

[1] *Autobiography*, 422-423.

on tea (from 2s. 2¼d. to 1s. per lb.). He forgave Ireland the famine-
debt of £4,500,000 ; he repealed the excise duty on soap ; he reduced
the tax on life assurance from 2s. 6d. to 1s. per £100, and simplified
many other taxes and duties.

This Budget debate afforded, as a colleague justly remarks, " one
of those rare occasions on which a really fine speech not only decides
the fate of a Government, but enlightens the mind of a people and
determines for an indefinite time to come the course of national
legislation ".[1] In one sense Gladstone's scheme never got its chance.
He budgeted for seven years of peace, and assumed that no increase
of expenditure would be demanded. His prescience was not equal
to his courage. In another sense the long view was justified ; the
scheme stood the unforeseen test uncommonly well ; the underlying
principles proved their adaptability to altered circumstances, and
although the 5th of April, 1860, did not witness the final extinction
of the income tax, and though some may deplore the increasing
reliance upon taxes which tend to the dispersion of capital, the fact
remains that the nation emerged financially unscathed from the
Crimean War and the Indian Mutiny.

Into these troubled waters we must now plunge.

There are two conflicting views as to the origin of the difficulties The Cri-
which issued in the Crimean War. Queen Victoria ascribed it to mean
the " selfishness and ambition of one man (the Czar Nicholas) and War—its
his servants," [2] Kinglake holds Napoleon III. primarily responsible. cause
Neither view can be accepted in its naked simplicity, though in
each there is a large element of truth. Napoleon III., if not the
primary cause of the war, was at least the immediate firebrand in the
Eastern conflagration. By a treaty of 1740 France had obtained
from Turkey the custody of several of the Holy Places in and near
Jerusalem. The Latins became neglectful of their rights in the latter
part of the eighteenth century, and the guardianship fell to Greek
monks. In May, 1850, however, Louis Napoleon anxious to conciliate the support of the Clericals in France, asserted his right to
place Latin monks in possession of the Holy Places. This demand was
supported by Austria, Spain, and other Roman Catholic powers, and
after some delay it was, in substance, conceded by the Sultan. The
concession roused bitter resentment in the mind of the Czar Nicholas,
whose dignity was already outraged by the establishment of the
democratic Empire in France. Not for the first time the Porte
found itself between the upper and the nether millstone, and, in
order to escape from that embarrassing situation, the Sultan played
an old diplomatic trick. His decision on the points at issue was
embodied in a letter to the French Chargé d'affaires, and in a Firman
addressed to the Greek patriarch at Jerusalem. The language of the
two documents was not identical : in the letter, stress was laid upon

[1] Argyll, i. 430.   [2] Q.V.L. iii. 25.

the substantial concessions to France ; the Firman dwelt upon the claims denied. In the upshot, France was satisfied, Russia was not. Accordingly, in March, 1853, the Czar despatched to Constantinople a rough and overbearing soldier, Prince Menschikoff, who was charged not only to obtain full satisfaction about the Holy Places, but to demand from the Sultan a virtual acknowledgement, embodied in formal treaty, of the Czar's protectorate over all the orthodox subjects of the Porte. On the question of the Holy Places the Czar had a strong case ; his claim to the protectorate over the Greek Christians in Turkey was, on the contrary, an extravagant extension of the vague and indefinite engagements contained in the seventh and fourteenth articles of the Treaty of Kainardji (1774). By Article VII. of that treaty the Sublime Porte " promises to protect constantly the Christian religion and its Churches, and it also allows the Ministers of the Imperial Court of Russia to make upon all occasions representation as well in favour of the new Church at Constantinople (' in one of the quarters of Galata, in the street called Bey Oglu,') . . . as on behalf of its officiating Ministers ".[1] In virtue of a right of interference on behalf of a given Church in a given street of Constantinople, Russia was now claiming a general protectorate over the Greek Christians in Turkey.[2] The demand was wholly inadmissible. " No Sovereign," wrote Lord Clarendon, " having a proper regard for his own dignity and independence could admit proposals so undefined as those of Prince Menschikoff and by treaty confer upon another and more powerful Sovereign a right of protection over a large portion of his own subjects. However well disguised it may be, yet the fact is that under the vague language of the proposed Sened a perpetual right to interfere in the internal affairs of Turkey would be conferred upon Russia, for governed as the Greek subjects of the Porte are by their ecclesiastical authorities, and looking as these latter would in all things do for protection to Russia, it follows that 14,000,000 of Greeks would henceforth regard the Emperor as their supreme protector, and their allegiance to the Sultan would be little more than nominal, while his own independence would dwindle into vassalage."

Inadmissible in substance, the Russian demand was urged upon the Sultan by Prince Menschikoff with insufferable insolence. By this time Menschikoff himself had to reckon with an antagonist in whose skilful and experienced hands the blustering Russian soldier was a mere child. On April 5th, Lord Stratford de Redcliffe [3] returned to Constantinople, and the whole diplomatic situation quickly underwent a complete transformation.

[1] Holland, *Treaty Relations between Russia and Turkey*, pp. 41, 42.
[2] Holland, *op. cit.* p. 9.
[3] For the relations between Stratford and the Home Government, *cf.* Maxwell's *Life of Clarendon*, ii. c. xiii.

The Czar Nicholas had never questioned the fact that Great England and Russia Britain was vitally interested in the solution of the Eastern question. But England herself had been curiously slow to manifest any jealousy of the advance of Russia in South-Eastern Europe. The younger Pitt was the first of English statesmen to awake to the fact that the decadence of the Ottoman power and the gradual absorption of her Black Sea Provinces by Russia was raising issues in the ultimate settlement of which England, as an Asiatic power, had direct concern. Pitt's fears found no echo in the House of Commons, and it was not until Canning plunged into the waters rendered turbid by the Greek revolt, that England perceived the true bearing upon English policy of the development of events in Eastern Europe. Owing to Canning's premature death Russia secured for herself all the advantages which otherwise she would have had to share with England, if not with Europe. The position attained by the Treaty of Adrianople (1829) was further strengthened by that of Unkiar Skelessi (1833), and but for Palmerston's accession to the Foreign Office the Black Sea would have remained a " Russian lake," and the Czar's fleets would have commanded the eastern waters of the Mediterranean. The Treaty of London (1841) tore up that of Unkiar Skelessi and intimated to Russia in unmistakable terms that in the ultimate settlement of the Eastern question England would demand an influential voice.

Three years later the Czar Nicholas paid his memorable visit to The Czar Nicholas and England the English Court. To Lord Aberdeen, then Foreign Secretary in Peel's Ministry, to other English statesmen and to Prince Albert the Czar opened his mind freely as regards the Eastern question and the relations of England and Russia in connection therewith.[1] Those views he actually embodied in a Memorandum preserved at the Foreign Office. He insisted : " that, in the event of the Porte giving to anyone of the Powers just cause of complaint, that Power should be aided by the rest in its endeavours to have that cause removed. That all the Powers should urge on the Porte the duty of conciliating its Christian subjects, and should use all their influence, on the other hand, to keep those subjects to their allegiance. That, in the event of any unforeseen calamity befalling the Turkish Empire, Russia and England should agree together as to the course that should be pursued." The Duke of Argyll goes so far as to assert with certainty " that if the Czar Nicholas had abided by the assurances of this Memorandum the Crimean War would never have arisen ". This at any rate may be conceded, that the personal relations established by the Czar in 1844 with English statesmen, and particularly with Lord Aberdeen, did predispose them to anticipate with some confidence a peaceful issue from the difficulties which had now arisen.

[1] For an admirable description of the Czar as he appeared to those who met him, cf. Argyll, Memoirs, i. 436 seq. See also Q.V.L. ii. 13-23.

More than this. In January and February, 1853, the Czar had two memorable interviews with Sir Hamilton Seymour, then British Ambassador in St. Petersburg. Once more he expressed his anxiety to come to an agreement with England in regard to the Eastern question, " lest the sick man should suddenly die upon our hands, and his heritage fall into chaos and dissolution ". He was prepared indeed with a specific scheme. Servia, Bulgaria, and the Danubian Principalities were to be erected into independent states under Russian protection, and England, to secure her route to the East, might annex Egypt, Crete, and Cyprus. Russia, he declared, did not desire permanently to occupy Constantinople ; but, if she did not, neither should England or France or any other great Power. Least of all would Russia permit a revival of the Byzantine Empire in favour of Greece, or the " breaking up of Turkey into little Republics, as an asylum for the Kossuths, Mazzinis, and other revolutionists ". The English Ministers refused to admit that the dissolution of the Ottoman Empire was imminent, or to discuss a partition of the inheritance.[1] The Czar, therefore, proceeded to plough his lonely furrow at Constantinople.

Lord Stratford de Redcliffe at Constantinople

Lord Stratford, meanwhile, did not allow the grass to grow under his feet. His first task was to persuade Menschikoff to separate the question of the Holy Places from that of a general Russian protectorate over the Greek Christians. This important distinction having been secured Stratford then induced the Porte to give satisfaction to Russia on the former point. The dispute as to the Holy Places was thus comfortably settled before the end of April. But the concession made by the Porte effected no improvement in the diplomatic situation. On the contrary, as the Porte became more conciliatory, Menschikoff became more menacing. But he was now on weaker ground, and he knew it. Too late he perceived that he had fallen an easy prey to Lord Stratford's astuteness. The latter advised the Porte to refuse the protectorate claimed by Russia, and on May 22nd Menschikoff and the staff of the Russian Embassy quitted Constantinople. A week later the Porte addressed to the Powers a Note announcing that " the question of the Holy Places had terminated in a manner satisfactory to all parties ; that nevertheless the Prince Menschikoff, not satisfied with that, had demanded from the Porte a treaty to guarantee the rights and privileges of all kinds accorded by the Sultan to his Greek subjects ". " However great," it continued, " may be the desire of the Porte to preserve the most amicable relations with Russia, she can never engage herself by such a guarantee towards a foreign Government, either concluding with it a treaty or signing a simple official Note, without compromising gravely her independence and the most fundamental rights of the Sultan over his own subjects." Despite all this, the Porte, though

[1] Q.V.L. ii 532-539.

bound to take measures of self-defence, did not abandon hopes of peace.

The hopes became fainter day by day. On July 21st a Russian army under Prince Gortschakoff crossed the Pruth and occupied the Principalities. Russia thereupon announced to the Powers that the occupation was not intended as an act of war, but as a "material guarantee" for the concession of her just demands. On the news of the impending occupation the combined fleets of England and France had been sent into Besika Bay, and Palmerston believed that the only chance of now convincing Russia that we were in earnest and thus averting war would be to order them up to the Bosphorus and if necessary into the Black Sea. This step would, among other advantages, "relieve England and France from the disagreeable, and not very creditable, position of waiting without venturing to enter the back door as friends, while the Russians have taken forcible possession of the front hall as enemies".[1] But Aberdeen still hung back, and the Sultan was advised not to resist the Russian invasion by force "in order to exhaust all the resources of patience". Palmerston was convinced that they were already exhausted, and that Russia was being led on by the apparent timidity of England.

Palmerston's policy

Meanwhile, an effort was made by the central Powers to avert the all but inevitable war. The representatives of England, France, Austria, and Prussia met at Vienna in July and agreed upon a "Note" which it was hoped might satisfy both Russia and Turkey. The Note simply reaffirmed the adherence of the Porte to "the letter and spirit of the treaties of Kainardji and Adrianople relative to the protection of the Christian religion". The Note was accepted by Russia, though not, as subsequently appeared, in the sense intended by the mediators. Turkey like Russia, perceiving its ambiguities, insisted on amending the Note. For the words above quoted the Porte proposed to read as follows : "To the stipulations of the Treaty of Kainardji, confirmed by that of Adrianople, relative to the protection *by the Sublime Porte* of the Christian religion". To a superficial view the amendment may appear a strangely inadequate reason for provoking a European War. But it is not too much to say that the addition of the words "by the Sublime Porte" revealed, in succinct epitome, the whole point at issue between Russia and Turkey. Did the Treaty of Kainardji give to Russia a general protectorate over the orthodox subjects of the Sultan ? Since Russia claimed that it did, the Vienna Note was sufficient for her purpose. The diplomatists at Vienna were simple enough to imagine that they had discovered a formula which might, by studied ambiguity, postpone or even avert war. Russia, putting her own interpretation upon the Note, was naturally willing to agree to it. Lord Stratford, however, was quick to perceive the ambiguity, and the addition of four

The Vienna Note, July 31st

---

[1] Palmerston to Aberdeen, July 4th, 1853 (Ashley, ii. 28).

words, seemingly unimportant, brought Russia out into the open. These words implicitly repudiated the Russian claim to a general protectorate over the Greek Christians. The latter were to be protected not by the Czar but by the Sultan. Russia, as was to be expected, promptly refused to accept the amendment, and her own interpretation of the original Note was, by an indiscretion, subsequently published. Despite her knowledge of the Russian gloss, Austria pressed the Porte to accept the original Note ; Prussia followed timidly in the wake of Austria ; England and France, undeceived by the Russian gloss, refused to press the Note upon the Porte.

Outbreak of war between Russia and Turkey

Meanwhile, Russia had declared (July 2nd) that the occupation of the Principalities was an answer to the presence of the combined fleets in Besika Bay, and that her troops would not be withdrawn until the fleets retired. Nothing could surpass the calm effrontery of this announcement. " It is," as Palmerston said, " the robber who declares that he will not leave the house until the policeman shall have first retired from the courtyard." But Palmerston was not master of the British Government ; still less was Aberdeen. The initiative was really in the hands of the Ambassador at Constantinople. On October 4th the Porte demanded from Russia the evacuation of the Principalities within fifteen days, and on October 23rd Turkey formally declared war. The British fleet had already been ordered up to the Bosphorus—an order of which Russia had some cause to complain as a technical infraction of the Treaty of 1841.

Nevertheless, Russia and the Western Powers still remained at peace, and the Czar declared that, despite the Turkish declaration of war, he would not take the offensive in the Principalities. The Turks, however, attacked vigorously on the Danube, and on November 30th the Russian Black Sea fleet retaliated by the entire destruction of a Turkish squadron in the Bay of Sinope.

The massacre of Sinope

That this was an act of " offensive warfare " cannot be denied ; that it might have been prevented by prompter action on the part of the combined fleet is equally certain, but nevertheless it is difficult to understand why " the massacre of Sinope " should have aroused so much indignation in England and France. The fact remains that it was the immediate prelude to the European War. " I have been," wrote Graham, " one of the most strenuous advocates of peace with Russia until the last moment ; but the Sinope attack and recent events have changed entirely the aspect of affairs. I am afraid that a rupture with Russia is inevitable." [1]

Dissensions in the English Cabinet

Graham had indeed been one of the staunchest friends of peace, but among the factors which contributed to war the dissensions in the English Cabinet cannot be ignored. One of the most brilliant of recent historians does not scruple to assert that the blame lies

[1] Parker, *op. cit.* ii. 226.

largely at Russell's door. " If Lord John had stood by his Chief instead of trying to supplant him, peace might have been maintained."[1] That Russell was from the first restless and uneasy in Aberdeen's Cabinet is certain. His sense of public duty, combined with the knowledge that the first place was not within his grasp, had induced him to accept the second. But he never forgot, nor permitted others to forget, the sacrifice he had thus made for his country's good. It is clear also that he regarded the arrangement as temporary and expected that Aberdeen would retire in his favour.[2] Aberdeen was entirely devoid of personal ambition ; he had accepted the leadership with reluctance, and would have gladly relinquished it. But to whom ? He was less blind than Russell to the latter's defects, but he would have resigned in August, 1853, could he have induced his colleagues to accept Russell in his stead. Many of them, however, perhaps most of them, would not entertain the proposal. Palmerston was equally impossible at the moment, and consequently, as the sky became more threatening abroad, Aberdeen, to the great comfort of the Queen, felt himself in honour bound not to abandon the helm.

It is far from certain that the cause of peace was served by his decision. Had the Cabinet been really homogeneous, and had Aberdeen been in a position to impose his own policy upon them from the first, war might have been averted. Lord Stratford would not have returned to Constantinople, Turkey would never have leant upon the support of England, and the Czar Nicholas might possibly have been induced to modify his demands. On the other hand, if Palmerston had been at the head of a united Cabinet and a united party in 1853, the Czar would have thought twice before sending Menschikoff to Constantinople and provoking a conflict in which Great Britain would have been certain to espouse the side of Turkey. Exasperated by the conduct of Napoleon III. and of Lord Stratford the Czar relied on Aberdeen and the peace party in England to extricate him from difficulties of his own creation. Even after war had been declared by the Porte, Aberdeen still continued to talk peace in London and St. Petersburg.

This was the moment appropriately chosen by Lord John Russell for pressing to the front the question of Parliamentary reform. In the details of the proposed measure Palmerston could not concur, and on December 15th he resigned. Lord Lansdowne would probably have followed him, but after ten days of suspense and negotiation Palmerston was induced to withdraw his resignation. Ostensibly, his consent to remain in office was due to the resolution of the Cabinet on the Reform question. But much more important was the fact

Lord Aberdeen

[1] Paul, *Modern England*, i. 311, 318.
[2] For conduct of Lord John during this autumn see Maxwell's *Clarendon*, ii. 21 and *passim*.

that the Cabinet " took a decision on Turkish affairs which Palmerston had long unsuccessfully pressed upon them ".[1]

The allied fleets in the Black Sea, Jan. 1854 The Cabinet decided that in consequence of the " massacre " of Sinope the allied fleets must enter the Black Sea. On January 4th, 1854, this momentous order was executed, and it was announced that the English and French admirals had instructions to " invite " all Russian ships in the Black Sea to withdraw into harbour. Even yet, the English Premier did not abandon his efforts for peace. On February 9th Napoleon III. was permitted, in his own name and that of Queen Victoria, to write an autograph letter to the Czar tendering his good offices towards the preservation of peace. The only response from St. Petersburg was a savage snub. On February 22nd, Austria, always anxious about the presence of Russian troops in the Principalities but not too straightforward in her diplomacy, intimated that if the Western Powers would present an ultimatum demanding the evacuation of Moldavia and Wallachia before a given date she would support tham. England and France promptly acted on this suggestion, and on February 27th Lord Clarendon informed Count Nesselrode that Great Britain, having exhausted all the efforts of negotiation, was compelled to call upon Russia " to restrict within purely diplomatic limits the discussion in which she has for some time been engaged with the Sublime Porte," and by return messenger to agree to the complete evacuation of the Provinces of Moldavia and Wallachia by the 30th of April.

Russia refused this ultimatum on March 19th, and on the 27th and 28th the Western Powers declared war. It was then made manifest that Austria's promised support was only diplomatic ; Prussia—to the great indignation of Queen Victoria—followed Austria's lead ;[2] the concert on which so much depended was broken, and England and France were left alone to sustain an exceptionally arduous struggle.

Was the Crimean War justified ? Can the Crimean War be justified before the tribunal of impartial history ? Retrospective criticism has tended to the view that the war, if not a crime, was at least a blunder, and that it ought to have been and might have been avoided. A great diplomatist has enshrined in classical phrase his deliberate opinion that in the Crimean War " England put her money on the wrong horse ". Other opinions suggest that England was dragged into war in defence of a Power notorious for oppression and misgovernment, at the heels of an overbearing diplomatist. The Duke of Argyll, on the contrary, writing at the close of the century, confessed himself as one of the

---

[1] Palmerston to Sullivan, December 25th, 1853, ap. Ashley, ii. 21. He also confirms the notorious fact (denied by *The Times*) as to dissensions in the Cabinet on Turkish affairs.

[2] See the remarkable letters of Queen Victoria to the King of Prussia in March and June, 1854, *Q.V.L.* iii. 21 , 39.

Cabinet responsible for the war " to this day wholly unrepentant ".[1]
Kinglake [2] has popularized the idea that England was an innocent
tool in the hands of an unscrupulous adventurer, anxious to establish
a throne unrighteously attained, by a brilliant war causelessly provoked.   That the Emperor Napoleon was anxious to point a contrast
between the glories of the Empire and the sordid failures of the
Citizen Monarchy is certain.[2]   To assert that either Stratford or
Aberdeen were the dupes of his ambition is grotesquely inaccurate.
The truth is that those sections of British opinion which Palmerston
so faithfully reflected were predisposed against the despotic ruler
who had abetted the Austrian Emperor in the congenial task of
suppressing a popular rising in Hungary, and who, but for the
protest of England and France, would have compelled the Sultan
to violate the right of political asylum.   More reflective opinion
inclined to the view that the time had come for vigorous resistance
to the secular ambition of the Russian Czar.   The bias of Russian
policy during the last century and a half was unmistakable.   From
the Treaty of Azov to that of Belgrade ; from Kainardji to Jassy ;
from Bucharest to Adrianople, and from that to Unkiar Skelessi, the
advance had been stealthy but continuous.   Was the dissolution of
the sick man to be hastened now to satisfy the impatient avarice of
the heir-presumptive ?   Was the Czar to be allowed to convert the
Black Sea into a Russian lake, and to establish an exclusive and
dangerous domination in the eastern waters of the Mediterranean ?
It was not a question as to the goodness or badness of Turkish
administration.   It was a question whether Europe in general, and
England in particular, was prepared to permit Russia to force upon
the Porte a " diplomatic engagement which would have made her
the sole protector of the Christian subjects of the Porte, and therefore
the sole arbiter of the fate of Turkey ".[3]   Rightly or wrongly England
came, slowly but steadily, to the conviction that the matter was one
of vital concern to Europe at large and to herself in particular ;
that the Czar was determined to assert his claims by force, and that
only by force could they be repelled.   Of this conviction the Crimean
War was the logical and inevitable result.

Treaties relative to the military assistance to be given to Turkey **The war**
were signed between England and France on April 10th, and between
the two Powers and Turkey on April 12th.   The latter affirmed the
conviction of the Western Powers that " the existence of the Ottoman
Empire in its present limits is essential to the balance of power among
the States of Europe ".   The first detachment of British troops
sailed on February 28th, and after a brief stay in Malta landed on

[1] *Our Responsibilities for Turkey* (1896), p. 10.
[2] For trenchant review of Kinglake, and for " the most authoritative vindication of the motives of the Aberdeen Government," see article in *Edinburgh Review*,
revised by Lord Clarendon himself (April, 1863).
[3] Argyll, *ibid.* p. 10.

April 5th at Gallipoli, where a French force had arrived a few days
earlier. The British Army, consisting of four divisions of infantry
and one of cavalry, some 28,000 men in all, was commanded by Lord
Raglan. The Earl of Lucan commanded the cavalry division, and
one of the infantry divisions was given to the Duke of Cambridge.
For the commander-in-chief no better choice could have been made
Lord Rag- than that of Lord Raglan. As Lord Fitzroy Somerset he had served
lan   with distinction under the Duke of Wellington both in the field and
as his military secretary at the Horse Guards. He was a brave man,
a perfect gentleman, and but for the hampering effect of the French
alliance would probably have won a reputation as a great strategist.
In a situation of great delicacy he displayed unfailing tact, and amid
circumstances profoundly depressing his courage remained unbroken.
The choice of Lord Lucan was less happy in itself, and that the
command of the light cavalry brigade should have been given to his
brother-in-law Lord Cardigan, with whom he was not on speaking
terms, is only one instance of the official ineptitude which was so
disastrously demonstrated during the early stages of the war. The command of the French Army, which was slightly bigger than our own,
was entrusted to Marshal Saint Arnaud, a brave soldier, but deeply
implicated in the fusillades of the *coup d'état*, untried in the conduct
of an elaborate campaign, and above all conspicuously lacking in the
qualities required in the joint commander of a combined expedition.

While a British army was sent to the Mediterranean a splendid
fleet was collected and despatched, under the command of Sir Charles
Napier, to the Baltic. The naval expedition failed to realize expectations, and contributed curiously little to the ultimate issue of the war.

Meanwhile, in the campaign between Russia and Turkey there
had been a considerable amount of fighting on the Danube. There,
for six months, the Turks had been giving fresh proof of their fighting
qualities. In vain had the Russians flung themselves against Silistra.
The prolonged defence of this weakly fortified town was due largely
to two English volunteers, Captain Butler and Lieutenant Nasmyth,
and in order to support it the allied army moved up from Gallipoli
to Varna. On May 19th a conference was held there between
Raglan, St. Arnaud, and Omar Pasha. On June 23rd, however, the
Russians raised the siege of Silistra, and in July they commenced
the evacuation of the Principalities. Before the end of the first week
in August there was not a Russian soldier to the west of the Pruth.

Already, however, a momentous decision had been arrived at by
Minis-   the English Government. Things had not been going smoothly in
terial dis- the Coalition Cabinet. Aberdeen's principal lieutenant was pre-
sensions occupied during the critical months at the beginning of 1854 with
and   two questions rarely absent from his mind, that of Parliamentary
changes   Reform and his own position in the Ministry. As to the latter it is
hardly too much to say that he was perpetually pestering his unhappy

chief.[1] He was convinced, and rightly, that administrative efficiency would be promoted by the separation of the functions of the Secretaryship of War and the Colonies.   By his insistence the salutary change was effected and a fourth Secretaryship of State came into being. Who was to fill it ?   As Lord John was himself tired of being without a portfolio, the Premier sensibly suggested that he should take the Colonies and leave the War Office to the Duke of Newcastle. But Russell was anxious to strengthen the Whig element in the Cabinet and proposed Sir George Grey, either for the Colonies or the Home Office. In the latter event Palmerston was to have the War Office. Much money might have been saved and much suffering and bloodshed avoided, had Aberdeen assented to this course. But he was unwilling to displace the Duke of Newcastle. The upshot was that Russell got his way as to Sir George Grey, who became Secretary for the Colonies ; Newcastle remained, to the great disadvantage of the public service, at the War Office, and Lord John's personal wishes were satisfied by his appointment to the high dignity of Presidency of the Council— an office which no commoner had held for nearly three centuries. To facilitate this arrangement Lord Granville amiably accepted the Chancellorship of the Duchy of Lancaster.

As to Parliamentary Reform Lord John was less successful. No one but a pedant or a fanatic would insist on spring cleaning while half the street is in a blaze. But the time was never unseasonable to Lord John for putting the Parliamentary house in order. Palmerston, whose enthusiasm for Reform lacked something of fervour, wanted to concentrate all the thought and energy of the Government and the nation on the war. Few people would now question the wisdom of this attitude ; not many people doubted it at the time. Lord John, however, so far prevailed with his colleagues as to be allowed, on February 13th, to introduce his Bill. Its reception was lukewarm ; the House and the nation were preoccupied. Nevertheless, Russell named a day for the second reading. Palmerston protested against this dissipation of the national energies ; and the break-up of the Ministry was, with the greatest difficulty, averted by Aberdeen. Russell eventually consented to postpone the Bill, but salved his sensitive conscience by resigning his seat in the Cabinet (April 8th). Palmerston, thereupon, generously insisted that he was the one to go. The Queen laboured assiduously to avert disruption ; she prevailed, and Russell gave way. On April 11th he announced to the House, in a speech broken by emotion, that his darling had been given to the lions. A question of momentous import demanded the attention of an individual Cabinet.

Parliamentary Reform

---

[1] *Cf.* Walpole, *Russell*, ii. 204-220.   It is only fair to add Walpole's excuse for this conduct : " Domestic trouble always produced a marked effect on Lord John's public course ; and those who think that in 1854 he was occasionally betrayed into an irritation which was unusual with him should recollect that . . . he was racked with public and private anxiety."—Walpole, ii. 211-12.

The invasion of the Crimea

War had been declared upon Russia, but where was the attack to be delivered ?   A blow at St. Petersburg might have been decisive, but Kronstadt was soon discovered to be too strong even for the fine fleet commanded by Sir Charles Napier.   The next most vital part was the great naval arsenal in the Crimean peninsula.   An expedition to the Crimea was strongly urged upon the Government, from without by *The Times*, from within by Palmerston.   Nothing would serve better to relieve pressure in the Balkans than an effective attack by land and sea upon Sebastapol.   Towards the end of June the Cabinet decided upon this course,[1] and orders were accordingly sent out to Lord Raglan.   They reached him at Varna, where the troops were suffering terribly from the ravages of dysentery, cholera, and malarial fever.[2]   Before the orders arrived in Bulgaria, the Russians had raised the siege of Silistra and were in retreat across the Pruth.   On July 26th the Turks reoccupied Bucharest.   Before leaving that city Prince Gortschakoff intimated that he was bidding its inhabitants *au revoir*.   It was in effect good-bye.   On June 14th Austria had concluded a convention with the Porte acknowledging the principle of the integrity of the Ottoman Empire, and pledging Austria to secure by negotiation or other means the evacuation of the Principalities.   In July they were evacuated by the Russians, and in August they were occupied by an Austrian army of observation.

The ostensible and immediate object of the European intervention might seem now to have been attained.   But the allies had already decided to take the offensive in the Crimea, and on July 22nd Lord Clarendon stated explicitly that they would no longer be satisfied by the restoration of the *Status quo ante bellum*.   They must at least secure guarantees on four points :—

1. Russia must be deprived of the Treaty Rights in virtue of which she had occupied the Principalities ;
2. Turkey must be guarded against attack from the Russian navy in the Black Sea ;
3. The navigation of the Danube must, in the interests of European commerce, be secured against the obstruction caused by Russia's " uncontrolled possession of the principal mouth of the Danube " ;   and
4. The stipulations of the Treaty of Kainardji relative to the protection of the Christians must be amended, since that treaty " has become by a wrongful interpretation the principal cause of the present struggle ".[3]

[1] The famous dinner at Pembroke Lodge at which the actual instructions were approved was on June 28th.   Russell confirms Kinglake's story that on that occasion many Cabinet Ministers slumbered peacefully : but the expedition had been decided upon, says Russell significantly, " in the daytime ".—Walpole, ii. 223.

[2] Cholera broke out on July 21st.

[3] Lord Clarendon to Lord Westmorland, Ambassador at Vienna, July 22nd, 1854.—*Eastern Papers*.

The CRIMEA

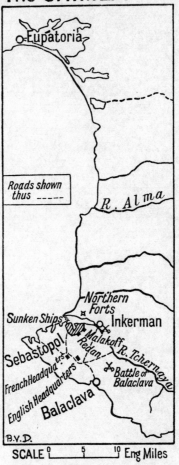

Eupatoria

Roads shown
thus -----

R. Alma

Northern
Forts

Sunken Ships

Inkerman

Sebastopol

Malakoff
Redan

R. Tchernaya

French Headquarters

Battle of
Balaclava

English Headquarters

Balaclava

B.V.D.

SCALE 0 — 5 — 10 Eng Miles

Lord Clarendon's despatch is of importance as defining at once the causes and the objects of the Crimean War.

The Crimean War proper began in September, 1854. On the 14th the allied army, more than 50,000 strong, disembarked in the Bay of Eupatoria to the north of Sebastopol. It was a fine army, but badly equipped. The tents had to be left behind for lack of transport, and the ambulances for lack of horses and drivers. On the 19th the march towards Sebastopol began. The French who had no cavalry were on the right wing next the sea ; with them were about 7,000 Turks under Selim Pasha ; the British were on the left. On the 20th Menshikoff in command of 40,000 troops tried to stop the advance of the allies on the Alma—a stream about fifteen miles north of Sebastopol. After three hours of severe fighting the Russians were routed. The allies, though victorious, suffered heavily. There were 619 killed and 2,860 wounded. The British force had been set to storm redoubts heavily manned, while their allies attacked the weaker left wing of the Russians. Consequently their losses were considerably heavier than those of the French. Raglan, despite the lack of transport and the ravages of cholera, wanted to make an immediate assault upon Sebastopol. Had his advice been taken, Sebastopol would almost infallibly have fallen. But St. Arnaud, in the grip of a mortal disease, opposed these bold councils, and the great opportunity was lost. The garrison of Sebastopol were not less amazed than delighted at their escape. After a three days' halt the army again began its march. Again Raglan, supported by Admiral Sir Edmund Lyons, wanted to make an assault upon the Star Fort to the north of the fortress. Again St. Arnaud vetoed the suggestion, and it was decided to march round the head of the harbour and approach Sebastopol from the south. This difficult operation was effected without resistance from Menschikoff who had withdrawn his main army into the interior, leaving the fortress under-garrisoned, and on the 26th Raglan occupied the harbour of Balaclava. Again Raglan and Lyons wanted to assault—this time from the south. St. Arnaud was now dying on board ship,[1] and the command of the French force devolved upon General Canrobert, a man of great personal bravery, but devoid of the moral courage essential for high command. Canrobert was not less strongly opposed than St. Arnaud to the idea of assault, and the allied forces, therefore, encamped to the south of the fortress, and made slow preparations for a regular siege. For such an enterprise their equipment was quite inadequate. The hope and intention of the British Government and the British General had been to carry Sebastopol by a *coup de main*. There is little doubt that it could have been done in September, 1854. That it was not done was no fault either of the Cabinet at home or of the English soldiers at the front.

The Crimea

Battle of the Alma

---

[1] He died on September 29th.

The hesitation of the allies gave the defenders of Sebastopol a chance which they seized with consummate adroitness and skill. They cleared the Russian ships of guns and men : sank some of the largest ships at the entrance to the harbour—thus rendering the allied fleets comparatively useless—and mounted the guns on shore ; Colonel von Todleben, the great engineer, and Admiral Korniloff worked with such energy and enthusiasm that the town was rapidly placed in a posture of defence. Menschikoff's army at Batchiserai was constantly receiving supplies and reinforcements from home, and the position of the allies became daily less advantageous. But the engineers worked with a will, siege guns were quickly landed and mounted, and on October 17th the bombardment began. The experience of the first day was sufficient to prove the inadequacy of the preparations for a siege. In order to arm three batteries we had to dismantle our ships and employ our seamen. Apart, therefore, from the fact that the sunken Russian ships blocked the way for an assault from the sea, the efficiency of the fleet was seriously impaired.

For a full week the fire of the besiegers was kept up, but no perceptible effect was produced upon the fortress, and on October 25th the allies were unpleasantly reminded of the dangers to which their position was exposed by Menschikoff's strategy. Reinforced from home Menschikoff, at the head of 30,000 men, re-entered Sebastopol, while a large detachment under General Liprandi delivered from outside an attack on the position of the allies, hoping to catch them between two fires and drive them out of Balaclava. The story of the fight of Balaclava has been endlessly retold, but no retelling is ever likely to dispel the mystery which still enshrouds the main incident of that brilliant but disastrous day. The first Russian attack was directed against some redoubts held by the Turks. The latter were compelled to retreat, leaving some English guns in the hands of the enemy. Liprandi then pushed forward his cavalry towards the harbour, but one of its columns was met and repulsed by Sir Colin Campbell, with the 93rd Highlanders in line. Only the brave Highlanders stood at that moment between the Russian cavalry and the harbour of Balaclava. Not less splendid than the feat of the 93rd was the dash of some squadrons of the Heavy Brigade under Scarlett against the main body of the Russian cavalry. Then followed the glorious tragedy of the charge of the Light Brigade. Lord Lucan, in command of the cavalry, was ordered by Lord Raglan, who was viewing the battle from distant heights, to aid the infantry in retaking the captured guns. Misunderstanding the order, he remained inactive. The order being repeated in hot temper by Raglan's aide-de-camp, Captain Nolan, Lucan sent the Light Brigade under his brother-in-law Lord Cardigan to certain destruction. Six hundred and seven men galloped to the attack, and captured the Russian batteries before them ; but only 198

Batchiserai

The Battle of Balaclava, Oct. 26th

returned, the rest were killed, wounded, or made prisoners. The comment of General Bosquet on the incident has become proverbial : *c'est magnifique mais ce n'est pas la guerre.* It was a gross and costly blunder, but it was not wholly wasted. The steadiness and dash of Colin Campbell's Highlanders combined with the reckless courage of the Heavy and the Light Brigades to put the fear of God into Cossack hearts. Lord Lucan's conduct, however, was inexcusable. " You have lost the Light Brigade," was the terse comment of his chief, and it was not a whit too severe. Lord Lucan was recalled ; Lord Cardigan was permitted to retire, and to his amazement found himself on his return to England a popular hero. That popularity he owed less perhaps to his own gallantry than to the genius of Tennyson.

Meanwhile, the enemy, though repulsed in their attack upon Balaclava, retained their position on the heights above. On the following day (Oct. 26th) the attack was renewed from another quarter. Six thousand men made a sortie from Sebastopol, and had they not been gallantly driven back by a far inferior force on the heights of Inkerman, the position of the allies, caught between the fires, would have been dangerous in the extreme. The besiegers were now, in fact, besieged, and ten days later they were made to realize the fact.

For a regular investment of Sebastopol our forces were hopelessly insufficient : for a bombardment the navy had been rendered useless by Menschikoff's ingenious device, and the army by itself could make little impression on a fortress which six weeks before might have been taken by assault, but which was rendered every day more proof against a siege by the greatest engineer of his day. All that the allies could do was to await the arrival of reinforcements, and meanwhile hold their position on the Bay of Balaclava and the ridges above it. From that position Menschikoff was determined to dislodge them. The attempt was made on November 5th. The Russians, 40,000 strong, concentrated their attack on the heights, at the extreme north-eastern corner of the ridge, known as Mount Inkerman. Another 20,000 Russians were massed in the valley of the Tchernaya. To these forces the English opposed about 8,000 men, the French about 6,000. Inkerman, fought in dense mist, was a series of almost isolated incidents ; regiment against regiment, fighting mostly at the point of the bayonet. Of such a battle no coherent account can be given except in such minute detail as cannot be attempted here. Enough to say that the English and French soldiers alike fought with splendid gallantry, and that the Russians were compelled to retire with the loss of 10,000 men. The allies lost 4,300 men, of whom over 2,500 were British. But now, if ever, was the moment for a storm. Raglan was in favour of it ; Canrobert, however, refused to concur, and the opportunity of dealing a really

Battle of Inkerman Nov. 5th

13

effective blow at Menschikoff's army was lost. On November 6th
the British and French commanders held counsel as to the possibilities of assault, but Raglan was obliged once more to acquiesce in
postponement. The " soldiers' battle " did little, therefore, towards
achieving the purpose of the campaign.

The great
gale of
Nov.
14th
On November 14th a terrible disaster befell the allies. A fierce
hurricane, accompanied with storms of rain and snow, sprang up,
swept down the tents on shore and destroyed much of the shipping
in the roads. Immense stores of food, medical comforts, beds,
blankets, and warm clothing for the men, of hay for the horses and
ammunition for the guns were still on board the transports. The
largest of them, *The Prince*, a new steamer of 2,700 tons, was driven
on the rocks and thirty others foundered in the gale. Stores to the
value of £2,000,000 were lost, and the men were deprived of all that
might have rendered tolerable the cruel Crimean winter.

The win-
ter of
1854-1855
The great gale was the real beginning of the sufferings which have
made the " Crimean Winter " a byword in the history of military
administration. Hitherto there had been hardships, incidental in
some measure to every campaign, but intensified in this case by in-
experience and mismanagement. But hardship is no word to apply
to the sufferings of those who endured the long agony of the winter
of 1854-1855. The camp before Sebastopol was six or seven miles
uphill from the port of Balaclava, but after the storm the road was
almost impassable ; the horses, weakened by want of fodder, could
hardly drag the waggons through the mud, and men and beasts alike
perished miserably from exposure. The stores, therefore, liberally
supplied from home could not be transported to the soldiers in the
camp. Wearied by incessant labour in the half-frozen trenches,
inadequately clothed, unsuitably fed, the men fell victims, by the
thousand, to fever, cholera, scurvy, and every other form of disease
familiar to dwellers in insanitary camps. Disease claimed nearly
9,000 victims during the autumn and winter months, and by the end
of February, 1855, no fewer than 13,000 men were in hospital. The
transport arrangements were no better than those of the commissariat,
and worst of all was the administration of the base hospitals at Scutari.

Rising in-
dignation
in Eng-
land
The public at home were not ignorant of these things. Mr.
William Howard Russell, first and greatest of war correspondents,
had gone out with the army to represent *The Times*. Russell was
no respecter of persons, and he took good care that the British public
should know the truth, so far as he was able to ascertain it. His
regular accounts, extraordinarily vivid, aroused bitter and clamorous
resentment against the military administration. *The Times* itself
opened a relief fund which was largely subscribed to, and a Patriotic
Fund was established under the presidency of the Prince Consort.
The Queen, rendered painfully anxious by accounts of misfortune
and mismanagement, allowed no detail to escape her watchful eyes.

More particularly was she grieved by the news as to the condition of the hospital at Scutari where the mortality in the early months of the war was 50 per cent. To the women of the country the Queen set the example of personal service by knitting comforters and mittens with her own hands. The example was quickly and splendidly followed. In October, Miss Florence Nightingale went out to Scutari at the head of a band of thirty-seven English ladies. Miss Nightingale and her comrades, skilled and devoted nurses, arrived at Scutari on November 5th, just in time to prepare for the reception of the men wounded at Inkerman. They quickly evolved order out of chaos, and transformed a chamber of horrors into a haven of comfort. They were joined a little later by Miss Stanley with an additional staff of fifty trained nurses,—an invaluable reinforcement, but none too many for the 4,000 sick and wounded already upon their hands.

Chiefly with a view to supplying the Crown with additional military resources Parliament was summoned to meet on December 12th. From many quarters the Ministry was assailed for its mal-administration of the war. But the centre of political interest was, for the moment, not in Parliament but in the Cabinet. For some time past Lord John Russell had been urging upon the Premier the necessity of superseding the Duke of Newcastle at the War Office by Lord Palmerston.[1] Aberdeen refused to put such a slight upon his colleague. But Lord John was looking to the possibility of other changes. " The drift of his observations tended to the substitution of himself as the Head of the Government rather than to any change of Department ; and this he did not deny, when Lord Aberdeen pointed out the inference to be drawn from his remarks." So the Prime Minister wrote to the Queen on December 7th. Two days later Prince Albert wrote : " There was no doubt that they could not go on with Lord John. The universal feeling of the Cabinet seemed to be one of indignation . . . at Lord John's conduct." [2] But there was no counting on Lord John even from day to day. On December 7th he had intimated to the Cabinet his definite resolve to retire at Christmas. By the 16th he had changed his mind, and went to the Cabinet as though nothing had happened.

Parliament meets, Dec. 12th

Parliament reassembled on January 23rd, 1855, and Mr. Roebuck at once gave notice that he intended to move for the appointment of a Select Committee " to inquire into the condition of our army before Sebastopol, and into the conduct of those departments of the Government whose duty it has been to minister to the wants of that army ". Lord John at once resigned on the ground that the motion could not be resisted, although it involved a censure " upon the War Departments with which some of my colleagues are

Mr. Roebuck's motion and fall of the Coalition Ministry

---

[1] See Maxwell's *Clarendon*, ii. 54.   [2] *Q.V.L.* iii. 74.

connected ".[1] His conduct was generally condemned as pusillanimous
and disloyal. Mr. Gladstone declared that " to escape punishment
he ran away from duty ". Palmerston told him without circum-
locution : " You have the appearance of having remained in office,
aiding in carrying on a system of which you disapproved until driven
out by Roebuck's announced notice, and the Government will have
the appearance of self-condemnation by flying from a discussion
which they dare not face ". The Queen expressed in a curt note
" her surprise and concern at hearing so abruptly of his intention to
desert her Government on the motion of Mr. Roebuck ". At this
letter Lord John was " very much excited and very angry," but
despite further explanation the Queen refused to withdraw her just
censure. On the 26th Mr. Roebuck brought forward his motion,
and on the 29th it was carried, to the amazement of both sides, by
305 votes to 148, over 100 Liberals voting in the majority. On the
following day Lord Aberdeen tendered to his Sovereign the resignation of the Cabinet, and the Coalition Ministry was at an end. From
Lord Aberdeen himself the Queen parted with deep regret, and insisted on giving him the vacant Garter as a mark of her esteem and
gratitude. To the Duke of Newcastle also she spoke kindly and
comforting words, assuring him of her sense of his " loyal, high-
minded and patriotic conduct as well as of his unremitting exertions
to serve his Sovereign and country ".[2] History is compelled to judge
both Ministers less leniently. Lord John's dissatisfaction with the
administration of the War Office must be shared by all who have had
occasion to investigate the history of the Coalition Ministry. Nor
can Lord Aberdeen, single-minded and high-souled patriot though he
unquestionably was, escape a share of the blame which must attach
to his colleagues. " Capax imperii nisi imperasset." His endowments were high and his character was unimpeachable ; but he
failed to overcome the difficulties of a difficult situation and a critical
time. As to Lord John's share in the overthrow of the Government
contemporary opinion was not equivocal, and it has been entirely
endorsed by posterity. The least uncharitable view of his conduct
is to ascribe it to super-conscientiousness, to the promptings of which
lesser men are, to the advantage of a work-a-day world, generally
deaf.

The new Government   That the vote on the Roebuck motion accurately represented the
feeling of the nation cannot be doubted. But it was one thing to
dismiss the Coalition, and it was another thing to replace them. The
Queen sent immediately for Lord Derby as the leader of the largest
group in the composite majority which had overthrown the Ministry.
Lord Derby was anxious to avoid the responsibility of office, and
consented to attempt the formation of a Cabinet provided Lord
Palmerston, Mr. Gladstone, and Mr. Sidney Herbert would join him.

[1] Letter to Lord Aberdeen, January 23rd.   [2] Q.V.L. iii. 101.

To facilitate such an arrangement Disraeli, whose behaviour at this crisis cannot be over-praised, was willing to surrender the lead of the House to Palmerston and the Exchequer to Gladstone. Palmerston might have yielded to persuasion had Derby been willing to retain Clarendon at the Foreign Office, and had Gladstone and Herbert come in also. But the latter were even more disinclined for office in a Conservative Ministry than Palmerston, and Derby therefore, with evident relief, relinquished his attempt. In Gladstone's opinion " Lord Derby's error in not forming an administration was palpable and even gross," and Disraeli seems to have shared it.[1] At any rate he told Derby " some very disagreeable truths ". Lord Malmesbury attributes Lord Derby's pusillanimity to the severity of recent attacks of gout.[2]

The Queen next sought the advice of Lord Lansdowne—the Nestor of the Whig party, and after much negotiation sent for Lord John. The latter, to his evident surprise and chagrin, found himself unable to form a Cabinet. Except Lord Palmerston, always good-natured and amenable, practically none of his late colleagues, either Whigs or Peelites, would serve under him. At last, therefore, the Queen turned to Lord Palmerston himself. With little difficulty he formed a Ministry, and thus at the age of 71 became, for the first time, Prime Minister. Lord Palmerston's Cabinet was virtually that of the Coalition without Aberdeen, Russell, and the Duke of Newcastle. The post of difficulty at the War Office was entrusted to Mr. Fox Maule (now Lord Panmure), who had been Secretary at War in Lord John Russell's Ministry, and who was now the first to combine that office with the Secretaryship of State. Lord Granville became leader in the House of Lords, Sir George Grey took Palmerston's place at the Home Office ; Sidney Herbert succeeded Grey at the Colonial Office, and Lord Canning was introduced into the Cabinet as Post-master-General. In little more than a fortnight the Cabinet was threatened with disruption. Roebuck, despite the reconstruction of the Ministry, pressed for the appointment of his Committee and Palmerston was convinced of the impossibility of resisting it. The leading Peelites, who had joined Palmerston only at the urgent request of Aberdeen, were peculiarly sensitive on any point touching the honour of their friends and former colleagues, Newcastle and Aberdeen. Moreover, they regarded the proposed investigation as " a dangerous breach of a great constitutional principle ". Consequently on February 22nd, Graham, Gladstone, and Sidney Herbert seceded from the Ministry.[3] With this secession the Peelites as a distinct parliamentary group ceased to exist. Sir George Cornewall Lewis succeeded Gladstone at the Exchequer ; Sir Charles Wood took the Admiralty from Graham, and Lord John, though already on

Lord Palmerston's Ministry

---

[1] Morley, i. 257.   Malmesbury, *Memoirs*, p. 35ύ.
[3] For the Peelite view *cf.* Parker, *Graham*, ii. 268 *seq.* ; and Morley, i. 537 *seq.*

his way to Vienna, accepted office as Colonial Secretary, but resigned on July 13th. During the same month Canning became Governor-General of India, and the Duke of Argyll exchanged the Privy Seal for the Post Office, Lord Harrowby succeeding him as Lord Privy Seal. After this reconstruction there was little change in the allocation of offices until the fall of the Government in 1858.

"I think our Government," wrote Palmerston to his brother, "will do very well. I am backed by the general opinion of the whole country. . . . As Aberdeen has become an impossibility, I am, for the moment, *l'inévitable*. We are sending John Russell to negotiate at Vienna."

To the history of those negotiations and the progress of the war we must now turn.

CHAPTER XIII

WAR AND PEACE. THE PALMERSTON MINISTRY
(1855-1857)

THOUGH peace was already in the air the new Prime Minister Adminis-
fully assented to the Queen's wish that until it was actually $\frac{trative}{Reform}$
signed the war should be prosecuted with vigour and determination.
To this end various administrative reforms were pushed on apace :
a special transport department was organized at the Admiralty ; the
commissariat arrangements at Balaclava were thoroughly overhauled
by Sir John McNeill, and a strong sanitary Commission armed with
comprehensive powers was sent out to the Crimea. Of still greater
permanent importance was the reorganization of the War Office at
home. Originally established in the reign of Charles II. the War
Office had always been conspicuous, even among Government
Offices, for maladministration. The nation had never taken the
department seriously and had always regarded it as a temporary
expedient with which it might be possible in time to dispense. There
was therefore an exceptional amount of overlapping and confusion.
" The soldier was fed by the Treasury and armed by the Ordinance
Board ; the Home Secretary was responsible for his movements in
his native country ; the Colonial Secretary superintended his movements abroad ; the Secretary at War took care that he was paid and
was responsible for the lawful administration of the flogging which
was provided for him by the Commander-in-Chief." [1] The Secretaryship of State for War was established under exigencies of the French
War in 1794, but its functions were complicated in 1801 by the
absorption of Colonial business, and still more by the survival of the
Secretaryship at War. The first of these confusions was determined
by the bifurcation of the Secretaryships of State in 1854, and in 1855
Palmerston decided that the Secretary of State for War should take
over the duties, mainly financial, of the Secretaryship at War.[2] At
the same time the War Office absorbed the Army Medical Department
and took over from the Treasury the control of the Commissariat.
The Board of Ordnance was abolished and its functions were similarly transferred to the War Office. That this process of simplification
and concentration contributed greatly to efficiency is not open to
question.

The effect was eventually perceptible even at the front. But Siege of
for many weary months the condition of the British force before $\frac{Sebasto-}{pol}$
Sebastopol had been deplorable. After the great fight of Inkerman
(Nov. 5th) there was no operation on a large scale in the field until

---

[1] Anson, *Law and Custom of the Constitution*, ii. 375.
[2] This office was finally abolished in 1863.

the middle of February. Nevertheless, the intermission of fighting brought no cessation of toil or suffering to the unhappy soldiers. The initial difficulty was the lack of transport facilities. Between the harbour, which was at once arsenal and storehouse, and the camp, there intervened some seven miles of almost impassible mud. There were stores in plenty in the holds of the Transports, but the men in the trenches were half-starved and in rags. " During the wet season, from November to December," said one of the witnesses examined, " and of the bitter cold from that to the end of February, the men had no other protection than that of the weather-worn circular tent. In rain, the ground inside was a mass of mud ; in snow, a mass of filth. From morning till night they sat in the mud of the trenches, from night till morning they lay in the mud of their tents." There was coffee in abundance, but it was served out green, and forethought had not provided means of roasting or grinding it. Scurvy was rampant ; but there was no lime juice, and the fresh vege-tables sent from home rotted in the Transports ; food, insufficient and wholly inappropriate, contributed to the prevalence of cholera and dysentery. Only the contractors grew fat. Boots were sent out, but many sizes too small, and one witness declared that he had seen men, during the coldest part of the winter, go into the trenches and on guard " with their feet on their boots, instead of in them ". Frost-bite was not the least of the miseries they had to suffer. Of the three battalions of Guards, representing 3,500 rank and file, less than 700 mustered on parade in January. Other regiments suffered in similar proportions. During the month of January alone 4,073 invalids were sent away to Scatari, and the daily average in camp hospital was over 3,000. Of the men on duty there were hardly any who " in a time of peace would have been considered fit to be out of hospital ". But the behaviour of the troops from first to last was magnificent. Witness after witness testified to their courage, constancy, and confidence. " Great Britain has often had reason to be proud of her army, but it is doubtful whether the whole range of military history furnishes an example of an army exhibiting, through-out a long campaign, qualities as high as have distinguished the forces under Lord Raglan's command. The strength of the men gave way under the excessive labour, exposure, and privation ; but they never murmured, their spirit never failed, and the enemy, though far outnumbering them, never detected in those whom he encountered any signs of weakness." Such was the official testimony of the Commissioners, Sir John McNeill and Colonel Tulloch.

Peace ne-gotiations at Vienna. The " Four Points "   While the soldiers were toiling in the trenches, the diplomatists were busy at Vienna. Austria, whose policy during this phase of the Eastern question was consistently subtle and crafty, had set negotiations on foot at the end of 1854, and on December 28th the allied Powers, in conjunction with Austria, presented to the Russian

Plenipotentiary a Memorandum, embodying the " Four Points ".
They were as follows :—

1. The exclusive protectorate exercised by Russia over Moldavia,
Wallachia, and Servia was to cease, and the privileges
accorded by the Sultan to the Principalities was henceforward to be guaranteed collectively by the Five Powers ;

2. The navigation of the Danube was to be free ;

3. The preponderance of Russia in the Black Sea was to be
terminated ; and,

4. Russia was to renounce all pretensions to a Protectorate over
the Christian subjects of the Porte ; and the Five Powers
were to co-operate in obtaining from the Sultan the confirmation and observance of the religious privileges of all
the various Christian communities without infringing his
dignity or the independence of his Crown.

The negotiations had proceeded so far that in February Lord John
Russell was sent out as British Plenipotentiary. He took Paris and
Berlin on his way. In his official instruction Lord Clarendon stated
the point to be aimed at with admirable explicitness : " The end in
view is the formal recognition of the Turkish Empire in its character
as an independent and self-existent state, as a member of the great
European family, and as an essential element of the balance of power
in Europe. One of the means by which that end is to be accomplished
is the abrogation of Russian supremacy in the Black Sea." The
Conference formally opened on March 15th, but before that date
arrived two events had occurred, each, in its way, of profound
significance.

On January 26th, 1855, Count Cavour appended his signature to Adhesion
a Convention with Great Britain and France, promising the adherence of Sardinia to
of Sardinia to the Alliance. Of good omen for the Western Powers, the Alli-
this step was incomparably the most momentous in the diplomatic ance, Jan.
history of modern Italy. Never was there a better example of the 26th,
1855
effective combination of reckless daring, and calculating prudence,
and the credit of it belongs to two men—Cavour and his King, Victor
Emmanuel. On the face of it, the resolution to take part in the war
was at once cynical and foolhardy. What business had the little
sub-Alpine Kingdom, reeling under the shock of the military disasters
of 1849, to send a contingent to the Crimea ? What part or lot
had she in the quarrel between Russia and the Western Powers ?
To Cavour such questions seemed " a surrender of our hopes of the
future ". Sardinia had first to prove " that the sons of Italy could
fight like brave men," and then to claim a place in the Councils of
Europe. Everything turned out as Cavour had foreseen. The war
restored the military prestige of Sardinia and Cavour took his place
in the Congress of Paris. By the end of April 18,000 Italians were
on their way to the Crimea, under the command of General Alphonso

La Marmora. " You have the future of the country in your haver-
sacks." Such was Cavour's parting injunction to the troops. The
response came from a soldier in the trenches : " out of this mud
Italy will be made ". It was.

Death of
the Czar
Nicholas,
March
2nd, 1855

The adhesion of Sardinia came as a timely encouragement to the
allies. To those who were longing and working for peace the death
of the Czar Nicholas seemed of still happier augury. Nicholas was
unquestionably the prime author of the war ; he had sustained it
with unflagging energy, and he was bitterly disappointed at his
failure to bring it to a rapid and brilliant termination. What Russian
arms failed to accomplish at the Alma, at Balaclava, and Inkerman,
" Generals January and February " might be trusted to achieve.
So thought the Czar. They had indeed inflicted terrible suffering
upon the besiegers. But the besiegers had command of the sea, and
the sea could bring them both reinforcements and supplies. What
of the besieged and Prince Menschikoff's army in the open ? True,
Sebastopol was not regularly invested, but supplies had to be brought
to the Russian armies over thousands of miles of road. The Crimean
snows descended impartially upon the just and the unjust, upon the
Orthodox, the Latins, the Protestants, and the Mussulmans. " General
February turned traitor," as *Punch* with its unfailing felicity pointed
out. The Czar was deeply chagrined, his fortitude gave way, and on
March 2nd, 1855, he succumbed to a pulmonary attack, following
upon influenza. The news of his death evoked profound emotion
throughout Europe, more particularly, of course, at Vienna.

Confer-
ence of
Vienna

The accession of the new Czar Alexander did not, however,
render the Russian Plenipotentiaries more pliable. On the first,
second, and fourth " Points " an agreement was reached without
much difficulty ; the crux lay in the third—the limitation of Russian
naval preponderance in the Black Sea. To that point Palmerston
in particular attached the greatest importance, and on it the negotiations ultimately broke down at the end of April. Had Lord John
Russell been left to himself he would probably have accepted the
proposals at the Black Sea put forward by Austria ; so would the
French representative M. Drouyn de Lhuys, who on his return from
the Conference resigned office. It would have been well for Lord
John had he taken the same course. It gradually leaked out that
the envoy's views as to the settlement suggested at Vienna were not
in accord with those of his colleagues, and on July 7th he himself
substantially confirmed the rumours from his place in Parliament.[1]
Thereupon Sir E. Bulwer-Lytton gave notice of a vote of censure
upon " the conduct of our Minister in the recent negotiations at
Vienna," and on July 16th Lord John announced his resignation to
the House. He was succeeded by Sir William Molesworth at the

[1] Clarendon speaks of Lord John's conduct at this time as " wilfully malevolent " (ii. 87).

Colonial Office, where the departmental work had been undertaken
in his absence by the Prime Minister, who with septuagenarian
enthusiasm was always anxious to familiarize himself with the work
of a fresh department.

Though peace was not concluded at Vienna, the end of the war *Progress*
was in sight. Nevertheless, there was a great deal of hard fighting *of the*
round Sebastopol during the spring and summer of 1855. On *war*
February 17th a Russian force, 40,000 strong, made a determined
effort to take Eupatoria by storm, but were gallantly repulsed by the
Turks under Omar Pasha, supported by a French detachment and
by five men-of-war in the roadstead. After four hours' continuous
fighting the Russians retired with considerable loss. In March, the
Russians advanced the defensive works of Sebastopol into the allied
lines by the seizure and fortification of a knoll known as the *Mamelon
Vert*, and the construction of a number of rifle pits. Desperate
efforts were made by the allies to dislodge them from these advanced
points but without avail.

In April, Napoleon III. and his Empress paid a visit to England,
when the tact of the former and the grace and beauty of the latter
went far to dissipate the prejudice of the Queen against the " man of
December ". Napoleon, to the horror alike of the English and
French Ministers, had announced his intention of going out to the
Crimea and taking the command in person. He was fortunately
dissuaded from this step,[1] though the mere suggestion exercised a
sinister effect upon the armies at the front. Towards the end of
May, however, the allies planned and executed a diversion in the
south-eastern extremity of the Crimea. A combined fleet, under Sir
Edmund Lyons and Admiral Bruat, with a considerable land force
of English, French, and Turkish troops left Sebastopol on May 22nd,
and three days later captured Kertch, and made themselves complete
masters of the Straits of Yenikale, which lead from the Black Sea
into the Sea of Azof. This expedition was brilliantly successful both
in design and execution and contributed in no slight degree to the
general purpose of the campaign. The stores destroyed at Kertch
were computed to amount to nearly four months' ration for 100,000
men—a very serious loss for the Russian army in the Crimea.

On May 16th Canrobert asked to be relieved of his command, but *Pélissier*
at the same time begged with rare gallantry, that he might be per- *succeeds*
mitted to serve as a General of Division under his successor. That *Canrobert*
successor was General Pélissier, who was not only a great soldier,
but was possessed of the moral courage which Canrobert lacked. He
soon infused fresh vigour into the operations before Sebastopol. On
June 18th a tremendous assault was delivered by the allies upon the
Russian position ; the French directed their attack upon the Malakoff,

---

[1] By Lord Clarendon, who was sent to Boulogne for this purpose.—Maxwell,
ii. 72.

the English upon the Redan, two formidable outworks on the east of the fortress. Both attacks were repulsed by the Russians with heavy loss. The failure of the attack upon the Redan was a bitter disappointment to Lord Raglan.

Death of Lord Raglan   A braver soldier and a more gallant gentleman never breathed. With splendid resolution he had faced all the privations and discouragements of an exceptionally strenuous campaign. He had seen St. Arnaud succeeded by Canrobert and Canrobert by Pélissier ; he had served under two Prime Ministers and two Secretaries for War ; he had witnessed the decimation of his army by disease ; he had been riddled with criticism ; [1] he had been pestered by Commissions and correspondents, and had submitted with perfect temper to the thwarting of his plans by his allies. Through it all, he had never lost courage and never faltered in the execution of the task entrusted to him. But he had now been for nearly two years at the front ; and, enervated by anxiety and worn out by ceaseless toil, he succumbed to an attack of cholera on June 28th at the age of sixty-eight. The maintenance of a difficult alliance was the best tribute to his tact, the fall of the great fortress to his persistency and courage. General James Simpson succeeded to the command, and reaped where Raglan had sown.

Fall of Sebasto-pol   Slowly but surely the allied armies pushed their lines towards the Russian fortifications. Once more, therefore, the covering army, under the command of Prince Michael Gortschakoff, made a desperate and gallant effort to raise the siege. On the night of August 15th-16th the Russians descended from the Mackenzie Heights upon the Tchernaya River. The brunt of the attack fell upon our allies, and after many hours of desperate fighting, the Russian army, 50,000 strong, was driven back with the loss of 3,000 killed, 5,000 wounded, and 400 prisoners. In this important engagement the Sardinian contingent, under General La Marmora, got their first real chance. Nor did they miss it. Fighting with the utmost gallantry they contributed in no small degree to the decisive repulse of the Russian army. Thus were Cavour's calculations precisely fulfilled. In the waters of the Tchernaya the stain of Novara was wiped out for ever ; out of the mud of the trenches was modern Italy built up. Henceforward Cavour could speak with his enemies in the gate. The victory of the allies at the Tchernaya shattered the last hopes of the besieged from the army in the field. For three weeks the allies kept up a continuous and terribly destructive fire upon the devoted fortress, and on September 8th the attack which had been foiled in June was renewed. The British, with a force miserably inadequate, again attacked the Redan and were again with great loss repulsed, but the Malakoff—the real key of the position—was already in the hands of their allies. The story of the final assault may be told in

[1] Cf. Panmure Papers, ii. 521-533.

the words of General Niel, the French Commandant of Engineers :
" At noon precisely our soldiers rushed forward on the Malakoff
from our advanced *places d'armes.* They crossed the ditches with
surprising agility ; and, climbing on the parapets, attacked the
enemy to the cry of ' Vive l'Empereur ! ' At the foot of the Malakoff
the slopes on the inside being very high, the first to arrive stopped
for a moment in order to form, and then mounted on the parapet
and leaped into the works. The contest which had commenced by
the musket-shots was continued with the bayonet, with the butt-
ends, and stones ; the Russian artillery-men made use of their
rammers as weapons ; but they were everywhere killed, taken
prisoners, or driven off, and in a quarter of an hour the French flag
was floating on the conquered Redoubt."

The storming of the Malakoff cost the French 7,500 in killed and
wounded, including fifteen generals, but it preluded the fall of
Sebastopol. Within a few hours the Russians blew up the magazines,
withdrew across the harbour to the north, and on September 9th,
after a siege of 349 days, the allies occupied the burning ruins of the
fortress that had been. The Russian garrison was unwisely permitted to make good its retreat, and thus the fall of Sebastopol did
not bring the war to an immediate conclusion.

On November 28th General Fenwick Williams was compelled to Fall of
surrender the fortress of Kars. He had been sent to reorganize the Kars
Turkish forces in Armenia, and with a small Turkish garrison had
been holding Kars for nearly six months against overwhelming odds.
It was an heroic defence and it won for Fenwick Williams undying
fame. A Turkish force had been sent too tardily to its relief, and
before it arrived the little garrison was starved out. General
Mouravieff's success at Kars had this much of significance ; it was
a slight set-off against the surrender of Sebastopol and it predisposed
the mind of the Czar Alexander to peace.

The Emperor Napoleon was equally ready for peace. He had Peace of
got all he could out of the war ; the French army had gained fresh Paris
lustre from the concluding passages of the war ; the English army
had not. His restless mind was already busy with the future disposition of Europe. He was looking towards Russia and towards
Italy ; for England he had no immediate use. Cavour too had got
all he wanted. The main obstacle to peace was Lord Palmerston.
His attitude is intelligible. England had made enormous sacrifices
in the war ; of men and money, and—most of all perhaps—of reputation. The failure of June 18th, repeated on September 8th, was
disheartening to the army and not agreeable to the Government.
Palmerston with a sportsman's instinct, would have liked to finish
strong. He was, moreover, gravely mistrustful of France, and still
more so of Austria. And he had reason. The part played by Austria
was crafty, selfish, and even treacherous. Her interest was

concentrated upon the Principalities. She had induced England and France to pick the chestnuts out of the fire for her there. Russia having been induced to withdraw from the Principalities, not by the words of Austria, but by the action of England and France, Austria had promptly occupied them, and had thus enabled Russia to concentrate her efforts upon the Crimea. Finally, as soon as there was a chance of peace, Austria spared no effort to detach Napoleon from the English alliance. And she nearly succeeded. In November, Persigny, the French Ambassador in London, attempted to persuade Lord Palmerston to accept Austria's suggestion that the Black Sea question should be settled by a separate treaty between Russia and Turkey. To this insidious proposal Palmerston offered a firm resistance, and on January 16th, 1856, the Czar (at the instance of his brother-in-law, the King of Prussia) virtually accepted as a basis of negotiation the " Four Points," including a stipulation for the neutralization of the Black Sea. On February 1st a Protocol embodying these terms was signed by the representatives of the Five Powers at Vienna. Palmerston, however, deeply resented the part played by Austria in the negotiations which led to this result. Sir Hamilton Seymour was now British Ambassador at Vienna and to him Palmerston wrote (Jan. 24th, 1856) : " Buol's statement to you the night before last was what in plain English we should call impertinence. We are happily not yet in such a condition that an Austrian Minister should bid us sign a Treaty without hesitation or conditions. The Cabinet of Vienna, forsooth, must insist upon our doing so ! Why really our friend Buol must have had his head turned by his success at St. Petersburg, and quite forgot whom he was addressing such language to. He should remember that he is a self-constituted mediator, but that nobody has made him umpire, arbiter, or dictator. . . . He may rest assured, however, that we have no wish to continue the war for the prospect of what we may accomplish another year, if we can now obtain peace upon the conditions which we deem absolutely necessary and essential ; but we are quite prepared to go on if such conditions cannot be obtained. The British nation is unanimous in this matter." Palmerston gauged public opinion to a nicety. The war was, at the moment of peace, more popular than it had ever been in England. But Napoleon was eager for peace, and if England had continued the war, it would have meant a serious quarrel with France. Nor had we any reason for further fighting. The definitive Peace signed at Paris on March 30th, 1856, contained all that we had any right to demand :—

   i. The Sublime Porte was formally admitted, on the invitation of the Six Powers (including the King of Sardinia), to " participate in the public law and concert of Europe," and the Powers engaged severally to respect, and collectively to

guarantee " the independence and the territorial integrity of
the Ottoman Empire ". (Art. vii.)

ii. The Sultan, " in his constant solicitude for the welfare of his
subjects," announced to the Powers his intention to amelio-
rate their condition " without distinction of creed or race " ;
but the Powers, while recognizing " the high value of this
communication," expressly repudiated the " right to interfere either collectively or separately " in the internal affairs
of Turkey. (Art. ix.)

iii. The Black Sea was neutralized, its waters and forts were to
be open to the mercantile marine of every nation, but permanently " interdicted to the flag of war," and there were to
be no arsenals, either Russian or Turkish, on its coasts.
(Arts. xi., xii., xiii., xiv., and attached convention.)

iv. Kars was to be restored to the Turks, and the Crimea to Russia.
(Art. iv.)

v. The navigation of the Danube was to be free, and Russia was
to retire from its shores by ceding a strip of Bessarabia to
Moldavia. (Arts. xv.-xxi.)

vi. The Principalities of Moldavia and Wallachia were to remain
under the suzerainty of the Porte ; Russia renounced her
exclusive protectorate over them, and the contracting Powers
collectively guaranteed their privileges. (Arts. xxii.-xxvii.)

vii. The liberties of Servia were to be similarly guaranteed.
(Arts. xxviii. and xxix.)

By an addendum to the treaty, known as the Declaration of
Paris, it was agreed to abolish privateering, and to proclaim as permanently accepted principles of maritime war the concessions to
neutrals made during the recent war by England and France ; (1)
a neutral flag was to cover an enemy's goods, except contraband of
war ; (2) neutral merchandise, except contraband, was not to be
seized under an enemy's flag ; and (3) a blockade was to be
" effective," *i.e.*, maintained by an adequate naval force. Such
were the terms of the treaty which crowned the conclusion of the
Crimean War. That war had cost England nearly 23,000 men, and
nearly £80,000,000. What had it achieved ?

The claim of Russia to an exclusive protectorate over Turkey or Results of
any part of it was definitely abandoned ; her ships of war were the war
driven from the Black Sea ; her arsenals were no longer to dominate
its coasts, and she herself was to retire from the shores of the Danube.
That these terms were highly advantageous to the Sultan is indis-
putable. Were they equally advantageous to his Christian subjects,
or to the Western Powers who had thrust back his hereditary foe ?
The neutralization of the Black Sea was a clear, though temporary,
gain to the Mediterranean Powers in general and, perhaps in particular, to Great Britain. But, repulsed at the Bosphorus, Russia

tried to force her way on to the Persian Gulf. Headed off again by
Great Britain from the Persian Gulf, she was driven still further east.
Whether to our ultimate advantage it is difficult to say. From a
selfish point of view England had better, perhaps, have accepted the
suggestions made by the Czar Nicholas to Sir Hamilton Seymour,
though captious critics of English policy will hardly fail to observe
that England is to-day in possession of Egypt and Cyprus, while
Russia is no nearer to Constantinople than she was in 1853.

France gained little from the war, but Napoleon gained much.
In 1853 his position in Europe was far from assured ; the Crimean
War established it, and until the advent of Bismarck his influence
upon the Continent was almost overwhelming. The war gained
him, paradoxically, the friendship of Russia : the peace lost him the
confidence of England.

The greatest gainer by the war, excepting the Porte, was Italy.
Cavour, despite the angry protest of Austria, took his place at the
Council Board in Paris, as the representative not merely of Sardinia
but of Italy. In the name of Italy he denounced the misgovernment
of the two Sicilies, and for Italy he conciliated the sympathy of
Great Britain and the active assistance of Napoleon. The intervention of Sardinia in the Crimean War gave to her a place in Europe
and rendered practically certain the war of Italian liberation.

Sequelæ of the Crimean War

There were other consequences of the war slightly more remote,
but not less significant. The alienation of the whilom allies was the
most obvious. That development was responsible for many things :
for a war scare which produced the volunteer movement ; for the
suspicion with which England regarded Napoleon's intervention in
the affairs of Italy ; for the impotence of the Western Powers in the
face of Bismarck's attack upon the Danish Duchies ; and thus, more
remotely, for the overthrow of Austrian power in Germany, and the
consequent war between Germany and France.

English finance

We must now turn to the effect of the Crimean War upon the
domestic politics of England. In Parliament there was almost
complete legislative stagnation. The interest alike of the Government and of the people was naturally and properly concentrated
upon the prosecution of the war. Other things could wait, the war
could not. There was, however, one department of domestic administration upon which the war powerfully reacted. The exchequer
had to bear an unusual strain and the fulfilment of Gladstone's
elaborate schemes was hopelessly impeded. But the author of the
Budget of 1853 was jealous of any infringement of its main principles.
And he had a right to be, for the results of his scheme were eminently
successful. Customs, notwithstanding remissions amounting to
£1,483,000, produced over £300,000 in excess of the previous year,
and Excise produced about £370,000 more. In the Budget of 1854,[1]

---

[1] The first Budget was produced on March 6th ; a revised edition on May 8th.

therefore he urged the House to adhere to the principles laid down in the previous year. The war expenditure he estimated at £8,100,000, and this he proposed to raise by doubling the income tax (from 7d. to 14d.), by raising the malt duty and the duties on Scotch and Irish spirits, and by a new scale of duties on sugar, adapted to a fresh and better classification. To borrowing for war purposes he was, both on moral and economic grounds, sternly opposed. " The expenses of a war," he characteristically said, " are a check which it has pleased the Almighty to impose upon the ambition and the lust of conquest that are inherent in so many nations. . . . The necessity of meeting from year to year the expenditure which war entails is a salutary and a wholesome check." Nevertheless, he was compelled to issue Exchequer Bills for £1,750,000 besides Exchequer Bonds to the amount of £6,000,000 in anticipation of revenue.[1]

Sir George Cornewall Lewis, who succeeded Gladstone, found himself unable to live up to this standard of financial virtue, and contracted a loan of £16,000,000 at £3 8s. 6d. per cent. But even this was insufficient to meet the estimated deficiency of £23,000,000. Sir George, therefore, proposed to issue £3,000,000 of Exchequer Bills ; to raise the sugar duties from 12s. to 15s. per cwt. ; the duty on coffee from 3d. to 4d., and that on tea from 1s. 6d. to 1s. 9d. per lb. He also put an extra 2d. on the income tax, and further increased the duties on spirits. Indirect taxation would thus yield an additional £3,300,000 and the income tax an extra £2,000,000. On August 2nd he had to take power to issue £4,000,000 additional Exchequer Bills to provide for supplementary estimates. A loan of £1,000,000 to the Sardinian Government was readily agreed to ; but the guarantee of a loan of £5,000,000 for the Turks was carried only by a majority of three.

The provision made for the war, ample as it seemed, proved insufficient ; the additional taxes yielded less than the estimate ; and in February, 1856, the Chancellor of the Exchequer had to raise an additional loan of £5,000,000. This was raised in 3 per cent. Consols at 90. A further loan of £5,000,000 was contracted in May to meet the estimated deficit in the accounts for 1856-1857.

The total addition to the National Debt, funded and unfunded, amounted to £42,000,000.[2] Nearly as much was raised by increased taxation. The whole cost of the war, therefore, was estimated by Lewis at £77,588,711. How far it is economically wise to pay for war out of income ; how far it is legitimate to pass on a large part of the burden to posterity ; whether loans, if raised at all, should be issued in stock of high or low denomination, whether it is better to

The War Budget of 1855

---

[1] The interest return on the Bonds was £3 11s. 6d. per cent. ; on the Bills £3 8s. 6d. Both were raised nominally at 3½ per cent.
[2] The American War had added £124,000,000, and the great French War £440,298,079.

14

pay a relatively high rate of interest, or to keep the rate nominally low at the expense of increased capital liabilities—these are questions which have exercised financial experts for the last two hundred years.[1] To them they must be left. One reflection may be permitted. However much the policy of the Crimean War may be approved, it is impossible not to deplore its financial results : the well-laid schemes of Gladstone were hopelessly frustrated, and an impetus was given to extravagant expenditure which has never since been arrested.

Proposed partition of Northern Africa The consequences of the Crimean War are discernible in directions far removed from domestic finance. Even after the signature of peace there were some awkward corners to be turned. There were difficulties in regard to the delimitation of the new Russian Frontier in Bessarabia, and more still about Serpent's Island at the mouth of the Danube. The noticeable point in regard to both is that France steadily supported the Russian view as against that of Lord Palmerston. The latter did not hesitate to charge Russia with deliberate bad faith in the execution of the treaty, and to accuse France of sustaining the former's baseless pretensions.[2] The attitude thus adopted by France did not predispose the British Minister to regard with favour the interesting suggestion put forward by the French that Northern Africa should be partitioned between England, France, and Sardinia. According to this plan France was to have Morocco, and England was to occupy Egypt and control the proposed canal through the Isthmus of Suez. On the moral aspect of the question Palmerston was very explicit. "The alliance of England and France," he wrote, " has derived its strength not merely from the military and naval power of the two States, but from the force of the moral principle upon which that union has been founded. . . . How, then, could we combine to become unprovoked aggressors, to imitate in Africa the partition of Poland by the conquest of Morocco for France, of Tunis and some other State for Sardinia, and of Egypt for England." Moreover, we did not want Egypt any more when offered to us by Napoleon than when offered by the Czar Nicholas. " We want to trade with Egypt, and to travel through Egypt, but we do not want the burthen of governing Egypt." For once Lord Palmerston spoke the language of the Manchester School. It was inspired largely by increasing mistrust of Napoleon. " The fact is that, in our alliance with France, we are riding a runaway horse, and must always be on our guard. . . . The danger is, and always has been, that France and Russia should unite to carry into effect some great scheme of mutual ambition." [3]

[1] Cf. Northcote, *Twenty Years of Financial Policy*, pp. 245-293 ; also Sir H. Parnell, *Financial Reform*, and Newmarch, *The Loans Raised by Mr. Pitt*, etc.
[2] Cf. an exceedingly frank letter to Count Walewsky ap. Ashley, ii. 117.
[3] Ashley, ii. 127.

In the Persian War of 1856-1857 we may discern another of the *sequelæ* of the Russian War. For many years past the English rulers of India had watched with alarm the stealthy advance of Russia in Central Asia, and particularly the growth of her influence in Persia. In 1837 the Shah of Persia attacked Herát, the strong city commanding the route through which an army must advance towards the invasion of India on the North-West. Russian diplomatists inspired the move, and Russian officers accompanied the Shah. Herát was defended, on behalf of its Prince Kamran, by Major Pottinger, an English officer. The defence was skilful and stubborn, and on the appearance of an English squadron in the Persian Gulf, and the withdrawal of the English envoy from Teheran, the Shah abandoned the siege, and the " Gate of India " was saved. Persia did not forget the disappointment of her hopes, nor forgave the Power by whom they had been thwarted. In 1851 the suspicions of the English Government were again aroused, and in 1853 the Shah bound himself by a Convention not to occupy Herát unless it was threatened by a foreign army. Both England and Persia, in fact, agreed to respect, and as far as possible to maintain, the indepence of Herát. The war between England and Russia ensued, and in December, 1855, the Persian Government declared that Herát was threatened by Dost Muhammad, Amir of Afghanistán, and once more advanced into the territory of Herát and laid siege to the city. Mr. Murray, the British Minister at Teheran, quitted the Embassy ; the Persian Government refused to withdraw from Herát, and on November 1st, 1856, the Indian Government declared war. A fleet was sent to the Persian Gulf ; Bushire was captured on December 10th ; a British force of 5,000 men was despatched from Bombay under the command of Sir James Outram and General Havelock. In February, 1857, there were two decisive victories, and on March 4th, 1857, a Treaty of Peace was signed in Paris. Persia renounced all claim over Herát or any part of Afghanistán, and agreed to refer any differences which might arise to the good offices of the British Government. The British public was disposed to regard lightly the Persian War. Palmerston, on the contrary, fully realized its significance. " We are beginning," he wrote, " to repel the first opening of trenches against India by Russia."

Before peace was signed with Persia we were already involved once more in hostilities with China. The dispute arose in the familiar fashion. Under existing treaties British vessels in Chinese waters were subject only to the jurisdiction of our own consuls. The *Arrow*, a lorcha or coasting schooner, was sailing, rightly or wrongly, under the British flag. The crew were Chinamen, and while the lorcha lay in the Canton river she was boarded from a Chinese warship, and the crew were carried off on a charge of piracy. The British Consul demanded their extradition, and Sir John Bowring,

The affair of the lorcha Arrow

the Governor of Hong Kong, supported him. The Chinese authorities refused reparation and Sir Michael Seymour, with the British fleet, proceeded to capture some of the forts on the Canton river. Bowring now seized the opportunity to demand the admission of foreigners to Canton, under the terms, hitherto neglected, of the Treaty of Nankin (1842). The Chinese made reprisals according to their wont; burnt down foreign factories, massacred European sailors, and set a price upon the heads of " the English and French dogs ". Things became so serious that early in 1857 troops were despatched from England, and Lord Elgin was sent out as plenipotentiary. The troops were diverted, as a later Chapter will disclose, to a more important duty, but Canton was taken in 1858 and the English and French fleets were sent up to Tiensten to enforce the demands of the Western Powers. Not until June, 1858, was peace finally concluded. China agreed to permit a permanent British Embassy at Pekin and establish one in London; to open the Yang-tse river and five more ports to foreign trade, and to protect the Christian religion.

Defeat of the Government
Before the Treaty of Tientsin was signed Lord Palmerston's Government had fallen, though not on their Chinese policy. That policy was not indeed unchallenged in Parliament. In February, 1857, Lord Derby moved the Lords to condemn it, but though supported by Lord Lynhurst he was defeated by thirty-six votes. In the Commons Mr. Cobden moved what was virtually a vote of censure, and was supported not only by Gladstone, Graham, and Russell, but by Disraeli. The motion was carried by sixteen votes, and the Government almost immediately announced their intention to appeal to the country as soon as the necessary financial business could be disposed of. This was rapidly done, and on March 20th Parliament was dissolved.

General Election of 1857
The issue as placed before the constituencies by Lord Palmerston was a simple one : did he or did he not possess their confidence ? The answer which they returned was unequivocal. The " fortuitous concourse of atoms " by which the Government had been defeated was scattered. The Cobdenites in particular were smitten hip and thigh ; in Manchester Bright was at the bottom of the poll ; Milner Gibson, his colleague, also lost his seat ; Fox was defeated at Oldham, Miall at Rochdale, and Cobden himself at Huddersfield. The result was a great personal and political triumph for Palmerston. The country believed that in him they had found a leader at once strong and patriotic ; he had " stood forth in the tempest of doubt and disaster " in the dark days of the Crimean War ; he had carried the war to a successful, if not a triumphant, issue ; he had stood firm for his country both against enemies and against allies ; he had faithfully supported her agents abroad—Bowring in China and Murray in Persia ; overbearing and high-handed he might be, but never pusillanimous, and the country rewarded him during the

remainder of his long life with its unstinted gratitude and confidence. In the new Parliament he found himself with a majority such as no Government had in recent years enjoyed.[1]

A strong hand was verily needed at the helm. One storm had been successfully encountered ; another of far greater severity was brewing. Before midsummer it burst. About the middle of June the news reached England that the Sepoy army had mutined in India, and that thousands of English lives, women's and children's no less than men's, were at the mercy of a pitiless and treacherous foe.

[1] His majority was eighty-five.

CHAPTER XIV

GROWTH OF THE BRITISH POWER IN INDIA
(1740-1856)

GREAT BRITAIN had barely emerged from the strain and stress of the Crimean War before she was called to confront still graver issues raised by a military revolt in India. The two events were not wholly unconnected, but neither exaggerated rumour as to British reverses in the Crimea nor any other single cause accounts for the outbreak of the Mutiny. The causes were, in part, immediate —almost accidental ; in part they were more general and remote. The latter cannot be understood without some reference to the historical development of British power in India. This would seem, therefore, to be the appropriate occasion for a brief but continuous sketch of a subject which has, up to the present, been deliberately postponed.

British merchants in India The English made their first appearance in India in the seventeenth century,[1] simply as traders, members of a Company incorporated under a Royal Charter by Queen Elizabeth (1600). They were not by any means the first representatives of the merchants of Western Europe. For a full century before Englishmen set foot in India the Portuguese had ruled a great Empire and carried on a large commerce in the East. After the absorption of Portugal into Spain (1580), the Portuguese power in India began to wane rapidly, and to the supremacy of the Portuguese there succeeded that of the Dutch. The Dutch established their great East India Company in 1602 ; they laid the foundations of Batavia in Java—henceforth the seat of their Government in the East—in 1619, and, in 1651, they made good the line of their communications by occupying the Cape of Good Hope. The Dutch concentrated their attention for the most part upon the rich islands of the Eastern Archipelago. Thither the English merchants followed them ; but the Dutch were intensely jealous of any interference with their valuable monopoly, and in 1623 the memorable massacre of Amboyna drove the English merchants —fortunately for their country—to seek refuge upon the continent of India. There in the course of the seventeenth century they established factories in Madras, Bombay, and Bengal. In 1689 the Company decided to take a further, and as it proved, a most momentous step. They deliberately resolved to try and obtain a territorial footing in India, and appointed Sir Josia Child as " Governor-General and Admiral of India ".

They had, however, to make good their position against European rivals. The Portuguese power was decadent ; the Dutch, though

---

[1] I ignore the visits of a few isolated Englishmen, such as Stephens (1579), at the close of the sixteenth century.

established at Chinsurah, near Calcutta, were intent, as we have Contest
seen, mainly on the Islands; our most serious European rivals, between
therefore, were the French. The French founded no fewer than English and
five Companies for trade in India between 1604 and 1664; ten years French
later they established their famous settlement of Pondicherri, and Com-
later still made secure their communications by the occupation of the panies, 1740-1763
Isle de France (1690) and the Isle de Bourbon (1720). Before the Dupleix
middle of the eighteenth century the representatives of the two great and Clive
Western Powers were locked in a desperate struggle for supremacy
in India, thus renewing in the Far East the grim contest they were
already waging in Europe and North America. That contest was
finally decided in our favour by the Treaty of Paris (1763). The
French were permitted to retain Pondicherri and, in Bengal
Chandenagore as trading settlements, but not to maintain any
military establishment, and from that day forward they ceased to
exercise—except for two fitful moments during the Wars of the
American and the French Revolutions—any political influence in
India.

Victorious over the French, the English Company now embarked, Contest
for good or evil, upon the turbid sea of Indian politics. The next half- with the
century witnessed a prolonged and desperate struggle for political "Native" Powers
supremacy between the English Company and various "Native" (1757-
Powers and Princes. The first round was decided by Clive on the 1818) (a) The
famous field of Plassey (June 23rd, 1757), a victory which definitely Marátha
established English supremacy in Bengal. The second consisted of a Wars, 1779-1818
series of wars against the great Hindu confederacy of the Maráthás.
The first war was waged under Warren Hastings (1779-1781); it
was brilliantly continued by the brothers Wellesley (1802-1804), but
the power of this formidable confederacy was not finally broken until
the third and last Maráthá War under the Marquess of Hastings
(1817-1818). The dominions of the Peshwá of Poona were then
annexed to the Bombay Presidency. The Peshwá himself retired on
a pension of £80,000 a year to Bithoor, near Cawnpúr, where he reared
an adopted son in the tradition of hatred against the British Government. That son—the notorious Náná Sáhib—flashed for a sinister
moment across the page of Indian history in the Mutiny, but with
his mysterious disappearance the tale of the Maráthá confederacy
dies down into silence.

Apart from the Maráthás the most imposing Powers in Southern (b) The
India were the Nizám of Haidarábad, and Haider Alí of Mysore. Mysore Wars,
The former was the greatest of the Muhammadan Viceroys of the 1780-1799
Mughal Emperor, ruling in the Emperor's name over a large Hindu
population. Almost from the earliest days the Nizáms formed a
friendly alliance with the English Company, and they remain to this
day the greatest and not the least loyal of the feudatory Princes
of the British Ráj. Haidar Alí of Mysore was one of the many

Muhammadan adventurers who at the dissolution of the Mughal Empire carved out for themselves great principalities by the power of the sword.

For more than twenty years Haidar Alí and his son Tipu maintained a fierce and not unequal contest with the English Company, nor was it until 1801 finally decided in our favour.

Consolidation of British India, 1805-1857 Upon the foundations well laid by Clive and Warren Hastings, by Cornwallis and Wellesley, a wonderful superstructure was, during the course of the next half-century, erected. But the expansion and consolidation of British power was due mainly to the logic of events and was effected in defiance of the declared policy of the Directors. The latter were frankly alarmed at the additional responsibilities thrust upon them by the enterprises of Lord Wellesley, and Governor after Governor was sent out with explicit instructions to put a peremptory stop to the progressive policy of his predecessor. Not one of them left India without having added substantially to the responsibilities he inherited. Lord Minto (1807-1813), for example, straitly charged to extricate the Company from political embarrassments and honestly intending to do so, was the first of the British rulers of India to open diplomatic relations with neighbouring States. Nor were his actual annexations, though small in extent, politically insignificant. For more than a century the Mauritius had been the principal connecting-link between France and the East. In 1810 it was captured and added to our chain. Java, which France had taken from the Dutch, was acquired in 1811, and in 1814 Cape Colony, which for one hundred and fifty years had served the Dutch voyagers as a half-way house to India, was finally and appropriately transferred to the Power which had succeeded to their supremacy in the East. But not for his annexations was Minto's rule memorable. In 1809 he concluded a treaty with Ranjít Singh, the famous ruler who had lately welded the religious bond of the trans-Sutlej Sikhs into a powerful confederacy and had erected a great power in the Punjab. That Treaty secured the Company against possible dangers from the North-West. A second embassy was despatched to the Court of the Amir of Afghanistán at Kábul and a third to the Court of Persia at Teheran. These missions, it is interesting to remember, were inspired primarly by mistrust not of Russia but of France. Napoleon, foiled in his scheme for the invasion of England, had come to terms with the Czar Alexander at Tilsit and was now contemplating an attack upon the North-West Frontier of India. His attention was fortunately diverted by the outbreak of the Peninsular War, but the fact that he seriously entertained the design is not devoid of significance.

Rule of Lord Hastings, 1814-1821 Lord Minto retired in 1813, and to him there succeeded Lord Moira, better known by his later title of Marquess of Hastings. Like his predecessor, he went out to India with a strong prejudice against the "aggressive" policy of Lord Wellesley. No sooner had he grasped the true position of affairs on the spot than he declared "that our object in India ought to be to render the British Government paramount in effect if not declaredly so; to hold the other States as vassals, though not in name, and to oblige them in return for our guarantee and protection to perform the two great feudatory duties of supporting our rule with all their forces, and submitting their mutual differences to our arbitration". During his long reign he went far towards giving effect to the principles thus enunciated.

His first war was forced upon him by the restlessness and encroachments of the "Highlanders of India," the Gúrkhas of Nepál. The Gúrkhas had long been a terror to all their neighbours in the Himalayan fastnesses. To the repeated remonstrances and warnings of Sir George Barlow and Lord Minto they had paid no heed, and in 1814 Hastings was compelled to declare war. The Gúrkhas—some of the best fighters among the hill-tribes—offered an obstinate resistance, but, after two years' hard fighting the brilliant campaign of General Ochterlony enabled Hastings to dictate the terms of the Peace of Segauli (Dec. 1816). That treaty has defined the relations of Nepál to the British Ráj from that day to this. The Gúrkhas, having made a splendid fight, frankly accepted defeat, and have since contributed some of the most valuable recruits to our Indian army. The Company acquired " a long strip of the lower Himalayas, with most of the adjacent forest lands extending from the present Western Frontier of the Nepál State north-westward as far as the Sutlej river ".[1] This acquisition, though not of great extent, has proved an immense boon to British administration in India, for within it are to be found the health-giving stations of Simla, Massuri, and Naini-tal. For the rest, the results of the expedition are thus summarized by Sir Alfred Lyall : "All the hill country that now overhangs Rohilcund and the North-West Provinces up to the Jumna river fell into our hands. The Anglo-Indian Frontier was carried up to and beyond the watershed of the highest mountains separating India from Thibet or from Kathay ; and the English dominion thus became conterminous for the first time with the Chinese Empire, whose Government has ever since observed our proceedings with marked and intelligible solicitude." [2]

Having dealt with the Gúrkhas, Hastings next turned his attention to the pacification of Central India. Life and property had long been rendered utterly insecure by the plundering raids by bands of freebooters known as the Pindárís. These "human jackals" represented the "débris of the Mughal Empire, the broken men who had not been incorporated by the Muhammadan or the Hindu powers, which sprang out of its ruins". No orderly administrator could tolerate the continued existence of a social pest of this character, and

Pindári War, 1817

---

[1] Lyall, *British Dominion in India*, p. 258.   [2] *Ibid.*

Hastings determined by one swift and strong blow to annihilate their power. The Pindáris enjoyed the sympathy, if not the avowed support, of most of the Maráthá chiefs, to whose trade they had succeeded. To proceed against them with anything less than over-whelming force would, therefore, have been simply to court disaster. Hastings accordingly collected a magnificent army of 120,000 men, and literally hunted down and cut to pieces these formidable marauders.

Third Maráthá War, 1817-1818 This done, he proceeded to deal a final blow at the Maráthás themselves. A confederacy formed between the Peshwá of Poona, Holkar of Indore, and the Rájá of Nágpur was defeated in detail, with results already recorded. Thus " did Lord Hastings carry to a successful conclusion the work begun by Lord Wellesley and establish the British Ráj as the Power Paramount in India ".

First Burmese War, 1824-1826 On the resignation of Lord Hastings in 1822, the Governor-Generalship was accepted by Mr. Canning, but the death of Lord Castlereagh detained that statesman in England, and deprived both India and Canning of an opportunity which would probably have been unique. In default of Canning, Lord Amherst was sent out. His rule (1823-1828) is memorable for the first Burmese War and the capture of the great fortress of Bhartpur. The Eastern frontiers of Bengal had for some time been threatened by the advance of the Kingdom of Burmah ; the intermediate tribes who had been taken under British protection were frequently annoyed by their encroach-ments, and in 1824 Amherst was forced to declare war. The war is notable for two reasons. It afforded, in the first place, a clear premonition of the Mutiny. The Bengal Sepoys were gravely dis-turbed by the prospect of an over-sea expedition ; they refused to cross the " black water " ; the 47th Native Infantry broke into open mutiny at Barrackpur and had to be ruthlessly shot down. The war itself lasted two years and cost us 20,000 lives and £14,000,000 sterling. The main expedition penetrated to Ava, and in 1826 Amherst dictated the Peace of Yandabu. The King of Burmah was obliged to cede the maritime provinces of Arakan and Tenasserim, and to recognize the English protectorate over Upper Assam, Cachar, and Manipur. Thus the war is memorable, in the second place, by reason of the fact that " it brought for the first time a non-Indian people within the jurisdiction of the Indian Empire ".[1]

Capture of Bhartpur In the year following the conclusion of the Burmese War Lord Combermere (the Stapleton-Cotton of the Peninsular War) was de-spatched in command of an expedition against the Ját state of Bhartpur. The storming of the capital city not only crowned a successful campaign but effaced the bad impression created by Lord Lake's failure in a similar enterprise in 1805. The idea had gained credence that the city was impregnable even against British arms.

[1] Lyall, *op. cit.* p. 267.

Combermere's timely victory served, therefore, to dissipate " a notion which had threatened to become a political danger ".[1]

Amherst's aggressive policy, though not lacking the justification of success, did not approve itself to his masters at home. The Directors were alarmed by rapidly increasing expenditure, the Board of Control were aghast at accumulating responsibility. Consequently Amherst was recalled in 1827, and there was appointed to succeed him a man who could be trusted to give a new turn to British policy in India. Twenty years before, Lord William Bentinck had been Governor of Madras, and had been recalled for lack of vigour in dealing with a serious mutiny at Vellore (1806). But the son of a former Prime Minister, and the kinsman of the Prime Minister of the day, got a second chance in 1827, and used it to the full. *The reforms of Lord William Bentinck, 1828-1835*

For close on a century the Company's territories in India had expanded with astonishing rapidity, and now as a result of almost continuous war and almost continuous annexation John Company had-become the the Lord Paramount in Hindustán. Two results only could justify that position : firstly, the suppression of the anarchy which prevailed on the dissolution of the Mughal Empire and the restoration of order and stable government to miserably distracted peoples ; and, secondly, the amelioration of the social and economic condition of our new subjects in India. The first task was to a large extent achieved under the rule of Lord Wellesley and Lord Hastings. Order was evolved out of chaos and legal rule was substituted for lawless violence. The second and even more difficult task was that to which Lord William Bentinck set his hand.

With his name no great extension of territory is associated. He was compelled, in 1830, to place Mysore under British administration and protection, and in 1834 he annexed the little territory of Coorg, in consequence of the flagrant tyranny of the Rájá, and " in consideration of the unanimous wish of the people ". But not by these things is the rule of Bentinck remembered. In 1833 an important change took place in the constitutional position of the Company. Its Charter was renewed by Parliament for another twenty years, but only on condition that it abandoned finally its commercial monopoly, and ceased to carry on trade at all. At the same time there was added to the Governor-General's Council a fourth (legal) member, who was not to be the servant of the Company, and the Governor-General of Bengal was transformed into the Governor-General of India with power to legislate, in Council, for the whole of British India. A Commission was also appointed to revise and codify the law. The first legal member of Council and the first President of the Law Commission was Macaulay. At last, therefore, the old confusion, deplored as long ago as 1776 by Adam Smith, was finally resolved. The Company ceased to be a Merchant, and was *Constitutional evolution of British India*

[1] Hunter, *op. cit.* p. 206.

henceforward only a Sovereign. But its sovereignty had long been shared with the Ministry of the day in England. In India itself the constitutional position of the Company had been first defined by Clive who established in 1765 the " Dual System ". Under this arrangement the Company took over, in return for a large annual tribute to the Emperor and to the Nawab of Murshidábád, the *Diwáni* or whole fiscal administration of Bengal, Behar, and Orissa. The system did not work and was terminated by Warren Hastings. His rule witnessed also the beginnings of parliamentary interference with the Company's affairs in India. The *Regulating Act* (1773) provided for the appointment of a Governor-General and Council for Bengal with loose powers of control over the other provinces ; it established a High Court of Justice—a first step towards the differentiation of the Judicature and Executive, and it stipulated that the British Ministry should be regularly supplied with information concerning the Company's correspondence with India. The daring defiance with which Hastings treated both Directors and Ministers combined with the inherent vices of the system itself to bring this provisional arrangement to an end. Pitt's India Act of 1784 established a dual control : it left the affairs of the Company untouched as regards trade, but it virtually transferred political responsibility to a Board of Control consisting of six Commissioners, all of whom were to be Privy Councillors, and among whom were always to be the Chancellor of the Exchequer and one of the principal Secretaries of State. The President of this Board (almost invariably a Cabinet Minister) was virtually, though not until 1858 in name, a Secretary of State for India, and controlled Indian Administration with the assistance of a Secret Committee of three Directors. Through this Secret Committee the orders of the Board were transmitted to India. The system thus established was frankly a compromise, but it worked well enough until the Mutiny, when John Company was abolished, and the administration of India was finally transferred to the Crown.[1]

Bentinck's reforms　Bentinck proved himself in many directions an intrepid and effective reformer. He extricated the finances from the chaos in which they had been left by Amherst ; he cut down the " allowances " of the military and civil servants of the Company ; he issued regulations for a new settlement of the revenue of the North-West Provinces ; he entirely reorganized the Provincial Judicature ; he abolished flogging in the native army ; he provided for the admission of natives to many offices in the Company's service, and he rendered a real service to social order by the suppression of the Thugs—a caste of hereditary assassins ; above all, with exemplary courage he grappled with the difficult problem of Satí. In the year 1817 no

[1] Sir Henry Maine holds that, except in regard to war and diplomacy, the Court of Directors was the efficient part of the " Dual System ". *Cf. Reign of Queen Victoria* (ed. Ward), p. 164.

AFGHANISTAN

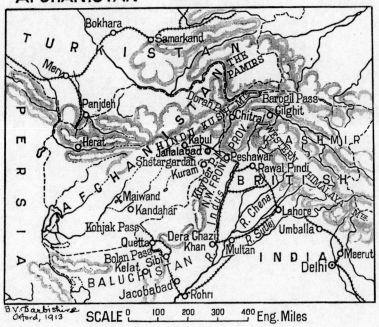

SCALE ⊢ 0   100   200   300   400   Eng. Miles

B.V. Darbishire
Oxford, 1913

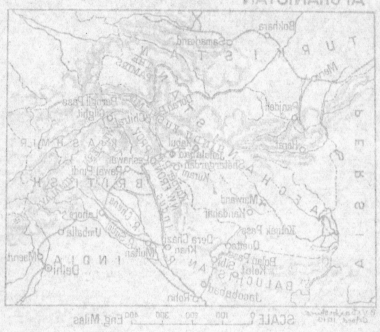

fewer than 700 widows, many of them mere children, had, according to this ancient custom, been sacrificed in Bengal alone, on the funeral pyres of their husbands. Vainly had the great Mughal Emperor Akbar attempted to abolish this cruel custom. It had acquired the sanctity of a religious rite, and it needed no ordinary resolution to interfere with it. Bentinck, however, was determined, and, in spite of opposition from Europeans and natives alike, he carried a resolution in Council, by which " all who abetted Satí were declared guilty of culpable homicide ".[1] Bentinck returned to England in 1835, leaving behind him in India the memory of a " wise, upright, and paternal administration ". Macaulay's well-known inscription on his statue in Calcutta has the rare merit of literal accuracy. " He abolished cruel rites ; he effaced humiliating distinctions ; he gave liberty to the expression of public opinion ; his constant study was to elevate the intellectual and moral character of the nations committed to his charge."

As to the wisdom of some of Bentinck's reforms—more particularly that for the admission of natives to office—opinions may possibly differ ; but it cannot be gainsaid that he gave to India a much-needed interval of repose. That repose was rudely and quickly broken by his successor. For some months after Bentinck's resignation, the reins of power were held by Sir Charles (afterwards Lord) Metcalfe as senior member of Council. Well had it been had he retained them. Peel appointed Lord Heytesbury to the office, but on returning to power, in April, 1835, the Whigs cancelled Heytesbury's appointment and sent out to India Lord Auckland. Auckland had served as First Lord of the Admiralty under Lord Grey, and had twice filled the office under Melbourne. He might be presumed, therefore, to know thoroughly the mind of the Government. He certainly knew the mind of Lord Palmerston, and Lord Palmerston's mind was filled with mistrust of the Eastern policy of Russia. He had good reason. By the Treaty of Unkiar Skelessi (1833) Russia had lately converted the Black Sea into a Russian lake, and had virtually established herself as Protector and patron of the Porte. She had lately won a diplomatic victory over England at Teheran, and had thwarted an English scheme for the establishment of a new Euphrates route to India. With all these things and with Palmerston's views on them Lord Auckland was familiar. *Lord Auckland, 1836-1842*

Consequently one of his first acts after arriving in India was to despatch Captain Alexander Burnes on a mission to Kábul. This mission was the prologue to a long series of the grimmest tragedies in the whole drama of Indian politics. A brilliant Afghán adventurer, Dost Muhammad, had by this time made himself master of the fierce tribes of Afghanistán and ruled them with an iron hand as Amír of Kábul. The North-Western frontier of British India rested on the *The opening of the Afghan question*

Sutlej ; the Amírs of Sind guarded the mouths of the Indus, while the Sikhs in the Punjab stood watch over the passes of the Himálayas.[1] The supreme ambition of Dost Muhammad was the recovery of Peshāwar, at one time the eastern outpost of the Afghán Empire, but now in the strong hands of Ranjít Singh. With Ranjít Singh we had no quarrel. He had faithfully observed the treaty concluded by Lord Minto in 1809, and a strong power in the Punjab was the best guarantee we could possess against hostile incursions from the north-west. Auckland's concern was not, therefore, for Peshāwar, but for Herát, which at the moment was seriously threatened by Persia. Dost Muhammad on his part was quite willing that Herát should fall to Persia, provided that Persia would help him to the recovery of Peshāwar. Such was the complicated situation by which Lord Auckland was confronted. Nor was it simplified by Burnes's mission, for Burnes found that he was not the only European diplomatist at Kábul. A Russian envoy, Vicovitch, was there also, and the advice of Vicovitch was far more palatable to the Amír than that of Burnes. " Let Persia have Herát, and Persia will help you to your eagerly desired revenge upon the Sikhs and the recovery of Peshāwar." That for " Persia " a suspicious eye might have read " Russia " mattered little to Dost Muhammad. What could Burnes offer against this ? Nothing but the platonic friendship and half-hearted diplomatic support of England. Vicovitch held all the cards, but Burnes had pluck and skill and might have won had he been supported from Calcutta. Auckland, however, haunted by the spectre of Russia at the gates of Herát and a Russian pawn in possession of Peshāwar, suddenly made an entirely new move. He decided to withdraw Burnes from Kábul, and to replace Dost Muhammad on the throne of Afghanistán by a puppet of his own. The puppet selected was Shāh Shujá, an aged grandson of Ahmad Shāh, the founder of the Durani dynasty in Afghanistán. Shāh Shujá had been expelled from the throne by Dost Muhammad, and was now living under British protection at Ludhiana. " His Majesty Shuja-ul-Mulk will enter Afghanistán surrounded by his own troops and will be supported against foreign interference and factious opposition by a British army." Such was the pretty make-believe solemnly put forward in Auckland's manifesto. To facilitate this " legitimist " restoration, a treaty was concluded between the British Government, Shāh Shujá, and Ranjít Singh. The latter was to be confirmed in possession of the provinces, which his sword had wrested from Afghanistán ; the integrity of Herát was to be respected, and Shāh Shujá, in return for a sum to be fixed by the British Government, was to relinquish all claim to tribute from the Amírs of Sind and to guarantee their independence (July, 1838). Ranjít Singh, despite the advantages secured to him by this alliance, wisely refused to

[1] The great province of Rajputana had passed into our protectorate in 1818.

allow the passage of a British army through the Punjab, and the advance, therefore, had to be made through Sind. The Amírs were not less reluctant than Ranjít Singh, but they were far less powerful, and though they imposed every obstacle they dared, a magnificent army started in December, 1838. Unfortunately for Auckland, one of his excuses for the invasion had already evaporated, for on October 9th the Persians inconsiderately raised the siege of Herát and agreed to molest it no more. But he was pledged to the restoration of a legitimate Sovereign to the throne of his immediate ancestors, and it seemed too late to draw back. The army, consequently, went on its way ; marched through Sind and thence by way of the Bolan Pass to Quetta, and on from there to Kandahár. Kandahár opened its gates, and there Sháh Shujá was enthroned (May 8th, 1839). Between Kandahár and Kábul lay the strong fortress of Ghazni. Ghazni was stormed in July and the road lay open to Kábul. On the approach of the British army Dost Muhammad fled, and in August Sháh Shujá was escorted in triumph into the Bala Hissár at Kábul.

By the Home Government the Afghan expedition was regarded as magnificent alike in conception, in execution, and in results. " By taking the Afghans under our protection," wrote Palmerston, " and in garrisoning (if necessary) Herát, we shall regain our ascendancy in Persia. . . . British security in Persia gives security on the eastward to Turkey and tends to make the Sultan more independent and to place the Dardanelles more securely out of the grasp of Nicholas." [1] No words could reveal more clearly the true inwardness of the policy for which Auckland and the British Cabinet were conjointly responsible.

In Afghanistán it soon became clear that the legitimate Sovereign could count upon the loyalty of his subjects only so long as he was protected by British bayonets, and for two years we remained in military occupation of the country about Kábul and Kandahár.

At length, however, it was decided to withdraw a portion of the army of occupation. Arrangements for the withdrawal were on the point of completion when the anger of the Afgháns, long pent up, suddenly burst forth,[2] and Sir Alexander Burnes, just appointed to succeed Sir William Macnaghten as Political Officer, was assassinated in Kábul (Nov. 2nd, 1841). General Elphinstone, no longer young, was in command of the British troops, and, owing to his inexplicable apathy, a riot was suffered to grow into an insurrection. The insurrection carried all before it and still Elphinstone did little or nothing to check it. On the contrary, he determined to evacuate the country. Akbar Khán, the eldest son of Dost Muhammad, appeared at Kábul at the end of November and with him was concluded, on December 11th, a treaty by the terms of which the Afgháns

The re-treat from Kábul

---

[1] Torrens, *Melbourne*, ii. 274.
[2] Kaye hints at private wrongs to be avenged, i. 614.

undertook to speed the departure of the British garrison by furnishing provisions and transport. Still there was delay. The Afgháns were slow in furnishing supplies, and Macnaghten occupied the interval by intrigues with rival chieftains. Invited to confer with Akbar Khán he walked into a trap and was murdered by Akbar's own hand (Dec. 23rd, 1841). No attempt was made to avenge him; Elphinstone's one anxiety was to get out of the country; and a further treaty, on terms perhaps the most humiliating ever imposed upon a British General, was concluded on January 1st, 1842. On the 6th the retreat actually began. Through the mountainous defiles between Kábul and Jalálábád the force made its way, in the depth of winter, and harassed perpetually by the attacks of the fanatical tribesmen of the hills. After two or three days the women and children were confided to the hands of Akbar Khán, and, later on, the aged and imbecile General, in the hope of saving the remnant of his force, surrendered himself and his staff as hostages. Each fresh humiliation was in vain. Out of 4,500 fighting men and 12,000 camp followers only one man, Dr. Brydon, reached Jalálábád in safety. A few prisoners were protected by Akbar Khán, but the rest perished miserably, having succumbed to the rigours of the march or been cut to pieces by the Afghán tribesmen. At Jalálábád Sir Robert Sale and his brigade had for two months been holding out; General Nott was holding Kandahár. Both Generals were ordered to withdraw the garrisons, and both, to the honour of the British name, refused. Meanwhile, in India, some efforts were made to retrieve the disaster. An attempt, under Brigadier Wild, to force the Khaibar Pass failed, but in February General Pollock reached Pesh, to take over the command. Not, however, until April was he in a position to take the field. Sale and Broadfoot were still holding out at Jalálábád and had actually beaten off Akbar Khán in a pitched battle, when, on April 16th, they were relieved by Pollock.

Lord Auckland succeeded by Lord Ellenborough, 1842

What was to be the next step? Were the garrisons to be summarily withdrawn from Kandahár and Jalálábád or was some retribution to be exacted from the Afgháns? The decision was no longer in Lord Auckland's hands. The Whig Government had fallen in 1841, and one of Peel's first acts was to send out Lord Ellenborough to supersede him (1842). For the policy which had been inaugurated so rashly and had failed so miserably the Whig Cabinet was not less responsible than Auckland. A change of Government in India was, under the circumstances, inevitable, but in his choice of a successor to Auckland Peel showed less than his usual discernment. A great orator and a skilled administrator, Ellenborough was nevertheless lacking in moral courage, and above all was self-conscious and bombastic.

In regard to Afghanistán he threw the real responsibility on to the Generals in command. They were ordered to withdraw, but by way of Kábul. Pollock and Sale fought their way from Jalálábád, Nott from Kandahár, and on September 16th they met at Kábul. The great Bazaar and the palace of the city were blown up ; the prisoners, including Lady Sale, were recovered ; and in October, 1842, the British force withdrew from Afghanistán. Our miserable puppet Sháh Shujá was murdered in 1843, and Dost Muhammad, released from India, was permitted to reseat himself upon the throne. That nothing might be wanting to this story of folly and humiliation, Lord Ellenborough thought fit to add a touch of ridicule and melo- drama. General Nott had been ordered to bring back with him as a trophy the gates of Somnáth from the tomb of the Sultan Mahmud at Ghazni. These gates were reputed to have been carried away from a great temple in India by Mahmud in the eleventh century. As a matter of fact they were a " modern forgery," [1] and their restora- tion with elaborate ritual and a vain-glorious proclamation added an element of farce to the grim tragedy so recently enacted.

Thirty years later it was revived, and every scene of the drama was, with singular precision, repeated on the same stage.

The results of the first Afghán War did not end with the with- drawal of the army, nor with Lord Ellenborough's famous proclama- tion. Two wars followed in the logic of history. The first was with the Amirs of Sind. Their independence had virtually disappeared with the passage of the British army through their territory in 1839. Throughout the subsequent period we had been obliged to maintain our line of communications by garrisoning the island of Bukkur, which commands the passage of the Indus, on the road to the Bolan Pass, and Kurrachi. When the Afghán War was over it seemed to Lord Ellenborough inconvenient to surrender these places. A pretext was soon found. Treaties imposed upon the Amirs had been indifferently respected. Further demands were made upon them, and in 1843 Major Outram, our political agent at Haidarábad, was attacked in the Residency. He held it gallantly with 100 men against 8,000, and safely withdrew his little garrison. Sir Charles Napier with 3,000 troops then flung himself upon an army of more than 20,000 Sindhis and Baluchis at Miáni, and achieved one of the most brilliant victories in the history of British arms in India. Three days later (Feb. 20th) he entered Haidarábad, and another victory in the neighbourhood of the capital brought the little campaign to a conclusion. Its inevitable consequence was the annexation of Sind. The territory of the Amirs, though not extensive, was of first-rate strategical importance. Its annexation gave us the command of the lower Indus valley and of the estuary of that river ; it completed our circuit of the sea-coast of Hindustán, and it gave Napier the opportunity of substituting for a cruel and grasping Government the unappreciated blessings of order and prosperity.

Conquest and an- nexation of Sind, 1843

---

[1] Hunter, *op. cit.* p. 212.

15

Expedition to Gwalior, 1843

Before the year was out Ellenborough had begun and successfully ended an expedition against the Maráthá State of Gwalior. Though left in the hands of Sindhia, Gwalior was under British protection. In consequence of domestic broils the Resident found it necessary in 1843 to withdraw. An army under Sir Hugh Gough was, accordingly, despatched to maintain order. The Maráthás opposed him at Máhárajpur, when he fought and won an important victory; General Grey won a victory on the same day at Panniár; and peace was promptly restored. The Márátha army was largely reduced, and a British force, maintained at the expense of Gwalior, was substituted for it.

The Gwalior campaign had two important results: it dissipated the danger of a possible coalition between the Maráthás and the Sikhs against the British Ráj; and it served to bring Ellenborough's reign to an end. His feverish activity alarmed both the Directors and the Cabinet, and in 1844 he was superseded by Sir Henry Hardinge.

The first Sikh War, 1845

Hardinge, though a veteran soldier, was sent out to India with a message of peace, and with definite instructions to pursue a policy of retrenchment. Before he had been a year in India he found himself, with an irony characteristic of British rule in India, involved in one of the most formidable wars of the century.

The Sikhs were not a distinct racial unit, but a religious sect, the disciples [1] of a prophet of the fifteenth century. On the break-up of the Mughal Empire they, like the Maráthás, emerged as a great territorial power. In the person of Ranjit Singh (1780-1839) they produced a great statesman. In his hands the loose confederation of the Sikhs was transformed into a compact nation, resting on the basis of an army, perfectly disciplined and organized by some of Napoleon's exiled veterans upon European models. Ranjít Singh, however, recognized the might of the British Ráj, and remained throughout life faithful to the treaty of 1809. By that treaty his activities were restricted to the Trans-Sutlej territory, but he added to his dominions Multán, Kashmir, and Pesháwar. The power which he had thus built up in the Punjab was exceedingly formidable. But it was subject to the defect common to all Oriental Principalities. Its basis was purely personal. On his death (1839) confusion quickly ensued, and his capital, Lahore, was the theatre of perpetual quarrels, intrigues, and assassinations. The only organized power was that of the army, and the army was bent on trying conclusions with the English Company. Ever since the close of the Afghán War the British Government had been fully alive to the danger threatened by the unsettled state of the Punjab and by the fixed ambition of the army, but they were determined to give the Sikhs no ground for offence. Hardinge, indeed, is accused by some critics of having gone

[1] Sikh = disciple.

so far in this direction as to have left the frontier inadequately guarded.

In December, 1845, the attack was delivered. On the 11th the Sikh army, 60,000 strong, with 150 guns, crossed the Sutlej near Firozpúr. The next few weeks witnessed some of the heaviest fighting in the history of British India. Sir Hugh Gough hurried up with 10,000 men, and on December 18th inflicted a crushing defeat on the Sikhs at Mudki. Then, picking up the garrison under Sir John Littler at Firozpúr, he attacked the fortified camp of the invaders at Firozsháh (Dec. 21st, 22nd). The Sikhs were far superior in numbers and guns and fought with the utmost determination. But again Gough was victorious. These victories were bought at a high price in wounded and killed, Sale and Broadfoot being among the latter. But they were decisive. India was saved from invasion and the Sikhs were compelled to recross the Sutlej. Not, however, for long. In the first month of the new year (1846) they were back again, moving on Ludhiana. Sir Harry Smith was accordingly despatched to support the little garrison with which Brigadier Godby held that post. Sir Harry relieved the garrison, and then, on January 28th, he inflicted a crushing defeat on the Sikhs at Aliwal. Meanwhile, Gough was watching the main body of the enemy, who had established themselves in a strongly fortified camp at Sobraon, guarding a bridge across the Sutlej. Sir Harry Smith rejoined the Commander-in-Chief on February 10th, and the two Generals, with their combined armies, carried the camp by storm, and drove the enemy with immense loss across the Sutlej. This was the crowning and conclusive victory of Sobraon. On the evening of the battle the advance on Lahore began. On February 20th the army was outside the walls of the capital, and Sir Henry Hardinge dictated the terms of a Peace which was concluded at Lahore on March 9th. The Sikhs agreed to cede the territory which lies between the Sutlej and the Beas rivers ; to cut down their army to limits prescribed by us ; to surrender all the guns used against us ; to pay an indemnity and receive a British garrison for eight years. There was to be no annexation of the Punjab ; Dhulip Singh, a reputed son of Ranjit, was recognized as Rájá, but the administration of the country was virtually committed to Major Henry Lawrence, who was to remain as British Resident at Lahore.

Sir Hugh Gough and Sir Henry Hardinge were rewarded with peerages, and in 1848 Hardinge handed over the reins to his successor with the cheering assurance that, so far as human foresight could predict, it would not be necessary to fire a gun in India for several years to come.

That successor was, perhaps, the greatest ruler ever given by Great Britain to India. During the eight years of Lord Dalhousie's reign modern India came into being, and to preside over such a

Battles of Múdkí, Firozsháh, Aliwal, and Sobraon

The rule of Lord Dalhousie, 1848-1856

transformation the new Governor-General, was pre-eminently well fitted. Politically he was Peel's disciple. He had served, in his Government, as President of the Board of Trade, and had commended his fiscal reforms to the House of Lords. He believed that in India he had a fair field for administrative reform. Others believed it too. " The youngest ruler who has assumed the responsibilities of this Empire, he receives it from his predecessor in a state of tranquility which has hitherto no parallel in our Indian annals. He arrived at a time when the last obstacle to the complete and apparently the final pacification of India has been removed ; when the only remaining army which could create alarm has been dissolved ; and the peace of the country rests upon the firmest and most permanent basis. The chiefs whose ambition or hostility have been the source of disquietude to his predecessors, have one and all been disarmed." [1]

Nowhere is fate more prone to mock than in India. Three months after these words were written a tragic outrage at Multán had reopened the question as to the future of the Punjab, and had involved Dalhousie in the difficult problems from which he never really emerged till he left India, a dying man, in 1856.

Sir William Hunter has summarized Dalhousie's work in India under three heads : the extension of our external frontier ; the internal consolidation and unification of our territory, and the development of national resources—the transformation of " the agricultural India of antiquity into the manufacturing and mercantile India of our own day ".[2]

The conquest and annexation of the Punjab, 1848-1849 In 1848 the map of India was divided into two portions : one was under the immediate government of the English Company ; the other consisted of the Feudatory States in which we exercised a greater or less degree of control, but without direct responsibility. The device was at best only a convenient makeshift, and the results were in some cases deplorable. British arms often maintained upon their thrones vicious and tyrannical Sovereigns, who, but for our support, would long since have paid the common and appropriate penalty of Oriental despotism. British Residents, though powerful to avert external interference, were impotent to secure good administration at home. On the contrary, their presence defended the " native " Prince from the consequences of his misrule. No ruler with an instinct for orderly administration could permit such a state of things to endure a day longer than was necessitated by the inadequacy of his own resources. Dalhousie's perception of this fact was largely responsible for the transformation of the map of India under his hand.

[1] The Friend of India, January 20th, 1848, ap. Sir Edwin Arnold, Dalhousie's Administration of British India, vol. i. pp. 59-60.
[2] Life of Dalhousie, p. 11. This is a brilliant, but in some details misleading book.

It was the Punjab which first demanded his attention. Lord Hardinge had rigorously curtailed its army and had placed the country under a regency of Sikh chiefs controlled by a British Resident at Lahore. The device was not to the liking of chiefs or people, and in April, 1848, the prevailing discontent blazed out. Two young officers, Mr. Vans Agnew, a civilian, and Lieutenant Anderson were sent to Multán to superintend a change in the government of the district, and while executing their mission were brutally assassinated. Their dying appeal for help reached Lieutenant Herbert Edwardes, stationed eighty miles away upon the Indus. Edwardes collected what forces he could, and on June 18th and July 1st won two brilliant victories over Mulráj, the deposed Governor of Multán. But it had already become clear that the local outbreak at Multán was developing into a general insurrection of the Sikhs. The Punjab would either have to be abandoned or reconquered. Edwardes appealed for immediate assistance, but Lord Gough refused to take the field with the inadequate force at his command, and during the hottest season of the year. His caution, though much criticized, approved itself both to the Governor-General and to the authorities at home. By November, however, he was ready to advance from Firozpúr with an army of 20,000 men ; and on the 22nd a dearly bought victory at Rámnagar enabled him to effect a crossing of the Chenab. It was an inauspicious beginning and there was worse to come. On January 13th, 1849, Gough was goaded into a rash and premature attack upon the Sikh position. Then ensued the battle of Chilianwála which a brilliant pen has described as " an evening battle fought by a brave old man in a passion and mourned for by the whole British nation ".[1] The British loss in killed and wounded reached the terrible total of 2,338 men ; four of our guns were captured by the Sikhs and three standards. It was not a defeat, but it needs some special pleading to claim it as a victory, and as soon as the news reached England there arose a loud clamour for the recall of Lord Gough. Sir Charles Napier was, accordingly, sent out to supersede him, but before Napier could reach India Gough won a brilliant victory at Gujrát (Feb. 20th). Multán had surrendered a month earlier (Jan. 22nd), and after Gujrát General Gilbert chased the Sikhs and their Afghán allies across the plains of the Punjab. At Ráwal Pindi the whole of the Sikh army surrendered (March 12th) and the Afgháns were hunted into the mountains. Thus was the second Sikh War brought to a triumphant termination, and the military power of the Sikh confederacy was for ever broken.

There could be but one sequel to the war. The half-measures of Lord Hardinge could not be repeated, and Lord Dalhousie, while

---

[1] Hunter, *Dalhousie*, p. 77. For an elaborate vindication of Gough, see Rait's *Life*, ii. pp. 211-245.

" deeply sensible of the responsibility " he assumed, determined that the Punjab must be annexed to British India. In this step Hardinge himself generously and cordially concurred. The young Mahárájáh Dhulip Singh received a pension of £50,000 a year, and the titular dignity of Prince. The administration of the newly conquered province was committed to a Board, consisting of the two Lawrences, Henry and John, and Mr. Mansel, acting under the immediate direction of the Governor-General. The Sikh army was disbanded; the Sikh confederacy was broken up, and the whole of the vast territory it had ruled was in a few years reduced to order and subordination by the genius of the Lawrences. How completely they gained the respect, if not the affection, of the Sikhs, the tale of the Mutiny was soon to prove, while no words can exaggerate the importance of the bulwark they thus erected on the most vulnerable frontier of British India.

The second Burmese War, 1852-1835 Lord Dalhousie's second annexation was the " submontane tract " of Sikkim in the Himálayas, due north of Bengal. Relatively small in extent, this annexation gave us an important tea-growing district and brought us into direct relations with Thibet. Much more important was the annexation of Pegu, a large tract of lower Burmah. This was the fruit of the second Burmese War.

The doctrine of " Lapse " More important still were the annexations in Central India rendered possible by a rigorous application of the doctrine of " Lapse ". When a Hindu had no lineal heirs it had long been the custom for him to " adopt " an heir and bequeath to him not merely his private possessions, but his principality as well. With the rights of "adopted" heirs to private inheritances Dalhousie had no wish to interfere, but he held that the interests of good government required that no rights of political succession should accrue without the sanction of the Paramount Power. This principle Dalhousie fearlessly applied. In deference to this doctrine the Maráthá principality of Sátára was annexed in 1849, and those of Jhánsi and Nágpur, in 1853. The last added to British India the great district known as the Central Provinces. The same doctrine is responsible for the less important annexations of Jaitpur, Baghát, Udaipur, and Budáwal. That these annexations were made with the most scrupulous conscientiousness on the part of the Governor-General, and that the result of them was to substitute good government for bad government is undeniable. But it is not less certain that in the aggregate they tended to create a feeling of unrest among the peoples of India which was among the contributory causes of the subsequent Mutiny.

The annexation of Oudh Most significant of all in this respect, and most direct in its bearing upon the Sepoy Mutiny, was the annexation of the Muhammadan kingdom of Oudh. In no district of India was the Government more notoriously and more heartlessly oppressive. The misrule had been persistent for half a century. Lord Wellesley had foreseen, as long ago as 1801, that the Paramount Power would be compelled to interfere. Thirty years later Lord William Bentinck, least ambitious and most humane of rulers, had solemnly warned the King that failure to amend his ways could have but one result. Lord Hardinge in 1847 definitely limited the period of grace to two years. In 1856 Dalhousie determined to act. It was his solemn conviction that " the British Government would be guilty in the sight of God and man if it were any longer to aid in sustaining by its countenance an administration fraught with suffering to millions ". But for that countenance the Kings would long since have paid the penalty for persistent oppression and misrule, and Dalhousie felt that the responsibility thus incurred by the British Government was too heavy to be borne any longer. Nevertheless, he shrank from the final and formal step. That the actual administration should be vested in the Company seemed to him inevitable, but he would have left the King his title, rank, and ample revenues. The Directors decreed otherwise, and on February 13th, 1856, the formal annexation of Oudh to the dominions of the Company was proclaimed. On the fallen dynasty no compassion need be wasted. They had been repeatedly warned, but despite warnings had persisted in their evil ways. As for their subjects, no one can doubt that in place of a bad government they got a good one. But it is none the less true that Oudh supplied a large proportion of the mutineers of '57.

The annexation of Oudh was the last official act of Lord Dalhousie. But to dwell exclusively upon the change he effected in the map of British India would be to present this administration in false perspective. That change was indeed stupendous. The British India of 1856 was " between a third and a half " larger than that of 1848. More than that, its " political centre of gravity had profoundly altered ".[1] Realizing this fact and all that it implied, Dalhousie promoted a series of consequential changes. Lower Bengal was placed under a Lieutenant-Governor, and the Governor-General was set free for his wider responsibilities.[2] The centre of military gravity was shifted steadily towards the north-west. The seat of the supreme Government was transferred, during the greater part of the year, to the Himalayan summer-resort of Simla, and thither, in 1865, the army head-quarters followed it. To bind together the old British India and the new, Dalhousie devised a comprehensive scheme of railway construction, basing it financially upon the system which he would fain have applied to England in 1844. Individuals were to find the capital, and the State was to guarantee a minimum rate of interest.[3] To the same source India owes the telegraphic system

Internal reforms

---

[1] Hunter, *Dalhousie*, p. 179.   [2] By an Act of 1853.
[3] Hunter describes Dalhousie's railway scheme set forth in the Minute of 1853 as " one of the most comprehensive and far-seeing which ever issued from a human brain," *op. cit.* p. 191.

and the halfpenny post, a wonderful expansion of trade, and the foundations of a national system of education. The work actually achieved by Dalhousie was stupendous : the face of the whole land was transformed, and much more than the face of it. We are not, even yet, perhaps, in a position to gauge accurately the full effect of the changes which Dalhousie initiated. " We are making," wrote Sir Edwin Arnold in 1865, " a people in India, where hitherto there have been a hundred tribes but no people ".[1] There could be no better summary of Dalhousie's work.

Whether Lord Dalhousie was fully conscious of the dangers implicit in his own handiwork is a question which cannot be decided. But to suggest that he was wrapped in any false security is a libel upon his powers of perception and of prescience. " No prudent man, having any knowledge of Eastern affairs, would ever venture to predict a prolonged continuance of peace in India." These were his parting words to the people of India. To his employers at home his warnings were equally candid and more specific. He protested strongly against the withdrawal of European troops from India, and earnestly warned the Government against the dangerously increasing disproportion between English and native troops. Even for the exigencies of the Crimean War India ought not to be depleted of British troops. " We are perfectly secure," he wrote, " so long as we are strong and are believed to be so." Between 1854 and 1857 reports were industriously circulated in India that the Crimean War had demonstrated to the world the military weakness of Great Britain. In many quarters those reports found ready credence. We were believed not to be strong. One of the main props of our security was thus rudely shaken and the result was seen in the outbreak of the Mutiny.

Quoted by Hunter, p. 209.

CHAPTER XV

THE INDIAN MUTINY

(1856-1858)

I N February, 1856, Lord Dalhousie handed over the reins of govern- Lord Can-
ment to his successor. The man selected for this arduous ning's
responsibility was Lord Canning, the third son of the great statesman India
who had himself, in 1822, accepted the office to which his son was
now called. A contemporary of Dalhousie's at Christ Church, Lord
Canning had, like his predecessor, served his political apprenticeship
under Peel. As Postmaster-General he had been a member of the
Coalition Ministry from 1853 to 1855.[1] From the moment of his
arrival in India he found himself confronted with difficulties : Herát
to be again defended from the attacks of Persia ; Oudh to be provided with a regular administration ; the native army to be reorganized. But he was hardly seated in the saddle when all other
anxieties were thrown into the shade by the outbreak of mutiny
among the sepoys of Bengal.

Historians are not, even now, agreed as to the precise scope and Causes of
nature of the rising of 1857. On the one hand it is described as a the
purely military revolt, on the other as an attempt at political revolu- Mutiny
tion. If it never actually engulfed India in revolution, that was
mainly because the revolt was subdued in time. For the causes
which contributed to the outbreak were not merely military. Mutinies
among the native troops were not indeed unknown in India. A
serious mutiny had broken out at Vellore in 1806 ; Lahore was the
scene of a less serious one in 1849, and many others had, during the
last thirty years, been hushed up by the authorities.[2] These facts
were known to all the responsible officials in India ; they were known
also to the native soldiers, to the native princes, and to the people at
large. From the latter nothing that happens in India can be concealed,
though their demeanour gives no hint of the knowledge they possess.
More particularly were they alive to the fact that in 1857 the native
troops outnumbered the British by seven or eight to one.[3] Of the
native army nearly half belonged to Bengal, and, of these, large
numbers were drawn from the Province of Oudh. The latter, as
we have seen, had a special and a recent reason, if not for disaffection,
at any rate for unrest. But all sections of the Bengal army were
unsettled. The unsettlement was due to many causes. The extension of the military responsibilities of the Indian Government ; the

---

[1] Admitted to the Cabinet by Lord Palmerston (1855).
[2] " For thirty years past the Bengal army had been in a state of quasi-
mutiny."—T. R. Holmes, *Indian Mutiny*, p. 63.
[3] The actual figures are very variously given : perhaps the most trustworthy
estimate gives the British troops at 39,500, the natives at 311,038.

over-sea expeditions to Burma and Persia ; the attempt to Europeanize discipline ; the diminution of the prestige of the regimental officers ; the passing of the Foreign Enlistment Act (1856) ; all these things contributed to the sense of impending change.

So long as the military reputation of England was undimmed this was of no great moment. But our prestige had lately waned. There were exaggerated rumours of reverses to English arms in the Crimea ; men talked of the success of Russia in sustaining the siege of Sebastopol against England and France in combination ; even young men had witnessed the disasters in Afghanistán and the questionable victories in the Punjab ; wars in China and Persia were likely to drain the strength even of a great military Power. There was not a bazaar in India in which such matters were not eagerly discussed.

It is doubtful, however, whether these things, taken by themselves, would have sufficed to produce a great revolt. Enough has been said already of the significance in this connection of Lord Dalhousie's policy. It is not easy to assign to that policy its precise weight as a factor in the problem. Unquestionably, however, the princes and peoples were alike filled with a sense of uneasiness by the rapidity with which Dalhousie had extended the dominions of the English Company. Nor was there a vestige of gratitude for the " blessings of good Government ". Oriental conservatism is strongly averse to change even if it be change for the better. This is a truth which the British mind finds it almost impossible to grasp ; but the neglect of it has more than once contributed to disaster. Never did it contribute more directly than in the Indian Mutiny.

Still more potent was the conviction which rapidly gained ground that the British Government were intent on religious proselytism. The Hindu feared for his caste ; the Muhammadan for his creed. Then, as often, there were isolated instances of tactless proselytism on the part of well-intentioned soldiers and civilians, but for the idea that there was any deep-laid plot to effect the conversion of the " heathen " there was not, of course, the least foundation.

The greased cartridges Upon materials thus highly inflammable a live spark was unfortunately dropped. A new weapon, the Enfield rifle, had lately been substituted, in the Indian army, for the old " Brown Bess ". It was rumoured that the new cartridges were greased with the fat of swine and cows. To load the new rifle the sepoy would have to bite the cartridge. This meant for the Hindu desecration, and for the Muhammadan contamination ; to the former the cow is sacred, to the latter the pig is pollution. The worst fears of both were apparently justified. The caste of the one was to be undermined, the creed of the other was derided. Both refused to touch the greased cartridges. Their officers, well knowing their prejudice, assured them that the rumour was baseless, and that they might safely use the new cartridges. The assurance did but inflame their terror and resentment. They felt themselves the victims of an accursed conspiracy, designed to effect their degradation in this world and their damnation in the next. For the sepoys were better informed than their officers. The story of the greased cartridges was true. With incredible folly and carelessness the fat of swine and cows *had* been used in glazing the paper which contained the powder. The officers never suspected it ; the men learnt it from the low-caste natives employed in the arsenal. The consequences of the initial blunder, and still worse the subsequent denial of the facts, can easily be imagined. The outbreak of mutiny was due in part to sheer terror ; in part to justifiable resentment against the fraud which, as the sepoys imagined, had been practised upon them by those in authority.

Personal influences were also working in the same direction. India was full of men with a grievance against the British Government : dispossessed princes, disappointed " heirs," greedy placemen deprived of comfortable jobs. Among these personal influences the most potent was that of the Náná Sáhib, the adopted heir of Báji Ráo the last of the Peshwás. The Peshwá died in 1851, and Dalhousie refused to renew to his adopted heir the pension with which since 1818 the Peshwá had been consoled. Second only to the Náná in malignant influence was Azimula Khan, a Muhammadan agent employed by the Náná to promote his suit in Europe.

Nevertheless, it is the opinion of Lord Roberts [1] that despite the accumulation of causes of discontent, personal and general, there would have been no mutiny had the warnings of Dalhousie received the attention they deserved ; had the British element in the Indian army been maintained in due proportion to the native ; [2] above all had the British officers been younger, more alert to observe the signs of disaffection, and more prompt to deal with its manifestations.[3]

Those manifestations became increasingly frequent in the early Outbreak months of 1857. On January 24th General Hearsey reported from of Mutiny Dum Dum the existence of an " unpleasant feeling " which he ascribed to rumours as to the preparation of the new cartridges. The 19th Native Infantry was stationed at Berhampur, a military station about 100 miles from Calcutta ; the 34th was at Barrackpur. These regiments were honeycombed with disaffection, and so quickly did the mutinous temper spread that it was thought desirable to disband the 19th on March 30th, and the 34th on May 6th.

[1] *Cf. Forty-one Years in India*, vol. i. c. xxx., an admirable analysis of the causes of the mutiny.

[2] Lord Roberts gives the figures in 1857 as 36,000 British against 257,000 natives, exclusive of armed police and Lascars.

[3] " Brigadiers of seventy, Colonels of sixty, and Captains of fifty. It is curious to note how nearly every military officer, who held a command or a high position on the staff in Bengal when the Mutiny broke out, disappeared from the scene in the first few weeks and was never heard of officially again."—Roberts, pp. 456-457.

It was, however, at Meerut that the first serious outbreak occurred. Eighty-five troopers of the 3rd Native Cavalry having been tried by a court-martial composed of native officers for refusing to touch their cartridges were sentenced to ten years' imprisonment, were publicly degraded and marched off to gaol. On the following day, Sunday, May 10th, the whole regiment mutinied, broke open the gaol, released their comrades and 1,200 other prisoners, gutted and burnt the European bungalows, and massacred every European man, woman, and child, on the outskirts of the cantonments. This done, the mutineers made off to Delhi. General Hewitt—one of Lord Roberts' " Generals of Seventy "—was in command at Meerut, and neither he nor Archdale Wilson, the Brigadier, made any effort to pursue the mutineers or to warn the garrison at Delhi. It is the opinion of Lord Roberts that " there was unaccountable, if not culpable want of energy displayed by the Meerut authorities on this disastrous occasion " : but that it would have been futile to pursue mutineers, even had their destination been ascertained, and that no action however prompt on the part of the Meerut authorities could, at this stage, have arrested the mutiny.[1] But the Government of India took a serious view of the conduct of affairs at Meerut and General Hewitt was removed from his command.

Delhi   Meerut is forty miles to the north of Delhi. On the morning of May 11th the mutineers reached unopposed the ancient capital of India. Their arrival was expected ; the native regiments in Delhi joined them ; the teeming inhabitants of the great city were on their side. They dragged forth from his retirement the old Mughál Emperor, and proclaimed the restoration of the Muhammadan dynasty to the imperial throne of India. Already a military revolt had developed into a political revolution.

Delhi thus became the centre of the insurrection. The fate of British India depended on its speedy recapture. Towards this end all energies were bent. General Anson, the Commander-in-Chief, was at Simla when the bad news reached him on May 12th. He collected what forces he could at Umballa, but found them insufficient for the task of retaking Delhi, and unequipped either with means of transport or with siege guns. He proposed, therefore, to wait until he could march with fair prospect of success. But time was of the essence of the situation. Lord Canning urged the General to immediate action. Sir John Lawrence wrote from the Punjab in the same sense. He admitted that on military principles the General's plea for delay was unanswerable. But political considerations should be paramount. " Pray only reflect," he wrote, " on the whole history of India. Where have we failed when we acted vigorously ? Where have we succeeded when guided by timid counsels ? " Anson yielded, arranged that two brigades should march from Umballa,

[1] Vol. i. pp. 87-91.

and, having united with one from Meerut, should try to carry out
their orders and " make short work with Delhi ".[1] Anson himself
started on May 24th, but succumbed to cholera at Kurnal on the
27th, and the command of the field force then devolved upon Sir
Henry Barnard.

Meanwhile, in the Punjab, Sir John Lawrence was straining every The
nerve for the fulfilment of a two-fold task : to secure the Punjab Punjab
itself, and to provide a force to assist in the recapture of Delhi.
Lawrence himself was a tower of strength, and was splendidly served
by his lieutenants Herbert Edwardes, John Nicholson, and Robert
Montgomery.   There was no panic, but at the same time no misplaced
reliance upon the loyalty of native troops.   Those troops were not
less mutinous in the Punjab than elsewhere.   But prompt action
rendered them impotent for mischief.   The great arsenal at Firozpur
was secured, and many of the native regiments were disarmed at
Mián Mir, Múltán, and Pesháwar.   These measures—exhibiting a
combination of calm courage and stern repression—deeply impressed
the Sikh population as well as those sepoys who were permitted to
retain their arms.   Thus Lawrence and his lieutenants saved the
Punjab, and in saving the Punjab succoured India.   On June 22nd
Nicholson was despatched in command of a strong force to Delhi,
and on August 14th he arrived before the town.

By that time the siege, if siege it may be called, had already been The Siege
in progress for two months.   Barnard, succeeding to the command of Delhi
on May 26th, was joined on June 7th by a brigade from Meerut, and
with this, and 500 Gúrkhas and a siege train, he marched on Delhi.
His total force was now about 3,800 strong.   On June 8th he met
the mutineers 8,000 strong, six miles outside the town, drove them
within the walls, and himself took up his position on the famous
ridge to the north of the city.   By the end of June the rebel army
had swollen to 30,000 ; the British force, therefore, had its work cut
out even to defend the ridge.   Barnard succumbed to cholera on
July 5th, and on the 17th General Reed, who had succeeded to the
command, was compelled through illness to give way in turn to
Archdale Wilson.   By the end of August the little force on the ridge
had been increased to 8,000 men fit for service, besides 3,000 men in
hospital.   No reinforcements could be looked for from the south, and
Lawrence told Wilson that he had sent the last man he could spare
from the Punjab.   It was decided, therefore, to deliver an assault
without delay.   The breaching batteries opened fire on September
11th, and in the early dawn of September 14th the assault was
delivered.   The Kashmír gate was blown in and two other breaches
were effected.   Immediately the ramparts were stormed and taken,

---

[1] Lord Roberts vindicates Anson from the charge of vacillation and lack of
promptitude. "The advice to march upon Delhi was sound, but had it been
rashly followed disaster would have been the inevitable result."—*Op. cit.* i. 105.

but for six days the British troops had to fight every inch of ground within the city. Nicholson, who had led the assault with splendid gallantry, was mortally wounded, but still the troops fought on. The magazine was taken after two days' hard fighting on the 16th and the imperial palace on the 21st. The old Mughál Emperor who thus fell into our hands was ultimately sent as a State prisoner to Rangoon where he died in 1862. His three sons, who had surrendered themselves, were shot down without a trial or any forms of arraignment by Hodson, the intrepid leader of the irregular horse. At last Delhi was ours.[1]

Cawnpúr

With the recapture of Delhi—" the scene of the essentially vital struggle " [2]—the curtain falls upon the first act of the drama of the Mutiny. But there were two other theatres of revolt where the tragedies enacted were even more grim. Grimmest was that at Cawnpúr. Cawnpúr is on the great trunk road between Delhi and Calcutta, 270 miles from the former and 684 from the latter. It contained a great native garrison, commanded in 1857 by Sir Hugh Wheeler, an aged officer. Early in May, Wheeler, anticipating mutiny, hastily fortified some buildings, and the British residents took refuge within the rough entrenchments. Near to Cawnpúr is Bithur where the Náná Sáhib lived in state. The native troops mutinied on June 6th, fled from Cawnpúr to Bithur, and the Náná, putting himself at their head, was proclaimed Peshwá of the Máráthás. The troops demanded to be led to Delhi, but the Náná persuaded them first to exterminate the vermin in Cawnpúr. Within the entrenchments were 870 non-combatants, and to defend them Wheeler had only 240 European soldiers and six guns. Without were 4,000 rebels led by the treacherous Náná. Unspeakable were the sufferings of the little garrison, huddled together under the burning June sun : with scant provisions, little water, and constantly exposed to the enemy's fire. For three weeks they held the enemy at bay, but on June 24th they surrendered on the sworn promise of the Náná that he would guarantee them safe escort by the Ganges to Allahábád. On the 27th they marched out, a miserable company of 450, fever-striken, wounded, and starving. Just as they were embarking the full measure of the Náná's treachery was revealed. A murderous fire was opened upon them ; the men were shot down or hacked to pieces before the eyes of their wives and children ; four only, the survivors of the single boat-load which actually got afloat, managed to escape ; the women and children, some 150 in number, were dragged back and thrust into captivity in Cawnpúr. General Havelock, hastily collecting a force of 1,000 men at Benares, advanced and defeated the rebels at Fathpúr on July

---

[1] The story of the assault is graphically told by Lord Roberts, *op. cit.*, i. c. xvii.-xix.

[2] McLeod Innes, *Lucknow and Oude in the Mutiny*, p. 25.

12th, and three days later inflicted upon them a second crushing defeat at Aoung. On that same day the Náná had every woman and child at Cawnpúr butchered in cold blood, and flung dead or dying into a well. With a force of 6,000 men the Náná then tried to stop the advance of Havelock. Once more, but too late to save the wretched captives, Havelock routed the Náná, and on July 17th the English were again masters of Cawnpúr. Havelock blew up the palace and magazines at Bithúr, and leaving Neill to occupy Cawnpúr, he started on July 25th for the relief of Lucknow.

Next to Delhi, Lucknow was the most important centre of the Lucknow Mutiny. It was indeed natural that the capital of Oudh should be the focus of unrest. In March, Sir Henry Lawrence had been appointed Resident. He clearly foresaw the coming storm, and did all he could to put Lucknow in a condition of defence, but the task was not easy. He had 700 British soldiers under his command, and 16,000 native troops. On May 30th the storm burst; five of the native regiments broke out, set fire to the cantonments, and murdered their officers, under circumstances of exceptional treachery. The outbreak at Lucknow gave the signal for revolt to every station throughout the old kingdom of Oudh. By the middle of June every regiment in the province was in a state of mutiny. As soon as Cawnpúr surrendered, the mutineers moved on Lucknow. On June 30th, Lawrence with a little force marched out to meet more than 6,000 rebels at Chinhut, a few miles outside the city. His native gunners cut the traces of their horses, threw the guns into a ditch, and Lawrence was compelled to retreat with heavy loss. He could no longer hold the city, and on July 1st he withdrew his little garrison into the Residency. Within the Residency were now confined 927 Englishmen, soldiers and civilians, 765 native troops, and 130 women and children. On July 2nd the Residency was invested, and two days later the garrison suffered an irreparable loss—Lawrence being killed by a bursting shell. The command devolved on Brigadier Inglis, and for eighty-seven days he sustained the siege with unflinching courage and marvellous resource. Again and again the rebels assaulted the Residency; again and again the assaults were repelled. All through the burning summer the sufferings of the besieged were intense: cholera, smallpox, and fever wrought deadly havoc upon a garrison confined within a narrow space and weakened by lack of food and ceaseless toil. Again and again the garrison Havelock learned that relief was at hand, only to be disappointed; but at last and on September 24th the news reached them that Havelock had arrived. Outram Ever since the recapture of Cawnpúr, Havelock had been trying, with a force miserably inadequate, to cut his way through the rebels at Lucknow. So far, however, he had failed. Immediately on arriving in India, Sir Colin Campbell, the new Commander-in-Chief, promised him reinforcements, but at the same time announced, to

Havelock's bitter chagrin, that the command would be given to Sir James Outram. On September 15th Outram joined Havelock at Cawnpúr, but with a chivalry rare even in the annals of the most chivalrous service in the world, he refused to supersede his comrade until the work for which he had so long and so splendidly laboured, should have been accomplished. " The Major-General (Outram) in gratitude for, and admiration of the brilliant deeds in arms achieved by General Havelock and his gallant troops, will cheerfully waive his rank on the occasion, and will accompany the force to Lucknow in his civil capacity as Chief Commissioner of Oudh, tendering his military services to General Havelock as a volunteer." So ran the general order of September 16th. Three days later Havelock recommenced his march at the head of 3,000 men. Barely sufficient, but splendidly handled, they won their way through, and after two days' continuous fighting on the outskirts of the city, Havelock joined hands with Inglis on September 25th. But the relief had cost him 700 men, including General Neill ; he was not strong enough to bring out the garrison with safety, and in his turn, therefore, Havelock found himself besieged in the Residency.

The re-conquest of India   When Sir Colin Campbell reached India in August to take over the supreme command the prospects for his countrymen looked black indeed. Delhi was untaken ; Lucknow unrelieved ; Cawnpúr doubtfully held by Havelock. For two months Campbell was busily employed in collecting men and transports and sending them to the front ; he left Calcutta himself on October 27th, and reached Cawnpúr on November 3rd. On the 9th he set out for the relief of Lucknow. He attacked the city with 5,000 men on the 14th, and after a series of difficult but brilliant actions, he joined hands with Outram and Havelock on the 17th. By the 22nd Campbell had withdrawn the garrison in safety, but the lustre of a great military achievement was dimmed by the death in the Palace of the Alambagh of the gallant Havelock (Nov. 24th). Leaving Outram to hold that strongly fortified post, Campbell then hurried back to Cawnpúr. He was only just in time to avert disaster. During his absence a large body of mutineers from the Maráthá State of Gwalior had joined hands with the forces led by two of the most formidable opponents we had ever to encounter in the Mutiny war. The one was Tantia Topí, the brilliant lieutenant of Náná Sáhib, the other was the Raní of Jhánsi, the Joan of Arc of the Hindu mutineers. The rebels attacked Cawnpúr in force, and General Windham, whom Sir Colin had left in command was driven back into his entrenchments. Urgent messages were despatched to the Commander-in-Chief. Impeded though he was by the sick and wounded rescued from Lucknow, the latter marched with all possible speed. On December 5th he sent off the convoy to Allahábád, and on the 6th he attacked the rebels in Cawnpúr, and smote them hip and thigh. Cawnpúr was saved, and the mutineers, flying before the vigorous pursuit of Sir Hope Grant, were dispersed far and wide.

Over Cawnpúr, as over Delhi, the British flag once more waved, never again to be lowered. But Lucknow was still untaken. The Governor-General urged the importance of retaking Lucknow with all possible speed, and thus dealing an effective blow at the growing disaffection in Oudh. Sir Colin retorted that the remnant of the cold season was insufficient for so great a task, and proposed instead an expedition for the reduction of Rohilkhand. On military grounds there was much to be said in favour of Sir Colin's view ; Lord Canning, however, was unquestionably right in insisting that political considerations pointed to the paramount necessity of reasserting British authority in Oudh. The Commander-in-Chief loyally gave way, and during the next three months the mutineers were gradually driven in upon Lucknow. Jang Bahádur, the loyal Prime Minister of Nepál, advanced from the north at the head of 9,000 Ghurkas ; General Franks drove in the rebels from the east, while Sir Colin himself, at the head of the finest British army which had ever been seen in India, swept up the whole country to the south and west of the city. Rejoining Outram at the Alambagh, he fought a series of severe engagements, and at last, on March 21st, 1858, Lucknow finally surrendered.

The recapture of Lucknow dealt a death-blow to any hope of victory which might still be entertained by the mutineers, and it ought to have ended the war. That it failed to do so was due primarily to the apathy which allowed a huge body of mutineers to escape, with their trusted leaders, from Lucknow, and secondly, to the unfortunate effect produced upon the tálukdárs, or chief land-owners of Oudh, by the issue of Lord Canning's proclamation. The terms of this famous proclamation aroused acute controversy both in India and at home.[1] Issued on the morrow of the recapture of Lucknow, it declared that all the chiefs, with six exceptions, having been guilty of rebellion against the Queen had forfeited all their proprietary rights ; that if they made instant submission their lives and honour should be safe, provided that their hands " were not stained with English blood murderously shed," but that for any further privilege " they must throw themselves upon the justice and mercy of the British Government ". Intended by Canning as a conditional offer of clemency it was interpreted in Oudh as a decree of confiscation. Sir James Outram and John Lawrence, to say nothing of Lord Ellenborough, now President of the Board of Control, regarded the proclamation as a grave error. Lawrence would have offered an amnesty to all who had not been guilty of murder. " No mutineer," he wrote, " ever surrenders ; for directly he is caught, he is shot or hanged."

[1] *Cf. infra*, p. 250.

16

The truth of his words was proved to the hilt during the next few months. Rohilkhand was reduced to submission by the end of May, but not until January, 1859, was the last of the organized force of the rebels finally dispersed. In Oudh, and in Oudh alone, did the Mutiny assume something of the character of a national insurrection, and there can be no question that this was due in large measure to the unfortunate terms of Lord Canning's proclamation. The chiefs believed, erroneously but not unnaturally, that they had little to gain by submission and everything to fear. Consequently they waged for months a guerilla war which caused infinite embarrassment to the British forces and their commanders, and yielded them little credit.

Reduction of the Central Provinces   While Sir Colin Campbell was busy in Rohilkhand, Behar, and Oudh, Sir Hugh Rose (afterwards Lord Strathnairn) was gradually reducing the Central Provinces to obedience. That the trouble was virtually confined to these Provinces and did not extend to the Bombay Presidency was due in the main to the firm and prudent statesmanship of the Governor, Lord Elphinstone, and of George Berkeley Seton-Karr, the political officer in charge of the Southern Maráthá country. The Central Provinces, the fruit of Dalhousie's doctrine of " Lapse," were less amenable to control, and their temper gave cause for much anxiety to the Government. On December 16th, 1857, Sir Hugh Rose arrived at Indore to take up his command, and during the next six months he gradually reduced the Central Provinces. Jhánsi was the centre of insurrection ; its leaders were Tantia Topí and the Raní of Jhánsi. Outside Jhánsi Sir Hugh won a brilliant victory over Tantia Topí at Betwá (April 1st, 1858), two days later he captured Jhánsi itself, the stronghold of the Raní, and on May 22nd the great fortress of Kalpí. The intrepid Raní then got possession of Gwalior and induced its inhabitants to proclaim the Náná Sáhib as Peshwá. On June 17th, however, the Raní was killed at the head of her troops, and on the 19th Gwalior was taken by Sir Hugh Rose. But as in Oudh so also in the Central Provinces the capture of the fortresses was followed by a prolonged period of guerilla warfare. For nine months Tantia Topí successfully eluded the British pursuit, doubling backwards and forwards with baffling rapidity, until at length in April, 1859, he was betrayed to his pursuers, and after due trial was executed (April 18th, 1859). With Tantia Topí's capture and death the long-drawn tragedy ends.

End of John Company. British India transferred to the Crown   Before the sword was actually sheathed, a change of momentous consequence was announced to the peoples of India. It was generally recognized that the rule of the Company could not survive the Mutiny. Pitt's dual system established as a makeshift in 1784 had worked unexpectedly well for nearly three-quarters of a century, but the theory was illogical and the machinery was cumbrous. The time had clearly come when the Crown must assume direct and formal responsibility for the government of the great Empire which had been gradually built up by the representatives of a commercial Company. Accordingly, a Bill, framed on a series of resolutions adopted by the House of Commons, was passed by both Houses and received the Royal assent on August 2nd, 1858. Under this Act the powers and territories of the East India Company were transferred to the Queen, and the actual administration of India was committed to a Secretary of State, assisted by the Council of India. This Council (to be carefully distinguished from that of the Viceroy) is no phantom board. It has consisted from the first of fifteen members, appointed by the Secretary of State. Nine of them must have recently served and resided for ten years in India, and all are paid. The Board meets weekly, and controls, in a large measure, the action of the Secretary of State.[1]

The transference of authority effected by this Act was formally announced to the peoples of India on November 1st, 1858. The terms of the proclamation were carefully revised by the Queen, who, from first to last, had taken the closest and keenest interest in the progress of events in India. With the original draft of Lord Stanley, who as President of the Board of Control became the first Secretary of State, she was far from satisfied. She wrote, therefore, to Lord Derby asking him to " write it himself in his excellent language, bearing in mind that it is a female Sovereign who speaks to more than one hundred million of Eastern people on assuming the direct government over them after a bloody civil war, giving them pledges which her future reign is to redeem, and explaining the principles of her government. Such a document should breathe feelings of generosity, benevolence, and religious feeling, pointing out the privileges which the Indians will receive in being placed on an equality with the subjects of the British Crown, and the prosperity following in the train of civilization."[2]

The Queen's wishes were respected, and with admirable results. More particularly were her personal views revealed in the passage with reference to religion : " Firmly relying," said her Majesty, " on the truth of Christianity, and acknowledging with gratitude the solace of religion, we disclaim alike the right and the desire to impose our convictions on any of our subjects. It is our Royal will and pleasure that no one shall in any wise suffer for his opinions, or be disquieted by reason of his religious faith or observance. We will show to all alike the equal and impartial protection of the law, and we do strictly charge and enjoin those who may be in authority under us that they abstain from all interference with the religious belief or worship of any of our subjects under pain of our highest

The Queen's Proclamation

---

[1] Of the fifteen members seven were in the first instance appointed by the Directors of the Company.

[2] *Q.V.L.* iii. 379.

displeasure. It is our further will that, so far as may be, our subjects, of whatever class or creed, be fully and freely admitted to any offices the duties of which they may be qualified by their education, abilities, and integrity duly to discharge." Finally, the Queen declared that the aim of her government should be the benefit of all her subjects resident in India. " In their prosperity will be our strength, in their contentment our security, and in their gratitude our best reward."

The proclamation produced the happiest effect in India, and the Queen's pleasure is reflected in a letter to the Viceroy (Dec. 2nd, 1858). " It is," she writes, " a source of great satisfaction and pride to her to feel herself in direct communication with that enormous Empire which is so bright a jewel of her Crown, and which she would wish to see happy, contented, and peaceful. May the publication of her proclamation be the beginning of a new era, and may it draw a veil over the sad and bloody past." [1]

The Queen's hope was realized ; the proclamation did inaugurate a new era—the direct government of India by the British Crown. This fact was further emphasized by the State Tour of the Prince of Wales (Oct. 1875—April 1876), and still more by the Queen's assumption of the new title of Empress of India. The latter step was severely criticized at the time, but it is now generally recognized to have been both opportune and appropriate. It gave great satisfaction to the ageing Monarch, and it served to cement the bond between the Queen-Empress and the Princes and peoples of the Indian Empire. To describe it as a piece of political charlatanry is merely to betray that lack of imaginative sympathy which cost us so dear at the time of the Mutiny. Almost every other gift, both of character and intellect, had been bestowed in full measure upon Lord Dalhousie ; had this been added, the Mutiny might never have occurred. Had the obverse gifts been lacking to his lieutenants and his successor the Mutiny might well have been more serious than it was. For, tragic as were many of its incidents, and critical as were many of its moments, the Mutiny was suppressed with relative ease. That this was so was due to many contributory causes ; primarily to the unruffled coolness and intrepid courage of Lord Canning himself ; to his promptitude in diverting to India the British reinforcements on their way to China, and his refusal to give way to panic ; to the skill with which Lord Elphinstone restrained the restlessness of Bombay ; to the combination of sternness and conciliation displayed by Lawrence and his colleagues in the Punjab ; to the loyalty of the ruling Princes, not one of whom espoused the cause of the mutineers, and to that of several powerful Ministers such as Jang Bahádur of Nepál and Sálar Jang of Haidarábad ; to the splendid services rendered at more than one important juncture by Captain Peel and his Naval Brigade, and not least to the heroic fortitude of thousands of individual English-

[1] *Q.V.L.* iii. 389.

men, known and unknown to fame. There were other factors in the suppression of the Mutiny, to which allusion has already incidentally been made. Of these, perhaps the most important was the lack of national unity in India. Thanks to this, the sepoy mutiny never developed, except in Oudh and in a less degree in the Central Provinces, into a national insurrection. Had it done so it could hardly have been quelled by the efforts, however splendid and heroic, of a handful of Englishmen, planted in the midst of a teeming population, alien to themselves in tradition, in race, and in creed.

The most momentous result of the Mutiny was to bring that teeming population, for the first time, into direct dependence upon the British Crown.

CHAPTER XVI

DOMESTIC ADMINISTRATION. ENGLAND AND ITALY
(1856-1860)

FOR half a decade—from the reopening of the Eastern question (1852) to the suppression of the Mutiny (1858)—the mind of the nation was concentrated upon affairs external to Great Britain. The Near East, the Middle East, and the Far East in turn demanded all but exclusive attention. It was not long before foreign policy was again the dominant interest. For a brief interlude, however, we must plunge into the vicissitudes of parties and recall the details of domestic administration.

Financial crisis, November, 1857 While Englishmen were still racked by anxiety as to the fate of their countrymen in India, they were called upon to face a financial crisis at home, which was sufficiently severe and might have been disastrous. It was due to causes which during the last century have periodically recurred and are now well ascertained. A period of overtrading and speculation is invariably followed by a cessation of demand, a consequent contraction of credit, and the failure of Banks and commercial Houses. The crisis of 1857 in Great Britain was due primarily to railway speculations in the United States. The effects made themselves felt on this side early in October. The Bank of England, in order to protect its gold reserve, put up the rate of discount to 8 per cent. and later on to 10. Private firms refused to discount bills at all. Banks of high standing closed their doors : the Bank of Liverpool, the Western Bank of Scotland, and the City of Glasgow Bank being among the victims. On the evening of November 11th the Government learnt that the reserve at the Bank of England had fallen to £1,400,000 ; that it had less than £8,000,000 in bullion, and that its liabilities exceeded £18,000,000. On the 12th, therefore, Lord Palmerston and the Chancellor of the Exchequer authorized the suspension of the Bank Charter Act, and gave the Directors permission to issue notes to an amount not exceeding £2,000,000 in excess of their legal maximum. This saved the situation. On December 3rd Parliament met for the purpose of passing an Act of Indemnity. Lord Palmerston's summary of the debate is characteristic : " George Lewis and J. Russell made good speeches. The others, not having a clear idea, conveyed none." No serious opposition was offered to the Bill of Indemnity. The Government had done the right thing and had done it promptly. They could not, of course, avert a considerable amount of commercial distress ; but they successfully allayed the incipient financial panic. As in 1847 the opponents of Bank restriction used the opportunity to point the moral of their argument, but they once more failed to convince the nation. The necessity for occasional suspension in times of panic is no proof of the futility of the restriction under normal conditions. From the standpoint of economic theory J. S. Mill's plea [1] against the Bank Charter Act is unquestionably powerful ; but it cannot stand against the advocacy of such practical experts as Lord Overstone and Sir Robert Peel.

All serious danger was at an end when, on February 4th, Parlia- The Orsini bombsment reassembled for the regular session of 1858. Its first business was to vote an address of congratulation to the Queen on the marriage of the Princess Royal to Prince Frederick William of Prussia. The marriage, which had taken place at the Chapel Royal, St. James', on January 25th, was cordially approved by the nation, though the European position of an heir to the Prussian throne was not, in 1858, what it is to-day. The affection manifested towards one who was looked upon as " *England's* daughter " (in Cobden's happy phrase) gave unfeigned pleasure to the Queen.[2] A little later Parliament voted its thanks to the statesmen and soldiers who had saved the situation in India. The Conservatives showed some disposition to resent the inclusion of Lord Canning's name, but fortunately for the reputation of the Party the point was not pressed. To Palmerston's India Bill considerable opposition was offered, but the first reading was carried by a majority unexpectedly large (145). The position of the Government seemed unassailable, and it was generally believed that Lord Palmerston was installed in the Premiership for life. Sir Richard Bethell, the Attorney-General, remarked to the Premier, as they left the House together after the division on the India Bill, that he ought, like the Roman Consuls in a triumph, to have somebody to remind him that, as a Minister, he was mortal.[3] Within a week Lord Palmerston was beaten on what was virtually a vote of no-confidence, and a few days later he resigned. Such is the irony of English politics. The circumstances which led to the sudden over-throw of a powerful Minister require explanation.

Felice Orsini was one of the many Italian exiles who found a temporary home in England. His lectures on Italian independence were received with enthusiasm by English audiences, and he imbibed the crazy notion that, but for the Emperor of the French, the English Government would be disposed to give active assistance to the Italian cause. He determined, therefore, to remove the obstacle. On January 14th bombs were thrown at the Emperor's carriage as he was driving with the Empress to the Opera. The Emperor and Empress were unhurt, but so severe was the explosion that 10 people were killed and 156 were wounded. The news of the crime was received with horror and indignation in France, and indeed through-out Europe. Orsini himself and one accomplice were executed ; two

---

[1] *Principles of Political Economy*, p. 397 seq.   [2] *Vide Q.V.L.* iii. 334.
[3] Ashley, *Life*, ii. 142.

others were sent to penal servitude for life. But it was against England that the anger of the French people blazed out most fiercely. Orsini's conspiracy was hatched in England ; here the bombs were manufactured. Napoleon III. and his Empress had paid a friendly visit to the English Court in the previous autumn, but Lord Palmerston's speech at the Lord Mayor's Banquet (Nov. 9th, 1857) had been gratuitously provocative in tone, and he noted with curious satisfaction that he had aroused French susceptibilities. The Orsini conspiracy opened the flood-gates of invective against England. The army demanded to be led against the den of assassins ; they urged that " the infamous haunt in which machinations so infernal are planned should be destroyed for ever ". Unfortunately these foolish vapourings, and many like them, were published in the official *Moniteur*. Count Walewski, on behalf of the French Government, expressed official regret, and pleaded inadvertence, but in a despatch (Jan. 20th) he affirmed the unquestionable fact that the Orsini conspiracy was the third which had been hatched in England against the person of the French Emperor, and propounded certain questions which could hardly, under the circumstances, be deemed impertinent : " Ought the right of asylum to protect such a state of things ? Is hospitality due to assassins ? Ought English legislation to contribute to favour their designs and their plans, and can it continue to shelter persons who by their flagrant acts place themselves beyond the pale of common right and under the ban of humanity ? " He pointedly refrained from indicating the steps which the English Government ought to take, but he expressed the opinion that France had a right to expect " from an ally " that the guarantees against a repetition of such outrages should be effectual. To this despatch no official reply was made, though Lord Cowley was instructed to communicate the sentiments of the English Cabinet to the French Government.

Con-
spiracy
to Murder
Bill

A more effective response was not long deferred. On February 8th Lord Palmerston moved for leave to introduce a Bill to amend the law in regard to conspiracy to murder. Hitherto it had been treated in England merely as a misdemeanour, in Ireland as a capital crime. He proposed to unify the law throughout the United Kingdom and to make conspiracy to murder a felony punishable with penal servitude. Mr. Kinglake moved as an amendment that it was inexpedient " to legislate in compliance with the demand made in Count Walewski's despatch of January 20th, until further information be obtained," but the amendment was withdrawn and leave to introduce the Bill was given by 299 votes against 99.

On February 19th the second reading was moved by the Prime Minister, but it was immediately apparent that in the interval opinion had developed against the Bill, or rather against the action or inaction of the Government. In particular, they were severely

criticized for not having replied, in formal manner, to Count
Walewski's despatch of January 20th. Mr. Milner Gibson moved as
an amendment " that this House hears with much concern that it is
alleged that the recent attempt upon the life of the Emperor of the
French has been devised in England, and expresses its detestation
of such guilty enterprises ; and that while this House is ready at all
times to assist in remedying any defects in the criminal law which,
after due investigation, are proved to exist, yet it cannot but regret
that Her Majesty's Government, previously to inviting the House
to amend the law of conspiracy at the present time, have not felt it
to be their duty to reply to the important despatch received from
the French Government dated Paris, January 20th, 1858, which has
been laid before Parliament ". Mr. Gladstone and Mr. Disraeli both
supported the amendment, and through a combination of Radicals,
Peelites,[1] and Tories the Government was beaten by 234 votes to 215.

Lord Palmerston at once resigned, and the Queen entrusted the
formation of a Ministry to Lord Derby. His first step was to invite
Gladstone's co-operation, but the latter, after consultation with
Graham, Sidney Herbert, and Lord Aberdeen, declined. Lord Grey
also refused to join him.[2] Once more, therefore, Derby was compelled to form a purely Conservative Cabinet and to take office in a
minority. He did not relish the task, and it proved to be not less
difficult of fulfilment than he anticipated. Eventually he was joined
by eight of his late colleagues ; [3] his son, Lord Stanley, came into
the Cabinet as Colonial Secretary, General Jonathan Peel as War
Secretary, Sir Frederick Thesiger (raised to the Peerage as Lord
Chelmsford) became Lord Chancellor in place of Lord St. Leonards,
and Lord Ellenborough went to the Board of Control.[4]

The sec-
ond Ad-
ministra-
tion of
Lord
Derby,
Feb. 22nd
1858-
June
11th,
1859

On March 12th Disraeli, who again led the House of Commons,
was able to announce that the " painful misconceptions," which had
for a time subsisted between the French and English Governments,
had " entirely terminated in a spirit friendly and honourable, and in
a manner which will be as satisfactory to the feelings, as it will be
conducive to the interests and the happiness of both nations ".
Lord Malmesbury's answer to the famous despatch of January 20th,
and Count Walewski's reply were alike admirable in tone, and the
incident was thus happily closed. But it left behind it an uneasy
feeling in both countries. This feeling found expression in England

---

[1] The opposition to the Bill was attributed by Palmerston to the concerted
action of Lord John Russell and Sir James Graham ; cf. Q.V.L. iii. 338. Graham
believed Palmerston " to be by far the worst Minister the country has had in our
time " (Parker, ii. 338), but Palmerston seems to have exaggerated the extent of
his interference though not of his influence.

[2] Morley, i. 578 ; cf. a remarkable letter from Bright to Gladstone.

[3] Lords Malmesbury, Salisbury, Hardwicke, and John Manners, Disraeli,
Walpole, Pakington, and Henley.

[4] The other principal Ministers were Disraeli (Chancellor of the Exchequer),
Lord Malmesbury (Foreign Secretary), Spencer Walpole (Home Secretary), and
Sir J. Pakington (Admiralty).

in the formation of a Volunteer Rifle Corps and of a Reserve Volunteer Force of seamen (1859),[1] and a year later in a special vote of £2,000,000 for the fortification of dockyards.

The government of India
The fall of Lord Palmerston interrupted his schemes for the better Government of India, but the matter once mooted could not be allowed to rest and the incoming Ministry proposed a measure known as " India Bill No. 2 ". Framed on the same general principle as that of Lord Palmerston, it contained a fantastic and pseudo-democratic device for the election of the India Council. All parties mistrusted it, but all agreed that the transference of India from the Company to the Crown must somehow be effected, and Lord John Russell, therefore, rescued the Government from a difficulty by suggesting that the House should proceed by way of resolution. Disraeli eagerly assented, and resolutions were brought forward on which the Bill, already described,[2] was framed.

Lord Ellenborough and Lord Canning
Before the Bill became law (Aug. 3rd), and while the debates on the resolutions were in progress, the whole question was hung up by the controversy which arose between Lord Ellenborough, now President of the Board of Control, and the Governor-General. Lord Canning's Oudh Proclamation [3] was a tempting opportunity for a man with Lord Ellenborough's turn for pompous phrasing and melodramatic effect. Lord Ellenborough was by no means alone in his disapprobation of the proclamation, and owing to an indiscretion on the part of Mr. Vernon Smith, his predecessor at the Board, it reached him without the explanatory letter addressed by Lord Canning to the late President. Thereupon Lord Ellenborough, without consulting his colleagues, and without taking the Queen's pleasure, addressed to Lord Canning a severe and scathing rebuke. However great Canning's mistake might have been, the terms employed by Lord Ellenborough admitted of no excuse. To make matters worse he actually made public his despatch. The Government declared, through the mouth of Disraeli, that they " disapproved of the policy of the proclamation in every sense ". Many other people did the same. But Lord Ellenborough's treatment of a public servant placed in such a situation as that of Lord Canning was regarded by every fair-minded man as intolerable. To rate the Governor-General like a schoolboy was bad enough, to publish the lecture to the world was worse still. To save his colleagues from inevitable defeat, Lord Ellenborough resigned (May 13th). Lord Derby made great efforts to induce Mr. Gladstone to accept the vacant post. These efforts were warmly seconded by Disraeli whose letter to his great rival remains a monument of ill-requited magnanimity.[4]

---

[1] 22 and 23 Vict. cap. 40.   [2] Cf. supra, p. 241.   [3] Cf. supra, p. 240.
[4] " None of us I believe " (writes Lord Morley) " were ever able to persuade Mr. Gladstone to do justice to Disraeli's novels. . . . In the comparative stiffness of Mr. Gladstone's reply on this occasion I seem to hear the same accents of guarded reprobation."—*Life*, i. 589.

Gladstone again consulted his Peelite friends, but again declined Lord Derby's overtures. The vacant post was filled by Lord Stanley, whose place at the Colonial Office was taken by Sir E. Bulwer Lytton.

Lord Ellenborough, after a generous eulogium from his Chief, disappeared from public life. Of him it may truly be said that nothing became him like the leaving of it. Everything that was possible to atone for his conduct he did. As for Lord Canning he met the attack with his invariable calmness and courage. " No taunts or sarcasms, come from what quarter they may, will turn me from the path which I believe to be that of my public duty. I believe that a change in the head of the Government of India at this time, if it took place under circumstances which indicated a repudiation, on the part of the Government in England, of the policy which has hitherto been pursued towards the rebels of Oudh, would seriously retard the pacification of the country. . . . Firm in these convictions, I will not, in a time of unexampled difficulty, danger, and toil, lay down of my own act the high trust which I have the honour to hold." Thus Lord Canning wrote to his masters in Leadenhall Street. He was sustained in his resolution by expressions of sympathy from many quarters. Lord Derby telegraphed an assurance of his personal confidence ; Lord Malmesbury wrote as a private friend, but with the cordial assent of the Queen, urging him not to resign : " neither Lord Derby," he wrote, " nor any of our party wish it, and the whole country is ready to give you all the credit you merit for having so well encountered the extraordinary difficulties of your position " ; [1] the Directors passed a special vote of confidence ; the Queen lost no opportunity of expressing her disapproval of Ellenborough's vanity and tactlessness,[2] and her " undiminished and entire confidence in Lord Canning ".[3] He was made an Earl and received the G.C.B. iu 1859 and the Garter in 1861.

In Parliament the attack on the Government was a complete failure. In the Lords, Lord Shaftesbury's motion was lost by a majority of 9 ; in the Commons Mr. Cardwell's motion was withdrawn and the attack unexpectedly collapsed. The Leader of the House described the scene to the Queen with evident but decorous glee : [4] to the electors of Slough he was less restrained. He compared the collapse of the opposition to an earthquake in Calabria or Peru. " There was," he said, " a rumbling murmur, a groan, a shriek, a sound of distant thunder. No one knew whether it came from the top or the bottom of the House. There was a rent, a fissure in the ground, and then a village disappeared, then a tall tower toppled down, and the whole of the opposition benches became one great dissolving view of anarchy." [5]

---

[1] Malmesbury, *Memoirs*, p. 438 (ed. 1885).   [2] *Cf. e.g. Q.V.L.* iii. 357, 363.
[3] *Q.V.L.* iii. 390, 516, 578.   [4] *Q.V.L.* iii. 368.
[5] *Speeches*, ed. Kebbel, ii. 487 *seq.*

The new Government had survived, not without an element of luck, its first great peril, and for twelve months more, despite the heterogeneous majority opposed to it, went on its way rejoicing.

Admission of Jews to Parliament

Over and over again, during the last quarter of a century, had the House of Commons attempted to induce the Lords to assent to the admission of Jews to Parliament. At last, in 1858, their persistence had its reward. Once again the Lower House passed a Bill, proposed to it by Lord John Russell, to alter the Oaths of Allegiance and Supremacy and to relieve Jews from the necessity of affirming " on the true faith of a Christian ". Once more the Lords refused to make the concession to the Jews. The Commons insisted and a deadlock seemed imminent, when Lord Lucan proposed that either House should be empowered to modify, by its own resolution, the form of Oath to be taken by its members. This ingenious compromise was accepted and a Bill to give effect to it was passed, together with Russell's Oaths Bill, by both Houses. In the Commons, a resolution was carried to enable Jews to omit the words objectionable to them and Baron Rothschild, who had been periodically elected to the City of London since 1847 was at last permitted to take his seat (July 26th). The same session witnessed, also, the abolition of the property qualification of members.

Parliamentary reform

This modest instalment of the Chartist programme must be credited to Mr. Locke King, a persistent reformer who tried also to effect an extension of the county franchise. He failed, not for the first time, in his immediate purpose. But in the following session the Conservative party, under the inspiration of their brilliant leader in the House of Commons, tackled this thorny question. The year 1859 opened with a renewed agitation for parliamentary reform led by Mr. Bright. Disraeli, anxious to prove that the Liberals had no monopoly in the subject, produced his Reform Bill on February 28th.

Disraeli's Bill

The new Bill was based upon the principle of representing not merely property and population but interests. " This House," declared Disraeli, " ought to represent all the interests of the country . . . after all, the suffrage and the seat . . . are only means to an end. They are means by which you may create a representative assembly that is a mirror of the mind, as well as of the material interests, of England. You want in this House every element that obtains the respect and engages the interest of the country." The central feature of the Bill was an attempt to realize this conception. It contained a small dose of redistribution : fifteen relatively unimportant boroughs were to lose one member apiece ; eight towns were enfranchised ; four additional members were given to the West Riding, two to South Lancashire and two to Middlesex ; there were to be increased facilities for polling, but the most interesting and most distinctive proposals were those connected with the franchise. The county franchise was to be assimilated to that of the boroughs ; the borough freeholders were to be deprived of their county vote, and a large number of new qualifications were created. A vote was to be given to University graduates, ministers of religion, lawyers, medical men, certain schoolmasters, and every one who had £60 in a savings bank, who had a naval, military, or civil pension of £20 a year, or who drew £10 a year from the Funds, Bank Stock or East India Stock. It was these "fancy franchises," as they were derisively termed, which ultimately killed the Bill, but, meanwhile, opposition developed in many quarters. Two members of the Cabinet, Mr. Walpole and Mr. Henley, refused to be responsible for its introduction and resigned office. That they reflected the mind of the Conservative party much more faithfully than its brilliant chief cannot be doubted. In particular they disliked the disfranchisement of the freeholders, an objection which they shared with Mr. Bright and Lord John Russell. The two latter also complained with Roebuck that nothing was done for the working classes. Nevertheless, the reception accorded to the Bill was not unfriendly, and it was defeated on second reading only by a majority of 39 (330-291). The Government thereupon decided to appeal to the constituencies, and after some necessary business was despatched Parliament was prorogued (April 19th) with a view to immediate dissolution. The General Election which ensued turned less upon Reform than upon Foreign Affairs. The Italian War had broken out, and the Conservatives were suspected of some leanings towards the Austrian cause—perhaps with justice. At any rate their neutrality was less benevolent towards Italy than that of their opponents. They gained twenty to thirty seats, but this was not sufficient to give them a majority,[1] and on an amendment to the Address moved by Lord Hartington [2] they were defeated in a full House by 13 (323-310).

Lord Derby immediately resigned, and the Queen, anxious to avoid the invidious task of deciding between the claims of two statesmen "so full of years and honours as Lord Palmerston and Lord John Russell," sent for Lord Granville. The two veterans had previously agreed to co-operate with each other, whichever of the two might be called upon to form a Ministry. That the Queen might select a third person had not entered into their calculations. Neither liked the solution, but Palmerston, always good-natured and complaisant, agreed to serve under Lord Granville, provided the latter could form a really strong Cabinet. Lord John, however, refused to occupy the third place in the Ministry,[3] and the negotiations, to the Queen's regret, broke down. The Queen then sent for Lord Palmerston. Lord John would have liked his rival to go to

---

[1] The estimated strength of parties was Liberals 348, Conservatives 305.
[2] Afterwards 8th Duke of Devonshire.
[3] Lord Palmerston was to have led the Commons.

the House of Lords and leave him the lead of the Commons. Failing that, he now agreed to serve under him provided he might have the Foreign Office. This demand, though not intrinsically unreasonable, had the unfortunate result of excluding from the Cabinet the soundest and safest of living diplomatists—Lord Clarendon. Lord John's terms were accepted, and Palmerston was able to form a Government of unquestionable individual strength. Lord Granville, the Duke of Argyll, Sir Charles Wood, and Mr. Gladstone returned to the posts they had previously held ; Sir George Grey, temporarily displaced at the Home Office by Sir G. C. Lewis, accepted the Chancellorship of the Duchy of Lancaster ; Lord Campbell became Lord Chancellor, and the Duke of Somerset took the Admiralty. Cobden was pressed to take the Board of Trade, and on his refusal it was given to Milner Gibson. But of the new appointments incomparably the most important was that of Lord John Russell to the Foreign Office.

Foreign affairs

Rarely has the interest in foreign affairs been more absorbing than during the Second Palmerston Ministry : the war of Italian Liberation ; the relations between England and Napoleon III. ; a new war in China (1860) ; the civil war in America, raising delicate diplomatic questions for Great Britain, and resulting in one of the severest commercial crises through which we ever passed ; finally, the fateful struggle for the Danish Duchies—upon these matters the attention of the country was for the next six years necessarily concentrated.

France, Austria, and Sardinia. The war of Italian Liberation

On January 1st, 1859, Napoleon III. startled the diplomatic world by an ominous speech to the Austrian Ambassador in Paris. " I regret that the relations between our two countries are so unsatisfactory." The echo came ten days later from Turin. " The situation," said Victor Emmanuel in opening the Piedmontese Parliament, " is not free from peril, for, while we respect treaties we cannot be insensible to the cry of anguish which comes to us from many parts of Italy." There was no mistaking the significance of either speech ; nor any doubt as to the source of their inspiration. Cavour, as we have seen, had gone away from the Congress of Paris a happy man. " What can I do for Italy ? " Napoleon had asked. Cavour told him, and the pact drafted at Paris was sealed at Plombières (1858). Austria was to be expelled from the Peninsula ; and Northern and Central Italy were to be united under the House of Savoy. In return, France was to get Savoy and perhaps Nice also. Queen Victoria was much exercised by the prospect of war and did her utmost to maintain peace. She personally addressed the Emperor of Austria [1] and sent Lord Cowley on a mediatorial mission to Vienna. But to no purpose. France refused the proffered mediation of England, and Austria accepted it only under the condition of

---

[1] Martin's *Prince Consort*, iv. 392, gives the material portions of the letter ; *cf.* also *Q.V.L.* iii. 411-413.

the disarmament of Sardinia.[1] On April 23rd Austria demanded, hastily and precipitately,[2] that disarmament ; Cavour gleefully accepted the challenge, and the Austrian troops crossed the Ticino. The Emperor of the French promptly fulfilled his engagement. On May 13th Victor Emmanuel met at Genoa the " magnanimous ally " who had come, at the head of a magnificent army, to liberate Italy " from the Alps to the Adriatic ". A brief but brilliant [3] campaign in North Italy was suddenly arrested, to the chagrin of Sardinia and the astonishment of Europe, by the armistice of Villa-Franca. On July 8th Napoleon came to terms with the Emperor Francis Joseph. Italy was to be free not to the Adriatic, but only to the Minico ; Austria was to retain Venetia and the Quadrilateral ; Leopold of Tuscany and Francis of Modena were to be restored to their ducal thrones, but " without recourse to force " ; Piedmont was to annex Lombardy, and Italy was to be federated under the Presidency of the Pope. Neither Napoleon's reasons for proposing, nor those of Austria for accepting, the armistice concern the argument of this chapter ; [4] both were largely influenced by the mobilization of Prussia. " The gist of the thing is," wrote Moltke, " that Austria would rather give up Lombardy than see Prussia at the head of Germany ". There can be no doubt that Napoleon preferred to leave his Italian mission half accomplished rather than see a Prussian army on the Rhine. As a matter of fact he had done more for Italy than he knew, perhaps more even than he meant. In 1860 Tuscany, Parma, Modena, and the northern half of the Papal States were united by plebiscite to Sardinia, and on April 2nd, 1860, a Parliament, representing 11,000,000 Italian people, met for the first time at Turin.

This result was achieved partly by the pluck and pertinacity of Victor Emmanuel, still more by the singularly adroit diplomacy of Cavour, but not least by the cordial sympathy and goodwill of the Liberal Ministry in England. That Ministry contained at least three men who were whole-heartedly devoted to the Italian cause : Lord John Russell, Mr. Gladstone, and Lord Palmerston himself.[5] During the months which followed upon the armistice of Villa-Franca the position was undeniably critical. It soon became clear that the Duchies of Central Italy were irrevocably determined upon union with Sardinia. This placed Napoleon in a difficult position both as

England and Italy

[1] Lord Derby to the Queen, *Q.V.L.* iii. 420.

[2] The phrase is Lord Derby's.

[3] Mr. Thayer, *Life and Times of Cavour*, vol. ii. p. 34 *seq.*, throws doubt upon the " brilliance " of the French victories. Unquestionably Napoleon had more than a small slice of luck.

[4] They are canvassed in detail by Thayer, *op. cit.* ii. p. 80 *seq.*, and briefly by the present writer in the *Quarterly Review*, No. 431, p. 388, from which a few sentences are here quoted.

[5] To their influence upon the Italian settlement Mr. Thayer pays a tribute which is not more warm than just (*op. cit.* ii. 123).

regards Austria and Italy, and he wished to thrust upon Great Britain the responsibility of proposing a revision of the terms agreed upon at Villa-Franca. England's position was not free from embarrassment. The Court was increasingly suspicious of the designs of Napoleon, and most anxious not to throw the weight of England into the scale against Austria. Lord Palmerston, on the contrary, stood where he had stood in 1848-1849. " I am very Austrian north of the Alps, but very anti-Austrian south of the Alps. The Austrians have no business in Italy, and they are a public nuisance there." [1] Gladstone and Russell entirely shared his views, but the Cabinet thought that these Ministers were " inclined to meddle too much in Italian affairs ".[2] Again and again the Queen was compelled to appeal to the Cabinet against the Prime Minister and the Foreign Secretary. And not infrequently with success. " Johnnie has had a lesson," wrote Lord Granville to the Duke of Argyll, " that the Cabinet will support the Queen in preventing him and Pam acting on important occasions without the advice of their colleagues." [3]

In the end, however, it was the view of Palmerston and Russell which prevailed. They insisted that the Italians must be left to settle their own affairs for themselves. " The people of the Duchies," wrote Palmerston, " have as good a right to change their Rulers as the people of England, France, Belgium, and Sweden, and the annexation of the Duchies would be an unmixed good for Italy, for France, and for Europe." [4] The Duchies expressed their will unmistakably, and Europe acquiesced. But if Sardinia was to be enlarged by the acquisition of Central Italy, the Emperor Napoleon must have his *quid pro quo*. Savoy and Nice was the price demanded, and paid.

Garibaldi and his Thousand   Still further shocks were in store for the apostles of " legitimacy ". As long ago as 1851 Mr. Gladstone had exposed the scandals of Bourbon rule in Southern Italy. Early in 1860 the great free-lance Giuseppi Garibaldi—the hero of the Defence of Rome in 1848—learnt that the standard of revolt had been raised by the Sicilians, and resolved to go to their assistance. Cavour did all he could to aid him, so far as the diplomatic proprieties permitted.[5] There was

---

[1] To Lord Granville, *Life*, i. 325.

[2] Granville to Lord Canning, Fitzmaurice, *Granville*, i. 355.

[3] On the friction between the Court and the Ministers *cf. Q.V.L.* iii. c. xxviii. ; Martin, *Prince Consort*, v. 44-60 ; Fitzmaurice, *Granville*, i. c. xiii. The relations between the Court and the Foreign Minister are sufficiently indicated by a letter from Lord John to the Queen beginning : " Lord John Russell unfortunately does not partake of your Majesty's opinion in regard to Italy," and covertly insinuating that the Queen was " no well-wisher of mankind and indifferent to his freedom and happiness ". The Queen sent the letter to the Premier, with an intimation—not uncalled for—that she " must demand that respect which is due from a Minister to his Sovereign " (Feb. 10th, 1860, *Q.V.L.* iii. 494-495). Lord John expressed his regret.

[4] Palmerston, *Life*, ii. 165.

[5] On the difficult question as to Cavour's attitude towards Garibaldi's Sicilian expedition, *cf.* Thayer, ii. 268   Trevelyan, *Garibaldi and the Thousand*, p. 162.

naturally much fluttering in the diplomatic dovecotes when it was known that Garibaldi and his " Thousand " had sailed from Genoa. Before Europe had recovered from the first shock of surprise, Garibaldi had made himself master of Sicily, had crossed to the mainland and was on his way to Naples. The Bourbon King fled from his capital on September 6th, and on the 7th Garibaldi entered it. Six weeks of intense anxiety ensued. Would Garibaldi insist on the perpetuation of the Dictatorship he had perforce assumed ? Would he consent to the annexation of the Two Sicilies to the new Kingdom of North Italy ? Would he defy Catholic Europe and march on Rome ? Garibaldi declared that he would not annex his recent conquests to the Italian Kingdom until he could proclaim Victor Emmanuel King of Italy in Rome itself. The moment was intensely critical for the future of Italy ; but Cavour was equal to the crisis. " Go to Naples," was Palmerston's advice to Cavour. To Naples Cavour went. Luckily for Italy the King of Naples held the Garibaldians in check for a fortnight on the Volturno. Before Garibaldi had scattered the Neapolitans (Oct. 1st), Victor Emmanuel and the Sardinian troops had marched south, and on November 7th Garibaldi and his King rode into Naples side by side. Naples and Sicily declared by plebiscite for annexation ; Garibaldi assented. On February 18th, 1861, a Parliament, for the first time representative of the whole of Italy, save Rome and Venice, assembled at Turin. Italy was all but made.

At this supreme crisis of her fate the support of England was of inestimable value to Italy. Napoleon would gladly have stopped Garibaldi if England would have joined him in the task. England refused to do so. Palmerston and Russell had always been warm friends to the cause of Italian liberty. They were now converts to the idea of Italian Unity. They had become convinced that " the only manner in which the Italians could secure their independence of foreign control was by forming one strong Government for the whole of Italy. . . . Her Majesty's Government," wrote Russell, instead of joining in the censure pronounced by the Powers against Victor Emmanuel, " will turn their eyes rather to the gratifying prospect of a people building up the edifice of their liberties, and consolidating the work of their independence." [1] Russell's famous despatch caused much heart-burning among the Chancelleries and Courts (not excluding our own) of Europe. " Ce n'est pas de la diplomatie," said Baron Brunnow, " c'est de la polissonnerie." At any rate it made it clear that Great Britain would brook no outside interference with the development of internal affairs in Italy. In this sense it was entirely effective. Nor have the Italians been slow

England and the making of Italy

---

[1] *Cf.* Russell's despatch of October 27th, 1860, a despatch which caused him to be " blessed night and morning by ' twenty millions ' of Italians ". The whole policy of Russell has been for the first time revealed in its entirety by Trevelyan, *Garibaldi and the Making of Italy,* pp. 27-30 105-108, and Appendix A.

17

to recognize the debt which they owe to British diplomacy. Lord Palmerston and Lord John Russell are enshrined, and justly, alongside Victor Emmanuel and Cavour, Mazzini and Garibaldi, among the " makers " of Italian Unity.[1]

England and France

The mistrust of Napoleon III. inspired by his Italian policy in 1859 was deepened by the events of 1860-61, nor was it really allayed either by the conclusion of the Cobden Treaty, or by the co-operation of the two countries in China. The absorption of Nice and Savoy by France was resented in England, and the more so when Palmerston failed to secure from Napoleon some consideration for the rights and susceptibilities of the Swiss Confederation—closely affected by the cession of Savoy.[2] Rumours—not groundless—that the annexation of Savoy and Nice was to be complemented by that of Genoa or Sardinia, and perhaps Geneva as well, served still further to increase English suspicions of France. A French expedition to the coast of Syria (1860-1861) on behalf of the Maronites tended in the same direction. " The Emperor's mind," wrote Palmerston, " seems as full of schemes as a warren is full of rabbits, and like rabbits, his schemes go to ground for the moment to avoid notice or antagonism." With such a restless neighbour no country could afford to be unprepared for contingencies. Palmerston held firmly to the maxim *si vis pacem, para bellum ;* the naval estimates accordingly rose from about £9,000,000 in 1859, to nearly £12,000,000 in 1860 : an additional million and a half was taken for the army (£14,000,000 instead of £12,500,000) ; 180,000 men were enrolled in the new Volunteer force, and an expenditure of £9,000,000 was authorized on the fortifications of Portsmouth, Plymouth, Chatham, and Cork. The last item nearly cost Palmerston his Chancellor of the Exchequer. But " better lose Mr. Gladstone," as he wrote to the Queen, " than run the risk of losing Portsmouth and Plymouth ". And the former risk was really more remote, for Lord Palmerston's desk was said to be nearly full before 1865 of Mr. Gladstone's resignations. As to the danger of attack from France, Palmerston was becoming increasingly apprehensive. " Of late," he wrote to Lord John, " I have begun to feel great distrust and to suspect that his formally declared intention of avenging Waterloo has only lain dormant and has not died away."[3] This feeling was largely responsible for Palmerston's refusal to encourage the scheme of M. Lesseps for the construction of a canal through the Isthmus of Suez. He saw in it a great "naval and military advantage to France in a war with England " (Dec. 8th, 1861).[4]

Chinese War, 1859-1860

The co-operation of the two countries in the Far East did not allay suspicion. The Chinese Government refused to ratify the

---

[1] Thus Mr. G. M. Trevelyan writes of " the action of Great Britain in this summer, without which Italy could not have been made."—*Op. cit.* p. 27.
[2] To Lord Cowley, April, 1860, ap. Ashley, ii. 182.
[3] Ashley, ii. 187.   [4] Ashley, Appendix ii.

conditions accepted in the Treaty of Tientsin (1858), and consequently it was found necessary to despatch a considerable force
under Sir Hope Grant and General Montauban. The Chinese treated
the European Envoys with treachery and brutality, and not until
severe fighting had taken place and the summer Palace at Pekin had
been sacked, did the Chinese give way. The Convention of Pekin
was signed on October 24th, 1860. The Treaty of Tientsin was
ratified ; the indemnity imposed by it was doubled, and the Port of
Tientsin was opened to British trade. Thus was the disagreeable
task of Lord Elgin and Baron Gros at last accomplished.

A similar difficulty was encountered two years later in Japan. Difficul-
In 1862 the murder of Mr. Richardson, a member of the British ties in
Agency established at Yokohama, compelled the English Govern- Japan
ment to extract by force the payment of an indemnity. The guilty
parties, after a brief struggle, gave way, and certain Japanese ports
were reopened to British trade.[1]

In January, 1860, a notable victory was won for the principle of The
Free Exchange by the conclusion of the " Cobden " Treaty between "Cobden"
England and France. In the autumn of 1859 Cobden was deeply Treaty
concerned at the increasing mistrust between the two Governments,
and volunteered to try to negotiate a commercial treaty. Gladstone
warmly approved the project, and after some months of direct
negotiation between Cobden and the Emperor, the treaty was concluded (Jan. 23rd, 1860). France agreed to substitute a moderate
tariff for virtual prohibition : gradually the duty was to be reduced
on British coal, iron, steel, tools, machinery, and all the staples of
British manufacture : yarns, flax, hemp, hair, wool, silk, cotton,
skins, wood, glass, and earthenware. On none of these articles was
the duty to exceed 30 per cent. England engaged to sweep away all
duties on manufactured goods, and to reduce the duties on wine and
brandy. But the concessions were not limited to the contracting
countries : they were to apply to all nations alike. " Our treaty
with France," said Mr. Gladstone, " was in fact a treaty with the
world, and wide are the consequences which engagements of that
kind carry in their train." In view of this fact, clearly insisted upon
by the authors of the treaty, it is grotesque to describe it as a departure
from the principles for which Cobden had always stood.[2] But
excellent as were the commercial effects of his intervention, it did
little to improve the international outlook.

The energies of Napoleon III. were, however, temporarily Napoleon
diverted to the other side of the Atlantic. In 1861 Benito Jaurez, III. and
the Republican Leader in Mexico, overthrew Miramon who repre- Mexico
sented the Clericals and Monarchists. Miramon appealed for help

---

[1] They had been originally opened in 1858.
[2] The straitest sect of the Free Traders have always denounced Tariff Treaties,
as tending to the heresy of " reciprocity ". But cf. Morley Cobden, ii. c. xiv., for
vindication.

to the great Catholic Powers in Europe, and in this appeal Napoleon's vivid and fantastic imagination saw an opportunity for killing several birds with one stone. He determined to place upon the throne of Mexico the Archduke Maximilian, brother of the Emperor Francis Joseph of Austria. His candidate was well chosen. Maximilian was not only the brother of the Emperor of Austria, but the son-in-law of King Leopold of Belgium, and had won personal reputation as the Governor of Lombardy and Venetia. His promotion might, therefore, be expected to gratify the French Clericals, and the powerful family interests of Hapsburgs, Orleans, and Saxe-Coburgs. Moreover, Juarez gave Napoleon a legitimate pretext for interference by the repudiation of the Mexican debt. England and Spain agreed to join France in enforcing payment, and in protecting the persons and properties of their subjects in Mexico. To the demand of the three Powers, backed up by imposing force, Juarez quickly assented. England and Spain, therefore, withdrew; Napoleon, whose ulterior designs had not been revealed to his confederates, did not. Alone he embarked on an enterprise destined to culminate in a terrible tragedy, to cheat all his hopes and to react disastrously upon his position in France.

CHAPTER XVII

THE RULE OF LORD PALMERSTON.   THE CIVIL WAR IN AMERICA. THE DANISH DUCHIES.   THE CLOSE OF AN EPOCH

(1861-1865)

SUCH temporary success as Napoleon attained in Mexico would The Civil not have been possible but for the preoccupation of the War in United States.   In the autumn of 1860 the States were in the throes America, 1861-1865 of a Presidential Election.   That contest was the most momentous in their history, for it resulted in the election of Abraham Lincoln. Lincoln had leapt into fame in 1858 as the opponent of Douglas in the Senatorial Election for the State of Illinois.   Douglas was successful, but two years later the tables were turned and Abraham Lincoln was elected President of the United States.   In the first speech of his Senatorial campaign Lincoln had said : " A house divided against itself cannot stand.   I believe that this Government cannot endure permanently half-slave and half-free.   I do not expect the Union to be dissolved : I do not expect the house to fall : but I do expect that it will cease to be divided.   It will become all the one thing or all the other.   Either the opponents of slavery will arrest the further spread of it and will place it where the public mind shall rest in the belief that it is in the course of ultimate extinction, or its advocates will push it forward until it shall become alike lawful in all the States, old as well as new, North as well as South."   Lincoln was no root and branch Abolitionist, but the election of this Western attorney to the Presidency was taken by the Slave States as a menace to the institution by which they stood.   In February, 1861, Georgia, Alabama, Florida, Mississippi, Louisiana, and Texas following the lead of South Carolina, formally seceded from the Union, organized a Government known as the " Confederate States of America " ; drafted a Constitution and elected, as their first President, Jefferson Davis.   It is difficult to deny the constitutional right of the Southern States to withdraw from a Federal Union formed by a contract between " Sovereign " States.   It is not less difficult to deny that, but for the supposed menace to the institution of slavery, this right would not have been exercised.   Least of all can it be doubted that secession was a tactical blunder on the part of the South.   Slavery would have been safer inside than outside the Union.   But the hot blood of the South was up.   On March 4th, 1861, Lincoln entered upon the high office to which he had been elected in November, and at once announced that he had neither the will nor the power to abolish slavery, but that no " secession " could be permitted.   The Confederates seized Federal forts and arsenals, the first shot being fired against Fort Sumter at Charleston (April 12th, 1861).   Lincoln then called for 75,000 volunteers and declared the seceding States to be under blockade. The great Civil War had begun. The varying fortunes of that war during the next four years (1861-1865) cannot be followed in these pages, except in so far as they react upon England and English policy. The British Government at once (May 8th) recognized the Confederate States as belligerents and issued (May 13th) the usual proclamation of neutrality. The recognition of belligerency was bitterly resented by the partisans of the North, but unreasonably, since it was logically necessitated by the proclamation of a " blockade ".

Opinion in England

Nevertheless, it was accepted as proof positive that English sympathies were with the South. As a fact opinion was divided. The Government maintained throughout a strict neutrality. Lord Russell,[1] it is true, committed one bad blunder, for which this country afterwards paid dearly, but the official attitude was not merely correct but dignified and calm. Nevertheless, the North had some ground for regarding England as a partisan of the South. " Society " in the narrower sense was all for the gentlemen of the cotton States against the commercial Yankees. The more influential organs of public opinion tended in the same direction. Palmerston, Russell, and Gladstone all said or did things which seemed to indicate similar sympathies, and would have done more had they not been restrained by a majority of their Cabinet colleagues. The Duke of Argyll and Lord Stanley, Cobden and Bright were, on the contrary, in favour of the North, and the working classes, despite the terrible sufferings inflicted on many of them by the conflict, were on the same side.

The affair of the *Trent*

The war had been in progress about seven months when an incident occurred which nearly brought Great Britain into the actual arena of conflict. The Confederate States were anxious to secure recognition from England and France. To that end they despatched two envoys, Mason and Slidell, to represent them, officially if it might be, in London and Paris respectively. The envoys successfully pierced the blockade, and at Havanna, a neutral port, took ship in an English mail steamer, the *Trent*. On November 8th, 1861, the *San Jacinto*—a Federal ship of war commanded by Captain Wilkes—intercepted the *Trent* on the high seas, fired a shot across her bows, and demanded the surrender of Mason and Slidell, who with their secretaries were carried off in custody to Fort Warren in Boston Harbour. The conduct of Captain Wilkes was, beyond all question, a flagrant violation of international law, and aroused the liveliest indignation in Great Britain. A reinforcement of 8,000 troops was immediately sent to Canada, and Lord Lyons, the British Ambassador at Washington, was instructed to demand the instant surrender of the prisoners, and an apology for the insult to the British flag. The

[1] In July, 1861, Lord John, now 69 years of age, had accepted a Peerage as Earl Russell of Kingston Russell and Viscount Amberley of Amberley and Ardsalla.

despatch containing these instructions was sent to Windsor for the Queen's approval on November 30th, 1861. The Prince Consort was gravely perturbed at the possibility of war, and saw clearly that Russell's diplomatic methods were only too likely to provoke it. No one could doubt that the Federal Government was in the wrong; but the highest function of diplomacy, as the Prince conceived it, is to build a golden bridge for discomfited opponents. Prince Albert, from his death-bed, built it. The despatch was remodelled, precisely on the lines suggested by him,[1] and a way of honourable retreat from a false position was offered to President Lincoln.

Would he seize the opportunity? For a month there was tense anxiety in England and indeed throughout Europe. The friendly offices of France and Russia at this juncture ought never to be forgotten. Both Powers warned the American Government that peace would be preserved only by prompt surrender. Mr. Thurlow Weed, an intimate friend of the Federal Secretary of State and then resident in London as his authorized but unofficial representative, warned Mr. Seward that feelings in England were deeply stirred, and urged him " to yield to the British demands absolutely and immediately ". If Prince Albert built the bridge, the tact of Lord Lyons induced the American Government to use it. On Christmas Day, 1861, President Lincoln agreed to hand over the prisoners to the British Government, and on January 9th, 1862, the good news reached England that Lincoln had disavowed the action of Captain Wilkes and that the immediate crises was at an end.

The Queen justly claimed this happy issue as a triumph for " her beloved Prince ". But the Prince himself did not live to see it. On December 14th, 1861, he succumbed to an attack of gastric fever complicated by congestion of the lungs. The grief of the whole nation was profound, that of the Queen was indescribable.[2] Those who were brought nearest to the Queen knew best what she and the country had lost. And the country came to know it too. At last the Queen's husband was known for what he was; at last his worth was recognized :— *The death of the Prince Consort*

> all narrow jealousies
> Are silent ; and we see him as he moved,
> How modest, kindly, all accomplished, wise,
> With what sublime repression of himself,
> And in what limits and how tenderly.

The war-cloud between England and the Northern States passed ; between North and South there was no cessation of conflict. In England there was a superstition that the shopkeepers of the North could never beat the gentlemen of the South. And for a time it seemed to be justified. As in our own Civil War, the first advantage *Progress of the war*

---

[1] The Prince's draft is reproduced in facsimile by Martin, *Life*, v. 422.
[2] *Cf. e.g.* Martin, v. pp. 440 *seq. ; Q.V.L.* iii. c. xxx.

lay with the aristocratic party. The North could produce, for a while, no General fit to cope with " Stonewall " Jackson and Robert E. Lee. And the South had the advantage of strategical position ; if they stood where they were, they won ; the North could win only by crushing their resistance and capturing their capital. But though the initial advantages were with the South, the odds were terribly against them. The North had the money, the men,[1] and the machinery of Government. Nevertheless, the dejection in their ranks was great as the second year of strife wore on without bringing them any nearer their main objective.

Attitude of the British Government ; the armed cruisers

The Confederate States, meanwhile, were desperately anxious to secure from the leading neutrals a recognition of their independence. And in the autumn of 1862 they were within measurable distance of getting it from France and England, if not from Russia. Napoleon III. would gladly have conceded it, and Palmerston and Russell had got as far (Sept. 1862) as to be willing to offer mediation. If mediation were refused by the North, the independence of the South was to be recognized. On October 7th, a third member of the Government, Mr. Gladstone, made a memorable speech at Newcastle : " We may have our own opinions about slavery ; we may be for or against the South ; but there is no doubt that Jefferson Davis and other leaders of the South have made an army ; they are making, it appears, a navy ; and they have made what is more than either, they have made a nation ". The sensation produced by these words was, says Lord Morley, " immediate and profound ".[2] They were taken to portend immediate recognition of Southern independence. Mainly, however, through the influence of Lord Granville, the Cabinet decided against an offer of mediation.[3] Nevertheless, the North had cause of offence against them. The South were making desperate efforts to repair the lack of a navy. They continued, by various devices, to acquire a small fleet of armed cruisers, which inflicted immediate damage on the merchant shipping of the North. Several of these cruisers were built in English yards. The most famous and the most destructive of them—the *Alabama*—was built by the famous firm of Laird at Birkenhead. More than once before she left the docks, Mr. Adams, the American Minister in London, warned Russell as to the real destination of the vessel, and begged him to stop her. Partly owing to his characteristic pedantry, partly to a series of accidents, Russell's intervention came too late, and the *Alabama* was let loose to prey upon American commerce.[4] Russell's blunder cost this country over £3,000,000 sterling and not a little humiliation.

[1] They numbered 22,000,000 against 9,000,000, of whom 3,500,000 were slaves.
[2] *Life of Gladstone*, ii. 79. It is fair to say that the words were bitterly repented of.
[3] Fitzmaurice, *Granville*, i. 443-444.
[4] *Cf.* Walpole's *Life of Russell*, ii. 352-367.

On the American Continent, meanwhile, things were beginning to march to their appointed end. Not hastily, and perhaps not willingly, Lincoln at last took the decisive step. On September 23rd, 1862, he issued a proclamation that in all States which should not by January 1st, 1863, have returned to their allegiance to the Union the slaves should be at once and for ever free. At last the true significance of the contest was clearly and unmistakably revealed. Lincoln himself was primarily and pre-eminently a Unionist. " My paramount object," he wrote, " is to save the Union, and not either to save or destroy slavery." The fortunes of war converted him into an Abolitionist. From January 1st, 1863, the cause of the Union was identified with the cause of human liberty. In 1864 the champion of both causes was re-elected President of the United States. On April 4th, 1865, the Confederate Government evacuated Richmond ; on the 9th Lee surrendered to General Grant at Appomattox. The Civil War was at an end. In less than a week after Lee's surrender, Lincoln was assassinated at Washington (April 14th, 1865).

Into the actual vortex of the struggle England, as we have seen, The cotton famine had been nearly engulfed ; some of its worst consequences she did not escape. In the year 1860-1861 the Lancashire cotton trade was unusually active and prosperous : wages were high ; profits good ; the supply of raw material was abundant. In the summer of 1861 Lincoln declared the blockade of the Southern ports, and for the next four years the prosperity of Lancashire was blasted. The Lancashire mills, then as now,[1] were almost wholly dependent for the raw material of their staple industry upon the plantations of the southern States of America. In 1861 the supply was suddenly cut off. Within a few weeks, thousands of spinners and manufacturers were thrown out of work ; savings were quickly exhausted, and by Christmas, 1861, signs of distress were manifest in many towns. The calamity was faced by Lancashire with a quiet courage that evoked the sympathy and admiration of the world. Early in 1862 a Central Relief Committee was established in Manchester under the Presidency of Lord Derby, with Sir James Kay-Shuttleworth as Vice-President. In every town and village in Lancashire sub-committees were established, and the Lord Mayor opened a fund in London. Subscriptions poured in from all parts of England, from India, the Colonies, and from many foreign countries. Even the United States, in the stress of their own difficulties, did their best to assuage the suffering for which they were directly responsible. The Lord Mayor ultimately collected over £500,000 sterling, and from other sources more than £2,000,000 in money and kind was subscribed. It is safe to say

---

[1] As early as June, 1861, Palmerston suggested to Milner Gibson the importance of stimulating supplies of raw cotton from Africa, India, Australia, Egypt, etc. (Ashley, ii. 211). The same subject is now (1912) engaging serious attention.

that no great charitable fund was ever administered with such economy and wisdom. All classes in Lancashire and the adjacent counties gave freely of their time and energy both to minimize immediate sufferings and to prevent permanent demoralization, while the behaviour of the operatives themselves was admittedly exemplary. In 1862 Cobden estimated the loss to them in wages at £7,000,000 per annum. But there was hardly any crime, and marvellously little imposition. Moreover, all through the famine the working men never wavered in their devotion to the North. They believed the Union to be fighting in the cause of righteousness and freedom, and to that cause they steadfastly adhered. By 1863 the worst was over ; a certain amount of cotton was smuggled by the " blockade-runners " through the northern fleets ; more was procured from Egypt and other formerly undeveloped markets, but not until 1866 did Lancashire get back to normal conditions.[1]

Polish insurrection, 1863 The American Civil War, with all its attendant anxieties for neutrals, was still unfinished when the English Ministry was confronted with difficulties in Northern and Eastern Europe. For a full century Poland had supplied a fruitful soil for the cultivation of international rivalries. The diplomatists imagined that the problem had been solved—somewhat roughly—in 1815, but the insurrections of 1830 and 1863 proved that the hope was vain. The latter rising was due to the seizure of 2,000 men—the flower of Polish manhood—as conscripts for the Russian army. The incident was described by the British Ambassador at St. Petersburg as " simply a plan, by a clean sweep of the revolutionary youth of Poland, to kidnap the opposition and to carry it off to Siberia or the Caucasus ". The action of the Russian Viceroy in Poland had singularly far-reaching results. Bismarck, who had lately come into power, utilized the situation with consummate but cold-blooded adroitness to conciliate the goodwill of Russia. He offered a free passage, through Prussian territory, to Russian troops, and refused an asylum to Polish refugees. Apart from his anxiety to gain the favour of the Czar, he could not afford to dally with revolution in Poland. His position is made clear in the following extract from a letter from King Leopold to Queen Victoria : " If a Poland such as the Garibaldians wish could be restored, *it would be in close alliance with France*, and Prussia particularly, between the French on the Rhine and a French province on the Vistula, *could not exist* ".[2] King Leopold's diagnosis of the situation, though coloured by German sympathies, was not inaccurate. Napoleon III. would gladly have done anything in his power to follow the traditional policy of France, but his power was for the moment limited by pre-occupation in Mexico. Palmerston and

---

[1] For the cotton famine *cf.* Watts, *Facts of the Cotton Famine ;* Arnold, *History of*, and article by E. Helm ap. Palgrave's *Dictionary of Political Economy*.
[2] Granville, *Life*, i. 446.

Russell were, as usual, all in favour of " oppressed nationalities," Foreign
and anxious to give every kind of moral support to their aspirations. policy of
Russell addressed to the Government of the Czar a characteristic the Whig-
homily on the sanctity of the Treaties of 1815 and the healing
virtues of Constitutional liberty. The Czar, in reply, politely told
him to mind his own business, and the Poles were left to their fate.
The whole incident has a significance quite apart from Poland. It
exhibited the foreign policy of the Whigs in its worst and weakest
aspect—a priggish and hectoring tone, combined with an unreadi-
ness to employ force in support of convictions ; it secured the benevolent neutrality of Russia towards the policy which Bismarck had
already in contemplation ; it led to the refusal of Great Britain to
join Napoleon in calling a European Congress to consider the European
situation at large, and thus weakened at a critical moment the
Anglo-French *entente* ; [1] above all, it enabled Bismarck to take the
measure both of Napoleon III. and of the Whig Government in
England. " I do not desire war, but neither do I desire peace."
Thus Napoleon to the French Senate (March 17th, 1863). Lord
Russell genuinely desired peace, but he desired also to secure the
results which only successful war could have given him. Neither
the Czar nor Bismarck was a man to concede anything except to
force, and the final result not only constituted a decided rebuff for
Russell, but reacted very unfavourably upon the position of England
and France in regard to the Danish Duchies.

This intricate and embarrassing problem was once more brought The
prominently to the front by the death in 1863 of King Frederick VII. Schles-
of Denmark. Frederick was not only King of Denmark but Duke Holstein
of Schleswig-Holstein and Lauenburg. His death, without heirs question
male, raised a question as to the continuance of the personal union
between the Crown of Denmark and the Duchies—a Union which
had subsisted since 1460. The problem thus presented to Denmark,
to Germany, and to Europe was one of admitted complexity. Holstein
was a German Duchy inhabited by Germans, and held as a fief of
the Empire until the dissolution of the latter body (1806). Since
1815 the Duke of Holstein and Lauenburg had been a member of
the Germanic Confederation. Schleswig was less exclusively German
in speech and blood than Holstein, but according to German theory
was " indissolubly united " to Holstein. This theory of indissolubility was denounced by the Danes, who had long been anxious for
the complete incorporation of both Duchies, and especially Schleswig,
in the Danish Monarchy. Such incorporation had, however, never
been permanently accomplished, and the question was further complicated by the fact that Salic law survived in the Duchies, while
the Danish Crown was, under the *lex regia* of 1665, transmissible
indifferently to males and females. In 1848 the Duchies rose in

[1] For Palmerston's reasons *cf.* his letter to King Leopold ap. Ashley, ii. 237.

insurrection under Prince Frederick of Augustenburg, who, under the Salic law, had strong prospective claims upon Schleswig and Holstein, though none upon the throne of Denmark. But for the armed assistance of the Germanic Confederation and the diplomatic intervention of the Powers, the insurrection would unquestionably have been suppressed by the Danes, and the Duchies would have been incorporated in the Danish Monarchy. As it was, the matter dragged on, war and diplomacy taking alternate parts, until a settlement was eventually reached, under the leading inspiration of Great Britain, in the Treaty of London (May 8th, 1852).

Treaty of London (1852) To that treaty, England, France, Austria, Prussia, Russia, Sweden, and Denmark were parties. The Duke of Augustenburg had already (March 31) renounced, for himself and his family, all claims upon the Duchies, and had accepted £400,000 in compensation. The Powers, therefore, recognized the right of Prince Christian of Glücksburg to succeed to the whole of the States then united under the sceptre of the Danish King, basing their recognition upon the importance to European peace of " the maintenance of the integrity of the Danish Monarchy ". They also affirmed that the reciprocal rights and obligations of the King of Denmark and the Germanic Confederation were not, as regards Holstein and Lauenburg, affected by the treaty.[1] To this treaty the Germanic Diet was not a party ; several of the individual States subsequently acceded to it, but others refused to do so until the views of the Germanic Diet were known. Austria and Prussia were among the original signatories.

Between 1852 and 1863 Denmark made further attempts to bind the Duchies to the Crown. Schleswig was originally incorporated, and a new Constitution was imposed upon Holstein without the assent of the Holstein Diet. The incorporation of Schleswig was a distinct breach of the pledge given by King Frederick to Austria and Prussia, while the Holsteiners sought the support of the Germanic diet against that part of the arrangement which especially affected them. Denmark, however, went on its way unheeding. The British Government made every effort to avert a complete rupture,[2] and in 1862 Russell suggested a somewhat clumsy compromise : the " integrity " of the Danish Kingdom, as guaranteed by the Treaty of London, was to be maintained ; Schleswig was to have " the power of self-government " ; and Holstein and Lauenburg were to have (of course under the Danish Crown) " all that the German Confedera-

---

[1] Art. iii. As this clause has been misunderstood by some writers I give the exact wording : " It is expressly understood that the reciprocal rights and obligations of His Majesty the King of Denmark, and of the Germanic Confederation, concerning the Duchies of Holstein and Lauenburg, rights and obligations established by the Federal Act of 1815 and by the existing Federal right, shall not be affected by the present treaty ".

[2] See *Parliamentary Papers re* Schleswig-Holstein, 1860-1863 ; *Germany and Denmark* (1864).

The CAMPAIGNS of 1864, 1866, 1870-71.

SCALE 0 100 200 300 Eng. Miles

tion asks for them ".[1]   The German Powers accepted Russell's suggestion as a basis for negotiation, but Denmark rejected it, and in 1863 repudiated the compact of 1852 and, by conferring autonomy upon Holstein, under the Danish Crown, separated the fortunes of that Duchy from those of Schleswig.   This was a direct challenge to the German theory of "indissolubility," and it was at once accepted by the Diet, which threatened "Federal execution" (Oct. 1st, 1863) unless the obnoxious Constitution were withdrawn before October 27th.   Russell, thereupon, urged Denmark to suspend or withdraw the Constitution, but declared that Great Britain "could not see with indifference a military occupation of Holstein which is only to cease upon terms injuriously affecting the Constitution of the whole Danish Monarchy ".[2]   But the control of events was already passing into hands stronger than those of Lord Russell.

Bismarck had made up his mind that the acquisition of the Danish Duchies—particularly the great harbour of Kiel—was essential to the future greatness of Prussia at sea.   He discerned moreover, in the complex situation a means of forcing a quarrel upon Austria.   That quarrel he believed to be unavoidable, unless the interests alike of Prussia and of Germany were to be permanently sacrificed.   But there were many obstacles in his path : the Danish nationalists ; the guarantors of the Treaty of London ; the Austrian Emperor, and the Germanic Diet.   On the death of King Frederick VII. (Nov. 15th, 1863) Prince Christian of Glücksburg was at once proclaimed King of Denmark as Christian IX.   As regards the Danish Kingdom the succession was undisputed ; to the Duchess the Germanic Diet immediately laid claim on behalf of Duke Frederick of Augustenburg, and on the refusal of Denmark to annul the new Constitution, a body of Saxon and Hanoverian troops occupied Holstein in the name of the Diet and its candidate.   This did not suit Bismarck's game ; he wanted the Duchies not for the Germanic Confederation but for Prussia.   In his refusal, however, to admit the claims of Duke Frederick he was virtually alone in Germany, perhaps in Prussia. With all the cards against him he played with consummate coolness and skill.   He had already taken the measure, accurately enough, of the Emperor Napoleon and of the English Whigs.   To Lord Russell's homilies on political morality he was indifferent, so long as they were not backed by force ; and he had good reason for his belief that Russell would not fight for Denmark.   Before Austria he dangled the red flag of the Democratic Revolution [3] and persuaded her to pull the chestnuts out of the fire for him in the Duchies. Upon Russia's benevolent neutrality he could confidently count. Early in 1864, therefore, Austria and Prussia occupied Holstein as

Bismarck and the Duchies

---

[1] *Parliamentary Papers*, lxxiv. 1863.
[2] Russell to Sir A. Malet, September 29th, 1863.
[3] See Malet, *Overthrow of the Germanic Confederation*, p. 75.

signatories of the Treaty of London, and pushed aside not only the Danish nationalists but the Germanic Diet and their candidate.

Policy of Great Britain

What was the policy of Great Britain in this serious European crisis ? Russell was anxious to impose mediation upon the combatants and, in the event of the refusal of the German Powers, to send an English squadron to the Baltic, and ask Napoleon to send a French army to the Rhine. Palmerston disliked the idea of a French army on the Rhine, and some of his younger colleagues, notably Lord Granville, were more conscious than the veterans of the Cabinet of the new forces which were already at work in Germany, and were soon to transform it. The Queen, too, was unwilling to discourage that rising German sentiment which had quickened the public imagination of her husband.[1] The English people, on the contrary, stimulated no doubt to sympathy with the Danes by the recent arrival in their midst of the " Sea-King's daughter from over the sea," the young bride of the Prince of Wales, regarded the German Powers as treaty-breakers and bullies. The fighting in the Duchies did not last long. The Danes, hopelessly outnumbered, were thrust out of them ; the Powers were induced (April 25th) to enter into a conference in London, and on May 12th the belligerents agreed to an armistice. The conference sat until June 25th, but it accomplished nothing. " The victorious Germans were exacting, the desperate Danes were obstinate." [2] Accordingly, the armistice lapsed ; fighting was resumed at the end of June, but in July the Danes sued for peace ; the preliminaries were signed on August 1st, and the terms were embodied in the Treaty of Vienna (Oct. 30th). The King of Denmark handed over the three Duchies to Austria and Prussia. Half Bismarck's task was accomplished ; but not the harder half. The Danes were pushed aside ; the Germanic Diet and Austria remained. The Diet still pressed the claims of " Frederick the Eighth " (the Duke of Augustenburg) ; Austria was virtually compelled to espouse them, and Bismarck agreed to recognize them on terms which would have made Frederick a vassal of Prussia. Frederick of Augustenburg refused to accept the Duchies on these terms, and Austria and Prussia were on the verge of war. Bismarck, however, was not quite ready, and at Gastein (Aug. 20th, 1865) he " papered over the cracks ". Lauenburg was sold to Prussia ; Holstein remained in the occupation of Austria ; Schleswig in that of Prussia. The cracks soon reappeared ; Bismarck completed his preparations ; at Biarritz he came to terms with Napoleon (Sept. 1865), and he promised Venetia to Italy (April, 1866). In June Prussia seceded from the Germanic Confederation ; war straightway broke out between herself and the " Bund," and within six weeks

---

[1] But she was convinced that it was in England's interest that she resisted " any attempt to involve this country in a mad and useless combat ". *Cf.* for Queen's correspondence with Lord Granville, Fitzmaurice, i. 456.

[2] Ashley, *Palmerston*, ii. 253.

not Austria only but Germany lay prostrate under the rapid blows which Prussia delivered. After the decisive victory of Königgratz, the Emperor gave up the game, and the Treaty of Prague was concluded on August 23rd, 1866. Bismarck, having thought out beforehand every move in the diplomatic game, treated Austria with leniency, though she was driven out of the Germanic body; Prussia enlarged and consolidated her own dominions by the annexation of Hanover, Hesse-Cassel, Schleswig-Holstein, Lauenburg, Nassau, and the free city of Frankfort-on-Main, and all the German States north of the Main accepted her hegemony.

England preserved throughout these events an attitude of correct neutrality. Palmerston and Russell were strongly tempted to side with Denmark, though the application of their favourite doctrine of " nationality " was not in this case free from ambiguity; public opinion inclined in the same direction, but the Queen laboured untiringly to keep this country out of war. The Queen was accused then, and frequently, of allowing her policy to be swayed by dynastic considerations. That she should be solicitous as to the prospects of the Princess Royal was natural; that she allowed her personal anxiety to influence her to the detriment of her own country is untrue. " Often," wrote Mr. Gladstone (Jan. 4th, 1864), " as I have been struck by the Queen's extraordinary integrity of mind . . . I never felt it more than on hearing and reading a letter of hers . . . about the Danish question. Her determination in this case, as in others, not inwardly to ' sell the truth ' overbears all prepossessions and longings strong as they are on the German side." [1] The seven weeks' war naturally caused the Queen intense anxiety. To avert it she had offered to act as mediator, but Bismarck roughly rejected the unwelcome suggestion. By the issue of it she was distraught. Her elation at the improvement in the prospects of the Crown Princess of Prussia were balanced by the regret at the extinction of her cousin's Kingdom of Hanover, by the curtailment of the rights of her son-in-law of Hesse, by sympathy with the Princess of Wales, and above all by increasing exasperation at the methods, if not the policy, of Bismarck.

England and Germany

How did England stand at the close of this period of continental turmoil ? " Lord Russell's fierce notes and pacific measures furnish an endless theme for the taunts of those who would gladly see the influence of England in the councils of Europe destroyed." [2] Thus wrote the late Lord Salisbury in 1864. Sir Alexander Malet, British Minister at Frankfort, held similar language when reviewing these events in 1869. It cannot be doubted, he affirmed, that England's " utter desertion of Denmark lowered her national reputation and left a stigma of egotism on the nation ".[3] That our national interests coincided with the dictates of national honour is no longer open to

Position of England

[1] Morley, ii. 192.   [2] Lord Salisbury, *Essays*, i. 145.   [3] *Op. cit.* p. 27.

question. "There is no use," said Palmerston in 1863, "in disguising the fact that what is at the bottom of the German design . . . is the dream of a German fleet and the wish to get Kiel as a German seaport. That may be a good reason why they should wish it ; but it is no reason why they should violate the rights and independence of Denmark. . . . If any violent attempt were made to overthrow those rights and interfere with that independence, those who made the attempt would find in the result that it would not be Denmark alone with which they would have to contend." Bismarck estimated Palmerston's brave words at their true value. With Denmark alone he had to contend ; Kiel passed into the hands of Prussia ; the dream of a German fleet has been realized, and the country which, in the view of contemporaries, deserted Denmark in 1864 is to-day compelled to concentrate her naval power in the North Sea and to pay nearly £50,000,000 a year to keep pace with the naval development of her most serious rival.

Before the Prussian triumph was assured, an epoch-making event had taken place at home. Lord Palmerston's long political career was terminated by his death on October 18th, 1865.

Home politics, 1860-1865 During the last five years of his life and Ministry interest in home politics was almost completely in abeyance, Lord John Russell, ever faithful to the enthusiasms of his political youth, introduced a Reform Bill in 1860, but presently withdrew it. The subject did not again figure in the ministerial programme during Lord Palmerston's life. Of the four seats vacated by the defranchisement of the boroughs of St. Albans and Sudbury, two were assigned in 1861 to the West Riding, and one each to South Lancashire and Birkenhead, while the franchise question was kept to the fore by periodical motions made by Mr. Locke-King and Mr. Baines. But nothing was done ; and it was tacitly assumed that so long as Palmerston lived nothing would be done.

Gladstone's finance The dead calm of domestic politics was ruffled only by Mr. Gladstone's Budgets, and a serious conflict, arising therefrom, between the two Houses of the Legislature.

The Budget of 1859 presented no feature of special interest. There was an increase of nearly £4,500,000 in the army and navy estimates, and of more than £500,000 for miscellaneous purposes. To meet this the income tax, which ought according to Mr. Gladstone's original purpose to have been on the point of extinction, was raised from 5d. to 9d. in the £. But if the Budget of 1859 was otherwise featureless, that of 1860 was one of the most important of the century. Mr. Gladstone himself spoke of 1860 as " the last of what I may call the cardinal or organic years ".[1] The dominating fact of the fiscal situation was the conclusion of the Cobden Treaty with France. But it was also influenced by the falling in of the long annuities

[1] Ap. *Nineteenth Century* for February, 1880.

which placed £2,100,000 at Gladstone's disposal.[1] He was resolved
that the opportunity should be taken of this happy conjunction to
" do something for trade and the masses ". For us the Cobden
Treaty meant in Mr. Gladstone's words " a sweep, summary, entire
and absolute, of the duty on what are known as manufactured goods
from the face of the British tariff ". Silk manufacturers, gloves,
watches, and artificial flowers were among the manufactured articles
entirely freed from duty. It meant also the removal of duty from
butter, cheese, eggs, tallow, oranges, nuts, and a number of articles
of food. In 1845, after Peel's reforms, there remained in the tariff
1,163 articles ; by 1859 these had been reduced to 419, the Budget
of 1860 made a clean sweep of 371 leaving only 48, of which no more
than 15 would contribute anything substantial to the revenue.
These were : spirits, sugar, tea, tobacco, wine, coffee, cocoa, currants,
timber, chicory, figs, hops, pepper, raisins, and rice. Thus the
Budget of 1860 gave " nearly universal effect" to the following
principles :

> " 1. That neither on raw produce, nor on food, nor on manu-
> factured goods should any duty of a protective character
> be charged.
> " 2. That the sums necessary to be levied for the purposes of
> revenue in the shape of customs duty should be raised upon
> the smallest possible number of articles." [2]

How would the application of these principles immediately affect
the revenue ? On Customs Mr. Gladstone anticipated a loss of just
over £2,100,000, a sum exactly equal to the sum saved on the payment of the annuities. But such a result was too easy and too tame
for the Chancellor of the Exchequer. He proposed to put an extra
1d. on the income tax, bringing it up to 10d., and to remit, at the
cost of £1,200,000, the duty on paper and other excise duties. The
principle of the Budget was not unchallenged in the House of
Commons, but a hostile resolution proposed by Mr. Duncan was
rejected on February 24th by the substantial majority of 116. When
the Paper Duty Repeal Bill came on for second reading (March 12th)
Sir William Miles moved : " That as it appears the repeal of the
duty on paper will necessitate the addition of 1d. in the £ to the
property and income tax, it is the opinion of this House that such
repeal is, under such circumstances, at the present moment inexpedient ". In view of the very substantial relief given to indirect
taxation, it is difficult to resist the conviction that Sir William Miles
was right ; but the second reading was carried by fifty-three. On
the third reading, however, the Government majority fell to nine.

[1] The National Debt was originally raised by the issue of terminable annuities,
and some of the longer ones had not until now fallen in.
[2] *Nineteenth Century*, February, 1880.

The Lords and finance

This gave the House of Lords its opportunity. The Commons were more than lukewarm about the repeal of the " taxes on knowledge," as Mr. Gladstone grandiloquently termed them. The Cabinet was notoriously divided on the subject.[1] On May 5th the Prime Minister spoke for forty-five minutes against the Paper Duties Bill in the Cabinet. Two days later he wrote to the Queen to say that if the House of Lords, encouraged by the narrow majority in the Commons, were to throw out the Bill they would " perform a good public service," and " the Government might well submit to so welcome a defeat ".[2] However questionable Palmerston's ideas of Cabinet loyalty, it is difficult, on the merits of the case, to disagree with him. Plainly, his Chancellor of the Exchequer wanted to go too fast. On May 21st the Lords rejected the Bill [3] by 193 to 104. Palmerston was all for acquiescence. But he reckoned without his fiery colleague. On May 26th and on June 30th Gladstone delivered to the Cabinet two elaborate lectures on the constitutional aspects of the case. " This proceeding of the Lords amounted," he affirmed, " to the establishment of a revisory power over the House of Commons in its most vital function, long declared exclusively its own, and to a divided responsibility in fixing the revenue and charge of the country for the year." And he declared : " I for one am not willing that the House of Commons should hold on sufferance in the nineteenth century what it won in the seventeenth, and confirmed and enlarged in the eighteenth ".[4] Accordingly Palmerston was obliged with very ill grace to submit, on July 6th, a series of resolutions to the House of Commons. The first affirmed that " the right of granting aids and supplies to the Crown is in the Commons alone, as an essential part of their constitution, and the limitation of all such grants as to matter, manner, measure, and time is only in them ". The second, while admitting that the Lords had sometimes exercised the power of rejecting Bills relating to taxation by negativing the whole, nevertheless affirmed that the exercise of that power " hath not been frequent, and is justly regarded by this House with peculiar jealousy as affecting the right of the Commons alone to grant supplies. and to provide the ways and means for the service of the year ", The third, grimly foreshadowing future action, stated " that to guard for the future against an undue exercise of that power by the Lords, and to secure to the Commons their rightful control over taxation and supply, this House has, in its own hands, the power so to impose and remit taxes, and to frame Bills of Supply that the right of the Commons as to the matter, manner, measure, and time may be maintained inviolate ".

The Commons, of course, assented to these Resolutions, and, for the moment, the excitement died down.

---

[1] *Cf.* Morley, *Gladstone*, 30.
[3] Not the *Budget* as some writers.

[2] Martin, *Prince Consort*, v. 100.
[4] Morley, ii. 32, 38.

But the Chancellor of the Exchequer was not content with the Platonic affirmation of a principle. To him the action of the Lords was a "gigantic innovation". In 1861 came the counter-stroke. By an innovation not less gigantic, he embodied the financial proposals of the year not as heretofore, in a number of separate Bills, but in a single Bill, in which he included the rejected Paper Duty Repeal Bill, and sent it up to the Lords for acceptance or rejection as a whole. This procedure was deliberately adopted in order to challenge and, if possible, to defeat the concurrent, though not co-ordinate rights of the Lords in regard to finance. This was the moment at which, if at all, the Lords should have made their stand. In 1860 the position they adopted was relatively weak. In 1861 they were challenged on grounds not merely defensible but constitutionally impregnable. "We have it in our power," said Lord Derby, "to divide the Bill which has been sent up to us by that House ; and so divided we have it in our power to adopt it, and to send it back to the Commons for acceptance or rejection." Nevertheless, despite the fact that the Commons had approved Gladstone's innovation only by a majority of fifteen, Lord Derby counselled acquiescence ; the Lords gave way, and permitted the Commons, henceforward, to wield a weapon forged by the indomitable will of the Chancellor of the Exchequer.

Apart from the revolution in procedure, the Budget of 1861 was remarkable only for the repeal of the " taxes upon knowledge ". **Finance, 1861-1865** One penny was also taken off the income tax, but, greatly to his chagrin, Mr. Gladstone was compelled to assent to a loan of £9,000,000 to be expended gradually upon fortifications. In the three following years he did but enlarge and extend the principles affirmed in 1860. The success of those principles was indubitable. Despite the cotton famine ; despite a reduction of no less than £8,000,000 in British exports to the United States,[1] both trade and revenue exhibited remarkable elasticity. In the triennium 1849-1852 British exports had averaged only £72,000,000 ; in 1853-1859 they averaged £119,000,000 ; in 1860-1866 no less than £149,500,000, while in the last year (1866) they reached a sum of £188,000,000. The total foreign trade which in 1860 was £375,000,000 was £534,000,000 in 1866. In times of such abounding national prosperity the people looked naturally for some relief from the burden of taxation ; and they did not look to Mr. Gladstone in vain. In 1863 he took 2d. off the income tax, thus reducing it to 7d., and at the same time he reduced the tea duty from 17d. to 1s. ; in 1864 the income taxpayers were relieved of another penny, and in 1865 of a further 2d., the tax being thus brought down to 4d. Simultaneously the tea duty was reduced from 1s. to 6d. The five years 1862-1866 showed aggregate remissions of no less than £13,500,000. But an abounding

[1] 1856-1859 they averaged £19,500,000 ; 1861-1862 only £11,500,000.

revenue did not make Mr. Gladstone careless either as to the equities
of taxation, or as to the objects and aggregates of expenditure.
Thus in 1863 he attempted, though unsuccessfully, to persuade the
House to bring charities within the sphere of the income tax. His
speech on that occasion contained one of the most closely reasoned
arguments ever addressed to the House of Commons, but reason
yielded to sentiment. More important was the establishment, in
1861, of the Post Office Savings Bank. Mr. Gladstone himself
classed this among the most notable achievements of his political
life, and its beneficent results none can question. It provided for
the savings of the people with safety, cheapness, and convenience;
and it provided " the Minister of Finance with a strong financial
arm," and secured his independence of the City " by giving him a
large and certain command of money ".[1] The Post Office Savings
Bank affords one more illustration of Mr. Gladstone's constant
solicitude for the promotion of private no less than public economy.
The growth of public expenditure he viewed with the gravest alarm.
between 1853 and 1861 it had increased from £56,000,000 to
£72,000,000. By 1866 he had the satisfaction of having reduced it
to £66,250,000. But it was a herculean task. " It is more difficult,"
he wrote to Cobden, " to save a shilling than to spend a million."
He was fighting, however, for a principle which to him was not
merely economic but ethical, and in such a crusade there was no
withstanding the fiery zeal of Mr. Gladstone. " All excess in public
expenditure beyond the legitimate wants of the country is," he
insisted, " not only a pecuniary waste, but a great political, and
above all a great moral evil," [2] and it was his firm conviction that the
" spirit of expenditure " would never be exorcised and " give place
to the old spirit of economy, so long as we have the income tax ".[3]
How accurate was his diagnosis, how shrewd his prediction is known
to all who have come after. But his was the voice of one crying in
the wilderness. Neither from his colleagues nor from the House at
large did he get effective support. Alone he did it. " The whole of
my action in 1859-1865," he wrote long afterwards, " was viewed
with the utmost jealousy by a large minority, and a section of the
very limited majority." One other reform effected by Gladstone,
though dating from 1866, may be conveniently noticed here. By the
Exchequer and Audit Act of that year he completed the circuit of
the control of the House of Commons not merely over revenue but
over expenditure. The Controller and Auditor-General, himself the
creature of this Act, is the pivot upon which the whole working of
the financial machinery now turns. He is a non-political official,
whose complete independence is secured by the fact that his salary
is charged upon the consolidated fund, and that he is not permitted

The Post
Office
Savings
Bank

The Ex-
chequer
and
Audit
Act, 1866

---

[1] See Gladstone's own Memorandum ap. Morley, ii. 52.
[2] Morley, ii. 53.   [3] *Op. cit.* p. 63.

to sit in Parliament. All money collected by the fiscal officials—
Inland Revenue, Post Office, and Woods and Forests Commissioners
—is paid into the Exchequer account at the Bank of England and
the Bank of Ireland. Not a penny can be withdrawn from that
account without the sanction of this potent individual, who presents
annually to Parliament an audited account together with a report,
in which it is shown that the sums voted by the House of Commons
to the several enumerated purposes have been expended strictly
upon them and not otherwise.

Before the *Exchequer and Audit Act* became law the régime The close
against which Mr. Gladstone had so long chafed had for ever passed of the
away. Parliament, having run for six years, was dissolved in July, Palmerstonian
1865. The General Election which ensued increased the normal era
majority of the Government from forty to sixty. But the numerical
results were less significant than the personal. Lord Palmerston
himself was returned for Tiverton, but the increase of strength on
the Ministerial Benches was more apparent upon the left than upon
the right wing. John Stuart Mill, a philosophical Radical, was
induced to become a candidate for Westminster, and was elected ;
the City returned four Liberals with Mr. Goschen at the head of
them ; and Thomas Hughes, author of *Tom Brown*, and a friend of
Kingsley and Maurice, was returned for Lambeth. Most significant
of all : Mr. Gladstone was defeated for the University of Oxford by
Mr. Gathorne Hardy, and was promptly elected for South Lancashire.
The last real tie between Mr. Gladstone and his pristine Conservatism
was thus abruptly severed ; he stood before the country an
" unmuzzled " Radical. Almost at the same moment there disappeared the most outstanding landmark of the passing era.

Not until the session of 1865 did Lord Palmerston exhibit any The death
palpable sign of failing health. In June, 1864, he rode down to of Lord
Palmer-
Harrow for the Speeches within the hour : and on his eightieth ston
birthday (Oct. 20th, 1864) he spent the greater part of the day in
the saddle, inspecting the Portsmouth fortifications. But in 1865
he was clearly failing. His old enemy the gout flew to the bladder.
He caught a chill while driving out, and within two days of completing his eighty-first year he suddenly passed away (Oct. 18th,
1865). On October 27th his body was committed to the companion-
ship of the mighty dead in Westminster Abbey.

The death of Lord Palmerston had a two-fold significance. In
the first place, it closed a great epoch in English history. More
distinctly even than the Reform Act of 1832 it ended the era of
Whig ascendancy—the period during which England was ruled by a
group of great families who, brought into power by the Revolution
of 1688, were nominally dethroned by that of 1832.

Not that Lord Palmerston was a typical Whig. He was not His place
concerned, like his colleague and rival, Lord John Russell, to exalt in English
politics

the glories of the Revolution of 1688, nor did he share his belief in the divine right of the Whig families to exclusive political power. Still less was he a typical Tory. Least of all was he a Radical. He had nothing in common with the priggish Liberalism of the Benthamites, nor with the more democratic sympathies of some of his younger colleagues.

Politically, indeed, it is not very easy to label him. Perhaps it is enough to say that his true political progenitor was George Canning; and that a corner of his own mantle fell upon Disraeli. Like Canning he was an ardent Liberal in foreign politics; a determined foe to continental absolutism. A devoted friend of oppressed or struggling nationalities, he was the creator of Belgium, the patron of Greece, the friend of Italy. Like Canning he was an intense believer in the might and the majesty of England, and in her obligation as well as her power to maintain the cause of justice among nations. Meddlesome, high-handed and overbearing—so he was regarded by the diplomatists, especially by the reactionary diplomatists of the Continent. It was the inevitable judgment on one who deemed it to be the mission of Great Britain, in season and out of season, to succour the weak and defend the right. That he failed to do this in 1862-1863 cannot be denied. But three things must be remembered: that Palmerston was not personally at the Foreign Office; that his powers were not what they had been in the 'forties; and, finally, that there had arisen in central Europe a diplomatist for whom Palmerston, even at his best, would have been no match. As regards domestic politics he was most in sympathy with the humanitarian Toryism of his friend, Lord Shaftesbury. To this fact his tenure of the Home Office bore testimony. It proved, too, his excellence as an administrator. But it is as a Foreign Minister, not as a domestic reformer, that Palmerston will be remembered. Nevertheless, his removal marks the close of a distinct era in our domestic history. His unquestioned personal supremacy, his superb common sense and his unfailing tact harmonized conflicting elements and checked the spirit of innovation. His death liberated forces which he had more or less consciously controlled, and left the door open to Gladstonian radicalism.

His character

Palmerston's death did more than close an epoch. It removed from the stage of English politics its most attractive, if not its most striking personality. As a man he was extraordinarily winning: perfect in temper, unfailingly good-humoured, splendidly courageous, invincibly optimistic. He never knew when he was beaten, and really beaten he never was. Confident in himself and proud of the confidence which he inspired in his countrymen, he was absolutely devoid of that self-consciousness and restlessness which tortured some of his more conscientious colleagues. He took all the blows of adverse fortune with equanimity, and he never bore a grudge.

Dismissed from the Foreign Office in 1851, he cheerfully accepted an inferior post in the Coalition of 1852. On the fall of Lord Derby in 1859 he was willing to serve under his young colleague, Lord Granville, though the latter had supplanted him at the Foreign Office. Such magnanimity is as rare in politics as it is admirable.

That Palmerston had the defects of his qualities is undeniable. Convinced of the justice of his own position, and conscious of the disinterestedness of England, he was too careless of the susceptibilities of other countries.

In his dealings with the Sovereign he was at times impatient and inconsiderate. Why any one—least of all a lady—should want to interfere with the business of the Foreign Office while Palmerston was in control, he was—quite honestly and simply—at a loss to comprehend. For the Queen's character and intellect he had a genuine respect, but he disliked her meddling in what he conceived to be his business. The Queen, on her side, deplored his levity and was probably misled by his manner. He had not the gravity of a Peel, or an Aberdeen, or a Gladstone. Like Canning he had too much of the Irishman in him, and to the last he never ceased to be a school-boy. But he was more serious than he pretended to be, or let others suppose. In Parliament for nearly sixty years, in office for nearly fifty, he was an indefatigable worker, and yet never let work damp his high spirits or affect his genial temper. That was surely a great achievement. It was better than an achievement : it was part of the endowment of the man : the Celtic admixture in his blood and his splendid physical equipment. Palmerston resolutely refused to grow old, and he died in harness. He was one of the happy few who are born young, and to the end he preserved the dew of his youth.

BOOK III

DEMOCRACY AND EMPIRE

CHAPTER XVIII

"THE LEAP IN THE DARK"—THE ADVENT OF DEMOCRACY

(1865-1868)

HAS England at any time enjoyed a better Constitution than that which subsisted between the Reform Bill of 1832 and that of 1867 ? Many competent judges [1] have answered this question with an emphatic negative. Nevertheless, that Constitution was about to undergo, with the concurrence of both the great Parties in the State, profound modification. For many years past the ascendancy of Lord Palmerston had imparted to English politics a sense of stability. This tranquillity was purchased, some would affirm, at the price of legislative sterility. Be that as it may, " sleeping dogs " were certainly allowed to lie.

The new epoch : characteristics. It was otherwise during the period upon which we now enter. The twenty years which followed the death of Lord Palmerston witnessed changes far-reaching in scope and bewildering in rapidity. Consequently, the England of 1885 was separated by a wide gulf from that of 1865. The most obvious change was the democratization of the electorate, if not of the legislature. The Reform Act of 1832 had added only 455,000 votes to the electoral roll and had in some cases actually operated as a measure of disfranchisement. The Acts of 1867 and 1884 added more than 3,000,000. Demos at last came into his Kingdom.

Not less remarkable was the way in which social and industrial problems gradually but insistently began to demand solution. To this fact the Statute-book bears eloquent testimony : the provision for elementary education (1870) ; the " legalization " of Trade Unions (1871-1876) ; Factory and Workshop Acts ; the Artisans' Dwelling and other Public Health Acts ; the Agricultural Holdings Acts (1875 and 1883) ; the Employers Liability Act (1880) are examples selected almost at random to illustrate this truth.

The Irish problem, also, enters upon a new stage. Almost quiescent since the fiasco of 1848, it thrusts itself into prominence again in 1865 under the guise of Fenianism. The Fenian movement inaugurates a period of remedial legislation, ecclesiastical and agrarian ; a period which culminates in the attempt, foiled by the electorate,

---

[1] See Lecky, *Democracy and Liberty*, i. 18, and *cf.* Gladstone, ap. *Nineteenth Century* (November, 1877) : " As a whole our level of public principle and public action were at their zenith in the twenty years or so which succeeded the Reform Act of 1832 ".

to alter fundamentally the constitutional relations of Ireland and the United Kingdom. All this is before us in the twenty years which ensued on Lord Palmerston's death.

Even more marked is the change in the sphere of foreign policy. This was peculiarly the domain of Palmerston. For more than thirty years he had dominated the Foreign Office. But the ensuing period witnessed more than the removal of a vigorous personality. It revealed a profound change in the centre of political gravity. From 1815 to 1865 Great Britain was pre-eminently a great European power. In the Settlement of 1815 she had played a great part. In the solution of the problems to which that settlement gave birth her voice was powerful if not predominant. By 1871 these problems were mostly solved. Greece and Belgium had been erected into independent Kingdoms ; France, after trying many experiments in Legitimacy, in Citizen Monarchy, and in Imperialism had settled down into Republicanism ; the House of Savoy had consolidated the disunited Kingdoms, Duchies and Republics of Italy into a unitary Kingdom ; all the German States, save only the German lands of Austria, had united in a Federal Empire under the Presidency of Prussia. These were the matters which bulked largest in the view of the diplomatists of the Palmerstonian era. Since 1871 the centre of gravity has shifted, more particularly for Great Britain. Our concern is less with Europe than with Asia, America, and Australia. We are absorbed in *Welt politik*. With the beginnings of these momentous changes, this and the succeeding chapters will be largely concerned.

The instability resulting from the removal of Lord Palmerston is strikingly illustrated by the rapid succession of Ministries. No fewer than four Prime Ministers held office in the three years following Palmerston's death. The first of these was Earl Russell to whom, as to " an old and tried friend," the Queen naturally turned. But the change of Premier involved few changes in the Cabinet. Lord Westbury had resigned the Chancellorship in July in consequence of a vote of censure passed against him by the House of Commons, for certain more than ordinarily disreputable jobs. The Great Seal had then passed to Lord Cranworth, who had held it in Palmerston's first Ministry and now retained it under Russell. The Foreign Office was once more committed to the safe and experienced hands of Lord Clarendon ; Mr. Gladstone became Leader of the Lower House ; and early in 1866 the Cabinet was reinforced by two recruits, both destined to eminence, Lord Hartington, who took the War Office, and Mr. Goschen, whose brilliant financial ability was recognized by the attainment of Cabinet rank at the early age of thirty-four.[1]

Earl Russell's second ministry, 1865-1866

---

[1] Mr. Goschen was not promoted as Mr. Paul suggests (iii. 3) " as a recognition of the Radicals ". On the contrary, he had offended Cobden and Bright by the Imperialist tone of his speech in seconding the Address in 1864, and they rather resented his early promotion. I state this on the authority of a letter written to me by Lord Goschen himself, and still in my possession.

It was assumed on all hands that Lord Russell's resumption of the first place in the Ministry would be signalized by an attempt to reopen the question of parliamentary reform. And not without reason. But the public mind was, in the first four months of the new Ministry, exercised far less about reform than about the cattle plague and the methods employed by Governor Eyre and his lieutenants for the suppression of insurrection in Jamaica.

Negro insurrection in Jamaica, October, 1865

In October, 1865, serious riots broke out among the negroes in the island of Jamaica. Martial law was promptly proclaimed, and the insurrection, if it can be dignified by the term, was speedily and effectively suppressed. The Governor, Mr. E. J. Eyre, had earned the reputation, by work among the aborigines of Australia, not merely of a just and capable but of a pre-eminently humane administrator. The methods employed in putting down the Jamaica insurrection were, however, of doubtful legality and unquestionable cruelty. Four hundred and thirty-nine persons, including a certain coloured Baptist preacher named Gordon, who had been a leading fomenter of the rebellion, were put to death under martial law ; 600 persons, including a number of women, were mercilessly flogged, and 1,000 houses belonging to negroes were burned. As soon as the news reached England a loud outcry arose, chiefly owing to the tone of unpardonable levity and callousness exhibited in the letters of the young officers employed in the suppression of the riots. A deputation of the usual sort, but of unusual size, waited upon Mr. Cardwell, the Colonial Secretary. Cardwell promptly sent out a strong Commission consisting of Sir Henry Storks, Governor of Malta, and two eminent barristers, and, pending the receipt of their report, superseded Governor Eyre. Parliament, at the request of the Colonial Legislature, suspended the Constitution of Jamaica and reduced the island to the status of a Crown Colony (Feb. 1866). The report of the Commissioners was published with commendable alacrity in April, 1866. They found that the rising had been of a serious character, but that martial law had been continued longer than was necessary, that the punishments inflicted were excessive, and the burning of houses wanton and even cruel. Eyre was consequently recalled : Sir John Peter Grant, a distinguished Indian Civil servant, was appointed to succeed him, and the island soon resumed its normal condition.

Governor Eyre

In August, 1866, Eyre arrived in England, and at once found himself the centre of a storm area : exaggerated abuse on one side, equally exaggerated adulation on the other. The House of Commons adopted a resolution embodying the findings of the Commission, but the Government wisely declined to prosecute Eyre. Outraged humanity could not, however, let the matter rest. A Jamaica Committee was formed under the Chairmanship of J. S. Mill, who was supported by Herbert Spencer, Huxley, and Goldwin Smith.

On the other side Carlyle, Ruskin, and Tennyson were prominent members of the Eyre Defence Committee. The Shropshire magistrates issued a warrant for the arrest of Eyre on a charge of being an accessory to murder, but refused to send him for trial. A London magistrate, however, sent for trial Lieut. Brand, R.N., who presided over the court-martial on Gordon, and Brigadier Nelson, who confirmed the sentence. But the Grand Jury, despite an exhaustive charge from Chief Justice Cockburn—described by Carlyle " as six hours of eloquent imbecility "—ignored the Bill. Not to be foiled of their vengeance, the Jamaica Committee at last (June, 1867) got a *mandamus* under which Eyre was brought up to Bow Street, and had the satisfaction of seeing him sent for trial. The Grand Jury ignored the Bill. In a civil action brought against him for damages Eyre was equally successful, and in 1872 the Government repaid him the heavy expenses to which he had been put by the various and protracted legal proceedings. Two years later he was pensioned, and his career as a public servant was thus abruptly terminated. The nett result was not unsatisfactory. The somewhat vindictive impulses of the obtrusive humanitarians were foiled, but, on the other hand, a salutary lesson was read to British administrators in distant lands. They learnt, once for all, that the constitutional rights of British subjects, even though they belong to an inferior race, are not to be overridden or ignored.

On February 6th, 1866, the Queen opened the first session of the new Parliament elected in the summer of 1865. This was the first occasion on which, since the death of the Prince Consort, the Queen had personally taken part in the ceremony. The Speech from the Throne was not a cheerful pronouncement. It referred not only to the troubles in Jamaica, but to the prevalence of cattle disease in England and the existence of a formidable conspiracy in Ireland. To the genesis and history of Fenianism reference will be made later. Here it must suffice to say that the session was barely a fortnight old before the Government deemed it necessary to hold a Saturday sitting of both Houses to pass a Bill for the suspension of the Habeas Corpus Act in Ireland. So pressing was the danger that the Bill passed through all its stages in both Houses in one day and received the Royal assent in the early hours of Sunday (Feb. 17th). *The new Parliament meets, February, 1866*

Hardly less alarming than the Fenian conspiracy in Ireland was the spread in England of the cattle disease or Rinderpest. This terrible scourge made its appearance among the cattle of some London dairymen in Midsummer, 1865. From London it spread with appalling rapidity : by the middle of October twenty-one counties in England were affected, two in Wales, and sixteen in Scotland. Before Parliament met in February, 120,000 cases had been reported, of which 90,000 had proved fatal. The measures taken by the executive under *Orders in Council* had proved wholly *Cattle plague* inadequate, and Parliament, therefore, was compelled to legislate. The most effective remedy would have been the absolute prohibition of the transfer of cattle by road or rail during the continuance of the epidemic, and the substitution of a dead meat trade for one in live cattle. But for so drastic a change of custom the country was not in the 'sixties prepared. In the event, the carriage of cattle by rail was prohibited until March 25th ; all imported cattle were to be slaughtered on landing, except those from Ireland, which was entirely immune from disease, and provision was made for the destruction of all beasts actually diseased or exposed to contact. On the subject of compensation there was a battle royal among the economists, J. S. Mill and Robert Lowe leading the rival factions. Ultimately it was decided that in the case of animals actually stricken with the plague half the value, not exceeding £20, should be paid, and in the case of contacts, three-quarters of the value, not exceeding £25. In both cases the charge was to fall upon the local rates. These measures were effective, and the grievous murrain gradually abated. It had affected different parts of the country in curiously varying degree. Ireland was totally exempt ; Wales almost entirely ; it was worst in the North-West, and on the dairy farms of Cheshire many ancient pastures had to be put under the plough. The total losses were estimated at no less than £3,500,000, but in the long run the visitation was not devoid of salutary results ; sanitary precautions were more generally enforced, and dairy cattle were placed under more effective supervision. Epidemic disease was not confined to the herds. Several of the months of 1866 proved exceptionally unhealthy for human beings, and the summer was marked by a serious outbreak of cholera.

The financial crisis of 1866   While the agricultural interest was suffering from the cattle plague, the financial world was plunged into gloom by a crisis of unusual severity. On Thursday, May 10th, a great firm of bill-discounters, Messrs. Overend, Gurney & Co., stopped payment with liabilities of £19,000,000. Dismay spread through the City, and the day following the failure of Overend & Gurney is still memorable as " Black Friday ". The crash was due to over-speculation stimulated by the facilities afforded by the legalization of the principle of limited liability. Between 1855 and 1862 there were passed a series of *Joint Stock Companies Acts* which have done much to revolutionize the conditions of English commerce and finance. Few Acts passed in the Victorian era have had more far-reaching and in some sense more unexpected results. The first effect was an immense stimulus to speculation. Overend & Gurney were only one—though the greatest—of some 250 firms which had recently registered themselves under the Joint Stock Acts. The rate of discount was raised from 3 per cent. in June, 1865, to 8 per cent. in the succeeding January. But the warnings of the Bank were vain ; the crash came in May.

The failure of Overend & Gurney was followed by a murrain of bankruptcies. The English Joint Stock Bank; the Imperial Mercantile Credit Association; the Consolidated Discount Company were among the earliest defaulters. Great railway contractors like Sir Morton Peto & Betts followed in the wake of the bankers and financiers. The Government, as in 1848 and 1857, was compelled to come to the rescue of the Bank. On May 11th the Bank had advanced over £4,000,000 to approved customers and its reserves were dangerously depleted. The Charter Act was accordingly suspended, but public confidence was rapidly restored, and the Bank found it unnecessary to act upon the permission accorded by the Executive. The discount rate of 10 per cent. imposed by the Government upon the Bank as the condition of additional powers of issue was maintained from May 11th to August 17th. Fortunately the crisis was financial rather than commercial, and the effects, therefore, were relatively transitory. But a severe shock was administered to the infant principle of limited liability from which it took time to recover. It might have been better had the recovery been even more gradual.

No disasters or alarms could quench the septuagenarian affection Parliaof Lord Russell for his first love. Firms might totter and herds be mentary decimated, Colonial Governors might execute negroes and Fenians reform might weave their webs of conspiracy, but the bounds of freedom must be widened and the House of Commons be reformed.

The question of parliamentary reform was, in the 'fifties and 'sixties, almost entirely academic. It was raised by the *a priori* speculations of philosophical liberalism, rather than by democratic demand. The machine was, by general consent, working well. Its legislative products, though sparse in quantity, were carefully conceived, and have, for the most part, stood the test of experience. But efficient machinery is not everything. Great urban populations were springing up, and little was being done for their education in citizenship. Mostly compound householders, they were serving no apprenticeship to the craft of politics by participation in local government. Out of a total of 5,300,000 adult males in England and Wales only 900,000 enjoyed the parliamentary franchise.

The new Reform Bill was introduced by Mr. Gladstone on March The Re-12th. It dealt only with the franchise and was commended to the form Bill House as a simple and modest measure. It proposed to reduce the of 1866 borough franchise to £7, estimated on the rental not the rateable value, and the county franchise to £14; to enfranchise lodgers, compound householders, and depositors in Savings Banks who had had £50 continuously to their credit for two years. Finally, it proposed to deal with a serious and increasing danger by the disfranchisement of Government employees in the dockyards. The estimate was that it would add 400,000 votes to the register. Moderate as the proposals appear in the light of later events, they were vehemently attacked at the time as dangerously democratic. It was Robert Lowe who, in Gladstone's phrase, " really supplied the whole brains of the opposition ". During this year, indeed, " and this year only he had such a command of the House as had never," even in Gladstone's experience, " been surpassed ".[1] Lowe gathered round him a band of stalwart critics nicknamed by Bright the " Adullamites " ; [2] and the " Cave " proved formidable. Lord Grosvenor, one of the leaders of the " Cave," asked the House to decline to proceed with the franchise Bill until the scheme for redistribution was laid before it. In a House of 631 members the Ministry escaped defeat on Lord Grosvenor's amendment only by a majority of five (April 27th). On this point, therefore, the Government gave way and carried to a second reading a redistribution Bill. It proved to be of a very unambitious character. Forty-nine small boroughs were to lose a member apiece ; the English county representation was to be increased by twenty-six ; four additional members were to be given to London ; seven to Scotland ; five of the largest cities were to get an extra member, and six new boroughs and the University of London were to be enfranchised for the first time. The aggregate number of members would, therefore, be unchanged.

There was no real driving power, either parliamentary or popular, behind the Bills, and on June 18th the Government were beaten by 315 against 304 on an amendment moved by Lord Dunkellin, who proposed to substitute rateable value for gross rental as a basis for the borough franchise. In consequence of this defeat the Ministry at once tendered their resignation to the Queen. The Queen saw matters in much truer perspective than the Prime Minister. On the very day on which Russell's Government was defeated, Prussia had declared war upon Austria and the German Bund. Central Europe was, in consequence, threatened with profound convulsion. In this war two of the Queen's sons-in-law, the Crown Prince of Prussia and the Duke of Hesse-Darmstadt, were fighting on opposite sides, and many others of her kinsmen were in the field. But it was not private anxieties which mainly oppressed her. Always averse to war, she perceived clearly the issues which this particular war must necessarily raise. She therefore urged her Ministers to reconsider their decision to resign. " In the present state of Europe," she wrote, " and the apathy which Lord Russell himself admits to exist in the country on the subject of reform, the Queen cannot think it consistent with the duty which Ministers owe to herself and the country that they should abandon their posts in consequence of their defeat on a matter of detail (not of principle) in a question which can never be settled

[1] Morley, ii. 201.

[2] From the Biblical phrase for the " broken men " who rallied around David in the cave of Adullam, " Every one that was in distress, and every one that was discontented ".

unless all sides are prepared to make concessions." Lord Russell
acknowledged the force of the Queen's objections to a change of
Ministry in the midst of a foreign crisis, but, overborne, perhaps by
Gladstone,[1] ultimately persisted in resignation. The Queen was
angry and hurt at what she regarded as a " desertion ".

Lord Russell's resignation brought to a close a long and dis- Earl
tinguished career. He survived, indeed, until 1878, but during the Russell
last twelve years of his life he took little part in public affairs, and
his death removed only the shadow of a mighty name. He had been
a member of the Legislature with brief intermissions for sixty-five
years : he was elected to the House of Commons two years before
the battle of Waterloo, he vacated his place in the House of Lords in
the year when Lord Beaconsfield brought back " Peace with Honour "
from Berlin. He was recognized as the leader of the Whigs on the
Reform question before George III. died, and was admitted to the
Cabinet in the second year of William IV.

Did the greatness of his achievements correspond to the length
of his service ? He was an admirable administrator, an extraordinarily copious legislator, and an effective debater. Nor can it
be questioned that he was at once a sincere friend of humanity and
a genuine patriot. " There is one thing worse," he said, " than the
cant of patriotism, and that is the re-cant of patriotism." This
brilliant epigram, flung out as a retort to Sir Francis Burdett, reflected Russell's genuine conviction. But with all his great qualities
and important achievements it is difficult to feel assured that the
ultimate judgment of history will give to Lord Russell a place in the
small " first class " of English statesmanship in which Walpole and
Chatham, Pitt and Peel are indisputably included. His domestic
life was happy, and he enjoyed the affectionate regard of kinsmen
and of friends. But to the world in general he gave the impression
of shyness and aloofness, and he was tortured by a self-consciousness
and restlessness which made him a difficult colleague.[2] He was a
keen student of literature, especially of constitutional history, and
his own contributions to it were not unimportant. His despatches
and more elaborate political memoranda are stiff and pedantic in
style, contrasting unfavourably with the trenchant directness, the
homely wit, and brusque common sense of Lord Palmerston. Nevertheless, he played for more than half a century a distinguished and
a transparently honourable part in the public life of England—

[1] Morley, ii. 207-211.
[2] Lord Selborne's admirable judgment is worth quoting ; Lord Russell was
" very much under the Government of popular impulses ; prone to sudden and
unexpected movements and stratagems in politics ; and not proof against the
craving for power. To serve under him was easy, for he was just and generous to
his followers ; but it was difficult for him, after he had once been a leader, to serve
under others . . . ambitious as he was . . . he had the self-command to apply to
himself the maxim that a wise man ought to retire voluntarily before others
perceive that he is too old to govern."—*Memorials*, part ii. vol. i. pp. 40, 41.

indeed of Europe—and his retirement created a void which was not soon or easily filled.

Lord
Derby's
third
Ministry,
July 6th,
1866-Feb-
ruary
25th,
1868
On Lord Russell's final resignation the Queen called upon Lord Derby to form a Ministry. For the third time he responded to the call. He could not command, any more than he could in 1852 or 1858, a majority in the House of Commons, and he sought therefore, with complete constitutional propriety, to form a Ministry not exclusively Conservative in composition. Lord Clarendon and the Duke of Somerset, though strongly appealed to, declined to retain office, and the Adullamites would not serve under Lord Derby, though they would have been willing to serve under Lord Stanley. An endeavour to secure the adhesion of Lord Shaftesbury was equally unsuccessful. In the event, Lord Derby was compelled to rely entirely on his own party. Nevertheless, the Cabinet was in personnel far stronger than that of 1858. Lord Stanley replaced at the Foreign Office Lord Malmesbury, who contented himself modestly with the Privy Seal, and four important recruits were included in the Cabinet : Lord Cranborne (the Lord Salisbury of after years) took the India Office ; Lord Carnarvon became Secretary for the Colonies ; Sir Stafford Northcote went to the Board of Trade, and Mr. Gathorne Hardy to the Poor Law Board. Disraeli again became Chancellor of the Exchequer and led the House of Commons.

Popular
agitation
for reform
No sooner were the Whigs out and the Conservatives in than the people, or a noisy section of them, awoke to the fact that they were being defrauded of their political rights. Associations and leagues for the promotion of parliamentary reform sprang into existence. The most important of them—the Reform League—having held a demonstration in Trafalgar Square on July 2nd, announced its intention of organizing another demonstration in Hyde Park on July 23rd. The police, acting on the orders of the Government, announced that the gates of the Park would be closed on that day at five o'clock. Accordingly, when the procession arrived at the Park they found it closed against them. The leaders, having demanded in vain that the gates should be opened, withdrew quietly to Trafalgar Square where the meeting was held. But, though the actual demonstrators departed, the mob lingered, broke down the railings, and swarmed into the Park itself. A conflict ensued between the mob and the police : the guards were summoned, but before they could arrive the riot was over and order was restored. The League and their chairman, Mr. Beales, were anxious to test the legality of the action of the Government. But no opportunity was given. The legal aspect of the matter is, however, clear enough. The Park is the property of the Crown, and the Crown can close it. If the public are admitted at all, there is nothing to prevent them from holding a " meeting " provided they do not otherwise bring themselves into conflict with the law. A Reform Demonstration

was held without interference in the Park in the following May. There was a general feeling that the Government had bungled on this question, and they found a scapegoat in the person of Mr. Spencer Walpole, the Home Secretary. In May, 1867, Walpole resigned his portfolio to Mr. Gathorne Hardy, a distinguished lawyer who had, in 1865, defeated Mr. Gladstone at Oxford.[1]

Meanwhile Mr. John Bright had been conducting a reform campaign in the Provinces. During the autumn great meetings were held at Manchester, Birmingham, Leeds, Edinburgh, Glasgow, and many other towns. In all, a thousand such meetings were held, and on every side there was a clamorous demand for " reform ". Bright spared no efforts to inflame it. The accession to office of Lord Derby, he affirmed, with questionable taste and truth, " is a declaration of war against the working classes ". *The Conservatives and reform*

Meanwhile the Derby-Disraeli Ministry was anxiously considering its position and its policy. There was nothing in the recent position of the party to preclude them from an attempt to settle the question of reform. But it was their belief, as it was that of the Queen, that it could be settled only by consent—by Parliament as a whole, not by either party. Accordingly the Speech from the Throne, in February, 1867, expressed a hope that the deliberations of Parliament on this matter would be " conducted in a spirit of moderation and mutual forbearance," and lead " to the adoption of measures which, without unduly disturbing the balance of political power, shall freely extend the elective franchise ". To give effect to these amiable aspirations the Cabinet decided to proceed not by Bill, but by resolution. The resolutions, thirteen in number, proved to be largely truistic. They affirmed that the number of electors for counties and boroughs ought to be increased ; that this should be done by reducing the value of the qualifying tenement, and " by adding other franchises not dependent on such value " ; that the occupation franchise should be based upon the principle of rating ; that the principle of plurality of votes should be adopted ; that " while it is desirable that a more direct representation should be given to the labouring class, it is contrary to the Constitution of this realm to give any one class or interest a predominating power over the rest of the community " ; that redistribution of seats was expedient, but that no existing parliamentary borough should be wholly disfranchised ; that registration should be improved ; bribery and corruption prevented, and further facilities for polling provided ; in particular, that voters should be permitted to use polling-papers for recording their votes.

How did the Government intend to translate these abstract resolutions into concrete proposals ? This was the question asked

[1] These events are described in detail and with special knowledge by Sir Spencer Walpole (a son of the Minister).—*The History of Twenty-five Years*, vol. ii. c. ix.

on every side, and not answered by Disraeli until February 25th.
On that day he introduced a Bill to give effect to them. The scheme
he then expounded was the more moderate of two schemes which
the Cabinet had for some time past been considering. On February
23rd—a Saturday—the Cabinet had agreed to the larger scheme.
During the leisure of Sunday Lord Cranborne had discovered that it
was too large for his taste, and on February 25th he and Lord Carnarvon refused to proceed with it. An explanation of the ministerial
scheme was promised for Monday afternoon. The Cabinet, therefore,
was hastily summoned. Disraeli produced his " smaller scheme " ;
the disruption of the Ministry was, for the moment averted, and the
smaller scheme was duly presented to the House.[1] It included four
new and " fancy " franchises ; a £6 rating franchise for boroughs
and the reduction of the county franchise from £50 to £20 occupiers.
The changes were estimated to add 400,000 voters to the register.
As for redistribution, thirty small boroughs were to lose one member
apiece ; two additional members were to be given to the Tower
Hamlets, twelve considerable towns such as Burnley, Barnsley,
Croydon, Darlington, and Middlesbrough were to be enfranchised :
fifteen additional members were to be given to counties, and one
member to London University.

The scheme embodied in this " Ten Minutes Bill " was virtually
still-born. It was coldly received by Parliament. The Conservative
party professed a preference for the larger scheme ; and upon the
larger scheme, therefore, Disraeli fell back. The " resolutions " were
formally withdrawn on February 26th ; the resignations of Lord
Cranborne, Lord Carnarvon, and General Peel were announced on
March 4th, and on the 18th Disraeli expounded to the House of
Commons the larger scheme which had been temporarily laid aside
in the hope of securing their adhesion.

It was admittedly a scheme of " checks and counterpoises ".
The borough franchise was to be associated with the direct payment
of rates ; every householder paying rates and having resided for two
years was to have a vote ; every one who paid £1 in direct taxes
(other than licenses) was to have a vote ; if he were also a rate-
paying householder he was to have two votes. Besides these qualifications there were to be three others : an education franchise, a
second based upon the possession of funded property, a third on that
The Bill of a deposit in a savings bank. It was estimated that more than
of 1867 1,000,000 voters would in all be added to the borough constituencies.
In counties the rating qualification was to be £15 in place of a £50
rental, which, together with the "lateral" franchises, would add, it was
estimated, 330,000 voters to the county register. The redistribution
proposals were identical with those propounded on February 25th.

---

[1] The inner history of these proceedings was blurted out by Sir John Pakington
when seeking re-election.—*Cf. Annual Register* (1867), p. 31.

These revised proposals were received with favour by the bulk of
the Conservative party, with caution by Mr. Gladstone, and with
strong opposition by Adullamites like Lowe and by the extremer
Tories such as Sir W. Heathcote and Mr. Beresford Hope. After
two nights' debate the Bill was read a second time without a division,
but not before Mr. Gladstone had indicated the scope of the amendments upon which he and his party would insist, if with their consent,
the Bill were to become law.

A lodger franchise must be inserted ; the fancy franchises and
the dual vote must go ; the distinction between classes of rate-paying
householders must be abolished ; the county franchise must be
further reduced ; the scheme of voting papers dropped, and the
redistribution part of the scheme enlarged.

The later parliamentary career of this famous measure is extra- The Bill
ordinarily complicated. The confusion arises mainly from the atti- in Com-
tude towards the question of the two protagonists. To the casual mittee
observer that of Disraeli appears simply reckless and unprincipled ;
that of Gladstone hesitating and cautious. Whether closer examination will confirm this view remains to be seen. This much at least
is certain : that the Radical leaders, Gladstone and Bright, were not
at that time prepared for household suffrage. " In all our boroughs,"
said the latter, " there is a small class which it would be much better
for themselves if they were not enfranchised, because they have no
independence whatever. . . . I call this class the *residuum*." [1] " We
did not wish," wrote the former in a retrospective Memorandum,
" to make at once so wide a change as that involved in a genuine
household suffrage (always in our minds involving county as well as
town) . . . so we adhered to our idea of an extension, considerable
but not violent, and performing all it promised.[2] Disraeli, on the
contrary, was not in the least afraid of a leap into the darkness of
household suffrage, provided he could carry with him a sufficient
number of his own party. With superb ingenuity, he led them to
the brink of the abyss by dangling before them the " checks and
counterpoises "—in other words the " lateral " extension of the
suffrage, and the exclusion of the compound householder. In tactics
he was always more adroit that his rival ; and never were the contrasted endowments of the two men more clearly displayed than in
this session of 1867.

Before the House got into Committee on the Bill the Radical
leaders decided to move an Instruction to the Committee which
would have had the effect of excluding Bright's *residuum* from the
suffrage. Such a motion was in complete accord with their settled
convictions, but it was a grave tactical blunder. A Radical " cave "
—known as the " Tea-room party "—rapidly formed itself, and the

---

[1] Speech on second reading.   Bright did not soon hear the last of the *residuum*.
[2] Ap. Morley, ii. 224.

Instruction had to be abandoned. But Mr. Gladstone was not to be moved from his set purpose. He tabled a series of amendments of which the two most important were : (1) to delete the distinction between direct and indirect ratepayers, and thus admit to the franchise " compound householders " ; and (2) to fix an inferior limit of £5 rating value and thus exclude all the householders, whether ratepapers or not, of the very lowest class. Gladstone moved the first of these amendments on April 11th, supporting it on the ground that the Bill as it stood would do little for the enfranchisement of the working classes in towns, since the occupiers of two-thirds of the houses under the value of £10 were compounders. The debate revealed the confusion and perplexity into which members of all parties were plunged by the cross currents of opinion, and particularly by the complications of the " compound householder ". On the one hand extreme Tories described their leader's proposals (not untruthfully) as at once niggardly and lavish, timid and rash. On the other, extreme Radicals resented the restrictive amendment, of which their leader had given notice. The House generally did not want a change of Ministry, involving an inevitable dissolution and did want the settlement of a tiresome and difficult question.

In the event, Gladstone was defeated on his first amendment by a majority of twenty-one. The result was a staggering blow to his personal prestige and was a conspicuous triumph for the tactics of his rival. But the irony of the situation was that the result was achieved merely by the action of the " Tea-room party," who defeated their leader's first amendment because they disliked his second.

The Easter recess

The Easter recess followed immediately upon the defeat of Mr. Gladstone. It was not unnatural that he should, for a moment, have contemplated retirement from the leadership of his party. The party was notoriously rent by insubordination and intrigue, while the leader exhibited a combination of profound earnestness and nervous irritability which matched ill with the sardonic imperturbability of his great rival. Two things, perhaps, dissuaded Mr. Gladstone from a step which at this stage of his career might have been irrevocable. One was the rising tide of democratic fervour in the country and the other was the generous encouragement of John Bright.[1]

The later stages of the Bill

The triumph of the Tories was short-lived. In the later stages of the Bill the Liberals had it all their own way. One by one the counterpoises went by the board ; the dual vote and the lateral or fancy franchises were abandoned ; the two years' qualifying residence was reduced to one ; a lodger franchise was inserted ; the rating qualification for the county franchise was reduced from £15 to £12 ; the voting paper device was deleted. One great difficulty remained ; one barrier still stood between the Bill and household

[1] See Morley, ii. 232.

suffrage *sans phrase*—the compound householder.[1] This was the last remnant of Conservatism left in the Bill.[2] On this point it seemed impossible that Disraeli could yield, nor did he. His face was saved by the amendment of Mr. Hodgkinson, who proposed to solve the difficulty by getting rid of " compounding " altogether. This solution was accepted by the Government and by the House ; the franchise was made in this way to rest upon the principle of personal rating.[3] Nevertheless, the Bill had become a Bill for " household suffrage, pure and simple," and there was justice in the plaint of Lord Cranborne that it represented a negation of all the principles professed by his party.

Several interesting amendments were proposed by J. S. Mill ; one for the enfranchisement of women was received with some hilarity, and was rejected by 196 to 73 ; but John Bright and Henry Fawcett were with Mill in the minority. Other amendments were intended to provide for the representation of minorities, and in particular to recommend Mr. Hare's scheme for proportional representation. The reception of these was sympathetic but discouraging and they were withdrawn. It was, however, decided to give a third member to Manchester, Liverpool, Leeds, Glasgow, and Birmingham, and a proposal, made in the House of Lords by Lord Cairns, that in these boroughs and in the three-member counties [4] electors should be permitted to vote only for two candidates was, despite the strong opposition of Mr. Bright, accepted by the Commons. But this was the only crumb of comfort vouchsafed to minorities.

The " Redistribution " clauses were also considerably amended. Taken in conjunction with the Reform Bills for Scotland and Ireland (1868) the nett result was that 6 boroughs returning two members each, and 5 boroughs returning one, were totally disfranchised, and 35 other boroughs lost one member each. Thus 52 seats were set free for redistribution. Of these the boroughs got 22 additional members, the counties 27, London University 1, and the Scotch Universities 2. The aggregate numbers of the House remained therefore constant.

The Representation of the People Bill received the Royal assent on August 15th, 1867.

A word may be added as to the Scotch and Irish Reform Bills which became law in 1868. The Scotch Bill followed the same lines as the English, except that the occupation franchise for counties

---

[1] I.e. a tenant whose rates are paid (under composition) by the landlord.

[2] The account given of the process of amendment is logical, but not chronological.

[3] Even this did not last more than two years. " Compounding " was restored in 1869 by 32 and 33 Vict. c. 41.

[4] It may be interesting to recall the fact that the effect of this provision was to give a " minority " Liberal to the seven counties concerned, and to Liverpool ; to give a " minority " Conservative to Manchester, and occasionally to Leeds and Glasgow. Birmingham regularly returned three Liberals.

was fixed at £14 instead of £12. In Ireland the county qualification already stood at £12, and was not, therefore, altered in 1868 ; the qualification in boroughs was reduced from £8 to £4, the latter being the inferior limit of direct ratepayers. Lodgers were admitted on the same terms as in England—£10 a year rental for unfurnished rooms.

The Reform Acts, 1867-1868 Such was the parliamentary reform legislation of 1867-1868. The magnitude of the change effected none can gainsay. In all some 1,080,000 persons were enfranchised. In the towns, notwithstanding the original disclaimer of the principle, the Act meant the adoption of " household suffrage pure and simple ". Loud were the predictions of impending disaster. " The bag which holds the winds," said Mr. Lowe, " will be untied, and we shall be surrounded by a perpetual whirl of change, alteration, innovation, and revolution." " Your repentance," he told Disraeli, " bitter as I know it will be, will come too late." Even the Conservative Premier admitted that the Act was " a leap in the dark ".

Disraeli's conduct His brilliant lieutenant was entirely unrepentant. There was indeed truth as well as point in General Peel's bitter avowal that the proceedings in reference to the Reform Bill " had taught him three things—first, that nothing had so little vitality as a ' vital point ' ; second, that nothing was so insecure as ' security,' and third, that nothing was so elastic as the conscience of a Cabinet Minister ". Similarly the splenetic sage of Chelsea might bewail the " shooting of Niagara " and might denounce " the superlative Hebrew conjuror, spell-binding all the great Lords, great parties, great interests of England to his hand and leading them by the nose like helpless, mesmerized somnambulant cattle to such issue ". Such tirades left Disraeli quite unmoved. His personal triumph was complete, and in his speech on the third reading that note is clear. Five Ministries —Lord John Russell's, Lord Aberdeen's, Lord Palmerston's, Lord Derby's, and Lord Russell's again—had attempted to settle the question and had failed. What was the position of the Conservative Government on taking office in 1866 ? They were unpledged as to details, but they had always claimed that the question of reform was open to them no less than to their opponents. In 1867, indeed, they had no choice. " Having to deal with this question and being in office with a large majority against us, and finding that Ministers of all colours of party and politics with great majorities had failed to deal with it successfully, and believing that another failure would be fatal not merely to the Conservative party, but most dangerous to the country, we resolved to settle it if we could." Under these circumstances was it not the only reasonable course " to take the House into council with us and, by our united efforts and the frank communication of ideas, to attain a satisfactory solution " ? [1] For himself Disraeli had always held

[1] Lord Beaconsfield, *Selected Speeches*, vol. i. pp. 607-623.

that if the question were tackled at all it must be tackled boldly :
that if the settlement of 1832 were upset there was no resting-place,
in the boroughs, short of the acceptance of " the principle of rated
household suffrage ". Can anyone now doubt that in this Disraeli
was right ? Why then did he not in the first instance produce a Bill
based on this principle ? This was obviously a question not of
principle, but of Cabinet and parliamentary tactics. His colleagues
were aware of his opinions ; they had accepted the principle of
household suffrage in 1859,[1] though it may well be that nothing but
a tactical movement would have induced either the party or the
House to take the final plunge. The Act of 1867 gave precise expression to Disraeli's life-long convictions. The peroration of his
third reading speech in 1867 echoes the language and reasserts the
principles of *Coningsby*. For an oligarchy, whether of landlords or
merchants, Disraeli had nothing but contempt ; like Bolingbroke, he
believed in a " Patriot King " and he desired to see his monarchy
" broad based upon the people's will ". That he was unscrupulous in
the choice of means may be admitted ; that he lacked principle, or
was false to his convictions, can be asserted only by those who have
not been at pains to understand the one or probe the other.[2]

It may be convenient before leaving the reform question to notice *Sequelæ*
briefly three changes of some importance which followed hard upon *of the*
the enactment of the Bill of 1867. In 1868 the Lords abandoned a *Act of*
privilege, long enjoyed, of voting by proxy, and concurred with the *1867*
Commons in transferring the trial of election petitions from the
House of Commons to the judges. In 1872 vote by ballot was
substituted for open voting.

Such were the questions upon which the minds of Englishmen *Canadian*
were for the most part concentrated in the late 'sixties. Relatively *Federa-*
unnoticed was the passage of a Bill of infinitely larger significance.[3] *tion*
While politicians at Westminster were wrangling over the £10 lodger
and the compound householder, men of English blood across the seas
were initiating an experiment, immensely important in its immediate
aspect, and pregnant with still wider possibilities for the future.
That experiment was embodied in the *British North America Act* of
1867, and laid the foundation of the Canadian Federation of to-day.
An achievement so remarkable demands a chapter to itself.

[1] *Ibid.* p. 610.
[2] Dr. J. F. Bright is an honourable exception to the historians of his school ;
cf. Growth of Democracy, p. 423 : *cf.* also Mr. Walter Sichel s brilliant study of
Disraeli (Methuen & Co., 1900).
[3] The *Annual Register* for 1867 devotes four pages to the *British North America
Act*, about 100 to " Reform ".

CHAPTER XIX

COLONIAL AND FOREIGN POLICY   THE DOMINION OF CANADA

Unique character of Canadian federalism
THE Constitution of the Dominion of Canada is, in one respect, unique among those of the federal type. It represents the result of forces in part centripetal, but in part also centrifugal. It satisfied the aspirations of the British Colonies in North America—or most of them—for closer union, and at the same time the separatist tendencies which had long been manifest in the two Canadas themselves. The two movements, the one disintegrating, the other federal, came to a head with curious simultaneity in 1864.

The two Canadas
Long before that time, however, it had become apparent that neither the Union Act of 1840 nor the attainment of responsible Government was destined to register the final stage in the constitutional evolution of British North America. For this lack of finality there were several reasons, among which two were of pre-eminent validity. On the one hand, there was obviously much in common between the disunited British Colonies : Newfoundland, Nova Scotia, Prince Edward Island, and, more particularly, New Brunswick and Upper Canada ; on the other hand, there were many elements of disunion between the united Colonies of Upper and Lower Canada. The latter were, as a candid historian puts it, " obviously ill-matched yoke-fellows ".[1] Lord Durham had perceived the fact twenty years earlier. But he found it an argument not for Federation but for Union. " The French," wrote Lord Durham, " remain an old and stationary society in a new and progressive world. In all essentials they are still French ; but French in every respect dissimilar to those of France in the present day. They resemble rather the French of the Provinces under the old régime." [2] But while Quebec was rigidly Conservative, not to say reactionary, Ontario was both, in a political and economic sense, eminently progressive. Ontario was anxious to attract population ; the French Canadians, though themselves prolific, were fearful of losing their identity, and discouraged immigration. Consequently the balance of population between the two Provinces rapidly shifted. Quebec in 1841 numbered 691,000 people, Ontario could claim only 465,000 ; by 1861 the latter had increased to 1,396,000, the former only to 1,111,000.[3] Race, religion, and tradition all combined to keep apart two peoples who had never really united.

The Maritime Provinces
Among the Maritime Provinces there was, on the contrary, a strong movement towards closer union, and in 1864 the Legislatures

---

[1] Greswell, *Canada*, p. 194.
[2] Durham, *Report*, vol. ii. p. 31 (ed. 1912, Clarendon Press).
[3] Greswell, *op. cit.* ,p. 194.

of Nova Scotia, Prince Edward Island, and New Brunswick agreed to hold a Convention for the purpose of discussing the project. Meanwhile in Canada a constitutional deadlock had been solved only by the formation in June, 1864, of a Coalition Ministry, pledged to address themselves in the most earnest manner to the negotiation for a federation of all the British North American Provinces. In pursuance of this pledge the Canadian Government sought and obtained permission to send delegates to the Convention called by the Maritime Provinces. It met at Charlottetown on September 1st. The project of the larger federation rapidly took shape, and in October a second Convention assembled at Quebec. Before the month was out the Delegates had agreed upon seventy-two resolutions, which formed the basis of the subsequent Act of Federation.[1] Alexander Galt, George Brown, and George Étienne Cartier must share with John A. Macdonald the credit of this remarkable achievement; but to Macdonald it belongs in pre-eminent degree. He himself would have preferred to go even farther, believing that " if we could agree to have one Government and one Parliament, legislating for the whole of these peoples, it would be the best, the cheapest, the most vigorous, and the strongest system of Government we could adopt." But he realized that his own ideal was unattainable. Neither Lower Canada nor the Maritime Provinces were willing to surrender their individuality; they were prepared for Union, but not for Unity; and Macdonald expressed his belief that in the resolutions they had " hit upon the happy medium," and had devised a scheme which would give them " the strength of a Legislative Union, and the sectional freedom of a Federal Union, with protection to local interests ".

Many difficulties were encountered, many jealousies had to be appeased, but the scheme was eventually approved by the two Canadas, Nova Scotia, New Brunswick; and in December, 1866, delegates from these Colonies met under the Presidency of Lord Carnarvon—then Colonial Secretary—in London. A Bill embodying the details agreed upon in this Conference was submitted to the Imperial Parliament, and on March 29th, 1867, the British North America Act received the Royal assent. It came into operation on July 1st of the same year.

The Canadian Dominion represents the first Federation in world history, under the ægis of a Constitutional Monarchy. The preamble of the Act lays it down that the Dominion Constitution was to be " similar in principle to that of the United Kingdom ". In other words, the Constitutional Conventions, attained after long centuries of evolution in the unwritten constitution of the motherland, were presupposed in the statutory Instrument devised for the daughterland.

Features of Canadian federalism

---

[1] Cf. Egerton, *Federations and Unions in the British Empire*, pp. 27 et seq.

The Ex-
ecutive
The executive power was " to continue to be vested in the Queen, and in the heirs and successors of Her Majesty, Kings and Queens of the United Kingdom of Great Britain and Ireland ". On this point Macdonald laid great stress. " With the universal approval of the people of this country we have provided that for all time to come, so far as we can legislate for the future, we shall have, as head of the executive power, the Sovereign of Great Britain." His hope was in this way to avoid " one defect inherent in the Constitution of the United States. By the election of the President by a majority and for a short period, he never is the Sovereign and chief of the nation. . . . He is at best but the successful leader of a party. . . . I believe that it is of the utmost importance to have that principle recognized, so that we shall have a Sovereign who is placed above the region of party ; to whom all parties look up ; who is not elevated by the action of one party, nor depressed by the action of another ; who is the common head and Sovereign of all."

The Sovereign of Great Britain was to be represented in the Dominion by a Governor-General, who was to have the ordinary powers of a " Constitutional " Sovereign in the English sense ; the command in chief of the armed forces of the Crown ; and the right to appoint and, if necessary, to remove the Lieutenant-Governors of the Provinces of the Dominion. He was to be aided and advised by the Queen's Privy Council of Canada. It was clearly understood that this body was to be a Parliamentary Cabinet on the English model ; homogeneous in composition, mutually responsible, politically dependent upon the parliamentary majority, and acting in subordination to an acknowledged leader. But though this was understood, and indeed implied by the terms of the preamble, it was not specifically set forth in the Constitution. There was not even a provision, such as that in the Australian Commonwealth Act, that the members of the Privy Council should be members of the Legislature. The number of this Cabinet has varied with the growth of new administrative departments, and now (1912) consists of fifteen members : a Premier-President of the Cabinet ; a Secretary of State (virtually Minister for Foreign Affairs) ; a Postmaster-General, and twelve ministerial heads of public departments such as Trade and Commerce, Justice, Finance, Railways and Canals, Labour, Militia, and Defence.

The
Legis-
lature
Legislative Power was vested in a Parliament for Canada, consisting of the Queen, an Upper House or Senate, and a House of Commons. The Governor-General was authorized to assent in the Queen's name to Bills presented to him in the two Houses, or to withhold the Queen's assent, or to reserve the Bill for the signification of the Queen's pleasure. Bills to which the Governor-General had assented might be disallowed by the Queen, by Order in Council, at any time within two years after the receipt of an " authentic copy of the Act " by the Secretary of State. Bills reserved for the Queen's

pleasure were not to come into force unless and until, within two years from the day on which it was presented to the Governor-General for the Queen's assent, the Governor-General signified, by speech or message to each of the Houses of the Parliament or by proclamation, that it had received the assent of the Queen in Council.[1] That such reservation was no mere form is clear from the fact that between 1867 and 1877 no less than twenty-one Bills were actually reserved.[2]

The Federal Parliament, like the Union Parliament erected in 1840, was to consist of two chambers. Under the Union Act the Second Chamber of Legislative Council was to consist of not fewer than twenty persons nominated by the Crown for life. But the nominated Second Chamber was not a success, and in deference to an agitation, more or less persistent, it was decided, in 1856, to abandon the nominee system. The existing members of the Council were to be left undisturbed, but vacancies as they occurred were to be filled by election. The experiment of 1856 was not more successful than the nominee system which it superseded.[3]

The Federal Act of 1867 reverted to the principle of nomination. The Senate, as then constituted, was to consist of seventy-two members, and was, like that of the United States, to embody and emphasize the federal idea. Quebec, Ontario, and the Maritime Provinces (Nova Scotia and New Brunswick) were to be equally represented in the Senate, twenty-four members being nominated from each. But in subsequent amendments this principle has not been maintained. An Act of Imperial Legislature, in 1871, authorized the Dominion Parliament to provide for the due representation in the Senate of any Provinces subsequently admitted to the Federation. Under these powers four Senators each have been assigned to Manitoba, Alberta, and Saskatchewan, and three to British Columbia. The Act of 1867 provided (§ 147) that Prince Edward Island, if it elected to join the Federation, should have four Senators, but in this event the senatorial representation of the other Maritime Provinces, Nova Scotia and New Brunswick, was to be automatically reduced to ten each. The contemplated event having since occurred, the Senate now consists of eighty-seven members apportioned to the several provinces in accordance with the Acts enumerated above.

Subject to this apportionment, Senators were to be nominated for life by the Governor-General—in practice on the advice of his responsible Ministers. A Senator was to be (a) of the full age of thirty years ; (b) a British subject ; (c) a resident in the Province for which he was appointed, and (d) possessed of real property of the nett value of not less than four thousand dollars within the Province.

The Senate (marginal note)

---

[1] _British North America Act_ (1867), iv. 56, 57.

[2] _Cf._ Egerton, _op. cit._ p. 137. After 1877 the practice was altered. For reasons, see _Can. Sess. Papers_, 1877, No. 13 (cited by Egerton).

[3] _Cf._ J. A. R. Marriott, _Second Chambers_, pp. 93 _seq._, from which this and the succeeding paragraphs are summarized.

He may at any time, and under certain contingencies must, resign his seat.

No direct provision was made in the Act for a deadlock between the two Houses, but power was given to the Crown to nominate three or six additional Senators, representing equally the three divisions of Canada. In 1873 the Canadian Cabinet advised the exercise of this power, but the Imperial Government refused to sanction it, on the ground that it was not desirable for the Queen to inferfere with the Constitution of the Senate, " except upon an occasion when it had been made apparent that a difference had arisen between the two Houses of so serious and permanent a character that the Government could not be carried on without her intervention, and when it could be shown that the limited creation of Senators allowed by the Act would apply an adequate remedy ".[1]

It will be observed that the Canadian Senate is a cross between several principles which, if not absolutely contradictory, are clearly distinct. Consequently, it has never possessed either the glamour of an aristocratic and hereditary chamber, or the strength of an elected assembly, or the utility of a Senate representing the federal as opposed to the national idea. Devised with the notion of giving some sort of representation to provincial interests, it has, from the first, been manipulated by party leaders to subserve the interests of the central Executive.[2]

The House of Commons
The House of Commons was to consist of 181 members, 82 being assigned to Ontario, 65 to Quebec, 19 to Nova Scotia, and 15 to New Brunswick. Quebec was always to retain 65 members ; the representation of the other Provinces was to be readjusted after each decennial census, but in such a way that the representation of each Province should bear the same proportions to its population as 65 bears to that of Quebec.[3] The House of Commons was to sit for five years, and was to have the right of originating money Bills, on the sole recommendation of the Executive. Otherwise the powers of the two Houses were to be co-ordinate.

Provincial Constitutions
In each Province there was to be a Lieutenant-Governor, appointed by the Governor-General and assisted by an Executive Council ; the Legislature was to consist of two Houses in Quebec, New Brunswick, Nova Scotia, and one in Ontario.[4] Certain matters were specifically assigned to the Provincial Legislatures, but the residue of powers was vested in the Dominion Parliament. This is a feature of primary importance, and it is one which differentiates the Canadian Constitution alike from that of the United States, and

---

[1] *Canadian Sess. Papers*, 1877, No. 68, ap Egerton, p. 129.

[2] The composition of the Senate was amended by the British North America Act (1915). For details see Marriott, *Second Chamber* (2nd edition, Oxford, 1927), pp. 94-104.

[3] The number is now 245.

[4] All the Provincial Legislatures are now (1912) unicamera. except those of Quebec and Nova Scotia.

from that of the Australian Commonwealth. In the latter it is the
federal authority to which certain special powers are delegated by
the constituent states, and any power which is not so delegated
remains vested in the State. The Canadian solution of this crucial
problem is an interesting memorial to the historical circumstances
under which the Constitution came to birth. Macdonald, as we
have seen, and many of his more influential colleagues would have
preferred a legislative union. They were baffled by " the centrifugal
nationalism of Quebec ".[1] But, though accepting the inevitable,
they were resolved to infuse into Canadian federalism as much of
unitary cohesion as Quebec would tolerate.

The original constituent Provinces of the Dominion were, as Growth of
already indicated, Quebec, Ontario, New Brunswick, and Nova the Cana-
Scotia, but provision was made in the Constitution for the admission Federa-
of other Colonies or territories ; in particular Newfoundland, Prince tion
Edward Island, and British Columbia. Newfoundland has continued,
in pride of birth, to stand aloof from her younger sisters,[2] but hardly
had the British North America Act come into force (July 1st, 1867)
when resolutions were adopted in the Dominion Parliament in favour
of the Union of Rupert's Land and the North-West Territory. Before
the Crown could give effect to these resolutions a preliminary arrangement had to be reached between the Dominion Government and the
Hudson Bay Company. The latter agreed, in consideration of the
sum of £300,000 and certain reserved tracts of land, to surrender its
territorial rights to the Crown, and by Order in Council (June 23rd,
1870) Rupert's Land and the North-West Territory were admitted to
the Union. In the same year the Province of Manitoba was carved
out of the Territory, and was formally admitted a member of the
Dominion, with representation according to population in the Canadian
House of Commons, and three Senators in the Upper House. These
arrangements were confirmed by an Act of the Imperial Parliament [3]
in 1871, and by the same Act the right of the Dominion Parliament
to establish Provinces in new territories forming part of the Dominion
was made clear. A subsequent Act of 1886 [4] gave the Canadian
Parliament power to provide representation in the Senate and House
of Commons for territories not yet included in any Province.[5] In
1905 two further Provinces, those of Alberta and Saskatchewan, were
carved out of the North-West Territory, and were admitted with
appropriate representation into the Dominion. Long before that, in
1871, British Columbia had taken advantage of the provision made
in the Act of 1867, for its admission to the Dominion, and by Order

[1] Goldwin Smith, *Canada and The Canadian Question*, p. 158.
[2] In 1895 Newfoundland made overtures for union, but they were not accepted
by the Dominion.
[3] 34 and 35 Vict. c 28   49 and 50 Vict. c. 35.
[5] Egerton, *op. cit.*, p. 167.

in Council (May 16th, 1871) its admission was formally ratified.
Prince Edward Island was similarly admitted in 1873.

The Red
River
Expedi-
tion, 1870

As yet, however, the Great Dominion was very loosely compacted.
Between the Maritime Provinces on the Atlantic littoral and the
Maritime Province which occupies the Pacific slope there intervened
more than 3,000 miles of territory. A word must be said presently
of the initiation and completion of the great Imperial enterprise
which has now linked these together in bonds of steel. Intermedi-
ately it is proper to notice a small military expedition arising out of
the incorporation of the Hudson Bay Territory. That incorporation
was not entirely popular with the French Canadians and half-breeds
who inhabited the country. In 1870, a young French Canadian,
Louis Riel, collected a band of Indians and half-breeds, attacked the
stores of the Company at Fort Garry on the Red River, and proclaimed himself President of the Republic of the North-West. It
was a transient ebullition of discontent, and it was dealt with
promptly and successfully. Colonel Garnet Wolseley was despatched
from Toronto in command of a mixed force of 1,400 men, composed
partly of Imperial troops, partly of Canadian Militia. The march
from Toronto to Fort Garry was a difficult one of more than 600
miles, but thanks to the foresight, caution, and skill of Colonel
Wolseley it was accomplished without the loss of a man. No fighting
was necessary ; the " President " fled into the United States before
Wolseley arrived at Fort Garry (August) ; order was completely
restored, and the objects of the expedition were fully attained at a
trifling cost of £100,000. The scale of the operations was small, but
the skill with which they were carried out gave promise of powers on
the part of the commander abundantly redeemed by a brilliant future.

The Cana-
dian
Pacific
Railway

The Red River rebellion did not interrupt the work of expansion
and consolidation in Canada. To that work the construction of a
trans-continental railway was an indispensable adjunct. It was
indeed a condition of the union between Canada and British Columbia.
" The Government of the Dominion," so the agreement ran, " undertake to secure the commencement simultaneously, within two years
from the date of the union, of the construction of the railway from
the Pacific towards the Rocky Mountains, and from such point as
may be selected east of the Rocky Mountains towards the Pacific,
to connect the seaboard of British Columbia with the railway system
of Canada ; and further, to secure the completion of such railway
within ten years from the date of such union."

The work of construction ought to have begun in 1873. As a
matter of fact various delays interposed, and it was not until 1880
that the great enterprise was actually initiated. The contract
stipulated that it should be completed by 1891, but so rapid was the
progress that the work was finished in half that time, and the line
was opened in 1886.

The Canadian Pacific Railway is from every point of view—political, economic, and strategic—of the highest significance, and deserves to rank among the most imposing Imperial achievements of the century. Its terminals are at Montreal and Vancouver respectively ; its total length of line is 2,909 miles, or about half the distance which separates Liverpool from Vancouver. Of the engineering difficulties encountered in its construction some idea may be gleaned from the fact that it crosses the Rocky Mountains at an elevation of 5,560 feet. It was the work of private enterprise, but in order to expedite and encourage its construction the Dominion Government granted to the Company a subsidy of £5,000,000, together with a land grant of 25,000,000 acres, and the privilege of permanent exemption from taxation. No privilege could, however, be too great for an enterprise of such high Imperial significance. To enable the farmers of Western Canada to feed the mill-hands of Lancashire and the miners of South Wales ; to bring Liverpool within a fortnight of Vancouver ; to unite in commercial and political bonds the Pacific slope and the Atlantic littoral—this was the purpose and this was the achievement of the Empire-builders who planned and constructed the Canadian Pacific Railroad. Of the work of federation that railroad was at once the condition and the complement.

A Government which could in one session place upon the Statute-book two such measures as the Reform Act of 1867 and the *British North America Act* had good reason to congratulate itself on its legislative record. Ministers were not less fortunate in their management of foreign affairs. *Foreign affairs*

The sequence of events which culminated in the Seven Weeks' War of 1866 has been indicated in a previous chapter. The rapid and overwhelming success achieved by the armies of Prussia took the world by storm. But the Prussian victory did more than exclude Austria from Germany, it profoundly affected the balance of power in Europe. France, in particular, was quick to realize its significance. In the autumn of 1865 the Emperor Napoleon and Bismarck had met in friendly conference at Biarritz. The French Emperor had then fallen an easy prey to the disarming bluntness of the German diplomatist.

At Biarritz Bismarck had secured Napoleon's benevolent neutrality in the coming struggle with Austria by the promise, not too definite, of territorial compensation—perhaps a Rhine Province, or Luxemburg, or even Belgium. Napoleon had swallowed the bait, and had allowed Bismarck to make his plans for the destruction of Austria. But the rapid and complete success of Prussia entirely upset his calculations. He imagined—as did every one else—that the contest would be prolonged and indecisive, and that, after the exhaustion of both combatants, he would be able to step in and secure the appropriate reward of a benevolent and impartial arbitrator.

Instead of this he found himself at the close of the brief but decisive conflict a humble suitor to Bismarck for an unconsidered trifle. His first suggestion was the Rhenish Palatinate. Bismarck laughed in his face, and sent the correspondence to Bavaria, to whom the Palatinate belonged. The only result was to detach from France an hereditary friend, and to cement a Prusso-Bavarian alliance, which proved its value in 1870. A demand for Belgium—perhaps stimulated by Bismarck himself—had no better results for Napoleon but was equally convenient for Bismarck. The correspondence, published at the psychological moment in 1870, served to alienate English sympathies from their whilom ally. Luxemburg remained.

Luxem-burg
The situation of the Grand Duchy of Luxemburg was peculiar. An integral part of the Germanic Confederation, it was ruled by the King of Holland whose possession of the Grand Duchy was guaranteed by a treaty, concluded in April, 1839, between Great Britain, France, Austria, Prussia, Russia, and the Grand Duke of Luxemburg. Its capital was a fortress of the first class, and the Grand Duchy occupied a strategic position of great importance. The presence of a Prussian garrison was a disquieting fact for Holland and Belgium, and a real menace to France. Foiled elsewhere by Bismarck, Napoleon opened negotiations with William of Holland as Grand Duke for the purchase of Luxemburg. The Grand Duke was not unwilling, but the Dutch Cabinet appealed to Prussia who referred them to the Treaty of 1839.

Confer-ence in London
The position of the signatory Powers was thus directly challenged, and in May a conference met in London. The tact and caution of Lord Stanley, backed by the Queen's personal intervention with the King of Prussia, brought about a speedy and satisfactory settlement. The Prussian garrison was to be withdrawn; the fortifications of the city of Luxemburg were to be demolished; no military establishment was to be maintained or created there for the future, and the Grand Duchy itself was to be neutralized under the joint guarantee of the five Powers.

An awkward corner had been skilfully turned. It would not have turned so easily had Bismarck been quite ready for the inevitable war. But if he was not ready, still less was Napoleon. The latter, baffled on every side, now tried to persuade himself and his friends that no territorial " compensation " was really necessary; and that Prussia had been in reality weakened rather than strengthened by recent events. The accuracy of his diagnosis was to be tested by happenings not distant. Meanwhile, his own prestige suffered a further and a staggering blow from the defeat, capture, and execution of his protégé the unhappy Emperor Maximilian in Mexico [1] (June 19th, 1867).

---

[1] In the foregoing paragraphs I borrow a few sentences from my *Remaking of Modern Europe* (Methuen & Co., 4th edn., 1911). Both there and here, I owe much to Lord Acton's brilliant Essay.

After a session unusually arduous and prolonged Parliament was prorogued on August 21st. The Royal Speech contained an ominous reference to communications " to the reigning Monarch of Abyssinia, with a view to obtain the release of the British subjects whom he detains in his dominions ". These communications proved ineffectual, and in less than three months' time the two Houses were summoned to meet for the purpose of making provision for an armed expedition to effect the release of the captives at Magdala.

The events which led up to this *dénouement* must be briefly related. The story is typical of English relations with semi-civilized potentates and peoples. An English traveller, Mr. Plowden, reported to the Foreign Secretary, Lord Palmerston, on the opening for English trade and on the opportunity for philanthropic effort offered by a neglected portion of the surface of the great sub-tropical continent. Caught by the idea of extending British interests, and at the same time of curtailing the traffic in slaves, Lord Palmerston appointed Mr. Plowden Consul at Massowah (1848). Not content with his routine functions in the island, Mr. Plowden plunged into the domestic politics of Abyssinia. For some ten years he was the right-hand man of the chief King or Negus of Abyssinia. The latter, King Theodore, an ambitious potentate, who claimed descent from King Solomon and the Queen of Sheba, desired the assistance of the Great White Queen against his Egyptian enemies, who threatened him on the north, and the Turks who were troublesome neighbours on the east. Plowden was killed in a fray in 1860, and a Captain Cameron was appointed to succeed him. Lord John Russell was less expansive than Lord Palmerston in his interpretation of Consular duties. He peremptorily forbade Consul Cameron to meddle in the domestic politics of Abyssinia, and ordered him to attend to his own business, or rather that of his employers, at Massowah. But King Theodore was still sanguine as to the results of an alliance with England, and in 1862 addressed a personal letter to the Queen requesting that he might be allowed to send a mission to her Majesty's Court. By an error destined to be costly, Lord Russell left the letter unanswered, contenting himself with renewed orders to Consul Cameron to mind his own business. Unluckily for himself and for his country, Cameron disobeyed orders, and in 1864 Theodore, impatient for an answer and deeply resentful of the slight involved in the neglect of his overtures, flung Consul Cameron and all the Europeans within his reach into captivity in the Rock Fortress of Magdala. Between this capital and the coast lay four hundred miles of mountainous and trackless country. A formal mission under Lieutenant Prideaux and Mr. Rassam, a Syrian Christian in the English service, was despatched to Magdala to demand the relief of the captives. But King Theodore was defiant, and the only

Expedition to Abyssinia

20

result of the mission was that Prideaux and Rassam joined the band of captives in Magdala.

The matter now began to assume a serious aspect.   The number of captives was insignificant—not more than thirty in all—but three of them were British subjects, and of these two at least had been entrapped in the execution of their duties as official representatives of the British Government.   To repeated remonstrances and requests King Theodore paid no heed, and in the spring of 1867 Lord Stanley sent an ultimatum to Magdala.   A preliminary survey of the ground which an expeditionary force would have to traverse was made, and in August, 1867, the Government decided to despatch it.   Abyssinia was treated as within the sphere of Indian politics.   Bombay was selected as the base of the expedition, and Sir Robert Napier, Commander-in-Chief at Bombay, was appointed to the command. No better choice could have been made.

In January, 1868, Napier landed near Massowah, at the head of a force of 12,000 men, of whom two-thirds were drawn from the Indian army.   The main difficulties ahead were those of country, climate, and transport, but no risks were taken ; the whole expedition was scientifically planned and carried through with exemplary attention to detail.   By April, 1868, Napier and an advanced force found themselves before Magdala, and on the 10th they swept aside the only serious opposition they encountered.   Five hundred of the enemy were killed and 1,500 were wounded.   Nineteen Englishmen were wounded, but not one was killed.   Theodore then released the captives unharmed, but refused to surrender his capital.   Napier was accordingly compelled to storm a fortress of immense natural strength. The assault was entirely successful.   Theodore died by his own hand, and Magdala was destroyed.

Napier's task was accomplished, British honour was vindicated, the captives were free.   Within a week the expedition was on its way back to the coast.   Abyssinia was left severely alone ; the army received the thanks of Parliament, and its Commander was raised to the Peerage as Baron Napier of Magdala.   The compliments were well deserved.   The scale of the expedition was relatively small, but the skill with which it was planned, and the precision with which it was carried through, reflect the highest credit upon the Commander and his subordinates.

A considerable portion of the cost was charged, not without protest from Mr. Henry Fawcett, upon the revenues of India ; but even so, the British taxpayer had to find £8,000,000 to extricate a meddlesome Consul from a pit digged by himself.

Disraeli succeeds Derby as Prime Minister   Before General Napier had reached Magdala a change of some significance had taken place in the English Ministry.   Lord Derby resigned office in February, 1868, and " Vivian Grey " reigned in his stead.   That Disraeli should be the next Premier was, after his long and brilliant services to his party, inevitable ; that he should ever have been called or permitted to render those services may well seem inexplicable. The changes in the Cabinet consequential upon Lord Derby's retirement were few. Lord Chelmsford was dismissed from the Woolsack " without ", as he complained, " even the usual month's notice," to make room for Sir Hugh Cairns, one of the greatest lawyers, and one of the most eminent statesmen, who ever filled that high office. Disraeli was replaced at the Exchequer by Mr. George Ward Hunt, a Tory Squire, with a fund of common sense and an excellent head for business.

Lord Derby survived his retirement little more than a year. His **Death of** death in 1869 removed from the stage almost the last of the early **Lord** Victorian veterans. A devoted Churchman ; an excellent scholar ; **Derby** a successful translator of Homer ; appropriately commemorated in the University of which he was Chancellor by a scholarship which is the guerdon of pure classical attainment ; a brilliant debater, and a sound administrator, Lord Derby never attained to the first rank of statesmanship. His best official work was done before he reached middle life : as Irish Secretary under Lord Grey, and at the Colonial Office under Grey and Peel. As Leader of the Conservative Party circumstances were against him. He stood for " Protection " in the heyday of the Manchester School, and although he was thrice Prime Minister of England he was never in power.

To his immediate successor he bequeathed no easy task. For **Disraeli's** about ten months Disraeli remained in office ; but as long as the **first** session lasted (until July 30) it was Gladstone who was in power. **ministry,** Reform Bills for Scotland and Ireland were, as already indicated, **February** added to the Statute-Book with the assent of both Parties. Apart **25th-** from this Disraeli could do little to guide the course of legislation. **December** It was Gladstone who proposed and carried a Bill for the abolition of **2nd, 1868** compulsory Church rates ; it was Gladstone who carried, against the whole strength of the Government, a resolution in favour of the disestablishment of the Established Church in Ireland.

That resolution marks the opening of a new epoch in the history of Ireland, and a new chapter in that of England.

CHAPTER XX

THE IRISH QUESTION : ECCLESIASTICAL—AGRARIAN—POLITICAL

The Irish
problem

FROM the days of Queen Elizabeth to those of Queen Victoria the Irish problem has resolved itself into three main factors : the constitutional relations between the larger and the smaller island ; the existence in Ireland of an established Protestant Church, powerless to conciliate the affection or even the goodwill of a population devoted to Roman Catholicism ; and an agrarian system, alien in origin, feudal in legal theory and superimposed upon tribal institutions deep-rooted in the memory and the instincts of the people. With all these factors British statesmen found themselves compelled to deal during the last decades of the nineteenth century.

The problem had already been attacked in fragmentary fashion in the first half of the century ; the removal of Roman Catholic disabilities (1829) ; the *Church Temporalities Act* (1833) ; the *Maynooth Act* (1845) ; the foundation of the Queen's Colleges (1845) ; the appointment of a Commission, under the chairmanship of Lord Devon, to enquire into the land question (1843) ; the *Encumbered Estates Act* (1849) ; the Repeal movement under O'Connell (1833 *et seq.*) ; the " Young Ireland " movement, culminating in the abortive rebellion of 1848—all these testified to the existence of a problem or a sheaf of problems still unsolved.

Calm surface of
Irish politics, 1848-
1865

Between the fiasco of 1848 and the Fenian conspiracy (1865-1867) there was a calm, almost continuous, in Irish politics. It was the calm, however, not of placid happiness and contentment, but of exhaustion and despair : of exhaustion due to the famine and the exodus ; of despair after the abortive rebellion of 1848. But though the surface was unruffled there was in old Ireland an unceasing ground-swell of discontent, and in the new Ireland which gradually grew up on the other side of the Atlantic there was an acute and dangerous agitation. In that agitation Fenianism had its birth. For the twenty years after the outbreak of Fenianism (1865-1887) the Irish question was never permitted to slumber : in Parliament legislative proposals of great complexity and importance almost continuously occupied attention ; in Ireland symptoms of unrest and disloyalty manifested themselves with alarming frequency, and baffled the efforts of well-meaning administrators. Essentially, the problem was the same as that which had distracted English counsels for three centuries : it revolved around the land, the Church, and the Constitutional relations.

Fenianism

The first guise under which the perennial problem obtruded itself was that of Fenianism. The genesis of the movement which, with characteristic felicity, adopted this Celtic label [1] is to be found in the exodus which followed close upon the great famine. Not all the benevolent, though sometimes misdirected activities of English administrators could induce Irishmen to regard the famine otherwise than as a crime perpetrated by England against Ireland. Coroners' juries were but re-echoing the sentiment of the people at large when they brought in verdicts of wilful murder against "John Russell, commonly called Lord John Russell". In 1841 the population of Ireland was 8,175,124 ; it is now less than 4,500,000, and it is undeniable that for good or ill, it was the famine which gave the initial impetus to this depopulating movement. In the half-decade between 1846 and 1851 nearly a million people died in Ireland, and over a million people left the country. In the decade between 1852 and 1861 another million (1,123,000) emigrated and found a home for the most part in the States of the American Union. How well they prospered and how tenderly their hearts turned towards the Ireland they had left behind is attested by the fact that between 1848 and 1864 the Irish-Americans sent home a sum of no less than £13,000,000 to enable their relatives to follow them to the United States.

Among the Irish emigrants were not a few fiercer spirits, who nourished feelings of bitter resentment against the stern step-mother who, as they believed, had made them exiles from their native land. These men kept alive the revolutionary temper in Ireland itself, and in many parts of the country, particularly in the small towns of the South and West, secret societies were established. In May, 1858, James Stephens, one of the survivors of the '48, who had for years been in exile, visited the little town of Skibbereen in the County Cork. At Skibbereen Jeremiah Donovan, afterwards known as O'Donovan Rossa, and other young men had lately founded the Phœnix National and Literary Society. The aims of the Society were revolutionary ; its members were pledged to work for the establishment of an independent Republic on Irish soil. The meetings and drillings which they organized in the West of Ireland were well known to the Government, and in December, 1858, twenty leading members of the Society were suddenly arrested. A special commission was issued for the trial of the prisoners ; one of them was sentenced to a long term of penal servitude, the others after some months' imprisonment were liberated on bail. The Phœnix conspiracy was scotched in Ireland, but operations were transferred to the other side of the Atlantic.

While James Stephens was busy in fomenting conspiracy in Ireland, another survivor of the '48, John O'Mahony, was actively organizing the Fenian Brotherhood in America. The Society was skilfully organized ; each member was acquainted only with his *The Irish-Americans*

---

[1] The " Fenians " were the warriors who in the prehistoric days of Irish legend followed the great tribal monarchs.

immediate superior in the hierarchy; secrecy was maintained and obedience was implicit.

The close of the American Civil War (1865) gave the signal, as it offered the opportunity, for the opening of the Fenian attack. In that war had fought, on both sides, thousands of Irish-Americans. Some had attained distinction, all had gained experience; that experience they were now burning to utilize in a cause more immediately their own.

Fenianism in Ireland   Meanwhile, the English Government had kept under close observation the doings of the Brotherhood in Ireland. In September, 1865, the Dublin police raided the offices of the *Irish People*, a paper devoted to the propaganda of Fenianism; they arrested the proprietor Donovan and the directors, seized the plant and suppressed the paper. Shortly afterwards Stephens also was arrested but, through the connivance of Fenian gaolers, he effected his escape from Richmond prison. He remained in hiding for some months in Dublin and was then smuggled out of the country and was never recaptured. Meanwhile, Donovan and his associates were arraigned, before a special Commission, on a charge of treason-felony, and were sentenced to long terms of penal servitude. That they were engaged in a conspiracy to " subvert the government of the country " is not open to question. After their arrest the police discovered abundant evidence that it was widespread and might become formidable. In February, 1866, the Irish Executive, Lord Wodehouse (afterwards Earl of Kimberley), Lord Chancellor Brady, and Mr. Chichester Fortescue, came to the conclusion that they could no longer be responsible for the government of the country unless they were entrusted with exceptional powers. The Cabinet concurred, and on February 17th, 1866, an Act for the suspension of the Habeas Corpus Act was passed through both Houses and received the Royal assent.[1] Events proved that the apprehensions of the Castle were well founded, nor can it be doubted that the prompt action of the Government averted both danger and suffering from Ireland. The Irish-Americans hastily decamped to pursue their activity elsewhere. As far as Ireland was concerned Fenianism was scotched if not killed. In February, 1867, there was an attempt at insurrection in County Kerry, and for a month or two there were sporadic outbreaks in different parts of Ireland; but the movement never attained serious dimensions. Some 300 Fenians were arrested, put on their trial for felony or treason-felony, and two of the leaders were sentenced to be " hanged, drawn, and quartered," but no one actually suffered death.

Fenianism in Canada   Ireland, however, was not the main theatre of Fenianism. A few months after Donovan and his companions had passed into the obscurity of penal servitude, 1,200 of their brethren raided the Canadian frontier, crossed the Niagara River and occupied Fort Erie.

[1] *Cf. supra*, p. 283.

The success of the enterprise depended entirely, of course, on the measure of sympathy and support it might obtain from the United States. Of support it received none. The behaviour of the Washington government was disappointingly " correct " ; strict neutrality was enforced, and the Canadian volunteers and police did the rest. The main body of raiders was driven back across the frontier ; six of the leaders were captured, tried by court-martial and shot. No further trouble was experienced in Canada.

Such importance as Fenianism really possessed lay in its influence In England : upon English opinion. That influence was powerfully exerted by Chester the events of 1867. The alarms were frequent throughout the year. Castle Of the first of the series Chester was the scene. The Castle contained 9,000 stands of arms, 4,000 swords, 900,000 rounds of ammunition, besides a large amount of powder in bulk and the armoury of the militia and volunteers. It was garrisoned by half a dozen soldiers of the 54th Regiment. It is supposed that the plan was to seize the Castle, to carry off the stores, arms, and ammunition ; to cut the telegraph wires and tear up the rails ; then make all speed for Holyhead, seize some vessels in the harbour, and descend upon the Irish coast. Had it not been for the promptitude of the police, magistrates, and citizens of Chester the plan might have succeeded, and the country would have incurred ridicule if not danger. From the early hours of Monday, February 11th, bands of young men, from eighteen to twenty-five years of age and " apparently of the labouring and operative class," [1] began to pour into the city by train from Liverpool, Preston, Manchester, Halifax, and other neighbouring towns. By Monday evening there were said to be 1,500 of them in the city. The authorities in Chester acted with commendable promptitude. By one o'clock on the afternoon of Monday a company of the 54th Regiment arrived from Manchester, the volunteers and other citizens were enrolled as special constables ; Lord Grosvenor left London by the mail on Monday night and put himself at the head of his Cheshire Yeomanry on Tuesday morning, and at 10.45 A.M. on the Tuesday (Feb. 12th) a battalion of Scots Fusiliers arrived by special train from Euston. After the arrival of this strong reinforcement the citizens of Chester breathed again : the mysterious strangers disappeared as quickly as they had come, and by Tuesday evening the scare was at an end.

Some of the Chester visitors may have taken boat for Ireland. At any rate, seventy suspected Fenians were arrested on their arrival in Dublin on board the *Alexandra* from Holyhead and the *S. Columba* from Liverpool, on the morning of Wednesday the 13th. On the 14th there was a rising in County Kerry, and for twenty-four hours there was much alarm at Killarney. But on the arrival of reinforcements the Fenians took to the mountains, and on Friday

[1] *The Times*, February 12th, 1867.

evening (Feb. 15th) *The Times* correspondent was able to telegraph from Dublin : " All danger is over and the country quiet ".

The Manchester affray   In the autumn of the same year (1867) Manchester was the scene of a Fenian outrage of exceptional audacity. Early in September the Manchester police had arrested two men suspected of intent to commit a felony, and subsequently identified as two notorious Fenian officers, Colonel Kelly and Captain Deasy. On the 18th they were remanded by the magistrates, and as they were being taken back to gaol the prison van was attacked by a band of forty to fifty Fenians armed with revolvers. Police-Sergeant Brett in charge of the van behaved with the utmost gallantry, refused to surrender his keys or his prisoners and was killed by a shot fired through the lock ; others were wounded. The rescue was successful ; Kelly and Deasy made good their escape, but of the rescuers twenty-nine were ultimately arrested. Five men, William O'Meara Allen, Michael Larkin, William Gould, Thomas Maguire, and Edwin Shore, were put upon their trial for the murder of Sergeant Brett. All five were convicted and sentenced to death ; Maguire and Shore were subsequently reprieved, but on November 23rd the other three **The " Manchester martyrs "** suffered the extreme penalty of the law. The trial and the execution excited an unusual amount of interest ; the youth of the prisoners ; the audacity of the deed for which they were to suffer ; the absence of any murderous intent ; the sorrow expressed by all for the fate of their innocent victim Brett ; their courageous demeanour in the dock ; the vigorous agitation for a reprieve ; the apprehension of an insurrection on a serious scale—all combined to invest the trial and execution of the " Manchester martyrs " with a halo of romance, and to remove from the ordinary category the crime for which they forfeited their lives. That the forfeiture was just none can deny. But the murder which in law they committed was neither intentional nor sordid, and the sentiment which still surrounds their memory in Ireland is, if not admirable, at least intelligible.

The Clerkenwell explosion   The execution of the Fenians at Manchester was followed early in December by a number of demonstrations in honour of the " Martyrs," at Manchester itself, at Dublin, Cork, Limerick, Mitchelstown, and other Irish towns. Much more important, however, than these " demonstrations," in its ultimate results, was the attempt to liberate two Fenian prisoners from the Clerkenwell House of Detention. Planned by the same organization as the Manchester outrage, the Clerkenwell explosion differed from it in callous indifference to human life. Here, as at Chester, the authorities were warned ; but in this case they culpably failed to avert the attack. On the afternoon of December 13th a terrible explosion occurred in Corporation Row overlooking Clerkenwell Gaol. A considerable length of the prison wall was blown down ; houses in the vicinity were destroyed ; several persons were killed outright ; several others died from shock, and

about one hundred were more or less severely injured. A number of
persons were charged with treason-felony and one man was ultimately
hanged.

The scare at Chester, the sporadic outbreaks in Ireland, the
audacious outrages in Manchester and London, operated powerfully
upon public opinion. On the one hand there was an unflinching
determination to maintain public order ; but on the other there was
an increasing disposition to inquire whether the Fenian movement,
though undeniably criminal in itself, might not be the outcome of a
discontent at once legitimate and remediable. One eminent statesman was, as the sequel will show, converted to this view.

The Government, however, were not in a position to deal effectu- The posi-
ally with any subtle or difficult problem. Mr. Disraeli was in office tion of the
on sufferance, and the debates in both Houses soon made him Ministry
acutely conscious of the fact.

The first business of Parliament after the Christmas recess was to
renew the suspension of the Habeas Corpus Act in Ireland. There
was, however, a consensus of opinion that remedies at once more
drastic and more curative would have to be applied. Speaking at
Bristol in January, Lord Stanley, whose position in the Government
was second only to that of Disraeli, had declared with emphasis that
" Ireland is the question of the hour ". Its material condition was
not bad, " yet it would be idle to deny that discontent is very widely
spread, that disaffection is not infrequent, and that there is a portion
of the population . . . who regard their connection with England as
a burden rather than a benefit ". On March 16th Lord Mayo, the
Chief Secretary, made to the House a statement of ministerial policy.
Like Lord Stanley he admitted that, despite a marked increase of
material prosperity, there was " much disaffection and even disloyalty ". To Fenianism he attached little importance ; it was not
a native but an American product. The Government intended to
bring forward an Irish Reform Bill (a promise speedily fulfilled) ; a
Land Bill, dealing with compensation for improvements, extended
forms of leasing for limited owners, and the encouragement of written
contracts between landlords and tenants ; a measure for the more
efficient management of Irish railways, and another for the improvement of elementary education and the establishment of a Roman
Catholic University. They also proposed to appoint a Commission
to enquire into the relations between landlord and tenant in Ireland.
As to the most difficult question of all, the position of the Established
Church in Ireland, the Government intended to await the Report of
the Commission appointed in 1867 at the instance of Lord Russell.
" But neither on this nor on the land question could a satisfactory
settlement be obtained by confiscation. Policy and justice might
demand the equalization of Church Establishments in Ireland, and
Protestants were not disinclined to consider any fair proposal for

that purpose. But it must be done by the process of levelling upwards, not downwards ; the destruction of the Irish Church would not conciliate one enemy, while it would alienate many friends."

Mr. Gladstone and the Irish Church

What precisely did Lord Mayo mean by " levelling upwards and not downwards " ? It was generally taken to point towards " concurrent endowment," though the interpretation was subsequently repudiated. But, whatever it meant, Mr. Gladstone would have none of it. He definitely told the House that in his opinion the time had come when the Anglican Church in Ireland must cease to exist as an Establishment, and the principle of religious equality must be definitely accepted. His mind had for some time been moving in this direction. In 1865, 1866, and 1867 the House had been asked to consider the question, and on the last occasion Gladstone declared that the " time is not far distant when the Parliament of England . . . will feel it its duty to look this question fully and fairly in the face ". It was not.

Mr. Gladstone's resolutions

On March 23rd, 1868, Mr. Gladstone gave notice of his intention to move three resolutions on the subject. The terms of the resolutions were as follows : " (1) That in the opinion of this House it is necessary that the Established Church of Ireland should cease to exist as an establishment ; due regard being had to all personal interests and to all individual rights of property. (2) That, subject to the foregoing considerations, it is expedient to prevent the creation of new personal interests by the exercise of any public patronage, and to confine the operation of the Ecclesiastical Commissioners of Ireland to objects of immediate necessity or involving individual rights, pending a final decision of Parliament. (3) That an humble address be presented to Her Majesty, humbly to pray that, with a view to the purposes aforesaid, Her Majesty will be graciously pleased to place at the disposal of Parliament her interest in the Temporalities in Archbishoprics, Bishoprics, and other ecclesiastical dignities and benefices in Ireland and in the custody thereof."

The Prime Minister at once agreed to afford facilities for the discussion of the resolutions, and on March 30th Mr. Gladstone moved that the House should go into Committee to consider them. As an amendment Lord Stanley moved that the question ought to be reserved for the decision of a new Parliament. The amendment was defeated by a majority of sixty (330 to 270), Gladstone's motion was affirmed by a majority of fifty-six, and exactly a month later (April 30th) the first resolution was carried by 330 votes against 265.

Position of the Government

The significance of this vote was clearly apprehended by Disraeli's Ministry, and on May 4th the Prime Minister made a formal, though not an unambiguous, announcement as to their position. He told the House that he had placed the resignation of his Ministry at the disposal of the Queen, and had suggested the alternative of a dissolution, that the Queen had refused to accept the resignation, but had promised to dissolve Parliament as soon as the interests of public business would permit. The announcement was received with marked disfavour. Gladstone hotly denied the right of the Ministry to force a dissolution, and deprecated the use made by Disraeli of the Queen's name. He was, in fact, all impatience to go through with the work to which he had now set his hand, and to the general principle of which the House of Commons had already assented. That the new constituencies, just coming to the birth, had not been consulted on this or any other question, seemed to him a matter of secondary importance. It was ultimately agreed, however, that the registration should be expedited and an election held on the new register in November.

To the second and third resolutions practically no opposition was offered, but the House awaited with some curiosity the answer which the Queen would be advised to make to the third. It was promptly forthcoming (May 12th) and proved to be entirely " correct ". " Relying," says the Queen, " on the wisdom of my Parliament, I desire that my interests in the Temporalities of the United Church of England and Ireland in Ireland may not stand in the way of the consideration by Parliament of any measure relating thereto in the present session." *The Suspensory Bill*

Thereupon, Mr. Gladstone in accordance with the terms of the third resolution, immediately (May 14th) introduced a Bill suspending until August 1st, 1869, the exercise of the public ecclesiastical patronage in Ireland. The second reading was carried (312 to 258) before the month was out, and the Bill after slight amendment was sent up to the Lords. There, after a brilliant debate in which Lord Derby took an animated part, the Bill was rejected by a majority of ninety-five (192 to 97). The decision on the whole matter would now rest with the electorate.

The verdict was pronounced with the least possible delay. Parliament was dissolved by proclamation on November 11th, and before the end of the month Demos had spoken. In the event, the Liberals found themselves in a majority of 115-120 in the new House of Commons.[1] Gladstone failed to secure re-election in South-West Lancashire, but had taken the precaution to be nominated for Greenwich, where he was returned. Lord Hartington was defeated in North Lancashire and had to take refuge in Wales. Disraeli accepted the verdict of the constituencies as final, and did not await the meeting of Parliament before placing his resignation in the hands of the Queen (Dec. 1st). The man who had " shot Niagara " was not afraid of setting a democratic precedent,[2] and it is undeniable that by prompt resignation he consulted both his own dignity and *General Election of 1868*

[1] Estimated strength of parties : Liberals 387, Conservatives 271, but some estimates give the Liberals a few more.

[2] Lord Goderich similarly resigned in 1828, but he never sat in Parliament at all as Prime Minister.

the interests of the country. It was high time that the Minister in
office should also be in power.

Glad-
stone's
first Min-
istry

The Queen charged Mr. Gladstone with the formation of a
Ministry (Dec. 2nd), and on December 5th he went down to Windsor
with a provisional list of the Cabinet colleagues. His first act was
to offer a place in the Cabinet, but without portfolio, to his old chief
Lord Russell, who declined it. The Cabinet as eventually formed
was one of great individual ability. Lord Clarendon returned to the
Foreign Office and remained there until his death (June 27th, 1870).
Lord Granville led the House of Lords, first as Colonial and afterwards as Foreign Secretary. Sir Roundell Palmer, with one exception
the greatest of living lawyers, disapproved of the disendowment,
though not of the disestablishment of the Church in Ireland. Pre-
ferring principle to place, he declined the Woolsack, which was
given to Sir W. Page Wood (Lord Hatherley). Earl de Grey and
Ripon became President of the Council ; Lord Kimberley, Lord
Privy Seal ; the Duke of Argyll, Secretary for India, and Lord
Hartington, Postmaster-General. Mr. Bruce went to the Home
Office, Mr. Childers to the Admiralty, and Mr. Goschen to the Poor
Law Board ; but perhaps the most interesting appointments were
Mr. Cardwell to the War Office, Mr. Robert Lowe to the Exchequer,
and Mr. Bright to the Board of Trade. The Premier was anxious to
have Bright at the India Office, but he was with difficulty persuaded
to take office at all, and two years later he was compelled, owing to
ill-health, to retire—not, however, before he had learnt to respect
and admire his Royal Mistress, and had inspired her with similar
sentiments towards himself. Mr. Chichester Fortescue, as Chief
Secretary for Ireland, was included in the Cabinet ; Lord Spencer,
who became Lord Lieutenant, was not, nor was Mr. W. E. Forster
who, as Vice-President of the Council, was to be responsible for one
of the most important legislative achievements of the new Government.[1]

The new
Parlia-
ment and
the new
Ministry

If it be true that the death of Lord Palmerston marked the close
of a great era in English history, it is not less true that a new epoch
was opened by the election of the Parliament of 1868 and the formation of Mr. Gladstone's first Ministry. The personnel of the new
House of Commons differed essentially from that which it displaced,
reflecting the change wrought by the Act of 1867 in the electorate.
Even more remarkable was the fact that the Act of 1832 was at last
beginning to tell on the personnel of the Executive. About half
Mr. Gladstone's Cabinet belonged to the class which had ruled
England since 1688 ; [2] it contained also one or two successful lawyers ;
but nearly half the Cabinet were men of different tradition and

[1] Admitted to the Cabinet, July 1st, 1870.
[2] An analysis of Cabinets down to 1867 will show how closely they conformed
to the oligarchal type of the eighteenth century.

environment : Goschen was personally a typical Oxonian, but in the councils of the nation he represented the City ; Bright and Forster were admirable specimens of the Northern manufacturers ; Cardwell and Lowe were alike Wykehamists, Oxonians, and barristers, but the latter's experience had been mainly Colonial and journalistic, while Childers owed his reputation almost entirely to administrative work in Australia.

" My mission," said Mr. Gladstone on being summoned to power, *The Irish* " is to pacify Ireland." He embarked upon the mission with char-. *Church* acteristic vehemence and vigour. He had already declared that the three branches of the " upas tree " were the Church, the land, and education. To the first he applied the axe in the session of 1869.

That he had received, in modern phrase, a " mandate " to deal with the Established Church in Ireland is not open to question. His conduct in the session of 1868, the tone of his speeches in Lancashire and elsewhere, made it abundantly clear that if the electors gave him a majority he would use it, in the first instance, to disestablish and disendow the Irish Church. With the single exception of the General Election of 1886, no contest has ever been fought on a more unclouded issue. It has been said that the Clerkenwell explosion sounded the knell of the Irish Establishment. Mr. Gladstone himself partly admitted the impeachment. " It has only been since the close of the American War and the appearance of Fenianism that the mind of the country has been greatly turned to the consideration of Irish affairs." [1] But while admitting that it was the Fenian outrages which " produced that attitude of attention and preparedness on the part of the whole population of this country which qualified them to embrace in a manner foreign to their habits in other times the vast importance of the Irish controversy," he vehemently denied that Fenianism had affected " in the slightest degree " his own convictions on the subject.[2] Fenianism did, in fact, merely suggest the occasion : the causes of the problem now to be solved lay deep in the historic past.

" The Irish Church," said Lord Lytton, " is the greatest Irish Bull in the world." " There is," said Sydney Smith, " nothing like it in Europe, in Asia, in the discovered part of Africa, or in all we have heard of Timbuctoo." [3] Without accepting literally the dicta of professional humorists, it may be admitted that the position of the Irish Establishment had always been anomalous. The Irish Reformation of the sixteenth century was a purely official movement. It corresponded to no instinct or tradition on the part of the people ; it did not even pretend to remedy a grievance or get rid of an abuse. From the first, Protestantism had been regarded by the mass of the

---

[1] Speech on March 30th, 1868, Hansard, vol. cxci. p. 491.
[2] Speech on third Reading, May 31st, 1869 ; *cf.* also O'Brien, *op. cit.* ii. 231.
[3] Ap. O'Brien, ii. 176.

Irish Celts as the symbol of Saxon ascendancy; it soon became associated with the policy of "plantations". Of this association Oliver Cromwell was the personal embodiment. The two main pillars on which his Irish policy rested were Protestantism and plantation. The Orange conquest of 1691 accentuated and perpetuated the connection; but as regards the conversion of the Celt, the Whigs of the eighteenth century were no more successful than the Puritans of the seventeenth. Penal laws were as ineffective as plantations. More and more obtrusive did the anomaly become with the weakening of the spirit of religious bigotry. The Act of Union was the last chance for the Church of the minority. Had Pitt's whole policy been adopted, instead of a mere torso; had tithe been abolished; had the Roman Catholic laity been admitted to full political rights; had their clergy accepted concurrent endowment, Pitt's policy would have had a real chance of success. It took thirty years of agitation to secure tithe commutation and Catholic emancipation, and by then the time for concurrent endowment had already passed, if indeed it had ever been. Without some such scheme the fate of the Established Church was sealed. At no period, probably, did the Episcopalians in Ireland number more than 1,000,000. In 1868 they were said to number less than 700,000—not one in eight of the whole population. In 199 parishes out of 2,428 there was said to be not a single Protestant Episcopalian.[1] The Church of this minority enjoyed a revenue of about £614,000 a year;[2] the twelve Protestant Bishops in Ireland divided between them a net revenue of nearly £60,000. This was the condition of affairs when Mr. Gladstone laid his axe to the root of the tree.

The Irish Church Bill, 1869   It was on March 1st, 1869, that the Prime Minister, in a speech of rare dignity, not to say solemnity, unfolded to the House his scheme for the disestablishment and partial disendowment of the Established Church in Ireland. As from January 1st, 1871, the Irish Church was to be disestablished: its connection with the English Church was to be dissolved; its Bishops were no longer to be represented in the House of Lords;[3] all ecclesiastical Corporations were to be abolished; ecclesiastical Courts were to cease and ecclesiastical laws to be no longer binding.[4] The Queen in Council was to have power to reorganize a representative Church Body which was to be elected by the clergy and laity and to be incorporated by Charter. Disendowment was to take effect at once after the passing of the Act. The Ecclesiastical Commission was to be dissolved immediately, and the property of the Church, secured by the Act, was to be vested for ten years in a new "Commission of Church

---

[1] Brady, *English State Church in Ireland*, p. 159.
[2] Gladstone put the gross revenue at £700,000.
[3] Under the Act of Union four Irish Bishops sat in the House of Lords.
[4] Temporary arrangements were provided for the interval to elapse between the passing of the Act and January 1st, 1871.

Temporalities ". With vested interests Mr. Gladstone proposed to deal equitably : all beneficed clergy, including bishops and other dignitaries, were to retain their net income for life, so long as they discharged their duties ; or they might commute their income for a life annuity and relinquish their cures. Permanent curates were to be treated on the same principles, but " transitory " curates were to be dismissed with a gratuity. Such private endowments as had come to the Church since 1660 were to be handed over intact to the new Commissioners ; churches actually in use, which the Church Body was willing to maintain for public worship, were to be handed over to them with the graveyards attached to the churches ; a few, such as St. Patrick's Cathedral, partaking of the character of national memorials, were to be maintained by the Commissioners ; the glebe houses were, like the churches, to be vested in the Church Body, which was to repay the building charges upon them, amounting to £250,000 : glebe land might be purchased at a fair valuation. The Maynooth Grant and the *Regium Donum* (or grant to Presbyterian ministers) were to be commuted for a sum of £1,100,000, on principles similar to those which governed the compensation to be paid to the clergy. The Tithe Rent charge was to be purchased by the landlords under an ingenious arrangement which provided for the extinction of the charge in forty-five years. The total value of Church property Mr. Gladstone estimated at £16,000,000. Of this, the Bill disposed of £8,650,000,[1] leaving a surplus of about £7,350,000, which was to be applied mainly to the relief " of unavoidable calamity and suffering, yet not so as to cancel or impair the obligations now attached to property under the Acts for the relief of the poor ".[2]

Such were the outlines of Mr. Gladstone's carefully conceived and comprehensive scheme. It was attacked vigorously by Dr. Ball and Mr. Gathorne Hardy and defended with genuine eloquence by Bright ; but, the debate as a whole, was half-hearted. The Bill was read a second time (March 24th) by 368 to 250, an unexpectedly large majority.[3] It was through Committee, without substantial amendment, before Whitsuntide, and on May 31st was read a third time by a majority of 114.

[1] Vested interests of Incumbents £4,900,000
    Curates 800,000
    Lay Compensation 900,000
    Private Endowments 500,000
    Building Charges 250,000
    Commutation of Maynooth Grant and *Regium Donum* . 1,100,000
    Expenses of Commission 200,000
[2] Lunatic Asylums . . . . . £185,000 per year
    Idiot Asylums . . . . . . 20,000 „ „
    Training Schools for Deaf, Dumb, and Blind . . 30,000 „ „
    Training of Nuns . . . . . . 15,000 „ „
    Reformatories . . . . . . 10,000 „ „
    County Infirmaries . . . . . 51,000 „ „
[3] Gladstone to Granville ap. Morley, ii. 264

Fortunate, both as to weather and pilotage, in its voyage through the Commons, the Bill encountered heavy storms in the Lords. Much depended on the attitude of the Bishops, and both the Queen and the Prime Minister had done their utmost to secure beforehand a favourable consideration at their hands. At Lord Granville's suggestion the Queen had given an interview to Dr. Magee, an eloquent Irishman who had been promoted by Disraeli, in 1868, to the See of Peterborough, and the Premier had, at the Queen's request, consulted the Primate. Fortunately for the Church, the Queen had insisted that the Archbishopric of Canterbury should be offered on the death of Archbishop Longley (Oct. 1868) to Dr. Tait, then Bishop of London and previously Headmaster of Rugby. Dr. Tait was one of the greatest of post-Reformation Archbishops : a man of genuine piety and profound learning, a proved administrator, a shrewd, cautious, broad-minded and far-seeing statesman. He was barely seated in the Chair of Augustine (Feb. 1869) when he was called to confront a great issue. After the Bill had passed the Commons, the Queen wrote both to Archbishop Tait and to Lord Derby, urging that the Bill should not be opposed on second Reading in the Lords. Her Majesty made no secret of her strong objection to the Bill, but she foresaw the probable consequences of rejection. " Carried as it has been by an overwhelming and steady majority through a House of Commons chosen expressly to speak the feeling of the country on the question, there seems no reason to believe that any fresh appeal to the people would lead to a different result. The rejection of the Bill, therefore, would only serve to bring the two Houses into collision, and to prolong a dangerous agitation on the subject." In her constitutional instinct and political perceptions the Queen was rarely at fault. But some of the lay Peers were obdurate, and determined (June 5th) to try to defeat the Bill on second Reading.

The debate was maintained at a level high even for the House of Lords. The most notable contributors to the debate were Dr. Thirwall, the learned Bishop of St. David's, and the only prelate who voted for the Bill ; two seceders from Lord Derby's last Cabinet —Lord Salisbury and Lord Carnarvon, who refused to vote against it ; a great Irish lawyer, Lord Cairns, and a great Irish Churchman, Bishop Magee. The debate was characterized not only by elevation of thought but by independence of argument. Dr. Magee, for example, derided the argument that the Bill was a violation of the Queen's Coronation Oath or of the Act of Union. Either might surely be modified by the assent of the parties. Lord Cairns, on the contrary, held that it was impossible to abrogate a single essential clause of the Act of Union without abrogating the whole. Both, however, concurred in the belief that the Bill would do nothing to pacify Ireland : it would exasperate the Protestants, the Catholics it would gratify but not pacify. " The Irish peasant," said the

Bishop, " has already given his answer to your offer of pacification
—pacification which consists in refusing him the land which he does
want, and giving him the destruction of the Church which he does
not." " The Roman Catholic population of Ireland," said Lord
Cairns, " merely look upon the destruction of the Establishment as
a preliminary to the destruction of the landlords." How truly they
both diagnosed the situation the sequel will tell. On June 19th,
however, in a House of 325 the second Reading was carried by a
majority of 33.

But the Bill was no sooner in Committee than it encountered **Amend-**
stormy waters. In the amendments which they proposed and **ments ii**
carried the opponents of the Bill concentrated on two points : (1) **Com-mittee**
better financial terms for the Church, and (2) such an alteration of
the preamble as would permit the surplus to be devoted to concurrent endowment instead of to secular purposes. Archbishop Tait
asked for an extra £3,000,000 " to float the new Church upon," and
the House of Lords gave him more. The effect of the amendments
with which the Bill returned to the House of Commons was, according
to Gladstone, to give the disestablished Irish Church an additional
solatium of nearly four millions. Relying largely for support on
Scotch Presbyterians, English and Welsh Nonconformists, and Irish
Roman Catholics, Gladstone dared not have accepted the amendment
even if he would. After much negotiation he agreed to give the
Church an extra £280,000 and some minor concessions, but struck
out the principle of concurrent endowment. The Lords refused to
give way, and a deadlock seemed to be imminent. That it was
ultimately averted was due to the genial and skilful diplomacy of
Lord Granville, to the courage and good sense of Lord Cairns, and
above all to the untiring efforts of the Queen. Her Majesty insisted
that negotiations between the Premier and the Primate should be
reopened through Dr. Wellesley, Dean of Windsor ; and, at the
height of the crisis, Lord Cairns, though doubtful as to the support
of his party, sought and obtained a private interview with Lord
Granville.[1] Mr. Gladstone's patience was exhausted, and had his
will prevailed the Bill would have been abandoned ; Lord Granville,
however, was determined to find a way out.[2] With the help of Lord
Cairns he found it. The surplus was to be used for the relief of
unavoidable calamity, but " in such a manner as Parliament should
hereafter direct," and the Church got further pecuniary concession
the precise money value of which is very variously estimated.[3] The
Bill received the Royal assent on July 26th.

[1] On these prolonged and difficult negotiations *cf.* Fitzmaurice, *Granville*, ii.
10-15 ; Morley, ii. 270-279, and especially Davidson and Benham, *Tait*, ii. 8-43,
where the correspondence is printed.
[2] See Morley, ii. 274-277.
[3] Anything between £250,000 and £850,000.

21

No sooner had the Bill become law than the friends of the disestablished Church set to work with a will to prepare for the inevitable, and to reorganize the Church. A representative Church Body
was at once formed, and duly incorporated. Fortunately it was able
to command the services, not only of men of piety, but of men of
business, and in all recent Irish history there is nothing more truly
remarkable than the wisdom and skill with which this Body evolved
order out of chaos, and saved and reaccumulated for the Church it
served a not inconsiderable proportion of its wealth.[1] That the
results of disestablishment to the Church in Ireland were in many
respects bracing and invigorating cannot be denied. Its sphere of
usefulness was obviously curtailed, but within that contracted sphere
its activity has been conspicuous and its zeal untiring.

To what extent did the Act fulfil the expectations of its author
in regard to Catholic and Celtic Ireland ? Did it heal wounds and
assuage bitterness ? In this regard it must be admitted that fulfilment was vouched not to the hopes of Mr. Gladstone, but to the
predictions of Lord Cairns and Bishop Magee.[2]

On its merits there was much to be said, even by the admission
of opponents, for the Act of 1869 ; but as a measure of pacification
it failed. It would be unfair to lay too much stress upon the prevalence of lawlessness and serious crime in Ireland during the later
months of the year. Nor was it surprising that the release of a
considerable batch of Fenian prisoners, so far from being accepted as
an act of clemency and goodwill, was derided as a sign of weakness.
Nevertheless, there was justification for the fears expressed by Cairns
and Magee. The disendowment of the Church proved to be the
prelude for the reopening of an agrarian agitation which convulsed
Ireland for a quarter of a century.

About the Anglican Church few people knew more than Mr.
Gladstone ; about Irish land tenure few people knew less. Yet, as
regards Ireland, the latter question was infinitely the more important.
" The question of central and paramount interest in Ireland is to-day,
as it has been for some centuries past, that of the land." Thus wrote
one who knew Ireland, as few men have known it, and who used
language with the accuracy of a great scholar.[3] Mr. Gladstone was
of course conscious of this truth, and took infinite pains to equip
himself for the task to which he now turned his hand, but, despite the
best intentions, the results, as the sequel will show, were not commensurate with the effort involved ; and for a simple reason. Knowing little of Ireland at first hand himself, he was curiously impatient

---

[1] For the details of the reorganization *cf.* Thom's *Official Directory* for 1888.
[2] It is fair to point out that Mr. Gladstone himself deprecated the notion that
" the settlement of the Church question in Ireland was to be a panacea for the evils
of that country ".—Hansard, cxci. p. 1667.
[3] S. H. Butcher, *Irish Land Acts and their Operation.* Glasgow, 1887.

of the advice of those who knew much. His agrarian legislation, therefore, was a progressive series of disappointments.

It was the publication of the Report of the Devon Commission The in 1845 which first made Englishmen realize that there existed in Devon Ireland an agrarian problem, which urgently demanded the attention mission of the Imperial Legislature. The Irish land system, like much else in Ireland, was the result of the super-imposition of English ideas upon an arrested native development. Early in the seventeenth century the English lawyers, by a stroke of the pen, substituted the principles of English land law for the traditional customs which prevailed in Ireland. The root blunder made by the English lawyers lay in regarding an Irish tribal chieftain as the proprietor of the soil tilled by the tribesmen. This initial blunder was never eradicated, nor even, until the close of the nineteenth century, repaired. The confiscations and plantations of the seventeenth century all proceeded on the erroneous assumption that the chieftain was a landlord. Not until the Devon Report did Englishmen begin to suspect that the Irish land system differed fundamentally from their own ; that the ordinary contractual relations of landlord and tenant—as understood in England—were entirely opposed to the genius of the Irish system ; that improvements were commonly effected not as in England by the " landlord," but by the tenant ; and that partly by virtue of those improvements, partly by immemorial tradition, the " tenant " regarded himself as possessed of customary rights in the soil which he tilled.[1] The Report of the Bessborough Commission did not go beyond the facts in saying : " there has in general survived to the Irish farmer, through all vicissitudes, in despite of the seeming or real veto of the law, in apparent defiance of political economy, a living tradition of possessory rights, such as belong, in the more primitive ages of society, to the status of the man who tilled the soil ".

This living tradition was first broken by the famine and by the Encumbered Estates Act. The latter, as we have seen, went far to substitute for the old proprietors, not less imbued with the living tradition than the tenants, a new race of commercial landlords who brought to the business of landowning the ethics and economics of the " Manchester School ". From this moment the acute difficulties began. Mr. Cardwell's Land Act of 1860 represented the attempt of one of the most capable of Peel's disciples to indoctrinate the Irish land system with the principle of Free Trade. In the forefront of the

[1] On the Irish land system *cf.* Richey, *Irish Landlords ;* Longfield ap. *Systems of Land Tenure* (Cobden Club) ; Montgomery, *Land Tenure in Ireland ;* Godkin, *Land War in Ireland ;* besides Reports of Devon, Bessborough, and other Commissions. The writer has also in his possession a large collection of pamphlets and MS. material, accumulated by his own personal investigations in Ireland. To such " authorities " detailed reference would obviously be impossible, and the reader must accept an assurance that the statements in the text, though unavoidably brief, are made on the authority of evidence laboriously acquired.

Act is was asserted that " the relation of landlord and tenant shall be deemed to be founded on the express or implied contract of the parties and not upon tenure or service ". But the Act of 1860 was a dead failure. So far as it was operative at all, it tended to encourage the evictions and to embitter the relations of owner and occupier.

The Land Act of 1870 The Act of 1870 was conceived on entirely different lines. It was intended to effect four main objects : (1) to deter the landlord from exercising a right of capricious eviction, by giving the tenant compensation for disturbance ; (2) to give the force of law to the Ulster custom of tenant-right, wherever such custom was recognizable ; (3) to secure to the out-going tenant compensation for unexhausted improvements effected by himself or his predecessor in title, and (4) by what were known as the Bright clauses, to facilitate purchase on the part of the tenants. The Bill passed both Houses with a modicum of opposition, but some of the best Irish opinion deplored the fact that no attempt was made either to provide against arbitrary raising of the rent, or to define the respective rights of owner and occupier.[1] The purchase clauses, popularly and rightly associated with the name of Bright, were unfortunately clogged with such complicated conditions as to render them practically inoperative. Nevertheless, it was on the lines suggested by Bright, not on those laid down by Gladstone, that the solution of the problem was ultimately to be found.

The Peace Preservation Act, 1870 It is not without significance that, long before the Land Bill emerged from Committee, an Act for the suppression of crime in Ireland should have been rapidly passed through both Houses. " The first effects of the stirring of the stagnant slough of Irish despond by the dredge of legislation had been to bring all the mud and refuse to the surface at once." [2] It was truly said, and not less true was Lord Salisbury's comment in the course of the debate : " You must teach the Irish people to *fear* the law before you can induce them to *like* it ". The Peace Preservation Act of 1870 forbade the use of fire-arms in any district proclaimed by the Lord Lieutenant ; required a licence for the possession of arms under any circumstances, and gave powers to the police to make domiciliary visits to search for arms or for evidence as to threatening letters, and to arrest any person wandering about at night in a suspicious manner. It also authorized a change of venue in trials, where justice was likely to be impeded by local prejudice ; authorized the grand jury, with the consent of the judge, to levy damages on the district for compensation in cases of agrarian murder ; gave increased powers of summary jurisdiction to magistrates, and empowered the Executive to suppress any newspaper which lent itself to intimidation.

So general was the conviction as to the necessity for strengthening the administration of the law in Ireland that only fifteen members

[1] *E.g.* Judge Longfield.   [2] *Annual Register,* 1870, p. 4.

opposed the Bill on the second Reading, and on April 4th it became
an Act.   Before the close of the year, however, Mr. Gladstone thought
it well to temper justice with mercy, by granting an amnesty to the
Fenian prisoners who still remained in penal servitude ; though the
amnesty was coupled with the condition of banishment from the
United Kingdom for life.

Firmness, mercy, and generosity seemed alike impotent to secure The
the peace and good government of Ireland.   Hardly six months had West-
elapsed after the passing of the Land Act before Lord Hartington, meath
who had become Chief Secretary in January, 1871,[1] moved for a 1871
Select Committee to enquire into the state of County Westmeath
and other adjacent districts.   The prevalence of agrarian crime more
than justified the enquiry, and the fact that the crime was a result
of organized conspiracy rendered the situation doubly serious.   " The
reports which we receive," said Lord Hartington, " show that such
a state of terrorism prevails that the (Ribbon) Society had only to
issue its edict to secure obedience. . . . Ribbon law and not the law
of the land appears to be that which is obeyed.   It exerts such
power that no landlord dare exercise the commonest rights of property ; no farmer or other employer dare exercise his own judgment
or discretion as to whom he shall employ ; in fact, so far does the
influence of the Society extend that a man scarcely dare enter into
open competition in the fairs or markets with any one known to
belong to the Society."   Such language was less familiar to the
Parliament of 1871 than it has since unhappily become ; the Committee was readily granted, and as a result of its enquiries the
" Westmeath Act " was passed.   Authority was given to the Lord
Lieutenant to proclaim a district ; to suspend the Habeas Corpus
Act for two years in any such district, and by warrant to commit for
trial suspected persons who were arrested in other parts of Ireland
if they had been in a proclaimed district since January 1st.   The
operation of the Act was limited to two years, but at the same time
the Peace Preservation was continued.[2]

With two factors of the Irish problem Gladstone had now dealt. The
There remained the third—the constitutional factor.   On May 19th, Home
1870, Mr. Isaac Butt and others [3] inaugurated, at a meeting held at move-
the Bilton Hotel, Dublin, the " Home Government Association of ment
Ireland ".   The Association was formed : " To obtain for our
country the right and privilege of managing our own affairs, by a
Parliament assembled in Ireland, composed of Her Majesty the
Sovereign, and her successors and the Lords and Commons of
Ireland ; to secure for that Parliament, under a federal arrangement,

----

[1] In succession to Mr. Chichester Fortescue, who succeeded Mr. Bright (resigned, December, 1870) at the Board of Trade.

[2] Until January 1st, 1873.

[3] Including Mr. King Harman and other Conservatives, who were disgusted
with the Imperial Parliament for " betraying " the Irish Church.

the right of legislating for and regulating all matters relating to the internal affairs of Ireland, and control over Irish resources and revenues, subject to the obligation of contributing our just proportion of the Imperial expenditure ; to leave to an Imperial Parliament the power of dealing with all questions affecting the Imperial Crown and Government, legislation regarding the Colonies and other dependencies of the Crown, the relations of the United Empire with Foreign States, and all matters appertaining to the defence and stability of the Empire at large ; to attain such an adjustment of the relations between the two countries, without any interference with the prerogatives of the Crown, or any disturbance of the principles of the constitution."

It has seemed well to record the *ipsissima verba* of the more important resolutions adopted at the Dublin meeting of 1870, for that meeting was the cradle of the Home Rule movement. The Association soon showed its practical efficacy. In 1871 and 1872 there were in Ireland twelve bye-elections, in eight of which the " Home Rule " candidates were successful, and in this way Isaac Butt and Mitchell Henry, Mr. Blennerhasset and Colonel Nolan found themselves in the House of Commons—a nucleus of a new party. In 1873 a Conference was held in Dublin to organize the forces of the new movement for the approaching General Election. It was then and there that the " Home Government Association " was transformed into the " Home Rule League ".[1]

Irish education Upon the new movement inaugurated by Butt, Gladstone poured undiluted scorn. " Can any sensible man, can any rational man," he asked, " suppose that at this time of day, in this condition of the world, we are going to disintegrate the great capital institutions of the country for the purpose of making ourselves ridiculous in the sight of all mankind, and crippling any power we possess for bestowing benefits, through legislation, on the country to which we belong ? "[2] Gladstone himself was by this time intent upon another piece of work for Ireland—the reorganization of higher education.

It stood badly in need of it. Since Sir Robert Peel's day nothing effectual had been done. In 1848 Peel had established the "Godless" Colleges at Cork, Galway, and Belfast, and in 1850 these Colleges were affiliated into the Queen's University of Ireland. But into the soil of Catholic Ireland the new institution never struck roots, and in 1851 the Catholic Bishops in the Synod of Thurles formally condemned the " mixed system ". Three years later a Catholic University was established under the presidency of John Henry Newman, and for years was maintained entirely by Catholic piety, unassisted by the State. Not until 1873 was any serious attempt made to deal,

---

[1] *Cf.* O'Brien, *Life of C. S. Parnell* (1910 ed.), pp. 56-59.
[2] Speech at Aberdeen, 26th September, 1871, quoted by O'Connor Morris, *Ireland from 1798 to 1898*, pp. 218, 219.

on broad lines, with the thorny question of University education for the Irish Catholics.

Mr. Gladstone's Bill was founded upon two propositions which Irish could hardly be disputed : (1) that the condition of the Irish Catholics University Bill, 1873 in respect of University education was " scandalously bad " ; and (2) that the Queen's Colleges had been a " comparative failure ". Mr. Gladstone, therefore, proposed to abolish the Queen's University altogether and to metamorphose the University of Dublin. Of late years the latter had contained but one college, the famous foundation of Trinity. Henceforth it was to be, not in name only, but in fact, *Matrix Collegiorum* ; and to it were to be affiliated Trinity College, the Queen's Colleges at Belfast and Cork, the Catholic University College, and other Colleges. The new University was to have both teaching and examining functions ; it was to be the sole degree-giving body in Ireland and to be liberally endowed—partly from the revenues of Trinity College ; but there were to be no chairs for Theology, Moral Philosophy or Modern History. The scheme was assailed from every quarter : English Nonconformists objected to State aid for denominational teaching ; Irish Protestants denounced the disendowment of Trinity College and attacked the " endowment of error " ; Catholics in both countries were firmly opposed, then, as always, to a mixed system of education. As to the parliamentary history of the Bill and its effects upon the fortunes of the Ministry something will be said later.[1] Its defeat on the second Reading was regretted by few. The measure was framed with perverse ingenuity so as to wound every susceptibility and to disturb every existing institution, without satisfying a single grumbler and without removing a single grievance. A much less pretentious measure introduced and passed by Disraeli in 1879 achieved a degree of success beyond all expectation.

Like so many Ministries before it, Mr. Gladstone's famous administration of 1868 was doomed to go to pieces on the Irish rocks. Not, however, before it had passed into law an extraordinary number of legislative projects and had effected administrative changes of far-reaching significance. To this tale of administrative and legislative work the next chapters must be devoted.

[1] *Infra*, p. 356.

CHAPTER XXI

NATIONAL EDUCATION

The Edu-
cation Bill
of 1870
" WE must induce our masters to learn their letters." Mr.
Lowe's aphorism will be remembered and quoted long after
his incisive arraignment of democracy has faded into oblivion.   The
following pages will disclose the first serious attempt made by the
State to follow his sage advice.   That attempt will be associated for
all time with the name of Mr. William Edward Forster, Vice-President
of the Council in Mr. Gladstone's first Ministry, but not until July,
1870, a member of the Cabinet.   Mr. Forster introduced his famous
Bill on February 7th, 1870.   Before we examine its provisions and
follow its parliamentary fortunes, it may be advisable to repair a
deliberate omission and cast a brief retrospective glance over the
history of elementary education in England.

Elemen-
tary edu-
cation in
England
It is a fact not without significance that the first State grant in
aid of elementary education was made the year after the first great
Reform Bill became law.   Down to 1833 the work of educating the
children of the poor in England had devolved wholly upon the
Churches.[1]   Something was done by this meagre dole to improve
matters, but not much, and in 1839 Lord John Russell expressed the
concern of Her Majesty at " the want of instruction which is still
observable among the poorer classes of her subjects ".   " All the
enquiries which have been made show," he added, " a deficiency in
the general education of the people which is not in accordance with
the character of a civilized and Christian nation." [2]   Lord Melbourne's
Government decided, therefore, to set up what was in effect a new
administrative department, though technically a Committee of the
Privy Council on Education.   They increased the Treasury Grant
from £20,000 to £30,000 and made a beginning with the appointment
of an Inspectorate.   The Inspectors were of two kinds : (1) clergymen
of the Church of England appointed under the sanction of the Archbishop of Canterbury to inspect Church schools, and reporting in
duplicate to the Archbishop and to the Committee ; and (2) laymen
appointed under the sanction of the British and Foreign School
Society to inspect and report upon their schools.   But the root of
the difficulty lay in the lack of trained and efficient teachers.   " Almost
the only teachers," wrote Matthew Arnold, " whom the Committee
of Council found at its disposal in 1839, were ' either untrained men
who, from some defect of body and health, had been driven from
the rougher struggles of life and muscular toil ; or self-taught

[1] See *supra*, p. 87.
[2] Letter to Lord Landsdowne, February 13th, 1839.

Sunday school teachers trained for three or six months in some central model school,' such, for instance, as the British and Foreign School Society had established in the Borough Road." [1]

Lord John Russell had in 1839 proposed to establish a Government Normal school for the training of teachers, but so fierce was the opposition of the Church party, that Lord Melbourne's Ministry was all but wrecked and the proposal had to be withdrawn. Four years later the Nonconformists had their revenge. Sir James Graham's Factory Act of 1843 originally contained a provision for the establishment of State-aided schools in manufacturing districts. The religious teaching was to be in accordance with the tenets of the Established Church, though Nonconformists were to be protected by a conscience clause. But the latter would have none of it, and the clause was deleted. Nevertheless, although Russell failed to establish a Government Training College, his proposal had the effect of stimulating voluntary effort, and by 1851 twenty-five such institutions had been established. By 1846 the Treasury Grant had risen to £100,000 and the Minutes of that year necessitated still further increase ; the remuneration and prospects of the teachers were much improved ; a system of apprenticeship—or pupil-teachers—was inaugurated, and provision was made for improving the Normal schools and the training of teachers. So rapidly, indeed, did expenditure increase, that in 1858 it was thought well to appoint a Commission under the chairmanship of the Duke of Newcastle to " enquire into the present state of popular education in England ".

The Commission reported in 1861, and it fell to Robert Lowe to carry into effect its main recommendations.[2] The Commissioners gave due credit to the results of voluntary effort, and in particular they emphasized the debt due to the labours and self-sacrifice of the clergy ; [3] they recommended an increase of State grants to properly inspected schools ; that inspection should take the form of individual examination, and that the Treasury Grant should be based upon the results of examination. Only by " payment by results " could the efficiency of the elementary teaching of every scholar be, in their opinion, secured. Lowe's *Revised Code* of 1861 gave effect to this principle. Henceforward, the grant was to be earned only by approved schools taught by a certificated teacher ; it was to be paid to managers who were to be responsible for the appointment and remuneration of the teachers ; the pupils were to be required to make a certain number of attendances, and the amount of the grant was to depend upon the result of the individual examination of the pupils in the three elementary subjects—reading,

The New castle Commission and the New Code of 1861

---

[1] Ap. Ward, *Reign of Queen Victoria*, ii. 244.

[2] As Vice-President of the Council—an office created in 1856.

[3] See remarkable figures given by Mr. Arnold (ap. Ward, p. 264), who adds : " In truth if there is a class in English society whose record in regard to popular education is honourable it is the clergy. Every inquiry has brought this out."

writing, and arithmetic. Mr. Lowe was at once an economist and a
humorist. " I cannot," he said in introducing his scheme to the
House of Commons, " promise you either efficiency or cheapness ;
but if the system is not efficient it will be cheap ; if it is not cheap
it will be efficient."

The system of " payment by results," thus introduced, was
bitterly assailed by educational experts, notably by one of the most
eminent inspectors who ever served the Committee—Matthew
Arnold. The Government so far gave way as to allow one-third
of the grant to be reckoned by individual attendances, and two-
thirds to depend upon the results of examination ; but the principle
survived for many years. Long before its final decease its enemies
had multiplied and its friends diminished. Nevertheless, much progress was made in the decades which followed upon the Newcastle
Commission.

Between 1861 and 1870 various attempts at legislation were made
from both sides of the House, but until Mr. Gladstone's advent to
power, nothing effectual was accomplished. By that time people
were gradually awakening to the folly of entrusting the political
destinies of the country to the manual workers, without taking the
precaution that they should be reasonably educated. The ground,
therefore, was prepared for Mr. Forster, and the seed he flung into it
was good.

The Edu-
cation
Bill of
1870
" The first problem to be solved is ' how can we cover the country
with good schools ? ' " No elaboration of phrase would have been
so effective as the direct and simple words with which Mr. Forster
introduced his great measure of 1870. To the solution of this
problem he bent all the capacities of a powerful intellect, a dogged
will, and a transparently simple and open mind. Forster had no
arrière pensée whatever in framing his Bill of 1870 ; he did not
desire to strike a back-handed blow at any Church or institution ;
his one and only object was to give to the children of the poor the
education they lacked, and thus lay securely the foundations of the
Democratic State to come. " Our object is to complete the present
voluntary system, to fill up gaps, sparing the public money where it
can be done without, procuring as much as we rightly can the assistance of the parents, and welcoming as much as we rightly can the co-
operation and aid of those benevolent men who desire to assist their
neighbours." The main provisions of the scheme were as follows :
The whole of England and Wales was to be divided exhaustively
into school districts and its educational needs and existing facilities
to be accurately ascertained. Each district was to have sufficient
public school accommodation for elementary scholars. " If in any
one of the districts we find the elementary education to be sufficient,
efficient, and suitable . . . we let it alone so long as it continues in
that state." All schools were to be open to Government inspection

and governed by the *Code*. The ordinary fee was not to exceed 9d. a week. When the supply of voluntary schools was defective a School Board, with power to levy a rate, was to be set up; the Board was to be elected in the towns by the Town Council, in rural districts by the Vestry. The cost of Board schools was to be borne in equal proportions by the parents, by the State, and by the local rates. The local rate was not likely to come near 3d. in the pound —a singularly unwise attempt to prophesy. In specially poor districts the Boards were to have power to establish free schools, and in any district they might pay the fees of very poor parents— without any stigma of pauperism applying to such payment. So far all was tolerably plain sailing. There remained, however, two knotty questions to be decided : Was elementary education to be compulsory ? And, what was to be the place in the curriculum of religious instruction ? Both difficulties were transferred to the shoulders of the local authorities. The School Boards were to be authorized—though not compelled—to frame bye-laws for the compulsory attendance of all children in the district between the ages of five and twelve. The penalty for non-attendance was not to exceed 5s. and not to be imposed if reasonable excuses were forthcoming, or if there were no school within a mile. As to religious teaching the Boards—subject in every case to a stringent conscience clause—were to have entire discretion; they might provide any or none.

The Bill as a whole was received with general approval ; but round the question of religious teaching the battle raged hotly. The Education League—an association whose stronghold was in Birmingham—had pronounced in favour of the dogma that education should be free, compulsory, and secular. On no single point was Forster willing to make concession to these *doctrinaires*. Among them were his own colleague in the representation of Bradford, Mr. Edward Miall, Mr. Henry Richard, a prominent liberationist, and Mr. George Dixon, one of the members for Birmingham. Some of these men were bitterly disappointed to find that the authors of the Bill had been so exclusively concerned for the welfare of the children, as to neglect the opportunity of striking an oblique blow at the Church of England. Forster himself they regarded as a renegade, and they pursued him and his measure, with undeviating hostility. Mr. Dixon moved, on the second Reading, an amendment to the effect that " no measure for the elementary education of the people could afford a permanent and satisfactory settlement which left the important question of religious instruction to be determined by the local authorities," and so threatening did the attitude of the Dissenters [1] become that Mr. Gladstone deemed it prudent to promise that the Government would not press the points to which special objection was taken until after full consideration in Committee.

The religious difficulty

[1] Mr. Dixon himself is said to have been a member of the Church of England. See *Birmingham Daily Post*, December 3rd, 1913.

Three months elapsed after the second Reading before the Committee stage was reached (June 16). The opposition of the Dissenters to the Bill centred on two points : the inadequacy of a conscience clause to prevent the virtual " re-endowment of Anglicanism " in the Board schools ; and the danger of leaving entire discretion to the School Boards as to rate-aid for voluntary schools. On going into Committee Mr. Gladstone at once announced some important concessions. The most important was the acceptance of Mr. Cowper-Temple's amendment which provided (1) that no catechism or formulary distinctive of any denominational creed should be taught in any Board school ; and (2) that no voluntary school should receive assistance from the rates. To soften the blow to the latter the State Grant to all schools, Board or voluntary, was increased from a third to a half. At the same time the conscience clause was strengthened by the introduction of a time-table which, by making religious instruction (if and when provided) the first lesson of the day, rendered it easier for parents to withdraw, or rather to withhold, their children from such instruction. The age for compulsory attendance was raised from twelve to thirteen, and the principle of direct election by the ratepayers was substituted for indirect election by Town Councils and Vestries. Voting was to be cumulative, and by ballot.[1] The Birmingham party would gladly have postponed all educational reform in the hope of converting the House and the country to their own extreme views. Mr. Lowe aptly compared the attitude of extremists (on both sides) to that of " a fine herd of cattle in a large meadow deserting the rich grass which is abundant around them, and delighting themselves by fighting over a bed of nettles in one corner of the field ". In the end, however, good sense prevailed. The principal amendment moved, on behalf of the Birmingham party, by Mr. Richard was defeated by 421 to 60, and, with the amendments noted above, the Bill went through Committee, was read a third time on July 22nd, and on August 9th received the Royal assent.

The Act of 1870 was one of the most splendid legislative achievements of the century. For his share in it—the giant's share—Mr. Forster received a vote of censure from his constituents at Bradford, and earned the unrelenting hostility of a section of his political friends. But he had the supreme satisfaction of knowing that he had laid broad and deep the foundations of a truly national system of elementary education. The citizen rulers of the greatest empire the world has seen were at last to be taught their letters. The quickening of educational activity was immediately apparent. In 1870 there were about 9,000 State-aided schools in England and Wales, with about 1,300,000 scholars in average attendance. During the next decade the voluntary schools increased to 14,370, and 3,692

[1] The ballot was applied in the first instance only to London.

Board schools came into existence with an aggregate of nearly 3,000,000 children in average attendance.

Since 1870 there have been two important legislative changes in regard to elementary education, while administration has been modified and adapted year by year under the annual *Code*.[1] In 1876 Lord Sandon, as Vice-President of the Education Committee in Disraeli's Ministry, carried an Act of considerable importance. It placed restrictions on juvenile employment, whereby no child might be employed at all under the age of ten, and not until the age of fourteen without a certificate of educational proficiency ; it set up School Attendance Committees in every district where no School Boards existed ; it gave to these Committees equally with the School Boards the power to frame bye-laws enforcing compulsory attendance ; and it repealed the provision in the Act of 1870 authorizing School Boards to pay the fees in certain cases. Instead of this, parents were permitted to obtain the fees for their children from the Guardians of the Poor, without incurring the disabilities of pauperism. The Act of 1876 marked a distinct step on the road towards compulsion. In 1880, under Mr. Mundella's guidance, the goal was reached and local authorities were not merely permitted, but obliged to frame bye-laws to enforce attendance. *{Enlargements of the Act of 1870 — The Act of 1876 — Compulsion adopted, 1880}*

Further steps were taken by Sir William Hart-Dyke who was Minister of Education in Lord Salisbury's administration (1886-1892). The *Code* of 1890 made it possible to establish evening continuation schools ; payment on the results of individual examinations was abolished, and there was substituted for it a " block " grant reckoned on the basis of average attendances. In the following year (1891) a still more important change was effected. The fees paid by the parents were abolished, and the State undertook to make good the deficiency, estimated at that time at £2,000,000 a year. Thus elementary education became not only compulsory, but gratuitous —or rather the charge was transferred from individual parents to the community at large. The change, due mainly to Mr. Goschen inside the Cabinet and Mr. Chamberlain outside it, was much criticized at the time, and is still a matter of controversy. It was said that the " pence " was hardly worth collecting, and that gratuitous service was the natural corollary of compulsion. Neither plea was conclusive, and neither perhaps would have prevailed but for the fears of the Church party that if the change were delayed it would be effected by their opponents and in such a way as to extinguish the Voluntary schools. That the apprehension was a natural one can scarcely be denied ; whether it was sufficient to justify the step taken by the Conservative Government of 1891 is more arguable.[2] *{The Code of 1890 — Gratuitous education}*

---

[1] The body of rules issued by the Central Authority.

[2] The important Act of 1902 is outside the purview of this volume. It went far to reverse the policy of the previous thirty years. It abolished School Boards ; transferred their functions to County, Town, and Urban Councils, and made the local rates available for " Voluntary " schools.

Secondary and higher education

The problem of elementary education does not, of course, stand alone. The solution attained by the Acts of 1870, 1876, 1880 and 1891 may indeed, in one sense, be said to have intensified and complicated the educational problem as a whole. " Elementary instruction," as a great scholar once said, " unless crowned by something higher, is not only barren but may even be dangerous. It is not well to teach our democracy to read unless we also teach it to think." [1] It was proper, therefore, that the generation which tackled the problem of primary instruction should have taken thought also for secondary and higher education. To this large question, however, limitations of space will permit only the most jejune reference.

Secondary education

In 1861 a Commission was appointed under the chairmanship of Lord Clarendon to enquire into the condition of the nine " chief Grammar schools " of the country, known distinctively as the " Public " schools. Of these, the seven boarding schools were

The Public Schools Act, 1868

brought under the operation of *The Public Schools Act* of 1868— Eton, Winchester, Westminster, Charterhouse, Harrow, Rugby, and Shrewsbury. New governing bodies were appointed and much-needed reforms of constitution and curriculum were effected. Nor were the beneficial results of Government enquiry confined to the selected schools. They extended to many other Secondary schools such as St. Paul's, Merchant Taylors,[2] Repton, Uppingham, Marlborough, Wellington, and Clifton, which, with several others, took rank among the great " Public " schools. But the vast improvement effected in such schools touched only the fringe of the problem of secondary education.

The Endowed Schools Act, 1869

In 1865 a Commission, of which Lord Taunton was chairman and Dr. Temple the most active member, was appointed to enquire into the education given in Secondary schools included neither in the purview of the Public Schools Commission, nor in that of the Newcastle Commission of 1859. They found at work 572 Endowed Grammar schools with a net income of £183,066, and exhibitions of the annual value of £13,897,[3] besides some 10,000 private schools. As a result of their *Report*, issued in 1867, *The Endowed Schools Act* of 1869 was passed. Three Commissioners were appointed to draw up schemes for the revision of the educational trusts of some 3,000 schools. The result of their labours was " a very extensive resettlement, for the benefit of secondary education, of charitable trusts," involving an income of over £600,000 a year.[4] But, although under the Acts of 1868 and 1869 existing educational funds were applied to better purposes, little was done towards evolving a coherent system of secondary education for the nation at large.

---

[1] Sir Richard Jebb, *The Work of the Universities for the Nation*, p. 49.

[2] Merchant Taylors and St. Paul's were included in the enquiry held by Lord Clarendon's Commission but being day schools were not included in the Act of 1868.

[3] Mr. Arnold ap. Ward, p. 276.   [4] *Report*, vol. i. App. p. 151.

The first really effective step in this direction was taken by the The Act which in 1888 established County Councils. *The Technical* Technical *Instruction Act* was passed in 1889, and gave power to the Councils Instruction Act, of counties and boroughs to supply or aid in supplying technical 1889 and manual instruction, and for this purpose to levy a rate not exceeding one penny in the pound. In the following year there fell to these authorities a veritable windfall in the shape of the " Beer and Whisky money ". Under the Local Taxation Act of 1890 an additional tax was imposed on spirits, and the proceeds of this and part of the existing tax on beer were to be applied to compensation for the extinction of publicans' licenses. Parliament was unwilling to appropriate it to the latter purpose, and in the event the greater part of the money, amounting to over half a million a year, was placed at the disposal of the Local Authorities with a strong hint that they should apply it to technical education. Most of the Councils took the hint; the term " technical " was generously interpreted by the Central authority, and the " Whisky money " thus provided the means by which something like a coherent system of secondary education has been gradually evolved.[1]

In the work of improving secondary education the Universities The Uni- have played a not unimportant part. The system of Local Examina- versities tions established by Oxford and Cambridge in 1858 has immensely and improved the standard of teaching in thousands of middle-class ary schools, and in 1873 the two Universities established a Joint Board educa- which has devised a system of examination for Secondary schools of tion the highest grade. Certificates granted in connection with the Local and Joint Board examinations exempt successful candidates from various professional and other examinations and from the preliminary examinations at the Universities themselves.

The attentions of the educational reformer were not confined to Higher primary and secondary instruction. For many years past the education position of things at the Universities had been in the highest degree anomalous. Oxford in particular, ever since the restrictive legisla- tion of the sixteenth and seventeenth centuries, had been " narrowed into an exclusively Church of England Institution ".[2] After the repeal of the Test and Corporation Acts of 1828, and the passing of the Catholic Emancipation Act in 1829, and the Reform Act of 1832, the injustice of the situation was increasingly felt. There were now many Nonconformists admitted not merely to the Legislature, but to a place in the inner councils of the Empire to whom the highest education was obstinately denied. At Oxford, both matriculation and graduation were burdened with a religious test ; at Cambridge Nonconformists might matriculate, reside and offer themselves for

---

[1] The Acts of 1902, 1918 and 1944 are in this connection of first-rate importance : nor should the exhaustive labours of the Bryce Commission (1894) be overlooked.
[2] Brodrick, *History of the University of Oxford.*

examination, but they could not proceed to a Degree. For twenty years an assault was maintained against the barriers erected by Elizabethan and Caroline legislation.[1] Mr. Gladstone consistently maintained the view that " the Universities were undoubtedly national institutions, but only in so far as they were connected with the national Church " ; even in 1850 he insisted that " as matters now stand there is not the shadow or the pretext of a case for enquiry ". But Lord John Russell thought otherwise, and in 1850 two Royal Commissions were appointed to enquire into the state, discipline, studies, and revenues of the University and Colleges of Oxford and Cambridge respectively. The *Reports* of these Commissions and the resulting legislation mark an epoch of first-rate importance in national education. In the forefront of the Oxford *Report* there was an emphatic assertion of the national character of the University : " Such an institution cannot be regarded as a mere aggregation of private interests ; it is eminently national. It would seem, therefore, to be a matter of public policy that . . . such measures should be taken as may serve to raise its efficiency to the highest point and to diffuse its benefits most widely." Many of the resulting reforms were primarily domestic in character, affecting the constitution and powers of the governing bodies within the University—Convocation, Congregation, and Council ; others were intended to facilitate the admission of a poorer class of students by giving permission to undergraduates to reside in licensed lodging, or even to become members of the University without incurring the expense of joining a College or Hall ;[2] of even wider significance were those which admitted Dissenters to Matriculation and the Bachelor's Degree at Oxford (1854), and which, at Cambridge, abolished the test for all Degrees except those in Divinity. But at both Universities Dissenters were still excluded from all share in the government and (virtually) from all part in the teaching work alike of the Universities and of the Colleges, as well as from the enjoyment of the more permanent emoluments. Between 1860 and 1870 there was almost continuous agitation for the complete and final abolition of all such restrictions, and on several occasions attempts were made to legislate in this sense. Of such legislation Mr. Gladstone was the most powerful opponent. " It was," he declared in 1863, " a fair and just demand on the part of the Church of England that the governing body in her University and her Colleges should be composed of her members." [3] But in 1865 Oxford unmuzzled her champion, and as member for

University Commissions of 1850 (side note)

---

[1] *Cf.* on the general subject Lewis Campbell, *The Nationalisation of the Old English Universities*, London, 1901. In 1834 no fewer than thirty-four pamphlets were printed on the question of University Reform, and *cf.* Sir W. Hamilton, articles in the *Edinburgh Review* for 1830, republished (1852) in his *Discussions*.

[2] The admission of Non-Collegiate or Unattached Students was the object of *The University Education Act* of 1867, a Statute due to the efforts of Mr. Ewart, an untiring worker in the cause of University reform.

[3] Quoted by Campbell, *op. cit.* p. 133.

Greenwich he carried the sweeping legislation of 1871. The Act of that year abolished all religious tests at Oxford and Cambridge, except in the case of College headships and clerical Fellowships and of Theological Chairs and Degrees in Divinity. The principles of the Act of 1871 were enlarged still further by the Executive Commissions appointed at Lord Salisbury's instance in 1876. By these Commissions, whose functions extended over several years, the Universities and their Colleges, their Degrees, prizes and endowments, their offices and their government were opened freely to all creeds and classes.[1] Apart from the removal of the Tests, the principal changes effected were : the limitation of the tenure of the ordinary Fellowships to seven years ; the abolition of restrictions upon marriage ; the equalization in the value of College scholarships, and the application of College endowments to the increase and a higher remuneration of the Professorate and other University purposes.[2] Mr. Jowett and others urged upon the Commission to enlarge the principle of Local Examinations and to make provision for the extension of University teaching to persons beyond the limits of the University. Cambridge had already made a beginning in this direction (in 1873), and Oxford followed suit. The ancient Universities thus show themselves " no longer content to be only in the strict sense of the phrase ' seats of learning ' ; they now desire to be mother-cities of intellectual colonies, and to spread the influence of their teaching throughout the land ".[3]

The Universities and the nation

This colonizing movement undertaken by the older Universities prepared the way for another remarkable development in higher education : the foundation of Universities and University Colleges in London and many of the great provincial towns. University Colleges were established in London in 1828, and in 1836 the University of London came into existence as a Degree-giving institution. In 1898 it was transformed into a teaching University. The Owens College, Manchester, the nucleus of the Victoria University, was founded in 1851 ; the Newcastle College of Science (in connection with the University of Durham) in 1871, and during the next thirty years similar Colleges were established at Leeds, Bristol, Sheffield, Birmingham, Nottingham, Liverpool, Reading, Southampton, Bangor, Cardiff, and Aberystwyth.[4]

From every point of view, therefore, the second half of the nineteenth century was fruitful in educational activity. In 1850 Higher

---

[1] A very few exceptions do not demand separate enumeration.

[2] Lord Selborne, one of the most loyal and distinguished of living Oxonians, was induced by Lord Salisbury to accept the chairmanship of the Oxford Commission. For some misgivings as to the effect of the changes effected—not wholly unjustified by the event—cf. Selborne, *Memorials*, ii. vol. ii. pp. 374-376.

[3] Jebb, *op. cit.* pp. 1-2, and cf. generally, Marriott, *Oxford*, pp. 177 f.

[4] Most of the English Colleges have, like Owens College, developed into Universities ; the Welsh Colleges have become Constituent Colleges of the University of Wales.

22

education was a preserve of Anglicanism, Secondary education was simply chaotic, and Primary education reached only a small proportion of the children of the poor. Before the close of the century the old Universities were completely nationalized ; Colleges of University rank were springing up in great centres of industry ; a coherent and comprehensive system of intermediate education was being gradually evolved, and primary instruction, without payment and without price, was within the reach of all. More important still, the different educational grades no longer existed in isolation ; they were closely correlated ; and for the boy or girl of promise the transition from one grade to the other was rendered easy and cheap. The nation had learnt the lesson that of all forms of national waste, the most extravagant is the waste of brains.

CHAPTER XXII

ADMINISTRATIVE REFORM AND FOREIGN AFFAIRS. THE CLIMAX OF THE CENTURY ON THE CONTINENT
(1868-1874)

THE disestablishment and disendowment of the Irish Church, the reform of Irish land tenure, the establishment of a national system of elementary education—these things, large and difficult as they were, did not exhaust the tireless energies of Mr. Gladstone's first administration. The Army and the Civil Service, the Judicial Bench and the licensed victuallers, trade-unionists and miners, were some of the people who came within the orbit of their reforming activities.

Down to the middle of the nineteenth century the principle The Civil prevailed that the Public Services existed, in large measure, in order Service to provide appropriate occupation for the cadets of the ruling families. Qualifying examinations for candidates were instituted in 1855, and a year earlier the places in the Civil Service of India were thrown open to competition. The same principle was applied, with few exceptions, to the Home Civil Service by an Order in Council in 1870. A very few of the highest posts may still be filled by nomination ; in the Foreign Office there is a combination of nomination and competitive examination ; the Education Department is recruited largely from the Universities by nomination ; but the great mass of Civil Service appointments are given exclusively on the result of an examination which is both open and competitive. Consequently, since 1870 the higher ranks of the Civil Services have commanded some of the best brains of the nation.

Much more thorny was the question of Army reform, but Mr. Army Gladstone had put at the War Office one of his ablest lieutenants. reform Mr. Edward Cardwell was, like his Chief, the son of a Liverpool merchant. Educated at Winchester and Balliol, he found a seat in the House of Commons [1] before he was thirty, and served his official apprenticeship under Peel. As President of the Board of Trade (1852-1855) he was responsible for the Merchant Shipping Act of 1854 ; in subsequent Ministries he served as Chief Secretary for Ireland and Secretary of State for the Colonies. He brought, therefore, to the War Office in 1868 wide administrative experience and a high reputation for firmness and tact. Like his colleague Lowe he was a stern economist of the Manchester School, and disliked the desertion of *laissez-faire* principles implicit in the Irish Land Act of 1870. But he had other opportunities of enforcing them.

[1] For Clitheroe in 1842.

It was a dominant maxim of the Manchester School that the Colonies should be gradually prepared for independence.[1] To this end the British garrisons had been already withdrawn from Australia and New Zealand. Mr. Cardwell carried the same principle much further. When he took office the number of British soldiers in the Colonies was 49,000 ; by 1870 he had reduced them to about 18,000 ; the military expenditure on the Colonies he reduced in the same period from £3,388,023 to £1,905,538. Of the latter sum a large proportion was expended on Imperial garrisons in stations such as Malta and Gibraltar, and Cardwell reckoned the strictly colonial expenditure in 1870 at less than £700,000.

The War Office   It was Cardwell's hope and belief that diminished expenditure might go hand in hand with increased efficiency. His first task, therefore, was to complete the reorganization of the War Office itself. Down to 1855 the confusion which characterized army administration was appalling. But the Crimean War necessitated a measure of reform, the main outlines of which have been already described.[2] Cardwell completed the process. He assigned the business of his office to three departments under the Commander-in-Chief, the Surveyor-General of the Ordinance, and the Financial Secretary respectively ; and all were brought under the control of the Secretary of State. The subordination of the Commander-in-Chief to the Parliamentary Minister was emphasized by the removal of the Headquarters' staff from the Horse Guards to the War Office. This change involved an encroachment upon one of the most cherished prerogatives of the Crown. The Sovereign had hitherto regarded the Army as peculiarly her own domain and the Commander-in-Chief as, in a special sense, her servant. His subordination to the Secretary of State terminated his immediate dependence on the Crown, and it was " with ill-concealed reluctance " [3] that the Queen signed the Order in Council (June 28th, 1870) which gave effect to the policy of her responsible advisers. It may be added that in 1904 the position was further simplified by the abolition of the office of Commander-in-Chief.

Reform of the Army   Having put in order the administrative machinery, Cardwell next turned to the reorganization of the Army itself. The success of Prussian arms in the wars against Austria and France naturally attracted the attention of military reformers to the system by which so brilliant a result had been achieved. It also raised anxious questionings as to the efficiency of our own system. The idea of compulsory service—the basis of the Prussian system—was considered, but only to be deliberately rejected. That point settled, Cardwell bent all his energies to making our small volunteer army as efficient as possible.

[1] *Cf. e.g.* Lewis, *Government of Dependencies,* or A. Mills, *Colonial Constitutions.*
[2] *Supra,* pp. 199.   [3] Lee, *Life,* p. 415.

In moving the Army Estimates for 1871 Mr. Cardwell put forward an elaborate statement of his scheme. The Estimates, which had shown considerable reduction in the two previous years, amounted to £15,851,700—an increase of nearly £3,000,000 over the vote for 1870. For this sum the country was to have 497,000 men under arms : 135,000 Regulars (of whom 108,000 would be in England), 9,000 First Army Reserve, 30,000 Second Army Reserve and pensioners, 139,000 Militia, 14,000 Yeomanry, and 170,000 Volunteers. The whole of this force was to be unified, and to be controlled by the War Office and the Commander-in-Chief. This process involved two changes of first-rate importance : the transference of the control of the auxiliary forces from the Lord Lieutenants to the Crown, and the abolition of the system by which commissions in the regular army were obtained by purchase. Vested interests were to be safe-guarded ; officers were to receive not only the regulation price they had paid for Commissions, but the additional price sanctioned by long usage. This would involve a sum of £7,000,000 to £8,000,000, but the House of Commons agreed to pay the price.

The Lords, however, accepted an amendment declining to give a second Reading to the Army Regulation Bill until they had before them the complete plan of Army reorganization. Avoiding a direct affirmation in favour of an intolerable abuse, the Lords had never-theless scotched the Government scheme. But they had not killed it. They had not reckoned on the constitutional (or unconstitutional) resourcefulness of the Prime Minister.

Mr. Gladstone met the action of the Lords by a startling *coup d'état*. On July 20th simultaneous statements were made by the Leaders of the two Houses that the Government had advised the Queen to " take the decisive step of cancelling the Royal Warrant by which purchase is legal " ; that her Majesty had agreed to sign a warrant to that effect, and that on November 1st, 1871, " purchase " would cease to exist. Meanwhile, Parliament would be invited to proceed with the compensation scheme contained in the Army Bill. The Bill duly became law, but the Lords in assenting to the second Reading added a resolution that the conduct of the Government was " calculated to depreciate and neutralize the independent action of the Legislature, and was strongly to be condemned ". *The Royal Warrant of July 20th, 1871*

That the Ministers were technically within their legal rights is undeniable ; equally undeniable is it that their use of executive authority was to the last degree daring, if not dangerous. That their action should have aroused intense excitement was only according to expectation. Mr. Disraeli denounced it as " part of an avowed and shameful conspiracy against the undoubted privileges of the other House of Parliament ". Others deprecated such a distorted abuse of the Royal Prerogative. Technically, however, the action involved neither the abuse nor the use of the *Prerogative*, as both

Lord Granville and Mr. Gladstone were careful to insist. This particular power of the Crown was statutory, action being taken under the provisions of 49 George III. c. 126. Nevertheless, as Mr. Freeman, the Constitutional historian said, " the thing had an ill look. . . . Mr. Gladstone had two courses before him : he might abolish purchase by a Royal Warrant—that is by using the discretion which Parliament had given to the Crown ; or he might bring a Bill into Parliament . . . what gave the thing an ill look was that, having chosen the second way and not being able to carry his point that way, he then fell back on the first way." " I believe," he added with shrewd insight, " that this is one of those cases in which a strictly conscientious man like Mr. Gladstone does things from which a less conscientious man would shrink ".[1]

Short service

Not less important than the change in the tenure of the officers was that in the enlistment of the men. In 1829 the principle of enlistment for life had been for the first time adopted. Recruits were, on these terms, difficult to get. A large portion of them " were obtained through the lying stories of recruiting sergeants poured into the ears of country yokels befuddled with drink. In fact they were to a large extent nothing more nor less than kidnapped." [2] In 1847 the term of enlistment was reduced to twelve years, in the first instance, but men were encouraged to re-enlist for a further period of nine years or even longer. The result was, naturally, a great deficiency of Reserves. This deficiency Mr. Cardwell attempted to supply by continuing enlistment for twelve years, six of which were to be spent with the colours,[3] and six in a special Reserve. Soldiers with the colours were to be taught a trade, and reservists were to receive fourpence a day. The scheme has proved a great success : a better class of men certainly was attracted to the ranks, and the reservists, whenever called upon to mobilize, responded with alacrity and enthusiasm. Another part of Cardwell's scheme was to evoke local patriotism by associating each regiment with a territorial district. The country was divided into districts, from each of which there was to be raised a regiment of the line, consisting of two " linked " battalions, one serving at home, the other abroad, while the Militia and the Volunteers were to be brought into close relation with the regular battalions. This portion of Cardwell's scheme proved only partially successful, but it cannot be denied that for the first time a great Army administrator had attempted to work out a far-sighted and comprehensive scheme, and with unusual persistence and skill to adapt limited means to illimitable ends.

[1] *Pall Mall Gazette*, February 12th, 1874, quoted by Morley, ii. 365 ; *cf.* also Selborne, *Memorials*, ii. 192. Sir Roundell Palmer's opinion expressed in a letter (which was read in the House of Commons) to Mr. Cardwell coincided precisely with Freeman's.

[2] Lord Wolseley ap. Ward's *Queen Victoria*, i. 163.

[3] Men might enlist in the line for three years.

The lot of an Army reformer is not a happy one. In military <sub/>Temper-<sub/>ance reform circles there was hardly a good word for the War Minister. Yet Mr. Cardwell achieved the most brilliant success of the session of 1871, though he achieved it at the cost of alienating a powerful section of society. The Home Secretary, Mr. Bruce, alienated another section even more powerful, and without anything to show for it. For the licensed victuallers, while not less articulate in their opposition than the colonels, were far more successful. The cause of their agitation was the abortive Licensing Bill of 1871. The Bill proposed that existing licensees should, subject to good conduct and the payment of a small annual sum, remain undisturbed for ten years. At the termination of that period, the magistrates were to determine the number of public-houses required for a district, put the privilege of conducting them up to auction, and apply the proceeds to the maintenance of a special public-house police force and other purposes for the benefit of the district. The Bill which was not very wisely conceived, seriously alarmed the " trade," and did not evoke enthusiasm among ardent temperance reformers. It had little hold on life and perished prematurely. A much more modest measure was placed upon the Statute-book in 1872. Public-houses were to be closed at twelve o'clock in London, and at eleven o'clock in the country, unless the Justices in the latter case fixed another time between ten o'clock and midnight, and during certain hours on Sundays. The Act also contained provisions to secure the purity of the liquor sold. But though modest it was not popular, and, taken in conjunction with its abortive predecessor, aroused against the Government the suspicious hostility of a powerful class.

The hostility of another class was aroused by Mr. Goschen's Bill for the reform of Local Government and the readjustment of local rates. The main feature of the Bill was the immediate transference of half the local rates from the occupier to the owner, but as it failed even to reach a second Reading the details need not detain us.

More serious for the prestige of the Ministry than the abandon-Lowe's ment of the legislative projects of Mr. Bruce and Mr. Goschen was Budgets the defeat sustained by the Chancellor of the Exchequer in regard to his proposed match tax. Lowe was a purist, not to say a pedant, in finance, but down to 1871 he had been, for so clever a man, unexpectedly successful at the Exchequer. In 1869 he had been able, by an ingenious alteration in the date of payment, to take a penny off the income tax, and had largely reduced the taxes on locomotion. He had also, with characteristic pedantry, abolished the one shilling registration duty on imported corn. The tax brought in nearly a million a year and hurt nobody. In 1870, thanks to diminished expenditure on armaments, he had taken a further penny off the income tax, thus reducing it to fourpence ; he had reduced the sugar duty by 50 per cent., and had abolished the newspaper stamp and the duty on railway passengers. But in 1871 fortune deserted him. Cardwell wanted an extra three millions for the Army, and this Lowe proposed to raise in three ways : by a complicated readjustment of the income tax, which would have increased the rate by slightly more than 1¼d. in the £ ; by an increase in the Probate and Succession Duties ; and by a small tax on matches—*ex luce lucellum*. All these proposals were unpopular, and the last raised an agitation out of all proportion to the intrinsic importance of the proposal. The Cabinet gave way ; all Mr. Lowe's over-ingenious devices were abandoned, and an extra 2d. on the income tax provided in hum-drum fashion for the estimated deficit. The 2d. came off again in 1872, and a third penny in 1873, but Mr. Lowe never recovered his prestige. In 1873 an administrative scandal [1] brought his own career at the Exchequer to an abrupt and inglorious close, and still further damaged the credit of the Cabinet in which he continued to sit as Home Secretary.

Unpopularity of the Ministry
Long before 1873, however, the tide had begun to turn against the Liberal Government. Their appetite for legislation had been prodigious, and the digestion of the country proved to be less robust than their own. Apart from the larger Statutes already described, there stands to the credit of their industry a long list of useful measures : The Trades Union Act of 1871 ; the Mines Act of 1872 ; the Extradition Act, the Naturalization Act, and the Foreign Enlistment Act—all part of the copious crop of 1870, and the Bank Holiday Act of 1871, the credit for which belongs, however, not to the Ministry but to one who attained eminence as a banker, a man of science, a social philosopher, and a legislator, Sir John Lubbock, afterwards Lord Avebury.

Ballot Act
To the above list must be added two other Acts of considerable importance—the Ballot Act of 1872 and the Judicature Act of 1873. " Vote by Ballot " had formed a part of the programme of the Society for Constitutional Information in 1780 ; the demand reappeared in a " Declaration of Rights " drafted in 1831, and again in the People's Charter in 1837 ; but there was a strong prejudice—not confined to Conservative politicians—against the principle of secret voting, and not until after the Election of 1868 did it become a question of practical politics. A Committee was appointed in 1869 to enquire into the whole subject of the conduct of parliamentary elections, and in 1870 Lord Hartington introduced a Bill to abolish public nomination and to establish secret voting. Withdrawn in 1870, an amended Bill was passed through the Commons in 1871. In the meantime an argument from experience had been furnished by the first election for the London School Board, which was elected by ballot. But the Lords, exacerbated by the Royal Warrant on Army Purchase, contemptuously rejected the Bill.

---

[1] Needless to state that Lowe was not personally involved.

Their attitude stiffened the back of Mr. Gladstone, hitherto luke-warm about the ballot, and in September, 1871, he declared that " the people's Bill has been passed by the people's House, and when it was next presented at the door of the House of Lords it would be with an authoritative knock ".[1] In 1872 the Lords gave way ; the Ballot Bill became law, but without the just and valuable provision contained in the original Bill of 1871, by which the expenses of parliamentary elections would have been thrown upon the rates.

The most important legislative achievement of the session of 1873 was an Act for the reorganization and simplification of the work of the Judicature. This was due to the initiative of Sir Roundell Palmer who, on the resignation of Lord Hatherley, had become Lord Chancellor and been elevated to the Peerage as Lord Selborne. Down to 1873 the judicial system was chaotic. There existed no less than eight superior Courts of First Instance : the King's (or Queen's) Bench, the Common Pleas, the Court of Exchequer, the Chancery Court, the High Court of Admiralty, the Court of Bank-ruptcy, the Court of Probate, and the Court for Divorce and Matri-monial Cases. Most of these Courts had separate staffs of judges. Lord Selborne's Act of 1873 was the first step in the evolution of order out of the chaos, which, however interesting to the antiquarian, was distracting to litigants, and lamentably wasteful both of time and money. Lord Selborne's Act was amended in 1875, 1876, and 1894, and was supplemented by an important Order in Council of December 16th, 1880. It may conduce to economy of space and to lucidity to omit the chronological details, and summarize the broad results.

In place of the numerous Courts mentioned above, with their varieties of procedure and conflict of jurisdictions, we have now got one Supreme Court of Judicature divided into (1) the High Court of Justice and (2) the Court of Appeal. The former has three divisions : (i) The King's Bench Division which now exercises the jurisdiction formerly exercised by the Courts of King's Bench, Common Pleas, and Exchequer, and the Court of Bankruptcy. The Lord Chief Justice acts as President assisted by a staff of fifteen Judges ; (ii) the Chancery Division under the Lord Chancellor and six other judges ; and (iii) the Probate, Divorce, and Admiralty Division under the President and one other Judge.

The Judges of the High Court act also as Judges of Assize on circuit.

From the High Court (including Courts of Assize) an appeal lies to the Court of Appeal. This Court consists of three ex-officio Judges : the Lord Chancellor, the Lord Chief Justice, and the President of the Probate, Divorce, and Admiralty Division, and six permanent Judges, namely, the Master of the Rolls and five Lords

The Judi-cature Act, 1873

---

[1] Morley, ii. 369.

Justices of Appeal. Finally, from this Court of Appeal, and from the Scotch and Irish Courts, an appeal lies to the House of Lords. In the course of the judicial reforms now under notice the Lords went near to losing their historic rights of Appellate Jurisdiction. By Lord Selborne's Act of 1873 those rights were extinguished and transferred to the new Court of Appeal. Before the Act came into operation, however, the clause relating to the House of Lords was rescinded, and by the Judicature Act of 1876, the Appellate Jurisdiction of the House of Lords was for the first time placed upon a statutory basis. Provision was made for the creation immediately of two, ultimately of four, salaried Law Lords, to be known as Lords of Appeal in Ordinary. Thenceforward no appeal was to be heard unless at least three Lords of Appeal were present ; such Lords including not only the salaried Law Lords but the Chancellor, ex-Chancellors and any other Peers who " hold or have held high judicial office ".[1] The right of lay Peers to take part in the judicial work of their House remains unaffected by the Act of 1876, but it is never exercised.[2]

The Judicial Committee of the Privy Council   The Act of 1876 also effected considerable changes in the Judicial Committee of the Privy Council.[3] The Lords of Appeal in Ordinary, designated primarily for work in the House of Lords, were to act also on the Judicial Committee. At the same time it was provided that the Archbishops and such Bishops as are members of the Privy Council should no longer be members of the Judicial Committee, though they might continue to be summoned as assessors, for the hearing of ecclesiastical appeals. To the same Committee the King may also appoint persons who have served as Indian or Colonial judges. In effect, however, the composition of the Judicial Committee is almost identical with that of the House of Lords sitting in a judicial capacity.[4]

Lord Selborne's Judicature Act, especially as amended later, was an exceedingly valuable instalment of administrative reform. It was not a party measure ; it was hardly a contentious one. Nevertheless, it contributed to an impression which was beginning to prevail that no institution, however venerable, was secure from the hands of the reformer. Ever since 1871 the tide of Government popularity had been unequivocally on the ebb. They had attempted not only to do too much, but to do it too quickly. In a telling phrase, Disraeli charged them with having " legalized confiscation, consecrated

---

[1] By an Act of 1887 the Law Lords (now seven in number) may retain their seats though not their salaries after resignation. They have, therefore, become Life-Peers.

[2] On the Judicature Act of 1873 and amendments, cf. Selborne, *Memorials*, ii. c. xiv., and Marriott, *Second Chambers*, p. 39.

[3] The judicial work of the Council was transferred to a Committee in 1833.

[4] For differences in procedure, cf. Marriott, *English Political Institutions*, p. 301, from which I have here incorporated one or two paragraphs.

sacrilege, and condoned high treason ". This was the criticism of a partisan. But many besides partisans were becoming uneasy. The repose of almost all the comfortable classes had, during the last five years, been rudely disturbed : landlords, churchmen, lawyers, brewers, all felt that the innovator was abroad in the land. And many who approved strongly of the domestic reforms of the Liberal Ministers were dissatisfied by their conduct of foreign affairs. To the latter question we must now turn.

The year 1870-1871 is frequently accounted the zenith of the European Liberal movement of the nineteenth century in England. It cer- politics tainly marked the climax of the century upon the Continent of Europe ; it witnessed the transference of the Italian capital from Florence to Rome and the consummation of Italian Unity ; the consolidation of Germany under a great Federal Empire ; the establishment of the Third Republic in France ; [1] the final assertion of Russian claims in the Black Sea, and the promulgation of the doctrine of Papal Infallibility by the Vatican Council. Such events, even had they stood alone, could not have failed to affect the position of Great Britain in the European economy. The sequel will show that they did not.

With the movement which culminated in the union of north and Italian south Italy under Victor Emmanuel we have already dealt.[2] On Unity February 18th, 1861, a Parliament which was for the first time representative of nearly all parts of Italy assembled at Turin. But the work was still woefully incomplete. In the web of Italian Unity there were still two gaping rents. The Austrians were still in Venetia ; French troops were still protecting the remnant of the Temporal Power in Rome. The mending of both rents modern Italy owes to Bismarck. Early in 1865 the Prussian Ambassador at Florence approached La Marmora, the Italian Minister, with reference to a possible combination of Italy and Prussia against the common enemy, Austria. La Marmora wisely refused to put himself unreservedly into the hands of Prussia, and after the conclusion of the Convention of Gastein (Aug. 14th, 1865), La Marmora sent an envoy to Vienna to sound the Emperor Francis Joseph as to the possibility of an amicable cession of Venetia to Italy. La Marmora offered to pay a large sum of money, and to assume part of the National Debt of Austria. The overture was haughtily declined by the Emperor. His decision at this moment proved to be of crucial importance. Had he accepted La Marmora's terms the whole course of European history might have been changed. The Seven Weeks' War and the Franco-German War might have been almost indefinitely postponed ; Austria might still be a part of Germany, Alsace and Lorraine might

---

[1] Proclaimed in 1870.

[2] *Cf. supra*, pp. 254-258. In the following paragraphs I quote a few sentences from an article of my own contributed to the *Quarterly Review*, No. 431.

still be in the hands of France. The last obstacle in Bismarck's path had in reality been removed.

The meeting at Biarritz
In September, 1865, the Prussian Minister met the French Emperor at Biarritz. The blunt German, regarded by his host as a mere amateur in diplomacy, simply played with the master of intrigue. Bismarck went to Biarritz with two objects : to induce Napoleon to help him to an alliance with Italy, and to secure Napoleon's benevolent neutrality in the coming struggle with Austria. He came away from Biarritz a happy man ; both objects had been attained and he had given in exchange nothing but verbal promises. On April 8th, 1866, Prussia concluded an alliance offensive and defensive with Italy. If within three months Prussia should take up arms for the reform of the Germanic *Bund* Italy undertook to declare war upon Austria. The price of the bargain was the cession of Venetia. Too late the Austrian Emperor perceived the blunder he had committed. At the eleventh hour he made a frantic effort to come to terms with Victor Emmanuel on the basis of the cession of Venetia ; but Italy had given Austria her chance ; she had now made her bargain with Prussia, and to that bargain she faithfully adhered.

The Seven Weeks' War
The consequence was that in the Seven Weeks' War Austria had not one enemy to confront, but two. The triumph of Prussian arms was so rapid and complete that Bismarck might have done without Italy. But in matters of moment he left nothing to chance. Italy reaped no glory from the war, but she got her price—Venetia—from the Peace. There remained only Rome.

Cavour had declared that " without Rome for a capital, Italy can never be firmly united ". But Cavour had appreciated the diplomatic difficulties ; Garibaldi and Mazzini never did. To them the remnant of the Temporal Power seemed like a spear-point embedded in a living body. Flouting all the worldly wisdom of the diplomatists, they had been eager, directly after the conquest of the two Sicilies (1861), to make an assault upon Rome. The story of Garibaldi's generous folly on the one side, and on the other that of the blunders of the Italian Government, deprived of the statesmanship of Cavour,[1] need not be re-told. Enough to say that with the opening of the Franco-German War in 1870 the long-drawn agony was ended. If Austria was obstinate in 1865, Napoleon was demented in 1870. On the eve of the Franco-German War he refused to abandon the cause of the Pope. " Better the Prussians at Paris than the Piedmontese in Rome," the Empress is reported to have said.[2] But the dilemma was fallacious. On August 19th the last French soldiers left Civita Vecchia. A month later (Sept. 20th) the Italians, beating down the weak resistance of the Pope's troops, entered Rome, and the Italian tri-colour floated from the Capitol. The Pope still refused to come to terms with Victor Emmanuel ; a

[1] Died 1861. [2] Bolton King, *Italy*, ii. 372.

plébiscite declared in favour of annexation ; on June 2nd, 1871, the King made his triumphal entry into his new capital, and on November 27th a Parliament, representative for the first time of every part of Italy, was opened in Rome. At last Italy was one.

Before Victor Emmanuel had entered Rome, the Second French Empire had ceased to be, and King William I. of Prussia had been proclaimed first German Emperor in the Hall of Mirrors in the Palace of Versailles. The immediate antecedents of these astounding events demand a brief note. " It is France," said Marshal Randon, " which has been conquered at Sadowa." It was true. The rapidity and completeness of the Prussian victories entirely upset the calculations of Napoleon, and his diplomacy between 1866 and 1870 was marked by a series of blunders, each of which served only to draw him more tightly into the coils prepared for him by Bismarck. The latter prepared grimly for the next step in his carefully premeditated diplomacy. So far back as 1866 he had avowed his conviction " that a war with France would succeed the war with Austria lay in the logic of history," and that such a war was a necessary preliminary to the construction of a United Germany. The Franco-German War

Napoleon also believed war to be inevitable ; the Empress believed it to be essential to the maintenance of the dynasty, and held that if war had to come the sooner the better for France. Napoleon's health was failing and he knew that the military strength of Prussia was increasing much faster than that of France.[1] Feverishly he sought alliances with Austria, with Italy, with Russia. The negotiations with Austria had gone far, but the Roman entanglement impeded negotiations with Italy, and when the war-cloud burst France was still without allies.

By 1869 Bismarck was ready, but he was anxious that the offensive should come from France. He found (or rather made) his opportunity in the Hohenzollern candidature for the throne of Spain. Having got rid of their disreputable Queen Isabella, the Spaniards in 1869 declared for a Constitutional Monarchy, and Bismarck contrived that the throne should be offered to a cadet of the Prussian House, Prince Leopold of Hohenzollern-Sigmaringen. Prince Leopold hung back ; but in 1870 £50,000 of Prussian bonds were transferred to Madrid.[2] The offer was renewed and on July 4th was accepted. The Hohenzollern candidature for the Spanish throne

It was perfectly well known in Berlin that Prince Leopold's acceptance of the Crown of Spain would be regarded as a *casus belli* by Napoleon, and on July 4th the latter sent a formal intimation to this effect. On July 12th Prince Leopold, at his own instance, withdrew his candidature and Bismarck's diplomatic structure tottered. Once more war seemed to have been averted. The

---

[1] *Cf.* Acton, *Historical Essays*, pp. 206 *seq.*
[2] *Cf.* Acton (p. 214), who knew the banker through whom the transaction was effected.

French Prime Minister M. Ollivier declared that the crisis was over, but there were at least two people in France who were not less eager for war than Bismarck himself. France, therefore, with incredible folly, required that the King of Prussia should not merely express his formal approval of Leopold's revocation, but should also promise " that he would not again authorize his candidature ". This insolent demand was presented to the Prussian King at Ems by Benedetti the French Ambassador (July 13th). The King courteously declined to go beyond his approval of the revocation, and as Benedetti was importunate sent him word through an *aide-de-camp* that he had nothing further to say to the Ambassador. The King telegraphed the news to Bismarck at Berlin and left it to his Minister to decide whether it should be communicated to the diplomatists and to the Press.

The "forged" telegram   Bismarck's opportunity had come. He took brief counsel with Moltke and Roon and showed them the telegram he had prepared for publication. " You have converted," said Moltke, " surrender into defiance." He had ; but to describe his telegram as " forged ", is an abuse of language. The terms in which he communicated his master's message to the Ambassadors and to the Press were deliberately designed to inflame passions both in Paris and Berlin. His object was attained. The Parisian populace demanded war, and the Empress Eugénie and the Duc de Gramont pressed it upon the Emperor and a reluctant Cabinet. Napoleon was not ready and he knew it. But on July 14th the French Cabinet by a majority of one vote decided on war. The French declaration reached Berlin on July 19th. With consummate adroitness Bismarck had exhibited France in the eyes of Europe as a wanton aggressor.

England and the Franco-German War   The rapid sequence of events took the English Cabinet completely by surprise.[1] The Prime Minister was absorbed in other matters, and the one member of his Cabinet who might have intervened with effect to avert war passed away on June 27th. Lord Clarendon was one of the safest, if not one of the most brilliant, Foreign Secretaries of the nineteenth century, and his death at this critical moment was an irreparable loss both to England and to Europe. His successor was Lord Granville, who received the seals of the Foreign Office on July 6th—on the same day that France publicly declared that she could not permit a foreign State to disturb the balance of power by placing one of her princes on the " throne of Charles V ". On the previous day Lord Granville had been informed by Mr. (afterwards Lord) Hammond, Under-Secretary at the Foreign Office, that, with the exception of the trouble caused by " the recent murder of British subjects by brigands in Greece, he had never, during his long experi-

---

[1] This statement perhaps requires modification in view of the correspondence between Lord Lyons and Lord Clarendon printed ap. Lord Newton's *Lord Lyons*, i., c. vi., vii.

ence, known so great a lull in foreign affairs ".[1] Within twenty-four hours Lord Granville was immersed in a desperate effort to keep the peace of Europe.

That effort was, of course, abortive. On July 20th Bavaria decided to join Prussia. The adhesion of South Germany not only added 150,000 men to the forces at the disposal of Prussia, but shut the door in the face of France. Within three weeks Roon had poured 500,000 troops into France, and had another 500,000 ready to start.

On August 2nd the war began. Exactly a month later (Sept 2nd), Napoleon surrendered to the King of Prussia at Sedan. The Emperor himself and 80,000 Frenchmen became prisoners of war. The first phase of the war had ended in a splendid triumph for the German arms.

The military débacle was immediately followed by a political revolution. The Empire collapsed ; a Republic was proclaimed (Sept. 4th), and the Empress fled to England. A Government of National Defence was hastily formed under Jules Favre, Gambetta, and General Trochu, the Governor of Paris. M. Favre declared that the Republic would not yield " a stone of a French fortress nor an inch of French soil ". This valorous declaration did not facilitate the conclusion of peace. The siege of Paris began on September 20th and, despite the desperate efforts of Gambetta to relieve it, the capital surrendered on January 28th, 1871. The Germans then granted an armistice to allow the election of a National Assembly which met at Bordeaux (Feb. 12th) and elected the veteran states-man, Thiers, head of the State. Preliminaries of peace were signed in February, and finally ratified at Frankfort on May 10th. France was compelled to cede to Germany the whole of Alsace (except Belfort) and Eastern Lorraine, together with the great fortresses of Metz and Strasburg, and to pay the vast indemnity of five milliards of francs within three years. Until the indemnity was paid German troops were to remain in occupation of the French fortresses. Lord Granville, as we have seen, had made every effort to avert war. When it was declared he announced and observed complete neutrality. By both parties, however, his attitude was suspected.

English opinion was at first profoundly hostile to France, who was regarded as the wanton disturber of European peace. These feelings were still further inflamed when, on July 25th, *The Times* published the text of a draft Treaty, which it was alleged had been submitted on behalf of the Emperor Napoleon to Bismarck in 1866. It virtually provided for the absorption of Belgium by France. Bismarck himself communicated the Treaty, from obvious motives, to *The Times*, and followed up the startling disclosure by an elaborate vindication of his own virtue. The French Government repudiated Bismarck's account of the matter, and the Emperor himself declared

The attitude of England

---

[1] Fitzmaurice, *Granville*, ii. 32, 33.

from his camp at Metz that it was Bismarck who offered him Belgium and that he had refused it.[1]

Whatever the truth as to the original transaction it was not easy to justify Bismarck's disclosure, nor the moment selected for it.

But the diplomatic controversy that ensued was not without advantage to Great Britain. It rendered both Prussia and France eager to assent to Lord Granville's suggestion that the Treaty of 1839, guaranteeing the integrity of Belgium, should be renewed, and in terms even more rigorous and specific. This revised treaty was signed on August 9th and, shortly afterwards, the terms were extended to include Luxemburg.

Meanwhile, no diplomatic assurances sufficed to convince Prussia that the neutrality of England was otherwise than malevolent towards her. " The English are more hated at this moment than the French, and Lord Granville more than Benedetti." Thus the Crown Princess wrote from Berlin to the Queen on August 9th, 1870.[2] At this moment there was no justification for these sentiments. A month later there was. After the fall of the Empire public opinion in England veered round in favour of the defeated combatant. On September 21st the Queen telegraphed to King William to express the hope that he would make peace " in a generous spirit ". Lord Granville sent a special envoy to the German head-quarters to persuade Bismarck to meet Jules Favre. The King and his Chancellor were equally unyielding. France was beaten and Germany must make herself secure, if possible, for all time. On September 13th M. Thiers arrived in London to beg Lord Granville to initiate a movement for European mediation on behalf of France. The English Minister received him cordially but sent him away empty. Nothing short of armed intervention, proposed to the combatants by all the great neutral powers acting in concert, would, as Lord Granville conceived, have been of the least avail. France, however, was convinced that England might have done more. Prussia thought that she ought to have done less. What chance there was of concerted action among the neutrals the next move in the diplomatic game will show.

Russia and the Black Sea

In October, 1870, Prince Gortschakoff addressed to the Powers a circular denouncing on behalf of Russia the Black Sea clauses of the Treaty of Paris (1856). Article XI. of that Treaty declared : " The Black Sea is neutralized ; its waters and its ports thrown open to the mercantile marine of every nation are formally and in perpetuity interdicted to the flag of war, either of the Powers possessing its coasts or of any other Power ". Certain unimportant exceptions were made by Articles XIX. and XX., but by Article XIII. the Czar and the Sultan engaged " not to establish or maintain upon that coast any military-maritime arsenal ". These were the famous

---

[1] Fitzmaurice, ii. 41.   [2] *Ibid.* 38.

articles which Russia now seized the opportunity, by her sole and individual action, to denounce. The step, if not actually suggested, was certainly approved beforehand by Bismarck. Nor was it really unexpected. Russia had long chafed under the restrictions, and it was reasonably certain that she would take the first chance of escaping from them. Gortschakoff cynically referred to the " infringements to which most European transactions have been latterly exposed, and in the face of which it would be difficult to maintain that the written law . . . retains the moral validity which it may have possessed at other times ". In plain English, the Czar saw no reason why he should observe treaties when other people broke them.

It ought not to escape notice that both for Russia and Great Britain the question of naval power in the Black Sea had acquired a new significance by the recent (1869) opening of the canal across the Isthmus of Suez. Even yet, perhaps, the world has hardly realized the profound influence that event is destined to exercise upon *Welt politik*. It certainly was not realized in 1870. Virtually, however, there were but two courses open to Great Britain : to acquiesce in the bold and cynical action of the Czar, or, without allies, to fight him. To declare war upon Russia, at this juncture, would be to provoke the Armageddon which England was using all her endeavours to avert. And was the game worth the candle ? Lord Derby said that " he would fight for the neutrality of Egypt, but not for the neutrality of the Black Sea ".[1] And he expressed the best opinion on the subject. In face of it, Lord Granville had no option but to get out of a disagreeable business with as little loss of prestige as possible. Bismarck was induced to invite the Great Powers to a conference to discuss the questions raised by Prince Gortschakoff's circular. Great Britain assented on condition that the conference met not at St. Petersburg but in London, and that it should not assume " any portion of the Treaty to have been abrogated by the discretion of a single Power ". This may be regarded as solemn farce ; the conclusion was foregone ; but it was making the best of a bad job. The conference met in London in December, and Lord Granville got all the satisfaction he could out of a solemn protocol, declaring it to be " an essential principle of the law of nations that no Power can liberate itself from the engagements of a Treaty . . . unless with the consent of the contracting Powers by means of an amicable arrangement ". For the rest, Russia got what she wanted : the modification of the Treaty of Paris was duly recorded in the Treaty of London (March 13th, 1871).[2]

That English prestige suffered from the tearing up of the Treaty of Paris can hardly be denied. But a still more difficult question *The Alabama Arbitration*

---

[1] Odo Russell to Granville ap. Fitzmaurice, ii. 72.
[2] *Cf.* Holland, *European Concert in the Eastern Question* (with texts in full), p. 272.

23

awaited solution. Ever since the American Civil War relations between Great Britain and the United States had been severely strained. Neither party to the war was satisfied with our attitude. The North regarded our neutrality as rather more than malevolent, the South thought it inadequately benevolent. More specifically, there was the question of the damage inflicted upon American commerce by the *Alabama* and other cruisers.

On this question the attitude of England had undergone some modification. Lord Russell, the Minister primarily responsible, had repudiated all responsibility, though he lived to make a manly confession that he had been to blame. Lord Clarendon, however, in 1869, concluded a convention which virtually admitted that the damage inflicted by the cruisers upon individuals was a matter for negotiation. But of this the American Senate would not hear. They persisted that between the two nations there was outstanding a national question which demanded speedy settlement. More than this. The most extravagant demands were put forward. Great Britain was to be held responsible not merely for provable damage inflicted upon individuals, but for the actual prolongation of the war and the expenses incidental thereto. These " indirect claims," as they came to be called, were roughly estimated at £400,000,000. Mr. Gladstone himself reckoned that four times that sum would have barely covered them. The Americans doubtless said a great deal more than they meant, but feelings were exceedingly bitter, and war might very easily have ensued but for the extraordinary forbearance and restraint of the English Cabinet and the English Parliament.[1] Early in 1871 the two countries agreed on a joint commission to discuss not only the *Alabama* claims, but all other questions outstanding between them. The English commissioners were Lord de Grey and Ripon,[2] Sir Stafford Northcote, Sir John A. Macdonald (representing Canada), Sir Edward Thornton, Minister at Washington, and Mr. Montagu Bernard, Professor of International Law at Oxford. The Commission opened at Washington on February 27th, and after more than two months of difficult and delicate negotiation the Treaty of Washington was signed. Nothing but great forbearance on the part of Lord de Grey and Ripon and his colleagues could have saved the situation. They proposed that all the questions not decided in the Treaty which they hoped to conclude should be submitted to a body of arbitrators. The Americans insisted that the arbitration should itself be governed by certain new principles of international law, which were to be propounded in the Treaty. Those principles were admittedly not accepted when the *Alabama* had escaped from Liverpool, and the American demand was, therefore,

[1] *Cf.* Gladstone's testimony to the admirable temper displayed by the Opposition, Morley, ii. 408.

[2] Created Marquis of Ripon for his successful conduct of this difficult matter.

illogical. But the Foreign Enlistment Act, passed in England in
1870, had made it a criminal offence to build a ship for use against
a friendly belligerent Power, and the English Commissioners therefore
agreed, as a friendly act, that the Arbitrator should " assume that
Her Majesty's Government had undertaken to act " upon the new
principles. The other ¦chief impediment to an agreement was the
question of the British counter-claims in regard to the Fenian raids
in Canada. But on this point, also, Great Britain gave way.

On May 8th, 1871, the Treaty of Washington—a portentious Treaty of
document consisting of forty-three articles—was signed. It expressed Washing-
" in a friendly spirit the regret felt by Her Majesty's Government ton
for the escape, under whatever circumstances, of the *Alabama* and
other vessels from British ports, and for the depredation committed
by those vessels ". It adjusted in minute detail outstanding disputes
as to fisheries between United States and Canada, and agreed to
refer the question of the Vancouver boundary (involving the possession of the Island of San Juan) to the arbitration of the German
Emperor, who ultimately decided against Great Britain. It accepted
new principles of international law, involving greater diligence in
preventing the equipment of ships in neutral harbours for use against
friendly belligerents, and finally it agreed to refer the *Alabama* claims
themselves to a tribunal of five persons nominated by Great Britain,
the United States, Italy, Switzerland, and Brazil.

One difficult corner had thus been deftly turned : another re- The
mained. The Arbitrators were to meet at Geneva on June 15th, Geneva
1872. The English Arbitrator was Chief Justice Cockburn, and Sir tion
Roundell Palmer acted as Agent or Counsel.[1] At one moment,
however, it seemed doubtful whether the Gevena tribunal would
ever meet. Before the end of 1871 the English Government learnt
that the American " case " insisted upon an adjudication " not only
upon the losses suffered by individual American citizens, but upon
the indirect constructive, consequential, and national claims first
propounded in their full dimensions by Mr. Sumner ".[2] The Government were not only disappointed but deeply incensed at the revival
of this preposterous demand. And none more so than Mr. Gladstone,
who declared that " we must be insane to accede to demands which
no nation with a spark of honour or spirit left would submit to even
at the point of death ". The Cabinet, though with varying degrees
of emphasis, were unanimous against the submission of the indirect
claims.[3] The point had really been slurred at Washington. If the
Americans had insisted on specific inclusion, or the English on specific
exclusion, there would have been no treaty of arbitration. The
moderate men on both sides hoped that they would be ruled out by

[1] One of the best accounts of the Geneva Arbitration may be found in his
Memorials, ii. c. xi.
[2] Morley, *Gladstone*, ii. 406.   [3] Morley, ii. 408.

the arbitrators themselves, and this was precisely what happened at Geneva. That it did happen was due to the high courage, the true dignity a ndperfect tact of one man, whose name should be held in everlasting remembrance, Charles Francis Adams, the American nominee. Thanks to Adams the tribunal met, and in September, 1872, it issued its award. It was unanimously against Great Britain as regards the *Alabama*, and, by a majority, on other claims. The sum awarded for damages, in final settlement, was about £3,250,000. It was " a good deal cheaper than war," was the characteristic comment of Mr. Lowe. Eight years afterwards Mr. Gladstone said : " Although I may think the sentence was harsh in its extent and unjust in its basis, I regard the fine imposed on this country as dust in the balance compared with the moral value of the example set when these two great nations of England and America . . . went in peace and concord before a judicial tribunal rather than resort to the arbitrament of the sword ". It was finely said, and impartial history may applaud the sentiment, but among contemporaries there was an uneasy sense that too many of the kicks had of late fallen to our share. As for the Government, the Geneva Award added another item to its rapidly accumulating burden of unpopularity.

Patronage   The appointment of Sir Robert Collier [1] to be a paid member of the Judicial Committee of the Privy Council, though in itself unexceptionable, was a flagrant violation of the spirit of the recent Act. The Act provided that the paid member should have served on the Bench. Sir Robert never had, but was appointed for a few days a Justice of the Court of Common Pleas, to give him the technical qualification. This was sailing too near the wind, and the Government escaped actual censure in the Lords by only two votes, in the Commons by only twenty-seven. The appointment of a Cambridge Graduate to the Rectory of Ewelme seemed to be another, though less important, violation of law. When the Rectory had been divorced from the Regius Professor of Divinity, it was provided that the Rector should be a member of the Convocation of Oxford.

Resignation of the Gladstone Cabinet   Such things, relatively unimportant in themselves, were not calculated to prop up a tottering Ministry. But the final blow came, perversely, from an Irish measure. Defeated on his Irish University Bill by a majority of three, Mr. Gladstone immediately placed his resignation in the hands of the Queen (March 13th, 1873). The Queen sent for Disraeli, but Disraeli had no desire for another term of office without power, nor did he wish to check the coming Conservative revival by a premature and purposeless dissolution. The pear, he judged in a party sense, was nearly, but not quite, ripe. He judged wisely. Mr. Gladstone resumed office with a very bad grace (March 20th).

[1] Afterwards Lord Monkswell.

A shifting of Cabinet offices did nothing to redeem the popularity The Ash-
of the Ministry,[1] and the credit for the success of a " little war," antee
accrued—justly enough—to the soldiers. A deal with the Dutch War
had lately transferred to Great Britain some forts on the African
Gold Coast. In June, 1873, the native Ashantees, disliking the
change, attacked the Protectorate in force. Sir Garnet Wolseley
was sent out in command of a punitive expedition, penetrated through
the unhealthy jungle to Coomassie, the Ashantee capital, burnt the
palace and town, imposed terms on King Koffee Kalkalee, and returned triumphant. The whole expedition was planned with the
forethought, and executed with the punctuality and success, which
the world had long since associated with the name of its commander.
Before he and his troops returned to England (March, 1874) the
Government which sent them out had fallen.

In January, 1874, Mr. Gladstone had informed the Queen that Fall of
the Cabinet had resolved to advise an immediate dissolution as " the the
best means of putting an end to the disadvantage and weakness of Govern-
a false position ". The position was possibly false ; it was certainly ment
weak, and its weakness was due to many causes in combination ; to
an over-loading and still more an over-weighting of the parliamentary
ship ; to several legislative failures ; to one administrative scandal,[2]
and more than one equivocal use of patronage ; to Cabinet divisions
which not even the high authority of the Premier could wholly
check ; to a sense of lowered prestige abroad and weakened vitality
at home ; to a remarkable series of Government defeats in bye-
elections, above all to the political anti-climax which had ensued on
the defeat of the Ministry in March, 1873. On the top of all this
Gladstone had made up his mind to the greatest financial plunge
of his career at the Exchequer—the abolition of the income tax.
This was no death-bed repentance or hustings' inspiration. But
for the Crimean War, he might have done it nearly twenty years
before. If he could obtain the assistance of Cardwell and Goschen,
now at the head of the two great spending Departments, he believed
himself to be at last in a position to accomplish it. Their help was
doubtful, but the Premier clearly hoped much from an appeal to the
country. " We dissolve," he wrote, " on finance." His programme
as put before the country was threefold : (1) repeal of the income
tax ; (2) relief and readjustment of local taxation ; (3) remission of
taxes on articles of general consumption. It was not for nothing
that Mr. Gladstone had gone back to the Exchequer.

The constituencies, however, refused the bait from Mr. Gladstone The
and they never got another chance of swallowing it. In England General
Election
[1] Lowe was transferred to the Home Office ; Gladstone himself took the Ex- of 1874
cheque. Ripon and Childers retired Bright came back as Chancellor of the
Duchy.
[2] *Re* the application of £800,000 which was applied without authority to the
purchase of telegraphs when it should have gone to the consolidated fund.

the Tories swept the country; even in Scotland and Wales there was some weakening of the Liberal defences; the Home Rulers came fifty-eight strong from Ireland.   In the event, the Tories had a clear majority of over fifty in the House of Commons, reckoning all the Home Rulers as opponents.[1]   Mr. Gladstone attributed his defeat, neither generously nor accurately, to " a torrent of gin and beer," and to the coil of the education controversy.   His colleagues preferred not to await the verdict of Parliament, and against his own judgment he gave way.   On his resignation the Queen sent for Mr. Disraeli.

[1] Other estimates put it eighty-three.   In England and Wales it was 105.— Morley, ii. 491.

CHAPTER XXIII

THE NEW TORYISM. *IMPERIUM ET SANITAS*
(1874-1878)

NOT for a whole generation had the Conservative party been in power. Three times since the great schism of 1846 they had been in office, but always in a minority. Mr. Disraeli was now at the head of a party which commanded not only a large but a compact majority. His success in 1874 was due, primarily perhaps, to the blunders, unpopularity, and internal dissensions of his opponents. But not wholly. It was due partly to a gradual inclination of the mind and instinct of the electorate towards the objects for which modern Conservatism was to stand. Those objects had been in the last few years clearly re-stated and defined by the leader who was now, in the late evening of his days, to reap the tardy reward of patience and sagacity. The Conservative revival

Disraeli was no mere opportunist. No one who takes the trouble to master the political philosophy which permeates his novels can accept that superficial view of his career. Those novels are at least as serious a contribution to political thought as the solemn treatises which Bolingbroke wrote for the instruction of his party in the first half of the eighteenth century. Bolingbroke is accounted the first great educator of the Tory party, and with reason. Compare the Toryism of Filmer with that of the younger Pitt and you have the measure of the influence of Bolingbroke.[1] George III. learnt from the *Patriot King* the principles which he practised until he found a master in Chatham's son. George III. may have been an indifferent King, but he was consummately successful as the reconstructor and leader of a party.[2] Canning, had he lived, might have performed a similar service after 1830, though he was hardly less mistrusted than Bolingbroke. Sir Robert Peel attempted it, but succeeded only in creating the party which bore his name until it was absorbed into the new Liberalism. Disraeli accomplished it; and alike in his novels and in his more elaborate speeches the influence of Bolingbroke is clearly traceable. " The State is become, under ancient and known forms, a new and undefinable monster; composed of a king without monarchical splendour, a Senate of Nobles without aristocratical ascendancy, and a Senate of Commons without democratical freedom." [3] Disraeli might have taken this passage from Bolingbroke as the text of his great discourse at Manchester. The Manchester speech (April 3rd, 1872) followed by one at the Crystal Palace Disraeli and the education of Conservatives

---

[1] *Cf.* Churton Collins's brilliant essay on *Bolingbroke.*

[2] Lord Hugh Cecil lays stress upon this in his *Conservatism* recently published (1912).

[3] *Dissertation on Parties.*

(June 24) may be said to have defined the principles of the New
Toryism and to have prepared the way for the victory at the Polls in
1874.[1] Those speeches demand close attention. In the forefront
Disraeli placed the maintenance of the historic institutions of the
country. His party had been accused of having no programme.
The retort was singularly effective. " If by a programme is meant
a plan to despoil churches and plunder landlords, I admit we have no
programme. If by a programme is meant a policy which assails or
menaces every institution and every interest, every class, and every
calling in the country, I admit we have no programme . . . the programme of the Conservative party is to maintain the Constitution
of the country." [2] In that Constitution Disraeli laid especial stress,
for reasons which will appear presently, on the upholding of the
" ancient Monarchy of England ". The second duty of the party
was to uphold " the Empire of England " ; and the third the elevation
of the social condition of the people. " Sanitas sanitatum omnia
Sanitas," was the text of his discourse at Manchester. Opponents
might deride it as a policy of sewage and shoddy, but " the Constitution, the Empire and Social Reform " represented not merely the
battle-cry of an opportunist, but the carefully considered and
coherent programme of one who aspired not merely to win a transient
victory at the polls, but to refound a party. The response and the
reward came not in the conspicuous yet transitory triumph of 1874,
but in the prolonged ascendancy of his party from 1886 to 1906.

**The new
Cabinet**
Disraeli himself could look forward to no prolonged tenure of
power. He was now seventy years of age, and he had been in
Parliament ever since the Queen came to the throne.[3] He gathered
round him a Cabinet of great business ability. The Foreign Office
was put in the safe and trusted hands of Lord Derby ; Lord Cairns
returned to the Woolsack ; the rebels of 1867 were rewarded with
two Secretaryships of State, Lord Carnarvon taking the Colonies and
Lord Salisbury India ; Sir Stafford Northcote, trained in the Peel-
Gladstone school, became Chancellor of the Exchequer, Mr. Ward
Hunt being transferred to the Admiralty ; Mr. Gathorne-Hardy, a
brilliant fighter, went to the War Office ; the Duke of Richmond led
the Lords as President of the Council ; Lord Malmesbury held the
Privy Seal, and Lord John Manners was Postmaster-General. The
twelfth member of the Cabinet was a recruit, Mr. Richard Assheton
Cross, a shrewd, level-headed Lancashire banker who, like so many
twelfth men, proved himself the success of the team. Sir Michael
Hicks-Beach, a country gentleman of great ability, became Chief
Secretary to the Lord Lieutenant of Ireland (the Duke of Abercorn),
and two other businesslike squires, Sir Charles Adderley and Mr.

---

[1] The new organization devised by Mr. (now Sir John) Gorst must have its
share of credit for the victory : cf. Harold Gorst's *Earl of Beaconsfield*, c. xiii.
[2] *Speeches*, ii. 491.
[3] Elected M.P. for Maidstone, 1837.

Sclater-Booth, presided respectively over the Boards of Trade and Local Government. But the three squires were not included in the Cabinet. Disraeli was determined, like all the best parliamentarians, that his Cabinet should be not a debating society but a consultative Committee and to compass that end he wisely kept it small.

The new Ministry began a little unsteadily, but soon settled down to work. Public interest centred during their first session on three ecclesiastical measures, the most important of which was not technically a Government Bill. Ecclesi-astical legisla-tion

The first was Lord Sandon's Bill for the amendment of the Endowed Schools Act of 1869.[1] Lord Sandon proposed (1) to abolish the Endowed Schools Commission and to transfer its functions to the Charity Commission ; and (2) to restore to the Church of England all schools which, according to the clear intentions of the founder, had been founded in connection with the reformed and Established Church. The Commission had made all schools founded prior to the Act of Uniformity of 1662 undenominational. The intention was to reverse this policy, but the proposal evoked an opposition so strenuous that Disraeli gave way, dropped the second half of the Bill, and contented himself with substituting the Charity Commission for the special Commission set up by the Act of 1869.

A second Bill proposed to abolish lay patronage in the Established Church of Scotland and to transfer it, with some compensation to such lay patrons as were willing to accept it, to the communicant members of the several congregations. This was the very point which had split the Presbyterian Church in twain forty years earlier,[2] and the members of the Free Kirk strongly opposed this concession to their brethren of the Establishment. Mr. Gladstone backed them and urged that such a measure logically involved re-union. But logic was ignored, Mr. Gladstone was over-borne and the Church of Scotland got its Bill. Lay Patron-age Act for Scotland

The turn of the Church of England came next. The Bishops were gravely concerned at the increase of lawlessness among a section of their clergy in regard to the services of the Church and particularly in regard to the celebration of Holy Communion. The Archbishops, therefore, introduced a Bill, infelicitously described as a Bill for the Regulation of Public Worship, but really intended to provide a summary method for the enforcement of the Act of Uniformity. Archbishop Tait was not the man to have moved causelessly in so important and delicate a matter. Indeed so loyal an Anglican as Lord Selborne confessed that it seemed to him impossible to deny that " there had been a considerable growth of innovations upon the Ritual authorized by the Book of Common Prayer not The Pub-lic Wor-ship Regula-tion Act

[1] See *supra*, p 334.
[2] Dating from the beginning of the ten years' conflict.

casual or sporadic, but systematic and with a tendency to increase
and of a nature dangerous to the order and security of the Church,
and that it was equally difficult for the Bishops to repress them
under the powers of the existing law and to leave them uncontrolled
without incurring great responsibility ".[1] Mr. Gladstone took an
opposite line and flung himself with ardour into the defence, as he
conceived it, of ecclesiastical liberty. As originally proposed by the
Archbishop, the Bill provided that judicial powers should be vested
in the Bishop of the diocese assisted by a Board of Assessors, lay
and clerical, with an appeal to the Archbishop, similarly assisted.
To the lay Peers this procedure seemed too ecclesiastical and,
prompted by Lord Shaftesbury, they substituted for the Bishop and
Assessors a special Judge for ecclesiastical causes appointed by the
Archbishops with the approval of the Crown, with an appeal to the
Judicial Committee of the Privy Council ; the Bishop retaining the
right to veto proceedings if they seemed to him frivolous. In the
Commons Disraeli practically adopted the Bill as a Government
measure and commended it to the House as a means for " the suppression of ritualism ". This description infuriated the High
Churchmen with Mr. Gladstone—drawn from semi-retirement—at
their head. The ex Premier tabled an elaborate series of resolutions
hostile to the Bill, but finding the sense of the House against him he
gave way and did not move them. Sir William Harcourt brought
all his Erastian zeal to the support of Disraeli and the Bill became
law. Lord Selborne was sounded as to his willingness to become the
Judge under the Act, but prudently declined the ungrateful task.
Lord Penzance accepted the post and lived to regret it.

Mr. Glad-   His conspicuous failure to avert ecclesiastical legislation which
stone's   was in the highest degree distasteful to him impelled Mr. Gladstone
retire-   to a step already contemplated. He was now sixty-five, wearied and
ment   worried by forty years of politics and six years of Premiership. His
physician, with shrewd insight, declined to encourage his retirement,
but he himself craved for an " interval between Parliament and the
grave ". Directly after his defeat at the polls he had intimated to
his followers that they must not look for continuous leadership from
him. But the " in and out " arrangement proved unsatisfactory
alike to them and to him. His incursions into the ecclesiastical fray
were embarrassing to his party and disappointing to himself. Accordingly, in February, 1875, he formally and definitely withdrew from
the leadership of the Liberal party and Lord Hartington was selected
to succeed him in the House of Commons. His only serious rival
was Mr. Forster, but the Birmingham League still pursued with
rancorous hostility the author of the Education Act and Forster's
claims were not pressed. But although Lord Hartington sat in
Mr. Gladstone's seat the latter looked to Lord Granville as his

_____
[1] *Memorials*, ii. 337.

destined successor in the leadership, as soon as the party should
return to power.

Meanwhile the Tories settled quietly down to a course of unheroic Social
but not the less useful legislation. Of Mr. Cross's Licensing Act of reform
1874 there is not much to be said. After their exaggerated denunciation of Mr. Bruce's Act the " trade " naturally looked to the Tory
party for legislation, but if they were satisfied with the Act of 1874
their expectations cannot have been high. Introduced with the
object of curtailing the discretion of the magistrates and fixing by
legislation the hours of closing in public-houses, its nett result was
to fix 10 P.M. for the country, 11 P.M. for towns or " populous places,"
but to leave it to magistrates to determine what was a " populous
place ".

When the Conservative party came into power in 1874 agriculture Land,
had not begun to fall on the evil days which marked the 'eighties. landlords
But then, as always, it was to the interest of the community that ants
the land of the country, limited as it is in amount, should be put to
the best possible economic use. To this end three things are especially important ; that there should be no artificial restrictions upon
the transfer of real property ; that the title to it should be cheaply
ascertainable and secure, and that every encouragement should be
given alike to owner and occupier to effect improvements. Lord
Cairns's *Leases and Sales of Settled Estates Act* (1875) [1] was intended
to simplify sales and leases and to encourage the registration of titles,
but its permissive character, coupled with the persistent opposition
of family solicitors, rendered it ineffectual. More effective was Lord
Cairns's *Settled Land Act* [2] which did not actually become law until
1882. The object of this Act was to render it possible for a limited
owner to sell his settled estates. Such sales were somewhat discouraged by the condition that the purchase money must be
reinvested for the benefit of the reversioner, but the Act has
undeniably facilitated a free market in land.

The Duke of Richmond's *Agricultural Holdings Act* of 1875 was
intended to give security to tenants for capital invested in the soil.
The chief objection urged against the Bill was that its provisions
were not made compulsory. Yet there is a great deal to be said for
making legislation of this character experimentally permissive, and
it is an argument not against but in favour of the ability of the
measure of 1875, to recall the fact that in 1883 it was found desirable
to strengthen its provisions and make compensation for improvements compulsory.

An *Enclosure of Commons Act* [3] passed in 1876 was of even wider
import. Previous Acts on the subjects while promoting cultivation
and providing for the compensation of " commoners " had ignored

---

[1] 37 and 38 Vict. c. 33.   [2] 45 and 46 Vict. c. 38.
[3] 45 and 46 Vict. c. 38.

the substantial though intangible interests of the public at large. It was the object of Mr. Cross's Act, while consolidating and simplifying the existing Acts, to remedy this defect. " They must," said Mr. Cross, " take into consideration that which the people of this country wanted almost as much as food—the air which they breathed and the health they enjoyed." His Bill, therefore, was intended less to facilitate enclosure than preserve Commons as open spaces in the interests of the community in general.

Another Act affecting the agricultural interest in particular, but hardly less vitally the community at large, was the *Contagious Diseases (Animals) Act* of 1878. The Act provided that all cattle should be slaughtered on landing from foreign countries, unless the country of export were known to be free from cattle disease. The extreme Free Traders scented " Protection " in the measure, but the agriculturists argued, with reason, that it was useless to take stringent and expensive precautions against the spread of infection at home, so long as diseased cattle could be imported from infected areas abroad.

Factory Acts

The solicitude of the Government was not, however, confined to rural interests and pursuits. During his career at the Home Office Mr. Cross succeeded in placing on the Statute-book two valuable measures for the further regulation of the work of women and children in factories and workshops. The Act of 1877 further reduced the hours of labour in factories, not without some protest from Mr. Henry Fawcett and other apostles of *laissez-faire*, and increased the responsibilities of inspectors.

The *Factory and Workshops Act* of 1878 was primarily a great work of codification and consolidation, totally repealing no less than sixteen Acts on the same subject, with parts of others. But it had also noticeable features of its own. It remedied a defect in the Act of 1871 by bringing the inspectorate once more under the control of the central authority. It absolutely prohibited the employment of any child under ten years of age, and limited other " children " to " half-time ". For women it fixed a maximum of 56½ hours' work per week in textile factories, and 60 hours in non-textile, and provided that no woman should be employed continuously for more than 4½ hours in the former, and 5 in the latter. It was this monumental piece of legislation which called forth from Lord Shaftesbury the declaration that " two millions of people of this country would bless the day when Mr. Cross was asked to be Secretary of State for the Home Department ". But the indefatigable Minister was determined to earn the gratitude not of two millions, but of twenty. From the regulation of the conditions of industry, he passed to the conditions of home-life.

The housing problem

Mr. Cross's *Artisans' Dwellings Acts* of 1875 was the first serious attempt on the part of the Imperial Parliament to grapple with the problem of the housing of the poor. Glasgow and Edinburgh [1] had proved what could be done by a local authority to clear insanitary areas and provide decent dwellings for the poor. Mr. Peabody and Sir Sydney Waterlow had shown what could be done by wealthy and enlightened individuals. It was left to a Conservative Home Secretary to invoke the heavy hand of the Imperial Legislature. Every local authority was required to appoint a medical officer of health and an inspector of nuisances.[2] On the report of the medical officer the authority was empowered to acquire compulsorily an insanitary area at its ordinary value, to demolish the buildings thereon, and either itself erect improved dwellings, or dispose of the site to those who undertook to do so. The Act was, in the first instance, confined to London and large towns, and local authorities were only empowered not compelled to act, but even so, the Act was an important instalment of the policy of " sewage ".

More significant, perhaps, but still in accord with general Con- Labour servative tradition, and with the principles recently enunciated by legisla- Disraeli was the labour legislation of 1875-1876. Three Acts, in 1875-1876 particular, deserve notice in this connection, though they may be conveniently considered together : the *Conspiracy and Protection of Property Act* (1875) ; the *Employers and Workmen Act* (1875), and the *Trades Union Act* (1876). Taken in conjunction with the *Trades Union Act* of 1871 passed by Mr. Gladstone's Government, these Acts constitute such a remarkable reversal of public policy as to demand a brief retrospect.

Down to the year 1871 Trades Unions had no legal existence or status. Brought into being by the sharp differentiation of industrial functions, and the still sharper antagonism of economic interests, which were the first and least fortunate results of the Industrial Revolution, these associations of workmen were frowned upon by the legislature.[3] The Common Law held all such combinations illegal as " conspiracies in restraint of trade," and to the Common Law were added innumerable Statutes passed by Parliament to prevent their formation. Under the law as it existed at the beginning of the nineteenth century " any artisan who organized a strike or joined a Trades Union was a criminal, and liable on conviction to imprisonment ; the strike was a crime, the Trade Union was an unlawful association ".[4] In 1824, however, a Royal Commission reported strongly against the Combination Laws as both ineffective and mischievous, and by an Act of that year they were repealed *en bloc*—alike for masters and men. The immediate consequences were so alarming that in 1825 the old law of conspiracy was reaffirmed, but

[1] By Private Acts, 1866 and 1867.
[2] Under the Public Health Act.
[3] There were many embryo Unions before the nineteenth century, but the statement in the text is nevertheless accurate.
[4] Dicey, *Law and Public Opinion*, p. 98.

a limited right of combination was permitted. The broad result
was that Trades Unions ceased to be necessarily criminal, but they
remained non-legal associations. Consequently their funds, unpro-
tected by the provisions of the Friendly Societies Act of 1855, were
at the mercy of any dishonest official. Despite this grave disadvantage, Trades Unions multiplied rapidly between 1825 and 1860.
Popular attention was first directed to this new Labour movement
in the year 1866 by the outrages committed by members of these
associations in Manchester, Sheffield, and other industrial centres.
These disturbances led to the appointment of a Royal Commission,
on whose report the legislation of 1871-1876 was largely based.

Trade Union legislation, 1871-1876

These Acts form the Charter of Trade Unionism. They not only
gave to Trade Union funds the benefit of the Friendly Societies Acts,
but relieved them, as was supposed, from liability to damages for
the tortious acts of agents. They legalized picketing so long as it
stopped short of violence or intimidation, and they placed Trades
Unions in a position of legal privilege by mitigating the law of conspiracy in their favour. Mr. Cross's Act of 1875 enacted that " an
agreement or combination by two or more persons to do or procure
to be done any act in contemplation or furtherance of a trade dispute
between employers and workmen shall not be indictable as a conspiracy, if such act committed by one person would not be punishable as a crime ". Thus combinations in furtherance of trade
disputes are legally privileged. Such was the effect and such doubtless
the intention of Mr. Cross's legislation. How far the State had
travelled since 1825, still more since 1800, it is not necessary to insist.[1]

Friendly Societies Act

Another item in the plentiful crop of 1875 deserves a passing
notice. The Chancellor of the Exchequer had presided over a
Commission appointed by the late Government to enquire into the
position of the Friendly Societies. The Commission found that
many of the Societies suffered from incompetent and some of them
from fraudulent management. The object of the Bill passed into
law by Sir Stafford Northcote was less to improve the Friendly
Societies than to encourage and help them to improve themselves.
Registration, though not made compulsory, was facilitated and
encouraged ; model tables of contributions and benefits were to be
prepared by the Government and issued to societies which desired
them ; additional facilities were given for adult and the periodical
re-valuation of assets. *The Times* described the Bill as " modest if
not timid ". But Northcote insisted that its tentative and permissive character was due not to timidity but to " a deliberate view
that the only and true way of bringing about a development of the
virtue of providence amongst the people was to make them work it
out for themselves, and that one great desire ought to be to give
fair play and full play to those institutions which have sprung from

[1] For a luminous discussion of the question *cf.* Dicey, *op. cit.* pp. 266-271.

the people themselves ".[1]   The sentiment is admirable, but it is of
the kind to appeal rather to responsible statesmen than to enthusiastic philanthropists.

It was the zeal of one such philanthropist which drove the Merchant
Government to deal with some of the more obtrusive scandals con- Shipping
nected with Merchant Shipping.   For some years Mr. Plimsoll, one
of the members for Derby, had been trying to attract the attention
of Parliament and the public to the sacrifice of life caused by un-
seaworthy, overloaded and over-insured ships.   A Royal Commission
was appointed to enquire into the matter, and on its Report the
Government in 1875 decided to legislate.   The session of 1875 was
however, a crowded one, and on July 22nd Disraeli announced that
he was regretfully compelled to drop the Merchant Shipping Bill
with a view to early legislation in the following year.   Thereupon
Mr. Plimsoll, moved, as every one realized, by generous but uncon-
trollable indignation, provoked a violent scene in the House.   He
declared that the action or inaction of the Government would
" consign some thousands of living human beings to undeserved and
miserable death," and declared his intention to " unmask the villains
who send men to death and destruction ".   Refusing to withdraw,
Mr. Plimsoll was reported to the House, but its leader readily consented, on the appeal of a sympathetic Irish member, to defer his
motion of censure for a week.   At the close of that time Mr. Plimsoll
tendered an ample apology.   He could afford to do so.   The battle
which he had fought so strenuously was won.   During the week's
interval, public opinion had manifested itself with unprecedented
force in his favour.   The Government, wisely bowing before the
storm, introduced and passed as a temporary measure the Unsea-
worthy Ships Act giving to the Board of Trade powers as to the
detention of ships, but throwing upon the shipowners the responsibility of fixing a loadline for each separate voyage.

The *Merchant Shipping Act* of 1876 incorporated, enlarged, and
rendered permanent the provisions of the temporary Act of 1875.
Plimsoll was anxious that the Board of Trade should fix the loadline
for each ship.   The Government, however, was firm in adherence
to the principle asserted in the temporary Act, and left the responsibility to the owners.

Of set purpose, a catalogic summary of legislation has been General
inflicted upon the reader.   Even so the summary is not exhaustive, character
but it may serve to indicate the general character of the work ac- tic legis-
complished in the domestic sphere by Disraeli's second Administra- lation of
tion.   Few Governments have earned a better record.   It is true the Tory
that critics of a later day, accustomed to bolder departures from the ment
principle of *laisser-faire*, are apt to deride the legislation of these
years as halting and indecisive, maimed by a too tender regard for

[1] Speech at Manchester ap. Lang, *Iddesleigh*, p. 252.

vested interests and the rights of individuals, and vitiated by reluctance to confer upon public authorities compulsory powers. Even if
it be admitted that the latter is the better way, it does not follow that
the former was not good in itself and at the time the best possible.
The legislative and administrative achievements of the first three
years of the Disraeli Government generously fulfilled, not the specific
promises, for these were notably absent, but the general spirit of the
programme laid before the electorate by the Tory leader.

Sir Staf-
ford
North-
cote's fin-
ance

It is not, however, for its legislation that Disraeli's régime is held
in remembrance. Nor even for its finance. The new Chancellor of
the Exchequer was a cautious and unimaginative man ; he succeeded
to a surplus of £6,000,000 and to a period of retrenchment and
prosperity. It was no fault of his that he had to provide for
increased expenditure out of a contracting revenue. His first
Budget (1874) called for no ingenuity. He had merely to spend his
predecessor's surplus. He did it by taking 1d. off the income tax
—thus reducing it to the lowest figure—2d.—at which it ever stood ;
he repealed the sugar duties and the tax on houses, and he made a
wise readjustment of the finance of the Post Office Savings Bank.
The most significant and the most questionable feature of the Budget
was a grant of relief of local taxation which cost the Exchequer over
£1,000,000 sterling. He increased the contribution of the Treasury
from one-third to one-half of the expenses of the police force, and
Northcote made a grant to the local authorities of 4s. per head for
each pauper lunatic maintained in a lunatic asylum. This grant
was undoubtedly a step towards the better classification of paupers
and the more humane and scientific treatment of the insane, but it
did not conduce to economy. Of Northcote's second Budget (1875)
the only noticeable feature was the inception of the New Sinking
Fund. Down to this time extinction of debt depended entirely upon
the amount of unexpended balances in the hands of the spending
Departments. These balances went automatically to the reduction

The New
Sinking
Fund

of debt. With this " Old Sinking Fund " Northcote did not interfere, but he contrived in addition a new one of his own. He proposed
to raise the debt charge by gradual stages from £27,215,000, the sum
at which it stood in 1875, to £28,000,000, applying the balance
remaining after the payment of interest to the gradual extinction of
the capital charge. The device was open to some, but not all of the
objections urged against the whole principle of the sinking funds so
dear to the minds of eighteenth-century financiers. But it held out
a realizable hope of the gradual extinction of a real burden, and it
was in the best sense Conservative finance. If Northcote had had
the courage to apply to the same purpose the whole of the " death
duties " (and it is the only purpose to which such duties can legiti-
mately and scientifically be applied), he would have set an even
better example. But his sinking fund policy, so far as it went, was

sound. After 1875 he had no more chances. In 1876 he had to
face an expenditure of over £78,000,000, an increase of over £5,500,000
over 1874 ; [1] and the ordinary sources of revenue were beginning to
show an ominous lack of elasticity. The anticipated deficit was met
by a reimposition of the 1d. on the income tax, but the increased
rate was accompanied by a readjustment of the incidence. The limit of
total exemption was raised, with questionable prudence, from £100
to £150, while the graduation principle was extended. Hitherto
£80 deduction had been allowed on incomes under £300; Northcote
allowed £120 on incomes under £400. " We have a Budget ready
made to our hands " reduces to a sentence the financial statement of
1877. There was neither remission nor imposition of taxation. The
Budget of 1878 involves a criticism, not of finance but of foreign
policy. To the Chancellor of the Exchequer it was " a necessarily
unpleasant statement ". Expenditure, as compared with 1874, was
up by nearly £9,000,000. For this increase the Civil Service had to
bear the heaviest responsibility (£3,500,000), but armaments cost
£2,000,000 more. The income tax was raised to 5d. ; tobacco had
to pay an additional 4d. per lb., and dog licenses were (with certain
exceptions) raised from 5s. to 7s. 6d. This was bad enough, but
worse was to come. August brought supplementary estimates of
over £3,000,000, and the situation which Northcote had to face in the
spring of 1879 was gloomy, not to say grave. On his own shoulders
there was now a heavy burden. He was not only the " watch-dog
of the Treasury," but for more than two years had been leading the
House of Commons, but he faced all his duties with quiet courage.
Extraordinary expenditure in the near and far East was met for the
most part, despite Gladstone's protest, by short loans ; the expenses
of the Zulu War Northcote expected to defray without recourse to
increased taxation. The country was in no mood and in no condition
to assume additional burdens. The portents were unmistakable.
Trade was depressed and falling prices were bringing ruin upon
agriculturists. Northcote's reign at the Treasury was nearly over.
The Budget of 1880 was introduced amid the turmoil of an impending
dissolution. Commercial depression, a declining revenue, and war
expenditure (in South Africa) combined to produce a large deficit ;
but there was to be no new taxation : equilibrium was restored by a
raid on the new sinking fund—the favourite child of Northcote's
finance. In that finance the Opposition had a legitimate object
of criticism, and they did not neglect it. But there was a general
disposition not to impute overmuch blame to the unfortunate
Chancellor of the Exchequer. Sir Stafford Northcote had—almost
too obviously—the aspect of a good man struggling with adversity,
and Mr. Gladstone generally treated him with a tenderness which

[1] Of this about £2,000,000 was due to armaments ; £1,000,000 to education,
nearly £1,500,000 to local taxation, and the rest to increased Civil Service charges,
incurred by recent legislation.

24

was not extended to his Chief. For finance after all depends upon policy, and if ever the policy of a Government was the policy of its Chief, it was so in the case of Lord Beaconsfield's Administration. To one aspect of that policy attention had been already drawn. *Sanitas sanitatum omnia sanitas.* That pledge was amply redeemed. We must now turn to *Imperium.*

Imperium   It is impossible to deny that with the author of *Sybil* social reform was a matter of long-standing conviction and genuine enthusiasm. " The lesson which Disraeli taught his party was the possibility, which he had long perceived, of an alliance between the Tories and English wage-earners ; and the true basis of this alliance was their common dissent from individualistic Liberalism." The words are those of a critic [1] not entirely friendly to Disraeli, but there is truth in them. Yet it is not the whole truth. It was another lesson enforced by Lord Beaconsfield [2] with which his name will be immemorially associated. " You have a new world, new influences at work, new and unknown objects and dangers with which to cope. . . . The relations of England to Europe are not the same as they were in the days of Lord Chatham or Frederick the Great. The Queen of England has become the Sovereign of the most powerful of Oriental States. On the other side of the globe there are now establishments belonging to her teeming with wealth and population. . . . These are vast and novel elements in the distribution of power. . . . What our duty is at this critical moment is to maintain the Empire of England." The passages here quoted are taken from three separate speeches, but they present in a concise form the ideas and principles which actuated Lord Beaconsfield as Minister of the Crown. He possessed in unusual degree the gift denied to most English Statesmen—the gift of imagination. His ideas and utterances were, even on the confession of opponents, " spacious ". He perceived that a vast change was taking place under the eyes of his contemporaries, but unperceived by most of them, in the centre of political gravity. " A new world, new influences at work." This new world Lord Beaconsfield hoped might be predominantly English, the new influences he tried to shape in the interests of the British Empire.

Suez
Canal
shares
          The first indication given to the world of the " new Imperialism " was the purchase of the Khedive's shares in the Suez Canal. On November 25th, 1875, the world was startled by the news that the British Government had purchased from the Khedive for the sum of £4,000,000 sterling his 176,000 shares in the Suez Canal. [3] The merit

[1] Dicey, *Law and Public Opinion*, pp. 251, 252.
[2] Disraeli, acting on urgent medical advice, accepted a Peerage and took the title of Earl of Beaconsfield (Aug. 18th, 1876).
[3] The total shares were 400,000. The idea of the purchase was said to have been suggested by Mr. Frederick Greenwood, a distinguished London journalist. See *The Times*, December 27th, 1905, and January 13th, 1906. But there are now (1912) other claimants to the distinction.

of the achievement was Disraeli's alone, and for him it was facilitated by his friendship with the " city " and particularly with the great house of Rothschild. If Disraeli had not stepped in the shares would have gone to France, who would then have held the whole share capital. The Rothschilds received 2½ per cent. as brokerage commission and 5 per cent. interest on the money they advanced for the purchase, until the Government could take up the shares. Some of Disraeli's less imaginative colleagues, notably his Chancellor of the Exchequer, did not like the transaction.[1] As a financial speculation, its success has long since been brilliantly demonstrated. The shares are now worth £37,600,000 sterling and yield a revenue of over £1,100,000, or about 25 per cent. on the purchase money. As a political move, it marks a new departure of the highest significance. England had been curiously blind to her interests in the Eastern Mediterranean, though they were clearly perceived by her enemies. " Really to destroy England, we must make ourselves masters of Egypt." Thus Napoleon had written in 1797 ; in 1798 he tried to do it. The Czar Nicholas I. of Russia had opened the question to English statesmen in 1844 and had pressed Egypt upon us in 1853.[2] To no purpose. Our blindness did not permit us to perceive, or perhaps our morality forbade us to consent. To Disraeli the purchase of the Canal shares was no isolated speculation, but a move in a coherent and preconcerted plan.

His next stroke had a twofold object. During the winter of 1875-1876 the Heir-Apparent had undertaken an extended tour in India. The visit, which was without precedent in the history of the Empire, proved an eminent success. On January 1st, 1876, the Prince of Wales held a Chapter of the Star of India in Calcutta. On February 8th the Queen's Speech at the opening of Parliament, read in the Queen's presence,[3] announced the intention of the Government to ask for a " formal addition to the style and titles of the Sovereign ". Before his last session in the House of Commons closed, Disraeli had the satisfaction of making his Sovereign Empress of India. The new style was bitterly opposed in Parliament, and evoked much dissatisfaction in the country. Time, however, has amply vindicated the wisdom and prescience of the Minister. His *coup* was not due to the brilliant inspiration of the moment. It was the expression of a policy long since predetermined. " You ought at once . . . to tell the people of India that the relation between them and their real ruler and Sovereign Queen Victoria shall be drawn nearer. You must act upon the opinion of India on that subject immediately, and you can only act upon the opinion of Eastern nations through their

The Royal Titles Bill

---

[1] *Cf.* Northcote's letter to his Chief ap. Lang's *Iddesleigh*, p. 275 (ed. 1891). The letter concludes " I don't like it ".

[2] See *supra*, pp. 181-182.

[3] Only once before since her widowhood had the Queen opened Parliament in person.

imagination." So Disraeli had spoken at the time of the Mutiny, and in Opposition. Thus he spoke in 1876 as First Minister of the Crown : " The Princes and nations of India . . . know in India what this Bill means, and they know that what it means is what they wish ".[1]

Resignation of Lord Northbrook

Meanwhile, an important change had taken place in the personnel of the Government of India. For some months past there had been friction between the Secretary of State and the Viceroy. Lord Salisbury not only disapproved of Lord Northbrook's fiscal policy, but raised an important question as to the constitutional relations which should subsist between the Viceroy and the Secretary of State. In a despatch dated November 11th, 1875, Lord Salisbury administered a severe rebuke to the Viceroy and the latter immediately resigned.

Lord Lytton appointed to succeed him

Mr. Disraeli's choice of a successor was characteristic. He selected as first Viceroy under the new régime one who shared his own imaginative faculties, a brilliant man of letters, and an experienced diplomatist. Lord Lytton was the son of his old friend, Bulwer Lytton, and was himself known in the republic of letters as " Owen Meredith ". The first task which awaited the new Viceroy was to prepare for the fitting proclamation of the Empress. A magnificent Durbar was held at Delhi in the closing days of the year 1876, and on January 1st, 1877, a series of celebrations culminated in the proclamation of Queen Victoria as Empress of India in the presence of sixty-three ruling Princes, and amid the acclamation of the most brilliant assemblage ever brought together in British India.

The monarchical revival

It was not, however, merely in order to " add security to the Empire " that Disraeli conferred upon his Mistress the Imperial Crown of India ; he hoped also to " add splendour even to her throne ". This, too, was part of a deliberate policy. " The principles of the English Constitution do not contemplate the absence of personal influence on the part of the Sovereign ; and if they did, the principles of human nature would prevent the fulfilment of such a theory." Disraeli's words were not a mere rhetorical flourish. They had conviction behind them and intention. The popularity of the Queen had touched its nadir in the last few years. During the decade which followed the Prince Consort's death the Queen's health was less robust than usual, and once (Sept. 1871) it gave cause for some anxiety. She felt constrained, therefore, to make her choice between assiduous attention to the routine business of the State and participation in public ceremonial. The latter was naturally distasteful to her in the early years of her widowhood, and for some time the nation was acquiescent and sympathetic. But as the years went on and the seclusion of the Sovereign seemed likely to be permanent, murmurings arose and grew louder and louder. *The Times* lent its weight to attacks of increasing vehemence. " The

[1] *Speeches*, ii. 239.

living," it wrote, " have their claims as well as the dead." A *Punch*
cartoon portrayed the Queen as Hermione, while Britannia, as Pauline,
was made to address the Queen, " 'Tis time ; descend ; be stone no
more ".[1] The Queen was deeply pained, but quite obdurate. She
was acting, as she believed, in accordance with the plainest dictates
of duty. " Very few people know how superbly she continued to
stand sentry to the business of her Empire." [2] The Queen deeply
resented the reticence of her Ministers on this delicate point. They
might and ought, in her opinion, to have explained the situation and
saved her from unmerited reproof. Mr. Gladstone, on the contrary,
felt it his duty to remonstrate with her.[3] He was genuinely alarmed
lest her persistence in seclusion should weaken the hold of the
Monarchy upon the nation. And his alarm was not groundless.
After the fall of the French Empire there was a clearly marked wave
of republican feeling in England. When the House of Commons in 1871 was asked to vote £15,000 a year to Prince Arthur (afterwards the Duke of Connaught) no less than fifty-one members voted in favour of reducing the grant to £10,000. There was a noisy and malignant attack on the reputed affluence of the Queen herself in the same year, and in 1872 Sir Charles Dilke, boldly avowing himself to be a convinced Republican, moved for a full parliamentary inquiry into the expenditure of the Crown. From that moment, however, the tide turned. The Queen's own illness in 1871, followed in the same year by the far more serious illness of the Prince of Wales, evoked profound sympathy among her people, and when in February, 1872, the Queen attended with the Prince a service of public thanks-giving at St. Paul's Cathedral, she received an enthusiastic welcome. The mists of prejudices were quickly dissipated, and a marked reaction in the Queen's favour set in. Her own spirits were much improved by the substitution of Disraeli for Gladstone as First Minister. Disraeli, though no sycophant, was a courtier, and the Queen gave him her confidence in a measure not bestowed upon any of his less tactful predecessors. With him, however, it was a question not of personal deference but of political principle ; and the reward which he sought, and found, was the revival, not only of the personal popularity of the Sovereign, but of the place of the Monarchy in the Constitution.
(marginal note: Republican feeling in England)

The purchase of the Canal shares, the assumption of the Imperial Crown of India, were parts of a coherent whole. Disraeli's attitude towards the complex problems roused into fresh life by events in the near East was determined by precisely the same considerations. Lord Palmerston was always ready and anxious to assert the rights of Englishmen the whole world over. But his outlook upon diplomacy was, if not insular, at least European. Disraeli was the first Minister
(marginal note: Reopening of the Eastern question)

---

[1] Lee, *Life*, p. 359.			[2] *Quarterly Review*, April, 1901.
[3] *Cf.* Morley, ii. 293, 427, etc.

since Canning, perhaps since Chatham, to " think imperially ". He never forgot that the Queen was the ruler of Muhammadans as well as Christians ; of Asiatics, Africans, Australians, and Americans, as well as Europeans. He regarded the Eastern question, therefore, with the eye of an Oriental as well as of an Occidental Statesman.

The ink was hardly dry on the Treaty of Paris (1856) before it became obvious that the Crimean War had not permanently solved the Eastern question. Among the divided and heterogeneous populations subject to the Turk, there was almost perpetual unrest. In 1858 there were insurrectionary movements in Bosnia and Herzegovina, and Montenegrin troops crossed the frontier into the latter province. Moldavia and Wallachia were anxious to unite, but the Powers, though assenting to their virtual independence, decreed that they must remain separate principalities. With great ingenuity, however, the two States cut the knot by electing the same ruler, Prince Alexander Couza. Europe wisely accepted the accomplished fact, and in 1859 recognized the union of the two Romanic Principalities under the title of Roumania. In 1862 Servia expelled the Turkish garrisons, and in the same year the Greeks broke out into revolt, expelled King Otho, and offered their uneasy Crown to Prince Alfred of England. But the protecting Powers, England, France, and Russia, had pledged themselves not to allow any of their cadets to accept the throne, and in 1863 England obtained for the Greeks the services of a Danish Prince (now King George), and at the same time presented them with the Ionian Isles. Crete was only kept quiet (1866-1868) by the intervention of the Powers, and in 1875 the whole Eastern question was again reopened by the outbreak of insurrection among the peoples of Bosnia and Herzegovina, supported by volunteers from Servia and Montenegro.

Attitude of Russia   Whether that insurrection was spontaneous, or whether it was stimulated from St. Petersburg, is a question which it is not easy to decide. Russia was, at any rate, not sorry to have the opportunity of fishing again in troubled waters. It had been plain, for some time past, that the Czar Alexander did not intend to accept as final the results of the Crimean War. He had, as we have seen, taken advantage in 1870 of the preoccupation of Europe to denounce the Treaty of Paris in regard to the neutrality of the Black Sea—a neutrality which Disraeli declared to be " the very basis and gist of the Treaty of Paris of 1856 . . . the main object of the war, the great result for the accomplishment of which this country and France and their Allies made the vast sacrifices now so freely acknowledged ".[1] The insurrection of 1875 gave the Czar a still larger opportunity.

Turkish misgovernment   Turkey had now had nearly twenty years of grace in which to put her house in order, but all the fair promises made in 1856 had gone to the winds. Admitted to the polite society of Europe by the

[1] February 24th, 1871, *Speeches*, ii. 138-139.

Treaty of Paris, the Porte had continued to behave as a barbarian. The lot of the Christians was no whit better than before the Crimean War, and all unofficial classes groaned under the oppressiveness and uncertainty of a fiscal system which nevertheless starved the Treasury. For it is one of the salutary paradoxes incidental to misgovernment that it is as ruinous to the Sovereign as it is hurtful to the subject. The inherent extravagance of a bad system combined with the peculation of an army of officials to bring disaster upon Turkey, and in October, 1875, the Sultan was compelled to inform his creditors that he could not pay the full interest on the debt. Partial repudiation complicated an international situation already sufficiently embarrassing. The three Emperors took counsel together, and on December 30th, 1875, the Austrian Chancellor, Count Andrassy issued from Budapesth the Note which bears his name.

The Andrassy Note expressed the anxiety of the Powers to curtail The Andrassy the area of the insurrection, and to maintain the peace of Europe ; it Note drew attention to the failure of the Porte to carry out reforms long overdue, and it insisted that pressure must be put upon the Sultan effectually to redeem his promises. In particular, he must be pressed to grant complete religious liberty ; to abolish tax farming ; to apply the direct taxes, locally levied in Bosnia and Herzegovina, to the local needs of those Provinces ; to improve the condition of the rural population by multiplying peasant owners, and above all to appoint a special commission, composed in equal numbers of Mussulmans and Christians, to control the execution not only of the reforms now demanded by the Powers, but also of those spontaneously promised by the Sultan in the decrees of October 2nd and December 12th. To this Note the British Government gave in their general adhesion, though they pointed out that the Sultan had, during the last few months, promised the more important of the reforms indicated therein.

The Note was accordingly presented to the Porte at the end of January, 1876, and the Sultan, with almost suspicious promptitude, accepted four out of the five points—the exception being the application of the direct taxes to local objects.

The friendly efforts of the diplomatists were foiled, however, by the attitude of the insurgents. The latter refused, not unnaturally, to be satisfied with mere assurances, or to lay down their arms without substantial guarantees. The Sultan insisted again, not without reason, that it was impossible to initiate a scheme of reform while the Provinces were actually in armed rebellion. Meanwhile, the mischief was spreading. Bulgaria broke out into revolt in April ; at the beginning of May a fanatical Muhammadan *émeute* at Salonica led to the murder of the French and German Consuls ; the Sultan Abdul Aziz was deposed on May 30th, and on June 4th was found dead, " having apparently committed suicide ". More drastic measures were obviously necessary if a great European conflagration was to be avoided.

The Berlin Memorandum
On May 11th the Austrian and Russian Chancellors were in conference with Prince Bismarck at Berlin, and determined to make further and more peremptory demands upon the Sultan. There was to be an immediate armistice of two months' duration, during which certain measures of pacification and repatriation were to be executed under the superintendence of the delegates of the Powers. If by the expiry of the armistice the object of the Powers had not been attained, diplomatic action would have to be reinforced. France and Italy assented to the Note, but the British Government regarded the terms as unduly peremptory ; they resented the independent action of the three Imperial Powers, and declined to be a party to the Memorandum. Accordingly the proposed intervention was abandoned.

Attitude of the English Government
Mr. Disraeli's refusal created, as was inevitable, profound perturbation abroad, and evoked a storm of criticism at home. Out of the welter of charges and countercharges some points have now emerged with tolerable clearness. The European concert, whatever it was worth, was broken by the policy of Great Britain. Had the British Cabinet gone whole-heartedly with the other Powers, irresistible pressure would have been put upon the Porte, and some terrible atrocities might, perhaps, have been averted. On the other hand, it is clear that the Imperial Chancellors were encouraged in an attitude which was almost insolent, by the belief that England would " never again commit the crime of the Crimean War ". They presumed upon the pacific tendencies manifested by Great Britain in recent years, and were misled, much as the Czar Nicholas was misled by the amiability of Lord Aberdeen, into the belief that Great Britain might be regarded as a *quantité négligible* in European diplomacy. If they sincerely desired the preservation of peace they committed an inexcusable blunder in not inviting the co-operation of England before formulating the demands of the Berlin Memorandum.

The Bulgarian atrocities
Events now moved rapidly. On May 24th the Government ordered the British Fleet in the Mediterranean to sail for Besika Bay. The disorder in Constantinople was in itself sufficient justification for this precaution, but by the Turks it was unhappily interpreted as an encouragement to defiance of the will of the continental Powers. Perhaps also as an indication that they might safely show themselves to be masters in their own house. They showed it in characteristic fashion. Some disorders in Bulgaria led to terrible reprisals. A horde of irregular soldiery—the Bashi Bazouks—was let loose upon a half-armed peasantry, and all Europe was made to ring with an account of the atrocities committed in the name of the Ottoman Sultan. How much of exaggeration there was in the accounts

published in England and elsewhere, it was and is impossible to say.
But something much less than the ascertained facts would be sufficient
to make the historian avert his own eyes and those of his readers
with all possible rapidity from a scene so terrible. In July Mr.
Walter Baring was sent by the British Government to Adrianople
to ascertain, if possible, the truth. His final report was not issued
until September, but preliminary reports so far substantiated the
accounts which had been published in the English Press as to move
the conscience of England to its depths. In a despatch [1] to Sir
Henry Elliot, British Ambassador to the Porte, Lord Derby gave
expression, in language not the less strong by reason of its restraint,
to the feelings of indignation aroused in England by the accounts of
the Bulgarian atrocities, and instructed him to demand from the
Sultan prompt and effective reparation for the victims.

But a voice more powerful than that of Lord Derby was already Mr. Glad-
making articulate the feelings of his countrymen. To Mr. Gladstone stone's
the tale of atrocities made an irresistible appeal. A pamphlet, pamphlet
published on September 6th, was circulated by tens of thousands. [2]
With voice and pen he vehemently demanded that the Turks should
be cleared out " bag and baggage . . . from the province they have
desolated and profaned ".

Long before this, however, another complication had arisen. In
June, Servia and Montenegro had declared war upon the Porte.
How far would that conflict extend ? Could it be confined within
the original limits ? These were the serious questions with which
diplomacy was now confronted. The Servian army consisted largely
of Russian volunteers and was commanded by a Russian General.
How long would it be before the Russian Government became a
party to the quarrel ? The Servian army, even reinforced by the
volunteers, could offer but a feeble resistance to the Turk, and in
August Prince Milan, acting on a hint from England, asked for the
mediation of the Powers. [3] England, thereupon, urged the Sultan
to come to terms with Servia and Montenegro, lest a worse thing
should befall him. The Sultan, however, declined an armistice, but
formulated his terms, and intimated that if the Powers approved
them he would grant an immediate suspension of hostilities. But
to Lord Derby's chagrin Servia would accept nothing less than an
armistice, and, after six weeks' suspension, hostilities recommenced.
Nevertheless, Lord Derby was untiring in his efforts to promote a
pacification, and suggested (Sept. 21st) to the Powers some heads of
proposals : the *status quo* in Servia and Montenegro ; local or administrative autonomy for Bosnia and Herzegovina ; guarantees
against mal-administration in Bulgaria, and a comprehensive scheme

[1] September 21st, 1876.
[2] *The Bulgarian Horrors and the Question of the East.*
[3] Parl. Papers, Turkey, 1877 (No. 1), p. 380.

of reform—all to be embodied in a protocol concluded between the Porte and the Powers.[1] Russia then proposed (Sept. 26th) that, in the event of a refusal from Turkey, the allied fleets should enter the Bosphorus, that Bosnia should be temporarily occupied by Austria, and Bulgaria by Russia. Turkey, thereupon, suggested an armistice of six months ; Russia demurred, and eventually six weeks was agreed upon.

Conference at Constantinople
Lord Derby was determined that the breathing space should be utilized for one more effort to preserve the peace of Europe. At his suggestion a conference met at Constantinople in December, and Lord Salisbury attended it as the chief representative of Great Britain. The Powers agreed to the terms suggested by Lord Derby in September, but the Porte was obdurate. Profuse in his professions and promises of reform, the Porte stubbornly refused to allow Europe to superintend their execution. General Ignatieff, the Russian delegate, thereupon withdrew from the conference, and Russia proceeded to mobilize her troops. Diplomacy, however, made one more effort to preserve peace. On March 31st, 1877, the Powers signed in London a Protocol put forward by Count Schouvaloff. Taking cognizance of the Turkish promises of reform the Powers. declared their intention of watching carefully " the manner in which the promises of the Ottoman Government are carried into effect ". If, however, the condition of the Christian subjects of the Porte should again lead to a " return of the complications which periodically disturb the peace of the East, they think it right to declare that such a state of things would be incompatible with their interests and those of Europe in general ". The Turk, in high dudgeon, rejected the Protocol (April 10th), and on April 24th Russia declared war. Single-handed the Czar intended to extort by force of arms those guarantees which the Sultan had refused to the collective demand of Europe.

The Russo-Turkish War
Russia, it must be confessed, had behaved, in face of prolonged provocation, with considerable patience and restraint, and had shown a commendable desire to maintain the European concert. The Turk had exhibited, throughout, his usual mixture of shrewdness and obstinacy. It is difficult to believe that he would have maintained his obstinate front, but for expectations based upon the supposed good-will of the British Government. The language of the Prime Minister [2] and the Foreign Secretary had unquestionably given him some encouragement. So much so that, before the break-up of the conference, Lord Salisbury telegraphed [3] to Lord Derby from Constantinople : " The Grand Vizier believes that he can count upon the assistance of Lord Derby and Lord Beaconsfield ". The

---

[1] Parl. Papers, Turkey, 1877 (No. 1), p. 380.
[2] *E.g.* at the Guildhall on November 9th.
[3] January 8th, 1877.

Turk, it is true, is an adept at diplomatic " bluff," and " assistance "
went beyond the facts. But this much is certain. If the English
Cabinet had, even in January, 1877, frankly and unambiguously gone
hand in hand with Russia there would have been no war.

The details of the campaign must not detain us—suffice it to say
that for Russia it was no mere military parade. The Russian army
crossed the Danube in June, but it was many months before their
main army could pierce the Balkans. In their path was the great
fortress of Plevna, and for five months Osman Pasha resisted all the
efforts made by the Russians to capture it. At last, on December
10th, Plevna surrendered to General Todleben ; before the end
of January (1878) the Russian army reached Adrianople, and in
February Constantinople itself was threatened.

A basis of agreement had already been reached at Adrianople *Treaty of*
(Jan. 31st) ; the terms were now embodied in a Treaty signed, on *San*
March 3rd, at a village not far from Constantinople. Montenegro, *Stefano,*
Servia, and Roumania were to be recognized definitely as independent *March,*
of the Porte, and certain frontier districts were to be ceded to them ; *1878*
the reforms recommended to the Porte at the Conference of Con-
stantinople were to be immediately introduced into Bosnia and
Herzegovina ; the Danubian fortresses to be razed ; reforms were
to be granted to the Armenians ; Russia was to acquire, in lieu of
the greater part of the money indemnity which she claimed, Batoum,
Kars, and other territory in Asia, and certain districts on the Rou-
manian frontier to be exchanged with Roumania for the strip of
Bessarabia retroceded in 1856. But the most striking feature of the
Treaty was the creation of a greater Bulgaria, which was to be
constituted an autonomous tributary Principality with a Christian
Government and a national militia, and was to extend from the
Danube to the Ægean Sea, nearly as far south as Midia (on the
Black Sea), Adrianople and Salonica, and to include, on the West,
the district round Monastir.[1] Bulgaria would thus have comprised
" more than half of the Balkan Peninsula ".[2] These terms excited
alarm and jealousy in Greece and in the Balkan States. How were
they regarded by Europe in general and Great Britain in particular ?

Ever since the outbreak of the Russo-Turkish War, the British *British*
Government had watched with deepening anxiety the development of *policy,*
events in Eastern Europe. Mr. Gladstone indeed identified the cause *1877-1878*
of Russia with the causes of freedom and justice, but among statesmen
he stood almost alone. The Government declared their policy to be
one of rigid neutrality so long as Egypt, the Suez Canal, and Constantinople were not threatened, and when that policy was formally
challenged by Mr. Gladstone, their majority rose far above their
normal figure—to 131. If the Cabinet were not wholly united at

[1] See Turkey Papers (No. 22), 1878 ; Holland, *European Concert*, pp. 335 *seq.*
[2] Rose, *European Nations*, p. 229.

this moment, neither were the Opposition leaders. Mr. Gladstone's vehemence on the Eastern question strained severely the loyalty of his late colleagues. " I feel certain," wrote Lord Hartington to Lord Granville, " that the Whigs and moderate Liberals in the House are a good deal disgusted, and I am much afraid that if he goes on much further, nothing can prevent a break-up of the party." [1] His opponents were not much better off. " In private conversation, Mr. Disraeli gave a humorous account of the six parties in the Cabinet. The first party is that which is for immediate war with Russia ; the second party is for war to save Constantinople ; the third party is the party of Peace at any Price ; the fourth party would let the Russians take Constantinople and would then turn them out ; the fifth party desires to plant the cross on the dome of St. Sophia ; and then there are the Prime Minister and the Chancellor of the Exchequer, who desire to see something done, but don't know exactly what." [2] The Russian victories at the end of 1877 deepened anxieties and accentuated differences. In January, 1878, Lord Derby warned Russia that an occupation of the Dardanelles by her army would endanger the good relations between herself and Great Britain, and three days afterwards thought it necessary to remind her that any treaty concluded between Russia and Turkey which affected the engagements of 1856 and 1878 " would not be valid without the assent of the Powers who were parties to those Treaties " (Jan. 14th).

Parliament, called together at an ominously early date (Jan. 17th), was informed by the Queen that " should hostilities be unfortunately prolonged, some unexpected occurrence may render it incumbent on me to adopt measures of precaution ". It was soon apparent what was in the mind of Ministers. Northcote gave notice that they would ask the House for an additional £6,000,000 for armaments, and on January 23rd the Fleet was ordered to sail for the Dardanelles. Upon the public announcement of this menacing step Lord Carnarvon and Lord Derby resigned. The former was succeeded at the Colonial Office by Sir Michael Hicks Beach, the latter withdrew his resignation when the Fleet was recalled to Besika Bay. On January 28th Northcote, in moving the vote, made public the terms demanded by Russia, which, in addition to the points subsequently embodied in the Treaty of San Stefano, included " an ulterior understanding for safeguarding the rights and interests of Russia in the Straits ". This was the point in regard to which she had already been warned by Lord Derby, and the situation became critical in the extreme. In the preliminary terms signed between combatants on January 31st this stipulation disappeared ; but, in consequence of excited telegrams from Mr. Layard, the British Ambassador in Constantinople, the Cabinet decided (Feb. 7th) to send a detachment of the

---

[1] December 18th, 1876, cf. Holland's *Devonshire*, i. 186.
[2] Northcote's Memorandum ap. Lang, pp. 288-289.

Fleet into the Sea of Marmora for the protection of British subjects in Constantinople. Russia retorted that if British ships sailed up the Straits Russian troops would enter Constantinople for the purpose of similarly protecting the lives of Christians of every race. The Sultan, however, withheld the leave necessary to enable ships of war to pass the Dardanelles.

On March 3rd tension was relieved by the signature of the Treaty of San Stefano. But only for the moment. The Austrian Government had been moving in the matter of a European Congress, and on March 4th Lord Derby informed Count Beust that Great Britain agreed to the suggestion, provided it were clearly understood that " all questions dealt with in the Treaty of Peace between Russia and Turkey should be considered as subjects to be discussed in the Congress ". This had been throughout " the keynote of our policy," " the diapason of our diplomacy ".[1] With regard to the Treaty of San Stefano the language of Lord Beaconsfield was emphatic : " It abolishes the dominion of the Ottoman Empire in Europe ; it creates a large State which, under the name of Bulgaria, is inhabited by many races not Bulgarian . . . all the European dominions of the Ottoman Porte are . . . put under the administration of Russia . . . the effect of all the stipulations combined will be to make the Black Sea as much a Russian lake as the Caspian ".[2] Whether this description were exaggerated or no, there can be no question that, in every clause, the Treaty was a " deviation " from those of 1856 and 1871, and as such required the assent of the signatory Powers.

To the demand that the Treaty in its entirety should be sub- Lord mitted to a Congress Russia demurred. Great Britain insisted. Derby resigns Again things looked like war. Lord Derby, the most pacific member of the Cabinet, resigned (March 28th) ; on April 1st Lord Beaconsfield announced that Parliament would be asked to authorize the calling out of the Reserves, and on April 2nd Lord Salisbury, the new Foreign Secretary,[3] issued a masterly memorandum, placing before the Powers the case of Great Britain.

Peace hung in the balance. Apart from the dispute between England and Russia there was a great deal of inflammable material about, to which a match would set light. Greece, Servia, and Roumania were all gravely dissatisfied with the terms of the Treaty of San Stefano. Greece had actually invaded Thessaly at the beginning of February, and had only consented to abstain from further hostilities upon the assurance of the Powers that her claims should have favourable consideration in the definitive Treaty of Peace.

[1] Lord Beaconsfield in House of Lords, April 8th, 1878, *Speeches*, ii. 163.
[2] *Ibid.*, p. 170.
[3] Mr. Gathorne Hardy succeeded him as Secretary for India, and Colonel Stanley (brother of Lord Derby) became Secretary for War.

Indian
troops
ordered to
Malta

Parliament adjourned for the Easter recess on April 16th, re-assured as to the prospects of peace by a speech from the Chancellor of the Exchequer. On the following morning *The Times* made the sensational announcement that Lord Beaconsfield had ordered 7,000 Indian troops to embark for Malta. That the *coup* was dramatic none will dispute : but it has been variously judged. The disciples of Disraeli contended that it revealed as by a flash-light the resources upon which England could draw, and thus powerfully contributed to the maintenance of peace. His enemies declared that it smacked of transpontine melodrama rather than of the sober traditions of English statesmanship. Mr. Gladstone impeached the policy as gravely unconstitutional : Lord Selborne declared it to be illegal.[1] The historical critic must admit that the move was con-sistent with the whole trend of Lord Beaconsfield's policy, and must insist that if it alarmed England it impressed Europe, and that it made for peace.

The
Treaty of
Berlin

Before the end of May the Indian troops began to arrive at Malta ; on the 30th Lord Salisbury and Count Schuvaloff came to an agreement on the main points at issue, and on June 13th the Congress opened at Berlin. Prince Bismarck, of course, presided : the English plenipotentiaries were the Prime Minister and the Foreign Secretary. The Congress marked the zenith of one of the most remarkable careers in English parliamentary history. Lord Beaconsfield figured for a moment as the dictator of Europe. " Der alte Jude, das ist der Mann." Such was Bismarck's pregnant summary of the situation. The day after the Congress met, the world was informed, through the fraud of a Foreign Office clerk, of all the details of the convention concluded between Lord Salisbury and Count Schuvaloff on May 30th. The critics of the Government pointed to this as one more instance of the shameless duplicity of English diplomacy at this juncture. " The Congress, after all, was a hollow sham," and much to the like effect. Reflection will surely reverse such contemporary criticism. No prudent diplomatist would go into open Congress without a clear understanding on the main points with his principal antagonist. Lord Beaconsfield and Lord Salisbury had not omitted this wise precaution, though in-sufficient care had been exercised in preserving official secrecy. They had taken, also, another precaution not prematurely disclosed. By a convention dated June 4th [2] they had agreed with Turkey that, so long as Russia retained Kars and other recent conquests in Armenia, the Island of Cyprus was to be " occupied and administered " by Great Britain. Turkey was to receive the surplus revenues of the Island, to carry out reforms in her Asiatic dominions, and to be protected in them by Great Britain.

[1] *Memorials*, ii. 451, 452.

[2] Supplemented by an annexe of July 1st. For text *cf.* Holland, *op. cit.* pp. 354-355.

The Treaty of Berlin was signed on July 13th. The great point
on which it differed from the Treaty of San Stefano was in regard
to " Greater Bulgaria ". " Bulgaria " as defined at Berlin was not
more than a third of the Bulgaria mapped out at San Stefano. It
was to consist of a relatively narrow strip between the Danube and
the Balkans, and to be an independent State under Turkish suzerainty. South of it there was to be a province, Eastern Roumellia,
which was to be restored to the Sultan who agreed to place it under
a Christian Governor approved by the Powers. By this change the
Sultan recovered 2,500,000 of population and 30,000 square miles of
territory. Bosnia and Herzegovina were handed over to Austrian
occupation—an occupation which has proved to be permanent.
The Greeks obtained (but not until 1881) an unimportant rectification
of their Northern frontier. For the rest, the terms of San Stefano
were confirmed.

The essential differences between the two Treaties consisted in
the aggrandisement of Austria-Hungary and the partition of " Greater
Bulgaria ". The latter arrangement was not permanent. In 1885
Prince Alexander of Battenberg, who had accepted in 1879 the
Principality of Bulgaria, yielded to the clearly expressed will of the
people and agreed to the union of the two Bulgarias. The diplomatic position was now entirely reversed : Russia was indignant ;
Great Britain not merely acquiescent but approving. The explanation is simple. Russia had played her cards in Bulgaria as badly as
they could be played. In opposition to her high-handed and self-
seeking methods there had grown up a strong national party. The
" Greater Bulgaria " of 1878 would have been a Russian Province,
within striking distance of Constantinople. The Bulgaria of 1885
was, as Lord Salisbury (again in office) clearly perceived, a sure
bulwark against Russia. " If," wrote Sir Robert Morier [1] to Sir
William White, [2] " you can help to build up these peoples into a
bulwark of independent States and thus screen the ' sick man ' from
the fury of the Northern blast, for God's sake do it." With Lord
Salisbury's help Sir William White did it, and thus in Morier's
words : " A state has been evolved out of the protoplasm of Balkan
chaos ". [3] It is fair to remember that but for Lord Beaconsfield's
action in 1878 that evolution would have been impossible.

On July 16th the British Ministers returned from Berlin and were " Peace
received with the wildest acclamations by the London crowd. Lord with
Beaconsfield clearly interpreted the feelings of London, if not of Honour"
England, when he declared, in historic [4] phrase, that he had brought
back " Peace with Honour ". " Peace " was indubitable : as to

[1] Ambassador at St. Petersburg.
[2] Ambassador at Constantinople.
[3] December 27th, 1885, quoted by Rose, to whose admirable essay on the
Making of Bulgaria, op. cit. pp. 251-288, reference should be made.
[4] But not original.

" Honour " opinion was divided. The envoys received the Order of
the Garter from their Sovereign and the Freedom of the City from
the merchants and bankers of the capital. But the public voice
was not unanimous in the endorsement of these honours.

The history of the Eastern question between 1875 and 1878 raises
many difficult problems in political ethics. The first and broadest
is the general right of intervention in the internal concerns of
Sovereign States. In opposition to the Holy Allies, Lord Castlereagh
had laid down the sound principle that " with the internal affairs of
each separate State we have nothing to do ". His protest was
addressed to absolute Monarchs, and it is worth recalling in order
to remind impatient philanthropists that intervention is necessarily
a double-edged weapon. Employed in the defence of oppressed
nationalities to-day, it may be used to-morrow in the interests of
autocracy. The only safe rule is clearly that of Lord Castlereagh.
But no rule is without exceptions, more especially in politics. Did
the condition of the Ottoman dominions in 1875 provide one ?

It is impossible to dismiss lightly the argument put forward by
Mr. Gladstone in 1876-1878, and by the Duke of Argyll in 1896.[1]
In the latter year they were the only two survivors of the Cabinet
which waged the Crimean War. That war, its conduct and its
issue, had, in their view, imposed upon Great Britain a peculiar
responsibility in regard to the government of the Turk in general,
and in particular his treatment of his Christian subjects. That
responsibility will hardly be denied ; but its existence does not
determine the manner and time of fulfilling it. Nor must it blind
us to another truth of equal weight. " We support Turkey," said
Lord Palmerston in 1853, " for our own sake and for our own
interests." The policy of Great Britain from first to last has been
that " of protecting Turkey with a view to the repulse of Russia
from an exclusive and dangerous domination over the East of
Europe ".[2] But the " buffer " consisted, after all, of human beings,
and to their well-being we could not be indifferent. One cardinal
mistake Lord Beaconsfield made—that of separating Great Britain
from the other Powers in the Berlin Memorandum. That separation
led, though not immediately, to the single-handed intervention of
Russia. But that intervention rendered it absolutely essential that
in any general settlement the influence of Great Britain should be
decisively exercised. The Treaty which closed this chapter of the
Eastern question may not have been ideal, it was not destined to
be final, but this at least may be said of it : it did not leave the
cat's paw of Russia within striking distance of Constantinople. The
Treaty torn up by Lord Beaconsfield did. Whether the difference
between them was worth the risk of a European war is a question
which posterity must decide.

[1] *Our Responsibilities for Turkey.*   [2] Argyll, *op. cit.* p. 3.

CHAPTER XXIV

AFGHANISTÁN, SOUTH AFRICA, AND IRELAND
(1878-1880)

IT is the fashion to deny that history ever repeats itself. Such denials are confronted with an awkward illustration in Afghanistán. The story to be disclosed in this chapter repeats with singular precision the experience of the preceding generation. With one characteristic and suggestive difference. The intertwining of events in Europe and Asia is much more intricate than was the case forty years earlier.

On the day when the diplomatists met in Congress at Berlin (June 13th, 1878) the Amír of Afghanistán learnt at Kábul that a Russian mission was on its way to his capital. A week after Lord Beaconsfield returned to London bringing back " Peace with Honour " from Berlin, General Stolietoff in command of the Russian mission reached Kábul, and was received with every possible mark of distinction by Sher Alí (July 22nd).[1] _{The Russian mission to Kábul}

English diplomacy had headed off Russia from the Dardanelles ; was Russian diplomacy going to take its revenge on the Kháibar ?

The disastrous events of the early " forties " had made, naturally enough, a profound impression upon British policy in India. Successive Governments had pursued since then a consistent policy of " masterly inactivity " in Central Asia. Russia employed the opportunity for steady though stealthy advance. Dost Muhammad did not understand the policy of " masterly inactivity ". Again and again he pressed Sir John Lawrence (1863-1869) to take under the protection of the British Government his designated heir Sher Alí. Lawrence persistently declined to interfere in the domestic politics of Afghanistán. By 1868, however, Sher Alí, without British assistance, had made himself master of his brethren and of the wild tribes who had owned his father's sway. Lawrence, thereupon, recognized the *de facto* ruler and sent him a congratulatory message and a present of money and arms. The Amír did not fail to perceive that these compliments coincided with the capture of Smarkand by Russia (1868). The Russian advance in Central Asia was now giving some uneasiness to Great Britain, and in January, 1873, the frontiers between the two Powers in Asia were formally defined by Treaty. The ink was hardly dry upon the Treaty when the news arrived that Russia had occupied Khiva (June, 1873). Count Schuvaloff assured the British Government that the occupation was a purely temporary expedient ; but the moment of evacuation has not yet arrived. At Khiva Russia was within 400 miles of the North-Western frontier of British India. By this time Lawrence had given _{Anglo-Afghan relations}

---

[1] Roberts, *Forty-one Years*, ii. 110.

place to Lord Mayo, and Mayo, struck down by the hand of a fanatic, had been succeeded by Lord Northbrook. On the eve of his departure from India (1869) Lawrence indited a despatch which indicates, not obscurely, some change of policy : advised a " clear understanding with the Court of St. Petersburg as to its projects and designs in Central Asia, and that it might be given to understand in firm and courteous language, that it cannot be permitted to interfere in the affairs of Afghanistán, or in those of any State which lies contiguous to our frontier ".[1] Such an intimation to Russia was clearly inconsistent with the policy of masterly inactivity to which Lawrence had throughout his long tenure of office adhered. But that policy still dominated the Council in Whitehall. Sher Alí was at least as much alarmed by the approach of Russia as was Lawrence. But he could get no effective assurance of support from Lord Mayo : still less from Lord Northbrook. In 1873 when the Russians were actually marching on Khiva, Sher Alí tried to persuade the Viceroy that " the interests of the Afghan and English Governments are identical," and that " the border of Afghanistán is in truth the border of India ".[2] Northbrook, obviously perturbed, telegraphed home for instructions. The reply is historic : " Cabinet thinks you should inform Amír we do not at all share his alarm and consider there is no cause for it, but you may assure him we shall maintain our settled policy in favour of Afghanistán if he abides by our advice in external affairs ".[3] This was one of the clear cases in which telegraphy has proved a curse to the Government of India. Lord Northbrook obeyed his instructions to the letter. The Amír got 20,000 rifles and a large present of money : he did not get the assurance he wanted. The year 1873 marks, as has been truly said, " a fatal turning-point in Anglo-Afghan relations ".[4] Northbrook's refusal " turned Sher Alí from a friend into an enemy, and he decided, as his father had done forty years before, to throw in his lot with Russia ".[5]

Lord Lytton's Vice-royalty, 1876-1880   In 1874 a new Government came into power. The boot was now on the other foot. Lord Salisbury was anxious to induce the Amír to accept a British Resident. Lord Lytton, who succeeded Lord Northbrook as Viceroy in 1876, endeavoured to persuade him to accept a comprehensive Treaty, but in vain. The Amír, repulsed by one Viceroy after another, had made up his mind to look for support in another direction. Meanwhile, the British Government concluded with the Khan of Kelat in Baluchistan the important Treaty of Jacobabad (Dec. 1876), a Treaty which gave us the right of garrisoning Quetta, a position which turns the flank of the Afghan frontier opposed to India along the mountain across the Indus.

[1] Quoted by Rose, *op. cit.* p. 371.   [2] Rose, p. 374.
[3] Argyll, *Eastern Question*, ii. 331   [4] Rose, p. 376.
[5] Roberts *op. cit.* ii. p. 108.

This diplomatic success alarmed the Amír, but not sufficiently to induce him to receive a British Resident. The reception of the Russian mission in 1878 compelled Lord Lytton to immediate and decisive action, though the opportune conclusion of the Treaty of Berlin led to amended instructions to the Russian envoy. General Stolietoff was bidden " not to go generally as far as would have been advisable if war with England had been threatened ".[1] Such instructions, however, could not, even had they been known, affect the policy of Great Britain. Lord Lytton took the only possible step in announcing to the Amír that a British Envoy of high rank, Sir Neville Chamberlain, would proceed to Kábul forthwith. The mission, with an escort of about 1,000 men, left Pesháwar on September 21st. Sir Neville took the precaution of sending forward Major Cavagnari to demand leave for the mission to proceed. Leave was refused : it was made clear to General Chamberlain that he would encounter armed resistance, and the mission was disbanded. " Nothing," as Chamberlain wrote, " could have been more humiliating to the British Crown and nation." [2]

To the refusal to receive an Envoy from the Queen-Empress—at Afghan a moment, moreover, when a Russian mission was actually in Kábul 1878-1879 —there could be but one answer. A large force was mobilized for the invasion of Afghanistán ; but before it marched an ultimatum was sent to Sher Alí to demand a full and immediate apology, and the reception of a permanent Embassy in Afghanistán.

On November 21st the force, 30,000 to 40,000 strong, advanced in three columns : one by the Kháiber Pass, under the command of Sir Samuel Browne ; another through the Kuram Valley, under Major-General Roberts ; the third, under Sir Donald Stewart, was to advance through the Bolan Pass on Kandahár. Before the end of December Browne had reached Jellalabad, Roberts had fought his way through the Shutargardan Pass, and in January Stewart entered Kandahár. Sher Alí, realizing the hopelessness of resistance, fled into Turkestan, with such members of the Russian mission as lingered at Kábul, and there in February, 1879, he died. His son, Yakub Khan, established himself in Kábul ; in May he presented himself in General Browne's camp at Gandamak, and terms of peace were quickly arranged.

By the Treaty of Gandamak Yakub Khan agreed to receive a Treaty of permanent British Embassy, with a suitable escort, at Kábul ; to Ganda- conduct his foreign policy under the advice of Great Britain ; to May give facilities for trade, and to allow such a rectification of the 26th, North-Western frontier as was demanded by the scientific school of 1879 British strategists. In return he was to be supported against external aggression and to receive an annual subsidy of six lacs of rupees.

[1] Roberts, ii. 111.   [2] Ibid. 116.

The news of the conclusion of peace was received with much satisfaction in England, and the Government congratulated itself and the country on the attainment of a scientific frontier. Lord Lawrence's warnings were ignored ; the advocates of the " forward " policy triumphed ; the Indian frontier was to rest not upon the Indus, but upon the command of the passes. One of the great soldiers who had made the war had forebodings about the peace. General Roberts thought that " peace had been signed too quickly," and that it ought to have been dictated in Kábul.[1]

Murder of Cavagnari in Kábul   The forebodings were only too sadly justified. Sir Louis Cavagnari, whose diplomatic tact had done so much to smooth the negotiations at Gandamak, accepted the mission to Kábul. Taking with him only a small escort, he reached the capital in July. In September he and all his comrades were murdered by the Amír's mutinous soldiery. The news reached Simla on September 4th, and two days later Roberts left to take command of the Kábul Field Force. Stewart's army had hardly left Kandahár, which was at once reoccupied. Roberts and his little force reached Kábul early in October. Yakub promptly abdicated and was deported to India. Efforts were made to discover Cavagnari's murderers, and the city and district around it were placed under martial law. Roberts found Kábul " much more Russian than English, the officers arrayed in uniforms of Russian pattern, Russian money in the treasury, and Russian wares in the Bazaars ". Before he left he brought to light much evidence as to Russian designs in Afghanistán, and he placed it on formal record that in his opinion the recent rupture with Sher Alí had " been the means of unmasking and checking a very serious conspiracy against the peace and security of our Indian Empire ".[2]

Meanwhile his own position in Kábul was far from secure. Again and again he had to beat off the tribesmen, and not until the end of December did reinforcements reach him from India. Early in May, 1880, Stewart and his division, after a successful engagement at Ahmed Khel, near Ghazní, joined him at Kábul.

Before this, an important political decision had been arrived at. To retain Afghanistán was out of the question. How could it best be made to contribute to the tranquillity of the Northern frontier of India ? There were only two alternatives. To erect Afghanistán into a strong, united, and friendly buffer State ; or to break it up and so render it impotent for mischief. Could the friendship of the tribesmen or of their ruler be really assured, the former was the obvious policy. But the tribesmen were hostile, and a ruler was still to seek. Lord Lytton decided therefore on the policy of disintegration. Kandahár or Western Afghanistán was promised to

---

[1] ii. 177.
[2] Cf. despatch dated November 22nd, 1879. printed in Forty-one Years, Appendix iv.

Sher Alí, a cousin of the late Amír, but Sher Alí declared, truly enough, that he could hold it only with the help of British troops. Northern Afghanistán was still unprovided for. Opportunely at this moment there appeared upon the scene the strong man so badly needed. A grandson of Dost Muhammad, Abdur Rahman, had been, for some years, a semi-captive pensioner of Russia in Turkestan. He no sooner reappeared than the tribesmen rallied round him, and Lord Lytton offered to make him Amír of Kábul. But Abdur Rahman wanted to be Amír, not of Kábul but of Afghanistán. He had not to wait long for the realization of his ambition.

The new Amír had just been installed in Kábul (July 22nd, 1880) and the British preparations for evacuation were all but complete when a new danger arose. Ayub Khan, a brother of the late Amír Yakub, gathered round him a large force of tribesmen in the Herát district, and announcing himself as a candidate for the throne, marched on Kandahár. General Primrose, left in command at Kandahár, sent out a brigade under Brigadier-General Burrows to stop him. With a totally inadequate force Burrows did his best to carry out his orders. But at Maiwand on July 27th his brigade was cut to pieces by a force overwhelmingly superior, and only a remnant got back to Kandahár. Primrose and his force in Kandahár were now in imminent danger. Kandahár itself was invested by the forces of Ayub Khan, flushed with recent victory. A notable resolution was now taken by the two great soldiers at Kábul. The Government was inclined to attempt the relief of Kandahár from Quetta. Stewart and Roberts, with their ultimate approval, decided to do it from Kábul. Roberts with 10,000 picked men was to succour Kandahár, Stewart was to lead back the rest of the Kábul garrison to India.

On August 9th Roberts's famous march began ; by the 31st he had covered the 318 miles of country that separate Kábul from Kandahár. On September 1st his triumph was confirmed and consummated by a brilliant victory over the Afghan forces outside Kandahár. Ayub's army was annihilated, and his political pretensions were destroyed. Roberts became the idol of the army and of his countrymen. The Afghan War was at an end.

Even Lord Lytton shrank from the task of a permanent occupation of Northern and Central Afghanistán. But the disposition of events no longer rested with that brilliant, though unlucky, Viceroy. On the defeat of the Conservative party at the polls (April, 1880) he at once tendered his resignation, and it was accepted. Lord Hartington reigned in Whitehall, Lord Ripon at Calcutta. The new Government, despite strong protest from the Queen, determined upon a complete and immediate reversal of the policy of their predecessors. On one point only was there momentary hesitation. Lord Ripon himself realized the difficulty of abandoning Kandahár.

Roberts's march to Kandahár

Mr. Gladstone in power

Roberts regarded its retention as of " vital importance ". All the soldiers in India and most of the civilians were with him. The Queen ardently supported his views at home. But there were strong arguments on the other side. Sher Alí proved himself to be a weak creature, incapable of maintaining the position in which we had placed him without our help. Abdur Rahman regarded Kandahár as essential to his hold on Herát. To retain it meant friction with the Amír, hostility wíth the tribesmen, perhaps war with both. Lord Hartington, though not without grave consideration,[1] decided that as soon as it could be done with dignity and safety Kandahár must be evacuated. Lord Ripon was brought round to the view that the retention of Quetta would give us all the strategic advantages we could desire without the certain expense and possible danger of garrisoning Kandahár. Quetta was retained, and in April, 1881, the evacuation of Kandahár was completed. Thus the Treaty of Gandamak was torn up, and Abdur Rahman ruled over " a friendly, strong, and independent Afghanistán ". The policy of disintegration was repudiated, and we reverted to that of a buffer State. Thanks to the timely emergence of a strong and exceptionally sagacious ruler that policy relieved us of danger, though not of anxiety, for twenty years.

Afghanistán was not the only problem bequeathed by the Beaconsfield Cabinet to their successors. The " forward " policy had been adopted in other parts of the world, and nowhere with more significant results than in South Africa. On April 12th, 1877, Sir Theophilus Shepstone, acting in accordance with the discretion allowed him by Lord Carnarvon, proclaimed the annexation of the Transvaal to the British Crown.

This history has hitherto been silent as to the progress of British rule in South Africa, and the omission must now be repaired. From the middle of the seventeenth century down to the close of the eighteenth, Cape Colony was a dependency of the Dutch East India Company, being utilized by their ships as a port of call and by their sailors as a vegetable garden. In 1795 the United Provinces became a dependency of the French Republic, and to save Cape Colony from a similar fate it was occupied by a British force. Handed back to the Batavian Republic in 1802, it was reconquered by England in 1806, and at the Peace of Paris (1814) it was purchased for £6,000,000 sterling from the Dutch Government and became the property of Great Britain. But though the Government was British, the white inhabitants were mainly Dutch. Not until after 1820 was there any considerable emigration from this country. Between the British Government, progressive in policy, and the Dutch farmers, strongly Conservative in instinct, causes of friction rapidly developed—notably in regard to the treatment of the natives. The zeal of the English

[1] *Cf.* Holland, *Devonshire*, i. 304-318.

Government and of the English missionaries was perhaps more obvious than their discretion, and with the enforcement of the Act for the abolition of slavery the cup of Dutch indignation overflowed. That Act was administered with flagrant disregard for the interests of the Dutch farmers and with scant respect for their vested rights. They consequently determined to shake off the dust of the British Government from their feet, and to seek freedom in the vast hinterland of South Africa. This was the meaning of the Great Boer Trek (1836-1840)—the cardinal fact of South African history, and a story, in some respects, curiously romantic and pathetic. The ultimate result of the Great Trek was the establishment of two Boer States virtually independent, the Transvaal and the Orange Free State.[1] *The Great Boer Trek*

Meanwhile, a handful of English colonists had established themselves at Port Natal (1824), but the Boers from the north and west of the Drakensberg range threatened their existence, and in the early 'forties it seemed probable that a third Boer State would be established between the Drakensberg and the sea. In 1843, however, Natal was formally proclaimed to be a British Colony, and the Boers after a brief struggle sullenly withdrew to the west of the Drakensberg. Down to 1856 Natal was regarded as forming part of Cape Colony, but in that year it was declared independent, and it attained to the full dignity of " responsible " government in 1893. *Natal*

What were the relations between Cape Colony and the Boer States to the north ? From the moment of the Trek there were two possible alternatives open to the English Government : either frankly to recognize the secession of the Boers, and in due time to acknowledge the existence of European States in South Africa independent of the British flag ; or, to make it clear from the outset, that no other power would be tolerated in South Africa, and that the Boer farmers, go where they would, must remain subject to the English Crown. For either policy there was something to be said. Unfortunately for the credit of British rule in South Africa we adopted neither, or, rather, we adopted both. Thus in 1848 Sir Harry Smith, the English Governor of Cape Colony, issued a proclamation to the effect that " the whole territory between the Orange and Vaal Rivers as far east as the Drakensberg was to be under the Sovereignty of the Queen ". The Dutch farmers under Pretorius protested against this " assumption " of Sovereignty, but they were worsted in battle at Boomplatz (Aug. 29th, 1848). Some of them fled to the north of the Vaal, the rest acquiesced, with no good grace, and accepted the authority of the Queen in the " Orange River Sovereignty ". The Home Government was lukewarm in its support of Sir Harry Smith. In 1851 the whole force of Cape Colony was engaged in one of the perennial struggles with the Kaffirs on the eastern frontier of the Colony, and Pretorius, then an outlaw beyond the Vaal, threatened *British and Boers*

---

[1] Slavery abolition was only one of many causes of the Great Trek.

to raise an insurrection in the Orange Sovereignty unless the independence of his countrymen to the north of the Vaal were recognized.

The Sand River Convention, June 17th, 1852
Consequently, in 1852, the Sand River Convention was concluded. Great Britain thereby conceded " to the emigrant farmers beyond the Vaal River the right to manage their own affairs, and to govern themselves, without any interference on the part of Her Majesty, the Queen's Government ". Thus the South African or Transvaal Republic came into being as an independent State. But with two reservations : it was to be open to all comers on equal terms, and no slavery was to be permitted or practised. Meanwhile, we were involved in troubles with the Basutos, the natives to the east of the Orange River Sovereignty, and, at the close of the war, General Cathcart, the officer in command, reported that it would be necessary to station 2,000 troops permanently in the Sovereignty. The Home Government were in no mind for the assumption of further military responsibilities, and preferred the alternative of withdrawal.

The Bloemfontein Convention, February 23rd, 1854
The Bloemfontein Convention was a counterpart of that concluded two years earlier with the Transvaal Boers. Thus the Orange Free State took its place side by side with the South African Republic, and it seemed as though definite limits were to be set to British Sovereignty towards the north-west.[1]

Sir George Grey
For nearly twenty years the policy of non-intervention was consistently maintained. Meanwhile, the Cape Colony itself advanced steadily towards the goal of self-government. During the vigorous and enlightened administration of Sir George Grey (1854-1861), Cape Colony was endowed with an elected Legislature and attained to " responsible " government in 1872. But Sir George Grey had a far wider vision than that bounded by the horizon of responsible government. Looking beyond the vacillating policy hitherto pursued by Great Britain in South Africa, he saw that the only possible path of safety lay in some form of federation. The State Paper in which, in 1858, he submitted his views to the Home Government is one of the ablest documents in the history of our Colonial Empire. Grey had the support of the Boers of the Orange River Sovereignty. Their *Volksraad* resolved in 1858 " that a union or alliance with the Cape Colony, either on the plan of federation or otherwise, is desirable ". But the only reply of the Colonial Office was to recall Grey for exceeding his instructions. He was restored by the personal intervention of the Queen, but he returned to Cape Town with tarnished prestige, and with gravely impaired authority. Had the Home Government grasped the problem as Sir George Grey grasped it, had they even had the sense to trust " the man on the spot," the whole subsequent course of South African history might have been

---

[1] For the remarkably interesting Constitutions evolved by the Boer Republics during the period of independence, see Bryce, *Studies in History and Jurisprudence*.

different. Mr. F. W. Reitz, the Transvaal Secretary of State in 1899, wrote to Sir George Grey in 1893 : " Had British Ministers in time past been wise enough to follow your advice, there would undoubtedly be to-day a British dominion extending from Table Bay to Zambesi ".[1] But the weary Titan was tired of the whole " burden " of colonial establishments and was looking forward to the happy day when " those wretched Colonies would no longer hang like millstones round our necks ".

Responsibilities once assumed are not, however, so lightly shaken Expan-off. Towards the end of the 'sixties the period of masterly inactivity sion in was drawing to a close in South Africa as in India. In 1868 the Africa Boers on the Orange River became involved in a dispute with the Basutos to the east of them. The Basuto Chief addressed a prayer to the British Government : " Let me and my people rest under the large folds of the flag of England ". His prayer was heard, and in 1869 British Sovereignty was proclaimed over Basutoland.

In 1871 Griqualand West, a native territory to the west of the Orange State, was similarly annexed to the Crown. This important acquisition gave us the diamond fields of the Kimberley district. But its importance was not measured only in diamonds. The annexation meant a new turn in the wheel of policy : the definite abandonment of the *laisser faire* attitude which for the last thirty years had been characteristic of British policy in South Africa, as elsewhere. The acquisition of the Kimberley diamond-field meant also a new strain in the social life of South Africa. " The digger, the capitalist, the company promoter jostled the slow moving Dutch farmer and quickened the pace of life." [2]

Such was the condition of affairs in South Africa when, in 1874, Lord Lord Carnarvon took up the reins at the Colonial Office. Lord Carnarvon was the Minister who had been officially responsible for policy, the enactment of a Federal Constitution for British North America, 1874-1877 and he was anxious to confer a similar boon upon South Africa. The moment appeared not inopportune, for in 1872 a Federation Commission had been appointed in Cape Colony. But Cape Colony was in the first flush of self-satisfaction at the attainment of responsible government and had no leisure for the larger problem.

Nevertheless, Lord Carnarvon wrote to the Governor of the Cape Attemp-in 1875 to propose that the several States of South Africa should ted con-be invited to a Conference to discuss native policy and other points tion of common interest, and to ventilate " the all-important question of a possible union of South Africa in some form of confederation ".[3] The proposal was not welcomed in Cape Colony, and Mr. Froude, the eminent historian, who had been sent out to represent the Colonial Office at the proposed Conference, found his position highly

---

[1] Quoted by Egerton, *Federations*, etc., p. 71.
[2] Lucas, *South Africa*, p. 246.   [3] Lucas, *op. cit.*, p. 264.

embarrassing both to himself and to his hosts.[1] Froude put his finger with great acuteness upon the root difficulty : " If we can make up our minds to allow the colonists to manage the natives their own way we may safely confederate the whole country." Of federation, however, imposed upon them from London, the colonists would hear nothing. The Conference in South Africa never met.

Lord Carnarvon, not to be foiled, invited various gentlemen interested in South Africa to confer with him at the Colonial Office (Aug. 1876). The Cape Premier, Mr. Molteno, happened to be in London but was forbidden to attend ; no delegate was present from the Transvaal ; and Mr. Brand, President of the Orange Free State (who greatly impressed Froude), attended under strict injunctions from his *Volksraad* not to take part in any negotiations respecting federation by which the independence of his own state could be endangered. Sir Theophilus Shepstone and two members of the Legislature represented Natal. As regards federation the meeting was entirely abortive.[2]

Despite this discouragement Lord Carnarvon sent out to South Africa (in Dec. 1876) the draft of a permissive Confederation Bill, which in the session of 1877 was passed into law by the Imperial Legislative. This enabling Act contained the outline of a complete Federal Constitution. It was for the South African Colonies to fill it in if they would. Lord Carnarvon, while insisting that the " action of all parties whether in the British Colonies or the Dutch States must be spontaneous and uncontrolled," informed the new Governor of the Cape that he had been selected " to carry my scheme of confederation into effect ".[3] The man chosen for this high task was one of the most trusted and experienced servants of the Crown, one to whose life-work the confederation of South Africa might form an appropriate and noble crown. It was the expressed hope of his Chief that within two years he would be " the first Governor-General of South Africa ". The words read ironically, for the reign of Sir Bartle Frere (1877-1880) coincided, through no fault of his own, with the darkest period in South African history.

Annexa-   Less than a month after Sir Bartle Frere reached Cape Town
tion of   (March 31, 1877), another agent of Lord Carnarvon's took a step
the   which opened a new chapter in British policy in South Africa. Sir
Transvaal   Theophilus Shepstone was Secretary for native affairs in Natal, and
1877   no man had more intimate knowledge of the native problem. In October, 1876, he was sent out by Lord Carnarvon as " Special Commissioner to enquire respecting certain disturbances which have taken place in the territories adjoining the colony of Natal," and he was authorized, at his discretion, and provided it were desired by the inhabitants, " to annex to the British dominion all or part of the

---

[1] *Cf.* Paul, *Life of Froude*, c. vii. Eight gentlemen invited to meet him at dinner at Government House refused.
[2] Lucas, *op. cit.* p. 265.   [3] Egerton, *Federations*, etc., p. 72.

territories which formed the scene of his enquiry ".[1]   The scene was
the Transvaal Republic.   At this moment the Boers of the Transvaal
were in serious danger of annihilation at the hands of their native
neighbours.   More than this.   The condition and policy of the
Republic constituted a serious menace to the reputation and even
the existence of the whole white population of South Africa.   The
Boers had incurred the bitter enmity of Cetewayo, King of the
powerful tribe of the Zulus, as well as of the Matabele Chief, Lobengula.
With another Chief, Sekukuni, they were, in 1876, actually at war.
Morally and materially the Boers were bankrupt, and their native
enemies were only awaiting the opportunity to " eat them up ".
That process might begin with the Boers ; it was not likely to end
with them.   Under these circumstances Shepstone, after three
months of careful enquiry, decided that annexation was the only
remedy for the disease, and, on April 12th, 1877, he took over the
administration of the Transvaal in the Queen's name, promising to
the Boers complete self-government under the British Crown.   The
President, Mr. Burgers, after a formal protest, retired to Cape Town
on a pension ; his rival, the Vice-President, Mr. Kruger, proceeded
to London and tried to persuade Lord Carnarvon to reverse the
policy of his agent.   This the Colonial Secretary declined to do.

That the annexation saved the Boers of the Transvaal from The Zulu
destruction is hardly open to question.   But it left the British War, 1879
Government face to face, in a more acute form than ever before,
with the native problem.   A series of disputes with the Zulus led
in January, 1879, to the outbreak of war.   The history of that war
may be thus briefly summarized : one grievous disaster, several
deeds of heightened heroism, one great and final victory.   At
Isandhlwana (Jan. 22nd) a British force of 800 whites and 500 natives
was literally cut to pieces.   This was the disaster more than half
redeemed by the heroic defence of Rorke's Drift.   For eleven and a
half hours, less than 100 men of the 24th, under two subalterns,
Bromhead and Chard, held the Drift against 4,000 Zulus.   The
defence of this post on the Buffalo River saved Natal.   The final
victory was won by Lord Chelmsford at Ulundi in the Zulu territory
on July 4th.   Cetewayo was afterwards captured and sent as a
prisoner to Cape Town and the power of his people was finally broken.
In the course of a war, brief but full of incident, the exiled Prince
Imperial of France, the heir of Napoleon III., who had volunteered
to serve with the British force, was unfortunately killed in a recon-
naisance (June 1st), owing to the carelessness of the officer who had
been entrusted with the operation.

Before the year 1879 closed, a British force destroyed the power
of Sekunkuni, and this inveterate enemy of the Boers joined Cetewayo
in captivity.

[1] Egerton, *Federations*, etc., p. 274.

The Boer War, 1880-1881

The Boers could now breathe freely ; the English had destroyed their enemies. The Dutch leaders had never ceased to protest against annexation, and their visits to London led them to hope much from the rapid vicissitudes of party government. Their hopes were not destined to disappointment. In the Transvaal, Frere found in 1879 that the Boers, despite official assertions in London, were confident that their country would be given back. The history of the retrocession of the Orange Free State had taught them a lesson. Most unfortunately, there had been grave procrastination in regard to the fulfilment of Shepstone's promise of self-government. In June, 1879, Sir Garnet Wolseley was sent out to take over, as High Commissioner, supreme civil and military command. Shortly after his arrival a Crown Colony Constitution was conferred upon the Transvaal. But this was far short of the legitimate expectations of the Boers, and their disappointment was great. The new High Commissioner declared in the Queen's name that it was the will and determination of Her Majesty's Government that the Transvaal should remain for ever " an integral portion of Her Majesty's dominions in South Africa ". Her Majesty's Government was about to change hands. In the autumn of 1879 Mr. Gladstone insisted in his Midlothian speeches on the insanity of " the free subjects of a Monarch going to coerce the free subjects of a Republic ". On coming into power in 1880 his Government declared that " under no circumstances can the Queen's authority in the Transvaal be relinquished ". Bitter was the disappointment of the Boers, and on December 16th, 1880, Messrs. Kruger, Pretorius, and Joubert issued a proclamation declaring the independence of the Transvaal Republic. The moment was well chosen. The Basuto rebellion was in full progress ; the Transvaal was almost denuded of British troops, and on December 10th some companies of the 94th were surprised and cut to pieces at Bronker's Spruit, a place about forty miles from Pretoria. Sir George Colley had succeeded Wolseley in July and with a small force he hurried up to Newcastle in January (1881). Checked with heavy loss at Laing's Nek (Jan. 28th) and again at Ingogo (Feb. 7th) he met his death in the disastrous defeat at Majuba Hill (Feb. 26th). Ireland combined with South Africa to compel an early meeting of Parliament (Jan. 6th, 1881), and the Queen's Speech emphasized " the duty of taking military measures with a view to the prompt vindication of my authority ". Sir Frederick Roberts was sent out in command of a considerable force, but he arrived in South Africa only to find that Sir Evelyn Wood, who succeeded Colley, had signed an agreement with the Boers acknowledging their right to complete self-government under the suzerainty of the Queen (March 23rd). The Pretoria Convention, in which these terms were embodied, was amended three years later by the Convention of London (Feb. 27th, 1884). The latter treaty acknowledged the

" South African Republic," and, while retaining the control of external relations, deleted all reference to the suzerainty of the Queen. The whole policy of retrocession was violently assailed by the Conservative opposition in England [1] and it signally failed to achieve a final settlement in South Africa.

Between 1881 and the close of the century a series of profound Epilogue changes passed over South Africa. British Sovereignty was extended over Bechuanaland (1885), over Zululand (1886), and in 1889 the British South Africa Company was incorporated by Royal Charter, and accepted the administration of Mashonaland. In 1894 the Company scotched the power of the Matabeles and annexed their territory.[2] The conclusion of a convention with Germany in 1890, and with Portugal in 1891, reminded us—and others—that we had European neighbours in South Africa.

Meanwhile, in the Transvaal itself, an event of first-rate import- Gold in ance had taken place. Gold in great profusion was discovered in the 1886 on the Witwatersrand,[3] and the discovery attracted a crowd of Trans- adventurers who introduced into the social and economic life of the vaal South African Republic an entirely new strain. The slow-moving, intensely conservative farmers deeply resented this intrusion. Oil would not mix with water. The new-comers demanded political rights commensurate with their contribution to the wealth of the community. The Boer Government refused to grant them. At the close of the year 1895 the " Uitlanders " attempted to take by force what was denied to argument. Dr. Jameson, the administrator of the British South Africa Company, raided with an armed force the Transvaal territory. His force was crushed ; his confederates in Johannesburg were imprisoned ; Jameson himself and his comrades were handed over to the British Government. The fiasco of the raid served only to increase the tension between the Boer oligarchy and the " Uitlanders " in the Transvaal,[4] and at the same time rendered it more difficult for the Paramount Power to interfere. In 1897 Sir Alfred (now Viscount) Milner was appointed to succeed Sir Hercules Robinson as High Commissioner ; in April, 1899, he forwarded to the Queen a petition, signed by 21,000 British subjects resident in the Transvaal, praying that the Queen would make enquiry into their grievances and secure for them an adequate and permanent remedy. In May, 1899, the High Commissioner met President Kruger in conference at Bloemfontein. The conference proved abortive, and on October 10th the two Boer Republics

[1] Cf. in particular the remarkable speech of Lord Cairns in the House of Lords, March 31st, 1881.

[2] That the power of the Matabeles was not finally broken was proved by the rebellion of 1896.

[3] This statement might seem to suggest that this was the first discovery of gold in the Transvaal. It had previously been discovered elsewhere.

[4] For the case of the " Uitlanders " cf. Fitzpatrick, Transvaal from Within, or V. R. Markham, South Africa, Past and Present.

declared war. The war opened disastrously for Great Britain, but the resistance of the Boers was gradually worn down, and in May, 1902, peace was concluded at Vereeniging on the Vaal.

The Union of South Africa

The long contest for supremacy in South Africa was at last ended, and ended in the only possible way. The two Burgher States were annexed to the British Crown. Peace was no sooner signed than matters began to settle down with remarkable rapidity, so rapidly that it was found possible to confer self-government upon the Transvaal in 1906, and upon the Orange River Colony in 1907. But, as in the case of Canada and Australia, the attainment of " responsibility " was but the prelude to a further development. The *Union Act* of 1909 brought the four self-governing Colonies into a political union. Thus was the dream of Sir George Grey and Lord Carnarvon more than fulfilled. They had dreamt of confederation. But while the Constitutions of Canada and Australia are genuinely federal, that of South Africa is unitary. The four colonies merge their identity in that of the United South Africa, and accept henceforward the status of *Provinces*. With the *Union Act* the final stage in the constitutional evolution of South Africa has, we may presume, been reached. " Spasmodic violence alternating with impatient dropping of the reins ; first severity and then indulgence, and then severity again, with no persisting in any one system—a process which drives nations mad as it drives children." Such was Froude's summary of England's dealing with South Africa in the nineteenth century. The twentieth opens with a happier prospect.

The fall of the Conservative Government

We must now return, after a prolonged parenthesis, to the closing days of the Beaconsfield administration. The threatenings of war in Eastern Europe, a forward policy eventuating in war both in Afghanistán and in South Africa—such were the questions which, to the casual observer, seemed to dominate the political situation. Not so did the Prime Minister read the signs of the times. On the eve of the election of 1880, Lord Beaconsfield indited to the Duke of Marlborough, then Lord Lieutenant of Ireland, a letter which was in effect a political manifesto. It sought to concentrate the attention of the electorate upon a single topic. Ireland was distracted by " a danger, in its ultimate results scarcely less disastrous than pestilence and famine," by an attempt " to sever the Constitutional tie which unites it to Great Britain in that bond which has formed the power and prosperity of both ".

The Irish policy of the Tories 1874-1880

Throughout the first years of Lord Beaconsfield's administration Ireland had enjoyed a spell of unusual prosperity and tranquillity. That spell was broken by agricultural depression in 1878, but the cardinal feature of the Irish question during the Conservative régime was not economic but political. The years between 1874 and 1880 witnessed the growth of a new Irish party, both in Ireland itself and at Westminster. Mr. Gladstone complacently believed that he had

discharged in full the debt of England to Ireland.[1] The majority of
the Irish electors did not share his optimism, and it is a grim com-
mentary upon this view that the first General Election after the
passing of the Acts of 1869 and 1870 should have resulted in the
return for the first time of a majority of Irish members pledged to
the repeal of the Union. But although the Home Rulers numbered
close on sixty in the Parliament of 1874, Mr. Butt's annual motion
was treated with contemptuous indifference. Legislation for Ireland
did not occupy much of the time of this Parliament. The Peace
Preservation Act was renewed in 1875, though with considerable
modification, for a further period of five years ; the Westmeath Act
was renewed until 1877 ; but the most important legislation of this
Parliament had reference to education. A million of money from
the Irish Church surplus was appropriated, in 1878, to the encouragement of intermediate education, and in 1879 a further million and a
quarter was taken from the same source to provide pensions for
elementary teachers. The same year witnessed successful legislation
on the question which had brought disaster upon Mr. Gladstone. If The
the scope of Lord Beaconsfield's Irish University Act has been, as a Royal
rule, misunderstood, if the criticism of it is generally distorted, the Univer-
fault lies partly with its author. Under a most unpretentious aspect, Ireland
the Act contained the germ of a great concession. The Queen's
University was abolished, and in its place the Royal University of
Ireland was set up. The new University was to be primarily an
examining body, but the point which has escaped attention is that
it was supplied with the means of rewarding merit by Fellowships,
Scholarships, and Prizes. Of this endowment the Roman Catholics
have freely availed themselves. Thus the difficulty as to the state
endowment of a sectarian institution was surmounted, or rather
circumvented, with singular adroitness. " This is done," said Lord
Beaconsfield in private conversation, " in such a way that it will not
be understood, and when in due time the people of Great Britain
find that they are accepting the principle of an endowment which is
quite inadequate, their sense of justice will cause them to admit that
the Irish Roman Catholics are entitled to a properly endowed University College. . . . In fact, what we are doing is to place the ball at the
feet of the Roman Catholics, and if they do not kick it the fault will
be theirs and not ours." The conversation is well vouched for,[2] and
is eminently characteristic. Disraeli was never happier than when
" educating " his party and his countrymen. The morality of his
methods might be questioned, but their ingenuity was undeniable.
During the period that followed, the Irish Catholics kicked the ball
to some purpose ; but it is questionable whether the people of Great

---

[1] *Cf. The Vatican Decrees*, p. 59.
[2] By Mr. Edmund Dease, a member of the University Senate ; *cf.* Mr. Dease's
letter to the *Spectator*, December 31st, 1898.

Britain ever realized that it had been placed surreptitiously at their feet.

Charles Stewart Parnell By this time, however, a new force had made itself manifest in Irish politics, and a new " movement " had been inaugurated. Isaac Butt passed away, a weary and disappointed man, in 1879. His nominal successor in the leadership of the Home Rule Party was Mr. Shaw, but sometime before Butt's death a new leader had leapt to the front in the person of Charles Stewart Parnell.

Mr. Parnell was an Irish landowner of gentle birth ; on his father's side an Anglo-Celt, on his mother's an American.[1] He had none of the gifts of the demagogue, least of all the Irish demagogue ; no natural gift of speech, no sensibility, no passion. But he was a born leader of men, and he acquired in high degree the art of parliamentary tactics. Watchful, acute, restrained, he rarely made a blunder in the House of Commons, and never missed an opportunity. For English politicians and English people he had a genuine contempt, mingled with a hatred which was as near passionate as any feeling he could entertain. To his Irish confederates his attitude was one of consistent hauteur and aloofness. Inscrutable as Disraeli, he was as absolute in authority as Gladstone. He was only just of age [2] when his sympathies were excited by the execution of the Fenian prisoners in Manchester.

A visit to America (1871) confirmed both his sympathy for Fenianism and his hatred of England. He entered Parliament in 1875, took the measure of that assembly in a moment, and within two years was one of the most powerful forces in the House. He decided from the first that Home Rule must be achieved by tactics at Westminster and by agitation in Ireland and America. For English opinion he cared nothing, and he set himself deliberately to defy and to degrade the House of Commons by a policy of obstruction. In 1878 he cemented an alliance with the Clan-na-Gael or " New Fenians " by a second visit to America, and convinced the Irish-Americans, for the first time, of the efficacy of parliamentary action. In the same year he found a valuable, though not entirely congenial, ally in an ex-convict, Michael Davitt, recently released on ticket-of-leave from Dartmoor where he had been serving a term of imprisonment for being concerned with the secret importation of fire-arms into the kingdom. Davitt was not only a separatist but a socialist, a disciple of Henry George,[3] and convinced that the sovereign remedy for the economic and social disease of Ireland was the nationalization of the land. With this particular prescription Parnell had no

---

[1] His mother, Delia Stewart, was a daughter of an American Commander who played a prominent part in the war of 1812 against England.

[2] Born at Avondale, 1846.

[3] I am not, of course, unaware of the fact that many of the disciples of Henry George disclaim for themselves and their master the term " socialist," and deny that their proposals tend to " nationalization ".

sympathy; but Davitt was a useful ally, and in 1879 the Land
League was founded, with Parnell as its first President. The avowed
objects of the League were to reduce rack rents, and to facilitate the
purchase of farms by the cultivators. The real object was " the
complele destruction of Irish landlordism . . . because landlordism
was a British garrison which barred the way to national independence ".[1] Circumstances were favourable to this new agrarian
campaign : the harvest of 1879 was the worst since the famine,[2] and
the distress in Ireland was so great that the Duchess of Marlborough
opened a special relief fund, and the Government advanced funds
from the Church surplus to be applied, through the landlords, to
reproducive works.

Lord Beaconsfield, therefore, was not merely attempting to divert General
attention from his own misdeeds when, in his historic letter to the Election
Duke of Marlborough, he directed the interest of his countrymen to of 1880
the condition of Ireland. But a voice much more powerful at the
moment that Lord Beaconsfield's was exposing from the house-tops
the dead fruits of Imperialism. The outstanding feature of the
General Election of 1880 [3] was beyond all question the Midlothian
campaign waged, in the district round Edinburgh, by Mr. Gladstone
with a vigour and resourcefulness wonderful for any man, miraculous
in a man of over seventy. The results were not incommensurate
with the effort : the campaign gave the Liberals a majority of nearly
120 over the Conservatives, of 50 over Conservatives and Home
Rulers combined.[4] But the campaign did more than give the
Liberals a large majority ; it put Mr. Gladstone in power. Since
his definite retirement in 1875, the party in the House of Commons
had been led, with excellent temper and dignity though not quite
effectively, by Lord Hartington. But it was Lord Granville whom
Mr. Gladstone invariably regarded as the leader of the party, and
his destined successor in the Premiership. Lord Beaconsfield accepted
his unexpected defeat with unruffled equanimity, and following the
precedent he had himself set in 1868, he resigned before the meeting
of Parliament (April 21st).[5]

The Queen immediately sent for Lord Hartington. Lord Forma-
Hartington had accepted the leadership with reluctance and had tion of a
been deeply embarrassed by the rôle which, after his retirement, Mr. Ministry
Gladstone felt it his duty to play. Against his will he retained the
leadership, but having done so, he looked forward to the fitting

---

[1] Davitt, see *Report of Parnell Commission*, iv. 485, quoted by O'Connor
Morris, *op. cit.* p. 239.
[2] Morris, p. 240, estimates the loss in 1878-1879 at £10,000,000.
[3] Parliament was dissolved on March 24th.
[4] Liberals 351 ; Conservatives, 237 ; Home Rulers, 65.
[5] He was staying at Hatfield during the elections, and his unmoved serenity
amid the defeat of his party and the disappointment of his hopes was noted by the
few who were with him at the time ; from one of these I learnt it.

reward on the victory of his party at the polls.[1] His advice to
the Queen, however, was to send for Mr. Gladstone. Her Majesty
demurred, and only consented when it was made clear to her by
Lord Hartington and Lord Granville conjointly that Mr.
Gladstone would accept no place but the first, and that they could not form a
Government without him. The Queen acquiesced, and on April
23rd Mr. Gladstone kissed hands as First Lord of the Treasury and
Chancellor of the Exchequer.[2] Lord Granville took the Foreign
Office, Lord Hartington the India Office.[3] Lord Selborne again
became Lord Chancellor ; Lord Kimberley, Colonial Secretary ;
Forster, Chief Secretary for Ireland ; Lord Northbrook took the
Admiralty, and Childers the War Office. Two recruits were brought
into the Cabinet : Sir William Harcourt as Home Secretary, and Mr.
Joseph Chamberlain as President of the Board of Trade.[4] Mr.
Henry Fawcett, though not in the Cabinet, made noteworthy his
tenure of the Post Office, and Sir Charles Dilke represented, with
uncommon ability, the Foreign Office in the House of Commons.

Causes of
Liberal
victory

Before we turn to the history of the Gladstone Ministry a word
may be said as to the causes of the Conservative débacle. The first
may be found in the law of anti-climax. Had Lord Beaconsfield
yielded to the temptation of dissolving in 1878, he would probably,
though not certainly, have secured a new term of office for his party.
Down to that time their record, both administrative and legislative,
was a good one. Mr. Cross had made a notable success at the Home
Office ; their finance was respectable, and their general administration was sound. After 1878 everything went wrong. Trade and
agriculture became increasingly depressed ; the impudent tactics of
Parnell in the House of Commons impaired the reputation of its
leader ; the defeat at Islandhlwana was followed by the tragedy at
Kábul. But while these things may account for the defeat of the
Conservatives, the victory of the Liberals was due to another cause.
It was the moral fervour of Mr. Gladstone which recaptured the
straying allegiance of the Nonconformists, and his resort to new
political methods which for the first time aroused the enthusiasm of
the newly enfranchised masses. It is easy to condemn those methods
as demogogic ; to lament the " degradation of British politics " ;[5]

[1] See Holland's *Life*, i. 271.
[2] For circumstances regarding this negotiation see the interesting account
written by Gladstone ap. Morley, ii. 621 ; and *cf.* Fitzmaurice, *Granville*, ii. 193,
and Holland's *Devonshire*, i. 270 *seq.* Gladstone thought the Queen wrong in
sending for Hartington on the ground that it was to Granville he had " resigned
his trust," but with respect I submit that it was not even for Mr. Gladstone, in
Opposition, to designate his successor to the Queen.
[3] This being in Mr. Gladstone's opinion " next to the Foreign Office, and as
very near in weight and perhaps the most difficult of all at this time "
[4] The other Cabinet Ministers were : Lord Spencer (Lord President) ; Duke of
Argyll (Privy Seal) ; Bright (Duchy of Lancaster), and Dodson (Local Government
Board).
[5] The expression is Lord Selborne's, *cf. Memorials*, ii. 470.

to sigh for the days of greater dignity, repose, and restraint. But the Midlothian campaign was more than the triumph of oratory, more even than the victory of personality ; it was the recognition of a stupendous change coming over the face of the political waters : the shifting of the centre of political gravity from Parliament to the platform, from the House of Commons to the constituencies, from the classes to the masses. That change was first registered by the plébiscite which, in 1880, placed Mr. Gladstone in power.

CHAPTER XXV

THE GLADSTONE ADMINISTRATION. IRELAND AND EGYPT
(1880-1885)

The
death of
Beacons-
field,
April
19th,
1881

THE General Election of 1880 turned largely upon questions of foreign policy. Mr. Gladstone himself framed a wholesale indictment against what he described as the " Beaconsfieldian system ". The verdict of the country was in his favour, and it was inevitable that effect should be given to that verdict. It has been already shown how that was done in Afghanistán and South Africa. Lord Beaconsfield did not long survive his defeat. Amid the ruin and reversal of his policy, he passed away on April 19th, 1881. His death, under circumstances almost tragic, aroused a wave of deep feeling in the country. The Queen felt it as a personal bereavement, and paid unique honour to his memory. With her own hands she placed a wreath upon his coffin, and erected in Hughenden Church a tablet bearing an inscription from her own pen.[1] There was no shrewder judge of character than Queen Victoria, and that she trusted Lord Beaconsfield is a high testimonial to his integrity and patriotism. But to the majority of his countrymen he remains, what throughout a long career he always was, an enigma. His enemies described him as un-English, his patriotism they declared was pinchbeck, and his sense of honour distorted. In home politics they believed him to be merely opportunist, self-seeking, and un-principled. Much of the adverse criticism was due to early prejudice which he never quite lived down. He was not born to the purple, and for the greater part of his life he had to fight, and fight hard, for his own hand. Nevertheless, inscrutable as he was, some things are clear. He was a man of unyielding courage, of wonderful temper, of intense concentration of purpose. A bitter antagonist, he had real magnanimity, and never bore a grudge. He was a skilful tactician, conciliatory as a colleague, and considerate as a chief. Can he be described as a patriot ? Patriotism is difficult of definition, but this at least may be said that no man since Chatham had a higher sense of the honour and greatness of England (as he understood those attributes) than Benjamin Disraeli, Earl of Beaconsfield.[2]

The
Parlia-
mentary
Oath

Apart from foreign policy the new Government was soon launched upon a sea of troubles. Of the most turbulent—Ireland—something

---

[1] " To the dear and honoured memory of Benjamin, Earl of Beaconsfield, this memorial is placed by his grateful Sovereign and friend, Victoria, R.I. 'Kings love him that speaketh right.' "

[2] Bishop Stubbs's masterly analysis of the character of Simon de Montfort comes irresistibly into mind, though the parallelism is far from complete : " He is scarcely a patriot—a foreigner could hardly be expected to be so ; he is somewhat more distinctly a hero, but he never quite rids himself of the character of an adventurer ".

will be said later ; but not even Ireland, perhaps, caused the Cabinet and its chief more worry than what was known as the Bradlaugh case. Charles Bradlaugh, a notorious and out-spoken atheist, was returned for Northampton at the General Election.   The Parliamentary Oath ran : " I will be faithful and bear true allegiance to Queen Victoria, her heirs and successors, according to law, so help me God ". Bradlaugh claimed, instead of taking this Oath, to be allowed under the Parliamentary Oaths Act of 1866 to make an affirmation.   A Select Committee decided that he was not entitled to do so.   He then offered to take the oath with its " meaningless addendum " in the usual form.   A second Select Committee decided that he could not do so.   The House then refused to allow him to affirm ; but under a new standing order he was subsequently allowed to affirm, subject to statute (July 1st).   The case was now transferred to the Courts, who decided against Bradlaugh's right to affirm, and vacated his seat.   Promptly re-elected by Northampton (April, 1881), he presented himself to take the Oath, and the House repeatedly refused him permission to do so.   In February, 1882, he administered the Oath to himself and was expelled from the House. Re-elected by his constituents he repeated the process.   The Government proceeded against him for illegally taking the Oath, and the Courts decided against Bradlaugh.   He then applied for the Chiltern Hundreds, stood again and was re-elected (1884).   He was again elected by Northampton at the General Election of 1885, and Mr. Speaker Peel then declared that he knew " of no right whatever to intervene between him and the form of legal and statutable obligation ".   Bradlaugh quietly took the Oath and remained until his death (1891) a highly respected member of the House.   In 1888 an Affirmation Act was passed, and in 1891 all the resolutions against Bradlaugh were expunged from the Journal.

The case is important for several reasons.   Like the case of Wilkes, it raised the question as to the relations between the House of Commons and a constituency, and also the relations between the House and the Courts of Law.   In 1884 the Court refused to interfere with the privilege of the House of Commons to control its own proceedings and its own members.[1]   The matter had a political as well as a constitutional significance.   It gave a very bad start to the new Parliament and the new Government ; it led to the virtual supersession of Sir Stafford Northcote as Leader of the Opposition ; it brought into existence a distinct group of young Conservatives— a " Fourth Party " of four members,[2] and into special prominence a new parliamentary personality—Lord Randolph Churchill.[3]

Bradlaugh v. Gossett, 46 and 47 Vict. 1883.   Cf. Robertson, Select Cases, pp. 406-415, and on the whole case, Anson, Law and Custom (Parliament), pp. 87-89, and Erskine May (continued by Holland), iii. 222-228.

[2] I.e. Churchill, Gorst, Balfour, and Drummond Wolff.

[3] Cf. Lang, Iddesleigh, c. xvi. and xvii. ;   W. S. Churchill, Lord R. Churchill, i. c. iii., and Gorst, Fourth Party.

Domestic
legisla-
tion

With the domestic legislation of this Parliament we must deal summarily. The *Burials Act* (1880) removed a grievance of Nonconformists, by permitting them to bury their dead in parish churchyards with religious forms selected by themselves, or without any at all. The *Ground Game Act* (1880), popularly known as the " Hares and Rabbits Act," allowed tenant-farmers to protect their crops from " vermin " and to share the sport of their landlords. The *Agricultural Holdings Act* (1883) strengthened the Act of 1875, by making compensation for improvements compulsory instead of permissive. More important was the *Employers Liability Act* (1880), which gave the workman a legal right to compensation from his employer for injury sustained in the course of his employment through negligent management. The *Bankruptcy Act*, passed by Mr. Chamberlain in 1883, was a bold assumption of responsibility on the part of a State Department. Its effect was to transfer the control over insolvent estates from the Court of Bankruptcy to the Board of Trade and its Official Receivers. Less successful was the *Electric Lighting Act* of 1882, passed by the same energetic administrator. The intention of the Act was to encourage municipal enterprise in the provision of electric light ; the result was to place serious obstacles in the path of private enterprise, and to keep Great Britain twenty years behind any other civilized country in regard to the commercial development of electricity. So disastrous was the Act that in 1888 Parliament thought it well to amend it, and to give rather more encouragement to private enterprise. But a powerful obstructive weapon still remained in the hands of the municipalities. By obtaining a Provisional Order they could block private competition, and yet do nothing themselves. That gas-owning Corporations should have sought to postpone the advent of a powerful competitor was natural, but this episode is an apt illustration of the evil that frequently arises from well-intentioned legislation. A useful Act was passed in 1883 to diminish corrupt practices at elections ; and in 1884 the Government reopened the whole question of parliamentary reform.

Parlia-
mentary
reform

During the previous decade repeated attempts had been made, notably by Mr. George Trevelyan, to assimilate the county franchise to that established in boroughs by the Act of 1867. From 1872 to 1879 an annual motion was defeated by considerable majorities. But in 1884 the Government, of which Trevelyan was now a member, made themselves responsible for the Bill. It passed through the House of Commons, but the Lords, on the motion of Lord Cairns, declined to assent to " a fundamental change in the electoral body " until they had before them the details of the promised scheme for the redistribution of seats. The action of the Lords aroused a violent agitation in the country and bitter attacks were made upon the Second Chamber. Their action had logic and

reason behind it, yet the country resented delay. The case was
eminently one for compromise ; but an impartial arbitrator was
needed to bring the parties together. Rarely in modern politics
has the Crown played a more useful part than in making peace
between the two Parties and the two Houses in the autumn of 1884.
The Queen was greatly impressed by the gravity of the situation,
and during the recess she laboured assiduously to bring the two
sides together. And not in vain. Mr. Gladstone met Lord Salisbury
and Sir Stafford Northcote, and discussed with them the details of
the Redistribution Scheme. Satisfied on the main points, the Conservative Leaders allowed the Franchise Bill to pass, and in 1885
the Redistribution Act also became law. By the former the county
was assimilated to the borough franchise, and some 2,000,000 voters
were added to the electoral register. The latter went some way
towards the principle of equal electoral areas. All boroughs with
less than 15,000 inhabitants [1] were disfranchised and merged in the
county districts ; boroughs with less than 50,000 inhabitants were
to lose one member. For the rest, with the exception of twenty-two
towns which retained two members apiece, and certain Universities,
the whole country, counties and boroughs alike, was divided into
single-member constituencies. In order to effect this twelve additional members were added to the House, bringing up the total
number to 670. A profound change was thus accomplished virtually
" by consent ". That consent, however, was obtained by the mediation of the Crown, and Mr. Gladstone had good reason " to tender
his grateful thanks " to the Queen " for the wise, gracious, and steady
influence on her Majesty's part," which had " so powerfully contributed to bring about this accommodation, and to avert a serious
crisis of affairs ".[2]

The imminent danger of a collision between the two branches of The Irish
the Legislature was only one of the many anxieties which pressed problem
upon the Prime Minister. Ever since the Liberals had returned to again
power they had been harassed by difficulties in Ireland. Lord
Beaconsfield had seen the cloud then no bigger than a man's hand.
Nobody at the time believed that his warning was other than an
election device. His opponents discovered to their cost how accurate
his diagnosis had been.[3]

The post of difficulty was assigned to Mr. Forster with Lord
Cowper as his Lord Lieutenant. They began their administration
valiantly ; they declined to renew the Peace Preservation Act, and
declared that they would try to govern Ireland under the ordinary
law. Within six months they discovered its insufficiency, and
besought their reluctant colleagues to call Parliament together and

---

[1] Of these there were thirteen returning two members apiece, and sixty-eight
returning one.
[2] Cf. Morley, Gladstone, iii. 129-139, and Lang, Iddesleigh, p. 352.
[3] Cf. e.g. Morley, iii. 48.

obtain for them further powers. In the meantime the Government had passed an Act for the relief of distress, and had attempted to pass a "Compensation for Disturbance Bill". More than one thousand evictions had taken place in the first six months of 1880; Lord Hartington, himself the heir to a great Irish property, declared that some landlords were taking advantage of the agricultural distress to clear their estates of poor tenants without expense to themselves. The Bill proposed that an evicted tenant should be entitled to "compensation for disturbance," if he could prove that he was unable to pay his rent owing to the bad harvests of the last three years ; that he was willing to continue his tenancy on just and reasonable terms, and that these terms had been unreasonably refused by the landlord. The Bill was to remain in operation only until the close of the year, but even so it had few friends. In its ultimate form the Parnellites declined to support it, and though it was carried in the Commons the Lords rejected it by 282 to 51 votes.

The Land League   Its rejection gave the signal, if not the excuse, for a terrible outbreak of lawlessness in Ireland. Speaking at Ennis in September, Parnell launched the "boycotting"[1] campaign. The man who took a farm from which the tenant had been evicted was to be put into a "moral coventry," to be isolated "from his kind as if he was a leper of old". The tale of agrarian outrages mounted higher and higher.[2] In October the Government resolved to prosecute Mr. Parnell, Mr. Biggar, Mr. John Dillon, Mr. Sexton and others for conspiracy to prevent the payment of rent. But the jury, as was foreseen, disagreed. Mr. Forster was convinced that further powers were necessary, but Mr. Gladstone, believing him to be a "very impracticable man," was slow to agree. His colleagues, however, were against the Prime Minister, and he "submitted".[3]

Coercion Acts, 1881   Parliament was summoned in the first week of 1881 and was at once asked to arm the Irish Executive with further powers. The *Protection of Life and Property* Bill gave the Lord Lieutenant power to detain in prison, without trial for a period not extending beyond September 30th, 1882, any person reasonably suspected of treasonable practices or agrarian offences. The proposal was drastic but not difficult to justify. "In Ireland," said Forster, "the *Land League* law[4] is supreme, and there is a real reign of terror over the whole country." "With painful and fatal precision," said Gladstone, "the steps of crime dog the steps of the Land League." The leaders of that League in the House of Commons used every art to obstruct the progress of the Bill. A sitting of forty-one hours was ended by

[1] So called from Captain Boycott, one of its first and most resolute victims and opponents.
[2] 2590 in 1880 as against 301 in 1878.
He seems to have been alone in his Cabinet.—Morley, iii. 50.
[4] *I.e.* the orders of an Association formed for the purpose of depriving the Irish landlords of their property.

the courageous action of Mr. Speaker Brand, who, on his own responsibility, stopped the debate and put the question. Thus was the first Reading carried. Thirty-six Irish members were suspended, and the powers of the Speaker in regard to the restriction of debate were enlarged. A second Bill prohibiting the possession of arms or ammunition in a " proclaimed " district was also passed before the end of March.

In April Mr. Gladstone himself introduced a Bill described by Lord Morley of Blackburn as giving the Irish peasant " the charter of his liberation ". As a fact, the Bill ignored the best Irish opinion of the day, and did nothing towards a permanent solution of the agrarian problem.

The Land Act of 1881

It was based upon the principle of the " three F's "—free sale, fixity of tenure, and fair rent. It gave to sitting tenants increased security of tenure, the right of selling their interest in the holding to the highest bidder, and the privilege of having a " fair " rent fixed for a period of fifteen years by a judicial tribunal. There were also clauses, which proved practically inoperative, for facilitating land purchase and the multiplication of occupying owners. The Bill was based, like the Act of 1870, on the assumption, denied by few genuine Irish landlords, that the Irish tenant possesses an interest in the soil quite unlike anything which could be equitably claimed for an English tenant. But it proceeded to recognize this right in the wrong way. It conferred a vast boon upon the sitting tenant at the expense not only of the landlord but of all future tenants. The consequence has been that the respective interests of landlord and tenant have varied not in concurrent but in inverse ratios. The lower the rent the higher the value of the Tenant Right, until the one threatens to absorb the other, and the fee simple is virtually transferred to the sitting tenant. Had Mr. Gladstone condescended to listen to the best Irish opinion,[1] or even to that of his own Irish law officers, the Tenant Right would have been fixed in the terms of the rent demanded or offered, and the worst results of the Bill would have been avoided. It was in fact a fair-weather Act ; it encountered storms of exceptional severity and it foundered. The solution of the problem has been found not in the recognition of " dual ownership," but in the creation of cultivating owners by means of state-aided purchase. The Bill cost Mr. Gladstone one of his ablest colleagues, the Duke of Argyll, but despite the Duke's vigorous opposition, the House of Lords, with some modifications, accepted the Bill and it passed into law.

It did nothing to improve the immediate situation in Ireland. The Parnellites spurned it ; outrages multiplied ; the gaols were

The autumn of 1881

---

[1] Such as that of Lord Monteagle, Mr. Richey, Mr. Bagwell, Judge Longfield, and others who, recognizing the necessity for legislation, formed in 1880 the *Land Tenure Reform Committee* and drafted a scheme.

filled with suspects. On October 7th Mr. Gladstone, much irritated
by the reception accorded to his remedial legislation, declared that
the " resources of civilization were not exhausted," and on October
13th Mr. Parnell was arrested and lodged in Kilmainham Gaol. On
October 18th the League issued a manifesto commanding that no
rent should be paid until the leaders were released, and two days
later the League itself was " proclaimed " as an " illegal and criminal
association ". Thus Forster waged his brave fight against the forces
of lawlessness in Ireland. " If I am arrested," Parnell had said,
" Captain Moonlight will take my place." He did. Forster, though
in great personal danger, never faltered.

The
Kilmain-
ham
Treaty

When Parliament met in February, the Queen was able with
truth to say that " the condition of Ireland showed signs of improvement," and had Forster been loyally supported he might have won
through ; but his Chief was already off on another tack. With
splendid courage Mr. Forster had personally visited the most disturbed districts in Ireland during the winter and had escaped unhurt.
On April 19th, 1882, he left Dublin to attend the Cabinet which was
to decide the future policy of the Government.   But for the fact that
he decided at the last moment to dine at Kingstown instead of in
Dublin, Forster would that night have been murdered by a band of
assassins known as the " Invincibles ".[1]   On April 28th the announcement of Lord Spencer's appointment as Viceroy, in place of Earl
Cowper, gave substance to rumours of a " change of policy ".   The
rumours had some foundation in fact.   The Cabinet learnt that, if
they would release Parnell and other suspects, " the conspiracy
which has been used to get up boycotting and outrages will now be
used to put them down ".[2]   On May 2nd the Prime Minister announced the release of all suspects not associated with the commission
of crime and announced also the resignation of the Chief Secretary.
The " Kilmainham Treaty," so called from the gaol in which the
Irish leaders were at that time confined, had been signed. " The
Prime Minister . . . had now flung the Irish agents of the Government
over and made peace with the invincible agitator." This is the
account of Parnell's brilliant biographer, and this his summary of
the terms : " The Government were to introduce a satisfactory
Arrears Bill, and Parnell was to ' slow down ' the agitation ".[3] To
such a Treaty a man of Forster's temper could be no party.

The
Phœnix
Park
murders

Mr. Forster's successor was not, as had been anticipated, Mr.
Chamberlain, the representative of the extreme left, but Lord
Frederick Cavendish, brother of Lord Hartington, the leader of the

[1] Reid, *Forster*, p. 557.   *Ibid.* p. 561.
[3] O'Brien, pp. 268-269. I have used the term " Treaty " as the phrase of the
day, but it is proper to add that Mr. Gladstone denied the existence of any " bargain ". " There has been no arrangement, no bargain, no negotiation. Nothing
has been asked and nothing has been taken " (Hansard, May 4th, 1882) ; *cf.* Lord
Hartington's *Memorandum* (ap. Holland, i. 351), " Although there was no pledge
there was no understanding ".

Whig section of the Cabinet, and himself an intimate friend of the
Prime Minister. On May 4th Forster made a statement explanatory
of his resignation. In the middle of a scene already sufficiently
dramatic Parnell entered the House and confronted his old adversary
and his new friends. On May 6th the new Viceroy made his State
entry into Dublin. Lord Frederick Cavendish arrived with him.
On the same evening the new Chief Secretary and Mr. Burke, the
Under-Secretary at the Castle, were stabbed to death by a gang of
" Invincibles " in Phœnix Park. The murder of Lord Frederick was
an accident ; the intended victim of the assassins was the faithful
agent of the " Castle," Mr. Burke. Mr. Forster immediately offered
to resume his post ; the offer was declined. In January, 1883, the
" Invincibles " were captured and brought to trial. James Carey,
one of the leaders in the plot, and a member of the Dublin Town
Council, turned Queen's evidence ; five of his associates were hanged,
and three were sent to penal servitude for life. Carey himself was
murdered on shipboard as he was flying to South Africa, and his
murderer was hanged. Thus ended this terrible episode in Irish
history.

Parnell expressed, and probably with sincerity, his detestation of Further
the dastardly deed which had taken place. It is in evidence that he legisla-
was, perhaps for the only time in his life, completely unnerved.[1] In tion
Ireland there was genuine lamentation over the fate of the " innocent
stranger," Lord Frederick Cavendish, profound sympathy for his
courageous widow, but little to spare for the devoted public servant
who perished with him. On the refusal of Sir Charles Dilke to take
the Chief Secretaryship without a seat in the Cabinet, it was accepted
by Mr. George Trevelyan who, with Lord Spencer, braced himself
bravely for one of the most difficult tasks that ever confronted
English statesmen. A *Crimes Act* passed in 1882 gave the Executive
power in serious cases to substitute a Commission of three judges for
trial by jury ; to prohibit meetings and suppress newspapers ; to
deport aliens ; to levy compensation on the districts for murders
and maiming ; and to search for the " apparatus of crime " by night
or day ; it also enlarged the summary jurisdiction of magistrates and
in other ways increased the efficiency of the law. But with coercion
conciliation was to go hand in hand and the *Crimes Act* was accompanied by an *Arrears Act* which, partly at the expense of the State
and partly of the landlords, relieved the tenants from a burden of
debt, and enabled them to go into the Land Courts to get a " fair
rent " fixed under the Act of 1881. Thanks to the increased powers
given to the Executive by the *Crimes Act*, the murderers of Lord
Frederick Cavendish and Burke were brought to justice and the
more serious kinds of agrarian crime were virtually stamped out.[2]

[1] He offered to resign his seat if Mr. Gladstone thought well.—Morley, iii. 70.
[2] Such crimes numbered nearly 3500 in 1882 ; 762 in 1884.

The calm, courageous, and impartial administration of Lord Spencer and Mr. Trevelyan gradually wore down their lawless opponents. At Westminster the obstructive tactics of the Parnellites compelled the House of Commons to spend an autumn session (1882) in revising its rules of procedure. The most important of these gave authority to the Speaker to closure debate. In Ireland Mr. Parnell launched a new association to take the place of the suppressed Land League to which he gave the name of the *National League* (Oct. 17th, 1882). The avowed object of the new League was to secure Home Rule for Ireland ; its methods were boycotting and intimidation ; but, guided with superb skill by Parnell, it generally contrived to keep on the right side of the law. Its power was much increased by the inclusion of Ireland in the Franchise Act of 1884. Household suffrage gave Parnell eighty-five followers in the Parliament elected in 1885. But we anticipate events.

England in Egypt   Apart from Ireland and the other topics already touched, public attention, during the Gladstone Government, was mainly concentrated upon Egypt.

The course of this narrative has already disclosed the consistent reluctance of English statesmen to recognize the importance of Egypt in the general scheme of English policy. Twice Russia had offered it to England, and at Berlin Bismarck, not perhaps without sinister design, pressed it upon Lord Beaconsfield. To Beaconsfield the offer must have been tempting, for he was the first of English statesmen to perceive its significance, but it was declined. From his purchase of the canal shares [1] a new era in our relations with Egypt dates. The sale of the shares was due to the increasing financial embarrassments of the Khedive Ismail.[2] The debt which at his accession (1863) stood at £3,293,000 had increased by 1876 to £94,000,000. To this " Carnival of extravagance and oppression " [3] we may trace the European intervention in the affairs of Egypt, and thus the whole of the latest phase in its long history. In 1876 Mr. Stephen Cave, who had been sent out to make a report upon Egyptian finance, described the country as suffering " from the ignorance, dishonesty, waste, and extravagance of the East . . . and at the same time from the vast expense caused by hasty and inconsiderate endeavours to adopt the civilization of the West ". No description could have been more apt. The English and French creditors of the Khedive, naturally alarmed as to the security of their loans, sent out Mr. Goschen and M. Joubert to look after their interests. The immediate result was the establishment of the *Caisse de la dette* (May 2nd, 1876). This international Commission was originally empowered only to receive the revenue set apart from the service of the debt, and to sunction or veto fresh loans ; but its functions were

---

[1] *Cf. supra*, p. 370.   [2] A grandson of the famous Mehemet Ali.
[3] The phrase is Lord Milner's.

rapidly enlarged to embrace the whole financial administration of the country. Lord Derby refused to nominate an English Commissioner, but Mr. Goschen, devoid of Lord Derby's official responsibility, suggested at the Khedive's request the name of Captain Evelyn Baring, a member of the famous financial House and until recently Private Secretary to Lord Northbrook in India. In this characteristic fashion there was introduced into Egypt the man destined to be the regenerator of the country, " the Great Pharaoh of Modern Egypt ".

By 1879 Ismail's tyranny and extravagance had become insupportable, and on June 26th his Suzerain the Sultan was induced by the Powers to procure his abdication. His abdication, writes Lord Cromer, " sounded the death-knell of arbitrary, personal rule in Egypt ".[1] But his son and successor, Tewfik, though honest and well meaning, was not the man to cope with the situation by which he was confronted.

The country and more particularly the army was seething with discontent. Of this discontent an obscure colonel, named Arabi Bey, became the mouthpiece and representative. It is not, even now, easy to determine the precise character and significance of the movement which Arabi led. Primarily a military revolt, it was directed partly against Turkish suzerainty, partly against occidental intervention. " Egypt for the Egyptians " was the battle-cry of the rebels, but how far either Egypt or the Egyptians would have been profited by their success it is difficult to say.

Rebellion of Arabi Bey, 1881

On September 9th, 1881, the Khedive found his Palace surrounded by a large force under the command of Arabi, and was compelled to assent to their demands. He promised to dismiss two of his leading Ministers, to accept a responsible Ministry, to convoke an Assembly of Notables before the end of the year, and to limit the functions of the *Caisse* to the service of the debt. Doctrinaire Liberals, particularly in England, hailed with enthusiasm Arabi's success, as portending an era of constitutional Government for Egypt. Most of those who had knowledge of the facts regarded it differently. The democratic catchwords adopted by Arabi and his faction were in reality a thin veneer, calculated to cover a movement of the regular Oriental type. Europe became more and more uneasy. Order must be restored in Egypt ; but how ? By Turkey ? By the European Concert ? By France and England conjointly, or by either of these alone ? To any of these alternatives there was objection from one quarter or another. In January, 1882, England and France in a joint note assured Tewfik of their support, and in May the combined fleet anchored in the roads of Alexandria. France then expressed a preference for a European Conference. The Conference met in Constantinople at the end of June and proved entirely abortive.

[1] *Modern Egypt*, i. 145.

Meanwhile, an *émeute* at Alexandria precipitated the crisis. On June 11th the Arabs attacked the European population and slaughtered fifty or more of them, mostly Greeks, in cold blood. " Manifestly," says Lord Cromer, " something had to be done, for the whole framework of society in Egypt was on the point of collapsing. By June 17th 14,000 Christians had left the country."[1] Tewfik was powerless to restrain the fanaticism aroused by Arabi, now one of his " responsible " Ministers. The Concert of Europe was equally impotent. Great Britain decided to act, if necessary, alone. Sir Beauchamp Seymour, commanding the British fleet off Alexandria, was instructed to demand that the construction of fortifications should cease.

Bombardment of Alexandria The demand being ignored the Admiral proceeded (July 11th) to bombard and demolish the forts. Arabi let loose the convicts, and then with his troops abandoned the town, which for two whole days was delivered up to fire, pillage, and massacre. At length the British Admiral landed a body of blue-jackets and marines, and order was tardily restored in the ruined city.

The Egyptian expedition From the moment it became clear that decisive action was necessary France refused to co-operate, and her Fleet left Alexandria for Port Said. England had, therefore, to go through with the task alone. The Government moved (July 24th) for a vote of credit for £2,300,000 ; the first army Reserves were called out on the 25th, and the first instalment of troops left Portsmouth on the 27th. Almost simultaneously troops were despatched from India, and among these the Government, following the precedent of Lord Beaconsfield, decided to include a native contingent. The command was entrusted to Sir Garnet Wolseley, who fulfilled his commission with extraordinary promptitude and skill. Debouching not from Alexandria but from Port Said, he landed in Egypt on August 19th, and marching on Cairo across the desert, he inflicted a crushing defeat on Arabi, storming the formidable lines of Tel-el-Kebir on September 13th. So masterly were his strategy and tactics that the total British loss in killed was only 54, and in wounded only 342. On September 14th, Cairo surrendered to a couple of squadrons of British cavalry. The " series of military operations," to adopt Mr. Gladstone's periphrasis, was now complete. Arabi was captured, brought to trial, sentenced to death, and finally deported to Ceylon.

The restoration of order A British army was left in occupation of Egypt in order to complete the restoration of order, or, in official phrase, the " authority of the Khedive ". When that task had been accomplished the occupation would cease. That such was the genuine desire and intention of the Government, there is not a shadow of doubt. " We shall not keep our troops in Egypt any longer than is necessary ; but it would be an act of treachery to ourselves, to

[1] *Op. cit.* i. 289.

Egypt, and to Europe if we withdrew them without having a certainty
—or . . . until there is reasonable expectation—of a stable, a permanent, and a beneficial Government being established in Egypt." [1]
Thus spoke Lord Granville in the House of Lords, and his famous despatch on January 3rd, 1883, announced that policy to the great
Powers. That despatch further intimated that " the position in which
Her Majesty's Government is placed towards His Highness (the Khedive) imposes upon them the duty of giving advice, with the object of
securing that the order of things to be established shall be of a
satisfactory character and possess the elements of stability and
progress ". " Giving advice " is, as Lord Milner observes, a
" charming euphemism of the best Granvillian brand," [2] but Lord
Granville was at one with his colleagues in his anxiety that the
function should be temporary.

The anomaly of the whole position was strikingly illustrated by The
the events which shortly followed in the Egyptian Soudan. The Soudan
Arabs of the South, as of the North, had long groaned beneath the
burdens imposed upon them by their Egyptian taskmasters. Colonel
Charles Gordon, who had acted as Governor of the Soudan under
Ismail, retired in 1879, and from that moment the condition of its
inhabitants was pitiful. Consequently, when Muhammad Ahmed
announced himself as the Mahdi or promised Messiah, the Soudanese
rallied to his standard, and drove the Egyptian troops into the
fortresses. In September, 1883, General Hicks was despatched by
the Khedive, in command of a wholly inadequate Egyptian force, to
reconquer the Soudan. In November Hicks Pasha, his European
staff, and his Egyptian soldiers were cut to pieces by the Mahdi near
Shekan. Sir Evelyn Baring, who in September, 1883, had returned
to Egypt as Consul-General, advised the abandonment of the Soudan.
Lord Dufferin, in his report of 1883, had advised that the Western
Soudan should be abandoned, and that Egypt should be content to
hold Khartoum and Sennaar. Lord Wolseley concurred in this
opinion. After the Hicks disaster, however, Lord Wolseley urged
upon Lord Hartington that a strong garrison should be established
at Assouan, and that reinforcements should be sent to Suakim,
Berber, and Khartoum. Lord Hartington agreed with him, and
had their advice been accepted one of the most disastrous episodes
in English history might have been avoided.[3] Sir Evelyn Baring
and the British soldiers in Cairo were convinced, however, that
Egypt could not, without assistance, hold Khartoum. The British
Cabinet were now face to face with a serious difficulty. " The
Soudan was no business of ours." Technically it was not. But
British officers had been killed there ; Egyptian soldiers were still

---

[1] Hansard, cclxxvi. 41.   [2] *England in Egypt*, p. 33.
[3] Holland, *op. cit.*, p. 411.

blockaded there ; and the Khedive, if he accepted our advice to evacuate, could not calmly leave them there to perish.

Gordon's mission, January, 1884

At this critical moment General Gordon was on the point of undertaking a mission for the King of the Belgians in the Congo. Asked what he would do in regard to the Soudan, he replied : " I should send out myself ". The distracted Cabinet caught at the idea, and on January 18th, 1884, General Gordon was sent out to Khartoum to report on the situation with a view to immediate evacuation.[1] The Khedive appointed him Governor-General of the Soudan, the Home Government acquiesced in the appointment, and in that capacity he started for Khartoum. Baring disapproved of the mission then and always,[2] but he agreed that if Gordon went at all it had better be as Governor-General. That this appointment altered the character of the mission cannot be denied ; still less can it be denied that the Imperial Government approved the alteration. But Ministers—especially Mr. Gladstone and Lord Granville—were already uneasy about it. Words—parliamentary words in particular —they could understand ; of decisive action they were afraid. Their hope now was that Gordon would himself decide upon the evacuation of Khartoum without explicit orders to that effect. Meanwhile, the facts of the situation were hardening. Gordon had hardly left Cairo for Khartoum when Colonel Valentine Baker, the head of the Egyptian Gendarmerie, was badly defeated in an attempt to relieve Tokar, near the Red Sea coast (Feb. 4th). Gordon now found himself besieged by the Mahdists in Khartoum. Lord Wolseley was quick to perceive the danger of the situation, and urged upon Ministers the immediate despatch of reinforcements to Suakim, and the advance of an English Brigade to Wady Halfa. Failure to take prompt action at once might force us into a big war " before many months elapsed ".[3] Sir Gerald Graham, despatched to Suakim, inflicted some losses upon the Arabs and held that place securely, but nothing further was done. Baring became insistent that relief should be sent to Khartoum, and in England there was one person in high place whose clear brain penetrated through all the sophistries and ambiguities in which Ministers—and especially their Chief— delighted to involve themselves. On March 25th, 1884, the Queen telegraphed to Lord Hartington : " It is alarming ; General Gordon is in danger ; you are bound to try and save him. Surely Indian troops might go from Aden and could bear climate though British cannot. You have incurred fearful responsibility." [4]

Gordon at Khartoum

What the Queen said, the country thought. Lord Hartington was obviously uneasy, but Mr. Gladstone's mind was intent upon

[1] There is still some confusion as to whether Gordon's orders were to " report " or to " evacuate ". For text of instruction cf. Morley, iii. 554.

[2] Cromer, op. cit. i. 438-439.

[3] For Lord Wolseley's masterly Memorandum cf. Holland, i. pp. 426-427.

[4] Holland, Devonshire, i. 434.

THE NILE

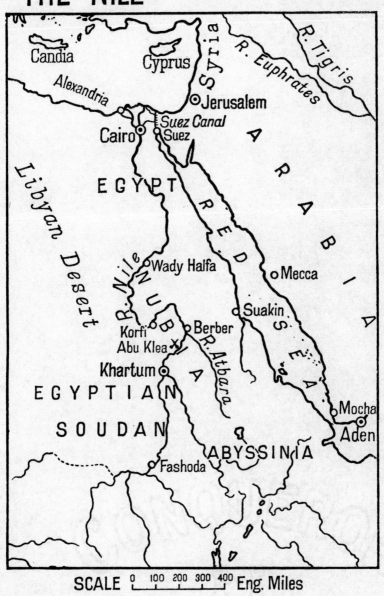

SCALE 0 100 200 300 400 Eng. Miles

domestic affairs and parliamentary tactics, and precious weeks and even months were allowed to pass before any decision was arrived at.   The miserable troops on whom alone Gordon could rely were defeated outside Khartoum on March 16th, and it became clear that if ever Gordon was to leave Khartoum alive he would have to be succoured by his own countrymen.   He himself had begun to realize that he was likely to be deserted.   On April 7th he telegraphed : " You state your intention of not sending any relief up here or to Berber and you refuse me Zobeir. . . .[1]   I shall hold out here as long as I can, and if I can supress the rebellion, I shall do so.   If I cannot, I shall retire to the Equator and leave you the *indelible disgrace* of abandoning the garrisons of Sennaar, Kassala, Berber, and Dongola, with the certainty that you will ultimately be forced to smash up the Mahdi under great difficulties if you would retain peace in Egypt." This telegram merely aroused Mr. Gladstone to the advisability of " sending a set of carefully prepared questions to Gordon about his future conditions and plans " (April 13th)   Baring warned the Government that they ought to begin immediate preparations for a relieving expedition in the autumn (April 14th).   Lord Hartington confesses, two days later, that he had " not the slightest idea what the Government proposes to do ".[2]   His ignorance was shared by all his colleagues, and the way was not made clearer by Gladstone's declaration (May 12th) that the reconquest of the Soudan " would be a war of conquest against a people rightly struggling to be free ".[3] Berber, the half-way house between Suakim and Khartoum, was captured by the Mahdi (May 26th)—an event which still further jeopardized Gordon's position in Khartoum.

Nevertheless, Lord Hartington still failed to bring the Cabinet to a decision.   Their procrastination was due to no lack of pressure from the ablest of their military advisers ; but despite the insistence of Lord Wolseley, nothing had been decided by the end of July.   A threat of resignation from Lord Hartington and the Chancellor, Lord Selborne, at last compelled the Premier to divert his attention from parliamentary tactics, and at the beginning of August Gladstone asked the House of Commons for the miserably inadequate sum of £300,000 to enable the Government " to undertake operations for the relief of General Gordon should they become necessary ".   Lord Wolseley was then appointed to command the expedition ; he left England at the end of August and started from Cairo to lead an expedition up the Nile at the beginning of October.   Gordon, asked by the Government why he did not leave Khartoum, replied, " I stay at Khartoum, because the Arabs have shut us up and will not

[1] He had begged the Government to appoint Zobeir Pasha Governor-General of the Soudan : but they demurred to the appointment of a slave dealer.

[2] Holland, i. 445.

[3] Morley, iii. 144, quotes this as an illustration of Mr. Gladstone's " curious instinct for liberty ".

27

let us out ". Lord Wolseley made all the haste possible under circumstances of great difficulty, but the procrastination of the Cabinet
had delayed the expedition until it was too late. On reaching Korti
(Dec. 29th) Lord Wolseley despatched Sir Herbert Stewart with a
small force by land to avoid the wide bend of the Nile. Stewart,
after a hard fight at Abu Klea (Jan. 17th, 1885), forced his way to
the Nile, not far below Khartoum, but on January 19th was mortally
wounded. The command then devolved on Sir Charles Wilson.
Exactly a week later (Jan. 26th) the Mahdi stormed Khartoum and
General Gordon was killed. Wilson came in sight of the City two
days after it had fallen.

Death of   The news of the tragedy reached London on February 5th, and
Gordon   on receipt of it the Queen despatched an angry telegram to Gladstone
declaring that " it was too fearful to consider that the fall of
Khartoum might have been prevented and many precious lives
saved by earlier action ". To Miss Gordon she expressed in an
autograph letter her grief and sympathy and her sense of " the stain
left upon England " by General Gordon's " cruel though heroic
fate ". The Queen exactly expressed the feelings of her people.
The House of Lords censured the Government by 189 to 68, and in
the Commons they were saved from similar condemnation only by
a majority of 14. Their first resolution was to send out large reinforcements to Lord Wolseley to enable him " to smash the Mahdi
at Khartoum ". By the middle of April other counsels prevailed.
The left wing of the Radical party brought pressure to bear upon
the Prime Minister, who was more than ready to be convinced. On
April 15th the Government decided to abandon the Soudan south
of Wady Halfa, and, though retaining the port of Suakim, to abandon
the construction, already commenced, of a railway from Suakim to
Berber. This sudden *volte-face* was due only partly to parliamentary
pressure ; serious danger was threatening in another quarter. On
March 30th Russia, quick to take advantage of England's preoccupation, had occupied Penjdeh on the frontier of Afghanistán.

The   The danger in Afghanistán passed, and with its passing there
sequel of was some disposition to modify the policy of complete evacuation of
the story
of the   the Soudan, and to retain the province of Dongola. Baring, Wolseley,
Soudan   and Kitchener were all strongly in favour of its retention, and the
Queen pressed it on her Ministers, but the will of Mr. Gladstone
prevailed. The British force was withdrawn in the summer of 1885,
and for another twelve years the Soudan was a prey to anarchy.
When the Mahdi was poisoned in 1885, the Khalifa whom he had
nominated as his successor continued his tyranny.

Meanwhile, thanks to the long and patient labours of General
Grenfell and General Kitchener, the Egyptian army was completely
reorganized, and in 1896 the Government of the Khedive determined
to attempt the reconquest of the Soudan. This decision coincided

with, and may have been precipitated by the withdrawal of the Italians from Kassala.[1] General Kitchener was appointed to the command of the Nile expedition, and slowly and patiently advanced towards the completion of his great design. Before the end of September, 1896, Kitchener was in possession of Dongola ; Abu Hamed was taken in August, 1897, and at the Atbara the Dervishes were scattered (April 7th, 1898) On September 2nd the power of Mahdiism was finally annihilated by the great victory of Omdurman. Two days later the British and Egyptian forces were paraded before the ruined Palace of Khartoum, and the shattered tomb of the Mahdi, and there, on the spot where Gordon had perished, a funeral service was held in solemn memory of the dead hero and saint.

The Queen conferred a peerage upon General Kitchener, and from Parliament he received £30,000 and formal thanks " for the distinguished skill and ability with which he planned and conducted the campaign on the Nile of 1896-1898 ". Never were honours and thanks better deserved.

Hardly, however, had General Kitchener reached Khartoum Fashoda when the diplomatic sky was suddenly overcast by a threatening cloud. The French Government had never forgiven themselves for their withdrawal from Egypt at the critical moment in 1882. For more than a dozen years they had impeded, in every way, the work of financial and political reconstruction undertaken by Great Britain in Egypt. That task, unwillingly assumed but patiently fulfilled, seemed now to be on the point of final triumph and consummation.

At the dramatic moment the French reappeared upon the scene. On July 12th, 1898, Major Marchand planted the French flag at Fashoda on the Upper Nile. For two years past, in the face of every difficulty, this intrepid soldier had been pushing his way from the French Congo across Central Africa. His arrival at Fashoda was well timed, but General Kitchener, steaming up from Khartoum, denied his right to be there as the political representative of France. The victory of Omdurman was a potent argument, but Marchand refused to yield even to it. The quarrel was then referred to the diplomatists. Lord Salisbury claimed for the Khedive all the lands over which the Khalifa had borne sway, and made it clear to the French Government that the claim would be asserted by the whole force of Great Britain. In the autumn of 1898 the two nations were on the brink of war. France, however, gave way, recalled Marchand, and in March, 1899, concluded with Great Britain a comprehensive agreement in regard to the Soudan. By this Treaty the rights of Great Britain over the whole Nile basin, from the source of that river to its mouth, were acknowledged ; France was confirmed in possession of a great West African Empire, but the whole of the Egyptian Soudan was to be subject to the power which ruled at

[1] Occupied by them after a successful encounter with the Khalifa (Dec. 1893),

Cairo. Thus the way to the Cape was still open, unblocked by any other European Power. From that moment Anglo-French relations rapidly improved, and in 1904 the diplomacy of the Salisbury-Balfour Government was crowned by the conclusion of the Anglo-French Agreement, whereby France agreed to give Great Britain for thirty years a free hand in Egypt. Thus closed the chapter which had opened in 1882.

England and Russia in Central Asia

British policy in the Soudan in 1885 was, as we have hinted, powerfully affected by the increasing tension of Anglo-Russian relations in Central Asia. In regard to Afghanistán the Gladstone Government had reverted in 1881 to the policy of the " Buffer State ". Given the maintenance of friendly relations with a strong Amír, there was little cause for apprehension in the advance of Russia. In 1884, however, it became doubtful whether the " buffer " could be kept intact. Early in that year Russia, conscious of England's preoccupation in the Soudan, occupied Merv and Saraks, and thus came within 200 miles of Herát. Such a step was in direct violation of Gortchakoff's assurance, given to Lord Granville in 1882, that Merv " lay outside the sphere of Russian influence ".[1] Nevertheless, Lord Granville assented, somewhat tamely, to the proposal of the Russian Government that a joint boundary commission should be appointed for the definitive delimitation of the frontier. Sir Peter Lumsden, the English Commissioner, reached the Afghan frontier on November 19th. His Russian colleague, M. Zelenoi, excused himself on the score of illness until February. February came but still no Zelenoi. The affront was unmistakable, and British patience was almost exhausted, the more so as the Russians usefully employed the interval by occupying various eligible points on the frontier. The situation could not endure. On March 6th, 1885, the Queen addressed to the Czar a personal appeal that he would assist her in maintaining the peace, but on the 29th Russians and Afghans came into collision at Penjdeh, and the Russians in consequence occupied the place. The Afghans felt that their " Protector " had deserted them. Fortunately, however, the Amír was at this moment at Rawal Pindi, where Lord Dufferin [2] had received him with splendid hospitality, and now smoothed his natural indignation with irresistible adroitness. At home, the Government acted with unusual decision and promptitude. The Reserves had already (March 26th) been called out in England, and the news of the seizure of Penjdeh aroused public excitement to the highest pitch. " We know," said Mr. Gladstone, " that the attack was a Russian attack ; we know that the Afghans suffered in life, in spirit, and in repute ; we know that a blow was struck at the credit and authority of a Sovereign, our protected Ally, who had

---

[1] Granville, *Life*, ii. 420.
[2] He succeeded Lord Ripon as Viceroy in 1884.

committed no offence. . . . We must do our best to have right done
in the matter."

This speech (April 27th) was the prelude to a motion for a vote
of credit of £11,000,000, £4,500,000 of which were for the Soudan
expedition. The vote was agreed without a dissentient voice, a
hint not lost upon Russia, who agreed to submit the questions in
dispute to the arbitration of the King of Denmark. In the event,
Penjdeh, for which Abdur Rahman cared little, was left in the hands
of Russia, but in compensation the Amír secured the exclusive
control of the Zulfillar Pass for which he cared much. There was
general satisfaction that peace had been preserved, but there was an
uneasy suspicion that it had been purchased at the price of a fresh
humiliation for British diplomacy.

That this impression contributed to the overthrow of the Govern- Over-
ment is undeniable. All through the session they were hard pressed throw of
by their opponents in Parliament, but their ultimate fall was due, Gladstone
in even greater degree, to their own internal weakness and dis- Govern-
sensions. With the greatest difficulty had they kept together ment
through the Soudan crisis in 1884, and between the middle of April
and the middle of May (1885), no less than nine members of the
Cabinet intimated, on one point or another, an intention to resign.[1]
In the last months of their existence the main cause of division in
the Ministry was not foreign policy but Ireland. The Crimes Act
was to expire in August. Was it to be renewed ? In whole or in
part ? The Whigs leaned towards partial renewal ; the Radical
wing insisted that if any portion of the Act were renewed it must
be accompanied by a reform of local government and perhaps by
the establishment of a central administrative board in Dublin. Mr.
Gladstone, whose supreme anxiety was to avert a rupture of the
Ministry and the Party,[2] was hopeful of adjustment of differences,
but nothing was actually settled, and on June 8th an amendment
to the Budget, moved by Sir Michael Hicks Beach, was carried
against the Government by 264 to 252. It was significant that 39
Home Rulers voted in the majority.

Mr. Gladstone tendered his resignation to the Queen on the The first
following day (June 9th). Several of his colleagues—notably Lord Salisbury
Hartington—were glad to be released from a task which had become tration
increasingly distasteful, but the Queen demurred to the necessity of
resignation. Lord Salisbury, summoned on the 11th, took the same
view, and pointed out the peculiarity of the circumstances. Two
million new voters had been enfranchised by the Act of 1884, but
the new Register was not ready, and an immediate dissolution was,
therefore, out of the question. Consequently, the Conservatives, if
they took office, would not command a majority in the House of
Commons, nor could they appeal to the country to give them one.

[1] See Morley, iii. 185.   [2] *Ibid*. 186.

If they were to come in, it must be on the understanding that the outgoing Ministry would assist them to obtain the necessary supplies and to carry on the routine business of State. Mr. Gladstone would give no pledge and the situation became tense. The crisis lasted from June 11th to June 23rd, and was terminated only by the good offices of the Queen. No less than six times in one day did her Private Secretary, Sir Henry Ponsonby, interview Mr. Gladstone.[1] At last an understanding was arrived at, and on the strength of it Lord Salisbury took office.

The revolt of the younger Tories against the leadership of Sir Stafford Northcote was rewarded by the latter's reluctant removal to the House of Lords, where, as Earl of Iddlesleigh, he served as First Lord of the Treasury. Lord Salisbury himself took the Foreign Office — an admirable arrangement, if there had been another Premier; Sir Michael Hicks Beach led the House of Commons as Chancellor of the Exchequer—until the leader of the Fourth Party was ready; Lord Randolph Churchill modestly contented himself, for the moment, with the India Office; Mr. W. H. Smith went to the War Office, Lord George Hamilton to the Admiralty, and Sir Richard Cross returned to the Home Office. Sir Hardinge Giffard became Lord Halsbury and Lord Chancellor; Mr. Gibson who in late years had done good service to the Party on the platform, became Lord Chancellor for Ireland with a peerage (Lord Ashbourne) and a seat in the Cabinet; but of all the appointments perhaps the most significant was that of Lord Carnarvon to be Lord Lieutenant of Ireland, with a seat in the Cabinet. Lord Carnarvon, a man of high integrity and great independence, made no secret of his leanings towards some form of extended local government for Ireland, and his appointment went far to secure the Irish vote for his party at the General Election. This took place, according to arrangement, in November.

The General Election of 1885   The English boroughs in the main returned Conservatives, but the new electors in the counties proved their gratitude to Mr. Gladstone by giving the Liberal Party a majority of eighty-six.[2] This figure exactly equalled the number of Mr. Parnell's followers. The strength of the Home Rule Party was the deciding factor in the situation. Before Parliament was opened the Conservatives shed their Lord Lieutenant, and in the first critical division on the Address (Jan. 26th, 1886) the Parnellites threw in their lot with the Opposition and left the Ministry in a minority of seventy-nine. Of the majority seventy-four were Parnellites. Lord Salisbury immediately resigned, and Mr. Gladstone was asked to form a

---

[1] The Queen pressed a peerage upon Gladstone in a letter which, as he wrote to Lord Granville, " moves and almost upsets me. It must have cost her much to write and is really a pearl of great price."—Morley, iii. 210.

[2] Including four Independents the Liberals numbered 335; the Tories 249; the Parnellites, 86.

Government. Lord Hartington declined to serve in it, and his example was followed by many of the most distinguished of his former colleagues. The old Liberal Party was rent in twain. A new issue of paramount importance was definitely raised—an issue destined to divide English Parties for at least a quarter of a century to come. That issue is not yet decided ; the chapter of history opened by Mr. Gladstone in 1886 is not yet concluded ; at this point, therefore, it is fitting that this detailed narrative should stop.

In more than one sense the year 1885-1886 marks the parting of the ways. The Reform movement, temporarily arrested by the French Revolution, but breaking forth after the Peace of 1815 with irresistible force, had now, for the time being, clearly reached its term. By successive stages the great mass of the manhood of the nation had been admitted to the responsibilities of citizenship. To the arbitrament of the new democracy a great issue was presented in 1886. They were invited to confer upon Ireland a separate Legislature with an Executive responsible thereto. The proposal seemed to them to be fraught with danger to the Commonwealth, and they installed, and for twenty years, with one short interval, maintained in power the Party which was pledged to preserve the integrity of the United Kingdom. Not, however, until the close of that period (1905) did the recently enfranchised voters realize the potency of the weapon placed in their hands. By that time the new ruling class had learnt more lessons than were dreamt of in the educational philosophy of Robert Lowe. Before the vast issues, social and economic, which gradually emerged as the century faded, even that of Legislative Independence for Ireland seemed to pale into insignificance.

These problems belong to the future ; the historian is concerned with the past ; truthful narration may be required of him, but not speculation. If the dead must bury the dead, the unborn must struggle in the womb of time.

CHAPTER XXVI

EPILOGUE. DEMOCRACY AND EMPIRE. THE CLOSE OF THE VICTORIAN ERA

(1885-1901)

THE formal argument of this work reaches its logical conclusion in the Parliamentary Reform Acts of 1884 and 1885. Nevertheless, in order to sketch the progress of events down to the close of the Victorian era, some words may be added by way of epilogue. To a period already regarded as " old-fashioned " the usage can hardly be deemed inappropriate.

The Irish Question

For nearly ten years Ireland continued to occupy the first place in political interest. On coming into office in 1885, the Conservatives deliberately declined to renew the expiring *Crimes Act*. This decision was admittedly a grave one,[1] and it did not stand alone. Combined with a virulent attack by Lord Randolph Churchill upon Lord Spencer's administration, it gave substance to the prevalent rumours that the Tory Government meant to come to terms with Parnell. A promised re-enquiry into a notorious murder case [2] and the passing of an Act to facilitate land-purchase seemed to afford further confirmation. The Land Act of 1885, popularly known as the Ashbourne Act, was one of the least pretentious, but, as far as it went, one of the most effective agrarian measures ever enacted for Ireland. By a simple use of State credit it made a real beginning with the work of converting tenant-cultivators into proprietors of the soil. A tenant desiring to purchase his holding and agreeing with his landlord to do so could borrow from the State the whole sum required at 4 per cent. By this means not only was his rent immediately reduced,[3] but at the end of a period of forty-nine years he became automatically the owner of his farm. The total sum to be advanced by the State was limited to £5,000,000,[4] but this modest experiment formed the basis of all subsequent land-purchase legislation down to the great measure of 1903.[5] Nothing could have been more consonant with the best Conservative tradition than the Ashborne Act. Can the same be said of the communications which, in the autumn of 1885, took place between Mr. Parnell and Lord Carnarvon ?

That the new Lord Lieutenant favoured the principle of federalism was well known : he had already applied it to Canada and had attempted to apply it to South Africa. Would he venture to re-

---

[1] *Cf.* Churchill, *Life of Lord R. Churchill*, i. 409.

[2] The Maamtrasna affair.

[3] By about 20 per cent. as compared with the " judicial " rent of 1881.—S. H. Butcher, *Irish Land Acts*, p. 20.

[4] Drawn from the Irish Church Surplus.

[5] The " Wyndham Act ".

commend to his colleagues its application to Ireland ? The happenings of 1885, though in the highest degree momentous, are still wrapped in some obscurity. But this much is certain. Within a few weeks of taking office Lord Carnarvon met Parnell and listened sympathetically to the statement of his views. The fact of these meetings was communicated to the Prime Minister, but not to the Cabinet.[1] In November the Irish vote in English constituencies was given, under orders from Parnell, to the Tory candidates. The result precisely fulfilled the astute anticipation of the Irish leader. In the new Parliament he held the balance between parties.[2] Had the Tories won a dozen more seats he could have kept them in power; as it was he could reduce the Liberals to impotence.

No sooner was the verdict of the electorate given than Mr. Gladstone sent up his famous " Kite ". It is now clear [3] that during the autumn of 1885, if not before, his own mind had been tending in the direction of Home Rule; but until the elections were over he gave no clear sign. To him Parnell's victory in Ireland appeared decisive; enfranchised Ireland had now spoken. But he would gladly have seen the question settled by the Conservatives, and he actually opened the matter to the Premier's nephew, Mr. Balfour. Lord Salisbury, however, was not prepared for the plunge. As soon as he was assured of this Mr. Gladsgone turned him out. The new Parliament met on January 12th, 1886. Before it was many days old the Lord Lieutenant of Ireland and his Chief Secretary, Sir W. Hart Dyke, resigned, and Mr. W. H. Smith succeeded the latter, with a seat in the Cabinet. On January 26th notice was given that the new Chief Secretary would promptly introduce a fresh Coercion Bill for Ireland, and on the same night the Salisbury Government found itself in a minority of seventy-nine. The immediate occasion was an amendment to the Address regretting that no announcement had been made as to the provision of allotments and small holdings; [4] but though the talk was of English labourers, the mind of the House was intent upon Ireland.

Lord Salisbury treated the vote as decisive, and Mr. Gladstone, for the third time, became Prime Minister. But he was no longer the leader of a united Liberal Party. Lord Hartington, Lord Selborne, Lord Northbrook, Mr. Goschen, and Mr. Bright were notable absentees from the new Cabinet; Sir Henry James refused the Woolsack, and Mr. Chamberlain and Sir George Trevelyan accepted office under protest and resigned [5] before the Home Rule Bill was introduced. In the task to which he now devoted himself

Gladstone and Home Rule

Mr. Gladstone's Third Ministry

---

[1] *Cf.* Disclaimer of Sir M. H. Beach in Hcuse of Commons; O'Brien's *Parnell*, p. 359.

[2] Liberals 335; Conservatives 249; Parnellites 86.

[3] *Cf.* Morley, iii. 234 *seq.*, and Holland, *Devonshire*, ii. 88 *seq.*

[4] This was Mr. Jesse Collings's famous " Three Acres and a Cow " amendment.

[5] March 27th.

Gladstone found his right-hand man in Mr. John Morley, a brilliant man of letters of advanced Radical views, who had lately entered the House of Commons ; and who now entered the Cabinet as Chief Secretary to the Lord Lieutenant. Other staunch adherents of the new policy were Lord Spencer, whose support was invaluable, and Mr. Childers (Home Secretary), whose conversion had preceded that of his Chief.

The first Home Rule Bill, 1886

Mr. Gladstone introduced the first Home Rule Bill on April 8th, 1886. There was to be a Legislative Body [1] in Dublin to deal with Irish affairs in strict subordination to the Imperial Parliament. In the Legislature there were to be two " Orders " : one consisting of the twenty-eight Representative Peers of Ireland and seventy-five members elected by select constituencies ; the other consisting of 206 members elected by the existing constituencies. The two " Orders " were to sit together, though either might demand a separate vote and thus exercise a suspensive veto upon the other.[2] The Irish Legislature was forbidden to make laws relating to the Crown, the Army, Navy, or defences, treaties, peace or war, trade and navigation, coinage, customs, excise, and many other matters ; nor was it to establish or endow any particular Church. Irish members were no longer to sit in the Imperial Parliament. As to the Executive, the Lord Lieutenant was to be converted into a Constitutional ruler, assisted by a Privy Council, but acting, ordinarily, on the advice of Ministers responsible to the local Legislature. This Executive was ultimately to control the Police, and to appoint the Judges.

Into the complicated financial proposals it is unnecessary to enter, except to recall the fact that alongside the Home Rule Bill was a Land Bill, giving to the Irish landlords the option of selling their estates normally at twenty years' purchase of the nett rental. That the terms of this latter Bill affected prejudicially the fortunes of the former is hardly open to doubt ; apart from this, however, Mr. Gladstone was leading a forlorn hope.

The Opposition

Against him was arrayed not only the regular Opposition in unbroken unity, but the flower of the Liberal Party in Parliament, and outside it, almost the whole aristocracy of intellect, of hereditary rank, and of commerce. In the House of Commons Lord Hartington led the opposition to the Bill, and powerfully supported by Mr. Chamberlain, defeated it on Second Reading by a majority of thirty. In that majority were no fewer than ninety-three Liberals.

General Election of 1886

Mr. Gladstone immediately decided upon an appeal to the constituencies, and their verdict was conclusive. The Gladstonian Liberals returned less than 200 strong ; Parnell had eighty-five

---

[1] For some occult reason Gladstone always avoided the use of the term " Parliament ".

[2] Ultimately the first Order would become elective.

followers ; the Unionists numbered close on 400.[1] Mr. Gladstone
resigned office before the meeting of the new Parliament. The old
Liberal Party was irretrievably shattered, and for twenty years—
with one brief and unimportant interlude—the Unionists retained
both office and power.

With characteristic modesty Lord Salisbury desired that the first Lord
place in the new Ministry should be taken by Lord Hartington. Salis-
But the Liberal Unionists, while promising unofficial support, were Second
not yet prepared for fusion with the Conservatives, and the new Ministry,
Cabinet was drawn entirely from the latter party.   Tardy and 1886-1892
transient amends were made to Lord Iddesleigh who became Foreign
Secretary ; Lord Randolph Churchill led the House of Commons as
Chancellor of the Exchequer, and Sir Michael Hicks Beach loyally
accepted the Chief Secretaryship to the Lord Lieutenant.

The task before him was no easy one. Twice within the last Unionist
twelve months had the enfranchised Celts of Ireland declared, with Policy
virtual unanimity, in favour of Home Rule. Their cause had now
been espoused with enthusiasm by the most conspicuous statesman
of the day. For a moment it had seemed not impossible that his
genius and vigour might prevail. Once again, as in the days of Lord
Fitzwilliam, their hopes had been raised only to be dashed to the
ground. How were the Unionists going to tackle the situation ?

Lord Salisbury had recently declared that what Ireland needed
was twenty years of consistently strong and resolute government.
The restoration of social order was, therefore, the first plank in the
Unionist platform. Sir Redvers Buller, a distinguished soldier, was
sent into the West of Ireland to suppress outrages and crimes,
whereupon Mr. Parnell produced, in his *Tenants' Relief Bill*, an
alternative prescription. In Ireland, as in England, there was
genuine distress among agriculturists, but whereas in England the
landlords behaved with extraordinary consideration towards their
tenants, in Ireland there were some landlords who were disposed to
press their legal rights to the uttermost. Parnell, therefore, proposed that rents fixed before 1885 should be reduced by the Land
Court, that leaseholders should be brought under the Act of 1881,
and that no tenant should be evicted who paid up his arrears and
half his rent. The Bill was rejected by a majority of nearly 100.

Prompt came the response from Ireland in the " Plan of Cam- The
paign ". This new strategical device was invented by Mr. Dillon " Plan of
and Mr. William O'Brien, and was frowned upon by their leader. paign "
The device was simplicity itself. The tenants of any given estate
were to agree on a " fair " rent ; should their offer be declined, the
money was to be paid into a war chest and spent on organized resistance to evictions. The " plan " was inaugurated in the autumn
of 1886, and throughout 1887 the campaign was vigorously sustained.

[1] Tories 316 ; Liberal Unionists 76 ; Gladstonians 192 ; Parnellites 86.

It was a direct challenge to the elementary principles of law, and no Government worthy of the name could have refused to take it up. Consequently, the first business of the new Session (1887) was a Bill to amend the Criminal Law in Ireland. Before this Bill was introduced the personnel of the Ministry had already undergone considerable modification.

Ministerial changes On the eve of Christmas (1886) the world was startled by the announcement that Lord Salisbury's principal lieutenant had resigned. Lord Randolph Churchill's ministerial career had scarcely begun. By a few months' tenure of the India Office he had established a reputation as a first-rate administrator; a few weeks' leadership of the House of Commons had convinced friends and foes alike that he would take rank among the great Parliamentarians of the Victorian era; he had earned the warm approbation of the Sovereign, and in the Party his supremacy was unquestioned. Well might he regard himself as not only omnipotent but indispensable. Some of his opinions may have sat lightly upon him; in regard to national economy he had genuine convictions. He believed, with Mr. Gladstone, that so far from being incompatible with efficiency, economy is the complement and test of it.[1] He was determined, moreover, to enforce his views upon his colleagues. Neither Mr. W. H. Smith at the War Office, nor Lord George Hamilton at the Admiralty, would abate materially their demands; the Prime Minister supported them and Lord Randolph resigned. That he expected to be recalled on his own terms can hardly be doubted; but he had made one grave miscalculation. He afterwards confessed to having "forgotten Goschen". Lord Salisbury's first impulse was to renew to Lord Hartington the generous offer declined in July. The latter adhered to his decision, but was willing that Mr. Goschen, who had held no office since 1874,[2] should enter the Conservative Government. Mr. Goschen, therefore, succeeded Lord Randolph at the Exchequer and proved a tower of strength to the Party with which he was henceforth associated. Mr. W. H. Smith resigned the War Office to Mr. Edward Stanhope, and himself became first Lord of the Treasury and Leader in the House of Commons. These changes involved others. Lord Iddesleigh, with characteristic unselfishness, had placed his seat in the Cabinet at the Premier's disposal in order to facilitate negotiations with the Liberal Unionists. It was, however, from the newspapers that he first learnt that his offer had been accepted and that Lord Salisbury had himself taken over the Foreign Office (Jan. 4th, 1887).[3] He declined the Presidency of the Council, and on January 12th the country was shocked to learn that he had died suddenly in the ante-room of the Premier's

---

[1] Cf. e.g. Speech at Blackpool, January 24th, 1884.—*Speeches*, p. 37.
[2] On account of his opposition to an extension of the franchise.
[3] Lang, *Iddesleigh*, p. 394.

official residence at 10 Downing Street. Thus closed, amid circumstances almost tragic, a life of high utility and complete blamelessness. Three months later Sir M. Hicks Beach was compelled, by temporary ill-health, to resign the Irish Office in which he was succeeded by Mr. A. J. Balfour.

It was Mr. Balfour who defined and carried through the Unionist policy in Ireland. A man of high courage, perfect temper, and winning personality he was admirably qualified for his difficult task. Neither lawlessness in Ireland nor abuse at Westminster disturbed his serenity or deflected his course of action. Having armed himself with a new and effective weapon he pursued the policy marked out for him without haste, without acerbity, and with unfaltering consistency. The new weapon was the Criminal Law Amendment Act (Ireland) of 1887. This Act differed from previous Coercion Acts in that its provisions were permanent. The Lord Lieutenant was authorized to declare an association to be " unlawful," and to proclaim a district as " disturbed ". The powers of the Resident Magistrates—" Balfour's removables " as they were nicknamed— were greatly enlarged ; in particular they were empowered to try summarily cases of conspiracy. The passing of this Crimes Act was much facilitated, on the one hand by the new rules of procedure adroitly carried through the House by Mr. Smith, on the other by the publication in *The Times* of a series of articles on *Parnellism and Crime*. The object of the articles was to establish the complicity of the Nationalist leaders in recent agrarian crime. On April 18th, 1887 — the date appointed for the Second Reading of the Crimes Bill—*The Times* printed what purported to be a letter from Mr. Parnell to an anonymous correspondent apologizing for having had to denounce the murder of Mr. Burke in Phœnix Park. This famous letter was subsequently proved to be a forgery ; but, at the moment, Parnell's denial of its authenticity was not believed, and the publication served its immediate purpose.

Coercion, however, was not to stand alone. A Land Act of 1887 gave power to the Court to revise the rents judicially fixed and admitted leaseholders to the benefits of the Act of 1881.

Lawlessness probably reached its acme in 1887. Balfour and his Crimes Act were defied by the Nationalist leaders ; but in July eighteen counties were proclaimed under the Act, in August the National League was proclaimed as an unlawful association, in September an affray at Michelstown resulted in the loss of several lives, and before the close of the year Mr. William O'Brien, and several other members of Parliament, and Mr. T. D. Sullivan, Lord Mayor of Dublin, were convicted under the Crimes Act and imprisoned. It was a struggle *à outrance* between the forces of order and disorder, but the law, thanks to the steady persistence of Mr. Balfour, slowly but surely won.

Mr. Balfour's rule in Ireland

Meanwhile, much discussion was taking place in the House of
Commons as to what action, if any, should be taken to sift the
allegations of *The Times* against Parnell and his colleagues. Mr.
Parnell asked for a Select Committee which the Government refused
to grant. In its stead they eventually appointed a Special Commission to investigate the charges. Three distinguished Judges,
Sir James Hannen, Sir John Day, and Sir A. L. Smith, consented
to serve, and on September 17th the Commission was opened. It
was in effect, if not in form, a State trial of high significance. The
Attorney-General was the principal counsel for *The Times*, Sir
Charles Russell, afterwards Lord Russell of Killowen and Lord
Chief Justice of England, for the defendants. The Commission sat
for 128 days,[1] and examined more than 450 witnesses. Only at one
moment during this protracted period was the dramatic interest
really tense. That was when, towards the end of February, an old
and broken man was put into the witness-box, and subjected to a
scathing cross-examination by Sir Charles Russell. The man was
Richard Pigott, a needy journalist, and now revealed to the world
as the forger of the famous letter. After enduring torture in the
witness-box for two days the miserable man fled the country, leaving
a full confession behind him. Before the police could execute a
warrant for his arrest he shot himself in Madrid (March 1st). *The
Times* offered an apology and withdrew the forged documents. With
this withdrawal much of the popular interest in the case evaporated,
but by no means all its significance.

Report of
the Com-
mission   On February 13th, 1890, the Commissioners presented their
Report. They found, of course, that the facsimile letter was a
forgery, and they acquitted Mr. Parnell and his colleagues of the
charge of insincerity in their denunciation of the Phœnix Park
murders. They found that the respondents collectively were not
members of a conspiracy having for its object the absolute independence of Ireland, " but that some of them had established the
Land League " with the intention by its means to bring about the
absolute independence of Ireland, and that they had conspired, by
means of an agrarian agitation, to " impoverish and expel from the
country " the Irish landlords who were styled the " English Garrison " ; that they had incited to the intimidation that produced crime,
and had promoted the defence of agrarian crime. What was to be
done with the Report ?

The Government moved that the House thank the Commissioners
for their just and impartial conduct, adopt the Report and enter it
upon the Journals. Mr. Gladstone, on the contrary, tried to persuade
the House to record " its reprobation of the false charges of the
gravest and most odious description, based on calumny and on
forgery, that had been brought against members of the House ".

[1] Until November, 1889.

It was clear that the terms of Gladstone's amendment went, in exculpation, far beyond the findings of the Commission ; it was rejected by a substantial majority, and the Government had its way.

No impartial person could interpret the findings of the Commission as a general acquittal for the Parnellites. Nevertheless, it was inevitable that the revelation of the carelessness and blunders of *The Times* and the exposure of Pigott's forgery should have caused some revulsion of popular feeling. Mr. Gladstone and his party were immensely elated by the issue, and the Unionists correspondingly chagrined. But the elation was short-lived. Mr. Parnell had entered an action for libel against *The Times* in 1888 ; in February, 1890, the case was compromised by the payment of £5000 damages. Before the compromise was reached Parnell was already involved in litigation of another kind. On November 17th, 1890, Captain O'Shea obtained a decree *nisi* against his wife, with Parnell as co-respondent.

Parnell affected to believe that the divorce suit was a matter of merely personal interest. The organs of Nonconformity sounded another note, and Mr. Gladstone quickly re-echoed it. On November 24th he expressed the view that Parnell's "continuance in the leadership would be productive of consequences disastrous, in the highest degree, to the cause of Ireland," but on the 25th the Irish Party, ignorant of Mr. Gladstone's letter, re-elected Parnell as Sessional Chairman of the Party.

Mr. Gladstone immediately published his letter, and the thunder- The Parcloud burst. For some weeks the utmost confusion prevailed in the nellite Home Rule camp. Mr. Dillon and Mr. O'Brien, then in the United split. States, called upon Parnell to resign ; Mr. Healy vehemently urged the same conclusion upon his colleagues in Committee Room No. 15 ;[1] the Roman Catholic Bishops issued a pronouncement of similar purport. But Parnell held grimly on. He would neither abdicate, nor submit to deposition. At length (Dec. 6th) a majority of his colleagues, forty-four in number, withdrew their allegiance and elected Mr. Justin McCarthy as their leader. Twenty-six remained faithful to the old Chief. For nine months Parnell made frantic efforts to maintain his position in Ireland. His pluck was superb, but all the cards were against him, and on October 6th, 1891, the painful struggle was terminated by his premature death.[2] Thus was removed from the political stage one of the great personalities of the century. " On the list of Irish patriots " Mr. Gladstone placed him " with or next to Daniel O'Connell," deeming him to be " of more masculine and stronger character than Grattan ". That he loved Ireland is certain ; whether his love for Ireland was as intense as his hatred of England is doubtful.

[1] Where the Irish Party met at this time.   [2] *Ætat* 45.

Interruption of the Unionist régime — Parnell's death overshadowed another event of some parliamentary significance. On the very same day that Parnell died, under circumstances almost tragic, at Brighton, there passed away, full of years and honour, Mr. W. H. Smith, the Leader of the House of Commons. Succeeding to the leadership at a critical moment Mr. Smith had done yeoman service to his party. Disarmingly simple, transparently honest, invariably courteous, he retained the respect of his opponents and won the affection of his friends. By universal acclaim the brilliant Chief Secretary was called to fill the vacant place. Mr. Balfour had accomplished the task to which he had set his hand in Ireland. He had shown himself sympathetic towards undeserved suffering, quick to devise healing remedies, but, above all, inflexibly firm in the vindication of law. He had greatly extended the operation of the Ashbourne Act, and had set up a Commission for dealing with congested districts. He proposed, in 1892, to crown his work by a large measure of Local Government, but the scheme was coldly received, and early in June it was abandoned. A few weeks later Parliament was dissolved.

Mr. Gladstone's Fourth Ministry — The General Election which ensued grievously disappointed the hopes of Mr. Gladstone. Instead of the majority of at least 100 on which he had confidently counted, the country gave him one of forty, and that highly precarious in composition. England was still staunchly Unionist, but was overborne by the " Celtic fringe ". In the new Parliament the Unionists numbered 315,[1] the Gladstonian Liberals 269, and the Irish Home Rulers 81.[2] In view of the composite majority opposed to him Lord Salisbury decided to meet Parliament, but, on an amendment to the Address, he was beaten by a majority of forty, and in August he gave way to Mr. Gladstone. The Cabinet of 1892 differed little in personnel from that of 1886, but was reinforced by Mr. H. H. Asquith, a young Oxonian who had quickly established a reputation at the Bar and in Parliament and now became Home Secretary ; by Mr. Bryce, a great jurist, by Mr. H. H. Fowler, a shrewd lawyer, who did admirable work at the Local Government Board, and others. The new Ministry at once (Sept. 1892) suspended by proclamation the operation of the Crimes Act in Ireland, and thus cleared the decks for the great measure of 1893.

The second edition of Home Rule, 1893 — The second edition of Home Rule was disclosed to the House by the Prime Minister on February 13th, 1893. In several important particulars it differed from the first. The single-chamber device with its two " Orders " was dropped, and the bicameral system was frankly adopted. The Legislative Council of forty-eight members was to be elected for eight years by persons who owned or occupied land of the rateable value of £20 per annum. The Legislative Assembly was to consist of 103 members, elected by the existing

[1] Of whom 269 were Conservatives.   [2] 9 Parnellites ; 72 anti-Parnellites.

constituencies, except Trinity College. Should the two Chambers disagree, the question was to be decided, but only after the lapse of two years, in joint session by a majority. In the original draft Irish members, to the number of eighty, were to be retained at Westminster, but not to vote on questions affecting Great Britain exclusively. This " in and out " clause was subsequently dropped, and the Irish members were retained for all purposes.

The Bill, after prolonged discussion, was pushed through the House of Commons by the amazing energy of Mr. Gladstone, but in the Lords it was thrown out by 419 to 41 (Sept. 8th). An immediate appeal to the country might have given Mr. Gladstone the mandate he wanted to deal with the House of Lords ; or it might not. Denied the opportunity of bringing the matter to an issue, Mr. Gladstone decided that his part in the great drama was played. Weighed down by increasing infirmity of sight and hearing, and sincerely desiring a quiet interval between the turmoil of politics and the grave, he resigned office in March, 1894. The interval he had craved lasted four years. He emerged from his retirement to plead the cause of the Armenian Christians in 1896, but on May 19th, 1898, after some months of suffering, he passed away.

Noble tributes were paid to his memory in both Houses of Parliament, his body lay in state in Westminster Hall, and was afterwards buried in the Abbey. One of the ablest of his lieutenants has since painted his portrait in colours which will never fade. For a final appreciation of a statesman who played so large a part in contemporary affairs, who excited in unusual measure alike admiration and detestation, the time has not, perhaps, arrived. But this much may be said. Though lacking the simplicity and directness characteristic of Bright, he was a consummate orator. Endowed by nature with a commanding presence and a sonorous voice, he acquired by art an extraordinary command of language and uncommon felicity of illustration. As a debater he was not equal to Disraeli, lacking his imperturbable temper and his sense of humour ; and although he could rouse intense enthusiasm among his followers, he cannot be said, like Peel, to have " played on the House like an old fiddle ". Great as an orator he was still greater as a man ; marvellous in the versatility of his interests, and touching life on many sides ; a genuine scholar of the old Oxford School, and a devoted son of the Anglican Church. As a statesman his greatest strength lay in finance. He had been admirably trained in the school of Peel, and he was, throughout his career, a jealous guardian of the public purse. Perhaps he spent too much of his ministerial life at the Treasury ; undoubtedly he spent too much of his public life in the House of Commons. Consequently his statesmanship was of the strictly parliamentary type ; his gaze was too closely concentrated upon tactics, sometimes, as in 1884-1885, with disastrous results. To say

Death of Gladstone

28

that his ontlook was insular would be untrue ; no man had a more vivid sympathy with oppressed nationalities, or a more touching faith in the universal efficacy of parliamentary institutions. But although he was frequently aroused to vehement speech by tales of oppression and occasionally to prompt action, as, for example, by the bad faith of Russia in regard to the Penjdeh incident, yet his interest in external affairs was intermittent, and his temper, in such matters only, was apt to be procrastinating. Nevertheless, no one could look upon him without a sense that here was a man cast in an heroic mould, and that whether he was right on a given question or wrong, in nothing was he less than great.

Lord
Rose-
bery's
Ministry
After Mr. Gladstone's resignation the Queen selected Lord Rosebery as his successor, and for fifteen months he carried on the government.[1] Sir William Harcourt succeeded to the leadership of the House of Commons, and the interest of the Session of 1894 centred on his Budget. The Queen's Speech of 1895 contained a portentous list of measures, including Welsh Disestablishment, Licensing Reform, and the abolition of Plural Voting, but no part of this ambitious programme was brought to legislative fruition ; on June 21st the Government was beaten on a War Office vote and promptly resigned.

The
Unionist
Ministry,
1895-1905
The Queen again sent for Lord Salisbury, who for the third time became Prime Minister. No longer, however, was he at the head of a purely Conservative Administration. Things had moved fast since 1886 when Lord Hartington had twice declined the generous offer of Lord Salisbury. He and Mr. Chamberlain now agreed that the time had come for an even closer alliance between the two wings of the Unionist Party. Early in 1887 an attempt had been made, by a round-table conference, to find a basis of compromise on Irish Government between Mr. Chamberlain and the Liberal Home Rulers. But the attempt proved abortive and was not renewed. On the other hand the working alliance between the Conservatives and the Liberal Unionists had now been maintained for nearly ten years. To Mr. Gladstone's second attempt to carry Home Rule in 1893 the latter had offered uncompromising opposition. On succeeding to the Premiership Lord Rosebery had made the significant admission that before Home Rule was conceded " England as the predominant member of the partnership of the three kingdoms will have to be convinced of its justice ". But the schism in the old Liberal Party was now too deep for healing, and unless the Liberal Unionist leaders were to renounce for ever the hope of official service, there remained to them no alternative but coalition with the Conservatives. One of those leaders conceived himself to be charged with a political

---

[1] There was virtually no change in the personnel of the Cabinet. The new Premier resigned the Foreign Office to Lord Kimberley, who was succeeded at the India Office by Mr. H. H. Fowler.

mission, far transcending the claims of party. He was quick, also, to discern the signs of the times. The centre of political interest was shifting rapidly from the centre to the circumference. The strong administration of Mr. Balfour, the repeated failure of Mr. Gladstone, the agrarian revolution now in quiet process of accomplishment—all these things seemed to promise an abatement in the acuteness of the Irish controversy. The majority given to Mr. Gladstone in 1892 was not only small but precarious ; the predominant partner remained wholly unconvinced ; the mind of the nation was turning in another direction. On the formation of the new Ministry some surprise was felt when Mr. Chamberlain selected the Colonial Office. It was, in fact, an unmistakable indication that he was conscious of the trend of opinion. Lord Hartington, who had now succeeded to the Dukedom of Devonshire, became President of the Council ; Lord Lansdowne, another Liberal Unionist, accepted the War Office ; Mr. Goschen the Admiralty, and Sir Henry James took a Peerage and the Chancellorship of the Duchy. Such appointments not only brought an immense accession of strength to Lord Salisbury's Ministry, but marked a notable stage in the evolution of a new political party.[1]

Of this evolution the country evidently approved. The new General Election of 1895 Ministry wound up the business of the Session with all possible speed, saved a few useful measures from the Liberal wreck, and in July made their appeal to the constituencies. The electorate was asked to confirm the verdict pronounced by the House of Lords upon the second edition of Home Rule. The reply was unequivocal. In the new Parliament Unionists numbered 411, Liberals 177, and Nationalists (of both sections) 82. The country had made up its mind on Home Rule, and wanted to hear no more of it. For a decade its wishes were respected. In 1898-1899 the Government carried two measures of first-rate importance. The Local Government Act of 1898 applied to Ireland the elective principle which was already revolutionizing local administration on this side of the Channel. That this Act opened out a " great vista of useful and patriotic work " [2] to Irishmen of all parties cannot be questioned. The second measure was of even greater significance. In form it only established " a Department of Agriculture and other Industries and Technical Instruction in Ireland ". In effect, it initiated a social and economic revolution. Worked in close connection with the Local Government Act of 1898, and interpreted and administered with rare wisdom and devotion by Sir Horace Plunkett, it has verily laid the foundations of a " new Ireland," and has taught some

---

[1] Lord Salisbury himself took the Foreign Office, and other important appointments were : Mr. Balfour (First Lord of the Treasury and Leader of the Commons), Lord George Hamilton (India), Sir M. Hicks Beach (Exchequer), Sir M. W. Ridley (Home Office), and Lord Halsbury (Lord Chancellor).

[2] The words are Sir H. Plunkett's, *Ireland in the new Century*, p. 88.

lessons which Great Britain has yet to learn.[1] With the enactment of legislation so full of happy augury for the future the historian of the nineteenth century may be well content to close an important section of his work.

Domestic affairs— 1886-1901   In contemporary interest South Africa was rapidly eclipsing Ireland. But before we pass to Colonial and Imperial topics, a word may be said as to domestic affairs. It is a grave, though common, misconception to suppose that the last years of the Victorian era constituted in this respect a period of stagnation. It is true that the fervour of Mr. Gladstone compelled the Liberal Party to concentrate their energies on a single issue. But except for an unimportant interlude administrative and legislative responsibility was not theirs, and the Tories, reinforced by the leader of the new Radicalism, betrayed no pedantic adherence to old-fashioned formulas. The *laisser-faire* doctrines of the Manchester School were light-heartedly jettisoned ; more and more reliance was placed upon the efficacy of the elective principle ; heavier and heavier functions were imposed upon the State, and municipalities invaded the sphere of commercial enterprise. This was one manifestation of the new spirit, but there were many others. Among them not the least significant was a rising of self-consciousness, or class-consciousness, in the ranks of the manual labourers. The last period of the nineteenth century was punctuated by a series of strikes and labour disputes. By no means all of them were due to disregarded demands for higher wages. The distribution of the product of industry was only one factor in the economic problem ; searchings of heart went deeper than that. " Fundamentals " as to the conduct of business and the organization of industry were called in question. The manual worker had not only learnt his letters but had attained to the full stature of citizenship. That this should react upon his industrial status was inevitable. He refused to be regarded as a mere " hand," a mechanical cog in the great wheel of industry ; he demanded recognition as a man, a workman, and a citizen.

Reorganization of Local Government   We have treated the evolution of representative democracy as one of the outstanding features of the nineteenth century. But the Acts of 1832, 1867, and 1884-1885 affected only Central Government. By the Act of 1835 the same democratic principle was applied to municipalities. The last years of the century witnessed the completion of the work by the democratization of Rural Government. Both the great Parties contributed to this development. The Act of 1888 provided for the creation of sixty-two " administrative counties," some of them co-terminous with the historic shires, some representing subdivisions of the same, and some sixty " county boroughs "—towns with over 50,000 inhabitants. In each county or county borough the Act set up a Council consisting in part of

[1] *Cf. e.g.* F. E. Green, *The Awakening of England.*

Councillors elected for a term of three years directly by the rate-payers, in part of Aldermen co-opted by the Councillors. To these Councils were transferred the administrative functions of Quarter Sessions, while the latter retained their judicial functions. The control of the Police was confided to a joint Committee of the County Council and Quarter Sessions. A similar Act was passed for Scotland in 1889, and in 1894 the elective principle was extended to parishes, and to intermediate areas known as urban or rural districts. These Acts did much to evolve administrative order out of the chaos which had been created by generations of piece-meal legislation ; authorities were concentrated ; areas were readjusted and simplified. More than this : the Acts provided a *cadre* and machinery for a number of social and economic reforms of far-reaching significance.[1]

The new Councils have proved themselves undeniably efficient, Finance but not economical. Local taxation and local indebtedness have increased with appalling rapidity : in 1875 the liabilities of local authorities in England and Wales stood, in round figures, at £92,000,000 ; in 1905 at £482,984,000. Not less appalling to old-fashioned economists was the growth of Imperial taxation. Sir Robert Peel's last Budget (1846) provided for an expenditure of £55,000,000; Sir Michael Hicks Beach in 1898 had to find £102,000,000; to-day the expenditure approaches £200,000,000.[2] These facts give additional significance to financial policy, but during the period now under review two Budgets only call for special notice. The first was Mr. Goschen's of 1888 ; the second was Sir William Harcourt's in 1894. In 1888 Mr. Goschen carried through a scheme for the " conversion " of the greater part of the funded debt of the country. The fact that " Consols " bearing interest at 3 per cent. stood considerably above par enabled Mr. Goschen to effect an immediate reduction of interest to $2\frac{3}{4}$ per cent., and a further reduction, after 1903, to $2\frac{1}{2}$ per cent. Mr. Goschen's " city " experience and connections stood him in good stead ; the hook was craftily baited and greedily swallowed. Nor did the policy of transaction lack justification at the time, or for some years to come. In 1897 " Goschens " touched $113\frac{7}{8}$. The South African War and the marked rise in the rate of interest which followed thereon put a different complexion on the matter. Sir William Harcourt's Budget of 1894 was notable for a marked increase in direct taxation in the form of " death " duties. The convenience of this method of raising revenue is unquestioned ; whether revenue so raised ought, in strictness, to be applied to any purpose save the extinction of capital liabilities is a much more doubtful point. The immediate justification was the fact that by both Parties social reforms were being pushed forward in hot haste and that reforms have to be paid for.

[1] For further detail, *cf.* Marriott, *English Political Institutions*, p. 260 *seq.*
[2] The estimate for 1913-1914 is £195,825,000.

The "con-   Throughout the greater part of this period social conditions
dition of   caused grave disquietude.   The agricultural depression which began
England" in 1879 became steadily worse ; trade was shifty ; employment was
precarious ; industrial disputes incessant.   The Capital was seriously
alarmed by labour riots in 1887 ; in 1889, 75,000 dock labourers
were on strike in London, the result being a notable improvement in
working conditions ; a prolonged strike among gas-workers (1889-
1890) led to the adoption in many gas-works of a system of profit-
sharing ; railway porters, brick-makers, boot and shoe makers,
colliers and iron workers followed suit in 1890.   Things were no
better in 1891, and the Government, therefore, appointed a strong
Commission to " inquire into questions affecting the relations between
employers and employed and the conditions of labour ".   This step,
wise in itself, had no immediate effect upon the situation.   The
cotton trade of Lancashire was paralysed by a dispute which lasted
from November, 1892, to March, 1893.   Hardly was this war ended
by the Brooklands agreement when the great coal strike of 1893
broke out and lasted for more than three months.   In 1895 there was
a long-drawn dispute in the shipbuilding yards of Glasgow and Belfast.

Social   The year which witnessed the great coal strike was noteworthy
Reform   for the foundation, under the presidency of an advanced socialist,
of the Independent Labour Party.   A year earlier (1892) the Government created at the Board of Trade a special Labour department
which has done useful work in the collection and dissemination of
statistical information.   A Board of Agriculture had been created in
1889.   Meanwhile, the Legislature was not idle in regard to economic
and social problems.   The establishment of a gratuitous system
of elementary education (1891)—another result of Mr. Goschen's
skilful finance—has been already noted.   An Act for the prevention
of cruelty to children and prohibiting their employment under the
age of ten was passed in 1889 ; local authorities were encouraged to
insist on the notification of infectious diseases (1889) and to prohibit
the sale of milk from dairies thus notified (1890).   In 1890 they
were empowered, under a drastic *Housing Act*, to purchase insanitary
areas, demolish unfit dwellings, and erect new ones.   In 1892 the
rural districts got their turn.   Under the *Small Holdings Act* County
Councils were empowered to purchase land, and re-sell in quantities
of not less than one and not more than fifty acres to actual cultivators,
to whom three-fourths of the purchase money might be advanced.
Holdings of not more than ten acres might be let to labourers.   The
money for the transaction was to be borrowed from the Public
Works Loan Commissioners.   Useful extensions of the acknowledged
principles of the Factory Acts were achieved in 1891 and 1895, and
in 1892 a *Shop Hours Act* was passed.   It prohibited the employment of persons under eighteen years of age for more than seventy-
four hours per week, including meal times, in shops.   Of much

wider scope and significance was the *Workmen's Compensation Act*
passed in 1897. This Act contained a new principle fearlessly
applied. Henceforward, employers were to be liable to pay compensation for death or injury, even though their workmen had been
guilty of " contributory negligence " and they themselves had not.
The operation of the Act was in the first instance confined to
mines, factories, railways, quarries, docks, and engineering sheds,
but nevertheless it registered an important stage on the road towards
compulsory insurance. The expenses of the Act were charged
wholly upon the employers.

These Acts, and others of like import, are sufficiently indicative
of the new spirit which was beginning to permeate the nation and
the Legislature. It was stimulated partly by an awakening of the
social conscience, and partly by outside pressure exerted by
organized bodies of manual workers. Among these the most
powerful were the Trade Unions, whose aims were now undergoing
considerable modification. That they should rely in increasing
degree upon political action was a natural result of the democratization of the parliamentary machine ; that their demands should
assume more and more socialistic hue was, perhaps, equally inevitable. In both respects the " New Unionism " owed much to the
powerful leadership of a new personality in English politics. This
was Mr. John Burns, a young engineer, who first obtained notoriety
in connection with the riots in Trafalgar Square, who then made his
mark on the London County Council, and before long impressed
himself upon the attention of the House of Commons. Great,
however, as was the awakening of the social conscience, it is not in
this direction that the historian must look for the characteristic
movement of the closing years of the Victorian era.

On June 21st, 1887, the ageing Sovereign celebrated the fiftieth Imperial-
anniversary of her accession to the throne. The occasion evoked a ism
remarkable demonstration of loyalty and affection among all classes
of her people at home and her subjects over-sea. The enthusiasm
was more than redoubled when, ten years later, she celebrated her
" diamond " Jubilee. On both occasions there was a solemn service
and a great review of battleships in the Solent. Yet there was a
difference between them. In the first procession the central feature
was the brilliant bodyguard of Princes : sons, sons-in-law, and
grandsons of the Queen. The second was, as a military spectacle,
even more splendid, but apart from the figure of the aged monarch,
touching in complete simplicity, public attention was riveted upon
a group of black-coated citizens who formed a part—to the outward
eye an incongruous part—of the superb pageant. These were the
Prime Ministers of the self-governing Dominions, and other representatives of over-sea Colonies. Their presence struck the keynote
of the Imperial Jubilee.

The Jubilees   The Jubilee celebrations had a threefold significance : they marked the zenith of the Queen's personal popularity among her subjects ; they were a recognition of her dynastic position in Europe ; and, above all, they forged fresh links between the Imperial Crown and the over-sea Dominions,—between the mother and the daughter lands. Lord Beaconsfield would have given much to have seen those days. In a remarkable degree they vindicated his prescience. As a factor in domestic politics the Crown had sensibly declined in importance during the last two hundred years. The Jubilees brought home to the imagination of the dullard that the Crown had a new function to fulfil, a new role to play, as the representative of Imperial interests and the embodiment of Imperial sentiment.

The Imperial idea   The increasing recognition of this sentiment was the characteristic differentia of the last years of the Victorian era. In the first decades of the reign the prevailing sentiment had been weary impatience of a useless though temporary burden. That the Colonies would in no short time sever the ties that bound them to the motherland was the hope of many and the expectation of all. The argument of Sir George Cornewall Lewis's *Essay on the Government of Dependencies* commanded in the 'forties all but universal assent.[1] So late as 1872 Tennyson had to rebuke *The Times* for having advised the Canadians to " take up their freedom as the days of their apprenticeship were over ". But *The Times* represented prevailing sentiment more truly than Tennyson.

The turn of the tide did not come until the 'eighties. Many things then contributed to swell it. The publication of Sir John Seeley's *Expansion of England* in 1883 was at once a cause and an indication of the change. The political future, he maintained, belonged to the " big states ". The Western Powers were quick to take the hint and the scramble for Africa began. That scramble was due essentially to a realization of the rapid shrinkage of the world. Science was annihilating time and space, and the remotest corners of the earth were being brought within the sphere of European politics. In Great Britain the new spirit was stimulated, partly by the apprehension of these facts, partly by the activity of neighbours and rivals, but, above all, by multiplied manifestations of the rising Imperial temper in the Colonies themselves.

Imperial co-operation   The year which witnessed the first Jubilee witnessed also, by a happy coincidence, the meeting of the first Colonial Conference.

[1] " If a dominant country understood the true nature of the advantages arising from the supremacy and dependence of the related communities, it would voluntarily recognize the legal independence of such of its own dependencies as were fit for independence ; it would, by its political arrangements, study to prepare for independence those which were still unable to stand alone ; and it would seek to promote colonization for the purpose of extending its trade rather than its empire, and without intending to maintain the dependence of its Colonies beyond the time when they need its protection."—Published in 1841.

The Conference was the outcome of the efforts of a band' of' enthusiasts among whom W. E. Forster, Edward Stanhope, and Lord
Rosebery were conspicuous. Its first-fruit was the *Imperial Defence
Act* of 1888 for the increase of the Australasian squadron. The
loyal and spontaneous offer of the Australasian Colonies to provide
military contingents for the war in the Soudan in 1885 had raised
the whole problem of Imperial co-operation for defence and war ;
the splendid services rendered by the Colonies in the South African
War (1899-1902) made a further and profound impression both upon
the Britons of the home-land and upon their neighbours. It was
manifest that for military purposes the Empire must henceforward
be regarded as an unit. Meanwhile, the experiment of a Conference
initiated in 1887 was repeated at Ottawa in 1894, and again in
London in 1897, 1902, and 1911.[1] These Conferences have touched
very cautiously, when at all, the larger question of constitutional
reconstruction for the Empire as a whole ; but in regard to defence,
communications, shipping, and many minor matters they have
rendered incalculable service to the cause of Imperial unity. Primarily, however, they have been valuable in bringing together, in
friendly and intimate communication, the responsible statesmen of
the mother and the daughter lands.

Meanwhile, the actual expansion of territory has been far from Terri-
insignificant. Communication with the Far East was rendered more torial
secure by the annexation of the island of Socotra in 1886 and by expansion
the establishment of a Protectorate over North Borneo in 1888.
More significant was the revival of a device which since the days of
Adam Smith had fallen into some discredit. The statesmen of the
seventeenth century cordially encouraged the concession of Charters
to companies of merchants. Such concessions brought to the
Crown a maximum of profit with a minimum of responsibility.
Adam Smith condemned the confusion between political and commercial purposes, holding that the function of a merchant was inconsistent with that of a Sovereign. None the less, this method of
colonization had solid advantages, and in the last decades of the
nineteenth century they became increasingly obvious. The " company of merchants " took risks and tried experiments, the Crown
and the nation reaped where the merchants had sown. The device
seemed to be particularly appropriate to Africa, upon which the
attention of the European Powers was largely concentrated during
the last fifteen years of the century.

The Berlin Conference of 1884-1885 initiated the scramble for Africa
African territory. British advance can here be indicated only by
a bare enumeration of dates. In the South a Protectorate was

---

[1] For history of the Conference, *cf. Responsible Government in the Dominions*,
vol. iii., and Jebb, *Colonial Conference ;* Marriott's *Evolution of the British Empire
and Commonwealth*, pp. 232:309.

established over Bechuanaland (1885).   On the West coast over the
Niger territory (1885), and, in the same year, a Charter was granted
to the Royal Niger Company.   But Chartered companies and Pro-
tectorates are, as a rule, transitory phases, and in 1900 Nigeria was
transferred to the Crown.   On the East coast the Chartered Company
of East Africa (1888) similarly prepared the way for the direct
sovereignty of the Crown (1896).   In 1889 a Charter was granted to
the South African Company, which has built up a great power in
Matabeleland and Mashonaland, and in the same year Central
Africa was declared to be under British protection.   In 1890 Lord
Salisbury concluded a comprehensive agreement with Germany, one
of the fruits of which was a British Protectorate over Zanzibar.
Germany herself was established on the East coast, in the hinterland
of Zanzibar, on the South-west from Angola to Cape Colony, while
in the North-west she acquired Togoland, a strip of territory between
the British Gold Coast and Dahomey, and the Cameroons, a large
tract to the south-east of Nigeria.   With Portugal Lord Salisbury
came to terms in 1891, and with France, in reference to West Africa,
in 1898.   Further treaties were concluded with Germany in regard
to Portuguese Africa in 1898, and to the Soudan in 1899.   It was
generally held that Heligoland—ceded to Germany in 1890—was a
cheap price to pay for the African agreement, and, in any case, the
partition of Africa will probably be accounted Lord Salisbury's
most enduring achievement in the domain of Foreign Policy.

The
Western
Powers
and the
Far
East

But it was not only Africa that was brought within the sphere
of Western statesmanship.   The attack of Japan upon Korea in
1894 proclaimed to the world the entrance of a new Power into
world-politics.   China intervened to save Korea from the grasp of
Japan, and the latter promptly turned upon the mediator, captured
Port Arthur, and imposed upon China the treaty of Shimonoseki
(1895).   China was obliged to cede the Lino-Tung peninsula, the
island of Formosa, and to promise a large indemnity.   But Europe
could not see with unconcern the rise of a new Power in the Far
East.   Russia, therefore, with France and Germany, stepped in to
deprive Japan of the fruits of victory, and, having come to the aid
of China, proceeded to claim her reward.   Germany obtained a
lease of Kiao-Chow in 1898 and Russia a similar lease of Port Arthur
in 1899.   England, fearful of being left in the cold, obtained Wei-
hei-Wei, and France got concessions near Tonkin.   These encroach-
ments roused into fresh life the old hostility of the Chinese to Western
influences, and in 1899 a national uprising, led by the " Boxers "
threatened the extermination of all foreigners in China.   Japan
joined the Western Powers in the task of rescuing their countrymen
from Pekin, and in 1901 peace was restored.   A year later the world
was startled to learn that Great Britain had so far emerged from her
traditional diplomatic isolation as to conclude an alliance with Japan.

To this significant step Great Britain was, perhaps, induced by Australia
a recognition of the vulnerability of her position in the Pacific.
The material development of the Australasian Colonies had not kept
pace with their constitutional evolution.   Between 1854 and 1890
all these Colonies—New South Wales, Victoria, Tasmania, South
Australia, Queensland, Western Australia, and New Zealand—
attained to the full dignity of responsible government.   What they
continued to lack was not government but subjects.   The vast
spaces of the great southern continents were virtually unpeopled.[1]
The spirit of high protection ran riot ; immigration was discouraged,
and Australasian democracy was primarily concerned to keep up the
price of labour.   Mingled with this motive was the laudable ambition
to preserve Australia as a white-man's country.   To the realization
of this and similar ambitions some closer form of political union was
essential.   But Federation was, in Australia, a plant of slow and
timid growth.   Ever since 1847 the project had been intermittently
discussed, but not until 1883 did it actually begin to take shape.[2]
Several things then combined to render the problem insistent : the
question as to the desirability of imported Chinese labour for the
mines ;   the escape of some French convicts from New Caledonia
into Australian territory ;   rumours that France was intending to
annex the New Hebrides ;   above all, Lord Derby's disavowal of the
action of Queensland in setting up the British flag in New Guinea.
Between 1883 and 1893 many conferences were held, and many
schemes were discussed, but in 1893 the question was temporarily
suspended by a severe financial crisis.   Between 1895 and 1899 the
draftsmen were again continuously at work, and in the latter year a
Bill, which expressed the mind of Australia, was sent home for the
approval of the Imperial Legislature.   Thanks to the tact of Mr.
Chamberlain, then Colonial Secretary, and of Mr. (now Sir Edmund)
Barton,[3] the Bill became law, with a single amendment, as the
Australian Commonwealth Act in 1900.   It was the last great statute
to which Queen Victoria gave her Royal assent, and in doing so she
expressed her fervent hope that " the inauguration of the Commonwealth may ensure the increased prosperity and well-being of my
loyal and beloved subjects in Australia ".[4]

Happy was the fate which permitted the venerable Sovereign to Death
watch over the cradle of a new Nation.   But this function, in- of
expressibly appropriate, was almost the last she performed.   Her Queen
Victoria
health, which throughout her reign had been remarkably robust,[5]
was now failing rapidly.   She felt acutely the humiliation inflicted
upon the country by the defeats to her arms in South Africa,[6] but

---

[1] The total population of Australasia in 1901 was only 4½ millions.
[2] I do not ignore the abortive measure of 1850.
[3] Afterwards first Prime Minister of the Commonwealth of Australia.
[4] For constitutional details, cf. Marriott, Political Institutions, pp. 326-327.
[5] With one short interval after the Prince Consort's death.
[6] Ap. Quarterly Review, No. 193.

never did she show herself more truly the mother of her people than in the dark days of the winter of 1899-1900. She it was who insisted, in December, 1899, that large reinforcements should be sent out, and that Lord Roberts should be entrusted with the command. Having thus made adequate, though tardy, preparation, she faced the issue with calm courage and complete confidence. Despite failing health she went in and out among her people : encouraging the fighters, consoling the wounded, comforting the mourners, warning and stimulating responsible Ministers. She followed closely all the efforts of her soldiers in South Africa and cordially commended their successes. Especially did she appreciate the gallantry of the Colonial contingents, and of the Irish regiments. The latter's services she acknowledged with more than words. She gave them permission to wear a sprig of shamrock on St. Patrick's Day, and when the time came for her spring holiday in 1900 she determined, instead of going to the South, to devote it to Ireland. In this determination there was perhaps a tinge of self-reproach. " She desired almost passionately," so we learn from one who knew her, " to be loved by the Irish," [1] but she had done little to win their love. Pathetically she strove, at the last, to make amends. Her last April she spent in Dublin, where she was enthusiastically welcomed by all classes. The strain of the effort was enormous, and combined with that of the South African war it hastened her end. On January 2nd, 1901, she welcomed Lord Roberts on his return from South Africa, and on the 19th the public learnt that she was seriously ill. On the 22nd, in the presence of two sons, three daughters, and her grandson, the German Emperor, she passed away. She was in her eighty-second year, and had reigned sixty-three years seven months and three days.

The close of a reign and an era

" A little figure in a great age," was Goldwin Smith's description of Queen Elizabeth. Untrue of Queen Elizabeth, it would be still less true of Queen Victoria. Her death marked the close of a great life, a great reign, and a great historical epoch. Her personal character was a compound of shrewdness, simplicity, and sincerity. She was, said John Bright, " the most absolutely truthful person I have ever known ". Her gift of sympathy was known to all, her punctuality in business and her devotion to duty could be known to comparatively few. Yet all men could see " how superbly she continued to stand sentry to the business of her Empire "—virtually to the end.[2] The building of that Empire was largely, as we have seen, the work of her reign, and she was unaffectedly proud of it.

Her reign had other claims to distinction which the foregoing pages have been intended to illustrate. Of the literature of the epoch no mention has been made, since the mention could only have

---

[1] Ap. *Quarterly Review*, No. 193.
[2] *Cf.* for a fine appreciation, *Quarterly Review*, No 193.

been catalogic and perfunctory. Nor of the achievements of science. Never were those achievements greater, and never were they applied with ampler generosity to the service of humanity. Whether regard be paid to the relief of human suffering, to the multiplication of utilities, or to the augmentation of wealth, the Victorian era incurred a heavy debt to the devoted workers in the scientific sphere.

Not less impressive were the changes in the economic and social structure : the enlargement of the bounds of commerce ; the genesis of new forms of industrial activity ; the development of the principles of co-operation and combination ; the deepening sense of social responsibility and social solidarity,—all these things were characteristic of the England of the nineteenth century.

Nevertheless, our survey would seem to have substantiated the claim put forward in the opening pages of this work. Great as were its achievements in the domain of pure intellect, of applied science, of social service, and of industrial development, the nineteenth century will take rank among the ages by virtue of its contribution to political experiment and to the art of government. The on-coming of Democracy, extension of the Overseas Empire and the evolution of the self-governing portions of that Empire into a Confederated Commonwealth, these are the things that will to all time distinguish the Victorian era.

SELECT BIBLIOGRAPHY

The assigned limits of this work do not allow for an exhaustive or critical bibliography, for which see Sir E. Ll. Woodward : *Age of Reform 1815-1870* and R. C. K. Ensor : *England 1870-1914.* For many aspects of the period there is still much work to do in the files of government departments in the Public Record Office and in the private papers of ministers, of which the British Museum has large collections.

The following rough working list of books has been drawn up since the text was last revised.

A. General :—

The Annual Register ; Hansard : *Parliamentary Debates* (compiled mainly from newspapers) ; *Statutes of the Realm ;* P. Ford ed. *Hansard's . . . Parliamentary Papers 1696-1834* and *Select List of British Parliamentary Papers 1833-1899.* The best histories are : Sir E. Ll. Woodward : *Age of Reform 1815-1870 ;* R. C. K. Ensor : *England 1870-1914 ;* and E. Halévy : *History of the English People in the 19th Century* (incomplete for 1841-1895). See also : Sir S. Walpole : *History of England* [1815-1856] and *History of 25 Years* [1856-1880] ; H. Paul : *Modern England* [1846-1895] ; J. McCarthy : *History of our Own Times* [1837-1897] ; *Political History of England :* 1801-1837 (G. C. Brodrick and J. K. Fotheringham) and 1837-1901 (Sir S. Low and Ll. C. Sanders) ; H. W. C. Davis : *Age of Grey and Peel ;* R. H. Gretton : *A Modern History of the English People 1880-1922* (based on newspapers) ; *History of " The Times " ;* Sir J. A. R. Marriott : *This Realm of England.*

B. Constitutional :—

W. Costin and J. S. Watson : *Law and Working of the Constitution* II, 1784-1914 ; Sir C. G. Robertson : *Select Statutes, Cases, and Documents ;* Sir D. L. Keir : *Constitutional History of Modern Britain* 1485-1937 ; with F. H. Lawson : *Cases in Constitutional Law ;* Sir T. E. May : *Constitutional History of England,* ed. F. Holland, and *Parliamentary Practice,* ed. Sir G. Campion ; W. Bagehot : *English Constitution,* ed. A. J. Balfour ; Sir H. Maine : *Popular Government ;* W. E. H. Lecky : *Democracy and Liberty ;* Sir W. R. Anson : *Law and Custom of the Constitution,* 2 ed. ; A. V. Dicey : *Law of the Constitution,* 9 ed., and *Law and Public Opinion ;* A. L. Lowell : *Government of England ;* E. and A. G. Porritt : *Unreformed House of Commons ;* J. R. M. Butler : *Passing of the Great Reform Bill ;* C. Seymour : *Electoral Reform in England and Wales ;* C. S. Emden : *The People and the Constitution ;* ed. *Selected Speeches on the Constitution ;* Sir W. S. Holdsworth : *History of English Law* XIII, XIV ; M. Ostrogorski: *Democracy and the Organization of Political Parties ;* K. B. Smellie : *100 Years of English Government,* 2 ed. ; N. Gash : *Politics in the Age of Peel ;* Marriott : *Mechanism of the Modern State ;* Sir W. I. Jennings : *Cabinet Government ;* S. and B. Webb : *English Local Government ;* J. Redlich and H. W. Hirst : *Local Government in England.*

C. Economic and Social :—

Sir J. H. Clapham : *Economic History of Modern Britain.*
The Economist (from 1844) ; *Economic History Review ;* G. R. Porter : *Progress of the Nation ;* C. R. Fay : *Great Britain from Adam Smith to the Present*

Day ; F. Engels : *Condition of the Working-Class in England in 1844 ;* T. Carlyle : *Chartism ;* M. Hovell : *Chartist Movement ;* J. L. and B. Hammond : *Town Labourer, Village Labourer, Skilled Labourer,* all 1760-1832 ; *Bleak Age ;* H. Mayhew : *London Labour and the London Poor ;* M. Beer : *History of British Socialism ;* B. Webb : *My Apprenticeship;* S. and B. Webb : *Trade Unionism ; Industrial Democracy ;* G. M. Young ed. *Early Victorian England ;* G. D H Cole : *Cobbett ;* ed. *Cobbett's Rural Rides ; Short History of the British Working Class Movement ; Chartist Portraits ; A Century of Co-operation ;* T. S. Ashton : *Industrial Revolution ;* R. J. Cornewall-Jones : *British Merchant Service ;* R. E. Prothero : *English Farming Past and Present ;* C. Booth : *Life and Labour of the People of London ;* W. Milne-Bailey : *Trade Union Documents.*

Vast stores of information lie in the decennial *Census* returns and in blue books, of which these *Reports* may be singled out : on agriculture, (*a*) select committees, 1814, 1821-1822, 1833, 1848 ; (*b*) royal commissions, 1879, 1881-1882, 1893-1897 ; on combination laws, 1825 ; poor law commissioners', 1834 and 1909 ; factory commissioners', 1833, 1842, 1876 ; on municipal corporations, 1835 ; on hand loom weavers, 1840 ; on trades unions, 1876 ; on trade depression, 1885 ; and on labour, 1893.

Excellent and imaginative pictures of ordinary life are to be found in the novels of Dickens, Trollope, Disraeli (*Sybil*), George Eliot, Kingsley, Mrs. Gaskell, Meredith, and Mrs. Humphry Ward, and in Kipling's stories.

D. Foreign Policy :—

R. W. Seton-Watson : *Britain in Europe* is the best guide, supplemented by H. W. V. Temperley and L. M. Penson : *Foundations of British Foreign Policy.* Their *A Century of Diplomatic Blue Books* lists all parliamentary papers on foreign affairs from 1814 to 1914. Sir E. Hertslet : *Map of Europe by Treaty* gives all treaty texts for 1814-1891 ; *British and Foreign State Papers* (indexes, vols. 64 and 93) cover 1815-1901. These two works, which overlap each other, are not confined to Great Britain. Nor are G. Weil : *L'Éveil des Nationalités* 1815-1848 ; C.-H. Pouthas : *Démocraties et Capitalisme* 1848-1860 ; H. Hauser, J. Maurain and P. Benaerts *Du Libéralisme à l'Impérialisme* 1860-1878 ; and M. Baumont : *L'Essor industriel* 1878-1904, the most recent general histories of Europe.

See also Marriott : *History of Europe 1815-1939 ; Makers of Modern Italy ; The Eastern Question ;* Sir C. K. Webster : *British Diplomacy 1813-1815* (texts) ; *Congress of Vienna ; Foreign Policy of Castlereagh 1815-1822 ; Foreign Policy of Palmerston 1830-1841 ;* Temperley : *Foreign Policy of Canning ; England and the Near East—the Crimea ;* B. K. Martin : *Triumph of Lord Palmerston ;* R. Cobden : *Three Panics ;* J. A. Hobson : *Cobden the international man ;* G. B. Henderson : *Crimean War Diplomacy ;* G. M. Trevelyan : *Garibaldi and the making of Italy ;* P. de la Gorce : *Histoire du second Empire ;* E. Eyck : *Bismarck* (better in German than in English) ; Newton : *Life of Lyons ;* Sir H. Maxwell : *Life of Clarendon ;* S. Lane-Poole : *Stratford de Redcliffe ;* Fitzmaurice : *Life of Granville ;* A. Ramm ed. : *Gladstone-Granville Correspondence 1868-1876 ;* Seton-Watson : *Disraeli Gladstone and the Eastern Question ;* W. Taffs : *Odo Russell ;* Acton : *Historical Essays ;* Mrs. R. Wemyss : *Memoirs and Letters of Morier ;* W. L. Langer : *European Alliances and Alignments* [1871-1890] ; *The Diplomacy of Imperialism* [1890-1902] ; A. J. Marder : *British Naval Policy 1880-1905.*

See also (G below) lives of other foreign secretaries.

E. The Empire :—

(I) *India.*

Cambridge History of the British Empire IV and V, with full bibliographies. A. B. Keith : *Constitutional History of India 1600-1935 ;* ed. *Speeches and documents on Indian policy ;* R. Muir : *Making of British India ;* Marriott : *English in India ;* D. C. Boulger : *Lord W. Bentinck ;* Hastings : *Private Diary ;* Colchester : *Administration of Ellenborough ;* Hardinge : *Viscount Hardinge ;* Sir W. Napier : *Conquest of Scinde ; Life of Sir C. Napier ;* Sir W. Lee Warner : *Protected Princes of India ; Life of Dalhousie ;* J. C. Baird : *Letters of Dalhousie ;* Sir H. S. Cunningham : *Earl Canning ;* Sir J. W. Kaye and G. B. Malleson : *History of the Sepoy War ;* T. Rice Holmes : *History of the Mutiny ;* Sir F. J. Goldsmid : *Outram ;* Sir H. B. Edwardes : *Sir H. Lawrence ;* R. B. Smith : *Lord Lawrence ;* L. Shadwell : *Life of Colin Campbell ;* J. C. Marshman ed. : *Memoirs of Sir H. Havelock ;* Sir G. O. Trevelyan : *Cawnpore ;* Sir H. Durand : *Afghan War ;* Sir W. W. Hunter : *Lord Mayo ;* L. Wolf : *Lord Ripon ;* Sir C. Ilbert : *Government of India ;* Sir A. Lyall : *Rise and Expansion of British Dominion in India ; Life of Lord Dufferin ;* Roberts : *41 Years in India ;* Curzon : *British Government in India ;* Sir W. S. Churchill : *With the Malakand Field Force ;* Sir R. Coupland : *Indian Problems 1833-1935 ;* R. Kipling : *Soldiers Three ; Plain Tales from the Hills;* etc. ; V. Garrett and E. Thompson : *Rise and Fulfilment of British Rule in India.*

(II) *The Dominions and the Colonies.*

Cambridge History of the British Empire II, VI-VIII, with full bibliographies, especially for each dominion. Sir C. P. Lucas : *Historical Geography of the British Colonies ;* and ed. *Durham Report ;* E. M. Wrong : *Charles Buller and Responsible Government ;* E. G. Wakefield : *Art of Colonization ;* Sir G. C. Lewis : *Government of Dependencies ;* Sir C. W. Dilke : *Greater Britain ;* Sir J. R. Seeley : *Expansion of England ;* J. van der Poel : *The Jameson Raid ;* B. Williams : *Rhodes ;* Sir C. Headlam ed. : *Milner Papers ;* E. Crankshaw : *The Forsaken Idea* [Milner's imperialism] ; J. A. Hobson : *Imperialism ;* L. S. Amery : *" The Times " History of the War in South Africa ;* H. E. Egerton : *British Colonial Policy ; Federations and Unions of the British Empire ;* Marriott : *Evolution of British Empire and Commonwealth ;* R. Muir : *Short History of the British Commonwealth* II ; Sir W. I. Jennings and C. M. Young : *Constitutional Laws of the British Commonwealth ;* A. B. Keith : *Speeches and Documents on British Colonial Policy* 1763-1917.

F. Ireland :—

J. L. Hammond : *Gladstone and the Irish Nation.*

J. C. Beckett : *Short History of Ireland* (introductory) ; J. E. Pomfret : *Struggle for Land in Ireland ;* Sir J. O'Connor : *History of Ireland ;* W. E. H. Lecky : *Leaders of Public Opinion in Ireland ;* Bryce ed. : *Two Centuries of Irish History ;* N. Mansergh : *Ireland in the Age of Reform and Revolution ;* F. S. L. Lyons : *Irish Parliamentary Party 1890-1910 ; Reports* of the Devon (1845), Richmond (1881), Bessborough (1881), Cowper (1887), and Special (1896) Commissions.

W. J. FitzPatrick ed. : *Correspondence of Daniel O'Connell ;* G. S. Lefevre : *Peel and O'Connell ; Gladstone and Ireland ;* Sir C. G. Duffy : *Young Ireland;* R. B. O'Brien : *50 Years of concessions to Ireland ; Life of Drummond ; Life of Parnell ;* J. Mitchel : *Jail Journal ;* H. Le Caron : *25 Years in the Secret Service ;* M. J. F. McCarthy : *The Irish Revolution ;* T. P. O'Connor : *The Parnell Movement ;* Sir H. Plunkett : *The New Ireland.*

G. Biographies, &c (short titles) :—

The Dictionary of National Biography (ed. Sir L. Stephen and Sir S. Lee) and its *Supplements* cover almost everyone of importance.

A. Aspinall ed. : *Letters of George IV ; Formation of Canning's Ministry ;* Buckingham : *Memoirs ;* C. C. F. Greville : *Journals* (best though rarest ed. Strachey and Fulford) ; Sir A. Alison : *Castlereagh Correspondence ;* W. R. Brock : *Lord Liverpool and Liberal Toryism ;* Temperley : *Canning ;* Sir H. Maxwell ed. : *Creevey Papers ;* J. W. Croker : *Correspondence and Diaries ;* G. M. Trevelyan : *Grey of the Reform Bill ; John Bright ;* G. Wallas : *Francis Place ;* Sir D. Le Marchant : *Althorp ;* Esher, A. C. Benson, and G. E. Buckle ed. : *Letters of Queen Victoria ;* L. Strachey : *Queen Victoria ;* R. Fulford : *Prince Consort ;* W. M. Torrens : *Melbourne ;* Disraeli : *Lord G. Bentinck ;* Sir R. Peel : *Memoirs ;* C. S. Parker : *Peel ; Graham ;* A. A. W. Ramsay : *Peel ;* I. I. Bowen : *Cobden ;* Lady F. Balfour : *Aberdeen ;* Sir G. O. Trevelyan : *Macaulay ;* H. C. F. Bell : *Palmerston ;* G. P. Gooch ed. : *Early Letters of Russell ;* Sir S. Walpole : *Russell ;* J. Bright : *Diaries ;* J. L. and B. Hammond : *Shaftesbury ;* Malmesbury : *Memoirs ;* Sir T. W. Reid : *Forster ;* W. F. Monypenny and G. E. Buckle : *Disraeli ;* J. Morley : *Gladstone ; Cobden ;* P. Guedalla: *Gladstone and Palmerston ; The Queen and Mr. Gladstone ;* Lady G. Cecil : *Salisbury ;* Lady F. Cavendish : *Diary ;* B. Holland : *Devonshire ;* A. R. D. Elliot : *Goschen ;* Rosebery : *Miscellanies ;* Crewe : *Rosebery ;* S. Gwynn and G. M. Tuckwell : *Dilke ;* Lady V. Hicks-Beach : *Hicks-Beach ;* Selborne : *Memorials ;* Argyll : *Autobiography ;* A. G. Gardiner : *Harcourt ;* Sir A. E. West : *Private Diaries ;* E. Marjoribanks and I. Colvin : *Carson ;* Sir W. S. Churchill : *Lord R. Churchill ;* J. A. Spender : *Campbell-Bannerman ;* J. L. Garvin and J. Amery : *Chamberlain ;* Newton : *Lansdowne.*

H. Thought :—

G. M. Young : *Victorian England Portrait of an Age.*

J. Bentham *Fragment on Government* (pubd. 1776, but important) ; J. H. Newman : *Apologia pro vita sua ;* J. S. Mill : *Utilitarianism ; On Liberty ; Representative Government ; Autobiography ;* C. R. Darwin : *Origin of Species ;* Sir H. Maine : *Ancient Law ;* T. H. Green : *Political Obligation ;* H. Spencer : *Principles of Ethics.*

INDEX

ABERDARE, Henry Austin Bruce, First Baron, Home Secretary, 316.
Aberdeen, George Hamilton Gordon, Fourth Earl of, 99 ; Foreign Secretary, 132 ; Prime Minister, 176, 196 ; and Crimean War, 185 ; resignation of, 196.
Abdur Rahman, 389, 421.
Abyssinia, expedition to, 305.
Acts of Parliament—
Affirmation, 96.
Agricultural Holdings (1875), 363 ; (1883), 406.
Arrears, 411.
Artisans' Dwellings (1875), 364.
Australian Colonies, 160.
Australian Commonwealth, 443.
Ballot, 295, 345.
Bank Charter (1833), 86 ; (1844), 138.
Bank Restriction Act, 32.
Bankruptcy, 406.
British North America, 297.
Burials, 406.
Catholic Emancipation, 69.
Charitable Bequests (1844), 150.
Combination, 62.
Conspiracy and Protection of Property (1875), 365.
Contagious Diseases (Animals) (1878), 364.
Crimes (1882), 411.
Criminal Law Amendment, Ireland (1887), 429.
Ecclesiastical Titles, 162.
Education of 1870, 330-332 ; of 1876, 333.
Electric Lighting, 406.
Employers and Workmen (1875), 365.
Employers' Liability (1880), 406.
Enclosure of Commons (1876), 363.
Encumbered Estates Court, 154.
Endowed School (1869), 334.
Exchequer and Audit, 276.
Factory, 87-88 ; (1844), 146 ; (1847), 159 ; 1878), 364.
Friendly Societies (1875), 366.
Ground Game, 406.
Housing (1890), 438.
Imperial Defence (1888), 441.
India Act (1858), 243, 250.
Irish Church (1869), 318-321.
Irish Land (1860), 324 ; (1870), 324 ; (1881), 409 ; (1885), 424.
Irish University (1879), 399.
Jamaica, 114.
Joint Stock Companies, 284.

Judicature of 1873, 345 ; of 1876, 345.
Lay Patronage, Scotland (1874), 361.
Leases and Sales of Settled Estates (1875), 363.
Licensing (1872), 343 ; (1874), 363.
Local Government (England) (1888), 436 ; (1894), 437.
Local Government (Ireland), 435.
Local Government (Scotland) (1889), 437.
Merchant Shipping (1876), 367.
Mines (1842), 146.
Municipal Corporations, 100.
Notification of Diseases, 438.
Parliamentary Reform (1832), 82 seq. , (1867), 289 seq. ; (1884), 406.
Peace Preservation, Ireland (1870), 324, 407.
Poor Law of 1834, 96.
Poor Law, Ireland, 104.
Poor Law Amendment, Ireland (1847), 154.
Protection of Life and Property (1881), 408.
Public Schools (1868), 334.
Public Worship Regulation (1874), 361.
Redistribution (1885), 407.
Royal Titles, 371.
Settled Land (1882), 363.
Shop Hours (1892), 438.
Six Acts, 291.
Slavery Abolition (1833), 88.
Small Holdings (1892), 438.
South Africa Union, 398.
Technical Instruction (1889), 335.
Test and Corporation, repeal of, 67.
Trade Union (1876), 365
" Westmeath," 325 ; (Ireland), 399.
Workmen's Compensation (1897), 438.
Adams, Charles Francis, 356.
Afghanistán, 221, 385, 420.
Africa, East, Company of, 442.
Africa, Partition of, 442.
Africa, South, 394. (See also Cape Colony.)
Africa, South British Company of, 397, 442.
Agnew, Patrick Alexander Vaus, 229.
Agriculture, 20.
Agriculture, Board of, 438.
Aix-la-Chapelle, Congress of, 38.
Akbar Khan, 223.
Alabama, the, 264, 353.
Alexander I., Czar of Russia, 36, 40, 42.